Social Processes
and Social Structures

Social Processes and Social Structures

An Introduction to Sociology

W. RICHARD SCOTT

STANFORD UNIVERSITY

Holt, Rinehart and Winston, Inc.

NEW YORK   CHICAGO   SAN FRANCISCO   ATLANTA

DALLAS   MONTREAL   TORONTO   LONDON   SYDNEY

301
S

5/25/71
febb

Library of Congress Catalog Card Number: 78-106599
SBN: 03-84413-4   (CI)
SBN: 03-084015-5   (Pa)
Printed in the United States of America
0 1 2 3 4   4   9 8 7 6 5 4 3 2 1

For my Mother

PREFACE

Many sociologists spend years describing and analyzing social structure without once asking themselves why it is that behavior persists long enough for them to describe and analyze it at all. Structure is not a given: it is itself the result of social process.[1]

Sociology has long devoted itself to the study of social structures and social processes. This being the case, there is perhaps nothing particularly novel about this volume. Books designed to introduce new students to a discipline should not be expected to be path-breaking but, rather, should be expected to give a balanced view of the current state of the field. But let us not become humble too quickly. A review of much of the current work in sociology suggests that although some sociologists focus on social structures and others on social processes, rarely do we find equal attention paid to both. If there is novelty in our approach, then, it is precisely in our attempt to present a *balanced* view that gives due consideration to both structure and process in a single volume.

The pendulum appears to swing back and forth between these twin emphases. In the 1920s, Park and Burgess' influential text stressed the centrality of such processes as competition and conflict, accommodation and assimilation.[2] In the following decades, the functionalist approach, with its emphasis on such structural concepts as role and social system, dominated the sociological landscape. And in recent years, largely in reaction to the problems of functionalism, we have seen the development (resurgence?) of the conflict school, social exchange theorists, and others who lament the long neglect of social process.

The present book is based on two premises to which many, but not all, sociologists would subscribe: (1) that it is possible to identify some of the basic social processes that must be understood if we are to understand how structures are created, maintained, and transformed and (2) that these social processes assume various guises, depending on the characteristics of the social structures within which they operate. A third premise implied by these two premises should be made explicit, namely, that the fundamental business of sociology is describing, analyzing, and developing explanations of these various processes and these diverse structural arrangements.

The five social processes on which this book will focus are integration, socialization, status, power, and adaptation. *Integration* refers to attempts to secure and maintain solidary relations among the members of a given social unit.

[1]George C. Homans, *Social Behavior: Its Elementary Forms*, New York: Harcourt, 1961, p. 99.
[2]Robert E. Park and Ernest W. Burgess, *Introduction to the Science of Sociology*, Chicago: University of Chicago Press, 1920.

Socialization refers to the process by which individuals or groups learn to play the social roles in the structures to which they belong or aspire to belong. *Status* processes entail the differential evaluation and rewarding of social units. *Power* processes include attempts to regulate and influence the attitudes and behaviors of other persons based on differential sanctioning ability. And *adaptation* refers to the process by which a given social unit attempts to survive and, if possible, thrive in its environment. There is no need for us to claim that these are the only important social processes; it is sufficient to say that they appear to us and to others to be quite important. We have simply selected five processes with which to illustrate the possibilities—and, inevitably, point up the difficulties—of our approach to the study of sociology. Other processes may be identified at approximately the same level of abstraction (for example, division of labor, goal setting, and coalition formation). However, within a single volume, some selectivity of focus is mandatory. It is also possible to identify more specific processes (for example, under the general heading "power" we can distinguish influence, authority, and other kinds of control attempts) as well as more general and abstract processes, such as role differentiation, exchange, and balance processes. Our attempt has been to chart a middle course between highly abstract formulations and more specific formulations.

All social processes operate within some specific structural context that they themselves help to create and to change. Social structures may be distinguished in a variety of ways, but for present purposes we have chosen to select a set of contexts that corresponds closely to traditional sociological categories as well as to somewhat familiar and recognizable social units. Thus, four structural settings are examined: the *small group*, the *formal organization*, the *community*, and the *society*. Note that, generally speaking, these settings are ranked from low to high with respect to such variables as number of participants and complexity of form. Other distinguishing variables will be discussed as these four settings are described and analyzed.

Here is the heart of our plan. By means of our commentary and our selection of readings, we will examine the operation of each social process as it occurs within each structural context. For example, our book includes selections on integration as this process operates in small groups, organizations, communities, and in the larger society. This approach does not allow us to systematically detail all that sociologists know about integration as a social process. Each article is necessarily selective in its approach so that, for example, we will learn about only a few aspects of social integration as it operates in the several settings. Also, this approach does not allow us to systematically relate all that sociologists know about each of the structural contexts. For example, even after we have explored integration, socialization, status, power, and adaptation processes in formal organizations, there are still other processes that must be analyzed, and there is as well the interaction of all the processes (their effect on each other) that must be considered in any reasonably complete analysis of this type of social structure.

What our approach does highlight are the two notions that essentially similar processes are to be found in each of these diverse social settings and that social processes oriented to the achievement of similar ends may assume very different forms, depending on the nature of the context within which they unfold. Our theme, then, is continuity in the midst of diversity, generic social processes shaping and shaped by distinctive structural contexts.

We have one final comment. It is our belief that sociology is effective as a scholarly pursuit and as an intellectual perspective to the extent that it is analytical. Sociologists should not be content with describing social phenomena, no matter how intrinsically interesting or fascinating the occurrence. Novelists and journalists are far better prepared to "hold the mirror up to nature." The task of the sociologist is to analyze such situations—to break them down into their component parts and processes. To emphasize the analytical nature of sociology is not to suggest a retreat from the study of contemporary problems. It is, rather, to call for a certain kind of approach to these problems. For example, we have not included in this book a separate part devoted to racial groups or ethnic relations. We believe that the behavior of various ethnic groups can best be understood by examining the distinctive normative and social structure of these groups—the values, norms, roles, and social relationships that characterize them and differentiate them from other groups. Interracial relations, we believe, can be fruitfully examined as instances of status relations and processes. At the very least, to do so is to raise questions and pose problems that are missed if only historical or descriptive accounts are presented.

This book is an attempt to introduce students to the discipline—and the fascination—of the analytical approach utilized by sociologists.

W. R. S.

ACKNOWLEDGMENTS

It is proper to at least acknowledge the debts that cannot be repaid. I am indebted to my former teachers at the University of Kansas and the University of Chicago for the richness of their insights and the generosity with which they shared them with me. I am indebted to my colleagues and students at Stanford University for many years of stimulating "postgraduate" education.

Even more obviously, I am indebted to the many authors and publishers who consented to having their works reprinted in this book. I trust that my editorial commentary in no way detracts from the value of their contributions.

Additional thanks are due to Rosalind Revell for expert secretarial and editorial assistance and to my wife, Joy Whitney Scott, for untold hours devoted to the preparation of "our book."

CONTENTS

Social Processes
and Social Structures

PART ONE

Introduction

SOME CHARACTERISTICS OF PRESENT-DAY SOCIOLOGY

Since ancient times, men have puzzled over the nature of social life and have tried in various ways to explain to themselves and others its seeming orderliness and its obvious defects. Some very perceptive insights about social life—along with much nonsense and prejudice—are contained in the folklore and the proverbs that are passed from one generation to another and in the writings of poets, philosophers, and social critics from the distant past down to the present. In what ways, if any, does the work of the modern-day sociologist differ from these attempts to understand and explain society?

Four attributes of the sociological approach help to distinguish it from earlier approaches and from other contemporary approaches to the study of society. Other characteristics could also be cited, but these four appear to us to be of central importance.

1. *Sociology aims at the formulation of general principles that can be used to explain certain features of social life.* This is neither the time nor the place for a general discussion of the philosophy and methodology of science, but a few comments are in order if the central features of the sociological enterprise are to be clarified. Sociology attempts to explain certain assertions or statements concerning a social phenomenon by showing that they can be deduced from more general principles or lawlike statements. The assertions to be explained may themselves be general statements believed to apply universally to phenomena of a given type, or they may be singular statements referring to a specific time or place. Thus, a sociologist might be concerned with attempting to explain why conformity is higher in more cohesive groups (a universal proposition) or why the Socialist party in the United States has been relatively unsuccessful in attracting the labor vote (a singular proposition). In approaching the latter type

1

of question, however, the sociologist who is true to his calling will be as interested in developing and refining the explanatory principles as he will be in explaining the singular predicament of the Socialists. It is this concern with the formulation of general principles that distinguishes sociology and the other social sciences from other disciplines like history, which is primarily occupied with the description and explanation of unique historical occurrences. It is true, of course, that insofar as a historian attempts to explain a particular historical occurrence, he must assume the existence of and make use of general laws; but, typically, "historians do not regard it as part of their aim to *establish* such laws."[1]

Before the reader's hopes and expectations for sociology are set impossibly high, however, we must hasten to point out that by no means all contemporary sociologists aim at the development of general explanatory principles. We see this as the most important task of sociology, but it is not the only one. Much of what goes on in sociology today may be accurately described as the writing of contemporary history, because its primary purpose is to describe and perhaps to explain a particular set of circumstances or events. It is to this type of activity that Hughes refers when he notes that "It has become a part of the mission of sociologists to catch the goings-on of people and institutions at the time; . . . ." (Reading 2) Thus, we have sociological studies of the Watts race riot and of the 1968 presidential campaign, of the hippie colony in San Francisco and of the taxicab driver in Chicago. Such studies are often enormously interesting and may be invaluable to members of special publics or to policy makers. However, from our point of view, they contribute but little to the central task of sociology: the building of sociological theory. Even in the cases where the investigators go beyond description and attempt to explain the phenomenon under investigation, the resulting theory is often unsatisfactory. Why is this so? One important reason is suggested by Cohen, who points out the necessity of distinguishing between the explanation of "events" and "statements about events."[2] To capture the uniqueness and complexity of a given event, a great many statements can and must be made—so many, in fact, that no single principle or set of principles can hope to adequately account for the complexity of the observed phenomenon. The investigator focusing on a particular event will often attempt to explain too much. And, as Cohen notes, "As the desire to explain more and more aspects of a single study, situation, or phenomenon increases, the possibility of using this explanation outside the situation for which it was created approaches the vanishing point."[3] By contrast, the sociologist interested in formulating general principles must be content to explain only a limited number of statements about the event; he must be selective in his approach to the phenomenon in question, recognizing the limitations inherent in applying any set of principles. His reward, however, may be the development and refinement of principles that are applicable to a variety of different situations, not just to a single time and place.

In a very real sense, the world is comprised of unique events and occurrences. No two events or situations are exactly alike in every respect. Hence, if the

---

[1] Ernest Nagel, *The Structure of Science*, New York: Harcourt, p. 550. Emphasis in oringinal.
[2] Bernard P. Cohen, "On the construction of sociological explanations," paper presented at the annual meeting of The American Sociological Association, Miami, Fla., 1966.
[3] Cohen.

sociologist is to attempt to develop generalizations based on descriptions of such events, he is obliged to be both *selective* and *abstract* in his approach to these materials. Similarly, if the sociologist hopes to apply generalizations in explaining certain phenomena in the world, he must selectively approach these materials and must treat the data as instances of his more general analytical categories.

Perhaps these observations may be clarified by an example. Suppose a historian and a sociologist both wish to examine the life of Lindbergh, the famous American aviator. The historian would probably attempt to carefully reconstruct the critical events in the life of this man, emphasizing the uniqueness of his background and experiences. The sociologist would be more apt to treat Lindbergh as an instance of a more general phenomenon—perhaps that of "hero"—in order to develop or apply certain general principles that would help to account for selected aspects of his career (as well as the careers of other similar personages) . The sociologist interested in heroes would not attempt to account for all that transpired in this man's life but would be highly selective in his approach. Thus, he might completely ignore the kidnapping episode, although the historian could hardly choose to ignore such a notorious event in his subject's life. The sociologist's approach would also be abstract. He might, for example, utilize the abstract concept of "charisma"—highly regarded abilities or qualities— which would allow him to treat as similar for purposes of analysis behaviors or characteristics that appear to be quite different. Thus, Lindberg's prowess as an aviator may be placed in the same category with General MacArthur's skills as a military leader or Roosevelt's oratorical skills.[4] Such abstractions allow the sociologist (1) to examine data on specific cases (Lindbergh, MacArther, Roosevelt) in order to develop general principles concerning the behavior of heroes and (2) to apply general principles concerning the behavior of heroes to specific cases, for example, by deducing certain statements that would be expected to apply to Lindbergh. It is the combination of selectivity and abstractness that allows sociologists to concentrate on the formulation of general principles, even when they are attempting to explain certain facets of a singular occurrence.

2. *Sociologists attempt to confront their generalizations with facts, that is, with empirical data.* Alfred North Whitehead, in his short classic *Science and the Modern World,* describes in general terms this combination of interests:

> This new tinge of modern minds is a vehement and passionate interest in the relation of general principles to irreducible and stubborn facts. All the world over and at all times there have been practical men, absorbed in "irreducible and stubborn facts": all the world over and at all times there have been men of a philosophic temperament who have been absorbed in the weaving of general principles. It is this union of passionate interest in the detailed facts with equal devotion to abstract generalization which forms the novelty of our present society. Previously it had appeared sporadically and as if by chance. This balance of mind has now become part of the tradition which infects cultivated thought.[5]

The sociologist shares with other scientists this "balance of mind." The empirical bent of the modern sociologist is one of the major characteristics that differenti-

---

[4]Of course, the sociologist would need to supply a set of statements that would serve to relate characteristics like aviation and military skill with the concept of charisma. Such statements are an important part of any theory and are often referred to as "initial conditions."

[5]Alfred North Whitehead, *Science and the Modern World,* New York: Macmillan, 1925, pp. 3-4.

ate him from past generations of "social thinkers" and "social philosophers." Sociological generalizations must be stated in a precise enough manner that they are subject—directly or indirectly—to refutation: a scientific generalization is one that can be proven false.

As the selection in this section by Hughes suggests, sociologists employ a wide variety of research techniques and gather their empirical data from a wide variety of settings. The techniques vary from informal observations of natural human groups at work or play to sophisticated experiments in which the investigator is able to control many aspects of the situation under study and to systematically vary others to determine their effects. It is certainly true that sociologists, along with other social scientists, are often guilty of employing techniques that are at best sloppy and ill-conceived; but it is also true, particularly in the last decade or two, that sociologists are becoming more skilled in the gathering and analysis of their materials. Nevertheless, for every piece of sociological research confronted, the discerning student should demand of the author "How do you know?" "On what evidence are your conclusions based?" Much of the material that passes for sociology cannot stand up under these basic queries, but a growing body of sociological research can.

The settings in which sociological studies are conducted should be selected on the basis of their relevance to the problems examined—not vice versa with the choice of setting determining the problems examined. There is an unfortunate tendency among sociologists to "specialize" in research settings rather than in theoretical problems. Thus, we have sociologists who specialize in "urban," or "industrial," or "medical" sociology. This basis of specialization may be useful for the transmission of knowledge to persons interested in these areas of endeavor; but it does not seem well calculated to advance sociology as a science because it does not encourage the formulation and testing of general principles. The limitations of "setting-specialization" include the following: (1) settings do not encourage a problem focus because a large range of sociological problems can be found in each of them, although, assuredly, such problems may take on different guises in the various settings; (2) very often, a given problem may be much more easily and directly researched in one setting rather than another; those sociologists committed to a given setting are less likely to exploit such advantages; and (3) a person who has investigated a given problem in only one kind of setting tends either to generalize his findings inappropriately to other settings or to limit his findings inappropriately to that setting when further studies in different settings would reveal them to be highly general across contexts.

Finally, while we are discussing methodological problems of our field, it is well to remind the beginning student that all problem areas of sociology are not equally well developed. Choice of research methods is dictated not only by the nature of the problem to be solved but also by how much is already known about the phenomenon in question. When little information of any kind is available, the appropriate sociological method may be the pedestrian exploratory observation of selected aspects of the phenomenon—a kind of glorified social bookkeeping. As more is learned, perhaps elementary distinctions can be introduced—the beginnings of a classification system. Later, as relationships among variables begin to become clear, more systematic data collection may be in order as simple hypotheses are checked. Then, as knowledge accumulates, it may be possible to formulate theories, to devise experiments, and even to construct rigorous mathematical models to represent the interrelation of the major variables present. The point is that any science develops in stages, and what is an appropriate technique at one stage may be inappropriate for another. It is essential to note at the outset of this book that most areas of sociology are at a relatively early stage of development.

3. *Sociologists strive for objectivity in their collection, analysis, and interpretation of data.* The sociologist's approach to his data is, insofar as possible, value-free: he attempts to describe and explain what is, not what he hopes for or would prefer to see occur.

The difficulties of achieving such dispassionate neutrality in sociology, or for that matter, in any of the social sciences, should not be discounted. As Kemeny notes in his chapter reprinted in this section (Reading 1), the emotional and ethical pressures on the investigator to arrive at "desirable" results come not only from the outside world but "from within the scientist" as well. Many psychological studies have demonstrated how the values and needs of an individual influence not only what he chooses to observe ("selective perception") but even cause him to distort what he does observe. Bertrand Russell has wryly noted such problems in commenting on the behavior of psychologists studying animal behavior:

> The manner in which animals learn has been much studied in recent years, with a great deal of patient observation and experimentation. . . . One may say broadly that all the animals that have been carefully observed have behaved so as to confirm the philosophy in which the observer believed before his observations began. Nay, more; they have all displayed the national characteristics of the observer. Animals studied by Americans rush about frantically, with an incredible display of hustle and pep, and at last achieve the desired result by chance. Animals observed by Germans sit still and think, and at last evolve the solution out of their inner consciousness [6]

Lord Russell has no doubt somewhat exaggerated the amount of distortion occurring, but there is no question that the problem described is a real one. And if the problem is present to some degree when animals are the object of study, how much more likely is it to occur when the subjects are human actors? A social scientist who attempts to behave as a "scientist" cannot completely overcome the fact that he is also "social" in his own makeup.[7] For example, a social scientist who examines the effects of "democratic" versus "dictatorial" leadership patterns on the behavior of groups may be constrained by the attitudes of his potential audience as well as by his own values to "see" the democratic pattern as the superior one. Numerous observers, noting such real problems, quickly conclude that a true social *science* can never be developed.

Such a conclusion, however, seems overly pessimistic. The sociologist has numerous aids to bolster his neutrality, chief among which is the scientific method. Scientific method is a vast and complex subject in its own right and cannot be discussed here in any detail except to note that it has been developed

---

[6]Bertrand Russell, *Philosophy*, New York: Norton, 1927, pp. 29–30.
[7]The physical scientist is also "social" in this sense. However, it is probably the case that his subject matter is less likely to be as emotion-laden as is that dealt with by the social scientist, although there are certainly important exceptions to this generalization.

over the years in large part as a means whereby an individual wanting to solve a problem can partially protect himself from his own biases, even from those of which he is not conscious. For example, in the collection of data, the use of random or representative samples protects the investigator from the biases that might affect his selection of cases; statistical techniques help to provide decision rules for determining whether or not an observed relationship is or is not likely to have occurred by chance, and various kinds of "self-blinding" techniques can be employed. As an illustration of the technique, suppose a social scientist wants to use IQ test scores to determine if there are differences in intelligence as measured by this instrument between white and black students; and suppose further that the scientist is politically a liberal who prefers that the results show no significant differences between the races. One technique he could employ to protect his data from the unconscious intrusion of his own liberal values is to ask his assistant to code each of the IQ tests in such a way that he will not know as he scores them whether a given test schedule was completed by a black or a white student. Only after the tests have been scored are they classified according to the race of the test subjects. The investigator thus "blinds" himself to the racial composition of his subjects and in this manner prevents his own racial attitudes from influencing his scoring of test performances.

The scientific method is only one of the mechanisms available for fostering objectivity on the part of the individual scientist. Another important support is provided by the structure of the scientific community. The community serves to develop and support basic scientific norms (rules) such as those forbidding the falsification of data or those emphasizing that all relevant data shall be reported, not just the portions that are consistent with the investigator's hypothesis. It also promotes the cause of truth by encouraging its members to find fault with the work of their colleagues: one of the most highly valued activities of a scientist is to reveal the mistakes and biases of his colleagues by reanalyzing their data, by repeating their studies, and so on. In general, little faith should be placed in any scientific finding until it has withstood over a period of time the efforts of these scientific wrecking crews.

Yet another support for dispassionate research is to be found in the institutional setting within which the scientist works. Although this may seem a controversial statement, we would argue that the more a scientist is removed from the immediate and direct pressures of the world around him, the more objective his work is likely to be. Thus, it would seem that the most conducive atmosphere for the development of a social science worthy of the name will be in a university or basic-science setting—an "ivory tower" far from the pressures of politicians and managers who want a solution for their problem "tomorrow" or who already have arrived at an answer and turn to the social scientist only for supporting evidence. And as universities increasingly become caught up in the day-to-day business of running a society, other kinds of scientific retreats may have to be devised where research can be carried on in a more politically neutral atmosphere.

4. *Sociology is distinguished from other approaches, and particularly from the other social sciences, by the specific concepts it employs.* A concept is simply a definition of what is to be studied or observed. Concepts are tools for sifting through the complex reality of social life. Thus, they are both devices for

learning more about the world, on the one hand, and devices for ignoring a great deal that we know but do not want to be bothered with, on the other hand. For example, when physicists study the motions of round metal objects, such concepts as mass and velocity focus the physicists' attention on certain of the objects' properties and help the physicists to ignore other properties the objects possess, such as color and chemical composition.

Any given phenomenon can be investigated in a large variety of ways, depending on which sets of concepts ("conceptual schemes") are brought to bear on it. Take, by way of illustration, the act of shaving performed by a man in the morning. A physician, particularly a dermatologist, might be concerned with evidence of skin irritation; a market researcher might be interested in why one type of razor was purchased rather than another; and the sociologist might prefer to speculate on the sorts of social norms that press on men to persuade them of the value and necessity of carrying out such an irksome daily ritual. This simple illustration points up two conclusions of importance: (1) "facts" do not select themselves—they are produced by the employment of one or another conceptual scheme and (2) "facts" do not speak for themselves—they must be interpreted in the light of some set of concepts. In short, there is a very close relation between theory and research. Theories are comprised of sets of concepts and statements about expected relations among these concepts under specified conditions. Selectivity is always involved in any perception of the empirical world; in the case of scientific observations, a more-or-less well-developed conceptual scheme furnishes the basis for making such selections. And scientists attempt to make explicit, for themselves and for their publics, the concepts guiding their observations.

Because concepts are merely definitions of what it is we wish to observe, they are not themselves subject to empirical test. One cannot say that a given concept is either true or false, only that it is a more or a less useful way of selecting and organizing the observations. Data are gathered to test hypotheses or statements made about the relations among concepts, considered as variables. Take, for example, the hypothesis that a high degree of task complexity within organizations is associated with a large administrative staff. Here the crucial concepts are "task complexity" and "size of administrative staff"; they are treated as variables in that we are concerned with differing amounts of each; and our hypothesis consists of a statement that with a given level of one variable will be found a given level of another. Such a statement obviously may be either true or false, and only observations of organizations with varying degrees of task complexity and varying sizes of administrative staffs will resolve the matter. Of course, two concepts and one hypothesis do not make a theory. Many abstract concepts, logically interrelated, together with interlocking sets of predictions, only some of which it may be necessary to empirically test, are required before one can properly speak of a theory. Nevertheless, concepts and hypotheses are the basic building blocks of any theory.

The concepts employed by the sociologist must be carefully defined to refer to selected aspects of the phenomenon on which he wishes to focus. The subject matter of the sociologist, however, is for the most part the familiar world of everyday social life. This poses yet another problem for the development of our field. The sociological analyst may choose to use familiar terms—the conventional language used by other members of his society—as his concepts, employing such terms as conformity, authority, loyalty, acceptance, family, and community. But in using these terms, the sociologist who attempts to define them precisely must expect to endure such criticisms as: "But, you have left out___!" "That's not what *I* mean by___!" or, "I know what___ is; let's get on with it!" Attempting another kind of solution, the sociologist may decide to avoid the associations and connotations of familiar terms by inventing new ones that he can then define to mean exactly what he wants them to. Neologisms like "tinsit," "syntality," and "satisfice" are the result. Far from pleasing everyone, however, such terms are attacked as barbarisms by the defenders of the king's English who see no point in adding new and tasteless words to our language (although the same individuals do not protest when the physical scientist coins his novel terms). Most sociologists have decided that old terms with all their problems are better than new terms, and the result is that we will be forced to spend a good deal of time in this book explaining the special meaning attached by sociologists to familiar terms. It is part of our fate to labor mightily to carefully define terms for which "everyone" knows the meaning.

THE AIM OF SOCIOLOGY

In order to decide whether any sociological concept is useful, it is necessary to have some general notion as to what it is that sociologists want to do. Although many definitions of sociology have been offered, it seems to us that the simplest and most satisfactory one is that sociology seeks to describe and explain the nature of social order and social disorder.

Many sociologists appear to be more intrigued with social order than with social disorder, and, when we stop to consider it, the amount of order exhibited by social phenomena is somewhat impressive. Every day, millions of individual members in many different societies perform billions of actions, and yet the outcome is not bedlam, not total confusion or chaos, but rather, a reasonable approximation of order. On the other hand, a sociologist cannot afford to overlook the real and powerful tendencies toward conflict, disruption, and disintegration. We must conclude that some natural forces work together to produce order and stability while other equally natural forces make for conflicts in and disruptions of existing social arrangements. Both kinds of forces must be of concern to us.

Some sociologists have probably put too much emphasis on social order in their analysis of a given society or social arrangement. They have sometimes assumed more integration and stability than is in fact present; they have emphasized the contribution a given belief or practice makes to the stability and continuity of the existing order without paying sufficient attention to the problems it may cause or the changes it may evoke; and they have given too much attention to the harmonious and consensual beliefs of participants in the social unit. Reacting and, indeed, often overreacting to these views of social unity and harmony, other sociologists have emphasized change, tension, conflict, and coercion as the bedrock of social life. Neither set of assumptions is universally valid and applicable; and some combination of them would seem to be called for if a complete and accurate view of the social world is to be gained. Furthermore, we must be careful not to attach ethical evaluations to either social order or disorder. Social order and disorder may result from tyrannical as well as democratic processes—to name two processes for which many of us have value preferences—and either form is equally grist for the sociologist's mill.

It is perhaps apparent that our sociological objective is not a particularly modest one: it means that all social activities are of potential interest to us. However, it must be emphasized that *not all aspects of all social activities* are of interest to the sociologist; we do not propose to encompass all of human existence in our formulations. Our sociological concepts, to be discussed in more detail later, allow us to select the phenomena of particular relevance for our purposes from the infinite varieties of social activities being carried on at any particular time or place.

Finally, we should point out that in examining the nature of social order and disorder it is not always necessary—and is often a tactical mistake—to seek answers by making an entire society our basic unit of analysis. The founding fathers of our discipline did, with a few notable exceptions, attempt to comprehend entire societies in their formulations. Such early sociologists as Auguste Comte, Henri de St. Simon, Vilfredo Pareto, Karl Marx, Emile Durkheim, Max Weber, and William Graham Sumner were primarily concerned with developing general laws applicable to whole societies or broad segments thereof. However, as the immense complexity of modern societies became apparent, the movement in sociology has increasingly been away from the study of macrosocial units to the study of microsocial units. Social relationships, small groups, and organizations are the constituent units out of which institutions and societies are composed. It is clearly an easier task—and, we would argue, a theoretical task of equal importance—to explore the bases of social order and disorder at these levels as at the macrolevel of the society as a whole. In the long run, studies of microstructure cannot substitute for analyses of macrostructure, but they can provide an important foundation for and supplement to such studies.

The flight of sociologists from large-scale to smaller-scale social units in which more rigorous analyses may be attempted has led some critics of the discipline to accuse our academic fraternity of cowardice. We are condemned for running away from the "really important" social problems and are said to spend our lives in the minute study of social "trivia."[8] In some instances these criticisms are undoubtedly justified. Sociology, like all professions, contains some overly cautious men who are all too willing to pull in their horns at the first sight of controversy or conclusions that depart from the majority opinion on some current issue. Such criticism, however, fails to take into account two considerations. The first is stressed by Kemeny, who, in effect, suggests that social scientists must learn to walk before they run, that the cause of science may be best served by those who begin by "finding laws describing extremely simple and basically uninteresting phenomena." Second, it fails to recognize that what may be trivial from an immediately practical perspective may have great theoretical significance and, hence, important practical implications in the long run. What could be more trivial than studies of fruit flies? But studies of the sex life of this insignificant insect have made important contributions to the development of genetic principles. And why should anyone have been concerned

---

[8]See, for example, the criticisms of C. Wright Mills in *The Sociological Imagination*, New York: Oxford, 1959, especially his chapter on abstracted empiricism.

with such trivial phenomena as dreams when there were really important things to study? But Freud, with his patient attention to detail and his keen mind, was able to demonstrate their nontrivial use as diagnostic and therapeutic tools. And can you imagine a professor from Harvard wasting years of his time by hanging out with a small band of disreputable men in a Boston slum? But William Foote Whyte was able to use his careful observations of this "street corner society" to make important contributions to our understanding of leadership behavior and social mobility. These few illustrations should serve to remind us that the dividing line between the important and the trivial is a somewhat uncertain one. In the final analysis, what a scientist looks at may not be nearly so crucial as what he sees.

1 The Social Sciences

John G. Kemeny

"Speak English!" said the Eaglet. "I don't know the meaning of half those long words, and, what's more, I don't believe you do either!"

The basic issue in the philosophy of the social sciences is the question of whether Man can be studied by the same methods that apply to lower beings or inanimate nature. This is perhaps the most debated question in the philosophy of Science . . .

THE STATUS OF THE SOCIAL SCIENCES

It is certainly true that the physical sciences have developed to a stage far beyond that of the social sciences of today and even of the anticipated future. If one examines the laws of the physical sciences and compares those with known laws in the social sciences, they seem to belong to a different species. A typical law in the physical sciences is stated precisely, usually in mathematical terms, and is quite free of ambiguity. It has been tested repeatedly and has withstood the tests. The usual law in the social sciences, on the other hand, is ordinarily couched in Big Words and a great deal of ambiguity. The law is usually presented with many qualifications and excuses. There are probably several exceptions known to the law, but the law still has its advocates as the best we know so far. The law in the physical sciences has enabled us to deduce precisely certain predictions which have been verified. While predictions have been attributed to the social law, the chances are that they simply reflect prejudices or commonsense knowledge of the authors of the law, and that these predictions have not been deduced from the law itself.

If we question the leaders of the field, it is quite likely that they will give us many reasons why the social sciences are so far behind the physical sciences. They will point out that the physical sciences deal with such simple objects as an atom, whereas the social sciences have to deal with human beings, singly or in groups. It will be pointed out that the basic tool of the physical scientist is the laboratory experiment, but such experiments are not permissible in the social sciences. Such reasons are legitimate methodological arguments. They may convince us that it is much harder to find laws in the social sciences than in the physical sciences.

In addition to methodological arguments we will also find frequent discussion of why, in principle, it is impossible for the social sciences to become truly scientific. We are told that inanimate objects obey laws, but human beings do not. We are told that within animate nature prediction is possible; with human beings, due to their free will, prediction is, in principle, impossible. Above all, we

Reprinted from John G. Kemeny, *A Philosopher Looks at Science*, Princeton, N.J.: Van Nostrand, 1959, pp. 244–258, by permission of the author and the publisher.

are told that social sciences must be basically different from physical sciences, since questions of value enter the former but not the latter. For these reasons, a purely scientific approach to the social sciences is supposed to be impossible.

However, we have already examined arguments of these sorts and found them untenable. The first argument is based on the mistaken belief that nature "obeys" laws in the sense in which human beings obey them. Due to this mistaken belief it is natural to suppose that human beings could disobey laws of nature in the same way that they disobey human laws. However, as soon as we realize that the laws of nature simply describe what actually takes place, this type of objection becomes absurd. Why should it be harder in principle to describe the actions of human beings than the actions of atoms? If anything, it should be easier, since we have direct experience of what it is like to carry out human acts. The second argument, concerning predictability, was considered in Chapter 13.[1] We found that free will is in no way incompatible with the possibility of prediction. Indeed, there have already been many fine examples of predictions in the social sciences. Yet none of us feel that our free will has been infringed upon.

The final argument, concerning value statements, is at the heart of a great many of these objections. This problem was considered in Chapter 14.[2] It is, of course, entirely possible to insist that the social sciences should deal with questions of value. If the purpose of this activity is to find answers to value questions, then it is certainly true that the social sciences will have to be fundamentally different from the physical sciences. However, this is a verbal argument. It cannot be denied that it is in principle

[1]Chapter dealing with the mind. [Ed.]
[2]Chapter dealing with science and values. [Ed.]

feasible and in practice important to find scientific laws which will enable us to correlate human means to human ends. This type of activity is appropriately described as social science, and it can be handled by the scientific method discussed in this book. It would seem to me most fruitful that only this activity should be called "social science," since the advocates of the other type of undertaking admit that it is not manageable by scientific methods. Of course, we run up against vested interests. There are many members of social science departments in our universities who teach what is right and what is wrong, and they would be afraid that, if these activities were labeled as unscientific, they might lose their positions.

Closely related to this debate is the question as to whether social sciences should deal primarily with historical laws. In this they would serve primarily to relate what has already taken place, to classify the various acts, and to try to rationalize the motives that led human beings to act in certain ways. In any science the gathering and classification of facts is an important first step. But if we can learn any lesson at all from the physical sciences, we must realize that this is a bare beginning. Real success comes only after this stage has been left for the higher activity of theory formation.

We have noted earlier that it is questionable whether classification of facts can ever take place without having some theory in mind. Indeed, historians usually have a thesis that they would like to establish, and they present historical facts to serve as evidence for their proposed hypothesis. In a field that is very unprecise, this is a dangerous kind of activity. The temptation is great to twist the historical facts to fit a proposed hypothesis. Indeed, we find social scientists constantly accusing each other of having done precisely this.

Let us, therefore conclude that in principle there is no difficulty in applying the scientific method to the social sciences, but in practice we run up against severe difficulties. Let us now turn to the consideration of these difficulties.

METHOD IN THE SOCIAL SCIENCES

We have analyzed the scientific method into three major stages: the formation of theories, the deduction of consequences, and the verification of predictions. We will consider how these activities take place in the social sciences, taking the activities in reverse order.

First, there are obvious difficulties confronting us in verifying a given prediction. Let us suppose that a given theory predicts that, when ten million people are isolated on a desert island for a hundred years, certain social phenomena will take place. Clearly there is no practical way to verify this prediction. One may have to wait for a historical accident for such an event to take place, and the waiting period may be forever. The social scientist is quite right in pointing out that the physicist has a great advantage with his controlled laboratory conditions and his ability to observe under ideal conditions.

Laboratories for the social sciences are now in existence at many universities throughout the world. However, it is a difficult question whether human beings isolated in a specially built observation room behave the way they would normally behave. The experimentalists among the social scientists have been accused of searching for laws that will apply only in these isolation booths. Nevertheless, it is reasonable to believe that, for certain simple types of actions, these experiments might be entirely satisfactory. The history of Science points out that each branch must start with the formation of simple laws which are later extended to cover the really interesting cases. But even among the experimental-

ists one finds that it is hard to reproduce an experiment exactly.

Take a specific example. A dispute has arisen among certain experimental psychologists as to how subjects behave under given conditions. An interesting experiment which is described by W. K. Estes, one of the pioneers in psychological learning theory, is the following: A subject is asked to guess whether a light in front of him will go on within the next five seconds. After he has guessed, the light may or may not be turned on, according to a predetermined pattern. Suppose that the experimenter turns on the light at random, with the light coming on 75 per cent of the time. If the subject would know this fact, and if he maximized his chances of guessing correctly on any one try, he would guess "Yes" each time. However, this is not what the subjects actually do. It was shown that, in the long run, the subject will guess "Yes" 75 per cent of the time and "No" the rest of the time. As a result of this, he will be right only 62.5 per cent of the time, thus doing considerably worse than is possible for him to do.

Other experimenters have carried out "the same" experiment and have found that the subjects eventually guess only "Yes." However, when we look into the experimental procedures, we notice certain differences. In the first group of experiments, the subject is asked to go on guessing and is not allowed time to consider the best way to proceed. In the second group of experiments, the subject is asked to pause after a certain number of trials and is given a chance to consider whether what he is doing is the best that he can possibly do. The real question now is whether the two experimenters have carried out the same experiment or not. I would certainly feel that these two sets of experiments are drastically different and that the results show reactions to different conditions; but the fact that eminent psychologists disagree on this point exemplifies a basic source of trouble in experimental social science.

Last but not least is the difficulty of trying to verify a prediction about the future. The fact that you are carrying out this verification may alter the actions of your subject, either to bring about verification or to destroy it.

The difficulties that have been given least thought are the difficulties in deducing consequences of laws in the social sciences. Of course, it has been pointed out frequently that precise deductions from vague laws are impossible. It is not worth dwelling on this question. Let us consider only those rare laws in the social sciences which have been precisely stated. We know that deduction in any science amounts to the solution of simple or complex mathematical problems. Since the social sciences are still in their baby shoes, it has been assumed that the solution of whatever mathematical problems may arise in the social sciences must be elementary. This has been the principal reason why most of the leading mathematicians have ignored applications to the social sciences. However, this is far from being the true picture.

To understand this assertion we must consider the nature of mathematical knowledge. In any actual application one deals only with a finite number of objects. Let us classify such applications typically into three categories: In the first category one deals with a small number of objects, let us say five. In the second category one may have 5000 or 50,000 objects. In the third category one would typically have five billion or five billion billion objects. The first type of problem is the kind which can be solved by elementary mathematical methods, by working through all possibilities one at a time. It might seem that the hardest type of question is that dealing with billions or billions of billions of objects; however, here is where the calculus has made a

tremendous contribution. We have found that for many such problems one may assume that there are infinitely many objects, and hence apply powerful mathematical tools developed just to answer such questions. For example, in physics, when we wish to measure the velocity of an object, we assume that, at least in principle, we can make infinitely many observations of the position of the object. Hence the methods of the calculus are applicable.

It is the intermediate region of five thousand to fifty thousand objects where neither of these methods is applicable. The numbers involved are too large to try all possibilities, and yet the numbers are too small for the analytic methods of the calculus to lead to accurate results. As a matter of fact, the only reasonable description of this mathematical situation is that we have not yet developed the kind of mathematics that is needed in the intermediate region. Because of this, problems in the social sciences are not easier than in the physical sciences, but actually considerably harder. Here we have a good example of progress in a branch of science having to await mathematical progress. Unless more of the really able mathematicians take an interest in these problems, this field will be very slow in developing.

Perhaps it is misleading to say that there are few really interesting and precise laws known in the social sciences. It may be quite unfair to the social scientist to say that he has developed only the most trivial theories. A fairer statement might be that only some of the more trivial theories have been treated to a degree where one can judge their adequacy. Many more laws have been proposed, but one very quickly runs into mathematical problems that exceed our ability for solving them.

Finally, we have the problem of theory formation in the social sciences. Here we run into the greatest difficulty facing the

social scientist, and this is a handicap in motivation. The physical sciences developed at a time when no one had any clear idea of the potential of Science. As a result, physicists were content in finding laws describing extremely simple and basically uninteresting phenomena. But since then the physical sciences have shown us that scientific development can lead to wealth and power for nations. The social scientists are understandably impatient in reaching a status where they themselves can make an active contribution to the development of civilization. It certainly takes remarkable human patience and humility to study the behavior of five human adults solving a childishly simple problem, when the social scientist has confronting him the problem of predicting inflations or financial crashes or of making predictions as to how a given nation can increase its wealth and position in the world. Yet all precedent points in the direction that it is the former that will lead to progress, and not the latter.

It is also difficult to keep emotional overtones out of hypotheses. Any human being is anxious about the ethical implications of actions. It is hard to formulate an unemotional version of the prospective results of human undertakings. In the history of the laws of celestial motion we realize how fortunate the astronomers were in not really caring what the exact paths of celestial bodies were, as long as they could describe them precisely. As a matter of fact, when some of these questions acquired political or religious overtones, they led to bad science. When it became a heresy for Galileo to maintain a view contrary to the accepted doctrine, it certainly had the effect of stifling the progress of physics. Fortunately, in this case there were scientists in other countries who could proceed in freedom. The difficulty in the social sciences is that the pressure to arrive at "desirable" results comes not from the outside but from within the scientist. He himself would like

to believe that certain kinds of actions will produce desired results. He cannot help but search for laws that will enable him to make these predictions.

The physical scientists also had the great advantage that no generally accepted terminology was available for the phenomena they were studying. In many cases they had to coin new terms, and it was a matter of little interest to their colleagues, and to the public as a whole, what words they used. The social scientists face the dilemma of either trying to describe well-known phenomena in technical terms, or of falling heir to all the vagueness and ambiguity of everyday language. There is some justice in accusing the scientist of coining a new word unnecessarily for something well known. But if this well-known act is tied up with prejudices, hopes, and fears, a technical term may turn out to be more suitable. Thus the social scientist must create his technical vocabulary not in a vacuum but in a space that has been filled by useless and dangerous words.

Above all, the social scientists are right in saying that the phenomena they study are basically more complex than the phenomena of the physical scientists. Because of this it is hard to see where to start in the formation of fruitful concepts. Although the distinction between inertial and gravitational mass is a subtlety to be mastered only by twentieth-century genius, it was clear from an early stage that somehow the weight of an object affected its motion. In the study of motion it must have been clear from the beginning that the speed with which an object moves was important, though it took centuries of progress to realize that acceleration was more basic than velocity. In the study of human beings it is difficult to find any clear-cut concept that is certain to play a basic role in the study of Man.

To summarize, we find that laws are harder to form because of the tradition of vagueness, ambiguity, and emotive over-

tones in the subject matter, and because of the inherent complexity of human beings. We find it difficult to make predictions, because we quickly run into mathematical problems that are too hard for us. Even if we are fortunate enough to make predictions, we are not in a position to carry out carefully controlled experiments. We may make predictions that will take a long time, if not forever, to verify. Even in the cases where verification is possible, the number of cases we can study will be of a much smaller order of magnitude than in the physical sciences. Considering all these factors, it is not surprising that the social sciences have developed much more slowly than the physical sciences.

AN EXAMPLE

To make the ideas here presented more concrete, let us consider an example of a theory in the social sciences. I will take this example from economics, choosing a model of an expanding economy due to the late, very noted mathematician, John von Neumann. This theory presents certain hypotheses as to how an expanding economy, such as the present United States economy, behaves in equilibrium.

The terms "expanding economy" and "in equilibrium" are used in a precise sense in the theory. They correspond reasonably well to the meanings of these words in everyday language, but there are also dangers in carrying everyday meaning too far. The economy is represented by certain production processes which enable it to produce various goods in varying quantities. The theory makes predictions as to the amounts of these goods produced, and as to the prices assigned to the goods. The basic theorem states that there is at least one way for the economy to expand in equilibrium. There are only a finite number, and usually a very small number, of different

ways in which it can function in equilibrium. The largest possible rate of expansion is presumably the one in which it will function under ideal circumstances. There are other theorems of considerable interest to the economist, such as: in equilibrium the rate of interest in the economy equals the rate of expansion.

This theory has been attacked on many grounds. For example, it presupposes that there is a single interest rate in the country. One can certainly show many examples where various interest rates will be applicable to different segments of the economy. Of course there are many ways of getting out of this difficulty. The simplest is to say that our economy is not in equilibrium. Or one can say that the United States is highly complex, and actually it is several economies in one, each of which may be in a different equilibrium. These explanations are both plausible and potentially dangerous. After all, if we carry this far enough, no matter what example is brought up in attempting to disprove the theory, we could talk our way out of it. It is not too unreasonable to maintain that whatever the sense of "equilibrium" is, no economy is exactly in equilibrium. But if we take this position, then the question arises as to whether such theories are of any value.

Let us compare this with Newton's Law of Inertia, which states how a body behaves if there are no forces acting upon it. It is certainly true that such a situation can never exist in practice. No matter what body there is, there are at least gravitational forces acting upon it at all times. The most one can maintain is that a body far enough from the major masses in the universe will be approximately free of forces, and hence Newton's law should apply to it approximately. The same is true for any oversimplified theory, as von Neumann's no doubt is. One should have a clear-cut notion of when an economy is approx-

imately in equilibrium, and then one could test whether von Neumann's predictions actually hold true. The danger in this is that one may have to wait forever for such an economy to exist.

Next let us consider the problem of prices in the economy. Under many circumstances the theory will give us a unique set of prices that must be applicable to each stage of the expansion. Yet it is entirely possible that, as a matter of fact, none of these prices correspond to actual sums of money paid out by purchasers. For example, this theory, as well as many similar theories, assumes that any item that is overproduced by the economy will have to be worthless. In practice we may find that these items are sold at a great discount, for "practically nothing," but they certainly would not be given away free. We immediately run across obvious oversimplifications in the theory. The act of giving away goods freely is a costly one in a complex civilization. A foundation whose sole purpose is to give away money may allocate up to 15 per cent of its budget for costs of giving the money away. The theory takes no account of these costs.

Again, let us consider the problem of the distribution of goods. In order to demonstrate the existence of an equilibrium, one must assume that the goods produced are divisible in arbitrary amounts. If the product should happen to be a house, it is most peculiar that equilibrium should take place when a fractional number of houses is produced each year. Naturally, one hopes that rounding these numbers off to integers will not materially affect the theory and will present a picture that is close to the actual facts. But even then the question of treating goods is a difficult one. For example, can one treat labor as goods? Or does this violate the facts? Can the theory take the amount of labor and its expense into account the same way as it counts the number of shoes or the amount of steel used in production, or must it somehow be treated as an essentially different item?

This last question gets us into technical, economic questions, which are beyond the scope of this book. However, it was brought up as an example where emotional overtones interfere with the formation of a scientific theory. An economist who tries to treat human labor in the same way that shoes and steel are treated may be ridiculed by his colleagues, or attacked for degrading the subject matter. Of course, it is true that the law of free fall applies equally well to a human being and to a stone, but the vast majority of cases it is applied to inanimate objects, and the physicists escape this particular difficulty. Here we have an example of the greatest intellectual courage being needed. to produce theories without regard to our own prejudices, or to the prejudices of our fellow man.

The greatest danger in a theory, such as the one we are considering, is in the way that it may be used. Suppose that a businessman discovers that the American economy is expanding at a rate of 7 per cent, while the interest rate is only 6 per cent. He may then try to use this theory as a reason why the interest rate should be raised. Of course, the theory says nothing about what *should* be done. It states that, under such-and-such assumptions concerning the behavior of an economy, a certain relation will hold between the expansion rate and the interest rate in equilibrium. If, as a matter of fact, the interest rate is lagging behind the expansion rate, and the economy is in equilibrium, then the assumptions of the theory were incorrect.

Equally dangerous is the question as to whether the economy "should" be in equilibrium. Naturally, this question could be given a precise scientific meaning in terms of human ends commonly derived. However, the chances are that the word "equilibrium" will raise emotional overtones. It suggests stability, and hence a desirable condition. The moment that word enters the scientific literature, the danger is great that social scientists will commit us to working for an equilibrium, without seriously considering the ends to which these means will lead us.

The silliest objection that I have heard to this theory is the following: A social scientist worked through an example of a hypothetical economy and found that the theory did not predict an expansion, but predicted that this economy in equilibrium must be contracting. It was then maintained that a theory that is proposed as a theory of expansion is useless if it sometimes predicts the exact opposite. Here, of course, we are in one of hundreds of verbal pitfalls in using everyday words in the social sciences. The word "expansion" was used by von Neumann to cover expansion, standing still, and contracting. This sort of convenience has been useful in the physical sciences, but has not yet been generally accepted in other fields.

The obvious way out is to replace controversial words by mathematical symbols and conduct the discussion entirely in terms of these symbols. However, this solution has its own inherent dangers. The literature of mathematical applications to the social sciences is full of worthless examples, where intricate mathematical computations have been carried out for quantities that have no application to the world as we know it. The proponents maintain that this is a steppingstone toward the building of a theory of the actual world. The opponents maintain, equally vigorously, that the theory, even if improved, would shed no light on actual applications. This danger is not peculiar to the social sciences but to any science that is just beginning. The question of when a theory is the beginning of great progress and when it is a complete dead end is unanswerable. In the last analysis one must trust to the intuition of the experts in the field and hope that at least some of them are following that rare path which leads to success.

THE FUTURE OF THE SOCIAL SCIENCES

Perhaps a philosopher of Science may allow himself the luxury of crystal-ball-gazing concerning the future of the social sciences. We have seen that the social sciences are just beginning. We have discussed many methodological difficulties in the way of progress in the social sciences. Yet we have felt that there is no essential difference in the scientific method as applicable in the physical sciences, in Biology, Psychology, or in the social sciences. We have noted that the social sciences have the peculiar difficulty of constantly running across ethical questions, which can serve as a great hindrance to progress, but also as a great motivating force. What can we guess as to the future of this humanly all-important field?

The history of Science indicates that most of the avenues explored in the early stages of a branch will lead nowhere. Since the social sciences are more complex than any branch previously attacked by the scientist, we have every reason to believe that most, if not all, present theories will lead nowhere. But this by no means indicates that these undertakings are worthless. Without these false beginnings we would never find a fruitful approach.

We already see many examples where the difficulties in the social sciences correspond to shortcomings in our knowledge of Mathematics. Therefore, the history of social science is bound to be paralleled by great progress in the development of Mathematics. Indeed, there are distinguished mathematicians who believe that the inspiration that Mathematics received from the physical sciences has nearly come to its end, and that the great new developments in Mathematics will be inspired by problems in the social sciences.

The history of Science certainly indicates that any branch which develops becomes more mathematical. Therefore, the student, who selected the social sciences as a career in the past in order to avoid taking a Mathematics course, may find himself studying more and more Mathematics with the progress of his field. Even now we find specialized journals in various social sciences dealing with the applications of Mathematics, and every indication is that these will grow and eventually take over the entire field. Today an article using mathematical formulas would be looked at askance by many social scientists, while physics has already reached the stage where an article without formulas is held in suspicion. Three hundred years ago physicists still conducted most of their discussions in ordinary language. Today it takes the combined genius of Einstein and Infeld to write a book on modern Physics without formulas. Perhaps the social sciences have just entered this stage.

It is to be expected that for a long time the fruitful results in the social sciences will come in areas of little direct interest to Mankind. But sooner or later results will be obtained from which humans can take guidance for their everyday activities. This will be the stage where the social sciences will have to face their major crisis. It is permissible today for a social scientist to give us advice on what to do, because we don't really feel that he knows what he is talking about. But when this branch reaches a stage where it can make predictions about our actions, and about the results of our actions, with good regularity, human beings will have to face the difficult question of how far the experts are to be trusted in the most basic decisions.

But this stage, too, must pass. Eventually the social sciences will acquire a respectability matching that of the physical sciences. Then human beings who are not experts in a certain field will have to realize that their free decisions lie only in choosing the ends to be achieved. The means are best determined by experts. At this stage an average human being would no more decide whether a certain form of taxation is desirable or not than he would dare pit his own opinion as to the best structure for an airplane against that of the expert engineer.

Without a doubt many of us shudder at the thought of giving up these decisions. However, a by-product of this development is bound to be that we will be forced to think about the ends to be achieved and, perhaps for the first time, be forced to do this in a precise and meaningful form. Ideally the progress of all of Science should reach a stage where the nonscientist would be relieved of all considerations of technical questions, and the sole decisions left up to him would be questions of right and wrong.

2 The Improper Study of Man

Everett Cherrington Hughes

The proper study of mankind is man. But what men shall we study to learn most about mankind, or simply about people? Those long dead, those now living, those unborn? The learned or the unlettered? The lowly, or those of high degree? Those nearby and of color and deportment like the student's own, or men of strange mien and demeanour? The men of the kraal, or those of the city? Faithful or infidel, the virtuous or the vicious? Are all equally human, or are some a little more so than others, so that what one learns about them is of wider application? Where should one start? At the earliest possible beginning, working toward the present by way of the peoples who were in some sense more directly our ancestors? Shall we produce the future from the lines of the past? Or should we, exploiting our experience of living men, apply to both past and future the lessons of the present?

And by what means shall we learn of those whom we choose to study? Suppose we elect to study living people. Shall we put our trust in studying great numbers, or at least such numbers as, properly selected, will represent all sorts and conditions of men in true proportion? Or shall we pick a few whose doings we observe as under a microscope and whose minds we probe for thoughts, desires, and memories, even for such as they themselves know not of? By what ideas, schemes, and formulae shall we reduce what we find to order? And, not least, how much of what we learn shall we tell those whom we have studied, the larger public, or our colleagues? What principles shall guide us in the discovery of men's secrets; what, in the telling of them?

Shall we wait for those crucial things to happen which offer most increase to our knowledge of this or that aspect of human life, and travel fast and far to catch events on the wing? Or shall we set up experiments, bringing people together under circumstances so controlled as to get precisely the answers we want next? Shall we study people in small groups and communities, and hope to find ways of expanding our findings without distortion to the big world? Shall we look at people where nothing happens save the turn of seasons and generations, and where men are of one breed and of one mind, taking that as man's normal state? Or shall we study men in the seething flux of cities, migrations, crusades, and wars, wherever breeds mingle and minds clash?

To what of people's doings shall we more closely attend: their politics, their religion, their work, their play, their poems, their philosophies, their sciences, their crafts? What, finally, should be the form of our questions: "What were people like and what did they do?" "What are they doing?" "What will they do?" or

"What would they do if—?"

The academic departments which study people are distinguished from each other by their choices from among these and similar possibilities. Some species of academic man insist on a single answer, explicitly stated. Most of us combine explicit answers with less conscious predilection for some kinds of human material rather than others. Some like to think of themselves as scientists; others as artists, critics, or moral judges. Some love the adventure of digging up manuscripts long buried in dust. Some like to crack a script, or to put together the fragments of ancient pots or temples. Others like to express behavior in mathematical formulae. Still others like to study living men, to discover new things about their own kind still warm, or to detect commonplace motives under the apparently strange ways of exotic people. But preference for one kind of study does not prevent scholars from having a try at other kinds and methods of study now and again. Again and again some academic people, or even rank outsiders, discontent with the set ways of academic study, go off on some new path of discovery, or simply take as their major preoccupation what others have considered a side issue.

So it was, in the century of evolution, that a number of naturalists, philosophers, historians, and students of the law assembled, classified and sought to put into "evolutionary" order the varied customs reported as practiced throughout the world, and especially by those peoples most removed from nineteenth-century Europe in time, distance, civilization, and race. Some of these men called their work *sociology*. Toward the end of the century English and American philanthropists and reformers visited the slums of the great and growing cities, described the ways of the people who lived there, counted and tabulated the things that appeared the best indicators of their misery. Their surveys were called *sociology*. Some French legal scholars sought explanations for the alleged penchant of modern people to follow the crowd rather than their ancestors in both virtues and vices. A sharp-tongued Yale professor, Sumner, and, a decade later, an Italian engineer and economist, Pareto, got concerned about those aspects of human social behavior—usages and sentiments—which did not yield good price curves. They wrote treatises on *sociology*.

In addition to a name, these varied pursuits had in common a concern with the classifying of human doings, with the relations of events rather than with the events themselves. They also cut across that organization of the academic studies of man by which the state, the church, economic life, literature, and the like, as well as the various periods of history and the various regions and countries of the world, were each the special domain of some organized group of scholars, and of one department of a university. As historians of human learning have been quick to say, others had gone off on these tangents before. What was new was that these *sociologists*, and people influenced by them, gained a footing in the universities, especially so in the newer American ones. The older scholarly guilds cried, "Trespass," and those of classical bent slew the sociologists with the true but irrelevant accusation that their name, although of noble lineage, was a bastard, being half Latin, half Greek. As do the members of any budding profession or academic specialty seeking access to the sacred precincts, the sociologists sought and found ancient and honored ancestors, founded a society and journals, and have since been arguing about what academic ways to get set in. In the debate and in their deeds they are moving toward a certain combination of answers to the questions raised about the proper study of mankind.

By predilection rather than by logic, most sociologists work on the here and now. Although vast apparatuses have been set up to catch and spread knowledge of current doings, not all is recorded; and of what is recorded, not all is spread abroad. There is an economy of observing, recording, and disseminating the news. There is also a politics of it, a balance between revealing and concealing, in which all people and all organized institutions are in some measure involved. It has become part of the mission of sociologists to catch the goings-on of people and institutions at the time; or at least to catch those parts of them which tend to be overlooked by students of politics and economics, and by those who report on and criticize what are considered the serious works of art and of the mind. The lives of the families across the tracks; the reactions of housewives to the morning soap opera; how the men down in the garage unconsciously weave their own inarticulate anxieties and yearnings into their talk of what happened to L'il Abner this morning; the slow moving changes in the level of schooling of those Americans who are called Negro. These things don't make the news, but they make the big story comprehensible when it breaks into the headlines. One might say that part of the calling of sociologists is to push back the frontier of the news so as to get at the news back of, or below the news, not in the sense of getting at the lowdown, but in that of giving the reported events another dimension, that of the perspective of culture and of social processes.

One part of this job is undertaken by the surveyors of opinion. They have invented all sorts of devices for getting at what people think and do about a great variety of matters, large and small. No one of the particular opinions or actions they report would make the news columns, as does the fiftieth home run of a big league player or the visit of a monarch to a country fair. Neither the actors nor the actions, taken singly, are thought worthy of note. Put together, they are the ground swell on which prominent figures and great projects rise and fall, run their courses or founder. Mr. Unnamed Millions is, as many have noted lately, more and more a gentleman of leisure, a grand consumer of goods and of the popular arts and of the innumerable "services" of our civilization. His choices make or break the great institutions and enterprises. Keeping abreast of him is a job which, like woman's work, is never done. Predicting what he will do, even in the short run, has some of the features of predicting the weather. Many sociologists specialize in these very jobs; they are the quantitative historians of their own times. One of the risks of their trade is that their errors of prediction are more quickly discovered than those of people in some other lines of human study.

Working on this frontier is not a matter merely of setting up machinery to watch people and to inquire of them what they do and think. For one immediately strikes that other frontier, that of conscious and unconscious secrecy. Even a willing informant seldom can or will tell all that he thinks, knows, or does about a matter; nor is he able to show or explain the many connections between his different thoughts and actions. He will tell more about some things than about others; more in some situations than in others; more to some people than to others. It is common knowledge that a human group —a family, school, business concern, a clique—keeps together and keeps going only by maintaining a delicate balance between discretion and frankness. Students of group behavior have achieved great skill in inserting themselves as participant observers into the interstices of groups so as to observe things which can be perceived only by an insider, but whose significance can be conceived only by an outsider free enough of emotional involvement to observe and report accurately and armed with concepts with which to relate what he sees to other groups. Learning the role of participant observer, including the subtle practice of its ethic, is a basic part of training people for social discovery. Each observer, himself a member of society, marked by sex, age, race, and the other characteristics by which people place one another in various roles or relations, must find out not merely what the significant kinds of people are in the groups and situations he wants to study; he must also learn to perceive quickly and surely what role he has been cast in by the people he is studying. He must then decide whether he can effectively and on honest terms get them to see him in such light that they will trust him.

The role of participant observer can be difficult and trying. A young sociologist spent a considerable time as observer in a public mental hospital. The patients would not believe he was not a physician; they pestered him to help them get out. The other doctors were somehow, they insisted, in a plot with relatives to keep them wrongly locked up. The attendants, accustomed to being spied upon, thought him another and more ingenious kind of detective sent to catch them breaking regulations or stealing public property. The physicians, although used to the idea of research and although briefed about his project, were a bit inclined to consider him a spy, too. Only by skillful and strict adherence to his role of seeing much and to his bargain of telling nothing that would harmfully identify any person, did he succeed in staying and in finding out the inward structure of the social groups which even the mentally ill and their keepers and therapists form.

The author of a well-known book on corner gangs "hung on the corner" with a group of young men in a New England city for three years, always torn between whether to get as involved as they wished, which would have bound him to secrecy; or whether to stay just on the edge, where there was a bit of a question whether they could trust him. Except for one essay into helping them get a man elected to public office by voting several times, he stayed on the edge. As it turned out, that was the way the gang wanted it. He wrote the book and is still friends with several members of the group.

It is conceivable that there are social groups so closed and so suspicious that they cannot be studied by participant observers. They may be so tight that they have no place for people of neutral role. Fanatical religious or political sects, criminal gangs, groups planning some secret strategy for either good or ill, bodies charged with knowledge which must be kept close for the common good, people living in great and vulnerable intimacy with each other, these do not welcome even the most trusted outside observers. However, a great deal can be learnt by projecting on these groups what is known of others which approximate them in some degree, and by setting up experiments which simulate them. A group of social scientists has indeed set up an organization to assemble, evaluate, and draw conclusions from the small amounts of information which can be got about people in the Iron Curtain regions. Some of them have written an intriguing book on how to study cultures from a distance. The problems are in part those of the historian, who is limited to the documents left around, since he cannot ask the dead to write documents to his order; but they are also in part the problems of evaluating the testimony of renegades and converts, people who have left some secret group and from various motives tell, or purport to tell, about what they have left. All of these are the problems of the social rhetoric common to all human intercourse.

The fears which lead people to make it difficult for investigators are often enough well-founded; more than that, they lie in the nature of social life. A family has secrets, or it is no family. It is not the public's business, ordinarily, what goes on in the bosom of a family; but it is a matter of basic human and scientific interest to know what kinds of families there are, what makes some hold together and others break up, and what happens to children brought up in one kind of family rather than another. The sociological investigator cracks the secrecy, but buries the secrets, one by one, in a tomb of silence—as do all the professions which deal with the problems of people. This means, of course, that the student of human groups must remain willingly and firmly a *marginal man* in relation to those he studies; one who will keep, cost what it will, the delicate balance between loyalty to those who have admitted him to the role of confidant and to his colleagues who expect him to contribute freely to the accumulating knowledge about human society and methods of studying it.

While some prefer to study people *in situ*, others take them aside and learn from them in long interviews, reassuring their subjects, showing sympathy for the problems of each, and refraining the while from even the gesture of censorship. One of the most powerful of modern social inventions is the psychoanalytic interview, in which the patient is led painfully through a maze of hindrances of conscience, shame, and fear to a fuller expression, hence to fuller knowledge, of his own mind. It is based on the assumption that the injunction to know one's self is one that few of us can follow without help. The prolonged sympathetic interview of the social investigator is less

dramatic, but is an effective instrument of social discovery. But every device must be valued by its results. Some students have found that there are situations in which contradiction, calling the subject's bluff, facing him with his own contradictions, and even questioning his sincerity bring out depths and ambivalences which might otherwise remain hidden. Some have undertaken experiments to discover how differences of tactical rhetoric on the part of the interviewer affect the rhetoric of the subjects.

Some investigators prefer to go even further than experimenting with methods of interviewing and observing; they set up their own situations and create their own groups. The social research of the University of Frankfort on the Main used such a method in a study of political attitudes in 1951. They got up a letter in which an American soldier who had spent some years in Germany tells the people back home in the United States what he thinks are the German attitudes towards the Nazis, Jews, Americans, and democracy. Germans of various backgrounds were called together in small groups to discuss social and political issues; the letter was read to them from a tape made by a speaker with an English accent. In the conversation following the reading, attitudes such as have not been caught by any political questionnaire in postwar Germany came to light.

Similar methods have been used in study of various matters in the U. S. A. A team of social scientists engaged to find out how juries arrive at their unanimous decisions, has had the record of a damage suit read on to tape, using different voices for the various persons in the court: the record is played to groups of twelve who are then left alone to decide the case as if they were a jury. A silent observer with a recorder sits unobtrusively in a corner. The subjects play the role of jurymen with great serious- ness. The doings of real juries are prop- erly kept secret; the experimental device provides an approximation with much better observation than one would in any case be likely to get by asking people what had happened in juries on which they had sat. For the observer keeps a record of those who talk the most, those who change their minds, and what alli- ances are made in the course of the wearing on of the argument. Combined with surveys of the ways in which people of various incomes, education, and other traits say they would judge various cases submitted to juries, these experiments are teaching us a great deal about the operation of one of our cherished institu- tions.

Some investigators would eventually replace all study of "natural groups" by experimental devices. Only so, they con- tend, can the many variable factors in social behavior be kept to such number that one can keep track of them and measure their influence. Some would go further than the Frankfort institute or the jury team. For in these projects, the experimenters were interested in the substance of their findings—the political attitudes of the Germans, and the opera- tion of juries in the United States, re- spectively. The pure experimenters make the substance suit the experiment. They assemble a group of people, and give them a problem to solve to which the experimenter and the subjects are alike utterly indifferent. It is the interaction between people, the influence they have on each other, the way and the mood in which they communicate with one an- other that is the object of study. For instance, what difference does it make in the interplay among a number of people whether one of them is so placed that the others can talk to each other only through him, or whether they can all talk to each other at once? One may study the forms of social interaction—social choreography—as a student of poetry may study meters and periods without attending to thought, or as the philologist may analyze grammatical forms and phonetic modulations free of concern for meaning and mood. It is but a narrow step from such study of form in human conduct to the study of form and style in art; one is on the fluttering edge between the abstractions of science and those of art. It is perhaps no accident that Sim- mel, the German philosopher who first proposed the study of pure interaction, attention to form rather than to content, as the basic concept of sociology, should also have written about money and about art in the same spirit. The more abstract one's way of conceiving things, the more likely one is to make generic discoveries which apply to many concrete fields of natural and human phenomena. As the experimenters penetrate further into the mathematical symmetries of human converse, they may well add to knowl- edge of other systems of things as well.

If men were gods, big gods with solar systems at beck and call, they might set up control planets, plant people on them, and reproduce millions of years of his- tory, intervening now and then to see what would happen. But students of human society are mortal; our subjects live as long as we do, and usually have as much power over us as we over them. One experimenter has seriously played god by pretending that, in his laboratory as in heaven, a minute is as a hundred years. His naivete only highlights the problem of translating the findings of small, limited experiments to larger or- ganizations and to the time-scale of history; it does not prove that the transfer cannot, with care and in limited degree, be made.

Social experimenting has also raised the problem, both ethical and practical, of manipulating other people. There has been quite a hue and cry about this lately. A psychologist "running rats" is playing a game; the rats play for keeps without even knowing that it is a game. I believe it is suspected that now and again a sly one makes a game of the experiments and laughs up his metaphoric sleeve at the serious psychologist. No one has objected to playing with the rat, but many believe that to manipulate people is an improper way of studying man. But, of course, all politics and much of social life consist of the more or less successful attempts of people to influence one another. Every profession that deals with people is suspected of looking with an experimental and manipulative eye at its clients; indeed, no one would think of going to a lawyer, physician, or even a clergyman who did not look upon his case as one among many from which they had learned their trades. The real problem of manipulating (hence of experimenting upon) humans is not that of manipulation or no manipulation, but that of the proper conditions, limits, means, and ends thereof.

Some sociologists combine the mood of the experimenter with the roving eye of the reporter. They frequent the places where events of the kinds they are interested in are bound to happen, or they get a wide knowledge of some order of human occurrences or problems, and chase down the crucial cases which will give them the combinations of circumstances on which a more general and abstract, yet more refined and useful, knowledge can be built.

Not long ago some social psychologists were studying what happens to a group of people when a great promised event does not occur as predicted by their leaders. When they were in the midst of their project, a small sect gathered about a man who was predicting an early end of the world. Now this has happened many times before, and there are some records of the cases. For instance, when the world didn't come to an end on the due date in 1843, the Millerites decided their arithmetic was wrong. A century later their successors, the Seventh Day Adventists (some of them at least) are beginning to say that while Jesus is indeed coming again in the flesh to establish his Kingdom on earth, it is sinfully presumptuous of men to think they can calculate the day and the hour. For did he not say, "Ye know not the day nor the hour"? But the team of psychologists mentioned above quite properly were eager to see a group of living people go through the experience of waiting for the world to end, and they did. Seldom do scholars have such luck.

We are in a time when we have more than common reason to want to know how people will react when disaster strikes. Flying squadrons have been sent in the wake of floods, tornadoes, explosions, and fires to find out tactfully, before memories are clouded and distorted, how people meet such adversity; who rises to the occasion to help others, and who must, on the contrary, be helped. Immediately after a great fire that destroyed half their town, the citizens told a field worker what a hero a certain obscure sister superior of a small convent-hospital had been. The nun, they said, had simply taken over and run the rescue services and the whole town. Sometime later the proper order of things had been restored; people appeared to believe that the mayor and an ecclesiastical dignitary had saved the day. In another disaster, the minister of one rather popular church went completely to pieces while the representative of a minority church and a school teacher saw the town through its tragedy. The minority minister's hair came out in handfuls some days later when reaction set in; it was the price of his courage. In many cases of such "firehouse" social research, two reports are issued. One is a newsy and perhaps immediately useful report, the other more general, and so phrased as to be useful to others who study human behavior.

If one frees his curiosity of the peculiarities of some one time and place by developing a good set of abstract ideas for comparing one case or situation with another, he will see many situations in various parts of the world comparable to those that originally aroused his interest. He will fall into the delicious conflict between wanting to learn more and more detail about the one dear case and the desire to go elsewhere to add both breadth and nuance to his knowledge. A number of students of American race relations have gone off to Africa, the most tumultuous and massive Negro-white frontier of these days. The relative numbers and the historical situations of people of Negro, European, and other ancestries on the racial frontiers of Africa are varied, and are everywhere quite different from the North American racial frontier. Race relations are still vivid in the United States, for we still consider a man's race an important thing about him. Furthermore, these relations are at a crucial point in which much of both practical and theoretical interest is to be learned. Adventure lies at our own door. But there is also much to be learned by going afield. Race relations have occurred in many historical epochs, in a great variety of circumstances, accompanied by various degrees of cultural differences; their course has been influenced by intervening events. Sometimes peoples meet who are alike in race, but different in almost all else. The irreducible core of race relations, as distinguished from the relations of peoples different from each other in other regards, might be found by comparing various communities.

To be sure, one's ability and will to learn languages, his health, the adaptability and sense of adventure of his wife, his knack for playing roles such that he can live among various peoples, not to mention the human life-span, limit the number of cultural situations one can study. On the whole, social science has suffered from too little rather than too much getting about (except to conventions). Anthropologists are great people to get around, but only lately have they begun to study the larger and more confused settings where races meet and where new nations are being made. The racially mixed locations and cities of Africa are places where the former subjects of the anthropologists are facing the favorite problems of the sociologist. In fact, sociologists and anthropologists are meeting there, too. In those cities, native prophets and evangelists preach half-Christian, half-tribal gospels and predict great events in which God's black people will come into their own while the white malefactors will be destroyed or driven back to their own land. Such prophets enjoin their people to make themselves pure and ready for their glorious future by a return to some idealized form of the ways of the past. One thinks of the Pharisees tithing mint and rue as part of their program of getting rid of Greek and Roman.

In the *Times* of New York or of London, one can follow from day to day the crises of a dozen interracial or intercultural conflicts; in most of them Europeans are reluctantly and bit by bit giving up political, economic, and social power over others. The underdog group is in most cases undergoing revolutionary changes in its culture and social structure and is awakening to a new group-consciousness on larger scale than in the past; it is usually rewriting its history, not because of Carbon 14 or new archaeological finds but because people with a new sense of unity and a new vision of the future seem always to need a new past different both from their traditional ones and from that given them by their foreign masters. Every rewriting of history—especially our own—is grist for the sociologist's mill. Racial and cultural frontiers are but one problem which can be understood only by wide-ranging about the world of the present, either in the flesh or in the mind's eye, and about the past, through the eyes of historians and through the works of art and literature in which men have expressed their hopes, hates, and aspirations.

A basic assumption of the study of mankind—hence of individual branches of study such as that called sociology—is that it is important and fascinating to find out what things do and what things do not repeat themselves in human history. Sociologists work rather more on those which are repeated. They assume that although the people of any race, culture, time, or place inherently merit study as much as those of any others, still each historic social time and place may show some special feature which may make it an especially fit laboratory for study of some problem or process of human society. Part of the adventure of the study of human society is the seeking out of the most intriguing living laboratory, prepared by the fortunes of history, for study of the problems we are especially interested in, for use of our particular skills, and for catering to our particular tastes, curiosities, and preoccupations. Our choices may spring from a sense of political and moral urgency, from a desire to advance knowledge for man's good, from some ill-defined identification with all that is human, or from some aesthetic sense.

Some of the students of man's doings should be creatures ready to invade the territory of others, both figuratively and literally, and to compare anything with anything else without shock or apology. It is a friction-generating and improper pursuit. Any social situation is in some measure dear to those in it. To compare it with others is to seem to dull the poignancy of the wrongs of the underdogs, and to detract from the merits of those who have the better place in it. Comparison may violate the canons of status and prestige, as when one compares the code of secrecy of the gentleman's gentleman with that of the lord chamberlain. Comparison of religion with religion appears to reduce the claim of each to a monopoly of truth. Such invasion is also dangerous and improper on the academic front, for any series of human events, any social time and place, and most of man's institutions are each thought to be the game preserve of one of the learned professions. Shoving over scholarly line-fences is even more dangerous than shifting boundary stones in Vermont.

Most perilous and improper of all is it to compare the academic disciplines with one another by pointing out that each is an historical entity which had a beginning and which will probably be superseded by others in the future. If we study man and his institutions with broad-sweeping curiosity, with the sharpest tools of observation and analysis which we can devise, if we are deterred from no comparison by the fallacy which assumes that some people and peoples are more human than others, if we do not allow loyalty to truth to take second place to department or academic guild, we will all be proper students of man. And when we become too respectable, too much bound to past methods, whenever our means show signs of becoming ends, may we all— even the sociologists—be succeeded by people to whom *nihil humanum alienum est.*

Further Reading

A very readable introduction to the philosophy of science that emphasizes some of the ethical issues posed by our new skills and rapidly expanding knowledge is John Kemeny, *A Philosopher Looks At Science*, Princeton, N.J.: Van Nostrand, 1959. And an excellent concise introduction to the philosophy of the social sciences is provided by Richard S. Rudner, *Philosophy of Social Science*, Englewood Cliffs, N.J.: Prentice-Hall, 1966. Among the best but technically more advanced treatments of this subject are Abraham Kaplan, *The Conduct of Inquiry*, San Francisco: Chandler Publishing Company, 1964; Ernest Nagel, *The Structure of Science*, New York: Harcourt, 1961; and Karl L. Popper, *The Logic of Scientific Discovery*, New York: Science Editions, 1961.

There are also numerous works describing the varied arsenal of research techniques developed by sociologists. Chief among these are participant observer techniques, more systematic observational methods, and interviews of various types. These methods are combined in various ways to collect data in natural settings, such as factories and communities; in field experiments, in which selected facets of a natural situation are systematically manipulated by scientists and the effects studied; in small and large scale surveys, where individual respondents are asked to describe their experiences, opinions, or present situation; and in laboratory experiments, in which individuals are asked to carry out specified tasks under highly controlled conditions. Among the many useful books describing methods in the social sciences are Leon Festinger and Daniel Katz (eds.), *Research Methods in the Behavioral Sciences*, New York: Holt, Rinehart and Winston, Inc., 1953; and Claire Selltiz, Marie Jahoda, Morton Deutsch, and Stuart W. Cook, *Research Methods In Social Relations*, New York: Holt, Rinehart and Winston, Inc., 1959. Slightly more advanced works that include discussions of appropriate statistical methods for summarizing and analyzing data are those of Hubert M. Blalock, Jr., and Ann B. Blalock, *Methodology in Social Research*, New York: McGraw-Hill, 1968; and Bernard S. Phillips, *Social Research: Strategy and Tactics*, New York: Macmillan, 1966. A recent book is notable for its attempt to more clearly relate research methodology with the process of theory building and verification. See Matilda Riley, *Sociological Research*, New York: Harcourt, 1967.

On the building of sociological theory, the reader may consult two brief but excellent volumes. Hans L. Zetterberg, *On Theory and Verification in Sociology* (rev. ed.), Totowa, N.J.: Bedminister, 1963; and Arthur L. Stinchcombe, *Constructing Social Theories*, New York: Harcourt, 1968.

The importance of objectivity in social science was asserted early by Max Weber, the great German social scientist, and his statement remains one of the best. Max Weber, "Science as a vocation," in Hans Gerth and C. Wright Mills (eds.), *From Max Weber: Essays in Sociology*, New York: Oxford, 1946, pp. 129–156. For a recent and readable statement on this problem see John Kemeny, "Science and Values," *A Philosopher Looks at Science*, Princeton, N.J.: Van Nostrand, 1959. A counterposition has recently developed in sociology that asserts our field cannot and should not be value-free. For numerous essays in support of this position see Irving Louis Horowitz (ed.), *The New Sociology*, New York: Oxford, 1964.

For a lucid and informative discussion of the scientific community and the role it plays in supporting and correcting the work of individual practitioners, see Bernard Barber, *Science and the Social Order*, New York: Free Press, 1952.

A good summary of the two views of society—of those who focus on social order and those who emphasize disorder and conflict—appears in Ralf Dahrendorf, *Class and Class Conflict in Industrial Society*, Stanford, Calif.: Stanford University Press, 1959, pp. 157 165. (See Reading 12) A recent collection of papers, many of them somewhat technical, summarizes this continuing debate. See N. J. Demerath III and Richard A. Peterson (eds.), *System, Change, and Conflict*, New York: Free Press, 1967.

The critics and criticisms of sociology are all too numerous, but even a short list would have to include the following: Joseph Wood Krutch, *The Measure of Man*, New York: Grosset & Dunlap, 1954; C. Wright Mills, *The Sociological Imagination*, New York: Oxford, 1959; and Pitirim A. Sorokin, *Fads and Foibles in Modern Sociology and Related Sciences*, Chicago: Regnery, 1956.

PART TWO

Some Basic Structural Concepts

Some concepts and ideas are sufficiently important and general that it is necessary to consider them before turning to examine the specific structures and the processes with which this book is primarily concerned. Because these notions are fundamental, they are among the most complex and difficult with which the sociologist must deal. (Why is it that the most difficult issues seem often to be among the first to confront us in any undertaking?) We will by no means dispose of them in this section. Rather, we will simply introduce them here and expect to see them returning again and again to puzzle and challenge us along the way.

Three pairs of concepts will be considered in these introductory readings: norms and values; positions and roles; and social organization and social disorganization. These concepts are primarily of value in describing and analyzing the structural aspects of social life, a point we will expand upon in Part Three.

Section I

NORMS AND VALUES

"The reason that sociology has given a great deal of attention to norms is clear. Human society, as distinct from insect and animal societies, is in part organized and made possible by rules of behavior."[1] Sociologists call such rules "norms." Man, with his enormous plasticity of response, receives but few behavioral cues from his innate characteristics; most of his responses are learned from the persons with whom he associates. This is not to say that all regularities of human behavior are socially determined. All men spend part of their time sleeping and part awake: this is a biologically determined regularity. But the circumstances of their sleep—where, with whom, how frequently, even how long—are in large measure determined by the normative expectations of the persons with whom men interact. Far from being biologically determined, many norms act in such a way as to curtail and restrict biologically induced drives by, for example, defining certain edible foods as inedible or forbidden. That cows are allowed to walk the streets of cities in which individuals lie dying of starvation is impressive testimony to the power of social norms.

Norms and values are an aspect of culture. Culture, as that term is used by the anthropologist, is a very broad concept indeed. Tylor's definition is quite adequate for our purposes: "Culture. . . is that complex whole which includes knowledge, belief, art, morals, law, custom, and any other capabilities and habits acquired by man as a member of society."[2] One way to visualize a particular culture in this broad sense would be to attempt to answer the question What is available to be learned by all the infants born in a given society? Interesting as such a topic might be, our concern now is not with all aspects of a given culture. Sociologists tend to emphasize the aspects that directly prescribe and orient social behavior—the portions of culture that present a "design for living" or a "blueprint for behavior." We focus now, in short, on norms and values.

Social Values   We must begin by recognizing that the line separating values and norms is a hazy one and that this distinction is often a difficult one to make. But let us try. A social value is an idea in the minds of the members of a group as to what objectives should be pursued, what goals are to be preferred over others. In some instances, when the goals being considered are quite immediate and concrete, it may be preferable to conceive of values as the

---

[1]Judith Blake and Kingsley Davis, "Norms, values and sanctions," in Robert E. L. Faris (ed.), *Handbook of Modern Sociology*, Chicago: Rand McNally, 1964, p. 457.

[2]Edward B. Tylor, *Primitive Culture*, New York: Brentano's, 1924, p. 1 (original publication, 1871).

criteria employed in the selection of goals rather than as the goals themselves. It is quite easy to give examples of contrasting social values said to be held by specific groups. Thus, individuals in the United States are often said to adhere to the value of individual freedom while individuals in Soviet Russia are believed to place more emphasis on the welfare of the state as a whole. This may or may not be true. It is often the case that assertions of this kind are based upon official ideologies or on the opinions of "experts" when the evidence required—namely, analysis of the actual beliefs of representative samples of Americans and Russians—is lacking. For example, it might be presumed that virtually all American citizens subscribe to the values and norms contained in the first ten amendments to the Constitution, the Bill of Rights. But research by Mack, who posed these beliefs as a series of questions asked of a sample of American students, found that several of the provisions were rejected by a majority of respondents and other provisions were upheld only by a slim majority.[3] Although individuals are assuredly guided by values in their social conduct, we should not too quickly assume that we know what they are.

How can we discover what values are held by a person or group of persons? One technique would be to examine situations in which individuals are forced to make choices among alternative courses of action. We can, for example, make some inferences about the values held by a person by noting how he spends his money. Does he buy a luxurious car, give large amounts to a charity organization, or save so that his son may go to college? We can also note how a person chooses to spend his time, to what kinds of groups and associations he belongs, and so on.

James Coleman, in his study of a sample of American high schools, illustrates one approach to the empirical study of values. (Reading 3) He obtained some interesting information on student values by asking questions like "How would you most like to be remembered in school: as an athletic star, a brilliant student, or most popular?" and "What does it take to get into the leading crowd?" Responses to such questions not only were used to give some indication as to the value preferences of a given student but also were combined to describe the value "subculture" of a school—that is, the value preferences prevailing among students in a given school. Coleman is able not only to describe student values as they vary from school to school but also to show that such subcultures have an impact on the behavior of individual students; that, for example, in schools where the subculture places more emphasis on academic achievement, brighter students are more likely to devote their efforts to gaining high grades than in schools where less emphasis is placed on academic values.

Social Norms   If values provide the criteria for selecting the goals of human conduct, social norms define what means are acceptable for pursuing these goals. In this sense, then, norms and values stand in a means-ends relationship. Means-ends distinctions are often difficult to make, and this is why we said at the outset of this discussion that this distinction was a somewhat hazy one. To illustrate the difficulty we can ask Is a belief in the freedom of the press a value or a norm? Is freedom of the press a means to some more ultimate value

[3]Raymond Mack, "Do we really believe in the Bill of Rights?" *Social Problems*, 3 (April, 1956), 264-269.

such as freedom of expression and communication, or is it an end in itself? Such questions are difficult but need not detain us long. Moral imperatives can frequently function as either norms or values; respondents in our studies can often help us decide how a particular imperative is being used, and so can our somewhat arbitrary choice as to the range and limits of our investigation.

George Homans, in his contribution to this section (Reading 4), provides us with a relatively precise definition of the concept of norm, stating that "a norm, then, is an idea in the minds of the members of a group. . . specifying what the members or other men should do, ought to do, are expected to do, under given circumstances." Further, "a statement of the kind described is a norm only if any departure of real behavior from the norm is followed by some punishment." Thus, the concept of norm contains two important components: first, that there exists some agreement among group members about the behaviors in which they or others of concern to them should or should not engage and, second, that there are mechanisms by which such agreements are enforced. Let us briefly consider each of these ideas.

Norms are shared agreements among group members; nevertheless, it is obvious that there will not be perfect consensus among members concerning all norms. Knowledge of group norms will vary from member to member, and not all members will agree as to which beliefs in fact constitute the norms of the group. We should not demand that all group members know of or accept a belief before concluding that the belief is a norm, but usually we should expect at least a majority of group members to do so. We employ the cautious "usually" here because we recognize that group members will differ in power and influence, and in some cases it may be more important to know who subscribes to the norm than to know how many do. In any event, the extent of knowledge and acceptance of a norm, and the kinds of group members subscribing to it, are important variables affecting its strength in a group. Finally, we should recognize that all norms are not of equal importance to the group. Such differential weighting was pointed to long ago by Sumner in his famous distinction between *mores*—norms that must be obeyed because they involve the welfare of the entire group—and *folkways*—norms that define appropriate conduct in areas less crucial to the group.[4] Many recent typologies of norms have also made use of similar distinctions with regard to importance.

One of the best indicators of the presence of a norm as well as its relative importance is the type of reaction that occurs among group members when a group prescription is violated by a member. When a norm has been violated we expect the offending individual to be sanctioned by his fellow members. A *sanction* is a behavior whose primary purpose is to provide rewards or punishments to some other.[5] Negative sanctions involve punishments or the removal of rewards; positive sanctions involve the lessening of punishments or the bestowing of rewards. Sanctions vary widely in intensity. For example, negative sanctions range from a slight reduction in the rate of interaction with the offender to ostracism and expulsion from the group. Indeed, certain groups, such as nation states, exercise the power of life and death over their member-

[4]William Graham Sumner, *Folkways*, Boston: Ginn, 1906.
[5]The concept of sanction is carefully defined and discussed by Gross, Mason, and McEachern in their analysis of positions and roles (Reading 6).

ship. The severity of the sanction provides some clue as to the importance of the norm that has been violated, although other factors may also influence the intensity of the reaction, such as consideration of the age, motives, or mental state of the offender.

As an example of the empirical study of social norms, we can find none better than that conducted by Roethlisberger and Dickson. (Reading 5) *Management and the Worker*, the larger volume from which this selection is taken, is one of the "classics" of the sociological literature. In their meticulous study of selected work groups in the Western Electric Company's Hawthorne plant in Chicago, Roethlisberger and Dickson laid to rest once and for all the ghost of "economic man" by demonstrating the operation of personal and social variables importantly affecting the behavior of workers in modern industry. In the particular reading we have included, the authors do not simply assert the presence of a work-group norm controlling individual productivity but reproduce much of the evidence on which their conclusion is based. Their report not only demonstrates the possibility of doing research on social norms but at the same time indicates the care that should be exercised in doing so.

Before completing our introductory comments on values and norms, it is important that we clear up a possible misconception that may be troubling some readers. In discussing the concepts of values and norms, we are not suggesting anything resembling a "group mind." Norms and values are nothing more than beliefs in the minds of individuals participating in groups. Nevertheless, for any particular group member, the norms and values are the shared beliefs of others to whom he must relate and, hence, may be said to be external to him. They are beliefs to which he is subject and which he will need to take into account as he interacts with other members. It is in this sense, then, that norms and values may be regarded as an important set of *social forces* that exert a constraining effect upon the conduct of all group members.

It should be emphasized again that we have only introduced the subject of norms and values, not exhausted it. Many important questions remain that we will want to consider throughout the remainder of this book. For example, we will want to seek answers to such questions as How do norms arise in a group? Why do some people conform to norms while others do not, and Why do people conform to some norms but not others? And, What in general are the functions (the positive consequences) of norms for groups?[6] Such questions as these are not easy, and one will find no simple or completely satisfactory answers to them in this or any other volume now written. They are nonetheless important questions to which we together will seek answers, however tentative and incomplete.

---

[6]It is well to note here that some of these questions can only be answered (and asked) if we forsake the structural perspective that asks What are the norms? or What individuals hold these norms? and assume the perspective of the process analyst to ask How did these norms develop? and How do norms change over time?

3   The Adolescent Subculture and Academic Achievement[1]

James S. Coleman

Industrial society has spawned a peculiar phenomenon, most evident in America but emerging also in other Western societies: adolescent subcultures, with values and activities quite distinct from those of the adult society—subcultures whose members have most of their important associations within and few with adult society. Industrialization, and the rapidity of change itself, has taken out of the hands of the parent the task of training his child, made the parent's skills obsolescent, and put him out of touch with the times—unable to understand, much less inculcate, the standards of a social order which has changed since he was young.

By extending the period of training necessary for a child and by encompassing nearly the whole population, industrial society has made of high school a social system of adolescents. It includes, in the United States, almost all adolescents and more and more of the activities of the adolescent himself. A typical example is provided by an excerpt from a high-school newspaper in an upper-middle-class suburban school:

Sophomore Dancing
Features Cha Cha

SOPHOMORES, this is your chance to learn how to dance! The first day of sopho-

more dancing is Nov. 14 and it will begin at 8:30 A.M. in the Boys' Gym....

NO ONE IS required to take dancing but it is highly recommended for both boys and girls....

If you don't attend at this time except in case of absence from school, you may not attend at any other time. Absence excuses should be shown to Miss —— or Mr. ——.

In effect, then, what our society has done is to set apart, in an institution of their own, adolescents for whom home is little more than a dormitory and whose world is made up of activities peculiar to their fellows. They have been given as well many of the instruments which can make them a functioning community: cars, freedom in dating, continual contact with the opposite sex, money, and entertainment, like popular music and movies, designed especially for them. The international spread of "rock-and-roll" and of so-called American patterns of adolescent behavior is a consequence, I would suggest, of these economic changes which have set adolescents off in a world of their own.

Yet the fact that such a subsystem has sprung up in society has not been systematically recognized in the organization of secondary education. The theory and practice of education remains focused on *individuals;* teachers exhort individuals to concentrate their energies in scholarly directions, while the community of adolescents diverts these energies into other channels. The premise of the present research is that, if educational goals are to be realized in modern society, a

[1]The research discussed in this paper was carried out under a grant from the United States Office of Education; a full report is contained in "Social Climates and Social Structures in High Schools," a report to the Office of Education. The paper was presented at the Fourth World Congress of Sociology, Milan, Italy, September, 1959.

fundamentally different approach to secondary education is necessary. Adults are in control of the institutions they have established for secondary education; traditionally these institutions have been used to mold children as individuals toward ends which adults dictate. The fundamental change which must occur is to shift the focus: to mold social communities as communities, so that the norms of the communities themselves reinforce educational goals rather than inhibit them, as is at present the case.

The research being reported is an attempt to examine the status systems of the adolescent communities in ten high schools and to see the effects of these status systems upon the individuals within them. The ten high schools are all in the Midwest. They include five schools in small towns (labeled *0-4* in the figures which follow), one in a working-class suburb (*6*), one in a well-to-do suburb (*9*), and three schools in cities of varying sizes (*5*, *7*, and *8*). All but No. 5, a Catholic boys' school, are coeducational, and all but it are public schools.

The intention was to study schools which had quite different status systems, but the similarities were far more striking than the differences. In a questionnaire all boys were asked: "How would you most like to be remembered in school: as an athletic star, a brilliant student, or most popular?" The results of the responses for each school are shown in Figure 3-1,[2] where the left corner of the triangle represents 100 per cent saying "star athlete"; the top corner represents 100 per cent saying "brilliant student"; and the right corner represents 100 per cent saying "most popular." Each school is representedly a point whose location relative to the three corners

[2] I am grateful to James A. Davis and Jacob Feldman, of the University of Chicago, for suggesting such graphs for presenting responses to trichotomous items in a population.

shows the proportion giving each response.

The schools are remarkably grouped somewhat off-center, showing a greater tendency to say "star athlete" than either of the other choices. From each school's point is a broken arrow connecting the school as a whole with its members who were named by their fellows as being "members of the leading crowd." In almost every case, the leading crowd tends in the direction of the athlete—in all cases *away* from the ideal of the brilliant student. Again, for the leading crowds as well as for the students as a whole, the uniformity is remarkably great; not so great in the absolute positions of the leading crowds but in the direction they deviate from the student bodies.

This trend toward the ideal of the athletic star on the part of the leading crowds is due in part to the fact that the leading crowds include a great number of athletes. Boys were asked in a questionnaire to name the best athlete in their grade, the best student, and the boy most popular with girls. In every school, without exception, the boys named as best athletes were named more often— on the average over twice as often—as members of the leading crowd than were those named as best students. Similarly, the boy most popular with girls was named as belonging to the leading crowd more often than the best student, though in all schools but the well-to-do suburb and the smallest rural town (schools 9 and 0 on Fig. 3–1) less often than the best athlete.

These and other data indicate the importance of athletic achievement as an avenue for gaining status in the schools. Indeed, in the predominantly middle-class schools, it is by far the most effective achievement for gaining a working-class boy entrée into the leading crowd.

Similarly, each girl was asked how she

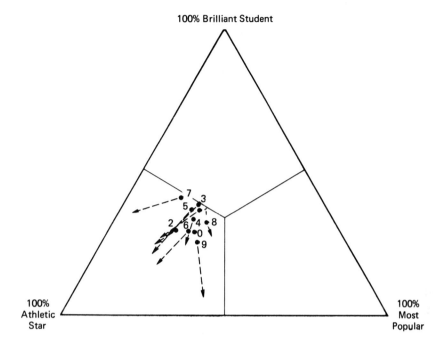

FIGURE 3-1. Positions of schools and leading crowds in boys' relative choice of brilliant student, athletic star, and most popular.

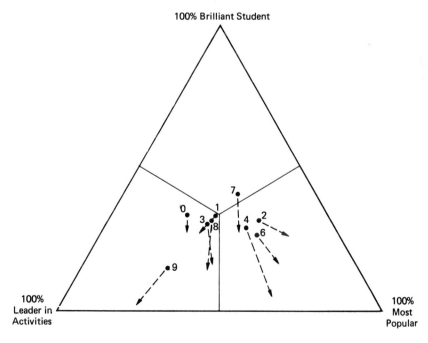

FIGURE 3-2. Positions of schools and leading crowds in girls' relative choice of brilliant student, activities leader, and most popular.

would like to be remembered: as a brilliant student, a leader in extracurricular activities, or most popular. The various schools are located on Figure 3–2, together with arrows connecting them to their leading crowd. The girls tend slightly less, on the average, than the boys to want to be remembered as brilliant students. Although the alternatives are different, and thus cannot be directly compared, a great deal of other evidence indicates that the girls—although better students in every school—do not want to be considered "brilliant students." They have good reason not to, for the girl in each grade in each of the schools who was most often named as best student has fewer friends and is less often in the leading crowd than is the boy most often named as best student.

There is, however, diversity among the schools in the attractiveness of the images of "activities leader" and "popular girl" (Fig. 3-2) . In five (9, 0, 3, 8, and 1) , the leader in activities is more often chosen as an ideal than is the popular girl; in four (7, 6, 2, and 4) the most popular girl is the more attractive of the two. These differences correspond somewhat to class background differences among the schools: 2, 4, 6, and 7, where the activities leader is least attractive, have the highest proportion of students with working-class backgrounds. School 9 is by far the most upper-middle-class one and by far the most activities-oriented.

The differences among the schools correspond as well to differences among the leading crowds: in schools 2, 4, and 6, where the girls as a whole are most oriented to being popular, the leading crowds are even more so; in the school where the girls are most oriented to the ideal of the activities leader, No. 9, the leading crowd goes even further in that direction.[3] In other words, it is as if a

pull is exerted by the leading crowd, bringing the rest of the students toward one or the other of the polar extremes. In all cases, the leading crowd pulls away from the brilliant-student ideal.

Although these schools vary far less than one might wish when examining the effects of status systems, there are differences. All students were asked in a questionnaire: "What does it take to get into the leading crowd?" On the basis of the answers, the relative importance of various activities can be determined. Consider only a single activity, academic achievement. Its importance for status among the adolescents in each school can be measured simply by the proportion of responses which specify "good grades," or "brains" as adolescents often put it, as a means of entrée into the leading crowd. In all the schools, academic achievement was of less importance than other matters, such as being an athletic star among the boys, being a cheerleader or being good-looking among the girls, or other attributes. Other measures which were obtained of the importance of academic achievement in the adolescent status system correlate highly with this one.[4]

If, then, it is true that the status system of adolescents does affect educational goals, those schools which differ in the importance of academic achievement in the adolescent status system should differ in numerous other ways which are

[3]This result could logically be a statistical artifact because the leaders were included among students as a whole and thus would

boost the result in the direction they tend. However, it is not a statistical artifact, for the leading crowds are a small part of the total student body. When they are taken out for computing the position of the rest of the girls in each school, schools 2, 4, 6, and 7 are still the most popularity-oriented, and school 9 the most activities-oriented.

[4]Parenthetically, it might be noted that these measures correlate imperfectly with the proportion of boys or girls who want to be remembered as brilliant students. These responses depend on the relative attractiveness of other ideals, which varies from school to school, and upon other factors unrelated to the status system.

directly related to educational goals. Only one of those, which illustrates well the differing pressures upon students in the various schools, will be reported here.

In every social context certain activities are highly rewarded, while others are not. Those activities which are rewarded are the activities for which there is strong competition—activities in which everyone with some ability will compete.—In such activities the persons who achieve most should be those with most potential ability. In contrast, in unrewarded activities, those who have most ability may not be motivated to compete; consequently, the persons who achieve most will be persons of lesser ability. Thus in a high school where basketball is important, nearly every boy who might be a good basketball player will go out for the sport, and, as a result, basketball stars are likely to be the boys with the most ability. If in the same school volleyball does not bring the same status, few boys will go out for it, and those who end up as members of the team will not be the boys with most potential ability.

Similarly, with academic achievement: in a school where such achievement brings few social rewards, those who "go out" for scholarly achievement will be few. The high performers, those who receive good grades, will not be the boys whose ability is greatest but a more mediocre few. Thus the "intellectuals" of such a society, those defined by themselves and others as the best students, will not in fact be those with most intellectual ability. The latter, knowing where the social rewards lie, will be off cultivating other fields which bring social rewards.

To examine the effect of varying social pressures in the schools, academic achievement, as measured by grades in school, was related to I.Q. Since the I.Q. tests differ from school to school, and since each school had its own mean I.Q. and its own variation around it, the ability

of high performers (boys who made A or A-average)[5] was measured by the number of standard deviations of their average I.Q.'s above the mean. In this way, it is possible to see where the high performers' ability lay, relative to the distribution of abilities in their school.[6]

The variations were great: in a small-town school, No. *1*, the boys who made an A or A - average had I.Q.'s 1.53 standard deviations above the school average; in another small-town school, No. *0*, their I.Q.'s were only about a third this distance above the mean, .59. Given this variation, the question can be asked: Do these variations in ability of the high performers correspond to variations in the social rewards for, or constraints against, being a good student?

Figure 3–3 shows the relation for the boys between the social rewards for academic excellence (i.e., the frequency with which "good grades" was mentioned as a means for getting into the leading

[5] In each school but 3 and 8, those making A and A- constituted from 6 to 8 per cent of the student body. In order to provide a correct test of the hypothesis, it is necessary to have the same fraction of the student body in each case (since I.Q.'s of this group are being measured in terms of number of standard deviations above the student body). To adjust these groups, enough 6's were added (each being assigned the average I.Q. of the total group of 6's) to bring the proportion up to 6 per cent (from 3 per cent in school *3*, from 4 per cent in school *8*).

[6] The I.Q. tests used in the different schools were: (*0*) California Mental Maturity (taken seventh, eighth, or ninth grade); (*1*) California Mental Maturity (taken eighth grade); (*2*) SRA Primary Mental Abilities (taken tenth grade); (*3*) California Mental Maturity (taken ninth grade; seniors took SRA PMA, which was tabulated as a percentile, and they have been omitted from analysis reported above); (*4*) Otis (ninth and tenth grades; taken eighth grade); Kuhlman Finch (eleventh and twelfth grades, taken eighth grade); (*5*) Otis (taken ninth grade); (*6*) California Mental Maturity (taken eighth grade); (*7*) California Mental Maturity (taken eighth grade); (*8*) Otis (taken ninth or tenth grade); and (*9*) Otis (taken eighth grade).

crowd) and the ability of the high performers, measured by the number of standard deviations their average I.Q.'s exceed that of the rest of the boys in the school. The relation is extremely strong. Only one school, a parochial boys' school in the city's slums, deviates. This is a

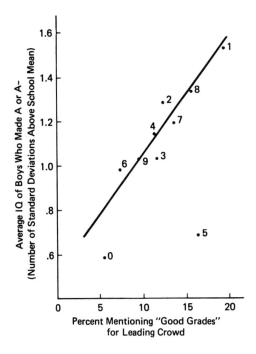

FIGURE 3-3. I.Q.'s of high achieving boys by importance of good grades among other boys.

school in which many boys had their most important associations outside the school rather than in it, so that its student body constituted far less of a social system, less able to dispense social rewards and punishments, than was true of the other schools.

Similarly, Figure 3-4 shows for the girls the I.Q.'s of the high performers.[7] Unfortunately, most of the schools are closely

bunched in the degree to which good grades are important among the girls, so that there is too little variation among them to examine this effect as fully as would be desirable. School 2 is the one school whose girls deviate from the general relationship.

The effect of these value systems on the freedom for academic ability to express itself in high achievement is evident among the girls as it is among the boys. This is not merely due to the school facilities, social composition of the school, or other variables: the two schools highest in the importance of scholastic achievement for both boys and girls are 1 and 8, the first a small-town school of 350 students and the second a city school of 2,000 students. In both there are fewer students with white-collar backgrounds than in schools 9 or 3, which are somewhere in the middle as to value placed on academic achievement, but are more white-collar than in schools 7 or 4, which are also somewhere in the middle. The highest expenditure per student was $695 per year in school 9, and the lowest was little more than half that, in school 4. These schools are close together on the graphs of Figures 3-3 and 3-4.

It should be mentioned in passing that an extensive unpublished study throughout Connecticut, using standard tests of achievement and ability, yielded consistent results. The study found no correlation between per pupil expenditure in a school and the achievement of its students relative to their ability. The effects shown in Figures 3-3 and 3-4 suggest why: that students with ability are led to achieve only when there are social re-

[7] For the girls, only girls with a straight-A average were included. Since girls get better grades than boys, this device is necessary in order to make the sizes of the "high-performer" group roughly comparable for boys and for girls. Schools differed somewhat in the proportion of A's, constituting about 6

per cent of the students in the small schools, only about 3 per cent in schools 6 and 7, 1 per cent in 8, and 2 per cent in 9. In 8 and 9, enough girls were added and assigned the average grade of the 7 (A –) group to bring the proportion to 3 per cent, comparable with the other large schools. The difference, however, between the large and small schools was left.

wards, primarily from their peers, for doing so—and these social rewards seem little correlated with per pupil expenditure.

So much for the effects as shown by the variation among schools. As mentioned earlier, the variation among schools was not nearly so striking in this research as the fact that, in all of them, academic achievement did not count for as much as other activities. In every school the boy named as best athlete and the boy named as most popular with girls was far more often mentioned as a member of the leading crowd, and as someone to "be like," than was the boy named as the best student. And the girl named as best dressed, and the one named as most popular with boys, was in every school far more often mentioned as being in the leading crowd and as someone "to be like," than was the girl named as the best student.

The relative unimportance of academic achievement, together with the effect shown earlier, suggests that these adolescent subcultures are generally deterrents to academic achievement. In other words, in these societies of adolescents those who come to be seen as the "intellectuals" and who come to think so of themselves are not really those of highest intelligence but are only the ones who are willing to work hard at a relatively unrewarded activity.

The implications for American society as a whole are clear. Because high schools allow the adolescent subcultures to divert energies into athletics, social activities, and the like, they recruit into adult intellectual activities people with a rather mediocre level of ability. In fact, the high school seems to do more than allow these subcultures to discourage academic achievement; it aids them in doing so. To indicate how it does and to indicate how it might do differently is another story, to be examined below.

Figures 3-1 and 3-2, which show the

way boys and girls would like to be remembered in their high school, demonstrate a curious difference between the boys and the girls. Despite great variation in social background, in size of school (from 180 to 2,000), in size of town (from less than a thousand to over a million), and in style of life of their parents, the proportion of boys choosing each of the three images by which he wants to be remembered is very nearly the same in all schools. And in every school the leading crowd "pulls" in similar directions: at least partly toward the ideal of the star athlete. Yet the ideals of the girls in these schools are far more dispersed, and the leading crowds "pull" in varying directions, far less uniformly than among the boys. Why such a diversity in the same schools?

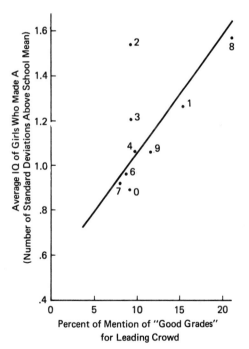

FIGURE 3-4. I.Q.'s of high achieving girls by importance of good grades among other girls.

The question can best be answered by indirection. In two schools apart from those in the research, the questionnaire

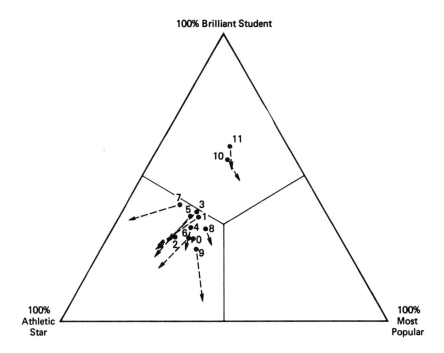

FIGURE 3-5.   Positions of schools and leading crowds in boys' relative choice of brilliant student, athletic star, and most popular (two private schools [10, 11] included).

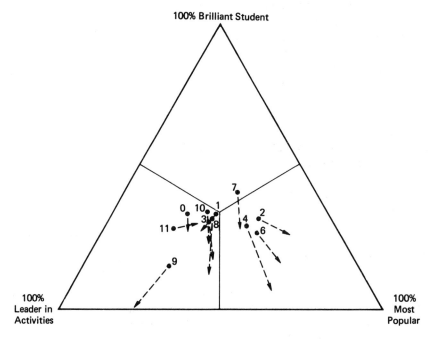

FIGURE 3-6.   Positions of schools and leading crowds in girls' relative choice of brilliant student, activities leader, and most popular (two private schools [10, 11] included).

was administered primarily to answer a puzzling question: Why was academic achievement of so little importance among the adolescents in school 9? Their parents were professionals and business executives, about 80 per cent were going to college (over twice as high a proportion as in any of the other schools) , and yet academic excellence counted for little among them. In the two additional schools parental background was largely held constant, for they were private, coeducational day schools whose students had upper-middle-class backgrounds quite similar to those of school 9. One (No. 10) was in the city; the other (No. 11) , in a suburban setting almost identical to that of No. 9. Although the two schools were added to the study to answer the question about school 9, they will be used to help answer the puzzle set earlier: that of the clustering of schools for the boys and their greater spread for the girls. When we look at the responses of adolescents in these two schools to the question as to how they would like to be remembered, the picture becomes even more puzzling (Figure 3-5 and 3-6) . For the boys, they are extremely far from the cluster of the other schools; for the girls, they are intermingled with the other schools. Thus, though it was for the boys that the other schools clustered so closely, these two deviate sharply from the cluster; and for the girls, where the schools already varied, these two are not distinguishable. Furthermore, the leading crowds of boys in these schools do not pull the ideal toward the star-athlete ideal as do those in almost all the other schools. To be sure, they pull away from the ideal of the brilliant student, but the pull is primarily toward a social image, the most popular. Among the girls, the leading crowds pull in different directions and are nearly indistinguishable from the other schools.

The answer to both puzzles, that is,

first, the great cluster of the boys and now, in these two additional schools, the greater deviation, seems to lie in one fact: the boys' interscholastic athletics. The nine public schools are all engaged in interscholastic leagues which themselves are knit together in state tournaments. The other school of the first ten, the Catholic school, is in a parochial league, where games are just as hotly contested as in the public leagues and is also knit together with them in tournaments.

Schools 10 and 11 are athletically in a world apart from this. Although boys in both schools may go in for sports, and both schools have interscholastic games, the opponents are scattered private schools, constituting a league in name only. They take no part in state or city tournaments and have almost no publicity.

There is nothing for the girls comparable to the boys' interscholastic athletics. There are school activities of one sort or another, in which most girls take part, but no interscholastic games involving them. Their absence and the lack of leagues which knit all schools together in systematic competition means that the status system can "wander" freely, depending on local conditions in the school. In athletics, however, a school, and the community surrounding it, cannot hold its head up if it continues to lose games. It *must* devote roughly the same attention to athletics as do the schools surrounding it, for athletic games are the only games in which it engages other schools and, by representation, other communities.

These games are almost the only means a school has of generating internal cohesion and identification, for they constitute the only activity in which the school participates *as* a school. (This is well indicated by the fact that a number of students in school 10, the private school which engages in no interscholastic games, has been concerned by a "lack of school spirit.") It is as a consequence of this that the athlete gains so much status: he is doing something for the school and the community, not only for himself, in leading his team to victory, for it is a school victory.

The outstanding student, in contrast, has little or no way to bring glory to his school. His victories are always purely personal, often at the expense of his classmates, who are forced to work harder to keep up with him. It is no wonder that his accomplishments gain little reward and are often met by ridiculing remarks, such as "curve-raiser" or "grind," terms of disapprobation which have no analogues in athletics.

These results are particularly intriguing, for they suggest ways in which rather straightforward social theory could be used in organizing the activities of high schools in such a way that their adolescent subcultures would encourage, rather than discourage, the channeling of energies into directions of learning. One might speculate on the possible effects of city-wide or state-wide "scholastic fairs" composed of academic games and tournaments between schools and school exhibits to be judged. It could be that the mere institution of such games would, just as do the state basketball tournaments in the midwestern United States, have a profound effect upon the educational climate in the participating schools. In fact, by an extension of this analysis, one would predict that an international fair of this sort, a "Scholastic Olympics," would generate interscholastic games and tournaments within the participating countries.

4   Norms

George C. Homans

What do we mean by norms? Sociologists and anthropologists are always saying that such and such behavior is, in a particular group, "expected" under such and such circumstances. How do they know what is expected? Sometimes the members of a group will state quite clearly what the expected behavior is, but sometimes it is a matter of inference. The process of construction by which social scientists determine the expectations of a group—and the process must be complex—seems to be taken for granted by the less sophisticated among them in their textbooks and popular works. Here we never take such things for granted, though we may not spend much time on them. Suppose, for example, three men are in a room. One goes out, and one of the two that remain says to the other, "I don't believe we've met. My name is Smith." Or, in another variation of the same scene, a man comes into a room where two others are already standing. There is a silence, and then one of the two says, "I'm sorry. I should have introduced you two, but I thought you had met. Mr. Jones, this is Mr. Smith." From observing several events of this kind, the sociologist infers that, in this

From *The Human Group* by George C. Homans, copyright 1950, by Harcourt, Brace & World, Inc., pp. 121-128, and reprinted with their permission and Routledge & Kegan Paul Ltd.

particular group, when two men are in the presence of one another and have not met before, the third man, if he has met both, is expected to tell each the other's name, but that, should he fail to do so, each is expected to act on his own account and tell the other his name. The sociologist's inference may be confirmed when he reads in a book of etiquette current in this group, "When two persons have not met before, their host must introduce them to one another." Inferences of this kind we shall call *norms*. Note that most norms are not as easily discovered as this rather trivial one, and confirmation by a book of etiquette or its equivalent is not always possible. The student should turn to *Management and the Worker* and run over the material from which the inference was reached that about 6,600 or, according to the type of equipment being wired, 6,000 completed connections were considered in the Bank Wiring Observation Room the proper day's work of a wireman. For example, Mueller (W_2) said in an interview:

Right now I'm turning out over 7,000 a day, around 7,040. The rest of the fellows kick because I do that. They want me to come down. They want me to come down to around 6,600, but I don't see why I should.[1]

In few works of social science are the norms, whose existence the sociologist often appears to assume so lightly, traced back to their referents in word and deed as carefully as they are in the Roethlisberger and Dickson book. We have already seen what some of the other norms of the Bank Wiremen were, in such matters as squealing, chiseling, and acting officiously.

A norm, then, is an idea in the minds of the members of a group, an idea that can be put in the form of a statement specifying what the members or other

men should do, ought to do, are expected to do, under given circumstances. Just what group, what circumstances, and what action are meant can be much more easily determined for some norms than for others. But even this definition is too broad and must be limited further. A statement of the kind described is a norm only if any departure of real behavior from the norm is followed by some punishment. The rule of the Bank Wiremen that no one should wire much more or much less than two equipments a day was a true norm, because, as we shall see, the social standing of a member of the group declined as he departed in one way or another from the norm. Nonconformity was punished and conformity rewarded. A norm in this sense is what some sociologists call a sanction pattern. But there are many other statements about what behavior ought to be that are not norms and are often called ideals. "Do as you would be done by," is an example. In an imperfect world, departure from the golden rule is not followed by specific punishment, and this is precisely what gives the rule its high ethical standing. If a man lives by it, he does so for its own sake and not because he will be socially rewarded. Virtue is its own reward.

We have defined norms as the expected behavior of a number of men. This is justified: each of the Bank Wiremen was expected to wire about 6,000 connections a day. But some norms, though they may be held by all the members of a group, apply to only one of them: they define what a single member in a particular position is supposed to do. A father is expected to treat his children, a host, his guests, a foreman, his men in certain special ways. A norm of this kind, a norm that states the expected relationship of a person in a certain position to others he comes into contact with is often called the *role* of this person.[2] The word comes,

[1]*Management and the Worker*, p. 417. (See Reading 5, pp. 51-57, this book. [Ed.])

[2]See *The Human Group*, p. 11.

of course, from the language of the stage: it is the part a man is given to play, and he may play it well or ill. A man's behavior may depart more or less from the role, and if the real behavior of enough persons in enough such positions over a long enough time departs far enough from the role, the role itself will change. For instance, our notion of the way a father ought to behave toward his children has changed greatly in the last century, as circumstances have made the patriarchal role of fathers on small, subsistence farms no longer appropriate for many fathers today.

One point must be made very clear: our norms are ideas. They are not behavior itself, but what people think behavior ought to be. Nothing is more childishly obvious than that the ideal and the real do not always, or do not fully, coincide, but nothing is more easily forgotten, perhaps because men want to forget it. A possible objection to the word *norm* itself is that we may easily confuse two different things: norm A, a statement of what people ought to do in a particular situation, and norm B, a statistical, or quasi-statistical, average of what they actually do in that situation. Sometimes the two coincide, but more often they do not. In the same way, the word *standard* suggests, on the one hand, a moral yardstick by which real behavior is judged and, on the other hand, in the phrase *standard of living*, a certain level of real behavior in the field of consumption.

CULTURE

By our definition, norms are a part, but only a part, of what social anthropologists call the *culture* of a group. Anyone who is interested in the various meanings that have been given to this famous concept should read the intelligent and witty discussion by Kluckhohn and Kelly. The definition they finally come out with themselves is the following: "A culture is a historically derived system of explicit and implicit designs for living, which tends to be shared by all or specially designated members of a group."[3] From this definition we might be led to believe that our norms are the same thing as culture, for designs for living suggest intellectual guides for practice rather than practice itself. The design of the ship is not the ship. But we should be mistaken. For Kluckhohn and Kelly, culture includes both theory and practice, ideal patterns and behavioral patterns, statements of what ought to be and modalities in what is done. Anthropologists are welcome to define *culture* as they wish, but we, interested in the relation between the two aspects of group life, must make it clear that our norms are statements of what ought to be, and only this. They are a part of culture, but not all of it.

THE RELATION OF NORMS TO BEHAVIOR

Our guiding principle throughout has been that unless things are kept separate in the beginning they cannot in the end be seen in relation to one another. We must not mix norms and actual behavior together in a shapeless mass if we are to examine the relations between the two, and the relations do confront us and demand analysis. It is clear, for instance, that norms do not materialize out of nothing, but emerge from ongoing activities. If the Bank Wiremen had not been doing the wiring job, and if their output had not reached the neighborhood of 6,000 connections per man per day (or about two equipments), it is hard to believe that this particular norm would ever have got itself established. If we think of a norm as a goal that a group wishes to reach, we can see that the goal is not set up, like the finish line of a race,

[3]C. Kluckhohn and W. H. Kelly, "The Concept of Culture," in R. Linton, ed., *The Science of Man in the World Crisis*, 78–106, 98.

before the race starts, but rather that the group decides, after it starts running, what the finish line shall be. Once the norm is established it exerts a back effect on the group. It may act as an incentive in the sense that a man may try to bring his behavior closer to the norm. But the norm can be a mark to shoot for only if it is not too far away from what can be achieved in everyday life. If it gets impossibly remote—and just how far that is no one can say—it will be abandoned in favor of some more nearly attainable norm. Society's preaching and its practice are elastically linked. Each pulls the other, and they can never separate altogether.

The really interesting question is, as usual, quantitative and not qualitative: not "Does behavior coincide with a norm?" but "*How far* does the behavior of an individual or a subgroup measure up to the norms of the group as a whole?" What, moreover, is the relation of this degree of coincidence to the sentimental process that we shall call *evaluation* or *social ranking,* by which individuals and subgroups are judged "better" or "worse" than others? What is the relation of evaluation to other aspects of the social system? These are questions we shall take up in the chapters that follow; the work we do now will help us then.

We have made an assumption without proof. In a chapter dealing with a single social unit, the Bank Wiring group, rather than the subgroups within this unit, we have talked about "the norms of a group as a whole." What do we mean? We mean that, the more frequently men interact with one another, the more nearly alike they become in the norms they hold, as they do in their sentiments and activities. But we mean still more than this. No doubt the norms accepted in a group vary somewhat from one person to another, and from one subgroup to another, and yet *the members of the group are often more nearly alike in the norms they*

hold than in their overt behavior. To put the matter crudely, they are more alike in what they say they ought to do than in what they do in fact. Thus the Bank Wiremen were more nearly, though perhaps not wholly, alike in what they said output ought to be than in what they actually turned out. Perhaps the explanation of this rule, if it is one, lies in the fact that a person's subjective recognition of a norm, although under influence from other aspects of the social system, is under less immediate influence than his social activity itself, and thus varies less than his social activity. Being an idea, the norm come closer to having an independent life of its own.

Norms do not materialize out of nothing; they emerge from on-going activities. This remark is true but needs to be amplified. The norms alive in a particular group do not all arise out of the activities of *that* group. Thus in the Bank Wiring Observation Room, the rule that about 6,000 connections should be wired in a day must have grown up in the main department from which the men came. The more general idea of restriction of output or, as labor sees it, "a fair day's work for a fair day's pay," is a part of the American, or Western, industrial tradition. That is, it is common to a large number of groups whose members have had some communication with one another. Again, the feeling that no man should act as if he had authority over someone else is an article in the democratic creed—and note that the creed is realized to some degree in American society and would not survive unless it were. Men bring their norms to a group; they work out new norms through their experience in the group; they take the old norms, confirmed or weakened, and the new ones, as developed, to the other groups they are members of. If the norms take hold there, a general tradition, the same in many groups, may grow up. The freight most easily exported is the kind carried in the head. In fact the environment determines the character of a group in two chief ways: through its influence on the external system, and through widely held norms.

ASSUMPTIONS OR VALUES

While we are speaking of the ideas that men bring to a group from the larger society of which the group is a part, we should not forget certain ideas that are closely akin to the norms: the unconscious assumptions the members of any society make or, as some sociologists would say, the *values* they hold. For instance, two such assumptions that the Bank Wiremen certainly brought with them to the Observation Room might be stated as follows: 1. A man who is paid more than another man has, in general, a better job than that man. 2. A man who can give orders to another man has, in general, a better job than that man. We can formulate these assumptions, but in everyday life they are not formulated, and for this reason we call them unconscious. Instead they are implied, over and over again, in actual behavior and in casual remarks. A man may in effect admit their truth even when he does not act upon them. He may turn down promotion to foreman because the job has too many "headaches," but he will concede that this job is somehow, on an absolute scale, better than his own. Perhaps the assumptions are so obvious that they do not need formulation—obvious, that is, to us who are also Americans, for the anthropologists have abundantly shown that what is obvious in one culture is not necessarily so in another. Note that these assumptions, including the two in our illustration, cannot be "proved." They are not propositions to be proved by logical processes, but premises from which logic starts, just as in geometry you do not prove that a straight line is the shortest distance between two points, you postulate it. From different premises different conclusions could be drawn. The social assumptions stand because a large number of people accept them and for no other reason. The Bank Wiremen brought many such premises with them to work. Some were and are a part of American democratic culture. Some may be found to contradict one another, which means that they are supposed to apply in different circumstances. And some may be unconscious assumptions of all human behavior. In their emphasis on cultural relativity, the anthropologists have almost—not quite—forgotten that there may be some premises held by all mankind.

INTRODUCTORY NOTE

The Bank Wiring Observation Room study was the last in a long series of studies conducted by the members of the Harvard School of Business during the late 1920s and early 1930s. The study was so named because the subjects of the research were engaged in wiring banks of telephone equipment. In this research, everything possible was done to keep the situation of the workers being studied as normal as possible. The major change made was to introduce an observer into the situation to record the activities and interactions of the workers. This, of course, is no minor change, but the researchers did much to minimize the effect of the observer's presence and to make as explicit as possible what changes his presence might have made (see pp. 379–408 of *Management and the Worker*). Workers were also interviewed about their attitudes toward their job and work situation.

Members of the work group were on a group incentive system such that each man's income was dependent on the productivity of the group as a whole. Each worker was paid an hourly rate that differed among the individual workers, and allocation of the weekly departmental earnings was based on this rate. To help increase productivity, a "bogey"—an output standard in terms of which each individual's efficiency could be measured—was established for each job. According to the authors: the bogey "was something 'to shoot at' and was intended to serve in much the same way as a record does for an athlete." But "the raising or lowering of the bogey would in no way affect earnings except in so far as it might influence output." (p. 410)

5 Beliefs of Employees Regarding Payment System

F. J. Roethlisberger and William J. Dickson

THE CONCEPT OF A DAY'S WORK

In interviews with the operators in the department before the study began, the investigators encountered certain beliefs which the employees seemed to hold in common. Chief among these was the concept of a day's work. This idea kept cropping up in interview after interview. Of the thirty-two men interviewed in the department before the study began, a group which included the nine wiremen later selected for the study, twenty-two discussed rates of output. Of these twenty-two, twenty said that the wiring of two equipments constituted a day's work. The other two men said they were supposed to try to make the bogey, which they correctly stated as 914 connections per hour. The following comments, quoted from interviews with members of the group under observation, are typical:

W_1: "6,600 is the bogey. You see, that's two sets. There are 3,300 connections on a set. Now on selector wiring the bogey is only 6,000, because there are only 3,000 connections on a set. In order to turn out 6,600

there, you have to wire three levels on a third set."

Int: "6,600 is your bogey then?"
W_1: "Yes, it's 6,600. You see they told us if we got out two sets a day it would be all right. That's a pretty good day's work too."

. . . .

W_2: "You know, some of those fellows stall around for three months before they turn out 6,000. There's no reason for that at all. I could turn out 6,000 in three weeks. I think the rest of them could if they wanted to. . . . I'm making around 7,000 every day. . . . I don't mind that [their fooling around] as long as it doesn't interfere with the work. I never fool around until I have my bogey out. That is the first thing. When I get my bogey out, then I don't mind loafing around a bit."

. . . .

W_3: "I turn out 6,600 regularly. That's about what is expected of us. Of course you could make out less and get by, but it's safer to turn out about 6,600."

Reprinted by permission of the publishers from F. J. Roethlisberger & William J. Dickson, *Management and the Worker*, pp. 412–423. Cambridge, Mass.: Harvard University Press, Copyright, 1939, '67, by the President and Fellows of Harvard College.

Int: "And is 6,600 your bogey?"

W₃: "No, our bogey is higher than that. It is 914 an hour."

. . . . . .

W₄: "I think connector wiring is the better job. The boards aren't as heavy [as on selectors] and you have an extra bank. You see, the rate on connectors is around 6,600 and on selectors it's only 6,000."

. . . . . .

W₅: "I turn out 100 per cent efficiency right along. That means I turn out 6,600 a day."[1]

Int: "Is the bogey 6,600 a day?"

W₅: "No, that's not the bogey. The bogey is 7,200, I think."

. . . . . .

W₆: "Well, the bogey is pretty high. I turn out 6,600 a day right along and that is pretty good, I think, for the average."

Int: "Is that the bogey?"

W₆: "I think it is."

Int: "Then you are making 100 per cent efficiency?"

W₆: "Well, I don't know about that. I don't think I am turning out 100 per cent. You see the bogey was 914 an hour for an 8¾-hour day, so I suppose it will be about 6,600 for an 8-hour day."

. . . . . .

W₇: "6,000 a day is the rate. I guess there's another rate that's higher than that, but the bosses tell us that 6,000 is a day's work."

. . . . . .

W₈: "I make between 5,500 and 6,000. On selectors they don't have to turn out as many. I think they are supposed to turn out 6,000 a day. We have an extra bank on each set so that if we wire two sets a day we would be making 6,600 a day."

Int: "Is that the bogey?"

W₈: "Yes, I think it is."

---

[1] In order to have an efficiency of 100 per cent, a wireman would have to wire 7,312 terminals a day.

From comments such as these it was apparent that the operators were accustomed to thinking of two equipments a day as a day's work. This was verified by the observer, who found that the operators frequently stopped wiring when they had finished their quotas even though it was not official stopping time. This concept of a day's work was of interest for two reasons. In the first place, it did not refer to the bogey or to any other standard of performance officially imposed. As compared with the day's work of which they spoke, which amounted to 6,000 or 6,600 connections depending upon the type of equipment, the bogey was considerably higher. If asked what the bogey was, some of the men could give the correct answer. Many of them, however, spoke of the day's work as being the bogey. Others said that they were supposed to turn out about two sets but they thought the bogey was higher. Still others spoke of the day's work as being the rate on the job, and the rate was held to be synonymous with bogey. Technically, the word "rate" had three quite different meanings depending on whether it referred to piece rates, hourly rates, or rates of working; yet frequently the employees made no distinction. Whatever else this confusion of terminology meant, one conclusion was certain. The bogey was not functioning as a competitive standard for this group.

In the second place, the idea of a day's work was of interest because it was contrary to one of the basic notions of the incentive plan. Theoretically, the incentive plan was intended to obviate the problems attendant upon the determination of a day's work. The chief drawback to paying stipulated monthly, daily, or hourly wages is that there is no accurate way of determining how much work should be done for the wages received. Some criterion there must be, but if its determination were left up to the workers it is possible that they might fix upon a low standard. On the other hand, standards arbitrarily imposed by the employer might possibly be too high and entail detrimental physiological results. Where the amount of work to be done in a given time for a given wage is determined by custom, such problems may be present but they do not come to the fore. In modern industry, however, jobs are subdivided and changed so frequently that whatever influence custom might bring to bear is lost. There is no customary standard to which to appeal. One of the chief arguments to be advanced in favor of incentive plans is that under an incentive system a day's work will be determined at that point where fatigue or "pain costs" balance the worker's subjective estimate of the added monetary return. The amount of work done by different individuals should, theoretically, vary as individual capacities vary, and for any one individual variations from day to day might be expected. Under such a system, the concept of a day's work, of a specified number of units to be completed each day by every worker, has, strictly speaking, no place. In the Bank Wiring Observation Room, then, there was evidence that the wage incentive plan was not functioning entirely as it was intended to function.

The question of how two equipments came to be fixed upon as a day's work is an interesting one, but it cannot be definitely answered. Among the possible explanations, four may be mentioned. First, it might be argued that the hourly rates of the people who wired 6,000 or 6,600 terminals a day were at the maximum of the labor grade established for this kind of work. If this were so, the supervisors could not offer the men, except in unusual cases, increases in hourly rates for further increases in output, and therefore the men would tend to fix their output at that level. This expla-

nation failed to be in any sense conclusive, however, simply because the majority of the people in the observation room had not reached the maximum of the labor grade.

Secondly, it might be argued that 6,000 or 6,600 terminals per day, or two equipments, represented the balance point between fatigue or s"pain costs" of work, on the one hand, and the satisfactions to be derived from the monetary returns for that amount of work, on the other. There were, however, no evidences of fatigue among the operators in the observation room. Furthermore, some of the operators wished to turn out more work, but they were reluctant to do so in the face of the attitudes prevailing in the group. Their concept of a day's work, in other words, did not represent a personally calculated equilibrium between work and monetary return.

A third explanation is that the supervisors might have mentioned some figure as a desirable day's work when attempting to stimulate some of the slower men. They might have said, for example, "Your output is too low, you should be turning out 6,000 connections a day." The figure thus mentioned might then have become, in the operators' thinking, the standard of acceptable performance. This explanation, however, fails to explain why the supervisors should have chosen this figure instead of some other or why the operators agreed among themselves that it was wrong to exceed it. In practice the supervisors did tell some of the slower men that they should have been turning out two equipments a day, but they also told some of the other wiremen that they should have been doing more. In view of the fact that different figures were given different operators, it is difficult to understand how this explanation could account for their concept of a day's work.

Finally, it might be claimed that the wiring of two equipments was a "natural" day's work in that a wireman could complete two but not three equipments. Rather than start on a third unit he might, for the sake of tidiness and good workmanship, prefer to complete only two and start out on a new one the first thing in the morning. Although some of the operators claimed that they did get a certain satisfaction out of finishing an equipment and seeing the resulting colorful pattern of interlaced wires before them (one of them likened it to the pleasure a woman must derive from knitting), the fact is that they stopped work during the wiring of an equipment more frequently than at the end.

None of these four explanations, then, is satisfactory. There is no way of telling whether one is more plausible than the others. For this reason, the question will be dropped from further consideration. It may be well to point out, however, that one could not hold to any one of the above explanations without admitting, implicitly, that the wage incentive was not functioning as it was supposed to. For, if it were functioning as it was supposed to, the conditions assumed in these arguments would not exist.

THE DAY'S WORK AS A GROUP STANDARD

As the study progressed, it became more and more apparent that the operators' conception of a day's work had a much wider significance than has thus far been implied. The interviewer, while inquiring further into this belief, found that it was related to other beliefs which the operators held quite generally. These other beliefs, which incidentally are quite common and more or less familiar to everyone, usually took the following form: "If we exceed our day's work by any appreciable amount, something will happen. The 'rate' might be cut, the 'rate' might be raised, the 'bogey' might be raised, someone might be laid off, or the supervisor might 'bawl out' the slower

men." Any or all of these consequences might follow. It is difficult to produce evidence in which such apprehensions were articulated as clearly as here represented. This statement represents the summation of a variety of employees' remarks in which these fears were more or less implied. The following quotations are given to show the type of evidence upon which the above observation is based:

W₂: (After claiming that he turned out more work than anyone else in the group) "They [his co-workers] don't like to have me turn in so much, but I turn it in anyway."

(In another interview) "Right now I'm turning out over 7,000 a day, around 7,040. The rest of the fellows kick because I do that. They want me to come down. They want me to come down to around 6,600, but I don't see why I should. If I did, the supervisors would come in and ask me what causes me to drop like that. I've been turning out about that much for the last six months now and I see no reason why I should turn out less. There's no reason why I should turn out more either."

. . . . . .

W₃: "No one can turn out the bogey consistently. Well, occasionally some of them do. Now since the layoff started there's been a few fellows down there who have been turning out around 7,300 a day. They've been working like hell. I think it is foolishness to do it because I don't think it will do them any good, and it is likely to do the rest of us a lot of harm."

Int: "Just how do you figure that?"

W₃: "Well, you see if they start turning out around 7,300 a day over a period of weeks and if three of them do it, then they can lay one of the men off, because three men working at that speed can do as much as four men working at the present rate."

Int: "And you think that is likely to happen?"

W₃: "Yes, I think it would. At present we are only scheduled for 40 sets ahead. In normal times we were scheduled for over 100. If they find that fewer men can do the work, they're going to lay off more of us. When things pick up they will expect us to do as much as we are now. That means they will raise the bogey on us. You see how it works?"

. . . . . .

Int: "You say there is no incentive to turn out more work. If all of you did more work, wouldn't you make more money?"

$W_4:$ "No, we wouldn't. They told us that down there one time. You know, the supervisors came around and told us that very thing, that if we would turn out more work we would make more money, but we can't see it that way. Probably what would happen is that our bogey would be raised, and then we would just be turning out more work for the same money.[2] I can't see that."

. . . . . .

$W_5:$ "There's another thing; you know the fellows give the fast workers the raspberry all the time. Work hard, try to do your best, and they don't appreciate it at all. They don't seem to figure that they are gaining any by it. It's not only the wiremen, the soldermen don't like it either. . . . The fellows who loaf along are liked better than anybody else. Some of them take pride in turning out as little work as they can and making the boss think they're turning out a whole lot. They think it's smart. I think a lot of them have the idea that if you work fast the rate will be cut. That would mean that they would have to work faster for the same money. I've never seen our rate cut yet, so I don't know whether it would happen or not. I have heard it has happened in some cases though."

. . . . . .

$W_6:$ (Talking about a relative of his who worked in the plant) "She gets in here early and goes ahead and makes up a lot of parts so that when the rest of the girls start in she's already got a whole lot stacked up. In that

way she turns out a great deal of work. She's money greedy. That's what's the matter with her and they shouldn't allow that. All she does is spoil the rate for the rest of the girls."

Int: "How does she do that?"

$W_6:$ "By turning out so much. When they see her making so much money, they cut the rate."

. . . . . .

$W_7:$ "There's one little guy down there that turns out over 7,000 a day. I think there's a couple of them. And we have to put up with it."

. . . . . .

$W_8:$ "Some people down there have had lots more experience than others and they can't possibly turn out the rate. I know a fellow who came in there just a few months ago and he is up above average already. It won't be long before he will be turning out 7,000 or 8,000 of them."

Int: "Do you think he will?"

$W_8:$ "Well, I think so. Some of them do it. Of course, the slower men don't like that so well."

Int: (After a discussion of a large vs. a small gang for purposes of payment) "Your earnings would probably increase as much under your present system of payment, provided everyone increased his output proportionately."

$W_8:$ "That would mean that somebody would be out of a job. We've only got so much work to do, you know. Now just suppose a person was doing 6,000 connections a day, say on selectors, that's two whole sets. Now suppose that instead of just loafing around when he gets through he did two more rows on another set. Well, then, when he comes to work the next morning he would have two rows to start with. Then suppose he did another whole set and two additional rows. On the third day, let's see, where would he be? On the third day he would start on the equipment that was already wired up six levels. Before long he would have an extra set done. Then where would you be? Somebody could be laid off."

Int: "Are you conscious of that when you

---

[2] It should be remembered that raising the bogey could not have this effect unless it resulted in lower output. See p. 410.

are working? Are you consciously thinking that if you turn out over a certain amount somebody will be laid off?"

W_8:   "That only stands to reason, doesn't it?"

Int: "That if you increase your output they're going to lay somebody off?"

W_8:   "Yeah. Now just suppose the fellows in that room could increase their output to 7,000. I think some of them can. That would mean less work for others."

Int: "On the same basis, why do you work at all? If you turn out only 3,000 a day, you're just doing work that someone else might do."

W_8:   "Yeah, but I think it should be spread around more."

Statements like these indicated that many apprehensions and fears were centered around the concept of a day's work. They suggested that the day's work might be something more than an output standard, that it might be a norm of conduct. The data obtained by the observer provided additional evidence in support of this interpretation. He found that men who persisted in exceeding the group standard of a day's work were looked upon with disfavor. This was manifested in subtle forms of sarcasm and ridicule which can best be illustrated by quoting from the observer's record:

W₆ and W₄ were kidding each other about working hard. W₆ was working very fast. W₄ was working faster than usual.

W_4:   (To W₆) "Go on, you slave, work. You're enough connections ahead now to take care of Friday."

Obs: (To W₄) "Is W₆ going too fast to suit you?"

W_4:   "He's nothing but a slave. A couple more rows and he'll have 8,000."

W_6:   "No, I won't. I haven't got today's work out yet."

W_4:   "You should have quit when you finished that set."

W_6:   "I'm good for another 6,000 connections. If they'd pay me for it, I'd turn 'em out."

. . . . . .

GC₂ was taking the output count.

W_4:   (To W₆) "How many are you going to turn in?"

W_6:   "I've got to turn in 6,800."

W_4:   "What's the matter—are you crazy? You work all week and turn in 6,600 for a full day, and now today you're away an hour and a quarter and you turn in more than you do the other days."

W_6:   "I don't care. I'm going to finish these sets tomorrow."

W_4:   "You're screwy."

W_6:   "All right, I'll turn in 6,400."

W_4:   "That's too much."

W_6:   "That don't make any difference. I've got to do something with them."

W_4:   "Well, give them to me."

W₆ did not answer.

. . . . . .

W_2:   (To S₁) "Come on, get this set."

S_1:   "All right." (To Obs.) "I want to introduce you to Lightning [W₂] and Cyclone [W₃]. When these two get going it's just like a whirlwind up here. Give W₂ a big chew of snuff and he just burns the solder right off the terminals."

. . . . . .

S_1:   (To Obs.) "What's a guy going to do if these fellows won't quit work?"

Obs: "That's it, what?"

S_1:   "Keep right on working."

Obs: "There you are. Now you've got it."

S_1:   "W₂ has got 8,000 and he don't know enough to quit. Well, if he wires 8,000, I must solder 8,000. That's it, isn't it?"

Obs: "Sure."

W₆ and W₂ were the first in output and it was toward them that most of the group pressure was directed. W₆ was designated by such names as "Shrimp," "Runt," and "Slave." Sometimes he was called "Speed King," a concession to his wiring ability. W₂ was called "Phar Lap," the name of a race horse. W₁ was nicknamed "4:15 Special," meaning that he worked until quitting time. W₅ was also called "Slave" occasionally.

One of the most interesting devices by which the group attempted to control the behavior of individual members was a practice which they called "binging." This practice was noticed early in the study. The observer described it as follows:

W7, W8, W9 and S4 were engaging in a game which they called "binging." One of them walked up to another man and hit him as hard as he could on the upper arm. The one hit made no protest, and it seems that it was his privilege to "bing" the one who hit him. He was free to retaliate with one blow. One of the objects of the game is to see who can hit the hardest. But it is also used as a penalty. If one of them says something that another dislikes, the latter may walk up and say, "I'm going to bing you for that." The one who is getting binged may complain that he has been hurt and say, "That one was too hard. I'm going to get you for that one."

In the following incident binging was being used as a simple penalty:

W9 suddenly binged W7.

Obs: (To W9) "Why did you do that?"
W9: "He swore. We got an agreement so that the one who swears gets binged. W8 was in it for five minutes, but he got binged a couple of times and then quit."
Obs: "Why don't you want W7 to swear?"
W9: "It's just a bad habit. There's no sense to it, and it doesn't sound good. I've been getting the habit lately and sometimes I swear when I don't want to. I never used to swear until I got next to W8, there, and now I find myself doing it all the time."

Another time binging was advocated as a means of expressing a mutual antagonism and settling a dispute.

W7 had his window open. W6 walked over and opened his window wide. W9 went over and closed W6's window. W6 ran over and grabbed the chain. He insisted that the window stay open. W9 insisted that it was too drafty.

W6: "You run your own window, I'll take care of this one."
W9: "It's too drafty. You leave that window closed or I'll bing you."
W6: "Go ahead, start."

W9 glanced up to see if he could take the chain off the top of the window. W6 held the chain tight so that W9 couldn't loosen it. They had quite an argument.

W6: (To W8) "How about it? Is it too drafty over there?"
W8: "No, it's all right."
W6: "There you are. Now leave the window alone."
S4: (To W8) "What's the idea of lying?"
W8: "I'm not."
S4: "You're lying if you say you don't feel the draft."

W8 did not answer.

W7: (Tired of the argument) "Why don't you bing each other and then shut up?"

In addition to its use as a penalty and as a means of settling disputes, binging was used to regulate the output of some of the faster workers. This was one of its most significant applications and is well illustrated in the following entry:

W8: (To W6) "Why don't you quit work? Let's see, this is your thirty-fifth row today. What are you going to do with them all?"
W6: "What do you care? It's to your advantage if I work, isn't it?"
W8: "Yeah, but the way you're working you'll get stuck with them."
W6: "Don't worry about that. I'll take care of it. You're getting paid by the sets I turn out. That's all you should worry about."
W8: "If you don't quit work I'll bing you." W8 struck W6 and finally chased him around the room.
Obs: (A few minutes later) "What's the matter, W6, won't he let you work?"
W6: "No. I'm all through though. I've got enough done." He then went over and helped another wireman.

From observations such as these and from interviews the investigators concluded that they had come upon a set of basic attitudes. Beliefs regarding a day's work and the dangers involved in exceeding it were not confined to a few persons but were held quite generally, both by the men in the observation room and in the regular department. It was apparent that there existed a group norm in terms of which the behavior of different individuals was in some sense being regulated.

Section II

POSITIONS AND ROLES

The types of values and norms with which we have been concerned to this point are those which apply to all members of the group in question. However, some values and norms are applicable only to certain members or categories of members. For example, newcomers in a group may be distinguished from regular or full-fledged members, with different expectations being held for their conduct in the group. Or one member may be singled out in the group as a leader, and expectations may be held for his behavior different from those held for other group members. Sociologists use the concepts of position and role to analyze normative expectations focused on selected group participants.

The concepts of position and role are carefully defined and discussed in the reading by Gross, Mason, and McEachern. (Reading 6) They define a *position* as "the location of an actor or class of actors in a system of social relationships" and define a *role* as "a set of expectations or . . . evaluative standards applied to an incumbent of a particular position." A role, then, is a set of shared expectations focused upon a particular position, these expectations including beliefs about what goals or values the position incumbent is to pursue and the norms that will govern his behavior. Like all such shared beliefs, there may be more or less agreement among group members as to what constitutes the "appropriate" set of expectations—how a given role is to be defined. And, as Gross, Mason, and McEachern note, such consensus may vary considerably, depending on the position occupied by the individuals whose beliefs help define the role in question. For example, certain beliefs may be widely shared by students as to how a professor should behave, but all these beliefs may not be shared by a dean, who stands in a different relationship to the professor and who will have his own beliefs regarding appropriate behavior for professors.

It is unnecessary to summarize here the many important distinctions that Gross and his associates suggest as they develop a language for role analysis. Some readers will undoubtedly find this reading difficult, but the student who studies it carefully will find it both clear and comprehensible. The authors have gone to great pains to define their concepts clearly and unambiguously, and they are also careful to note when their use of a concept departs from that of other influential social analysts.

Beginning students of sociology may be irked by differences that exist among sociologists in terminology and in the definitions of the terms employed. Thus, some sociologists use the concept of role to refer to the behavior of an incumbent of a social position while others, sharing the perspective of Gross and the editor of this volume, define a role as the set of normative expectations applied to the position incumbent. The former definition of the concept focuses attention on how the position holder *does* behave; the latter, on how others believe he *should* behave. Although such disagreements may be annoying and can lead to misunderstandings, they are not lethal for the science. As we noted in our introduction, the definitions given to concepts are neither true nor false, but only somewhat useful in focusing attention on selected aspects of some phenomena. Therefore, how a sociologist defines his concepts will depend in large part on the purposes for which he expects to use them. Nevertheless, some consistency in the defining of concepts is helpful for communication among scientists and between scientists and laymen, so we will endeavor to stick closely to a single vocabulary in this volume and, when discrepancies in usage do occur, call attention to them.

Some students after reading this selection by Gross, Mason, and McEachern may argue that it does not go anywhere, that it is nothing but a "bunch of definitions." In defense of Gross and his associates, we would point out that this selection is taken from an early chapter of a book in which they proceed to employ and refine their concepts in an empirical investigation of the role of school superintendent. In defense of ourselves for including this reading in our volume, we would point out that the concept of role is perhaps the single most used—and hence misused and abused—concept employed by the sociologist. It is the critical concept by which individual behavior is linked to social organization. It provides a kind of theoretical bridge between the individual actor and larger social units. Hence, it is very important that we clearly define this concept and that we develop a language for sorting out and taking into account its complexities. Gross, Mason, and McEachern have gone a long way toward the construction of such a language.

Roles and Role Conflict   Given that occupants of a particular focal position are typically confronted with expectations from the occupants of not one but a number of other counter positions, and given that these expectations are sometimes at variance with one another, what is the occupant of the focal position to do? He cannot conform to the expectations of others when these expectations are mutually incompatible. Stouffer has conducted a study of this situation where the focal role involved is that of the student and the counterroles are those of university administrators and fellow students. (Reading 7) The conflicting expectations concern the appropriate behavior for a student proctoring an examination who detects a fellow student engaged in cheating. Conformity to one set of expectations rather than another is shown to be influenced by such situational factors as (1) the observability of the behavior to members of one counterrole group, (2) the severity of the sanctions that the focal role is expected to administer, (3) the nature of the relationship between the student proctor and the offender, and (4) the extent to which occupants of the focal role *perceive* a conflict in the expectations of the counterrole groups. Further, the study emphasizes that the norms involved in the defining of roles are not necessarily perceived to call for *a* specific behavior on the part of the focal position occupant but are often seen to define a *range* of acceptable behaviors, thus giving the role occupant some measure of freedom in selecting his action.

After exposure to the readings in this section, the student should be in a position to pose some rather sophisticated questions when he undertakes to examine a given social role. Instead of the blunt and oversimplified question What is your role in this group? he may seek answers to such questions as:

1. To what other social positions is this position related?
2. What normative expectations do the incumbents of these several counter positions hold for the occupant of the focal position?
3. Do the expectations pertain to both role behaviors and role attributes of the occupant of the focal position?
4. Are the expectations specific or diffuse; that is, do they allow for a relatively narrow set or a broad set of alternative behaviors?
5. How much agreement is there concerning these expectations among the occupants of a given counterposition?
6. Do some of the expectations held by occupants of one counterposition conflict with those held by occupants of a second counterposition?
7. How do occupants of the focal position typically deal with conflicting expectations directed at them from two or more counterpositions?

This list illustrates the range and type of questions that might be asked in attempting to describe one position and its associated role. The matter becomes infinitely more complex, and more interesting, when we add the fact that a given individual typically occupies not one but several social positions simultaneously. The same individual may be a professor, a sociologist, a husband, a father, a church member, a member of a political party, and a member of the local board of the YMCA, to name only some of his more significant positions. Obviously, the previous set of questions is applicable to any and all of these social roles. In addition, it is clear that there are new possibilities for conflicts among the role definers because that set is now greatly enlarged. In addition to the conflicts that may be present in the expectations held by incumbents of the various counterpositions associated with a given position—which we may now identify as *intrarole conflicts*—there may be expectations held for the behavior of an individual by the occupants of counterpositions associated with one of his positions that may conflict with those held by others associated with another of his positions. We may refer to this latter type as *interrole conflict*. To illustrate this type, consider a professor who is expected by his departmental chairman to participate in commencement exercises on the weekend for which his wife had planned a family camping expedition. It goes without saying that this sort of conflict is not uncommon.

We should not, however, overestimate the extensiveness of interrole conflict. As Newcomb notes, "Most of us, most of the time, manage to take quite different roles, as prescribed by the same or by different groups, without undue conflict. . . . Indeed, it is rather remarkable how many different roles most of us manage to take with a minimum of conflict."[1] This is the case, of course, because many roles prescribe behavior in different provinces of a person's life. Most roles are played sequentially, so that an individual can fulfill his work, family, community, and

[1]Theodore Newcomb, *Social Psychology*, New York: The Dryden Press, Inc., 1950, p. 449.

other obligations each at its proper time and place. However, there is the ever-present danger of time conflicts; many role obligations are not inherently incompatible but become so when they must be carried out at the same time. The professor's dilemma in being caught between work demands and family demands for the same weekend is a perhaps trivial illustration of this situation. A more graphic example is provided by Killian, who examined role conflicts occurring during a crisis period: the Texas City disaster.[2] When oil-loaded tankers began to explode in the harbor, refinery workers and public officials were faced with the choice of staying on their jobs to prevent further explosions and deal with the aftermath of those which had already taken place or leaving their positions to look out for the safety and well-being of their own families. Although there were many important exceptions noted by Killian, he concludes that

The great majority of persons interviewed who were involved in such dilemmas resolved them in favor of loyalty to the family, or, in some cases, to friendship groups. Much of the initial confusion, disorder, and seemingly complete disorganization reported in the disaster communities was the result of the rush of individuals to find and rejoin their families.[3]

The term *conflict* has a nasty ring to it, and there is a tendency to assume all too readily that role conflict is an unpleasant condition to be avoided whenever possible. Before this conclusion is accepted, however, it would be well to review briefly a recent study that suggests the benefits accruing to individuals subjected to role conflict. Stanley Elkins has carried out an imaginative historical analysis comparing the position of the Negro slave in North America with his counterpart in South America.[4] Why was it, he asks, that in North America the transition from slave to freeman was such a difficult one, brought about only by violence and civil war, whereas in South America the transition from slavery to emancipation occured much more easily? In seeking an answer to this question, Elkins focuses on differences in the social position of the slave in the two situations. In North America, the slave occupied a single social position whose role was defined by counterpositions located within the plantation itself. Other institutions such as the church were too weak to interfere with this essentially economic relation, and U.S. political institutions were "liberal," stressing noninterference in the private and business affairs of citizens. By contrast, in the South American countries, other institutions competed with the plantation for the control of the slave. Specifically, "What it came to was that three formidable interests—the crown, the planter, and the church—were deeply concerned with the system, that these concerns were in certain ways competing, and that the product of this balance of power left its profound impress on the actual legal and customary sanctions governing the status and treatment of slaves."[5] The powerful Catholic Church, for example, insisted on bringing the union of slaves under the Holy Sacraments, with the result that slave marriages were protected

[2]Lewis M. Killian, "The significance of multiple-group membership in disaster," *American Journal of Sociology*, 57 (January, 1952), 309–314.

[3]Killian, p. 311.

[4]Stanley M. Elkins, *Slavery: A Problem in American Institutional and Intellectual Life*, Chicago: University of Chicago Press, 1959. Available in a paperbound edition published by the Universal Library, Grosset & Dunlap, New York.

[5]Elkins, Universal Library edition, p. 71.

by law, while various medieval codes, backed by the authority of the Spanish king, assured to the slave certain legal protections unavailable to his North American counterpart. In sum, South American slaves occupied several positions in addition to that of slave, including subject of the king, church member, and marital partner, whereas North American slaves were restricted for the most part to the single position of slave.

We may conclude that from the standpoint of gaining freedom and autonomy of action, it is better to have several masters than one, because their conflicting claims will set limits on the powers exercised by each. Hence, it may be advantageous for an individual to occupy several social positions rather than a single position and to be subject to conflicting role expectations rather than to a single set of consistent expectations. In much less extreme circumstances than that confronting the slave in the Americas, conflicts in role expectations can be used by an individual to his own advantage as he plays off one set of counter-roles against another. Further, because the occupant of the position subject to role conflict cannot possibly conform to the inconsistent expectations to which he is subject, he may be able to exercise discretion in selecting the set of expectations to which he will respond.

Status and Status Crystallization   We have been considering the situation in which a single person occupies more than one social position in the society and is thereby subject to the possibility of conflicting role expectations. Yet another source of potential conflict is created if we introduce the concept of social status. By *social status* we shall mean the evaluation of the characteristics of a given position relative to other positions with which it is compared. "Evaluation" in this context means that an individual can rank the positions or characteristics of positions as being higher or lower, better or worse, more or less desirable, relative to one another. As always when we consider the attitudes or beliefs of individuals, there will be some variation from person to person in the evaluation they make of one position as compared with another; but, it is also true that for some kinds of positions the consensus among persons as to their relative ranking may be quite high. For example, studies have shown that there is great similarity in the way in which individuals in this society rank the prestige of various occupations, even across a period of almost forty years[6], and that there is a striking uniformity of occupational prestige rankings from country to country among the countries that have undergone industrialization.[7]

Status is one of the most important concepts employed by the sociologist, and we shall be concerned with some of its many facets throughout this volume. At this point, however, our concern is primarily with the phenomenon variously referred to as "status consistency," "status crystallization," and "status congruence." This area of study emphasizes that it is overly simplistic and inaccurate to conceive of the status of an individual as consisting of "a single position in a

[6]See Robert W. Hodge, Paul M. Siegel, and Peter H. Rossi, "Occupational prestige in the United States: 1925–1963," *American Journal of Sociology*, 70 (November, 1964) , 286–302.

[7]See Alex Inkeles and Peter H. Rossi, "National comparisons of occupational prestige," *American Journal of Sociology*, 61 (January, 1956) , 329–339; and Robert W. Hodge, Donald J. Treiman, and Peter H. Rossi, "A comparative study of occupational prestige," in Reinhard Bendix and Seymour M. Lipset (eds.) , *Class, Status, and Power* (2d ed.) , New York: Free Press, 1966. Pp. 309-321.

uni-dimensional hierarchy" ranging from low to high evaluation. Rather, because a given individual will occupy several social positions simultaneously, as we have already noted, the status of an individual should be viewed as "a series of positions in a series of related vertical hierarchies." This is the point of view advanced by Gerhard Lenski in Reading 8. For example, a person holding the occupational position of physician may also hold the ethnic position of Negro. This combination of positions may create problems, as pointed out by Hughes:

Membership in the Negro race, as defined in American mores and/or law, may be called a master status-determing trait. It tends to overpower, in most crucial situations, any other characteristics which might run counter to it. But professional standing is also a powerful characteristic. . . . In the person of the professionally qualified Negro these two powerful characteristics clash. The dilemma, for those whites who meet such a person, is that of having to choose whether to treat him as a Negro or as a member of his profession.[8]

It goes without saying that there are also problems and dilemmas for the Negro physician who cannot predict with any certainty how he will be treated and, hence, how he should behave.

The concept of *status crystallization* focuses on the extent to which there is consistency in the evaluations made of the various positions that an individual occupies. The situation in which an individual occupies some positions that are relatively highly evaluated and some that are evaluated relatively low is defined as one of "low" crystallization. And the individual who occupies a series of positions all of which are relatively highly evaluated or all of which are evaluated relatively low is said to be in a state of "high" crystallization.

Because the low status crystallization of an individual presents conflicting social stimuli to others, they are not certain how to treat him, and he, in turn, is not certain what is expected of him or how he should respond. Low status crystallization, in short, is similar in many ways to role conflict. And like role conflict, many kinds of reactions and attempted resolutions are possible. Lenski focuses on one reaction of considerable interest. He examines individuals with varying degrees of status crystallization and relates this to their political attitudes. Lenski finds that individuals characterized by low crystallization are more likely to express liberal attitudes than those who are in a state of high crystallization. He suggests that, in general, persons for whom the status order creates problems are more willing to support programs of social change.

Lenski's data suggest, and it seems sensible to argue, that what kind of response is generated by low status crystallization will depend in good measure on what positions are involved and on what kinds of positions receive low or high evaluations. To give a specific example, we would expect greater dissatisfaction with the status structure in the cases where an individual is high on some ranks because of his achievements but low on others that he is powerless to change by his own efforts. Thus, the individual who climbs in large part by his own efforts to the position of physician (an achieved status) will be justifiably upset if respect and prestige are denied him because of his ethnicity (an ascribed status), which he as an individual cannot change. Such a person is likely to join together with others in efforts designed to change the evaluations

[8]Everett C. Hughes, "Dilemmas and contradictions of status," *Men and Their Work*, Glencoe, Ill.: Free Press, 1958, p. 111.

made of his ethnic group, as, for example, a civil rights group. Indeed, one can argue that the current, powerful movement toward civil rights in this country could not have developed until large numbers of Negroes were in a state of low status crystallization caused by their slow but steady upward movement on status dimensions such as occupation, income, and education. Their relative advance on these dimensions has made their lack of progress in changing evaluations of their ethnicity increasingly intolerable and, hence, has thrust them into the struggle for reevaluation of the position of the Negro.

Turning briefly to a contrasting situation, we may note that the individual who enjoys high ethnic status but low occupational status may not need to join with others in an attempt to reform the status structure in order to improve his own position, but instead may attempt to improve his occupational status by, for example, undergoing further training. We would argue, then, that where individual social mobility is possible, low status crystallization would not necessarily be associated with political liberalism or attempts to change the status order.

An attempt to examine the differential reactions of individuals and groups to the problems posed by low status crystallization leads us quickly away from a concern with social structure to an emphasis on social process. (This is also the case when one examines attempts to resolve role conflicts.) Social mobility processes and reform movements aimed at structural change are but two examples of social processes that may have their roots in a social structure that places some of its participants in a situation of low status crystallization. This illustrates the extremely close connection between social structure and process, a connection that we will continue to explore throughout this book.

Positions, Roles, and Persons   There is an important additional question that can be posed by the role analyst that has not yet been considered. This concerns the extent to which it is possible, for analytical purposes, to separate specific individuals from the positions they occupy and the role expectations to which they are subject.[9] Some positions clearly predate and postdate their individual incumbents. Many such positions exist independently of their occupants in the sense that one can describe the characteristics of such positions—for example, a job description in an organization—even when they are unoccupied. At the other extreme, we know of many situations in which an individual has, in effect, created his own position in some group and where to describe the characteristics of the position and role is simply to describe the relevant characteristics of the person involved.

In both cases, we are talking about positions (locations in a set of social relationships) and about roles (expectations focused upon the person occupying the position). The difference between these types of positions may be recognized by distinguishing between formal and informal positions and roles. A *formal* position is a position that can be defined independently of the character-

---

[9]An equally important question asks how individuals get assigned to a given position. The question of role or position allocation, however, clearly implies a process perspective because it asks how individuals are chosen and prepared for occupancy of a given position and what are the consequences for the individual of a given position assignment. These matters will be discussed in Part Three where we consider status processes.

istics of any particular occupant of that position, while a position is *informal* to the extent that it is impossible to separate position characteristics from those of the specific individual occupying the position.

We speak of "informal positions" rather than "individuals" to emphasize two important sociological premises: (1) that in any given situation only some subset of an individual's many characteristics are salient (are taken into account by those interacting with him) and (2) that individuals occupy different positions in different groups; that is, characteristics possessed by an individual may be emphasized by one group and become the basis for establishing particular relationships with him while another group completely ignores these same characteristics, selecting a different set as the basis for defining and relating to him. In the case of "formal positions," a set of characteristics is specified without regard to any particular individual. A formal definition of a position is an attempt to specify which characteristics are most salient; these characteristics are then used as the basis for selecting incumbents of the position. It often happens that an individual occupying a formal position has characteristics attributed to him that he does not in fact possess. There are cases known, for example, where an individual has successfully masqueraded as a physician and has had attributed to him by others all the appropriate characteristics associated with occupancy of this position.

Obviously, what is introduced here as a dichotomy is in reality a continuum for which our definitions may serve as the polar types. Thus, certain expectations will be held concerning the attributes and behavior of Supervisor Joe Jones both because he is a supervisor (the formal component of the role) and because he is Joe Jones (the informal component of the role). We can only loosely speak of formal and informal positions and roles. When we are being careful, we will talk about the extent to which a given position and role is formalized or the extent to which it is informally defined. These distinctions are merely introduced at this point. We will pick them up again at the point where we examine differences between informal groups and formal groups or organizations.

6　A Language for Role Analysis

Neal Gross, Ward S. Mason, and Alexander W. McEachern

The purposes of this chapter are to present a body of concepts that may be useful for students of role analysis and to consider some of their implications for empirical inquiry. Our objective has been to develop a "role" language that may be applied to individual, cultural, or social phenomena and one that makes possible the investigation of the problem of role consensus. We have attempted to intro-

Reprinted from Neal Gross, Ward S. Mason, and Alexander W. McEachern, *Explorations in Role Analysis*, New York: Wiley, Inc., 1958, pp. 48–69, by permission of the author and the publisher.

duce the minimum number of concepts and, as much as possible, to limit consideration to those concepts which are capable of operational definition. Some special terms used only in the discussion of role conflict are not considered here.[1] Those which are considered constitute the basic language of the research to be reported in this book. They are presented under four main headings: Position; Expectations; Role, Role Behavior, and Role Attributes; and Sanctions.

POSITION

The term *position* will be used to refer to *the location of an actor or class of actors in a system of social relationships.* The general idea of social location has been represented by some authors with the term status, and by others with position. The two terms have about equal precedent. We have chosen position for this purpose because status connotes the idea of differential ranking among a set of persons or social locations, whereas the more neutral term, position, does not.

The meaning of location in a system of social relationships is not, however, entirely self-evident. It is difficult to separate the idea of location from the relationships which define it. Just as in geometry a point cannot be located without describing its relationships to other points, so persons cannot be located without describing their relations to other individuals; the points imply the relationships and the relationships imply the points. In a system of social relationships, however, the points acquire labels or identities which may come to have an almost autonomous significance. People may recognize that some identities are located in a relationship system, but have only a rudimentary conception of what

[1]See Gross, Mason and McEachern, chapter 15.

those relationships are. For example, many people who recognize that there is such an occupation as school superintendent may understand only that it is found in the school system and has a higher rank than the occupation of teacher or principal.

People do not get sorted out into different locations in systems of social relationships at random. Certain characteristics of actors come to have relationship patterns associated with them. In his analysis of the social system Parsons has developed an elaborate classification of the "modalities of objects as foci of role expectations," the principal differentiation being that between the performances and qualities of actors.[2] Linton speaks of four "reference points for the ascription of status": age, sex, family (biological) relationships, and birth into a particular socially established group.[3] Similarly, Bennett and Tumin list the "raw materials of status" as (1) the wide variety of biologically determined kinship relations, (2) the biological attributes of man, (3) the great number of human and personality traits, and (4) the literally infinite number of situations of interaction possible between human beings.[4]

Of course not all characteristics of actors have social relationships associated with them. Whereas the sex of individuals constitutes the basis for certain relationship patterns, eye color, at least in American society, does not. The labels assigned to positions, as distinguished from the bases for these positions, serve the cognitive function of differentiating among them. In the case

[2]Talcott Parsons, *The Social System* (Glencoe: The Free Press, 1951), pp. 88-96.
[3]Ralph Linton, *The Study of Man* (New York: D. Appleton-Century Co., 1936), pp. 115–116.
[4]John W. Bennett and Melvin M. Tumin, *Social Life, Structure and Function* (New York: Alfred A. Knopf, 1948), p. 87.

of ascribed[5] positions, the labels which refer to them are generally derived from the "presocial system" characteristics on which the patterns are based. We speak directly of such positions as child or male, for example. Achieved positions are entered through performance and competition, and the labels chosen for them usually have a different derivation. They may refer to what the incumbent does either apart from the relationship system (for example, carpenter), or in terms of social relationships (for example, employer); they may refer primarily to rank in a hierarchic system (for example, lieutenant); or possibly to a combination of these. Whatever the source of the labels which allow cognitive discriminations among actors, identities do not become positions until they are placed in a relationship system.

Since positions have been defined as locations of actors in systems of social relationships, they can be completely described only by an examination of the content of their interrelationships. However, before investigating *how* positions are interrelated, we must go a step further in designating the position to be studied. Clarity in this respect is necessary for the selection of appropriate research procedures and for the statement of the universe of phenomena to which research findings may be generalized.

When an investigator uses a sampling procedure in his research, it is necessary that he specify precisely the population from which he is sampling and to which his findings may be generalized. Public opinion poll findings, for example, may be considered meaningless without this specification. However, in addition to specifying the population of respondents, for many types of social science inquiry it is just as necessary to specify the phenomena to which they are responding; it is necessary to specify not only a *subject* population but also an *object* population.

Similarly, in the analysis of a particular position certain specifications are necessary in order that the object of analysis will be clear. We propose to examine two aspects of position specification, the relational and the situational.

The Relational Specification of Positions

Nearly every role theorist, regardless of the frame of reference in which his analysis is couched, adopts the view that a position is an element or a part of a network or system of positions. In *The Study of Man* Linton says that statuses are the "polar positions" in reciprocal behavior patterns.[6] In *The Cultural Background of Personality* he says: "The place in a particular system which a certain individual occupies at a particular time will be referred to as his *status* with respect to that system."[7] For Parsons a status is a ". . . place in the relationship system considered as a structure, that is a patterned system of *parts*."[8] In Newcomb's scheme this point is given especial emphasis:

Thus the positions, which are the smallest element—the construction blocks—of societies and organized groups, are interrelated and consistent because they are organized

[5]Linton defines ascribed statuses as ". . . those which are assigned to individuals without reference to their innate differences or abilities." Achieved statuses on the other hand ". . . are left open to be filled through competition and individual effort." (Linton, *op. cit.*, p. 115.) Although Parsons claims indebtedness to Linton he uses the term with a somewhat different meaning: "Achievement-oriented roles are those which place the accent on the performances of the incumbent, ascribed roles, on his qualities or attributes independently of specific expected performances." (Parsons, *op. cit.*, p. 64.) We are following Parsons' usage.

[6]Linton, *op. cit.*, p. 113.
[7]Ralph Linton, *The Cultural Background of Personality* (New York: D. Appleton-Century Co., 1945), p. 76.
[8]Parsons, *op. cit.*, p. 25.

to common ends. From one point of view, then, societies and organized groups are structures of positions which are organized to reach certain goals. Since every position is a part of an inclusive system of positions, no one position has any meaning apart from the other positions to which it is related.[9]

The last sentence in the statement from Newcomb suggests the nature of the present problem. If a particular position has no meaning apart from other positions, it is necessary for an investigator, in focusing on one position, to specify the other positions with which his analysis will be concerned. Some positions in our society seem at first glance to be associated with only one other position, for example, the positions of mother or employer. The terms themselves seem to imply only one "opposite number" or reciprocal position, which are for these examples child and employee, respectively. Some theorists, moreover, define their terms to refer only to dyadic relations of this sort.[10] Closer inspection will usually reveal that such positions are related to more than one other position. When a mother consults a teacher about her son's progress in school she is still acting in the mother position, and when the employer deals with the labor union's business manager he is still acting in the position of employer. Other positions, such as college president, may not have implications for any dyadic relationships. Whatever the implications of the label, a position cannot be completely described until all the other positions to which it is related have been specified. Of course a complete relational specification is a limiting case with which it would be impossible to deal empirically. For a given research problem it may be necessary to

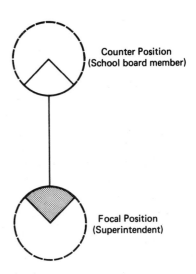

FIGURE 6-1.   A dyad model.

take into account only a limited set of counter positions.

In studying a particular position (a *focal* position), it may for some purposes be adequate to consider its relationship to only one other position (a *counter* position). This could be termed a *dyad* model, and is represented by Figure 6-1.

A more complete specification of the focal position of superintendent might include its relationships to teachers and principals as well as school board members, as in Figure 6-2.

In Figure 6-2, which shows what might be termed *a position-centric model*, the focal position is specified by its relationships to three counter positions. In the dyad model a position is specified by its relationship to only one counter position. In the position-centric model the position is specified by its relationships to a number of counter positions. The elements of this more complex specification are the relationships of the focal position to the different counter positions. In referring to these *elements of relational specification*, we will use the concept of positional sectors. A *positional sector* is specified by the relationship of a focal position to a *single* counter position and

[9]Theodore M. Newcomb, *Social Psychology* (New York: Dryden Press, 1951), p. 277.

[10]E. T. Hiller, *Social Relations and Social Structures: A Study in Principles of Sociology* (New York: Harper and Brothers, 1947).

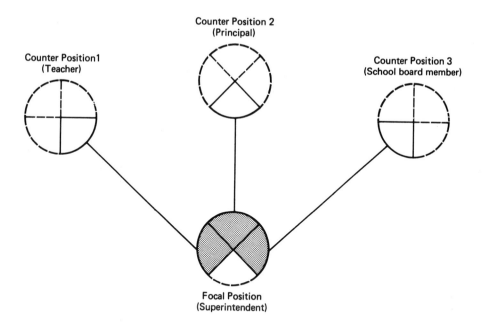

FIGURE 6-2. A position-centric model.

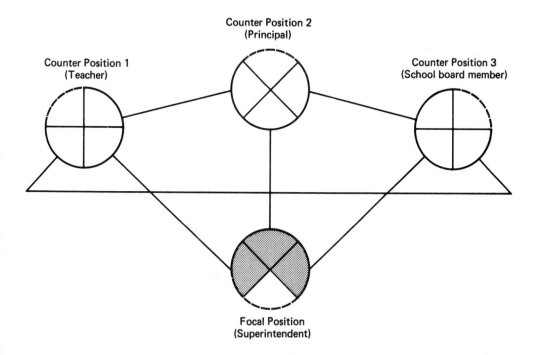

FIGURE 6-3. A system model.

is defined as an element of the relational specification of a position. Studying the superintendency in its relationship to the school board member position is quite a different unit of analysis from the superintendency in its relation to the principal position.

Some authors would treat each sector of the focal position as a different position. To some extent this may be a matter of arbitrary usage, but those who view each sector as a separate position generally fail to consider the problems of anything more complicated than a dyadic relationship. For certain analysis problems the more meaningful unit of analysis may be the position as defined by multiple relationships. In the first place, the indentities of actors can refer to their positions in all relevant relationships, not to just selected ones. This is obviously the case with such identities as school superintendent which implies relationships with many other positions, such as, school board member, principal, teacher, parent, local government official, and so on. It is also the case, though less obviously so, with positions like mother and employer as we tried to show earlier. In the second place, the relationship between the sectors of the total position may be of prime importance. That is, to understand the relationship of position X to Y, it may be necessary to know about the relationship of X to Z; to understand a superintendent's relationship to teachers it may be necessary to have some understanding of his relationship to his school board.

The position-centric model provides a framework for focusing on one position and examining its relationships to a series of counter positions. This model does not consider the relationships among the counter positions. If these relationships are added, we have what might be termed *system model*. By

including the relationships among the counter positions an important addition has been made. The object of study which Figure 6-3 represents may be viewed as a system in the scientific sense, that is, as a series of interdependent parts. A position can be completely described only by describing the total system of positions and relationships of which it is a part. In other words, in a system of interdependent parts, a change in any relationship will have an effect on all other relationships, and the positions can be described only by the relationships.

Usually, it is only possible to deal with partial systems. In Figures 6-1, 6-2, and 6-3 one sector of the focal position was

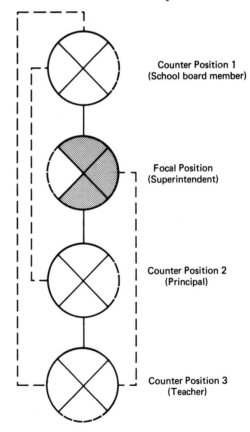

Counter Position 1
(School board member)

Focal Position
(Superintendent)

Counter Position 2
(Principal)

Counter Position 3
(Teacher)

FIGURE 6-4.   A hierarchic system model.

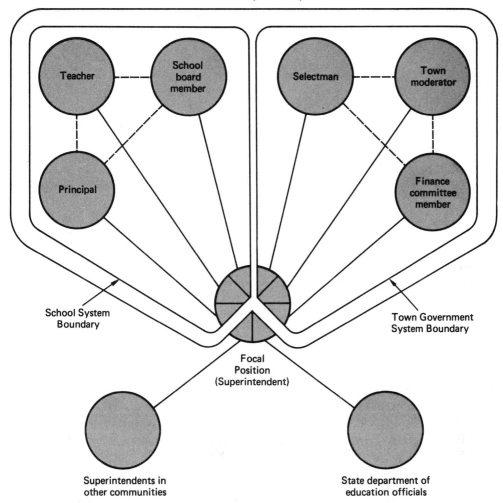

FIGURE 6-5.   A multiple systems model.

left blank to show that only a limited set of positions selected from all possible related positions have been considered. If we add another position, like student, the system, and consequently the specification of each position, will be more complete.

It may be possible to simplify this partial system model if the relationships place the positions in a hierarchical series, as in Figure 6-4. Even in this situation the relationships between non-adjacent positions in the series, although not necessarily of prime importance, are essential to the full understanding of this series of positions as a system. In addition, other positions, like supervisor, may not fit neatly into the series.

A final elaboration might be described. A focal position may be involved in several different systems of positions, as in Figure 6-5. Using the superintendency as a focal position, the system of educational positions which we have been considering can be thought of as one system among a number of systems. Superintendents are involved in many systems, such as, professional organizations and local and state government. Some of these systems are within the local community and some are not. When we observe the relationships between a superintendent and superintendents in other communities, the boundary between the local community and a larger social system has been crossed.

These superintendent-superintendent relationships suggest that relationships among the incumbents of the same position may be investigated. Teachers interact with other teachers, and doctors interact with other doctors. This type of relationship has been largely ignored in the literature.

The difference among these models might better be viewed as one of degree than of kind. In any of them we may pick one position to focus on, and all of these models, including the dyad, can be analyzed as a system. The differentiation is chiefly in terms of the completeness with which we wish to or can make an analysis. No matter how complete the analysis, there are always some things which must be left out; we must always select and abstract. How simple or how complex a relational system must be depends on the given problem. In general, the more complete the relationship system studied, the more completely can a given position be described.

The Situational Specification of Positions

In the preceding sections we have tried to show that a particular position has relationships with a set of positions and that clarity of analysis demands a precise specification of the positional sector or sectors which will be treated in a particular inquiry. A second specification which is required concerns the situational context in which the position will be examined.

The first type of situational specification required is almost geographical in nature. It describes the *scope of the social system* in which the position is to be studied. For example, shall we study the superintendency position in a specific community, in the state of Massachusetts, or in the United States? Positions may be studied at various levels of situational inclusiveness, but it is necessary to specify at which level one intends to work.

The specification of the scope of the social system designates the boundaries of the situation within which the position is being studied. Within these boundaries, however, the situation may include a number of different elements. If we choose a specific community in which to study a given position a complex set of situational factors is implied, for example, the size of the community, the resources available to it, and so on. If we were to study the superintendency in the Commonwealth of Massachusetts this would imply, for example, a study of the status of education in the General Laws of Massachusetts, how the State Department of Education is run, and the structure of town and city government in the Commonwealth. Within a state these factors would be constant. As we enlarge the scope of the system the situational specification of the position becomes more general, for fewer of the situational elements are constant within a larger system. For example, certain types of local government organization in Massachusetts do not exist in other parts of the United States.

At times it may be desirable to study positions in terms of a situational element which cuts across the scope of the system specification. For example we might wish to compare the superintendency in the suburbs of metropolitan areas with the superintendency in central cities.[11] Just what situational elements modify given positions will, of course, vary a great deal with the type of position. Although no attempt will be made here to present a general classification of them, it is necessary for an investigator to specify what situational elements he has used in describing the position which is his focus of interest.

One of the concepts in the literature which might be placed under the general rubric of situational specification is that of *office* as a type of position. For example, Kingsley Davis states:

The term status would then designate a position in the general institutional system, recognized and supported by the entire society, spontaneously evolved rather than deliberately created, rooted in the folkways and mores. Office, on the other hand, would designate a position in a deliberately created organization, governed by specific and limited rules in a limited group, more generally achieved than ascribed.

.   .   .   .   .   .

Occupational position, for instance, is often a status and office both, the first when viewed from the standpoint of the general public, the second when viewed from the standpoint of the particular business or agency.[12]

As an example of status (position) Davis uses "professor" and of a corresponding office, "professor of government at the University of Arizona." The concept of office makes a special kind of situational specification of the position; it implies that the position is to be viewed in the context of all the special situational features of a given organization. Davis'

distinction between status and office makes it clear that the same position can be studied at more than one level of situational specificity.

We have considered two aspects of the specification of positions: the relational and the situational. It should be pointed out that the two kinds of specification crosscut each other. A position with a certain relational specification may be studied in several situational contexts, and a position in a certain situational context may be viewed with several different relational specifications. For example, we might study the superintendency as specified relationally with the school board member and teacher counter positions at the community, state, or national level of situational specificity; or, given a level of situational specificity, such as the superintendency in Massachusetts, we might study the position under a variety of relational specifications, for example, in dyadic relation to the school board member position, or as part of a more complete system of educational positions.

EXPECTATIONS

We have defined position as the location of an actor or class of actors in a system of social relationships. The concept refers only to the location itself and not to the expectations and behaviors by means of which the position is described. This distinction is made for analytic purposes since concretely we never have a position without expectations and behaviors. We point this out because some authors have combined the idea of location with at least the normative aspect of the relationship structure. Thus for Linton a status is "simply a collection of rights and duties,"[13] and for Sarbin a position is equivalent to "a system of rights and

[11]We are still talking about the superintendency as an *object* of study. We might ask superintendents in both suburbs and central cities to consider both types of superintendency positions.

[12]Kingsley Davis, *Human Society* (New York: The Macmillan Company, 1948 and 1949), pp. 88–89. See also Everett Cherrington Hughes, "Institutional Office and the Person," *American Journal of Sociology*, XLIII (1937), pp. 404–413.

[13]Linton, *Study of Man*, p. 113.

duties."[14] In our scheme "position" is simply a social location.

Networks of positions can be analyzed with respect to either how the incumbents of the positions *should* interact with each other or how they actually *do* interact with each other. We shall consider the behavioral analysis problem later. If the analysis is concerned with how actors should behave, it will deal with *expectations*. An expectation will be defined as an *evaluative standard applied to an incumbent of a position*.

Before elaborating on certain aspects of this definition, two special points deserve emphasis. The first is that the term expectation has been used in role formulations in at least two different senses. In one, it refers to a prediction as in the case of the statement, "My expectation is that he *will* arrive at nine o'clock." In the other, it refers to a normative criterion or standard of evaluation: "My expectation is that he *should* arrive at nine o'clock." When Newcomb views a role as "the ways of behaving which are expected of any individual who occupies a certain position."[15] he is using the word "expected" in its normative sense. Similarly, Parsons and Shils view role-expectations as "patterns of evaluations."[16]

Sarbin uses expectation in its predictive sense when he says, ". . . a position in a social structure [is] a set of expectations or acquired anticipatory reactions. That is to say, the person learns (*a*) to expect or anticipate certain actions from

other persons, and (*b*) that others have expectations of him."[17] That stability in the prediction of behavior may be of importance in the development of evaluative standards is probably a correct assumption. Analytically, however, the two ideas are quite distinct. A man may predict that small boys will steal apples from his orchard, but he does not necessarily condone it. What will happen and what should happen in a situation are quite different ideas. The meaning of expectations in our definition is normative rather than predictive. For the predictive sense in which the term "expectation" is used, we would suggest the more general and precise term *anticipation* which would denote statements or feelings with respect to the probability of future events.

Another special point is that an expectation, as we have defined it, may be applied to all incumbents or to a particular incumbent of a specified position. Whether an expectation applies to all incumbents or to a particular incumbent is dependent on how the position has been specified. For example, a position, such as superintendent, could be specified to include only one incumbent, such as the superintendency in New York City. It could also be specified to include all the superintendents in the United States. We have tried to define the concept of expectation so that it could be used in studies dealing with either of these problems.

From the standpoint of actors in social situations, the same distinction can be made. For example, school board members can evaluate their superintendent on the standards they would apply to all superintendents in the United States, general standards modified to fit the local situation, or standards they would hold only for the superintendent in their

[14]Theodore R. Sarbin, "Role Theory," in Gardner Lindzey (Editor), *Handbook of Social Psychology*, Vol. I (Cambridge: Addison-Wesley Publishing Company, 1954), p. 225.

[15]Newcomb. *op. cit.*, p. 280.

[16]Talcott Parsons and Edward A. Shils with the assistance of James Olds, "Values, Motives, and Systems of Action," in Talcott Parsons and Edward A. Shils (Editors), *Toward A General Theory of Action* (Cambridge: Harvard University Press, 1951), p. 190.

[17]Sarbin, *op. cit.*, p. 225.

own community. In concrete interaction situations the expectations that one actor holds for a specific incumbent of a position are in part a function of his relational and situational specifications of this position. In addition, they may be partly a function of his perception of the other positions the incumbent occupies. For example, one actor may see another as the incumbent of only the position of teacher. Another actor may see the same person as an incumbent of the positions of teacher and female. These different perceptions may result in different expectations. Another set of conditions that may influence the expectations one actor holds for a position incumbent is the incumbent's personal characteristics: a teacher may have somewhat different standards for "bright" and "dull" pupils.

Our definition of expectations refers to evaluative standards, not to anticipations. Whereas it is commonly accepted that the behavior of position incumbents is affected by the complex set of conditions in which it takes place, the point we have been trying to make is that expectations held for position incumbents in concrete situations may be similarly a function of many conditions.[18]

Dimensions of a Single Expectation

If we ask individuals to tell us whether they feel that a particular behavior is expected of a position incumbent (for example, a school superintendent), we may find some respondents who reply that it is required whereas another might say that it is prohibited. Two other respondents may agree that a superintendent should engage in a certain behavior, but one may say he *absolutely must* do it and the other may give a more permissive response such as he *preferably should*. These responses suggest two dimensions of a single expectation: direction and intensity.[19]

One question that may be asked about an expectation, then, is about its *direction*. Every expectation can be reduced to a statement for or against something. Whether a particular expectation is a prescription or a proscription is an operational rather than a theoretical problem. The empirical reference of the expectation must be introduced before its direction can be specified.

The second dimension of an expectation is its intensity. Any expectation can be placed somewhere on a continuum which ranges from the completely permissive, through the preferential, to the mandatory. For example, a school board might hold the expectation that its superintendent *absolutely must* attend school board meetings, that he *preferably should* attend meetings of the local teachers' association, and that he *may or may not* attend the meetings of the state superintendency association.

ROLE, ROLE BEHAVIOR, AND ROLE ATTRIBUTES

In the second chapter we considered some of the different definitions of the term role which have been presented in the social science literature. It was

---

[18]Davis seems to be making a similar point when he says, "The essence of any social situation lies in the mutual expectations of the participants. These expectations rest to a great extent on the norms applicable in the situation." (Davis, *op. cit.*, p. 83.) However, later paragraphs indicate that he is using "expectations" in a predictive as well as a normative sense.

[19]Other dimensions of single expectations are suggested by several treatments of related concepts. See Clyde Kluckhohn, "Values and Value-Orientations in the Theory of Action," in Parsons and Shils, *op. cit.*, pp. 412–421; Robin M. Williams, Jr., *American Society* (New York: Alfred A. Knopf, 1952), pp. 24–29; Louis Guttman, "The Principle Components of Scalable Attitudes," in Paul F. Lazarsfeld (Editor), *Mathematical Thinking in the Social Sciences* (Glencoe: The Free Press, 1954), pp. 216-257.

pointed out that there was a certain amount of unity within the diversity. Most authors, in discussing roles, consider the ideas of social location, expectations, and behavior. These notions are integral to our own research problems, and we have so far given considerable attention to the concepts of position and expectation in this chapter. We propose to restrict our definition of role to a set of expectations: *A role is a set of expectations,* or in terms of our definition of expectations, it is *a set of evaluative standards applied to an incumbent of a particular position.*

This definition of role depends on the previous definition of position as a location of an actor or class of actors in a system of social relationships. We have defined role so that it can be used as a concept at any of the various levels of relational and situational specificity which can be applied to positions. Defined in this way, the role concept may be used in studies of dyadic or more complicated relational systems, formal and informal organizations, as well as of the structure of a total society. This means that the concept is not restricted to the situations or relationships which are of interest to a particular set of investigators but can be used in the analyses of problems at different levels.

In addition, no restrictions are placed by this definition on the definers of the expectations. The concept may consequently be used in analyses in which the incumbents of the position as well as nonincumbents of the position are the definers of the role or, in general, in analyses of a role as defined by any population an investigator wishes to specify.

In studying a particular role an investigator would presumably try to elicit from the members of a specified population the expectations which they hold for incumbents of a specified position. While it would be possible to proceed simply on this basis, it would seem to be helpful to have some way of organizing or differentiating among these expectations. A collection of expectations, while providing substantive information, would not allow any more detailed analysis of a role than its simple description. If we assume that the expectations applied to a position are not simply a random collection but are themselves organized, the role may be said to have an "internal organization." Consequently, the problem of *role segmentation,* or categorizing the expectations, becomes relevant to role analysis.

It may be helpful to distinguish role segmentation from a problem treated earlier, the distinction between dimensions of a single expectation. Our consideration of the dimensions of a single expectation was an attempt to point out certain questions that could be asked about a single expectation. It was suggested that a particular expectation includes the dimensions of direction and intensity. The focus was on the categorization of a *single* expectation along these two dimensions.

Role segmentation, however, is concerned with the classification of a group or *set* of expectations that individuals may hold for an incumbent of a specified position. Whereas the dimensions were components of expectations, segments are parts of roles. *Multiple* expectations are involved and we wish to consider how they may be categorized on socially relevant criteria. Three categorizations of expectations will be presented which can be applied in the analysis of any role. Each of these categorizations has received consideration by one or another of the social scientists whose definitions of role we examined earlier, and they may be implicit in the formulations of every one of them. It is important to make them explicit. The first categorization differentiates among *role sectors,* the second between *rights and obligations,* and the third between *behaviors and attributes.*

Role Sectors

In our examination of the problem of the relational specification of a position, we pointed out that to study one position it is necessary to consider one or more related positions. An empirical study concerned with the expectations applied to a particular position can focus on the expectations which are involved in any one or all of the relationships by means of which the position has been specified. This implies that the question "What expectations are attached to the position?" cannot be answered until the position has been relationally specified.

The concept of positional sector was introduced to refer to the elements of the relational specification. To correspond to these "parts" of the position, the concept of role sector will be introduced. *A role sector is defined as a set of expectations applied to the relationship of a focal position to a single counter position.*

To categorize expectations on the basis of role sectors is one basis of role segmentation. In an empirical inquiry the analysis may be concerned with one or more role sectors. The variety of possible relationships in which a specific position may be involved requires, therefore, that in the analysis of the set of expectations associated with it the investigator needs to specify precisely what role sectors will be examined.

The concept of role sector suggests certain interesting research questions. For example, for the study of role consensus, we may ask: Is there more consensus among a set of role definers on one role sector than another? Is there more consensus among one set of role definers than among another on a particular role sector?

Rights and Obligations

If the expectations applied to a position are classified according to its relationship with specific counter positions, then we may ask, for each expectation, if it is applied to the incumbent of the focal position or to the incumbent of the counter position. *Rights of the incumbent of a focal position are defined as expectations which are applied to an incumbent of a counter position. Obligations of the incumbent of a focal position are defined as expectations which are applied to the incumbent of the focal position.*

The distinction between rights and obligations implies that the description of the expectations associated with a position in its relationship with another position must include "what is due" the incumbent of the focal position from the incumbent of the counter position (rights) and what the incumbent of the focal position "owes" the occupant of the counter position (obligations). For a given role sector, the question of which expectations are called rights, and which are called obligations, depends, of course, on which position is "focal" for any analysis.

This distinction is clearly implicit in many role formulations and explicit in a number of them. That it is not central to all of them, however, can be seen from Linton's reference to "rights" in his volume, *The Cultural Background of Personality.* After stating that a role "includes the attitudes, values, and behavior ascribed by the society to any and all persons occupying the status," he adds, "It *can even be extended* to include the legitimate expectations of such persons with respect to the behavior toward them of persons in other statuses within the same system." (Italics ours.) [20]

This segmentation of a role into rights

[20]Linton, *Cultural Background*, p. 77.

and obligations suggests certain additional problems pertaining to role consensus. For example, using incumbents of a focal position as role definers the following questions might be raised: Will the incumbents of a position have more consensus on their rights in one role sector than on their rights in another role sector? Will there be more consensus on some obligations than on others in a single role sector?

Expectations for Behaviors and Attributes

This basis of role segmentation provides concepts by means of which an investigator can distinguish between what incumbents of positions *should do* and what incumbents of positions *should be,* or the characteristics they should have. A role can be segmented into *expectations for behaviors* and *expectations for attributes.*

Most authors have restricted their treatment of expectations to those in the first category, for behavior. Parsons, however, does make exactly this distinction when he says, "In orienting to an actor as object . . . primacy may be given . . . to his attributes or qualities, independently of specific expected performances, or . . . to his performances, completed, in process, or expected in the future."[21] Linton and those who derive directly from him, on the other hand, seem to neglect the possibility that one person may hold expectations for another's attributes. One reason why Parsons appears to be almost alone in making this distinction may be that he is one of the few authors for whom "role expectation" is an elemental concept.

In considering problems that arise in the use of the concept of position in empirical inquiries, we maintained that both relational and situational specifica-

[21]Parsons, *Social System*, p. 88. See also Sarbin, *op. cit.*, p. 227 for a similar distinction.

tions of the position are required. Since a role analysis is concerned with a set of expectations applicable to incumbents of a particular position, these same specifications are necessary. That is, in specifying the position, we are also specifying the role. However, the expectations which describe the role can be categorized into role segments, and in empirical analysis it is also necessary to say what segments are under examination. The role segments which have been differentiated imply that it is necessary to say, first, what role sectors will be analyzed, second, whether rights, obligations, or both will be included in the analysis, and third, whether the expectations considered will include those for attributes or behaviors, or both. Only some of the phenomena to which these specifications of positions and of role segments apply would probably be considered in any role analysis, but it is our suggestion that the specifications themselves must be made.

We have suggested that one of the ways of segmenting a role, or categorizing the expectations which comprise a role, is into expectations for behavior and expectations for attributes. So far, however, we have not presented concepts for the actual behaviors or attributes, as distinguished from the expectations for them. Although it is possible to conduct role analyses without reference to *actual* behavior or attributes, for some problems concepts to describe them are necessary. The problems of conformity-deviance, for example, imply a comparison of expectations and the behaviors and attributes to which they refer.

In addition to the definitions of role behavior and role attributes, terms parallel to "role sector" will be presented for both behavior and attributes.

A *role behavior* is an actual performance of an incumbent of a position which can be referred to an expectation for an incumbent of that position.[22]

A *role attribute* is an actual quality of an incumbent of a position which can be referred to an expectation for an incumbent of that position.

A *role behavior sector* is a set of actual behaviors which can be referred to a set of expectations for behaviors applied to the relationship of a focal position to a single counter position.

A *role attribute sector* is a set of actual attributes which can be referred to a set of expectations for attributes applied to the relationship of a focal position to a single counter position.

SANCTIONS

In the previous sections we have been concerned with two aspects of social relationships, the normative and the behavioral: what the actor is *supposed to do* and what he *actually does*. The dimension of conformity-deviance is inherent in such a scheme. In studying interactional systems an important question is whether or to what degree the actors are conforming to the roles for their positions. This in turn raises the problem of social control: Is there anything in the system which tends to maintain conformity? We will introduce the concept of sanctions to deal with this problem: *A sanction is a role behavior the primary significance of which is gratificational-deprivational.*

[22]It should be noted that this definition of *a role behavior*, as well as the definitions of *role attribute, role behavior sector,* and *role attribute sector,* does not specify who holds the expectation to which the actual performance of the position is referred. For different research problems variant role definers may be employed, for example, the incumbent of the focal position or incumbents of counter positions. This is an operational question, one that will be considered in the next chapter. The special point to be noted is that in the proposed conceptual scheme these terms refer to actual performances or qualities to which evaluative standards held by some role definer(s) for incumbent(s) of the position may be applied.

It is useful to differentiate between two "modes of significance" which either expectations or behavior may have, namely, instrumental significance and gratificational significance. The instrumental significance of an act refers to its consequences for some end or goal. The gratificational significance of an act refers to its consequences for some actor's gratification or deprivation. Similarly, expectations can be categorized according to the instrumental and gratificational significance of the behaviors to which they refer.

Any act has both types of significance (or can be analyzed in terms of each), and for certain purposes the relative importance of the two modes might be crucial. Some acts may be almost purely gratificational in significance, as when an actor responds by saying "I think it is wrong for you to do that." Other acts may appear to have only instrumental significance, as when each man operating a two-man saw responds to or follows the other's pull with a pull of his own. However, it could be argued that no act has only one type of significance. In the first example the expression of the negative attitude may also be seen as an interruption of an instrumental sequence; in the two-man saw example, the fact that the interaction continues in orderly fashion means that there is some kind of tacit approval implicit in the interaction. It was for these reasons that in defining the term *sanction* we said its *primary* significance was gratificational. An *instrumental act* is one in which the *primary* significance is instrumental. Corresponding terms on the normative side would be *expectations for sanctions* and *expectations for instrumental acts*. Since a sanction is a role behavior whose primary significance is gratificational, it can be viewed as falling along a positive-negative or reward-punishment dimension. . . .

To provide both a summary of and a convenient reference to the concepts which have been presented, they are listed with their definitions here. This list represents the basic language for the empirical analyses to be presented in this volume.[23]

A *position* is the location of an actor or class of actors in a system of social relationships.

A *positional sector* is an element of the relational specification of a position, and is specified by the relationship of a focal position to a single counter position.

An *expectation* is an evaluative standard applied to an incumbent of a position.

A *role* is a set of expectations applied to an incumbent of a particular position.

A *role sector* is a set of expectations applied to the relationship of a focal position to a single counter position.

A *right* of an incumbent of a focal position is an expectation applied to the incumbent of a counter position.

An *obligation* of an incumbent of a focal position is an expectation applied to the incumbent of a focal position.

A *role behavior* is an actual performance of an incumbent of a position which can be referred to an expectation for an incumbent of that position.

A *role attribute* is an actual quality of an incumbent of a position which can be referred to an expectation for an incumbent of that position.

A *role behavior sector* is a set of actual behaviors which can be referred to a set of expectations for behaviors applicable to the relationship of a focal position to a single counter position.

A *role attribute sector* is a set of actual attributes which can be referred to a set of expectations for attributes applicable to the relationship of a focal position to a single counter position.

A *sanction* is a role behavior the primary significance of which is gratificational-deprivational.

[23]For another set of concepts that embrace somewhat theoretically similar ideas see Robert K. Merton, *Social Theory and Social Structure* (Glencoe: The Free Press, 1956), pp. 368–370. For other recent efforts to develop a language for role analysis see Frederick L. Bates, "Position, Role, and Status: A Reformulation of Concepts," *Social Forces*, XXXIV (1956), pp. 313–321 and W. B. Brookover, "Research on Teacher and Administrator Roles," *Journal of Educational Sociology*, XXIX (1955), pp. 2–13.

7   An Analysis of Conflicting Social Norms

Samuel A. Stouffer

This paper illustrates an empirical procedure for studying role obligations, with particular reference to simultaneous role obligations which conflict.

The writer became especially interested in the problem when considering the strains to which the non-commissioned officer in the Army was subjected. On the one hand, the non-com had the role of agent of the command and in case the orders from above conflicted with what his men thought were right and necessary

Reprinted from Samuel A. Stouffer, "An analysis of conflicting social norms," *American Sociological Review*, 14 (1949), 707–717, by permission of the publisher, The American Sociological Association.

he was expected by his superiors to carry out the orders. But he also was an enlisted man, sharing enlisted men's attitudes, often hostile attitudes, toward the commissioned ranks. Consequently, the system of informal controls was such as to reward him for siding with the men in a conflict situation and punish him if he did not. There was some evidence that unless his men had confidence that he could see their point of view, he was an ineffective leader; on the other hand, open and flagrant disobedience by him of an order from above could not be tolerated by the command.[1]

The general theoretical viewpoint behind this paper involves several propositions:

1. In any social group there exist norms and a strain for conformity to these norms.

2. Ordinarily, if the norms are clear and unambiguous the individual has no choice but to conform or take the consequences in group resentment.

3. If a person has simultaneous roles in two or more groups such that simultaneous conformity to the norms of each of the groups is incompatible, he can take one of only a limited number of actions, for example:

(1) He can conform to one set of role expectations and take the consequences of non-conformity to other sets.

(2) He can seek a compromise position by which he attempts to conform in part, though not wholly, to one or more sets of role expectations, in the hope that the sanctions applied will be minimal.

It need hardly be pointed out that conflicts of role obligations are a common experience of all people, especially in our complex Western society. The foreman in industry, like the non-com in the Army, is an obvious example; the "marginal man," as represented by the second-generation foreign born, for example, has

been much studied. But role conflicts are not limited to such situations. Every adolescent is certain to experience situations in which his family and his peer group are in conflict, such that conformity to the norms of the one is incompatible with conformity to the norms of the other. Most adults are subject to strains to conformity to norms incompatible from one group to another; although, often enough to make life tolerable, either the conflicts do not arise simultaneously or there is a broad enough range of tolerated behavior to provide some flexibility.

In any authoritarian situation, it is axiomatic that adherence to the rules prescribed by the authority depends to no small extent on the compatibility of the rules with dominant values of those who must obey them. It is likely, in most social situations, that the compatibility is not absolute but a matter of degree. There may be variability among members of the group in the extent to which a given value is held in common. The existence of such variability if a factor which should weaken the sanctions against any particular act and facilitate compromise solutions.

With respect to any social value, there are at least two classes of variability which need to be distinguished:

(1) Each individual may perceive a narrow range of behavior as permissible, but for different individuals the ranges, though small, may constitute different segments of a continuum.

(2) Each individual may perceive a rather wide range of behavior as permissible, even though there is considerable consensus as to the termini of this range.

It is the viewpoint of this paper that the *range* of approved or permissible behavior as perceived by a given individual is an important datum for the analysis of what constitutes a social norm in any group, and especially for the analysis of conflicting norms.

---

[1]Stouffer, Suchman, DeVinney, Star, Williams, *The American Soldier*, Vol. I, Chapter 8.

In order to illustrate some of these concepts and to make some preliminary attempts to define them such that statistical operations could be performed with them, an empirical study was made of conflicting role expectations in a sample of 196 Harvard and Radcliffe students, mostly undergraduates. Since the concern was wholly methodological, no effort was made to obtain a random or representative sample of the student body, and the data here reported can not necessarily be regarded as typical of how a properly drawn sample would respond. The students were all taking the same course, Social Relations 116. The data were collected on the first day of the course, without any explicit prior discussion of the theoretical problems involved.

Each student filled out a brief questionnaire, anonymously. He was told first:

"Imagine that you are proctoring an examination in a middle-group course. About half way through the exam you see a fellow student openly cheating. The student is copying his answers from previously prepared notes. When he sees that you have seen the notes as you walked down the aisle and stopped near his seat, he whispers quietly to you, 'O. K., I'm caught. That's all there is to it.'

You do not know the student. What would you as proctor do:

"If you knew that, *except for your action*, there could be very little chance that either the authorities or your student friends would hear about your part in the incident, which of the following actions (*see Table* 7–1) would you as proctor be most likely to take? Next most likely? Least likely? Next least likely?"

After he had finished checking these questions he was presented with a new complication, as follows:

"Now, assume that *except for your action*, there could be very little chance that your student friends would hear about your part in the incident. But assume that, for some reason, there is a good chance, whatever you do, of the authorities finding out about it. Which of the following actions would you as proctor be most likely to take? Next most likely? Least likely? Next least likely?"[2]

This was followed by exactly the same check list as before.

Next the respondent was asked to fill out the following check list:

A. Suppose now that a proctor's action would be: *Take away his notes and exam book, dismiss him, and report him for cheating.*

How would the university authorities feel if they knew you as proctor did this? (check one)

——— Would expect one to do something like this

——— Would not necessarily expect one to do this, but would not disapprove

——— Would disapprove

——— Would not tolerate it

How would your friends in the student body feel if they knew you did this? (check one)

——— Would expect one to do something like this

——— Would not necessarily expect one to do this, but would not disapprove

——— Would disapprove

——— Would not tolerate it

[2]The questionnaire also contained a parallel set of answer categories for the situation where he was asked:

Now assume that, *except for your action*, there could be very little chance that the authorities would hear about your part in the incident. But also assume that there is a good chance that whatever you do your student friends would hear of it. Which of the following actions would you as proctor be most likely to take? Next most likely? Least likely? Next least likely?

However, only the situations indicated above will be used in the present paper.

TABLE 7–1

	Check One in Each Vertical Column			
	My Most Likely Action (Check One)	My Next Most Likely Action (Check One)	My Least Likely Action (Check One)	My Next Least Likely Action (Check One)
A. Take away his notes and exam book, dismiss him and report him for cheating	_____	_____	_____	_____
B. Take away his notes, let him finish the exam, but report him for cheating	_____	_____	_____	_____
C. If he can be led to withdraw from the exam on some excuse, do *not* report him for cheating, otherwise report him	_____	_____	_____	_____
D. Take away his notes, but let him finish the exam, and *not* report him for cheating	_____	_____	_____	_____
E. Act as if nothing had happened and *not* report him for cheating.	_____	_____	_____	_____

B. Suppose that a proctor's action would be: *Take away his notes, let him finish the exam, but report him for cheating.*

C. Suppose now that a proctor's action would be: *If he can be led to withdraw from the exam on some excuse, do not report him for cheating; otherwise report him.*

D. Suppose now that a proctor's action would be: *Take away his notes, but let him finish the exam, and not report him for cheating.*

E. Suppose now that a proctor's action would be: *Act as if nothing had happened and not report him for cheating.*

(For B, C, D, and E, the same check lists were used as for A, but are here omitted to save space.)

Next the respondent was confronted with what it was hoped, for the methodological purposes of this illustrative study, would be more of a dilemma. He was told:

"Now suppose the facts in the case in which you as proctor see a fellow student are exactly the same as in the first case, except for one difference. The student you as proctor see cheating is *your own roommate and close friend.* You know that your roommate is a hard working, though not a brilliant, student and desperately needs a good grade in this course.

"If you knew that, *except for your action,* there could be very little chance that either the authorities or your student friends would know about your part in the incident, which of the following actions would you as proctor be most likely to take? Next most likely? Least likely? Next least likely?"

The check list was the same as in the ordinary case presented first. This was followed by:

"Now assume that *except for your action*, there could be very little chance that your student friends would hear about your part in the incident. But assume that, for some reason, there is a good chance, whatever you do, of the authorities finding out about it. Which of the following actions would you as proctor be most likely to take? Next most likely? Least likely? Next least likely?"

Again the check list was the same.

Finally, the identical series of questions about expectations on the part of authorities and students was repeated for this roommate-friend situation.

The five actions described were designed to constitute, from A to E, an ordered sequence along a dimension of *degree of punitiveness*. That they were so perceived generally by the respondents can be shown easily. To illustrate: If a person said that the authorities, for example, would expect or approve more than one act, it is necessary for unidimensionality that the two or more acts be contiguous (for example, A and B, or B and C, or A, B, and C, but not A and C only). Actually, as we shall see, most students reported at least two acts which would be either expected or approved by the authorities; likewise most reported at least two acts which would be either expected or approved by their friends in the student body. In all, there were 4 chances for each respondent to designate such ranges. Of the 744 responses designating ranges of two or more, the acts checked were entirely contiguous in all but 41; in other words, 95 per cent of the

responses were consistent with the perception of the sequence of acts as a continuum.[3]

Attention should be called to the likelihood that the responses as to the approval or disapproval of the authorities or of one's friends in the student body to a given act have an intrinsic merit which for our purposes could be superior to the merit of the estimates of one's own probable action in a hypothetical case. In any social situation, we have some kind of awareness of the group expectations as to an act affecting the group. We can verbalize those, and these responses when tabulated are *primary data* as to the agreement among group members concerning such expectations. On the other hand, a guess as to what one would do one's self in a particular hypothetical conflict situation has a more "iffy" quality which, though possibly quite highly correlated with actual behavior, need not necessarily be so correlated. The main stress in the present paper, it will be seen, is on the reported *role expectations*. The hypothetical personal action is introduced mainly to suggest how concepts like role expectations, when adequately measured, can be applied in the study of an individual's behavior in that role. Ideally, in place of the individual s hypothetical behavior we would like to substitute actual behavior, either in a natural or experimental situation, or reported past behavior. Studies may be devised in the future with such improve-

[3]To simplify the subsequent presentation the inconsistencies are here treated as checking errors, although in some cases the respondent may actually have perceived an act as not fitting into an ordered sequence (for example, when he said A and C would be approved, but B would be disapproved, he may really have viewed B in a different way from other respondents). Fortunately, the inconsistencies were so few that it is possible to edit them without appreciable effect one way or another, except to simplify the ensuing presentation materially.

CASE OF ORDINARY STUDENT

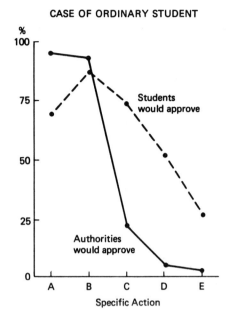

CASE OF ROOMMATE-FRIEND

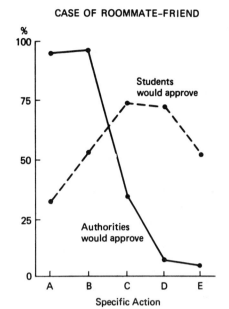

FIGURE 7–1. Percentage saying that a specific action as proctor would be approved by authorities and by fellow students, respectively.

ments, but in any case the basic sorting variables would be the reported role expectations as perceived by different group members.

Figure 7–1 is a picture of social norms, as perceived and reported by the respondents in this study. At the left, we see (heavy line) that almost all of the respondents thought the authorities would approve acts A and B, about a fifth thought the authorities would approve act C, and almost nobody thought the authorities would approve acts D and E.[4] Also at the left we see (dotted line) that the majority of the respondents felt that their friends in the student body would approve the most punitive acts, namely, A and B. But, in addition we see that three-fourths of the respondents thought act C would be approved and a bare

[4] To simplify the presentation, "approval" is here taken to mean that the respondent checked either of the following categories:
–Would expect one to do something like this
–Would not necessarily expect one to do this, but would not disapprove

majority said the same for act D. Only a few felt E would meet student approval. In other words, if a proctor took action consistent with the authorities' expectations he would not be in conflict with student expectations, although the range of expectations is wider for students than for the authorities.

The left diagram in Figure 7–1 portrays the estimate of the situation where the offender was an ordinary student. By contrast, the right-hand diagram shows far less overlap in expectations imputed to authorities and students respectively. The offender in this case was one's roommate and friend. Feelings that the proctor in punishing an ordinary offender was behaving consistently with the long-range interest of the students are now overshadowed by the obligations involved in codes of personal friendship: "You can't rat on a friend; you can't let a friend down."

In the case of the friend, the respondents perceived the authorities' position to be about the same as in the case of the ordinary student, except that about a third now thought the authorities might let the proctor get away with C in view of the proctor's personal dilemma. But only a third of the respondents thought the students would approve act A. The modal acts are C and D. About half believed that the least punitive of all, E, would be approved by most of the students.

In Table 7–2 each act (separately for the case of the ordinary student and the friend, respectively) is broken down according to the percentage who think it would be approved by (a) the authorities only, (b) both the authorities and students, (c) students only, and (d) by neither the authorities nor students.

Let us now examine the relationship

between these role expectations and the respondent's own hypothetical behavior as proctor. It will be recalled that in both the case of the ordinary student and the roommate-friend, the respondent was asked what he personally would do under two hypothetical conditions: (1) if neither the authorities nor his student friends would hear about his part in the incident; and (2) if there could be very little chance that the authorities would hear about his part in the incident.

In Table 7–3 we have a percentage distribution of the acts which each student said he would be *most* likely to choose in the given situation. In the case of the ordinary student, as Table 7–3 shows, the majority of respondents say they would be most likely to employ acts

TABLE 7–2 Percentage Who Attribute Given Role Expectations on the Part of Authorities and / or Students with Respect to Each Specific Act

	Percentage Distribution for Each Specific Action					
	A	B	C	D	E	All Actions
Case of Ordinary Student						
Think given action would be approved by:						
Authorities only	28	12	3	—	—	9
Both authorities and students	68	81	19	4	2	35
Students only	1	6	55	48	24	27
Neither authorities nor students	3	1	23	48	74	29
	100	100	100	100	100	100
Case of Roommate-Friend						
Think given action would be approved by:						
Authorites only	63	44	9	1	—	24
Both authorities and students	33	53	25	6	4	24
Students only	—	—	49	66	48	33
Neither authorities nor students	4	3	17	27	48	19
	100	100	100	100	100	100

N = 196

A or B, the most punitive. There is not a large difference between the hypothetical behavior in private or in public (public only in the restricted sense that the authorities would hear about it in any case, though students need not). The main difference is a small increase, from a private 21 per cent to a public 30 per cent, in first choices for the most severe act A. However, the hypothetical behavior in the roommate-friend case shows a very different pattern. As can be seen in Table

entered earlier in this paper against taking reports on such hypothetical behavior too literally. But the main purpose for introducing the material in Table 7–3 is to enable us to see how such hypothetical behavior is related to the reported perceptions of authorities' and students' expectations, respectively, of proper behavior from a proctor. The data in Table 7–3 are, therefore, next broken down according to the categories used in Table 7–2. Here we see in Table 7–4,[5] as we

TABLE 7–3 Percentage Distribution of Hypothetical Actions Which the Respondents Say They Would Be Most Likely to Take as Proctor

Action	In Case of Ordinary Student		In Case of Roommate-Friend	
	Private*	Public†	Private	Public
A	21	30	4	6
B	47	48	12	34
C	16	13	18	31
D	15	7	38	18
E	1	2	28	11
	100	100	100	100
		N = 196		

*"If you knew that *except for your action* there could be very little chance that either the authorities or your student friends would hear about your part in the incident."

†"If you knew that, *except for your action* there could be very little chance that your student friends would hear about your part in the incident, but that there is a good chance, whatever you do, of the authorities finding out about it."

7–3, nearly two-thirds of the respondents elect acts D or E as their first preferences in private action, and only 16 per cent say they would employ as first choice punitive acts A or B. But if the authorities were sure to find out about it, the picture changes. Less than a third would elect D or E as first choice and 40 per cent would prefer A or B. Yet this is still only about half as large as the proportion who would prefer A or B in comparable circumstances in the case of the ordinary student.

Table 7–3, while of a good deal of interest in itself, is subject to the caveats

doubtless would expect to see, that most students who chose acts A or B as their first preference if they themselves were proctors, also tended to perceive such acts as one which *both* the authorities and students would approve. But that tended to be true of several of the respondents who would take less punitive action—they had a different perception of expectations and thus thought they were avoiding conflict. In the case of the ordinary student, only 43 of the 196

[5]Table 7–4 has not been reprinted here because the major results are summarized in the text. [Ed.]

respondents indicated a private action which was perceived to be acceptable to students only, and only 27 a public action. Contrast this with their hypothetical behavior when the offender was a roommate-friend. Of the 196 respondents, 118 preferred a private action tolerated by the students only. This number was reduced to 74, who would still stick by their friend even if they knew the authorities would find out about their action, or rather, inaction.

Figure 7–1, it will be recalled, indicated quite a marked range of tolerance in imputed student expectations, especially in the roommate-friend situation. But it is not possible to tell directly from Figure 7-1 the extent to which this is due to (a) different respondents visualizing different role expectations, or to (b) respondents generally agreeing that a wide range of role expectations existed. Let us now look at Table 7–5,[6] where the frequency with which each range of expectations was indicated is shown. We see here quite clearly the degree of consensus among respondents as to what the authorities would approve. Among the 196 respondents, 134, or two-thirds, checked A, B identically for the case of the ordinary student; 120 checked A, B, for the case of the roommate-friend. The majority of the remainder checked A, B, C, in both cases.

Far different is the picture from Table 7-5 in the case of imputed student expectations. The Majority settled for a range of either two or three acts in both of the situations, but within a given range there were all possible variations. For example, in the roommate-friend situation there were 80 who indicated a range of student approval covering 3 acts, but of these, 20 perceived the range as A, B, C; 18 perceived it as B, C, D; and 42 as C, D, E. Clearly there is an absence of consensus here, and it is not a mere uniform coverage of the whole range of possibilities by all individuals.

If we take, for illustration, the 120 respondents who perceived the range of acts approved by the authorities in the case of the roommate-friend as A, B, and order the ranges approved by students, according to these same respondents, we see in Table 7–6 the ways in which these different specific ranges are related to one's personal hypothetical behavior as proctor.[7] Here we show for *each pattern* of role expectation the hypothetical private and public behavior respectively. For convenience, these hypothetical acts A, B, C, D, E have been ranked 1, 2, 3, 4, and 5, respectively, and average ranks computed.

As we move from role expectations A to E we see how the average ranks of the students' hypothetical behavior increase. It is interesting to note that, at least in the present example, this progressive increase seems to depend more on the midpoint of the range than on the termini. For example, if the expectation is BC the average rank of the hypothetical behavior is just about the same as when the expectation is A, B, C, D. In some cases the pattern with the longer range has higher average rank than its counterpart with the same midpoint but shorter range; in other cases the reverse is true. The number of cases available in the present data is, however, exceedingly small for this kind of comparison.

While the average rank of hypothetical acts did not tend to differ consistently when we compared two or more ranges with the same midpoint in Table 7–6, there is a hint that differences in the *range* of hypothetical acts vary with the *range* of the role expectations which have the same midpoint. It doubtless would be expected that if a respondent perceived

⁶Table 7–5 has not been reprinted here because the major results are summarized in the text. [Ed.]

⁷Table 7–6 has not been reprinted here because the major results are summarized in the text. [Ed.]

the range of approved behavior to be B, C, D, he would be more likely to choose *either* B or D for his own act than if he perceived the range to be only C. Take the following from Table 7–6:

	A	B	C	D	E	
C	—	—	2	—	—	2
BCD	—	4	1	8	—	13
ABCDE	—	3	1	7	3	14

Most of the other examples in Table 7–6 are less neat than this and the number of cases in distressingly few, but if we form other tables like Table 7–6 for other values of the range of expected approval by the authorities and take all possible matched comparisons thus available (for example, authorities ABC; students BC vs. ABCD) we obtain a rather convincing overall result, in the room-mate-friend situation: See Table 7–7.

The same tendency is also seen, though somewhat less strikingly, in the case of the ordinary student.

While interpretation of such a finding should be indulged in only with caution, the results are sufficient to suggest the importance of taking into account not only the midpoints of a given range of role expectations, but the magnitude of the range as well.

We have now completed the analysis of the present data except for one further observation which has implications for further research.

TABLE 7–7 Severity of Public and Private Acts, as Related to Student Expectation with Identical Midpoints but Different Ranges

	Student Expectations Which Have Identical Midpoints but Different Ranges	
	Those with Minimum Range	*Those with Greater than Minimum Range*
Private Act		
Own behavior more severe than any act within the *minimum* range of student expectation	2	12
Own behavior within *minimum* range	31	20
Own behavior less severe than any act within *minimum* range	8	34
	41	66
Public Act		
Own behavior more severe than any act within the *minimum* range of student expectation	5	29
Own behavior within *minimum* range	32	21
Own behavior less severe than any act within *minimum* range	4	16
	41	66

In such a study as this, it would be interesting first to differentiate individuals into types according to the way they perceive conflicting role expectations and then to ask how these different types of persons vary according to other social and psychological characteristics. Information of the latter type was not collected in the present study. However, the foregoing analysis has suggested how typologies could be set up and related to such outside variables. To take a simple illustration from the roommate-friend situation:

One could classify most of our respondents into three main types according to how they perceived the role conflict.

Type I—Those who thought the range of approved acts identical from the point of view of authorities and students. (21 cases) For such respondents the problem of conformity in their own hypothetical acts could not have been difficult.

Type II—Those who thought the range of acts approved by the authorities did not overlap in any way with the range of acts approved by the students. (56 cases) For them simultaneous conformity to both was impossible. It is noteworthy, parenthetically, that 51 of the 56 said their own private act would be one conforming to student expectation, though 16 of these 51 shifted their act to a non-student position in the public situation.

Type III—Those who perceived a difference in the range of authorities' and students' expectations but who found at least one act which would be tolerated by both. (119 cases) Privately, only 36 of these individuals would take an action satisfactory to both. Publicly, however, 73 out of the 119 were able to find in an act perceived to be mutually acceptable the basis for their own hypothetical solution.

Why did these three types differ so markedly in their definition of the situation? Why, within these types did different subtypes prefer different solutions? These are the kinds of questions which subsequent research can explore. But first we must have a way of defining and classifying the role expectations relevant to our problem and the purpose of the present study is to illustrate a technique for accomplishing this first step.

From the theoretical standpoint, the most important implication of this paper may stem from its stress on variability. In essay writing in this field it is common and convenient to think of a social norm as a point, or at least as a very narrow band on either side of a point. This probably is quite unrealistic as to most of our social behavior. And it may be precisely the ranges of permissible behavior which most need examination, if we are to make progress in this realm which is so central in social science. For it may be the very existence of some flexibility or social slippage—but not too much—which makes behavior in groups possible.

8   Status Crystallization: A Non-vertical Dimension of Social Status *

Gerhard E. Lenski

In recent years there have been numerous indications that, in the analysis of social stratification, sociology is rapidly outgrowing the classical conceptual schemes inherited from the past. Critically inclined students have come increasingly to recognize the inability of the older schemes to incorporate many of the findings of present day research, or to adapt themselves to newer theoretical concerns.

This trend is evident even with respect to such a basic matter as the manner in which the vertical structure of groups is conceived. From Aristotle to Marx to Warner, most social philosophers and social scientists have described the vertical structure of human groups in terms of a single hierarchy in which each member occupies a single position. Different exponents of this traditional scheme have not always agreed regarding the nature or characteristics of this hierarchical structure. Nevertheless, all have shared the common conception of a uni-dimensional structure.

Since Max Weber's day, however, this traditional approach has come to be criticized by a growing number of sociologists, who have argued that the uni-dimensional view is inadequate to describe the complexities of group structure. These critics have maintained that the structure of human groups normally involves the coexistence of a number of parallel vertical hierarchies which usually are imperfectly correlated with one another.

If this newer approach is sound, the traditional conception of individual or family status will require radical revision. Instead of being a single position in a uni-dimensional hierarchy, it becomes a series of positions in a series of related vertical hierarchies.

An important question which is raised immediately by such a view is the question of how these several positions are interrelated. Theoretically it becomes possible to conceive of a non-vertical dimension to individual or family status—that is, a consistency dimension. In this dimension units may be compared with respect to the degree of consistency of their positions in the several vertical hierarchies. In other words, certain units may be consistently high or consistently low, while others may combine high standing with respect to certain status

*This article is the first of a projected series on status and class crystallization growing out of a research project conducted jointly by Professor Werner S. Landecker and the present writer. Grateful appreciation is expressed to Professor Ronald Freedman and his Detroit Area Study Staff for their assistance in collecting the data, and to the Horace H. Rackham School of Graduate Studies of the University of Michigan for financial assistance.

Reprinted from Gerhard E. Lenski, "Status crystallization," *American Sociological Review*, 19 (1954) 405–513, by permission of the author and the publisher, The American Sociological Association.

variables with low standing with respect to others.[1]

While it is one thing to conceive of new theoretical models, it is another matter to demonstrate their utility. This article reports the results of an empirical study designed to test the significance and utility of this non-vertical dimension of status. More specifically, this study was designed to discover whether an analysis employing this new dimension would be capable of accounting for some of the variance in political behavior which is left unexplained by traditional methods of stratification analysis.

THE RESEARCH DESIGN

The basic hypothesis tested in this study is as follows: *individuals characterized by a low degree of status crystallization[2] differ significantly in their political attitudes and behavior from individuals characterized by a high degree of status crystallization, when status differences in the vertical dimensions are controlled.*

The data were gathered in the first Detroit Area Study.[3] In the spring of 1952, a random sample of the residents of the metropolitan Detroit area was

interviewed.[4] A total of 749 interviews was obtained. Comparisons with 1950 census data indicated that the sample obtained was highly representative of the total population of the metropolitan area.[5]

Two basic variables employed in the present study require operational definition. These are (1) social status, and (2) status crystallization.

SOCIAL STATUS   For operational purposes, the statuses of respondents were defined in terms of their relative positions in four vertical hierarchies: the income hierarchy; the occupation hierarchy; the education hierarchy; and the ethnic hierarchy. These four were chosen both because of their great importance and also because of the relative ease with which necessary information relating to them could be obtained.

With respect to income and education, there was no problem in defining the structure of the hierarchy. Both hierarchies are quantitative in nature. With respect to occupation and ethnic background there was, unfortunately, no such built-in scale. Thus, the construction of scales of relative rank had to be undertaken.

In ranking occupations, the Edwards classificatory scheme was considered and rejected on the grounds that it does not constitute a sufficiently precise scale of status. Top business executives, for

---

[1]This possibility has also been noted in recent years by Emile Benoit-Smullyan, "Status, Status Types and Status Interrelationships," *American Sociological Review,* 9 (1944), pp. 151-61; Pitirim A. Sorokin, *Society, Culture, and Personality,* New York: Harper & Brothers, 1947, pp. 289-94; Harold F. Kaufman, *et al.,* "Problems of Theory and Method in the Study of Social Stratification in Rural Society," *Rural Sociology,* 18 (1953), p. 15; and Stuart Adams, "Status Congruency as a Variable in Small Group Performance," *Social Forces,* 32 (1953), pp. 16-22.

[2]The term "status crystallization" will be used throughout the remainder of the article as a synonym for "status consistency."

[3]For details regarding the Detroit Area Study, see Ronald Freedman, "The Detroit Area Study: A Training and Research Laboratory in the Community," *American Journal of Sociology,* 59 (1953), pp. 30-33.

[4]Respondents were selected by the area sampling method. In general, the sampling procedure involved: (1) random selection of a sample of blocks in the community; (2) within these blocks a random selection of households; and (3) within each household a random selection of persons to be interviewed. For a more detailed description of the methods employed, see Leslie Kish, "A Two-Stage Sample of a City," *American Sociological Review,* 17 (1952), pp. 761-69, and Kish, "A Procedure for Objective Respondent Selection Within the Household," *Journal of the American Statistical Association,* 44 (1949), pp. 380-87.

[5]For detailed comparisons with census data, see *A Social Profile of Detroit: 1952,* Ann Arbor: University of Michigan Press, 1952, pp. 34-37.

example, enjoy greater prestige than many professional men. At the same time, very small proprietors (who are classified with top executives in the Edwards scheme) may enjoy no more prestige than skilled workers. Furthermore, recent empirical studies indicate that skilled workers today enjoy greater prestige than many clerical and sales workers.[6] In short, the overlap between occupational categories when judged by the criterion of relative prestige seemed too great in the Edwards scheme.

The best empirical basis for constructing a scale of occupational rank seemed to have been provided by the National Opinion Research Center's study of occupational prestige.[7] Using the occupations evaluated in that study as a basis, five occupational prestige levels were defined, and an attempt was made to extrapolate from the rated occupations to others not rated in that study. Slightly over 50 per cent of the occupations of the family heads in the Detroit sample required such extrapolation. Coding reliability in these cases was better than 90 per cent.[8]

No national sample of public opinion was available for the construction of the ethnic scale. In the circumstances, the best solution seemed to be an evaluation of the various ethnic groups by Detroit-area residents. For this purpose a sample of 195 Detroit area students enrolled in introductory sociology courses at the University of Michigan was obtained during the academic year 1951–52. These students were asked to rate all of the major ethnic groups found in the Detroit area on the basis of what they thought to be the general community evaluation, as distinguished from their own personal evaluation.[9] As was expected, the northwest European groups were ranked ahead of the south and east European groups, and these in turn were generally ranked ahead of the colored groups.[10]

For respondents who were not themselves the family head, the status characteristics of the head were used to define their position in the four hierarchies. This procedure was followed for two reasons. First, current literature, both theory and research, indicates that the family is normally a status unit and that the social attributes of the family head are the chief determinants of status for all dependent relatives in the domicile.[11] Second, this procedure rendered the data collected from wives and other dependent relatives comparable with that for individuals who were themselves family heads.[12] This latter consideration was quite important due to the relatively small size of the sample.

STATUS CRYSTALLIZATION Having established the structure of these vertical hierarchies, the next problem was to establish common scales for all of them, so that the relative position of respondents

[6]See "Jobs and Occupations: A Popular Evaluation," *Opinion News*, 9 (1947), p. 3 ff.

[7]*Op. cit.*

[8]Admittedly this technique was not wholly satisfactory. It seemed, however, the most satisfactory approximation which could be achieved within the financial and temporal limitations of the project.

[9]Student evaluations of their own ethnic group were not included, in order to minimize personal biases which might not be consistent with community biases.

[10]Separate ranks were determined for each of the specific groups within these general categories. In the case of respondents of mixed ethnic backgrounds, the scores of the several ethnic groups (see below) were averaged.

[11]See, for example, Talcott Parsons, "A Revised Analytical Approach to the Theory of Social Stratification," in *Class, Status and Power*, edited by Reinhard Bendix and Seymour Lipset, Glencoe: The Free Press, 1953, pp. 166-67; Kingsley Davis, *Human Society*, New York: The Macmillan Company, 1949, p. 364; W. Lloyd Warner and Paul S. Lunt, *The Social Life of a Modern Community*, New Haven: Yale University Press, 1941, p. 90.

[12]If this were not done, comparisons of nonemployed dependent relatives would be most difficult, since such respondents could not be ranked in terms of income and occupation.

TABLE 8–1 Frequency Distribution of Respondents by Income of Family Head, and Assigned Percentile Scores for Each Income Range

Annual Income of Family Head	Number of Respondents	Cumulative Percentile Range	Assigned Score
$10,000 or more	29	95.4–100.0	98
8,000–9,999	15	93.0– 95.3	94
7,000–7,999	19	90.0– 92.9	91
6,000–6,999	58	80.7– 89.9	85
5,000–5,999	82	67.6– 80.6	74
4,000–4,999	137	45.6– 67.5	57
3,000–3,999	191	15.0– 45.5	30
2,000–2,999	57	5.9– 14.9	10
1,000–1,999	21	2.5– 5.8	4
1– 999	10	0.9– 2.4	2
No income	5	0.0– 0.8	0
Total	624°		

° This figure includes only those who were themselves currently in the labor force or respondents who were members of families in which the head was in the labor force, and for whom income data were available.

in the several hierarchies might be compared. Without common scales, a measure of status crystallization would be impossible.

To this end, frequency distributions were established for each hierarchy. Using these distributions as a basis, scores were assigned for each of the various positions (or intervals) in each hierarchy on the basis of the midpoint of the percentile range for that position (or interval). Table 8–1 below illustrates the procedure as it was employed in assigning scores to the various income intervals.[13]

[13]In computing the educational scores of the respondents, one variation was introduced. Respondents forty years of age and over were separated from those younger. This was considered necessary in view of the rapid changes in educational expectations and attainments in American society in recent times. Direct comparisons of older persons with younger persons in terms of educational attainments would be unrealistic, since failure to complete high school, for example, is a far more serious handicap for members of the younger generation than for members of the older. Some allowance for this difference is usually made in the

Having obtained comparable scores for the four hierarchies, the last remaining step was to establish the quantitative measure of status crystallization. This was accomplished by taking the square root of the sum of the squared deviations from the mean of the four hierarchy scores of the individual and subtracting the resulting figure from one hundred.[14] The more highly consistent or

evaluative process in contemporary society. The division of the sample at age forty seemed the most effective simple method for taking recognition of this fact, since by this means the sample was divided into approximately equal halves.

[14]The use of squared deviations from the mean rather than simple deviations was employed to emphasize the effect of larger deviations and to minimize the effect of smaller deviations. This was considered desirable since the techniques employed in quantifying positions (or intervals) in the several hierarchies were sufficiently crude so that no great importance could be attached to small deviations.

The technique of subtracting the resulting figure from one hundred was employed so that respondents whose status was highly crystallized would have numerically higher crystallization scores than those whose status was poorly crystallized. This was done solely to avoid semantic difficulties.

crystallized an individual's status, the more nearly his crystallization score approached one hundred; the less consistent or crystallized his status, the more nearly his crystallization score approached zero.

THE STUDY GROUP   Of the original 749 respondents, it was necessary to eliminate 136 from the study group, either because of incomplete or inadequate data on one of the four key status variables, or because the family head was not in the labor force.[15] Due to the small number of cases, it seemed advisable to divide the study group into only two crystallization categories—a high crystallization category and a low crystallization category. Those with crystallization scores of 53 or more were placed in the former category (N=439) while those with scores of 52 or less were placed in the latter category (N=174). This line of division was selected because in the course of the analysis it was discovered that something roughly approximating a natural breaking point was discernible here.

FINDINGS

As a first test of the basic hypothesis, the voting behavior and preferences of the two categories of respondents were compared. Data relating to three elections were used: (1) the 1948 presidential election; (2) the 1950 Michigan gubernatorial election; and (3) the 1952 presidential election. For the first two elections comparisons were made on the basis of the respondents' reports of their behavior. For the 1952 election, it was necessary to make the comparison on the basis of the respondents' indications of

[15]It seemed desirable to remove those respondents in families in which the family head was not currently in the labor force due to retirement, prolonged illness, or extended unemployment, since serious difficulties arose in any attempt to compare them with the remainder of the sample with respect to their position in the occupational hierarchy.

their party preferences, since the interviews were conducted eight to ten months before the election.

In each election, the proportion of respondents supporting the Democratic party was substantially greater in the low crystallization category than in the high crystallization category. As may be seen from Table 8–2, below, these differences were significant at the five per cent level in all but the 1952 election.[16]

TABLE 8–2 Voting Behavior and Preferences in the 1948, 1950, and 1952 Elections, by Degree of Status Crystallization

	Per Cent of Voters Supporting Democrats		
Election Year	Low Crystal-lization	High Crystal-lization	Prob. Less Than
1948	81.3°	69.0°	.03
1950	84.0	68.4	.01
1952	73.2°°	64.7°°	.11

°Includes supporters of the Progressive party, since 70 per cent of these individuals (N=10) were normally Democratic voters; none gave any indication of ever having supported a Republican candidate.

°°Refers to the percentage expressing a *preference* for the Democratic party.

[16]It will be noted in Table 8-2 that the proportion of persons supporting the Democratic party is far above the national average in all three elections. Some difference in this direction was to be expected, since the sample was drawn from the metropolitan Detroit area, which is the stronghold of the Democratic party in Michigan. This, however, does not entirely account for the preponderance of Democratic voters. In the 1948 election, for example, slightly less than 60 per cent of the major party vote in the metropolitan Detroit area went to the Democratic party. However, slightly more than 70 per cent of the respondents in the study group reported that they voted for the Democratic party that year. This discrepancy seems to be due to the fact observed by polling organizations that many persons report on interviews that they voted in a previous election, when careful checking of the voting lists reveal they did not. This seems to be more frequently a character-

TABLE 8–3 Mean Income Occupation, Ethnic, and Education Scores by Crystallization Categories, Before and After Correction to Control Status Differences in the Vertical Dimensions

Crystallization Category	N	*Mean Income Score*	*Mean Occupation Score*	*Mean Ethnic Score*	*Mean Education Score*
Uncorrected:					
Low crystallization	174	46.6	49.5	50.1	54.1
High crystallization	439	51.3	50.2	50.0	46.1
Corrected:					
Low crystallization	166	48.6	50.0	49.7	53.7
High crystallization	413	48.4	48.2	48.4	44.1

Although the data in Table 8–2 suggest that the basic hypothesis is sound, no conclusions can be drawn until controls are established for status differences in the four vertical dimensions. This is necessary in the present problem because of the well established fact that variations in these four dimensions are

closely associated with variations in political behavior and attitudes. Thus, the variations between the two crystallization categories observed in Table 8–2 might be due simply to failure to control vertical status differences between the two categories.

A check of the mean scores of the two categories of respondents in the four vertical dimensions revealed, as shown in the upper half of Table 8–3, that low crystallization respondents had higher *mean* education and ethnic scores than high crystallization respondents. At the same time, however, high crystallization respondents had higher *mean* income and occupation scores.

This latter fact is important, since it might be argued that income and occupation are the chief determinants of political behavior, while education and ethnic background are of negligible importance. If this were so, the tendency of high crystallization respondents to favor the Republican party might then be simply a function of their higher average income and superior occupational status.

To test this alternative hypothesis, 26 respondents with the *highest* incomes in the high crystallization category and eight respondents with the *lowest* in-

---

istic of Democrats than of Republicans of the larger cities.

Some evidence of this tendency was discovered in the present study. In cases where the respondent resided at the same address in 1948 or 1950, the accuracy of his response was checked. Such checks revealed that at least 13 per cent of those who claimed to have voted in 1948, had not, in fact, voted. Eighty-five per cent of those who erroneously claimed to have voted reported voting for either the Democratic or Progressive parties, while only 15 per cent reported voting for the Republican party. While these respondents were not counted as voters in Table 8-2, others undoubtedly remained who gave erroneous reports, but for whom no check was possible due to a change in residence during the intervening period.

Among the erroneous reports discovered, the proportion of erroneous Democratic reports was somewhat greater in the high crystallization category while the proportion of erroneous Republican reports was somewhat greater in the low crystallization category. If it is assumed that comparable proportions of Republican and Democratic voters would be found in the undiscovered erroneous reports, this would mean that the present uncorrected error in the data works *against* the basic hypothesis, since it tends to make the difference in voting behavior between the two categories of respondents appear less than it actually was.

comes in the low crystallization category were dropped from the study group. The elimination of these respondents had the effect of controlling status differences simultaneously in *all* of the four vertical dimensions as shown in the lower half of Table 8–3. In other words, after the elimination of these 34 cases, respondents in the low crystallization category had a higher mean score than respondents in the high crystallization category with respect to *each* of the four status variables. Thus, any Democratic bias remaining after the elimination of these respondents could not be attributed to a failure to control status differences in these vertical dimensions. On the contrary, whatever differences might remain after this control was applied would remain *in spite of the fact* that respondents in the low crystallization category had slightly higher mean scores than respondents in the high crystallization category.

As may be seen by an inspection of Table 8–4, the application of this rigorous control tended to reduce the margin of difference in political behavior between the two crystallization categories. With

TABLE 8–4 Voting Behavior and Preferences in the 1948, 1950, and 1952 Elections, by Degree of Status Crystallization, After Correction

Per Cent of Voters
Supporting Democrats

Election Year	Low Crystalli- zation	High Crystalli- zation	Prob. Less Than
1948	82.2°	71.4°	.05
1950	83.5	71.4	.04
1952	72.2°°	68.0°°	.46

° Includes supporters of the Progressive Party.
°° Refers to the percentage expressing a *preference* for the Democratic Party.

the exception of the 1952 election, however, a statistically significant margin of difference remained. Even in the 1952 election, the direction of the difference was consistent with the pattern observed in the other two elections.

The significance of the differences between the two crystallization categories became more apparent when a further test of the basic hypothesis was made, using other data. A 50 per cent subsample of the respondents (N=311) were asked their views on (a) a government-sponsored health insurance program, (b) price controls, and (c) a general extension of governmental powers. As shown in Table 8–5 below, respondents in the low

TABLE 8–5 Frequency of Strongly Liberal Responses on Controversial Issues, by Degree of Status Crystallization

	Per Cent Strongly Liberal		
Issue	Low Crystal- lization	High Crystal- lization	Prob. Less Than
Government health insurance	26.7	14.9	.02
Price controls	31.1	25.8	.35
Extension of government powers	40.0	25.8	.02

crystallization category took a more liberal (i.e. leftist) stand on each of these questions than did respondents in the high crystallization category. In two of the three cases, the difference was significant at the two per cent level.

As in the analysis of the data on voting behavior and preferences, the application of controls for differences in the four status hierarchies reduced slightly the margin of differences between the two crystallization categories. It should be noted, however, that even with the application of these controls, the difference between the two categories was still significant at the five per cent level for both the health insurance question and the question regarding the extension of governmental powers.

On the basis of the data described above, it would therefore appear that a definite association existed between low crystallization and political liberalism among respondents in this cross-section sample of metropolitan Detroit. Before such a relationship could be asserted with confidence, one further problem required examination. Briefly stated, the problem was whether the differences observed between the two crystallization categories were due to the lack of status crystallization *per se*, or rather were a function of particular patterns of status inconsistency which were present in large numbers in the low crystallization category. Thus, for example, it might be argued that the combination of extensive education and limited income is associated with strong liberal biases, while the reverse combination is not, and that the differences observed in Tables 8–4 and 8–5 were due to the fact that persons possessing the former combination were extremely numerous in the low crystallization category, giving the category as a whole a liberal bias which was not due to lack of status crystallization *per se*.

To test this alternative hypothesis, a detailed analysis of the low crystallization category was made. All of the respondents in this category were classified on the basis of the various relationships between the income, occupation, education, and ethnic hierarchies. Thus, for example, respondents whose income score was markedly higher than their education score (*i.e.*, 30 or more points higher) were placed in one category, while those whose education score was markedly higher than their income score were placed in a second category. Each of

the twelve resulting categories of low crystallization respondents were then compared with high crystallization respondents in terms of their voting record and their views on the three controversial issues.[17] The results of this analysis are shown in Table 8–6.

Two tentative conclusions may be drawn from a careful analysis of Table 8–6. First, *liberal political tendencies are associated with a low degree of status crystallization regardless of the specific relationship of the status variables.* This conclusion seems justified in view of the fact that despite the relatively small number of cases involved, 23 out of 24 of the comparisons made yielded differences in the predicted direction. In short, regardless of whether income rank was high and educational rank low, or the reverse, or what the particular nature of the status inconsistency was, the fact of imperfect status crystallization *per se* seems to have been related to political liberalism.

The data in Table 8–6 also suggest the tentative conclusion that *certain types of status inconsistencies are more closely related to political liberalism than others.* For example, relatively low ethnic status in combination with relatively high income, occupational, or educational status was more closely associated with liberal tendencies than the reverse. Also, the data suggest that status inconsistencies involving high occupational rank and low educational rank are more closely associated with liberal tendencies than the reverse. However, in view of the small number of cases in each cell, it is necessary to use considerable caution in drawing conclusions from the present data regarding which patterns of relationships are most closely associated with political liberalism.

---

[17]This comparison was made *after* the correction to control for status differences in the four hierarchies.

TABLE 8–6 Summary Comparison of Voting Records and Attitudes on Controversial Issues of Twelve Categories of Low Crystallization Respondents with High Crystallization Respondents

Paired Variables[1]		Complete Sample		Subsample	
High	Low	N	Per Cent Strongly Democratic[2]	N	Per Cent Strongly Liberal[3]
Income ——— Ethnic		53	56.6	23	34.8
Occupation ——— Ethnic		53	50.9	28	39.3
Education ——— Ethnic		68	50.0	34	32.4
Occupation ——— Education		36	47.2	16	25.0
Education ——— Occupation		56	42.8	28	17.8
Income ——— Occupation		28	39.6	21	4.8
Education ——— Income		67	38.8	31	25.8
Income ——— Education		41	36.6	21	28.6
Ethnic ——— Occupation		53	35.8	29	17.2
Ethnic ——— Education		48	35.4	26	19.2
Ethnic ——— Income		63	34.9	32	21.9
Occupation ——— Income		32	34.4	17	29.4
All high crystallization		413	34.2	207	15.5

[1]In the case of each comparison respondents had an assigned percentile score 30 or more points higher for the high variable than for the low variable.

[2]Includes all those who supported Democratic (or Progressive) candidates at least twice between 1948 and 1952.

[3]Includes all those who took strongly liberal stand on at least 2 of the 3 controversial issues.

DISCUSSION

Not only do the findings in the preceding section suggest that a recognition of this non-vertical dimension of social status may help account for some of the previously unexplained variance in political behavior, but also they hint at a more basic relationship between social structure and social change. Extrapolating from these findings, one might predict that the more frequently acute status inconsistencies occur within a population the greater would be the proportion of that population willing to support programs of social change.[18]

Apparently the individual with a poorly crystallized status is a particular type of marginal man, and is subjected to certain pressures by the social order which are not felt (at least to the same degree) by individuals with a more highly crystallized status. Conceivably a society with a relatively large proportion of persons whose status is poorly crystallized is a society which is in an unstable condition. In brief, under such conditions the social system itself generates its own pressures for change.

Some insight into the manner in which such pressures for change may be generated by status inconsistencies has been supplied by Hughes in his excellent discussion of "Dilemmas and Contradictions

[18]It might be argued that conservatives advocate programs of social change just as do liberals, especially in periods of liberal control. Strictly speaking, this is true, but it must be noted that such changes are usually put forward as a program of return to former conditions. Although experts might challenge this claim in many respects, it is a claim which is accepted by the general public. Thus, in the public mind the liberal or left-wing parties are usually thought of as the parties advocating change, while the conservative parties are thought of as the supporters of the present order (or the old order).

of Status."[19] The Negro doctor, by virtue of the fact that in his person he combines two roles of grossly discrepant status, is apt to be subjected with some frequency to social experiences of an unpleasant or frustrating nature. The same will tend to be true of the highly educated man with limited income, or the business executive with a grammar school education.

Not all such individuals would be expected to react against the social order which produces such unpleasant experiences in their lives. For various reasons the individual may develop other reactions. For example, the individual may react by blaming other individuals *as individuals* rather than as agents of the social order. Such a reaction might be common among persons raised in an individualistic tradition or who, because of limited educational opportunities, have not learned to relate individual experiences to the social order. Another possibility open to the individual with a poorly crystallized status is that he will react to resulting unpleasant experiences by blaming himself. Finally, there is the possibility that the individual may withdraw in such a manner as to diminish the frequency and the seriousness of the socially disturbing experiences which arise as a result of his status inconsistencies. Such alternative types of reactions may very well explain a part of the variance in responses among individuals in the poorly crystallized category in the present study. It should be noted, however, that the tendency to react by advocating change in the social order seems to have been a frequent type of reaction in the present sample.

Building on this foundation, the politi-cal liberalism of several diverse groups in American society begins to appear as a common expression of a common social experience. In recent years political observers have reported relatively strong support for liberal political programs from such diverse groups as college professors, Jewish businessmen, Hollywood actors, and the Protestant clergy. All four of these categories of persons, it must be noted, are characterized by a relatively low degree of status crystallization. Professors and clergymen enjoy high occupational and educational rank, yet their income is sometimes less than that of skilled manual workers. Screen stars frequently combine high income rank with low educational rank, and sometimes with low ethnic rank as well. Jewish businessmen combine high income and occupational rank (and often high educational rank) with low ethnic rank. If the foregoing analysis is sound, one would be led to expect a relatively high frequency of liberal biases among the members of such groups, and for the same fundamental reason.

Building on the present foundation, it also becomes possible to predict one of the sources of leadership of successful revolutionary movements. Years ago Marx and Engels noted that successful revolutionary movements are usually characterized by the combination of broad support from the masses or lower strata, and leadership recruited from the higher strata in the old order.[20] The present study suggests that persons of poorly crystallized status may be an important source from which such leadership is recruited. Quite often such persons combine the personal skills necessary for effective leadership with the equally necessary motivation.

Finally, it may be noted that if the

[19]*American Journal of Sociology*, 50 (1944), pp. 353–57. It should be noted that Hughes uses the term "status" differently from the use made in this article. It is not difficult, however, to relate his discussion to the present problem if this fact is kept in mind.

[20]*Manifesto of the Communist Party*, New York: International Publishers, 1932, p. 19.

conception of social status presented in this paper is as fruitful as the findings of this pilot study would seem to indicate, some considerable modification of the traditional conception of social class will also be required. This point will be developed more fully in subsequent papers based on the present project.

One methodological implication of the present study remains to be discussed. During the past two decades it has become fashionable in social science circles to construct indices of socio-economic status by averaging up in some manner several status variables.[21] The findings of this present study indicate that such constructions are seriously deficient in characterizing the social status of a significant minority of the population. Such techniques for classifying individuals fail to take into account what appears to be an important dimension of status, and thus may frequently fail to account for an important part of the variance in the phenomena under investigation.

[21]See, for example, W. Lloyd Warner, *et al.*, *Social Class in America*, Chicago: Science Research Associates, 1949, Part 3; or Clyde V. Kiser and P. K. Whelpton, "Social and Psychological Factors Affecting Fertility, IX. Fertility Planning and Fertility Rates by Socio-Economic Status," *Milbank Memorial Fund Quarterly*, 27 (1949), pp. 214–16.

CONCLUSIONS

The conclusions which are drawn from a pilot study such as the present one should be concerned primarily with questions of the advisability of pursuing further the projected line of research, and the methods appropriate to further research, if such is warranted. Conclusions concerning the validity of given hypotheses about social relationships are hardly warranted, except insofar as they relate to the question of the advisability of further research.

In the present case the writer feels that the findings fully warrant further exploration of the crystallization dimension of status. This view seems justified not only on the ground that status crystallization seems a useful tool for reducing the range of unexplained variation in American political behavior, but also because of the broader theoretical and methodological implications which were outlined in the preceding section.

Future research in this area should be directed not only to the checking and rechecking of the relationship of status crystallization and political liberalism, but also to the exploration of the relationship of status crystallization to variations in other areas of behavior, and in personality development as well. Possibly fruitful new discoveries will result.

SOCIAL ORDER AND SOCIAL DISORDER

. . . always in human society there is what may be called a double reality—on the one hand a normative system embodying what *ought* to be, and on the other a factual order embodying what *is*. In the nature of the case these two orders cannot be completely identical, nor can they be completely disparate.[1]

We will label the two components distinguished by Davis in this passage as the normative structure and the social structure. Considered as an interrelated whole, they constitute the social order. Let us consider each of these important concepts in turn.

The Normative Structure   To this point, we have defined and briefly discussed the concepts of value, norm, and role. These concepts may be regarded as comprising the basic elements of the normative structure. The term *structure*, however, suggests more than the mere presence of these elements; it implies that they are arranged as a somewhat organized set of beliefs. A given group, or an entire society, for that matter, will not be characterized by a random collection of values, norms, and roles but will organize them so that they constitute a relatively coherent set of beliefs and rules governing the behavior of participants. Some values, for example, will be seen as more general or important than others, so that we may speak of a hierarchy of values. To illustrate this, we may say that most of us in this society would recognize as an important value maintaining the security of our country from hostile forces, both internal and external. Most of us would also recognize as an important value freedom of thought and expression for individual citizens and groups of citizens. Clearly, however, groups in this society differ in their ranking of these values: the more conservative groups would be likely to place more emphasis on maintaining the security of the country, even at the cost of limiting freedom of thought and speech, while liberal groups would be apt to reverse these priorities. As has already been noted, norms, too, are ranked by groups in terms of their importance, and this ranking will vary from group to group. And we have already seen in our consideration of roles how they are interrelated in specific ways so as to constitute systems of roles. Hence, in attempting to describe the normative structure of a given group, it is not sufficient merely to list the values, norms, and roles that are present. One will also want to describe the ways in which these expectations about behavior are organized so that they provide a particular cultural arrangement that makes this group somewhat distinctive from all other groups. As Mary Parker Follett reminds us, we must be prepared to examine

[1]Kingsley Davis, *Human Society*, New York: Macmillan, 1949, p. 52.

not merely the totalness of the situation, but the nature of the totalness . . . what you have to consider in a situation is not all the factors one by one, but also their relation to one another. This means, among other things, that when a factor is added to or subtracted from a situation, you have not that situation minus or plus that factor, for all the rest will be changed. [Further,] . . . the whole is determined also by the relation of whole and parts.[2]

Although we may define a *normative structure* as an integrated set of values, norms, and roles characterizing a particular group, it is clear that some normative structures are more integrated than others. Some groups will exhibit a much more coherent and consistent pattern of norms, values, and roles than will others. We cannot assume that all groups will exhibit a highly consistent normative structure, but we will want to examine the extent to which the normative elements are integrated into a consistent system. And we will also want to examine the determinants and consequences of varying degrees of integration.

The Social Structure   Although some readers may have begun to suspect otherwise, there is more to the study of sociology than the examination of beliefs about behavior. Sociologists are also interested in analyzing social behavior itself. However, because we are here considering the social structure, we are not concerned with all and any kind of behavior. Rather, our interest is in behavior that takes place within a normative structure and is oriented by its existence. This focus is clearly stated by the eminent social anthropologist S. F. Nadel:

Conceivably, in theory, there might be as many such ways of acting as there are situations in which people meet, practically an infinite number. But we are here speaking of ways of acting governed by rules and hence in some measure stereotyped (or rendered "determinate"). And of the ways of acting so understood it is true to say that they are finite and always less numerous than the possible combinations of people: which means that the same ways of acting are repetitive in the population.[3]

Nadel's point is one we have already emphasized. Namely, that an important consequence of the normative structure—in his terms, the "rules" for social behavior—is that it renders the latter more predictable, more determinant. However, this effect can be too easily overstated. To say that behavior is oriented to or governed by a normative structure is not to say that behavior always conforms to or is consistent with norms. Behavior can deviate from that prescribed by the normative structure and still be oriented to that structure to the extent (1) that the actor is aware that his behavior is in violation of the norms and that he structures his behavior accordingly, perhaps by attempting to consequence of the normative structure—in his terms, the "rules" for social behavior—is that it renders the latter more predictable, more determinant. evaluations.

Just as we have identified the basic elements of normative structures, we should now, in fairness, attempt to identify the basic elements of social structures. These elements are, simply put, *social relationships*. And, as Nadel explains, we have already defined them in our previous discussion:

[2]Mary Parker Follett, *Dynamic Administration: The Collected Papers of Mary Parker Follett*, edited by H. C. Metcalf and L. Urwick, New York: Harper & Row, pp. 192, 195.
[3]S. F. Nadel, *The Theory of Social Structure*, Glencoe, Ill.: Free Press, 1957, p. 8.

For "determinate ways of acting toward or in regard to one another" we usually say "relationships," and we indicate that they follow from rules by calling them "institutionalized" or "social" (as against "private" or "personal" relationships). We identify the mutual ways of acting of individuals as "relationships" only when the former exhibit some consistency or constancy, since without these attributes they would merely be single or disjointed acts.[4]

Interactions between and among persons, then, constitute social relationships to the extent that they exhibit some consistency or constancy. The relationship that is termed "friendship," for example, is comprised of many behaviors that exhibit certain common features, including mutual attraction, sharing, and assistance. It is important to note that the individual acts making up the relationship are never identical—no single act is ever exactly like any other act—but are only sufficiently alike that they may be identified as similar or of the same general character. To speak of a particular kind of social relationship is to move to a higher level of abstraction. We are no longer talking about raw behavior but are abstracting certain of its properties that allow us to regard one act as like another in that both exhibit certain common characteristics or properties.

Some social scientists have been so bold as to suggest that for some purposes any behavior involving two people can be regarded as similar to any other behavior. Making this assumption allows the simple counting of interactive behaviors occurring among individuals and allows relationships between pairs of persons to be characterized by a single property: the *frequency* of interaction. This observational technique was first suggested by Chapple and Arensberg[5] and has been employed by many investigators, including Blau, whose research is reported in this section. (Reading 9) Blau systematically observed the interactions occurring among a small group of officials who composed one department of a Federal law enforcement agency. Recording all contacts that occurred among the members of the group without taking into account the content or the length of the interaction, Blau devised a number of simple indicators with which to characterize the participation of each member. These indicators, together with other information on group members, such as competency ratings made by their supervisor, are ingeniously employed to characterize the social relationships—and more specifically, the status structure—present in this group. (We will have more to say about the specific subject matter of this article when we consider status processes in small groups.)

Many other schemes have been developed by social scientists to describe and examine the behavior of individuals and groups and to chart the social relationships that develop. One of the most frequently employed schemes is the sociometric technique developed by Jacob Moreno.[6] This method enables the investigator to focus on the emotional bonds that link persons, whether these feelings be positive, negative, or neutral. One other method that has received considerable attention may be briefly mentioned. Robert Bales has developed a system of twelve categories that may be employed by a trained observer to

---

[4]Nadel, p. 9.

[5]E. D. Chapple, with the collaboration of C. M. Arensberg, *Measuring Human Relations*, *Genetic Psychology Monographs*, 22 (1940).

[6]Many examples of the use of this technique may be found in J. L. Moreno *et al.* (eds.), *The Sociometry Reader*, Glencoe, Ill.: Free Press, 1960.

systematically record ongoing behavior.[7] Interaction process analysis, as this method is called, allows the observer to record who behaves, to whom the behavior is directed, and the significance or meaning of the behavior for the group situation in which it occurs. A study by Bales making use of this method is reprinted in this book in the section on the small group. (Reading 24)

Social relationships are the basic elements of social structure, but, again, the notion of structure suggests more than a casual assortment of these elements. To be able to speak of structure, the elements (in this case, the social relationships) must comprise some sort of orderly arrangement or pattern. Nadel suggests a musical analogy as being helpful in making this very point:

> Think of a piece of polyphonic music: any two tones in it are positioned relative to one another by the intervals they describe; but the total design or structure of the piece clearly lies not in the mere presence and collection of all these intervals but in the order in which they appear. Though this analogy has drawbacks, it illustrates the point I wish to make if for intervals we read relationships and for musical structure, social structure.[8]

Consider the article by Blau in this connection. He begins by charting interaction rates among individual workers, but these data are used not to describe a series of isolated social relationships but a pattern of relationships that comprise a status structure linking together all the members of the department. The status structure is one of the important aspects of any social structure.

The Social Order   Having described the two components of the social order—the normative structure and the social structure—we are better able to comment on the social order itself. In doing so, let us consider a specific example of social order: a football team during the playing of a game.

Players on a football team will hold certain values in common: perhaps, a desire to win games, respect for athletic prowess, and a desire to manifest sportsman-like conduct on the field. Norms are represented by the formal rules of the game that are modified and supplemented by informal player understandings about how one behaves as a member of the team, both on and off the field. All players are not expected to behave alike: normative expectations are held for each participant, depending on which position he plays (formal role expectations) and what special characteristics he exhibits (informal role expectations). These numerous values, beliefs, and understandings are somewhat codified and organized so as to form a more-or-less consistent system of formal and informal rules and of formal and informal expectations that orient and are expected to govern the behavior of all participants. In short, football teams exhibit a normative structure.

In addition to sharing certain beliefs and expectations, members of the football team also interact with one another and with members of the competing team. Although it is possible to emphasize the uniqueness of each individual action exhibited by a team member, the concept of social structure focuses on

---

[7]This technique is fully described in Robert F. Bales, *Interaction Process Analysis*, Reading, Mass.: Addison-Wesley, 1950. A more concise introduction to the technique is provided by Bales in his article "A set of categories for the analysis of small group interaction," *American Sociological Review*, 15 (1950), 146-159.

[8]Nadel, p. 11.

the extent to which the actions and interactions of members exhibit regularity and order. One notes certain activities occurring among particular pairs of participants that are similar in character and recurrent over time, for example, blocking or tackling an opposing player and centering or passing the ball to a member of one's own team. (Coaches apparently recognize the importance of these recurrent interactive activities, as they put their teams through tedious drills designed to stress the "fundamentals" of the game.) These relationships linking particular players do not occur in isolation but are themselves arranged into more complex action patterns as defensive and offensive "plays" are executed. The individual plays are likewise often organized into larger sequences of behavior when they reflect some more general strategy to be followed during a series of downs or even during the whole game—a "game plan." Without knowing anything at all about the beliefs and rules that govern the activities of players, a naive observer watching his first football game can see these unmistakable signs indicating the presence of social structure.

We have just attempted to distinguish the normative and social structures for analytical purposes, but when we consider a concrete example of social order, it becomes readily apparent that this distinction is in many ways an artificial one. Why are the actions of the individual players somewhat regular and patterned? Why do the multitudes of actions and interactions that occur on the playing field give evidence not of chaos and confusion but of a semblance of order? It is largely due, of course, to the existence of the normative structure.[9] Much of the consistency and stability exhibited by individuals in their behavior toward others is a reflection of the beliefs and understandings held by these individuals that define what they and others to whom they are related are expected to do.

We must be careful, however, not to push this idea too far. It reflects far too simple a view to say that the normative structure determines the social structure. After all, people who enjoy football will not be satisfied to read rule books or even to attend "skull" practice: they want to see football games. The behavior of the individual team members is not completely determined by the rules and expectations governing their behavior. The runner who is expected to make an end sweep may slip or fumble the ball; the receiver who is expected to catch the pass may drop the ball; and although players may understand the rules governing their conduct during the game, referees are hired to detect and punish infractions of the rules. Once again, we see that the existence of a rule or a normative expectation does not guarantee conformity to it. The truth of the matter is that deviant behavior accounts for much of the color and excitement of a football game. Part of the reason why athletic contests—and competitive and conflicting situations in general—are interesting is that participants are pitted against one another so that for one player to succeed in fulfilling his role expectations another must often fail. A pass successfully caught is a pass that was not knocked down or intercepted; a good run occurs when opposing tacklers have not successfully carried out their role assignments. A player who

---

[9]All regularities of behavior are not to be attributed to the effects of the normative structure. Some are due to the stable personality and physical characteristics of the individual players; others are accounted for by the physical characteristics of the playing field, and so on.

drops a ball passed to him on a given occasion may not immediately be defined as "deviant" by other participants; but a player who drops several passes in succession is likely to be so defined and to be removed from the game (sanctioned) by his coach.

We have noted the effect of the normative structure on the social structure while we have cautioned that this effect should not be overestimated. Now we must comment on forces moving in the opposite direction and must briefly examine the effect of the social structure on the normative structure. For, in a very fundamental sense, norms arise from ongoing behavior, and behavior patterns exert a continuing influence on the normative structure. The rules governing football games today are not the same as those in force one or two decades ago, because such rules gradually change and evolve to keep abreast of current practices. Such rule changes do not occur instantaneously, however, so that there are sometimes areas in which legislation lags behind practice. The lapse of time between behavior and norm changes can be seen even more clearly in areas such as sexual conduct and drug usage. Particularly with respect to premarital sexual practice, formal codes and informal community and group standards are only gradually beginning to reflect the "revolutionary" changes in behavior that began late in the nineteenth century and that have proceeded at an accelerated rate since World War I.[10] Although some people have long been aware of the gaping disparities between public definitions of morality and sexual behavior, studies such as the two Kinsey reports have made glaringly apparent to a large sector of the public the extent of these departures, in terms of both the frequencies of discrepant acts and the numbers of persons involved. Although many individuals and groups in U.S. society still profess and adhere to earlier and more rigorous standards of sexual conduct, there seems to be little question that the general normative structure governing sexual behavior in this society—legal statutes as well as informal "community standards"—is changing to correspond more closely with current practices.

Yet another area where the behavior of increasing numbers of persons is discrepant with present codes is that of drug use. With increasing numbers of people experimenting with an increasing variety of drugs, public officials are attempting to adjust legislation and police actions to fit the changed circumstances. The use of weaker drugs such as marijuana will probably cease to be a felony offense in most states and may, over time, cease to be an offense at all. Such changes occur in part for the practical reason that no society can afford for very long to enforce laws that define as criminals a substantial part of the population. Remember the fate of the Volstead Act, which brought on the prohibition era in this country!

Normative structures do exert important influences on social behavior, but it appears that the reverse is no less true: behavior discrepant with normative standards engaged in long enough by large enough groups of individuals can bring about changes in the normative structures themselves. As Davis observes:

. . . the factual order exercises an influence on the normative system for the norms must always refer to events in the real world and take into account the factual

---

[10]See, for example, W. Ehrmann, "Changing sexual mores," in E. Ginzberg (ed.), *Values and Ideals of American Youth*, New York: Columbia University Press, 1961, pp. 53-70; and I. L. Reiss, *Premarital Sexual Standards in America*, Glencoe, Ill.: Free Press, 1960.

situation. Although norms represent in a sense an imaginary construct, although they are matters of attitude and sentiment, they must nevertheless if they are to have any effect represent correctly the relations between real events . . . . The normative system, since it aims to achieve results in the factual world, is subject to constant modification by events in that world.[11]

How, then, shall we define social order? We shall say that a *social order* exists to the extent that behaviors occurring and relationships present in the social structure are to a relatively high degree oriented to the existence of a normative structure. This does not mean that deviant behaviors and relationships are not a part of the social order. Many such behaviors are oriented to the normative structure in the sense that they are defined by and evaluated in terms of this structure. The opposite of social order, then, is not deviance but *social disorder* or *social disorganization.* In a social order, behavior occurs that is covered by the rules constituting this order. The behavior may conform or deviate from the normative prescriptions, but it is considered to be a part of this order. Returning to our football game, certain behaviors such as catching and missing the ball and tackling an opposing player or clipping him are defined as being a part of the game and are covered by the rules of the game; other behaviors, such as players running through the stands or mobbing the referee, are not. To the extent that the latter types of behavior occur, we regard the game—the social order established by the rules of the game—as disorganized.

This definition is equally applicable to other types of situations that most observers would want to characterize as disorganized. As Cohen states the case:

> In describing military routs and natural disasters—situations in which there is consensus that the word disorganization is relevant—we say that persons "freeze," "panic," "flounder," "give up," "run away," "change their plans," or "stand around helplessly." All these behaviors disrupt or at least threaten the constitutive order of the ongoing activity; therefore, they are themselves, or at least they precipitate, disorganization.[12]

Cohen goes on to suggest that there are two basic conditions under which social disorganization is likely to occur. First, it may be the case that the rules of the social order are sufficiently unclear or conflicting that they provide no basis for orienting one's actions. This is the condition of *anomie*, usually defined as normlessness. Two somewhat contrasting views have developed of anomie, one advanced by the great French sociologist of the nineteenth century Emile Durkheim[13] and another by the American sociologist Robert Merton in his classic article "Social Structure and Anomie."[14] Both these conceptions are described in the article by Cloward, reprinted in this volume. (Reading 11) The second condition leading to disorganization, according to Cohen, occurs when the rules are unambiguous but when there is a failure of motivation to produce the required behaviors.[15] Such failures may be brought about through deficien-

[11]Davis, pp. 52–53.

[12]Albert K. Cohen, "The study of social disorganization and deviant behavior," in Robert K. Merton, Leonard Broom, and Leonard S. Cottrell, Jr. (eds.), *Sociology Today: Problems and Prospects*, New York: Basic Books, 1959, p. 479.

[13]Emile Durkheim, *Suicide* (tr. John A. Spaulding and George Simpson), Glencoe, Ill.: Free Press, 1951, pp. 241–276 (originally published 1898).

[14]Robert K. Merton, "Social structure and anomie," *Social Theory and Social Structure* (rev. ed.), Glencoe, Ill.: Free Press, 1957, pp. 131–160.

[15]Cohen, pp. 480–483.

cies in the socialization processes that prepare individuals to assume selected social roles or may be brought about because of breakdowns in the structures of power and authority that support and sustain a given order. The processes of socialization and power will be examined in greater depth in subsequent parts of this volume.

The Problem of Deviance   We have tried to emphasize that deviant behavior should be viewed as an integral part of the social order, not as behavior set apart or as behavior that necessarily gives evidence of disorder or disorganization. This view of deviance has only recently been developed by sociologists and represents an important break from an earlier theoretical tradition that associated all deviance with the breakdown of the social order. Deviant behavior has been invited into the house of order on two somewhat different bases. First, it has become increasingly clear that some amount of deviant behavior is an inevitable part of any ordered system. Further, although deviance creates important problems for the existing order, such as threatening the atmosphere of trust that others will do their fair share, it also makes important contributions to the maintenance of the order, as the discussion by Erikson makes clear. (Reading 10)

Second, early sociologists examining the world of thieves, prostitutes, delinquents, or drug addicts expected to see chaos and disorder, but instead, invariably, they turned up order—order that was based on norms, values, and social relationships viewed as deviant by members in the larger society, to be sure, but order, nonetheless. This discovery has led to the belated realization that one cannot speak simply of "deviant behavior" without specifying with respect to which set of rules the behavior is deviant. Berger underlines this point nicely with the following example:

Take a settlement house in a lower-class slum district trying to wean away teen-agers from the publicly disapproved activities of a juvenile gang. The frame of reference within which social workers and police officers define the "problems" of this situation is constituted by the world of middle-class, respectable, publicly approved values. It is a "problem" if teen-agers drive around in stolen automobiles, and it is a "solution" if instead they will play group games in the settlement house. But if one changes the frame of reference and looks at the situation from the viewpoint of the leaders of the juvenile gang, the "problems" are defined in reverse order. It is a "problem" for the solidarity of the gang if its members are seduced away from those activities that lend prestige to the gang within its own social world, and it would be a "solution" if the social workers went way the hell back uptown where they came from.[16]

This view, which emphasizes the existence of deviant subcultures and social orders, is amplified by the final selection in this section contributed by Cloward. (Reading 11) Cloward examines the situation of those in our society who for circumstantial reasons are unable to conform to the dominate societal norms, and he asks under what conditions they may become recruited into organized deviant subsystems. The answer in large part leads us back to role theory and on to socialization processes, because it has to do with what roles are available to be learned in a given location in the social structure and what opportunities there are to play out the roles that have been learned.

[16]Peter L. Berger, *Invitation To Sociology*, New York: Doubleday, 1963, p. 37.

Deviant behavior, then, may exhibit all the characteristics of socially organized behavior. These subcultures are deviant only in that the normative order on which they are based is not acceptable to some other group—often a majority group—from whose perspective the behavior is viewed. But it should always be kept in mind that deviant behavior, when engaged in long enough by enough people, can become the basis for a new social order supported by a newly constituted majority.

We cannot refrain from making one final comment. We have just indicated that sociologists have had a difficult time separating deviant behavior from social disorder. Part of the difficulty, we would argue, was due to a failure of objectivity on the part of sociologists.[17] Early sociologists had a difficult time believing that behavior of which they disapproved as individuals was nonetheless organized behavior, exhibiting the laws of social order. Bad behavior, they felt, must be different from good behavior; it must reflect the absence of social order. For a time, the analysis by sociologists of deviant groups reflected their own value judgments of deviance more than it did the characteristics of the phenomena under study.

We may conclude that there are at least two problems with this situation so far as the progress of sociology is concerned. First, value judgments can bias what one sees, as was noted in our introduction to this Part, so that what is seen and reported is often as much or more a reflection of the observer as it is of the observed. Second, value judgments are, in fact, judgments; they are conclusions. And such conclusions are the enemy of open-minded investigation and, hence, of science.

[17]See the remark by Edwin Sutherland quoted by Cloward in Reading 11 (p. 134). Sutherland was one of the first sociologists to see that the term *disorganization* was used more as an ethical judgment than as a descriptive scientific concept when applied to areas characterized by deviant normative structures.

9   Patterns of Interaction Among a Group of Officials in a Government Agency

Peter M. Blau

The analysis of small groups has received increasing attention in sociological research during recent years. One type of these studies focuses upon the normative orientations that arise in "natural" groups, as exemplified by investigations of restriction of output among factory workers. Another type is primarily interested in developing methods of observation and analysis of interaction, and usually deals with "artificial" groups in laboratory situations.

Reprinted from Peter M. Blau, "Patterns of interaction among a group of officials in a government agency," *Human Relations*, 7, No. 3 (1954), 337-348, by permission of the author and the publisher, Plenum Publishing Corporation.

This paper is concerned with a systematic analysis of the processes of interaction in a "natural" group of officials in a government agency,[1] and the status differences that emerge in this process. It focuses upon three problems: (1) The interdependence between the way an official performs his duties and his interpersonal relations with his colleagues. (2) The usefulness of observable interaction as an index of status in the group. (3) The relationship between interaction in "pair-events," contacts between two individuals, and "set-events," social situations involving more than two participants.

THE SETTING

The peer group studied consisted of 16 agents,[2] who, together with a supervisor and a clerk, composed a department in an agency of law enforcement. Their principal duty was the investigation of business establishments to determine whether any violation of the laws the agency administered had occurred. Each agent worked by himself on the cases assigned to him by the supervisor. Processing a case involved an audit of the books of the firm, interviews with the employer and a sample of employees, negotiation with the employer if violations were found, and writing a full report. Agents spent slightly more than half their working time in the field, and the remainder of it in the large office this department shared with another, similar, department.

Problems often arose in the course of making difficult legal decisions. When an agent could not solve such a problem, he was expected to consult his supervisor for advice. However, the supervisor also evaluated the performance of his subordinates on every case, and his annual official rating influenced their promotion chances. Agents were therefore reluctant to expose their ignorance to the supervisor by asking him often for advice. The comment of one of them was typical: "I try to stay away from the supervisor as much as possible. The reason is that the more often you go to the supervisor, the more you show your stupidity."

Officially, agents were not permitted to consult each other; but their need for advice from a source other than the supervisor induced them to ignore this rule. All agents, including the most competent ones, often discussed their problems with colleagues. This unofficial practice reduced their anxiety over making correct decisions, and thus improved their performance. The knowledge that he could obtain advice without exposing his difficulties to the supervisor enhanced the agent's ability to make accurate decisions, even when no consultation took place.[3] The existence of this cooperative practice basically influenced the relationships between officials. This therefore is a study of social interaction in a cooperative group.

Social Interaction and Competence

To obtain quantitative indices of interaction, all contacts any member of this department had with anyone else in the office during 30.5 hours of observation

---

[1]The method of observation used was suggested by E. D. Chapple and C. M. Arensberg, "Measuring Human Relations," *Genetic Psychology Monographs*, Vol. XXII, 1940, pp. 3-147. I am indebted to Professor Arensberg for his helpful comments on the study of social interaction in this group.

[2]Data for only 15 agents are available for most tables.

[3]This practice of unofficial consultation is analyzed in the author's doctoral dissertation at Columbia University, *The Dynamics of Bureaucracy*, [Chicago: University of Chicago Press, 1955; rev. ed. 1963] a study of this and another agency. A fellowship of the Social Science Research Council, which made this study possible, is gratefully acknowledged.

were recorded. On the average, an official had 8.3 contacts per hour; 5.1 of these were associations with other agents in this department. Of course, not all of these interactions were consultations. Many, such as greetings or brief private conversations, were not related to official business. Neither the length of the exchange nor its content were given consideration in this count. The total number of contacts observed was 2,189.

Four simple indices can be derived from this record: (1) The total number of contacts an individual had per hour. (2) The number of contacts an individual originated per hour. (3) The number of contacts an individual received per hour, that is, those originated by the other participant in the exchange. (4) The proportion of an individual's total contacts that he originated, which provides an index of his initiative in social interaction.

Competence in performing the duties of an agent was related to participation in the interaction of this group. The supervisor's rating of the performance of his subordinates provides an index of their relative competence.[4] The more competent agents had a disproportionately large number of contacts, but they did not originate more contacts than others. The positive relationship between proficiency and frequency of interaction was entirely due to the fact that the highly competent agents tended to *receive* more contacts from their colleagues than those who were less proficient,[5] as Table 9–1 shows.[6]

[4]The official rating of the supervisor divided agents into three groups. For purposes of this study, the supervisor ranked agents individually in terms of their competence.

[5]The relation between rank and received contacts corresponds to the conclusions reached by George C. Homans, but the absence of a relation between rank and originated contacts does not. See *The Human Group* (New York: Harcourt, Brace, 1950; London: Routledge & Kegan Paul), pp. 145, 181–82.

[6]All relationships discussed in this paper are significant on the .05 level.

TABLE 9–1 Contacts Received per Hour and Competence

Contacts Received	Competence		
	High	Low	Total
Many	5	1	6
Few	2	7	9
	–	–	–
Total	7	8	15

It is not surprising that the experts were frequently contacted in this situation. They could furnish the best advice, and they were highly esteemed in this group where competence was greatly valued. The rank correlation between esteem and competence was .93.[7] Their colleagues approached these experts disproportionately often, not only to ask their advice, but also to seek their companionship, since associating with a respected person tends to be especially desirable. Their frequent participation in interaction made most experts well integrated members of this group.

Superior ability alone, however, did not assure an integrated position. The two highly competent agents who were considered uncooperative by their colleagues were generally disliked and received only few contacts. To become accepted, an expert had to share the advantages of his superior skill with his colleagues. Provided that he was willing to help others with their problems, the highly competent agent was often drawn into discussions, and thus became an integrated member of the group without having had to exercise much social initiative.

Competence and Informal Relationships

The less competent agent did not become integrated without special effort.

[7]The members of this group were asked to rank their colleagues in terms of their ability as agent. An official's average rank is defined as the esteem he enjoyed among colleagues. In a two-by-two table, the relationship between esteem and competence is perfect.

Since he was initially less attractive an associate than the expert, he received fewer contacts, and probably experienced a greater need for improving his interpersonal relationships. As a result, the less competent agents exercised relatively more initiative in their social interaction in the office, as Table 9-2 shows,[8] and they also cultivated informal relations with colleagues in their free time.

TABLE 9–2 Social Initiative and Competence

Social Initiative	Competence		
	High	Low	Total
Much	2	7	9
Little	5	1	6
	—	—	—
Total	7	8	15

The major opportunity for relaxed informal contacts between agents was provided by the daily lunch hour. Most officials valued this period of companionship greatly, and sometimes returned to the office from the field just before noon in order to join some colleagues for lunch. Since about one half of the agents were usually in the field, even those persons who had regular partners often lunched with other colleagues. An index of the extent of the informal relations of each official was constructed on the basis of a record of all his lunch partners in a two week period.[9]

[8]The less competent agents tended to exercise more initiative than the experts partly because they were more likely to request advice, but also partly because they were more concerned with improving their position in the group.

[9]The agents kept this record themselves at the request of the observer. If a luncheon engagement is defined as eating with one colleague once, the total number of engagements reported (which often included several colleagues on the same day, and the same colleagues on repeated days), divided by the number of days on which the respondent went to lunch from the office, defines the value of this index.

Table 9–3 shows that the least competent agents tended to have more extensive informal relations at lunch than those whose competence was average or high. This appears, at first, to contradict the previous conclusion that most experts were well integrated. However, their less extensive informal relations do not indicate that these experts were excluded from the fellowship at lunch. Generally, they as well as other agents lunched in the company of colleagues.[10] But the greater need of the less competent agents to improve their position in the group, since they did not become as easily integrated through interaction in the office as the experts, induced them to maintain particularly extensive informal relations with their colleagues in their free time.

TABLE 9–3 Extent of Informal Relations and Competence

Informal Relations	Competence		
	High or Average	Low	Total
Extensive	2	5	7
Less extensive	7	1	8
	—	—	—
Total	9	6	15

Informal Relationships and Social Interaction

The interpersonal relations an agent had established at lunch influenced his participation in social interaction in the office. Most of the agents who had very extensive informal relations received many contacts from others, as Table 9-4 indicates. On the other hand, neither the total number of contacts, nor the number

[10]Only two agents. one of the least and one of the most competent members of the group, lunched alone more than once during two weeks of observation (excluding days when agents were in the field at noon).

TABLE 9–4 Extent of Informal Relations and Contacts Received per Hour

Informal Relations	Contacts Received		
	Many	Few	Total
Extensive	6	1	7
Less extensive	2	6	8
Total	8	7	15

of originated contacts, was related to extent of informal relations.

The more extensive an individual's interpersonal relations are, the better integrated a member of the group he will be. Further, in a group in which most members strive to become highly proficient, and in which they have occasion to appreciate the superior advice experts give them, a close association between integration and competence is to be expected. Since the number of received contacts was the only index of interaction related both to extent of informal relations and to competence, it may be considered an index of integration, that is, of an agent's unofficial status in this group.[11]

It will be noted that competence and extent of informal relations, although each was directly related to integration, were inversely related to each other. (Compare Tables 9–1 and 9–4 with Table 9–3.) This suggests the existence of two alternative means of becoming an integrated member in this group. Experts attracted their colleagues through their

[11] Why was the total frequency of interaction not related to integration in a cooperative situation? Possibly, because the very knowledge that interaction is integrative induces those members of a group not yet fully integrated but trying to improve their position to originate especially many contacts. For example, the newest member of this group (assigned to the department two months prior to observation) ranked third in the number of originated contacts, first in social initiative, but fourteenth in the number of received contacts.

superior ability, and became integrated by merely being cooperative, without having to exercise much social initiative. Less competent agents were more likely to establish extensive informal relations, since such extensive relations also made an individual a desirable companion for many colleagues, and thus an integrated member of the group. The existence of two alternative mechanisms of integration contributed to the high social cohesion in this department.[12]

The Process of Integration

The preceding interpretation of the relationships between competence, informal relations, and integration raises two questions. First, did these agents actually find their highly competent colleagues particularly attractive? To be sure, their estimation of an individual's ability was closely related to his competence. But was this rationally defined esteem related to social attractiveness? Second, is there any evidence that some agents experienced a need to improve their integration in the group and met this need by establishing especially extensive informal relations in their free time? The analysis of inaccuracies of interview responses concerning lunch partners suggests answers to these questions.

A card with the names of all members of this group was given to each one of them in the course of an interview in his home, and he was asked to divide his colleagues into those with whom he had and those with whom he never had spent a lunch period. Responses from 15 officials were obtained. Every fact,

[12] In a competitive group of officials observed in another agency, both mechanisms of integration were greatly impaired. Interaction in the office was largely disintegrative, and the resulting strained relations between officials discouraged them from spending their lunch periods together. As a result, the social cohesion of this group was low.

whether two officials had or never had lunch together, was independently reported by two individuals. Of the 105 pairs of statements, 41 did not coincide. This large proportion of discrepancies—39 per cent—indicates that such interview responses provide a very unreliable index of social contacts.[13] However, these very discrepancies do reveal differences in the interpersonal attitudes of these officials and their roles in the group.

Positive discrepancies, the number of colleagues whom an official named but who did not name him, can be considered an index of "role distortion." An individual who claims to have established informal relations with several other members of the group who disclaim these relations has a distorted image of his role in that group.[14] Negative discrepancies, the number of colleagues whom an agent failed to mention but who mentioned him, may be used as an index of "social attractiveness." If an individual does not recall several associations with colleagues which these colleagues report as having occurred, the others are more attracted to him than he is to them.

Table 9–5 indicates that social attractiveness was related to esteem, as has been assumed. The attractiveness of the esteemed expert, which found expression in his colleagues' remembering occasional contacts with him that he had forgotten, or perhaps reporting associations that had never occurred, induced the others to originate disproportionately

TABLE 9–5 Esteem and Social Attractiveness

Esteem	Social Attractiveness		
	High	Low	Total
High	6	2	8
Low	1	6	7
	—	—	—
Total	7	8	15

many contacts with him. The fact that the expert therefore became integrated without exercising much social effort may well have made his interpersonal relations *appear* less important to him, and thus account for his tendency to forget meetings with colleagues.

Role distortion, on the other hand, was inversely related to extent of informal relations, as Table 9–6 shows.[15] Agents who had established extensive informal relations only rarely reported having lunched with colleagues who failed to remember such engagements. Those whose interpersonal relations were less extensive often adapted to an insecure position by maintaining a distorted image of their role in the group. This adaptation

[13]Accuracy can be somewhat increased by asking for contacts during a limited time only. The number of colleagues who mentioned an agent as their lunch partner seems to provide a valid index of scope of partners, but the number of colleagues named by an agent does not. Only the former index was significantly related to an index of scope of lunch partners based on observation.

[14]It is not known whether a lunch engagement remembered by one agent but not by the other participant actually had taken place, but many positive discrepancies indicate role distortion

whether this had been the case or not. Either an individual imagined contacts that never had occurred, or he accurately remembered contacts that had taken place so rarely and so long ago that the other participants had forgotten them. Even the latter indicates that his interpersonal relations have assumed greater significance in his thinking than they warrant. It is also not known whether an individual whose statement was incorrect *remembered* or only *reported* inaccurately. Even if he did not deceive himself, but told the interviewer of contacts that he knew had never occurred, this would indicate that he felt it necessary to present a distorted image of his role in the group to others. The same considerations, *mutatis mutandis*, apply to many negative discrepancies; they indicate social attractiveness, as discussed in the text, regardless of which one of the participants was factually correct.

[15]Role distortion was not related to esteem (and neither to competence), whereas social attractiveness was not related to the extent of informal relations. This indicates that role distortion and social attractiveness measure two different dimensions.

**TABLE 9–6 Extent of Informal Relations
and Role Distortion**

Informal Relations	Role Distortion		
	High	Low	Total
Extensive	2	6	8
Less extensive	6	1	7
	–	–	—
Total	8	7	15

suggests that these agents experienced a need for improving their position. The existence of this need helps to explain why the less competent agents, who were originally less attractive to their colleagues, usually tried to become better integrated by cultivating informal relations with the other members of the group.

Interaction in Group Situations

The unofficial status of an agent, indicated by the number of contacts he received, influenced his behavior in group situations, his interaction with outsiders, and his performance of his duties.

Departmental meetings, held every other week, were the only occasions when all members of the department were assembled as a group. These meetings were largely devoted to explanations of new regulations and changes in enforcement practice by the supervisor, and the discussion of problems related to new procedures by the agents. Those whose status was secure, who received many contacts throughout the day, tended to participate more in these discussions than their less well integrated colleagues, as Table 9-7 shows.[16]

By raising a question, an agent could clarify an issue that was doubtful in his

[16]On the basis of observation during five departmental meetings, agents were divided into those who spoke three times or more and those who spoke less than three times per meeting. This index was also positively related to esteem.

mind. By making an intelligent comment, he enhanced his prestige in the eyes of his supervisor and his colleagues. But by participating in the discussion he also risked exposing his ignorance and being ridiculed. The group often responded to a remark with derisive laughter and comments, because it seemed irrelevant or obvious, and the participation of the least integrated agents was most often discouraged in this fashion. In effect, the group permitted only its integrated members to enhance their knowledge and prestige in these discussions.

The superior status of agents who received many contacts also manifested itself in the dominant roles they assumed when a small group of agents was engaged in a joint undertaking. They made most suggestions, and their suggestions were most often followed. For instance, they assumed command on the few occasions when several agents worked together on a project; they usually decided to which restaurant a group went for lunch. The fact that dominance in group situations is associated with the number of received contacts further justifies the use of the latter as an index of status.

**TABLE 9–7 Contacts Received per Hour
and Participation in Discussion
at Departmental Meetings**

Contacts Received	Agent Participated in Discussion		
	Often	Rarely	Total
Many	5	1	6
Few	2	7	9
Total	7	8	15

Interaction with Outsiders

The better integrated agents had a disproportionately large number of contacts with members of *other* departments.[17] Agents who received relatively few contacts in the course of social interaction tended to confine their associations to members of their own department. An insecure position apparently discouraged ventures into untried social situations. This relationship between status and ease of interaction with out-group members is exemplified by the contacts of agents with stenographers.

Agents could dictate their reports and letters to stenographers, but they did not always avail themselves of the opportunity to do so. Some agents usually wrote their difficult reports in long-hand and had them typed, and some typed an occasional brief report themselves. The extent to which an agent utilized stenographic assistance was related to his status.[18] Table 9-8 indicates that agents who received many contacts from their

TABLE 9–8 Contacts Received per Hour and Dictation Time

	Dictation Time		
Contacts Received	Much	Little	Total
Many	6	1	7
Few	2	7	9
	—	—	—
Total	8	8	16

[17]This is in agreement with William F. Whyte's finding that the leaders of gangs are the channels of communication between gangs. See *Street Corner Society* (Chicago: University of Chicago Press, 1943), pp. 259-60.

[18]The index of utilized dictation time is: the amount of time stenographers spent taking dictation from an agent during an eight-month period, divided by the number of cases he had completed in that period. By holding the number of cases constant, the amount of dictation time required is roughly held constant. Although the value of this index is influenced by dictation speed, it is primarily a function of the proportion of his reports an agent failed to dictate. Data for all 16 agents were available for this index.

colleagues dictated more often to stenographers than agents who were not as well integrated.

Composing the final report of a complex case was a difficult task, and an enervating one, since this report provided the basis for the supervisor's evaluation of the agent's performance. Two agents explained their failure to dictate some of their reports in the following terms:

If it's exceptionally hard; I actually write it out with pencil and paper, and turn it into the pool for typing . . . It's easier for me to write than to dictate. Often, I don't use quite the right word. I notice it a few seconds later, but I let it go. What shall I do? Ask the girl to go back and change it? I'd rather not. . . .

If I dictate directly, I worry about not getting everything in the report. This way, if I leave something out, I can go back and put it in. It would be a nuisance to tell the stenographer to go back and make such insertions.

An agent found the presence of the stenographer disturbing if he worried about the impression he made on her—for instance, when he had to tell her to correct a mistake he had made. Agents who received social recognition from their peers in the form of being often approached by them, either because their competence was respected or because their company was valued for personal reasons,[19] were relatively unconcerned with the opinion of stenographers. Agents who felt insecure in the peer group, on the other hand, were probably more eager to receive, at least, the respect of the stenographer, and were at the same time less confident of doing so. Their consequent preoccupation with the impression they made on her prevented them from concentrating their thoughts upon composing the report. This disturbance often induced the less integrated agents to forego the advantages of dictating.

Their status in the group also influenced the interaction of agents with the

[19]Both esteem and the extent of informal relations were also positively related to dictation time.

employers of the firms they investigated. Observation indicated that the agents who were well integrated, although not necessarily the most effective negotiators, tended to remain more detached in their negotiations with employers. Apparently, the recognition they received from their colleagues made it easier for them to disregard the personal attitudes of clients toward them, and thus to remain unperturbed even in the face of an excitable employer.[20] Such detachment improved the quality of an agent's performance, just as the ability to dictate difficult reports to stenographers enhanced his working efficiency. His status therefore influenced an agent's performance.

CONCLUSIONS

Unofficial status and quality of performance were mutually related in this department of a government agency. Superior competence usually produced an integrated status in this group, since its members were especially attracted to those colleagues whose ability they respected. A substitute means for attaining this end, which enabled the less proficient agents also to become integrated, was the establishment of extensive informal relations with colleagues, since this also made many others value the companionship of an individual. Agents who were highly competent, and those who had particularly extensive informal relations, received a disproportionately large number of contacts in the course of social interaction.

The relative number of contacts an agent received from his colleagues constituted the *actual*—to refrain from coining a new term by calling it the "interactual"—expression of their evaluation of

his role in the group. It provided him with concrete evidence of his significance for the group. Being approached often gave an agent a feeling of security in social situations which facilitated his interaction with outsiders as well as with members of his own group. In contrast, the insecurity of the agent who was rarely approached by others made his interpersonal relations on the job problematical for him. The number of contacts an agent received per hour indicated his status in the group.

The competence of an agent influenced his unofficial status, which, in turn, influenced the quality of his performance, especially because it affected the social relationships into which he entered in the course of discharging his duties. The concern of the insecure agent with his position in these relationships distracted his attention from his work. On the other hand, the agent whose status gave him confidence in being socially accepted and respected, could concentrate his energies upon the problems of his job, in work situations involving social interaction. Typically, he was more detached in negotiations with clients, less disturbed by the presence of stenographers, and less hesitant to clarify a problem in a discussion. All of these factors contributed to his efficiency as an agent.

Agents who were disproportionately often approached in the course of interaction between individuals tended to assume the dominant roles in group situations, for instance in the discussions at departmental meetings, or when a small group of officials engaged in a common undertaking. In other words, those agents who *received* relatively many contacts in "pair events" were most likely to take the *initiative* in "set-events."[21] The social recognition an agent

---

[20]For a full report on the relationship between an agent's role in this group and his role as an investigator, the reader is referred to the author's study cited above.

[21]Whyte also found that the leaders of a group originated most activities in "set-events"; p. 262.

received in the form of being approached, often gave him a feeling of security that enabled him to make recommendations freely in group situations. Simultaneously, the same regard for an agent that led others to seek to associate with him also induced them usually to follow his recommendations.

The designation of the frequency of received contacts as index of unofficial status is by no means arbitrary. The recipients of many contacts occupied a superordinate status in the group in the conventional meaning of the term; they could, and did, exercise social control over their colleagues. The members of this group, who were originally peers, became differentiated in status as the result of interacting with each other at different rates. By originating a disproportionately large number of contacts with one of its members, the group expressed their collective regard for and deference to him, and thus bestowed superior status, power as well as prestige, upon him. The frequency of the contacts an agent received therefore not only expressed but also helped to determine his status in the group.[22]

[22]In this group of peers, differences in power, the ability to control others, emerged in the process of co-operative, voluntary interaction. Even here, the intellectual resources of an individual, his competence, influenced his interaction and his status. Initial differences in status, of course, also influence interaction. The conclusions of this paper are not meant to imply that the process of voluntary interaction in a group is the source of all differentials in power. For example, the superior status of the supervisor did not originate in the interaction in this department. It found expression in his interaction with subordinates, and was modified through this interaction, but its source was his official authority over subordinates, including his right to administer sanctions to them. For a discussion of authority, see the author's study cited above.

10 Notes on the Sociology of Deviance

Kai T. Erikson

It is general practice in sociology to regard deviant behavior as an alien element in society. Deviance is considered a vagrant form of human activity, moving outside the more orderly currents of social life. And since this type of aberration could only occur (in theory) if something were wrong within the social organization itself, deviant behavior is described almost as if it were leakage from machinery in poor condition: it is an accidental result of disorder and anomie, a symptom of internal breakdown.

The purpose of the following remarks will be to review this conventional outlook and to argue that it provides too narrow a framework for the study of deviant behavior. Deviation, we will suggest, recalling Durkheim's classic statement on the subject, can often be understood as a normal product of stable institutions, a vital resource which is guarded and preserved by forces found in all human organizations.[1]

[1]Emile Durkheim, *The Rules of Sociological Method* (translated by S. A. Solovay and J. H. Mueller), Glencoe: The Free Press, 1958.

Reprinted from Kai T. Erikson "Notes on the sociology of deviance," *Social Problems*, 9, No. 4, (1962), 307–314, by permission of the author and the publisher. The Society for the Study of Social Problems.

I

According to current theory, deviant behavior is most likely to occur when the sanctions governing conduct in any given setting seem to be contradictory.[2] This would be the case, for example, if the work rules posted by a company required one course of action from its employees and the longer-range policies of the company required quite another. Any situation marked by this kind of ambiguity, of course, can pose a serious dilemma for the individual: if he is careful to observe one set of demands imposed upon him, he runs the immediate risk of violating some other, and thus may find himself caught in a deviant stance no matter how earnestly he tries to avoid it. In this limited sense, deviance can be regarded a "normal" human response to "abnormal" social conditions, and the sociologist is therefore invited to assume that some sort of pathology exists within the social structure whenever deviant behavior makes an appearance.

This general approach is clearly more concerned with the *etiology* of deviant behavior than with its continuing social *history*—and as a result it often draws sociological attention away from an important area of inquiry. It may be safe to assume that naive acts of deviance, such as first criminal offenses, are provoked by strains in the local situation. But this is only the beginning of a much longer story, for deviant activities can generate a good deal of momentum once they are set into motion: they develop forms of organization, persist over time, and sometimes remain intact long after the strains which originally produced them have

disappeared. In this respect, deviant activities are often absorbed into the main tissue of society and derive support from the same forces which stabilize other forms of social life. There are persons in society, for example, who make career commitments to deviant styles of conduct, impelled by some inner need for continuity rather than by any urgencies in the immediate social setting. There are groups in society which actively encourage new deviant trends, often prolonging them beyond the point where they represent an adaption to strain. These sources of support for deviant behavior are difficult to visualize when we use terms like "strain," "anomie," or "breakdown" in discussions of the problem. Such terms may help us explain how the social structure creates fresh deviant potential, but they do not help us explain how that potential is later shaped into durable, persisting social patterns.[3] The individual's need for self continuity and the group's offer of support are altogether normal processes, even if they are sometimes found in deviant situations; and thus the study of deviant behavior is as much a study of social organization as it is a study of *dis*organization and anomie.

II

From a sociological standpoint, deviance can be defined as conduct which is generally thought to require the attention of social control agencies—that is, conduct about which "something should be done." Deviance is not a property *inherent in* certain forms of behavior; it is a property *conferred upon* these forms by the audiences which directly or indirectly witness them. Sociologically, then, the critical variable in the study of deviance

[2]The best known statements of this general position, of course, are by Robert K. Merton and Talcott Parsons. Merton, *Social Theory and Social Structures* (revised edition), Glencoe: The Free Press, 1957; and Parsons, *The Social System*, Glencoe: The Free Press, 1951.

[3]Cf. Daniel Glaser and Kent Rice, "Crime, Age, and Employment," *American Sociological Review*, 24 (1959), pp. 679-686.

is the social *audience* rather than the individual *person,* since it is the audience which eventually decides whether or not any given action or actions will become a visible case of deviation.

This definition may seem a little indirect, but it has the advantage of bringing a neglected socialogical issue into proper focus. When a community acts to control the behavior of one of its members, it is engaged in a very intricate process of selection. Even a determined miscreant conforms in most of his daily behavior—using the correct spoon at mealtime, taking good care of his mother, or otherwise observing the mores of his society—and if the community elects to bring sanctions against him for the occasions when he does act offensively, it is responding to a few deviant details set within a vast context of proper conduct. Thus a person may be jailed or hospitalized for a few scattered moments of misbehavior, defined as a fulltime deviant despite the fact that he had supplied the community with countless other indications that he was a decent, moral citizen. The screening device which sifts these telling details out of the individual's over-all performance, then, is a sensitive instrument of social control. It is important to note that this screen takes a number of factors into account which are not directly related to the deviant act itself: it is concerned with the actor's social class, his past record as an offender, the amount of remorse he manages to convey, and many similar concerns which take hold in the shifting moods of the community. This is why the community often overlooks behavior which seems technically deviant (like certain kinds of white collar graft) of takes sharp exception to behavior which seems essentially harmless (like certain kinds of sexual impropriety) . It is an easily demonstrated fact, for example, that working class boys who steal cars are far more likely to go to prison than upper class boys who commit the same or even more serious crimes, suggesting that from the point of view of the community lower class offenders are somehow more deviant. To this extent, the community screen is perhaps a more relevant subject for sociological research than the actual behavior which is filtered through it.

Once the problem is phrased in this way, we can ask: how does a community decide what forms of conduct should be singled out for this kind of attention? And why, having made this choice, does it create special institutions to deal with the persons who enact them? The standard answer to this question is that society sets up the machinery of control in order to protect itself against the "harmful" effects of deviance, in much the same way that an organism mobilizes its resources to combat an invasion of germs. At times, however, this classroom convention only seems to make the problem more complicated. In the first place, as Durkheim pointed out some years ago, it is by no means clear that all acts considered deviant in a culture are in fact (or even in principle) harmful to group life.[4] And in the second place, specialists in crime and mental health have long suggested that deviance can play an important role in keeping the social order intact—again a point we owe originally to Durkheim.[5] This has serious implications for sociological theory in general.

III

In recent years, sociological theory has become more and more concerned with the concept "social system"—an organization of society's component parts into

[4]Emile Durkheim, *The Division of Labor in Society* (translated by George Simpson) ,Glencoe: The Free Press, 1952. See particularly Chapter 2, Book 1.
[5]Emile Durkheim, *The Rules of Sociological Method, op. cit.*

a form which sustains internal equilibrium, resists change, and is boundary maintaining. Now this concept has many abstract dimensions, but it is generally used to describe those forces in the social order which promote a high level of uniformity among human actors and a high degree of symmetry within human institutions. In this sense, the concept is normatively oriented since it directs the observer's attention toward those centers in social space where the core values of society are figuratively located. The main organizational principle of a system, then, is essentially a centripetal one: it draws the behavior of actors toward the nucleus of the system, bringing it within range of basic norms. Any conduct which is neither attracted toward this nerve center by the rewards of conformity nor compelled toward it by other social pressures is considered "out of control," which is to say, deviant.

This basic model has provided the theme for most contemporary thinking about deviance, and as a result little attention has been given to the notion that systems operate to maintain boundaries. Generally speaking, boundaries are controls which limit the fluctuation of a system's component parts so that the whole retains a defined range of activity—a unique pattern of constancy and stability—within the larger environment.[6] The range of human behavior is potentially so great that any *social* system must make clear statements about the nature and location of its boundaries, placing limits on the flow of behavior so that it circulates within a given cultural area. Thus boundaries are a crucial point of reference for persons living within any system, a prominent concept in a group's special language and tradition. A juvenile gang may define its boundaries by the amount of territory it defends, a profes-

[6]Cf. Talcott Parsons, *The Social System, op. cit.*

sional society by the range of subjects it discusses, a fraternal order by the variety of members it accepts. But in each case, members share the same idea as to where the group begins and ends in social space and know what kinds of experience "belong" within this domain.

For all its apparent abstractness, a social system is organized around the movements of persons joined together in regular social relations. The only material found in a system for marking boundaries, then, is the behavior of its participants; and the form of behavior which best performs this function would seem to be deviant almost by definition, since it is the most extreme variety of conduct to be found within the experience of the group. In this respect, transactions taking place between deviant persons on the one side and agencies of control on the other are boundary maintaining mechanisms. They mark the outside limits of the area in which the norm has jurisdiction, and in this way assert how much diversity and variability can be contained within the system before it begins to lose its distinct structure, its unique shape.

A social norm is rarely expressed as a firm rule or official code. It is an abstract synthesis of the many separate times a community has stated its sentiments on a given issue. Thus the norm has a history much like that of an article of common law: it is an accumulation of decisions made by the community over a long period of time which gradually gathers enough moral influence to serve as a precedent for future decisions. Like an article of common law, the norm retains its validity only if it is regularly used as a basis for judgment. Each time the community censures some act of deviance, then, it sharpens the authority of the violated norm and re-establishes the boundaries of the group.

One of the most interesting features of

control institutions, in this regard, is the amount of publicity they have always attracted. In an earlier day, correction of deviant offenders took place in the public market and gave the crowd a chance to display its interest in a direct, active way. In our own day, the guilty are no longer paraded in public places, but instead we are confronted by a heavy flow of newspaper and radio reports which offer much the same kind of entertainment. Why are these reports considered "newsworthy" and why do they rate the extraordinary attention they receive? Perhaps they satisfy a number of psychological perversities among the mass audience, as many commentators have suggested, but at the same time they constitute our main source of information about the normative outlines of society. They are lessons through which we teach one another what the norms mean and how far they extend. In a figurative sense, at least, morality and immorality meet at the public scaffold, and it is during this meeting that the community declares where the line between them should be drawn.

Human groups need to regulate the routine affairs of everyday life, and to this end the norms provide an important focus for behavior. But human groups also need to describe and anticipate those areas of being which lie beyond the immediate borders of the group—the unseen dangers which in any culture and in any age seem to threaten the security of group life. The universal folklore depicting demons, devils, witches and evil spirits may be one way to give form to these otherwise formless dangers, but the visible deviant is another kind of reminder. As a trespasser against the norm, he represents those forces excluded by the group's boundaries: he informs us, as it were, what evil looks like, what shapes the devil can assume. In doing so, he shows us the difference between kinds of experience which belong within the group and kinds of experience which belong outside it.

Thus deviance cannot be dismissed as behavior which *disrupts* stability in society, but is itself, in controlled quantities, an important condition for *preserving* stability.

IV

This raises a serious theoretical question. If we grant that deviant behavior often performs a valuable service in society, can we then assume that society as a whole actively tries to promote this resource? Can we assume, in other words, that some kind of active recruitment process is going on to assure society of a steady volume of deviance? Sociology has not yet developed a conceptual language in which this sort of question can be discussed without a great deal of circularity, but one observation can be made which gives the question an interesting perspective—namely, that deviant activities often seem to derive support from the very agencies designed to suppress them. Indeed, the institutions devised by human society for guarding against deviance sometimes seem so poorly equipped for this task that we might well ask why this is considered their "real" function at all.

It is by now a thoroughly familiar argument that many of the institutions built to inhibit deviance actually operate in such a way as to perpetuate it. For one thing, prisons, hospitals, and other agencies of control provide aid and protection for large numbers of deviant persons. But beyond this, such institutions gather marginal people into tightly segregated groups, give them an opportunity to teach one another the skills and attitudes of a deviant career, and even drive them into using these skills by reinforcing their sense of alienation from the rest of society.[7] This process is found not only in the institutions which actually confine the deviant, but in the general community as well.

The community's decision to bring deviant sanctions against an individual is not a simple act of censure. It is a sharp rite of transition, at once moving him out of his normal position in society and transferring him into a distinct deviant role.[8] The ceremonies which accomplish this change of status, usually, have three related phases. They arrange a formal *confrontation* between the deviant suspect and representatives of his community (as in the criminal trial or psychiatric case conference); they announce some *judgment* about the nature of his deviancy (a "verdict" or "diagnosis," for example); and they perform an act of social *placement*, assigning him to a special deviant role (like that of "prisoner" or "patient") for some period of time. Such ceremonies tend to be events of wide public interest and ordinarily take place in a dramatic, ritualized setting.[9] Perhaps the most obvious example of a commitment ceremony is the criminal trial, with its elaborate ritual and formality, but more modest equivalents can be found almost anywhere that procedures are set up for judging whether or not someone is officially deviant.

An important feature of these ceremonies in our culture is that they are almost

irreversible. Most provisional roles conferred by society—like those of the student or citizen soldier, for instance—include some kind of terminal ceremony to mark the individual's movement back out of the role once its temporary advantages have been exhausted. But the roles allotted to the deviant seldom make allowance for this type of passage. He is ushered into the special position by a decisive and dramatic ceremony, yet is retired from it with hardly a word of public notice. As a result, the deviant often returns home with no proper license to resume a normal life in the community. From a ritual point of view, nothing has happened to cancel out the stigmas imposed upon him by earlier commitment ceremonies: the original verdict or diagnosis is still formally in effect. Partly for this reason, the community is apt to place the returning deviant on some form of probation within the group, suspicious that he will return to deviant activity upon a moment's provocation.

A circularity is thus set into motion which has all the earmarks of a "self-fulfilling prophecy," to use Merton's fine phrase. On the one hand, it seems obvious that the apprehensions of the community help destroy whatever chances the deviant might otherwise have for a successful return to society. Yet, on the other hand, everyday experience seems to show that these apprehensions are altogether reasonable, for it is a well-known and highly publicized fact that most ex-convicts return to prison and that a large proportion of mental patients require additional treatment after once having been discharged. The community's feeling that deviant persons cannot change, then, may be based on a faulty premise, but it is repeated so frequently and with such conviction that it eventually creates the facts which "prove" it correct. If the returned deviant encounters this feeling of distrust often enough, it is understandable that he too

---

[7]For a good description of this process in the modern prison, see Gresham Sykes, *The Society of Captives*, Princeton: Princeton University Press, 1958. For views of two different types of mental hospital settings, see Erving Goffman, "The Characteristics of Total Institutions," *Symposium on Preventive and Social Psychiatry.* Washington, D.C.: Walter Reed Army Institute of Research, 1957; and Kai T. Erikson, "Patient Role and Social Uncertainty: A Dilemma of the Mentally Ill," *Psychiatry*, 20 (1957), pp. 263–274.

[8]Talcott Parsons, *op cit.*, has given the classical description of how this role transfer works in the case of medical patients.

[9]Cf. Harold Garfinkel, "Successful Degradation Ceremonies," *American Journal of Sociology*, 61 (1956), pp. 420–424.

may begin to wonder if the original verdict or diagnosis is still in effect—and respond to this uncertainty by resuming deviant activity. In some respects, this solution may be the only way for the individual and his community to agree what forms of behavior are appropriate for him.

Moreover, this prophecy is found in the official policies of even the most advanced agencies of control. Police departments could not operate with any real effectiveness if they did not regard exconvicts as an almost permanent population of offenders, a constant pool of suspects. Nor could psychiatric clinics do a responsible job if they did not view former patients as a group unusually susceptible to mental illness. Thus the prophecy gains currency at many levels within the social order, not only in the poorly informed attitudes of the community at large, but in the best informed theories of most control agencies as well.

In one form or another, this problem has been known to Western culture for many hundreds of years, and this simple fact is a very important one for sociology. For if the culture has supported a steady flow of deviant behavior throughout long periods of historical evolution, then the rules which apply to any form of functionalist thinking would suggest that strong forces must be at work to keep this flow intact. This may not be reason enough to assert that deviant behavior is altogether "functional"—in any of the many senses of that term—but it should make us reluctant to assume that the agencies of control are somehow organized to prevent deviant acts from occurring or to "cure" deviant offenders of their misbehavior.[10]

This in turn might suggest that our present models of the social system, with their clear emphasis on harmony and symmetry in social relations, only do a partial job of representing reality. Perhaps two different (and often conflicting) currents are found within any wellfunctioning system: those forces which promote a high over-all degree of conformity among human actors, and those forces which encourage some degree of diversity so that actors can be deployed throughout social space to mark the system's boundaries. In such a scheme, deviant behavior would appear as a variation on normative themes, a vital form of activity which outlines the area within which social life as such takes place.

As Georg Simmel wrote some years ago:

An absolutely centripetal and harmonious group, a pure "unification," not only is empirically unreal, it could show no real life process. . . . Just as the universe needs "love and hate," that is, attractive and repulsive forces, in order to have any form at all, so society, too, in order to attain a determinate shape, needs some quantitative ratio of harmony and disharmony, of association and competition, of favorable and unfavorable tendencies. . . . Society, as we know it, is the result of both categories of interaction, which thus both manifest themselves as wholly positive.[11]

V

In summary, two new lines of inquiry seem to be indicated by the argument presented above.

First, this paper attempts to focus our attention on an old but still vital sociological question: how does a social structure communicate its "needs" or impose its "patterns" on human actors? In the present case, how does a social structure enlist actors to engage in deviant activity? Ordinarily, the fact that deviant behavior is more common in some sec-

---

[10]Albert K. Cohen, for example, speaking for most sociologists, seems to take the question for granted: "It would seem that the control of deviant behavior is, by definition, a culture goal." In "The Study of Social Disorganization and Deviant Behavior," Merton, *et al.*, editors, *Sociology Today*. New York: Basic Books, 1959, p. 465.

[11]Georg Simmel, *Conflict* (translated by Kurt H. Wolff), Glencoe: The Free Press, 1955, pp. 15–16.

tors of society than in others is explained by declaring that something called "anomie" or "disorganization" prevails at these sensitive spots. Deviance leaks out where the social machinery is defective; it occurs where the social structure *fails* to communicate its needs to human actors. But if we consider the possibility that deviant persons are responding to the same social forces that elicit conformity from others, then we are engaged in another order of inquiry altogether. Perhaps the stability of some social units is maintained only if juvenile offenders are recruited to balance an adult majority; perhaps some families can remain intact only if one of their members becomes a visible deviant or is committed to a hospital or prison. If this supposition proves to be a useful one, sociologists should be interested in discovering how a social unit manages to differentiate the roles of its members and how certain persons are "chosen" to play the more deviant parts.

Second, it is evident that cultures vary in the way they regulate traffic moving back and forth from their deviant boundaries. Perhaps we could begin with the hypothesis that the traffic pattern known in our own culture has a marked Puritan cast: a defined portion of the population, largely drawn from young adult groups and from the lower economic classes, is stabilized in deviant roles and generally expected to remain there for indefinite periods of time. To this extent, Puritan attitudes about predestination and reprobation would seem to have retained a significant place in modern criminal law and public opinion. In other areas of the world, however, different traffic patterns are known. There are societies in which deviance is considered a natural pursuit for the young, an activity which they can easily abandon when they move through defined ceremonies into adulthood. There are societies which give license to large groups of persons to engage in deviant behavior for certain seasons or on certain days of the year. And there are societies in which special groups are formed to act in ways "contrary" to the normal expectations of the culture. Each of these patterns regulates deviant traffic differently, yet all of them provide some institutionalized means for an actor to give up a deviant "career" without permanent stigma. The problem for sociological theory in general might be to learn whether or not these varying patterns are functionally equivalent in some meaningful sense; the problem for applied sociology might be to see if we have anything to learn from those cultures which permit re-entry into normal social life to persons who have spent a period of "service" on society's boundaries.

11 Illegitimate Means, Anomie, and Deviant Behavior

Richard A. Cloward

This paper[1] represents an attempt to consolidate two major sociological traditions of thought about the problem of deviant behavior. The first, exemplified by the work of Emile Durkheim and Robert K. Merton, may be called the anomie tradition.[2] The second, illustrated principally by the studies of Clifford R. Shaw, Henry D. McKay, and Edwin H. Sutherland, may be called the "cultural transmission" and "differential association" tradition.[3] Despite some reciprocal borrowing of ideas, these intellectual traditions developed more or less independently. By seeking to consolidate

them, a more adequate theory of deviant behavior may be constructed.

DIFFERENTIALS IN AVAILABILITY OF LEGITIMATE MEANS: THE THEORY OF ANOMIE

The theory of anomie has undergone two major phases of development. Durkheim first used the concept to explain deviant behavior. He focussed on the way in which various social conditions lead to "over-weening ambition," and how, in turn, unlimited aspirations ultimately produce a breakdown in regulatory norms. Robert K. Merton has systematized and extended the theory, directing attention to patterns of disjunction between culturally prescribed goals and socially organized access to them by *legitimate* means. In this paper, a third phase is outlined. An additional variable is incorporated in the developing scheme of anomie, namely, the concept of *differentials in access to success-goals by illegitimate means.*[4]

[1]This paper is based on research conducted in a penal setting. For a more detailed statement see Richard A. Cloward, *Social Control and Anomie: A Study of a Prison Community* (to be published by The Free Press).

[2]See especially Emile Durkheim, *Suicide*, translated by J.A. Spaulding and George Simpson, Glencoe, Ill.: Free Press, 1951; and Robert K. Merton, *Social Theory and Social Structure*, Glencoe, Ill.: Free Press, 1957, Chapters 4 and 5.

[3]See especially the following: Clifford R. Shaw, *The Jack-Roller*, Chicago: The University of Chicago Press, 1930; Clifford R. Shaw, *The Natural History of a Delinquent Career*, Chicago: The University of Chicago Press, 1931; Clifford R. Shaw et al., *Delinquency Areas*, Chicago: The University of Chicago Press, 1940; Clifford R. Shaw and Henry D. McKay, *Juvenile Delinquency and Urban Areas*, Chicago: The University of Chicago Press, 1942; Edwin H. Sutherland, editor, *The Professional Thief*, Chicago: The University of Chicago Press, 1937; Edwin H. Sutherland, *Principles of Criminology*, 4th edition, Philadelphia: Lippincott, 1947; Edwin H. Sutherland, *White Collar Crime*, New York: Dryden, 1949.

[4]"Illegitimate means" are those proscribed by the mores. The concept therefore includes "illegal means" as a special case but is not coterminous with illegal behavior, which refers only to the violation of legal norms. In several parts of this paper, I refer to particular forms of deviant behavior which entail violation of the law and there use the more restricted term, "illegal means." But the more general concept of illegitimate means is needed to cover the wider gamut of deviant behavior and to relate the theories under review here to the evolving theory of "legitimacy" in sociology.

Reprinted from Richard A. Cloward, "Illegitimate means, anomie, and deviant behavior," *American Sociological Review*, 24 (1959), 164–176, by permission of the author and the publisher, The American Sociological Association.

**PHASE I: UNLIMITED ASPIRATIONS AND THE BREAK-
DOWN OF REGULATORY NORMS**   In Durkheim's work, a basic distinction is made
between "physical needs" and "moral
needs." The importance of this distinction was heightened for Durkheim because he viewed physical needs as being
regulated automatically by features of
man's organic structure. Nothing in the
organic structure, however, is capable of
regulating social desires; as Durkheim
put it, man's "capacity for feeling is in
itself an insatiable and bottomless
abyss."[5] If man is to function without
"friction," "the passions must first be limited. . . . But since the individual has no
way of limiting them, this must be done
by some force exterior to him." Durkheim viewed the collective order as the
external regulating force which defined
and ordered the goals to which men
should orient their behavior. If the collective order is disrupted or disturbed,
however, 'men's aspirations may then
rise, exceeding all possibilities of fulfillment. Under these conditions, "deregu-
lation or anomy" ensues: "At the very
moment when traditional rules have lost
their authority, the richer prize offered
these appetites stimulates them and
makes them more exigent and impatient
of control. The state of de-regulation or
anomy is thus further heightened by
passions being less disciplined precisely
when they need more disciplining." Finally, pressures toward deviant behavior
were said to develop when man's aspirations no longer matched the possibilities
of fulfillment.

Durkheim therefore turned to the
question of *when* the regulatory functions
of the collective order break down. Several such states were identified, including
sudden depression, sudden prosperity,
and rapid technological change. His ob-

[5] All of the excerpts in this section are from
Durkheim, *op. cit.*, pp. 247–257.

ject was to show how, under these conditions, men are led to aspire to goals
extremely difficult if not impossible to
attain. As Durkheim saw it, sudden depression results in deviant behavior because "something like a declassification
occurs which suddenly casts certain individuals into a lower state than their
previous one. Then they must reduce
their requirements, restrain their needs,
learn greater self-control. . . . But society
cannot adjust them instantaneously to
this new life and teach them to practice
the increased self-repression to which
they are unaccustomed. So they are not
adjusted to the condition forced on them,
and its very prospect is intolerable; hence
the suffering which detaches them from a
reduced existence even before they have
made trial of it." Prosperity, according to
Durkheim, could have much the same
effect as depression, particularly if upward changes in economic conditions are
abrupt. The very abruptness of these
changes presumably heightens aspirations beyond possibility of fulfillment,
and this too puts a strain on the regulatory apparatus of the society.

According to Durkheim, "the sphere of
trade and industry . . . is actually in a
chronic state [of anomie]." Rapid technological developments and the existence
of vast, unexploited markets excite the
imagination with the seemingly limitless
possibilities for the accumulation of
wealth. As Durkheim said of the producer
of goods, "now that he may assume to
have almost the entire world as his
customer, how could passions accept
their former confinement in the face of
such limitless prospects"? Continuing,
Durkheim states that "such is the source
of excitement predominating in this part
of society. . . . Here the state of crisis and
anomie [are] constant and, so to speak,
normal. From top to bottom of the ladder,
greed is aroused without knowing where

to find ultimate foothold. Nothing can calm it, since its goal is far beyond all it can attain."

In developing the theory, Durkheim characterized goals in the industrial society, and specified the way in which unlimited aspirations are induced. He spoke of "dispositions . . . so inbred that society has grown to accept them and is accustomed to think them normal," and he portrayed these "inbred disposition": "It is everlastingly repeated that it is man's nature to be eternally dissatisfied, constantly to advance, without relief or rest, toward an indefinite goal. The longing for infinity is daily represented as a mark of moral distinction. . . ." And it was precisely these pressures to strive for "infinite" or "receding" goals, in Durkheim's view, that generate a breakdown in regulatory norms, for "when there is no other aim but to outstrip constantly the point arrived at, how painful to be thrown back!"

PHASE II: DISJUNCTION BETWEEN CULTURAL GOALS AND SOCIALLY STRUCTURED OPPORTUNITY

Durkheim's description of the emergence of "overweening ambition" and the subsequent breakdown of regulatory norms constitutes one of the links between his work and the later development of the theory by Robert K. Merton. In his classic essay, "Social Structure and Anomie," Merton suggests that goals and norms may vary independently of each other, and that this sometimes leads to malintegrated states. In his view, two polar types of disjunction may occur: "There may develop a very heavy, at times a virtually exclusive, stress upon the value of particular goals, involving comparatively little concern with the institutionally prescribed means of striving toward these goals. . . . This constitutes one type of malintegrated culture."[6] On

[6]For this excerpt and those which follow immediately, see Merton, *op. cit.*, pp. 131-194.

the other hand, "A second polar type is found where activities originally conceived as instrumental are transmuted into self-contained practices, lacking further objectives. . . . Sheer conformity becomes a central value." Merton notes that "between these extreme types are societies which maintain a rough balance between emphases upon cultural goals and institutionalized practices, and these constitute the integrated and relatively stable, though changing societies."

Having identified patterns of disjunction between goals and norms, Merton is enabled to define anomie more precisely: "Anomie [may be] conceived as a breakdown in the cultural structure, occurring particularly when there is an acute disjunction between cultural norms and goals and the socially structured capacities of members of the group to act in accord with them."

Of the two kinds of malintegrated societies, Merton is primarily interested in the one in which "there is an exceptionally strong emphasis upon specific goals without a corresponding emphasis upon institutional procedures." He states that attenuation between goals and norms, leading to anomie or "normlessness," comes about because men in such societies internalize an emphasis on common success-goals under conditions of varying access to them. The essence of this hypothesis is captured in the following excerpt: "It is only when a system of cultural values extols, virtually above all else, certain *common* success-goals for the population at large while the social structure rigorously restricts or completely closes access to approved modes of reaching these goals *for a considerable part of the same population*, that deviant behavior ensues on a large scale." The focus, in short, is on the way in which the social structure puts a strain upon the cultural structure. Here one may point to diverse structural differentials in access to culturally approved goals by legitimate means, for example, differentials of age, sex, ethnic status, and social class. Pressures for anomie or normlessness vary from one social position to another, depending on the nature of these differentials.

In summary, Merton extends the theory of anomie in two principal ways. He explicitly identifies types of anomic or malintegrated societies by focussing upon the relationship between cultural goals and norms. And, by directing attention to patterned differentials in the access to success-goals by legitimate means, he shows how the social structure exerts a strain upon the cultural structure, leading in turn to anomie or normlessness.

PHASE III: THE CONCEPT OF ILLEGITIMATE MEANS

Once processes generating differentials in pressures are identified, there is then the question of how these pressures are resolved, or how men respond to them. In this connection, Merton enumerates five basic categories of behavior or role adaptations which are likely to emerge: conformity, innovation, ritualism, retreatism, and rebellion. These adaptations differ depending on the individual's acceptance or rejection of cultural goals, and depending on his adherence to or violation of institutional norms. Furthermore, Merton sees the distribution of these adaptations principally as the consequence of two variables: the relative extent of pressure, and values, particularly "internalized prohibitions," governing the use of various illegitimate means.

It is a familiar sociological idea that values serve to order the choices of deviant (as well as conforming) adaptations which develop under conditions of stress. Comparative studies of ethnic groups, for example, have shown that

some tend to engage in distinctive forms of deviance; thus Jews exhibit low rates of alcoholism and alcoholic psychoses.[7] Various investigators have suggested that the emphasis on rationality, fear of expressing aggression, and other alleged components of the "Jewish" value system constrain modes of deviance which involve "loss of control" over behavior.[8] In contrast, the Irish show a much higher rate of alcoholic deviance because, it has been argued, their cultural emphasis on masculinity encourages the excessive use of alcohol under conditions of strain.[9]

Merton suggests that differing rates of ritualistic and innovating behavior in the middle and lower classes result from differential emphases in socialization. The "rule-oriented" accent in middle-class socialization presumably disposes persons to handle stress by engaging in ritualistic rather than innovating behavior. The lower-class person, contrastingly, having internalized less stringent norms, can violate conventions with less guilt and anxiety.[10] Values, in other words, exercise a canalizing influence, limiting the choice of deviant adaptations for persons variously distributed throughout the social system.

Apart from both socially patterned pressures, which give rise to deviance,

[7]See, e.g., Seldon D. Bacon, "Social Settings Conducive to Alcoholism—A Sociological Approach to a Medical Problem," *Journal of the American Medical Association*, 16 (May, 1957), pp. 177-181; Robert F. Bales, "Cultural Differences in Rates of Alcoholism," *Quarterly Journal of Studies on Alcohol*, 16 (March, 1946), pp. 480–499; Jerome H. Skolnick, "A Study of the Relation of Ethnic Background to Arrests for Inebriety," *Quarterly Journal of Studies on Alcohol*, 15 (December, 1954), pp. 451–474.

[8]See Isidor T. Thorner, "Ascetic Protestantism and Alcoholism," *Psychiatry*, 16 (May, 1953), pp. 167–176; and Nathan Glazer, "Why Jews Stay Sober," *Commentary*, 13 (February, 1952), pp. 181–186.

[9]See Bales, *op. cit.*

[10]Merton, *op. cit.*, p. 151.

and from values, which determine choices of adaptations, a further variable should be taken into account: namely, *differentials in availability of illegitimate means.* For example, the notion that innovating behavior may result from unfulfilled aspirations and imperfect socialization with respect to conventional norms implies that illegitimate means are freely available—as if the individual, having decided that "you can't make it legitimately," then simply turns to illegitimate means which are readily at hand whatever his position in the social structure. However, these means may not be available. As noted above, the anomie theory assumes that conventional means are differentially distributed, that some individuals, because of their social position, enjoy certain advantages which are denied to others. Note, for example, variations in the degree to which members of various classes are fully exposed to and thus acquire the values, education, and skills which facilitate upward mobility. It should not be startling, therefore, to find similar variations in the availability of illegitimate means.

Several sociologists have alluded to such variations without explicitly incorporating this variable in a theory of deviant behavior. Sutherland, for example, writes that "an inclination to steal is not a sufficient explanation of the genesis of the professional thief."[11] Moreover, "the person must be appreciated by the professional thieves. He must be appraised as having an adequate equipment of wits, front, talking-ability, honesty, reliability, nerve and determination." In short, "a person can be a professional thief only if he is recognized and received as such by other professional thieves." But recognition is not freely accorded: "Selection

[11]For this excerpt and those which follow immediately, see Sutherland, *The Professional Thief*, pp. 211–213.

and tutelage are the two necessary elements in the process of acquiring recognition as a professional thief. . . . A person cannot acquire recognition as a professional thief until he has had tutelage in professional theft, *and tutelage is given only to a few persons selected from the total population.*" Furthermore, the aspirant is judged by high standards of performance, for only "a very small percentage of those who start on this process ever reach the stage of professional theft." The burden of these remarks—dealing with the processes of selection, induction, and assumption of full status in the criminal group—is that motivations or pressures toward deviance do not fully account for deviant behavior. The "self-made" thief—lacking knowledge of the ways of securing immunity from prosecution and similar techniques of defense—"would quickly land in prison." Sutherland is in effect pointing to differentials in access to the role of professional thief. Although the criteria of selection are not altogether clear from his analysis, definite evaluative standards do appear to exist; depending on their content, certain categories of individuals would be placed at a disadvantage and others would be favored.

The availability of illegitimate means, then, is controlled by various criteria in the same manner that has long been ascribed to conventional means. Both systems of opportunity are (1) limited, rather than infinitely available, and (2) differentially available depending on the location of persons in the social structure.

When we employ the term "means," whether legitimate or illegitimate, at least two things are implied: first, that there are appropriate learning environments for the acquisition of the values and skills associated with the performance of a particular role; and second, that the individual has opportunities to discharge the role once he has been prepared. The term subsumes, therefore, both *learning structures* and *opportunity structures*.

A case in point is recruitment and preparation for careers in the rackets. There are fertile criminal learning environments for the young in neighborhoods where the rackets florish as stable, indigenous institutions. Because these environments afford integration of offenders of different ages, the young are exposed to "differential associations" which facilitate the acquisition of criminal values and skills. Yet preparation for the role may not insure that the individual will ever discharge it. For one thing, more youngsters may be recruited into these patterns of differential association than can possibly be absorbed, following their "training," by the adult criminal structure. There may be a surplus of contenders for these elite positions, leading in turn to the necessity for criteria and mechanisms of selection. Hence a certain proportion of those who aspire may not be permitted to engage in the behavior for which they have been prepared.

This illustration is similar in every respect, save for the route followed, to the case of those who seek careers in the sphere of legitimate business. Here, again, is the initial problem of securing access to appropriate learning environments, such as colleges and postgraduate schools of business. Having acquired the values and skills needed for a business career, graduates then face the problem of whether or not they can successfully discharge the roles for which they have been prepared. Formal training itself is not sufficient for occupational success, for many forces intervene to determine who shall succeed and fail in the competitive world of business and industry—as throughout the entire conventional occupational structure.

This distinction between learning structures and opportunity structures was suggested some years ago by Sutherland. In 1944, he circulated an unpublished paper which briefly discusses the proposition that "criminal behavior is partially a function of opportunities to commit specific classes of crimes, such as embezzlement, bank burglary, or illicit heterosexual intercourse."[12] He did not, however, take up the problem of differentials in opportunity as a concept to be systematically incorporated in a theory of deviant behavior. Instead, he held that "opportunity" is a necessary but not sufficient explanation of the commission of criminal acts, "since some persons who have opportunities to embezzle, become intoxicated, engage in illicit heterosexual intercourse or to commit other crimes do not do so." He also noted that the differential association theory did not constitute a full explanation of criminal activity, for, notwithstanding differential association, "it is axiomatic that persons who commit a specific crime must have the opportunity to commit that crime." He therefore concluded that "while opportunity may be partially a function of association with criminal patterns and of the specialized techniques thus acquired, *it is not determined entirely in that manner,* and consequently differential association is not the sufficient cause of criminal behavior." (emphasis not in original)

In Sutherland's statements, two meanings are attributed to the term "opportunity." As suggested above, it may be useful to separate these for analytical purposes. In the first sense, Sutherland appears to be saying that opportunity consists in part of learning structures.

[12]For this excerpt and those which follow immediately, see Albert Cohen, Alfred Lindesmith and Karl Schuessler, editors, *The Sutherland Papers,* Bloomington: Indiana University Press, 1956, pp. 31–35.

The principal components of his theory of differential association are that "criminal behavior is learned," and, furthermore, that "criminal behavior is learned in interaction with other persons in a process of communication." But he also uses the term to describe situations conducive to carrying out criminal roles. Thus, for Sutherland, the commission of a criminal act would seem to depend upon the existence of two conditions: differential associations favoring the acquisition of criminal values and skills, and conditions encouraging participation in criminal activity.

This distinction heightens the importance of identifying and questioning the common assumption that illegitimate means are freely available. We can now ask (1) whether there are socially structured differentials in access to illegitimate learning environments, and (2) whether there are differentials limiting the fulfillment of illegitimate roles. If differentials exist and can be identified, we may then inquire about their consequences for the behavior of persons in different parts of the social structure. Before pursuing this question, however, we turn to a fuller discussion of the theoretical tradition established by Shaw, McKay, and Sutherland.

DIFFERENTIALS IN AVAILABILITY OF ILLEGITIMATE MEANS: THE SUBCULTURE TRADITION

The concept of differentials in availability of illegitimate means is implicit in one of the major streams of American criminological theory. In this tradition, attention is focussed on the processes by which persons are recruited into criminal learning environments and ultimately inducted into criminal roles. The problems here are to account for the acquisition of criminal roles and to describe the social organization of criminal activities.

When the theoretical propositions contained in this tradition are reanalyzed, it becomes clear that one underlying conception is that of variations in access to success-goals by illegitimate means. Furthermore, this implicit concept may be shown to be one of the bases upon which the tradition was constructed.

In their studies of the ecology of deviant behavior in the urban environment, Shaw and McKay found that delinquency and crime tended to be confined to delimited areas and, furthermore, that such behavior persisted despite demographic changes in these areas. Hence they came to speak of "criminal tradition," of the "cultural transmission" of criminal values.[13] As a result of their observations of slum life, they concluded that *particular importance must be assigned to the integration of different age-levels of offenders.* Thus:

Stealing in the neighborhood was a common practice among the children and approved by the parents. Whenever the boys got together they talked about robbing and made more plans for stealing. I hardly knew any boys who did not go robbing. The little fellows went in for petty stealing, breaking into freight cars, and stealing junk. The older guys did big jobs like stick-up, burglary, and stealing autos. The little fellows admired the "big shots" and longed for the day when they could get into the big racket. Fellows who had "done time" were the big shots and looked up to and gave the little fellow tips on how to get by and pull off big jobs.[14]

In other words, access to criminal roles depends upon stable associations with others from whom the necessary values and skills may be learned. Shaw and McKay were describing deviant learning structures—that is, alternative routes by which people seek access to the goals which society holds to be worthwhile. They might also have pointed out that, in

[13]See especially *Delinquency Areas*, Chapter 16.
[14]Shaw, *The Jack-Roller*, p. 54.

areas where such learning structures are unavailable, it is probably difficult for many individuals to secure access to stable criminal careers, even though motivated to do so.[15]

The concept of illegitimate means and the socially structured conditions of access to them were not explicitly recognized in the work of Shaw and McKay because, probably, they were disposed to view slum areas as "disorganized." Although they consistently referred to illegitimate activities as being organized, they nevertheless often depicted high-rate delinquency areas as disorganized because the values transmitted were criminal rather than conventional. Hence their work includes statements which we now perceive to be internally inconsistent, such as the following:

This community situation [in which Sidney was reared] was not only disorganized and thus ineffective as a unit of control, but it was characterized by a high rate of juvenile delinquency and adult crime, not to mention the widespread political corruption which had long existed in the area. Various forms of stealing and many organized delinquent and criminal gangs were prevalent in the area. These groups exercised a powerful influence and tended to create a community spirit which not only tolerated but actually fostered delinquent and criminal practices.[16]

Sutherland was among the first to perceive that the concept of social disorganization tended to obscure the stable patterns of interaction among carriers of criminal values. Like Shaw and McKay, he had been influenced by the observation that lower-class areas were organized in terms of both conventional and criminal values, but he was also impressed that these alternative value systems were supported by patterned systems of social relations. He expressly recognized that crime, far from being a random, unorganized activity, was typically an intricate and stable system of human arrangements. He therefore rejected the concept of "social disorganization" and substituted the concept of "differential group organization."

The third concept, social disorganization, was borrowed from Shaw and McKay. I had used it but had not been satisfied with it because the organization of the delinquent group, which is often very complex, is social disorganization only from an ethical or some other particularistic point of view. At the suggestion of Albert K. Cohen, this concept has been changed to differential group organization, with organization for criminal activities on one side and organization against criminal activities on the other.[17]

Having freed observation of the urban slum from conventional evaluations, Sutherland was able to focus more clearly on the way in which its social structure constitutes a "learning environment" for the acquisition of deviant values and skills. In the development of the theory of "differential association" and "differential group organization," he came close to stating explicitly the concept of differentials in access to illegitimate means. But Sutherland was essentially interested in learning processes, and thus he did not ask how such access varies in different parts of the social structure, nor did he inquire about the

---

[15]We are referring here, and throughout the paper, to stable criminal roles to which persons may orient themselves on a career basis, as in the case of racketeers, professional thieves, and the like. The point is that access to stable roles depends in the first instance upon the availability of learning structures. As Frank Tannenbaum says, "it must be insisted on that unless there were older criminals in the neighborhood who provided a moral judgement in favor of the delinquent and to whom the delinquents could look for commendation, the careers of the younger ones could not develop at all." *Crime and the Community*, New York: Ginn, 1938, p. 60.

[16]Shaw, *The Natural History of a Delinquent Career*, p. 229.

[17]Cohen, Lindesmith and Schuessler, *op. cit.*, p. 21.

consequences for behavior of variations in the accessibility of these means.[18]

William F. Whyte, in his classic study of an urban slum, advanced the empirical description of the structure and organization of illegitimate means a step beyond that of Sutherland. Like Sutherland, Whyte rejected the earlier view of the slum as disorganized:

It is customary for the sociologist to study the slum district in terms of "social disorganization" and to neglect to see that an area such as Cornerville has a complex and well-established organization of its own. . . . I found that in every group there was a hierarchical structure of social relations binding the individuals to one another and that the groups were also related hierarchically to one another. Where the group was formally organized into a political club, this

[18]It is interesting to note that the concept of differentials in access to *legitimate* means did not attain explicit recognition in Sutherland's work, nor in the work of many others in the "subculture" tradition. This attests to the independent development of the two traditions being discussed. Thus the ninth proposition in the differential association theory is stated as follows:

(9) *Though criminal behavior is an expression of general needs and values, it is not explained by those general needs and values since non-criminal behavior is an expression of the same needs and values.* Thieves generally steal in order to secure money, but likewise honest laborers work in order to secure money. The attempts by many scholars to explain criminal behavior by general drives and values, such as the happiness principle, striving for social status, the money motive, or frustration, have been and must continue to be futile since they explain lawful behavior as completely as they explain criminal behavior.

Of course, it is perfectly true that "striving for status," the "money motive" and similar modes of socially approved goal-oriented behavior do not as such account for both deviant and conformist behavior. But if goal-oriented behavior occurs under conditions of socially structured obstacles to fulfillment by legitimate means, the resulting pressures might then lead to deviance. In other words, Sutherland appears to assume that the distribution of access to success-goals by legitimate means is uniform rather than variable, irrespective of location in the social structure. See his *Principles of Criminology*, 4th edition, pp. 7–8.

was immediately apparent, but for informal groups it was no less true.[19]

Whyte's contribution to our understanding of the organization of illegitimate means in the slum consists primarily in showing that individuals who participate in stable illicit enterprise do not constitute a separate or isolated segment of the community. Rather, these persons are closely integrated with the occupants of conventional roles. In describing the relationship between racketeers and politicians, for example, he notes that "the rackets and political organizations extend from the bottom to the top of Cornerville society, mesh with one another, and integrate a large part of the life of the district. They provide a general framework for the understanding of the actions of both 'little guys' and 'big shots.'"[20] Whyte's view of the slum differs somewhat from that conveyed by the term "differential group organization." He does not emphasize the idea that the slum is composed of two different systems, conventional and deviant, but rather the way in which the occupants of these various roles are integrated in a single, stable structure which organizes and patterns the life of the community.

The description of the organization of illegitimate means in slums is further developed by Solomon Kobrin in his article, "The Conflict of Values in Delinquency Areas."[21] Kobrin suggests that urban slum areas vary in the degree to which the carriers of deviant and conventional values are integrated with one another. Hence he points the way to the development of a "typology of delinquency areas based on variations in the

[19]William F. Whyte, *Street Corner Society*, (original edition, 1943). Chicago: The University of Chicago Press, 1955, p. viii.

[20]*Ibid.*, p. xviii.

[21]*American Sociological Review*, 16 (October, 1951), pp. 657–658, which includes the excerpts which follow immediately.

relationship between these two systems," depicting the "polar types" on such a continuum. The first type resembles the integrated areas described in preceding paragraphs. Here, claims Kobrin, there is not merely structural integration between carriers of the two value systems, but reciprocal participation by each in the value system of the other. Thus:

Leaders of [illegal] enterprises frequently maintain membership in such conventional institutions of their local communities as churches, fraternal and mutual benefit societies and political parties. . . . Within this framework the influence of each of the two value systems is reciprocal, the leaders of illegal enterprise participating in the primary orientation of the conventional elements in the population, and the latter, through their participation in a local power structure sustained in large part by illicit activity, participating perforce in the alternate, criminal value system.

Kobrin also notes that in some urban slums there is a tendency for the relationships between carriers of deviant and conventional values to break down. Such areas constitute the second polar type. Because of disorganizing forces such as "drastic change in the class, ethnic, or racial characteristics of its population," Kobrin suggests that "the bearers of the conventional culture and its value system are without the customary institutional machinery and therefore in effect partially demobilized with reference to the diffusion of their value system." At the same time, the criminal "value system remains implicit" since this type of area is "characterized principally by the absence of systematic and organized adult activity in violation of the law, despite the fact that many adults in these areas commit violations." Since both value systems remain implicit, the possibilities for effective integration are precluded.

The importance of these observations may be seen if we ask how accessibility of illegal means varies with the relative integration of conventional and criminal

values from one type of area to another. In this connection, Kobrin points out that the "integrated" area apparently constitutes a "training ground" for the acquisition of criminal values and skills.

The stable position of illicit enterprise in the adult society of the community is reflected in the character of delinquent conduct on the part of children. While delinquency in all high rate areas is intrinsically disorderly in that it is unrelated to official programs for the education of the young, in the [integrated community] boys may more or less realistically recognize the potentialities for personal progress in local society through access to delinquency. In a general way, therefore, delinquent activity in these areas constitutes a training ground for the acquisition of skill in the use of violence, concealment of offense, evasion of detection and arrest, and the purchase of immunity from punishment. Those who come to excel in these respects are frequently noted and valued by adult leaders in the rackets who are confronted, as are the leaders of all income-producing enterprises, with problems of the recruitment of competent personnel.

With respect to the contrasting or "unintegrated area," Kobrin makes no mention of the extent to which learning structures and opportunities for ciminal careers are available. Yet his portrayal of such areas as lacking in the articulation of either conventional or ciminal values suggests that the appropriate learning structures—principally the integration of offenders of different age levels—are not available. Furthermore, his depiction of adult violative activity as "unorganized" suggests that the illegal opportunity structure is severely limited. Even if youngsters were able to secure adequate preparation for criminal roles, the problem would appear to be that the social structure of such neighborhoods provides few opportunities for stable, criminal careers. For Kobrin's analysis—as well as those of Whyte and others before him—leads to the conclusion that illegal opportunity structures tend to emerge in lower-class areas only when stable patterns of accommodation and integration arise between the carriers of conventional and deviant values. Where these values remain unorganized and implicit, or where their carriers are in open conflict, opportunities for stable criminal role performance are more or less limited.[22]

Other factors may be cited which affect access to criminal roles. For example, there is a good deal of anecdotal evidence which reveals that access to the upper echelons of organized racketeering is controlled, at least in part, by ethnicity. Some ethnic groups are found disproportionately in the upper ranks and others disproportionately in the lower. From an historical perspective, as Bell has shown, this realm has been successively dominated by Irish, East-European Jews, and more recently, by Italians.[23] Various other ethnic groups have been virtually excluded or at least relegated to lower-echleon positions. Despite the fact that many rackets (especially "policy") have flourished in predominantly Negro neighborhoods, there have been but one or two Negroes who have been known to rise to the top in syndicated crime. As in the conventional world, Negroes are relegated to the more menial tasks. Moreover, access to elite positions in the rackets may be governed in part by kinship criteria, for various accounts of the blood relations among top racketeers indicate that nepotism is the general rule.[24] It has also been noted that kinship criteria sometimes govern access to stable criminal roles, as in the case of the pickpocket.[25] And there are, of course, deep-rooted sex differentials in access to illegal means. Although women are often employed in criminal vocations—for example, thievery, confidence games, and extortion—and must be employed in others—such as prostitution—nevertheless females are excluded from many criminal activities.[26]

Of the various criteria governing access to illegitimate means, class differentials may be among the most important. The differentials noted in the preceding paragraph—age, sex, ethnicity, kinship, and the like—all pertain to criminal activity historically associated with the lower class. Most middle- or upper-class persons—even when interested in following "lower-class" criminal careers—would no doubt have difficulty in fulfilling this ambition because of inappropriate preparation. The prerequisite attitudes and skills are more easily acquired if the individual is a member of the lower class; most middle- and upper-class persons could not easily unlearn their own class culture in order to learn a new one. By

[22]The excellent work by Albert K. Cohen has been omitted from this discussion because it is dealt with in a second article, "Types of Delinquent Subcultures," prepared jointly with Lloyd E. Ohlin (mimeographed, December, 1958, New York School of Social Work, Columbia University). It may be noted that although Cohen does not explicitly affirm continuity with either the Durkheim-Merton or the Shaw-McKay-Sutherland traditions, we believe that he clearly belongs in the former. He does not deal with what appears to be the essence of the Shaw-McKay-Sutherland tradition, namely, the crucial social functions performed by the integration of offenders of differing age-levels and the integration of adult carriers of criminal and conventional values. Rather, he is concerned primarily with the way in which discrepancies between status aspirations and possibilities for achievement generate pressures for delinquent behavior. The latter notion is a central feature in the anomie tradition.

[23]Daniel Bell, "Crime as an American Way of Life," *The Antioch Review* (Summer, 1953), pp. 131–154.

[24]For a discussion of kinship relationships among top racketeers, see Stanley Frank, "The Rap Gangsters Fear Most," *The Saturday Evening Post* (August 9, 1958), pp. 26ff. This article is based on a review of the files of the United States Immigration and Naturalization Service.

[25]See David W. Maurer, *Whiz Mob: A Correlation of the Technical Argot of Pickpockets with Their Behavior Pattern*, Publication of the American Dialect Society, No. 24, 1955.

[26]For a discussion of racial, nationality, and sex differentials governing access to a stable criminal role, see *ibid.*, Chapter 6.

the same token, access to many "white collar" criminal roles is closed to lower-class persons. Some occupations afford abundant opportunities to engage in illegitimate activity; others offer virtually none. The businessman, for example, not only has at his disposal the means to do so, but, as some studies have shown, he is under persistent pressure to employ illegitimate means, if only to maintain a competitive advantage in the market place. But for those in many other occupations, white collar modes of criminal activity are simply not an alternative.[27]

SOME IMPLICATIONS OF A CONSOLIDATED APPROACH TO DEVIANT BEHAVIOR

It is now possible to consolidate the two sociological traditions described above. Our analysis makes it clear that these traditions are oriented to different aspects of the same problem: differentials in access to opportunity. One tradition focusses on legitimate opportunity, the other on illegitimate. By incorporating the concept of differentials in access to *illegitimate* means, the theory of anomie may be extended to include seemingly unrelated studies and theories of deviant behavior which form a part of the literature of American criminology. In this final section, we try to show how a consolidated approach might advance the

understanding of both rates and types of deviant conduct. The discussion centers on the conditions of access to *both* systems of means, legitimate and illegitimate.

THE DISTRIBUTION OF CRIMINAL BEHAVIOR   One problem which has plagued the criminologist is the absence of adequate data on social differentials in criminal activity. Many have held that the highest crime rates are to be found in the lower social strata. Others have suggested that rates in the middle and upper classes may be much higher than is ordinarily thought. The question of the social distribution of crime remains problematic.

In the absence of adequate data, the theorist has sometimes attacked this problem by assessing the extent of pressures toward normative departures in various parts of the social structure. For example, Merton remarks that his "primary aim is to discover how some social structures exert a definite pressure upon certain persons in the society to engage in non-conforming rather than conforming conduct."[28] Having identified structural features which might be expected to generate deviance, Merton suggests the presence of a correlation between "pressures toward deviation" and "rate of deviance."

But whatever the differential rates of deviant behavior in the several social strata, and we know from many sources that the official crime statistics uniformly showing higher rates in the lower strata are far from complete or reliable, *it appears from our analysis that the greater pressures toward deviation are exerted upon the lower strata. . . .* Of those located in the lower reaches of the social structure, the culture makes incompatible demands. On the one hand they are asked to orient their behavior toward the prospect of large wealth . . . and on the other, they are largely denied effective opportunities to do so institutionally. *The consequence of this structural inconsistency is a high rate of deviant behavior.*[29]

---

[27]Training in conventional, specialized occupational skills is often a prerequisite for the commission of white collar crimes, since the individual must have these skills in hand before he can secure a position entailing "trust." As Cressey says, "it may be observed that persons trained to carry on the routine duties of a position of trust have at the same time been trained in whatever skills are necessary for the violation of that position, and the technical skill necessary to trust violation is simply the technical skill necessary to holding the position in the first place." (Donald R. Cressey, *Other People's Money*, Glencoe, Ill.: Free Press, 1953, pp. 81–82.) Thus skills required in certain crimes need not be learned in association with criminals; they can be acquired through conventional learning.

[28]Merton, *op. cit.*, p. 132.
[29]*Ibid.*, pp. 144–145.

Because of the paucity and unreliability of existing criminal statistics, there is as yet no way of knowing whether or not Merton's hypothesis is correct. Until comparative studies of crime rates are available the hypothesized correlation cannot be tested.

From a theoretical perspective, however, questions may be raised about this correlation. Would we expect, to raise the principal query, the correlation to be fixed or to vary depending on the distribution of access to illegitimate means? The three possibilities are (1) that access is distributed uniformly throughout the class structure, (2) that access varies inversely with class position, and (3) that access varies directly with class position. Specification of these possibilities permits a more precise statement of the conditions under which crime rates would be expected to vary.

If access to illegitimate means is *uniformly distributed* throughout the class structure, then the proposed correlation would probably hold—higher rates of innovating behavior would be expected in the lower class than elsewhere. Lower-class persons apparently experience greater pressures toward deviance and are less restrained by internalized prohibitions from employing illegitimate means. Assuming uniform access to such means, it would therefore be reasonable to predict higher rates of innovating behavior in the lower social strata.

If access to illegitimate means varies *inversely* with class position, then the correlation would not only hold, but might even be strengthened. For pressures toward deviance, including socialization that does not altogether discourage the use of illegitimate means, would coincide with the availability of such means.

Finally, if access varies *directly* with class position, comparative rates of illegitimate activity become difficult to forecast. The higher the class position, the less the pressure to employ illegitimate means; furthermore, internalized prohibitions are apparently more effective in higher positions. If, at the same time, opportunities to use illegitimate methods are more abundant, then these factors would be in opposition. Until the precise effects of these several variables can be more adequately measured, rates cannot be safely forecast.

The concept of differentials in availability of illegitimate means may also help to clarify questions about varying crime rates among ethnic, age, religious, and sex groups, and other social divisions. This concept, then, can be systematically employed in the effort to further our understanding of the distribution of illegitimate behavior in the social structure. . . .

SUMMARY

This paper attempts to identify and to define the concept of differential opportunity structures. It has been suggested that this concept helps to extend the developing theory of social structure and anomie. Furthermore, by linking propositions regarding the accessibility of *both* legitimate and illegitimate opportunity structures, a basis is provided for consolidating various major traditions of sociological thought on nonconformity. The concept of differential systems of opportunity and of variations in access to them, it is hoped, will suggest new possibilities for research on the relationship between social structure and deviant behavior.

Further Reading

One would be hard pressed to pick up any book or article written by a sociologist and not find there some treatment or use of the concepts with which this section has been concerned. Therefore, our suggestions for further reading must be highly selective.

One of the earliest and most influential treatments of social norms is to be found in Muzafer Sherif, *The Psychology of Social Norms*, New York: Harper & Row, 1936. Richard T. Morris has attempted to construct a useful typological approach to norms in his article "A typology of norms," *American Sociological Review*, 21 (October, 1956), 610–613. Also, there is a very interesting and more advanced treatment of this topic in R. Rommetveit, *Social Norms and Roles*, Minneapolis: University of Minnesota Press, 1955. Additional references to the formation and enforcement of social norms from the small group literature will be described in a later section.

Among the first of the social scientists to employ the concept of role was Ralph Linton, *The Study of Man*, New York: Appleton, 1936. A useful analysis of the concept of role is provided by Frederick L. Bates, "Position, role, and status: A reformulation of concepts," *Social Forces*, 34 (May, 1956), 313–321. A very useful summary and guide to the literature on roles is provided by Theodore R. Sarbin and Vernon L. Allen, "Role Theory," in Gardner Lindzey and Elliot Aronson (eds.), *The Handbook of Social Psychology* (2d ed.), vol. I, Reading, Mass.: Addison-Wesley, 1968, pp. 488-567. Finally, a collection of readings on role theory has been edited by Bruce J. Biddle and Edwin J. Thomas, *Role Theory: Concepts and Research*, New York: Wiley, 1966. In addition to bringing together in one place some of the most important writings on social roles, Biddle and Thomas also provide a very detailed analytical introduction to the subject, treating such topics as the nature and history of role theory and basic concepts for describing the properties and the variables of role phenomena.

In addition to developing a language for role analysis, Neal Gross, Ward S. Mason, and Alexander W. McEachern have also proposed a schema for analyzing role conflict and its resolution in *Explorations in Role Analysis*, New York: Wiley, 1957, pp. 244-318. Robert K. Merton in *Social Theory and Social Structure* (rev. ed.), Glencoe, Ill.: Free Press, 1957, pp. 368-384, speculates on some of the ways in which intrarole conflict may be resolved. And a recent study by Robert L. Kahn *et al.*, *Organizational Stress: Studies in Role Conflict and Ambiguity*, New York: Wiley, 1964, examines the social and psychological consequences of role conflict in organizational settings.

The phenomenon of status crystallization was first described and examined by E. Benoit-Smullyan, "Status, status types, and status interrelations," *American Sociological Review*, 9 (April, 1944), 151–161. This subject has received a great deal of attention in recent years. Representative articles include Irwin W. Goffman, "Status consistency and preference for change in power distribution," *American Sociological Review*, 22 (June, 1957), 275–281; and Elton F. Jackson, "Status consistency and symptoms of stress," *American Sociological Review*, 27 (August, 1962), 469–480.

An enormous number of schemas for describing and analyzing social organization have been proposed. Among the more recent influential systems are those proposed by Talcott Parsons, *The Social System*, Glencoe, Ill.: Free Press, 1951; George C. Homans, *The Human Group*, New York: Harcourt, 1950; Peter M. Blau, *Exchange and Power in Social Life*, New York: Wiley, 1964; and Walter Buckley, *Sociology and Modern Systems Theory*, Englewood Cliffs, N.J.: Prentice-Hall, 1967.

An excellent short introduction to the field of deviant behavior is contained in Albert K. Cohen, *Deviance and Conformity*, Englewood Cliffs, N.J.: Prentice-Hall, 1960. Among the important recent contributions to the study of deviance are Howard S. Becker, *Outsiders: Studies in the Sociology of Deviance*, New York: Free Press, 1963; Richard A. Cloward and Lloyd E. Ohlin, *Delinquency and Opportunity*, Glencoe, Ill.: Free Press, 1960; and David Matza, *Delinquency and Drift*, New York: Wiley, 1964.

PART THREE

Selected Social Processes

To separate the notions of social structure and social process is no easy task, as we will soon discover. The concepts of "structure" on the one hand and "process" on the other are themselves highly complex and abstract, and this accounts for a part of the problem. Also, sociologists have not devoted as much time or energy to the systematic study of social processes, so that the concept of process is less well understood than that of structure; hence, we are still hesitant and uneasy in trying to talk about it. Nevertheless, with the reader's indulgence, we will attempt to wrestle with the problem of distinguishing process from structure as a necessary preliminary step toward the examination of a set of selected social processes.

STRUCTURE AND PROCESS

It has been argued that to separate social process from social structure is not to focus on two distinct kinds of phenomena but is to look at the same phenomenon from two different points of view. Thus, the operation of social processes gives rise to social structures; and social structures are comprised of the "residues" or traces of social processes viewed at one point in time. From this perspective, then, the central variable separating structure from process is time: does one look at social phenomena as they change and develop over time, or as they appear at one point in time? For example, we can talk about the division of labor as a social process occurring over a specified time period, as specialty groups emerge and one set of actors comes to be differentiated from another by the kinds of activities they perform; and we can talk about division of labor as one specific aspect of a particular social structure—as the number of different kinds of activity sets (for example, the number of occupations) present and the distribution of persons across those sets at one point in time. In this view, structure and process are but two sides of the same coin.

On closer examination, this conception appears to be oversimplified if not incorrect. To view structure as static and process as dynamic is to overlook the fact, as Nadel reminds us, that our definition of structural elements is built up by noting regularities persisting *over time*. "In brief, the terms 'invariance' or 'continuity' in fact refer to recurrence and repetitiveness. Social structure as Fortes once put it, must be 'visualized' as 'a sum of processes in time.' "[1] The difference is not, then, whether one's observations are made over time as against one point in time. Observation through time is necessary to arrive at characterizations of both structure and process. Rather, the difference is one of selective emphasis. Does the analyst look for and emphasize continuity and regularity or does he focus on variation and change?

There is no doubt that a focus on social structure yields a selective and partial view of the phenomena under study. As noted in our introduction, the concepts we choose to employ in large part determine what questions we are led to ask and, hence, what we see and report. Nadel, for example, recognizes that "structural analysis does lend itself to oversimplification in the sense that we are apt to concentrate on averages or typical situations."[2] Such selective attention can have far-reaching consequences for one's view of social reality, as the critics of structural-functional analysis in sociology have noted. The structural-functionalists, whose leading spokesman in this country is Talcott Parsons, work primarily with concepts similar to those described in Part Two—namely, values and norms, roles, and behavioral regularities.[3] Critics have correctly pointed out that the interest of structural-functionalists in structure leads them to be concerned with "the dominant, legitimized, institutionalized structure, or at least with those characteristic structures that *do not include* patterned strains or structured deviance and disorder."[4] To be more specific, structural analysts of society have been inclined to focus on the structures of dominant majorities as opposed to those of deviant minorities; they have emphasized value and role consensus more than value and role conflict; they have focused on persistance and integration to the neglect of change and maladjustment; and they have been more apt to see similarity and harmony of interest among participating members of the structure than they have differences and coercion.[5] (See Reading 12)

These emphases should not surprise us. A social analyst can only speak of social roles to the extent that he looks for and finds substantial agreement among participants concerning the appropriate behavior for the occupant of a given position. And he cannot examine social values and norms unless he focuses on consensus among group members as to ends and means. And the central

[1]S. F. Nadel, *The Theory of Social Structure*, Glencoe, Ill.: Free Press, 1957, p. 128. The quotation is from Meyer Fortes, *The Web of Kinship among the Tallenski*, London: Oxford, 1949, p. 342.

[2]Nadel, p. 137.

[3]See, in particular, Talcott Parsons, *The Social System*, Glencoe, Ill.: Free Press, 1951.

[4]Walter Buckley, *Sociology and Modern Systems Theory*, Englewood Cliffs, N. J.: Prentice-Hall, 1967, p. 25. Emphasis in original.

[5]See Ralf Dahrendorf "Out of Utopia: Toward a reorientation of sociological analysis," *American Journal of Sociology*, 64 (September, 1958), 115–127.

concepts of normative structure and social structure are dependent on observations concerning patterning and consistency in the beliefs and behaviors of the persons and groups studied. In sum, the concepts employed by the structural theorist help him to examine certain aspects of social reality but, by the same token, keep him from noticing or, at least, concentrating on other aspects.

We can go one step further in our discussion of the differences between these perspectives of society. In one sense, it is not true that structural analysts have overlooked the importance of social processes. But it is true that they have tended to focus on the processes that maintain a given structural arrangement rather than on the processes that change it. Processes that maintain the structure in its present form include those of socialization (the process by which new members learn to play their appointed roles), role allocation (the process by which members are assigned different positions in a social structure), and social control (the process by which members who deviate too far from the norms of the group are brought back into line or, if such efforts fail, are excluded from the system). Such processes in their "system maintaining functions" are not unlike the physiological processes of respiration, metabolism, and circulation operating in the human body.

Although biological organisms are subject to the operation of some processes, such as maturation or aging, that gradually change their structure, unlike social systems, they do not undergo changes that fundamentally alter their structural arrangements. This difference has been graphically pointed to by the great social anthropologist Radcliffe-Brown, who notes: ". . . an animal organism does not, in the course of his life, change its structural type. A pig cannot become a hippopotamus . . . On the other hand a society in the course of its history can and does change its structural type without any breach of continuity."[6] This is, in fact, one of the most important characteristics of a social organization. As Buckley states the matter, ". . . sociocultural systems are inherently structure-elaborating and changing . . . societies and groups continually shift their structures as adaptations to internal or external conditions."[7]

In his later discussion of social organizations as "open systems" (systems that engage in interchanges with their environment as an essential condition of their survival and development), Buckley supplies us with a vocabulary to distinguish the two types of processes we have been considering: *morphostasis* and *morphogenesis*. These terms are defined as follows:

> The former refers to those processes in complex system-environment exchanges that tend to preserve or maintain a system's given form, organization, or state. Morphogenesis will refer to those processes which tend to elaborate or change a system's given form, structure, or state. Homeostatic processes in organisms, and ritual in sociocultural systems are examples of "morphostasis"; biological evolution, learning, and societal development are examples of "morphogenesis."[8]

It appears, then, that we have arrived at the view that all is process. An emphasis on social structure is simply a concentration on morphostatic processes, while a concern with structural change is simply a concentration on

[6]A. R. Radcliffe-Brown, "On the concept of function in social science," in *Structure and Function in Primitive Society*, Glencoe, Ill.: Free Press, 1952, p. 220.
[7]Buckley, p. 18.
[8]Buckley, pp. 58–59.

morphogenic processes. This is, we believe, an essentially correct and useful perspective. At the same time, we do not want to completely forsake the vocabulary—which is second-nature to most sociologists—and the insights of the structuralist position. We will use their vocabulary when summarizing the differences and similarities among small groups, organizations, communities, and societies. Even more important, we will not forsake the interests of those concerned with social structure. In our examination of social process, we will be giving attention to morphostatic as well as morphogenic processes.

SELECTING THE SOCIAL PROCESSES

Sociology's major concern is with the exploration of social processes and structures. But we must recognize that other processes and variables profoundly affect their characteristics and operation. Some processes and variables help to determine the characteristics of individual actors and, hence, influence the ways in which the actors enter into social relationships with their fellows. Chief among these are the psychobiological processes, such as maturation, perception, and learning capacity. Other variables shape social processes and structures by their effect on the larger context within which these processes operate and within which these structures emerge. Of primary importance at this level are demographic variables, particularly group size and composition (for example, age distribution, sex ratios, and ethnic groupings) and ecological variables, including spacial patterning, characteristics of the physical environment, and the state of technological development. Psychobiological, demographic, and ecological variables and processes do not constitute the central focus of our concern, but they will enter into our discussion of social processes and structures as important conditioning and contextual variables.

An important decision confronting us at this point is a determination of the level of our analysis. We have chosen to pursue a middle course: we will focus neither on the highly specific nor on the very abstract and general social processes. Two examples of specific processes have already been briefly considered in the previous section, namely, the resolution of role conflict and responses to low status crystallization. We have noted that in some instances these processes have the effect of protecting existing structures by adjusting individuals to them. However, in other cases, role conflict and low status crystallization set in motion morphogenic processes that result in the elaboration or transformation of existing structures. General social processes may include cooperation and conflict, accommodation and assimilation, or social differentiation and social exchange. Such processes are important and are continuously operating in the maintenance and change of social organization but are too vague and ubiquitous to be prime candidates for our analysis.

Rather, we will concentrate on five social processes to which sociologists have devoted considerable attention: *integration, socialization, status, power,* and *adaptation.* Let us not make the mistake of assuming that these are the only processes worth investigating or even that these constitute the most important set. We have simply selected five important social processes that will allow us to focus on some of the major concerns of present-day sociologists. Our approach is selective rather than exhaustive. We hope to illustrate the types of processes to which sociologists have given attention, the sorts of questions they have raised in examining the operation of these processes, and the kinds of techniques employed in finding answers to the questions posed.

Processes do not occur in a social vacuum but in some kind of social context. We have chosen to focus on the operation of social processes within four structural contexts: *small, informal groups*; *formal organizations*; *communities*; and *societies*. As with our selection of social processes, we make no special claims for the importance of the structures selected except to say that each represents a type of social unit to which sociologists have devoted much attention and that each constitutes a familiar social unit of generally recognized importance.

We will take pains to show through both our commentary and readings that the same five processes operate within each structural context. Integrative processes, for example, operate within small groups, organizations, communities, and societies. However, the *way* in which they operate and the kinds of structures that shape their operation (and which, in turn, are shaped by the unfolding of the process) differ from setting to setting. This is the unifying theme of our book: generic social processes shaped by and shaping distinctive social structures.

We proceed now to define and discuss each of the five processes. Then we shall observe them in each of the four structural contexts.

Section I

INTEGRATIVE PROCESSES

The first process to be introduced is that of social integration. This is not a single process but is a whole family of processes, the members of which assume a variety of forms. In general, we will define integrative processes as concerned with the attainment of coherence and unity among the units comprising the social organization. Integration mechanisms, for example, enable individuals to behave as members of a common group—to exhibit unity of vision or community of activity. Groups will vary not only in degree of integration but also in type of integration.

Without attempting a complete or rigorous classification of types of social integration, let us briefly examine some of the forms that these integrative processes may take. Two broad categories of processes may be identified by returning to a distinction first made in Part Two when we introduced the two components of the social order—the normative structure and the social structure. As Dahrendorf notes in Reading 12, sociologists have emphasized two types of cohesive or integrative focus: (1) those based on the normative elements of social order and (2) those based on the "institutional elements" of social order.

Normative integration is brought about as normative expectations produce pressures toward uniformity on individual members. It is expected that group members will see things the same way or that they will think the same way. Such pressures to adopt common perceptual standards, common normative standards, and common values or opinions, are found in many groups and are among the most interesting social forces examined by sociologists. However, according to Dahrendorf, it is possible to overemphasize the importance of these normative forces. People do not always share the same expectations as to how they and others should behave; people do not always hold the same attitudes and opinions concerning some issue and may disagree on the norms or rules governing conduct.

Recognizing this, the sociologist may sometimes need to focus on the institutional order—the social structure—rather than on the normative order. That is, unity and integration may not be produced by the normative structure but, instead, may come from the institutional structure. For example, integration may be produced by a power structure with the social order "held together by force and constraint." Or the most important integrative bonds may be produced by the interpersonal attractions linking group members—the sociometric structure. Or, to cite one final example, members may be separated from some and joined to others because of certain interests they have in common, interests that provide the basis for coalitions and exchange relationships. Such commensalistic relations may be an important basis for the integration of the members of certain types of social organizations.

In short, very different kinds of processes may lead to the integration of a social order, and, in fact, there are a variety of types of integration to be considered. At this point we will only introduce the general topic with Dahrendorf's remarks. In later parts we will examine more carefully some of the different types of processes producing integration in differing social contexts.

12   Integration and Values versus Coercion and Interests: The Two Faces of Society

Ralf Dahrendorf

Throughout the history of Western political thought, two views of society have stood in conflict. Both these views are intended to explain what has been, and will probably continue to be, the most puzzling problem of social philosophy: how is it that human societies cohere? There is one large and distinguished school of thought according to which social order results from a general agreement of values, a *consensus omnium* or *volonté générale* which outweighs all possible or actual differences of opinion and interest. There is another equally distinguished school of thought which holds that coherence and order in society are founded on force and constraint, on the domination of some and the subjection of others. To be sure, these views are not at all points mutually exclusive. The Utopian (as we shall call those who insist on coherence by consensus) does not deny the existence of differences of interest; nor does the Rationalist (who believes in coherence by constraint and domination) ignore such agreements of value as are required for the very establishment of force. But Utopian and Rationalist alike advance claims of primacy for their respective standpoints. For the Utopian, differences of interest are subordinated to agreements of value, and for the Rationalist these agreements are but a thin, and as such ineffective, coating of the primary reality of differences that have to be precariously reconciled by constraint. Both Utopians and Rationalists have shown much ingenuity and imagination in arguing for their respective points of view. This has not, however, led them more closely together. There is a genuine conflict of approach between Aristotle and Plato, Hobbes and Rousseau, Hegel and Kant, and this conflict has grown in intensity as the history of thought has advanced. Unless one believes that all philosophical disputes are spurious and ultimately irrelevant, the long history of the particular dispute about the problem of social order has exposed—if not solved—what appear to be fundamental alternatives of knowledge, moral decision, and political orientation.

Conflicting philosophical positions must inevitably, it seems to me, reappear constantly in theories of science. Even if this should not generally be the case, I would claim that the philosophical alternative of a Utopian or a Rational solution of the problem of order pervades modern sociological thinking even in its remotest manifestations. Here, as elsewhere, philosophical positions do not enter into scientific theories unchanged. Here, as elsewhere, they pass through the filter of logical supposition before they become relevant for testable explanations of problems of experience. The sociological Utopian does not claim that order *is based on* a general consensus of values, but that it *can be conceived of in terms of* such consensus, and that, if it is conceived of in these terms, certain propositions follow which are subject to the test of specific observations. Analogously, for the sociological Rationalist the assumption of the coercive nature of social order is a heuristic principle rather than a judgment of fact. But this obvious reservation does not prevent the Utopians and the Rationalists of sociology from engaging in disputes which are hardly less intense (if often rather less imaginative and ingenious) than those of their philosophical antecedents. The subject matter of our concern in this study demands that we take a stand with respect to this dispute.

Twice in our earlier considerations we have been faced with differences in the image of society—as I then called it— which correspond very closely to the conflicting views of Utopians and Rationalists. I have tried to show that, at least in so far as historical societies are concerned, Marx subscribed to an image

of society of the Rational variety. He assumed the ubiquity of change and conflict as well as domination and subjection, and I suggest that this view seems particularly appropriate for the analysis of problems of conflict. In any case, it seems more appropriate than the Utopian view implicit in the works of Drucker and Mayo, according to which happy cooperation is the normal state of social life. Marx, or Drucker and Mayo, may not be especially convincing representatives of these views,[1] but the distinction with which we are concerned here is, in any case, not tied to their names. Generally speaking, it seems to me that two (meta-) theories can and must be distinguished in contemporary sociology. One of these, the *integration theory of society*, conceives of social structure in terms of a functionally integrated system held in equilibrium by certain patterned and recurrent processes. The other one, the *coercion theory of society*, views social structure as a form of organization held together by force and constraint and reaching continuously beyond itself in the sense of producing within itself the forces that maintain it in an unending process of change. Like their philosophical counterparts, these theories are mutually exclusive. But—if I may be permitted a paradoxical formulation that will be explained presently—in sociology (as opposed to philosophy) a decision which accepts one of these theories and rejects the other is neither necessary nor desirable. There are sociological problems for the explanation of which the integration theory of society provides adequate as-

[1]This would be true, of course, for rather different reasons. Drucker and Mayo are rather lacking in subtlety, and it is therefore too easy to polemicize against their positions. Marx, on the other hand, is certainly subtle, but his notions of the "original" and the "terminal" societies of (imaginary) history demonstrate that he was but a limited Rationalist with strong Utopian leanings. Such mixtures of views really quite incompatible are in fact not rare in the history of social thought.

sumptions; there are other problems which can be explained only in terms of the coercion theory of society; there are, finally, problems for which both theories appear adequate. For sociological analysis, society is Janus-headed, and its two faces are equivalent aspects of the same reality.

In recent years, the integration theory of society has clearly dominated sociological thinking. In my opinion, this prevalence of one partial view has had many unfortunate consequences. However, it has also had at least one agreeable consequence, in that the very onesidedness of this theory gave rise to critical objections which enable us today to put this theory in its proper place. Such objections have been stimulated with increasing frequency by the works of the most eminent sociological theorist of integration, Talcott Parsons. It is not necessary here to attempt a comprehensive exposition of Parsons' position; nor do we have to survey the sizable literature concerned with a critical appraisal of this position. To be sure, much of this criticism is inferior in subtlety and insight to Parsons' work, so that it is hardly surprising that the sociological climate of opinion has remained almost unaffected by Parsons' critics. There is one objection to Parsons' position, however, which we have to examine if we are to make a systematic presentation of a theory of group conflict. In a remarkable essay, D. Lockwood claims "that Parsons' array of concepts is heavily weighted by assumptions and categories which relate to the role of *normative* elements in social action, and especially to the processes whereby motives are structured normatively to ensure social stability. On the other hand, what may be called the *substratum* of social action, especially as it conditions interests which are productive of social conflict and instability, tends to be ignored as a general determinant of the dynamics of social sys-

tems".[2] Lockwood's claim touches on the core of our problem of the two faces of society—although his formulation does not, perhaps, succeed in exposing the problem with sufficient clarity.

It is certainly true that the work of Parsons displays a conspicuous bias in favor of analysis in terms of values and norms. It is equally true that many of those who have been concerned with problems of conflict rather than of stability have tended to emphasize not the normative but the institutional aspects of social structure. The work of Marx is a case in point. Probably, this difference in emphasis is no accident. It is nevertheless as such irrelevant to an understanding of or adoption of the alternative images of society which pervade political thought and sociological theory. The alternative between "normative elements in social action" and a factual "substratum of social action," which Lockwood takes over from the work of Renner, in fact indicates two levels of the analysis of social structure which are in no way contradictory. There is no theoretical reason why Talcott Parsons should not have supplemented (as indeed he occasionally does) his analysis of normative integration by an analysis of the integration of social systems in terms of their institutional substratum. However we look at social structure, it always presents itself as composed of a moral and a factual, a normative and an institutional, level or, in the doubtful terms of Marx, a superstructure and a substratum. The investigator is free to choose which of these levels he wants to emphasize more strongly—although he may be well-advised, in the interest of clarity as well as of comprehensiveness of his analysis, not to stress one of these levels to the exclusion of the other.

At the same time, there is an im-

[2]David Lockwood, "Some remarks on 'The Social System,'" *British Journal of Sociology*, 7 (June, 1956). 134–146.

portant element of genuine critique in Lockwood's objection to Parsons. When Lockwood contrasts stability and instability, integration and conflict, equilibrium and disequilibrium, values and interests, he puts his finger on a real alternative of thought, and one of which Parsons has apparently not been sufficiently aware. For of two equivalent models of society, Parsons has throughout his work recognized only one, the Utopian or integration theory of society. His "array of concepts" is therefore incapable of coping with those problems with which Lockwood is concerned in his critical essay, and which constitute the subject matter of the present study.

For purposes of exposition it seems useful to reduce each of the two faces of society to a small number of basic tenets, even if this involves some degree of oversimplification as well as overstatement. The integration theory of society, as displayed by the work of Parsons and other structural-functionalists, is founded on a number of assumptions of the following type:

1. Every society is a relatively persistent, stable structure of elements.
2. Every society is a well-integrated structure of elements.
3. Every element in a society has a function, i.e., renders a contribution to its maintenance as a system.
4. Every functioning social structure is based on a consensus of values among its members.

In varying forms, these elements of (1) stability, (2) integration, (3) functional coordination, and (4) consensus recur in all structural-functional approaches to the study of social structure. They are, to be sure, usually accompanied by protestations to the effect that stability, integration, functional coordination, and consensus are only "relatively" generalized. Moreover, these as-

sumptions are not metaphysical propositions about the essence of society; they are merely assumptions for purposes of scientific analysis. As such, however, they constitute a coherent view of the social process[3] which enables us to comprehend many problems of social reality.

However, it is abundantly clear that the integration approach to social analysis does not enable us to comprehend all problems of social reality. Let us look at two undeniably sociological problems of the contemporary world which demand explanation. (1) In recent years, an increasing number of industrial and commercial enterprises have introduced the position of personnel manager to cope with matters of hiring and firing, advice to employees, etc. Why? And: what are the consequences of the introduction of this new position? (2) On the 17th of June, 1953, the building workers of East Berlin put down their tools and went on a strike that soon led to a generalized revolt against the Communist regime of East Germany. Why? And: what are the consequences of this uprising? From the point of view of the integration model of society, the first of these problems is susceptible of a satisfactory solution. A special position to cope with personnel questions is functionally required by large enterprises in an age of rationalization and "social ethic"; the introduction of this position adapts the enterprise to the values of the surrounding society; its consequence is therefore of an integrative and stabilizing nature. But what about the second problem? Evidently, the uprising of the 17th of June is neither due to

[3]It is important to emphasize that "stability" as a tenet of the integration theory of society does not mean that societies are "static." It means, rather, that such processes as do occur (and the structural-functional approach is essentially concerned with processes) serve to maintain the patterns of the system as a whole. Whatever criticism I have of this approach, I do not want to be misunderstood as attributing to it a "static bias" (which has often been held against this approach without full consideration of its merits).

nor productive of integration in East German society. It documents and produces not stability, but instability. It contributes to the disruption, not the maintenance, of the existing system. It testifies to dissensus rather than consensus. The integration model tells us little more than that there are certain "strains" in the "system." In fact, in order to cope with problems of this kind we have to replace the integration theory of society by a different and, in many ways, contradictory model.

What I have called the coercion theory of society can also be reduced to a small number of basic tenets, although here again these assumptions oversimplify and overstate the case:

1. Every society is at every point subject to processes of change; social change is ubiquitous.
2. Every society displays at every point dissensus and conflict; social conflict is ubiquitous.
3. Every element in a society renders a contribution to its disintegration and change.
4. Every society is based on the coercion of some of its members by others.

If we return to the problem of the German workers' strike, it will become clear that this latter model enables us to deal rather more satisfactorily with its causes and consequences. The revolt of the building workers and their fellows in other industries can be explained in terms of coercion.[4] The revolting groups are engaged in a conflict which "functions" as an agent of change by disintegration. A ubiquitous phenomenon is expressed, in this case, in an exceptionally intense and violent way, and further explanation will

have to account for this violence on the basis of the acceptance of conflict and change as universal features of social life. I need hardly add that, like the integration model, the coercion theory of society constitutes but a set of assumptions for purposes of scientific analysis and implies no claim for philosophical validity— although, like its counterpart, this model also provides a coherent image of social organization.

Now, I would claim that, in a sociological context, neither of these models can be conceived as exclusively valid or applicable. They constitute complementary, rather than alternative, aspects of the structure of total societies as well as of every element of this structure. We have to choose between them only for the explanation of specific problems; but in the conceptual arsenal of sociological analysis they exist side by side. Whatever criticism one may have of the advocates of one or the other of these models can therefore be directed only against claims for the exclusive validity of either.[5] Strictly speaking, both models are "valid" or, rather, useful and necessary for sociological analysis. We cannot conceive of society unless we realize the dialectics of stability and change, integration and conflict, function and motive force, consensus and coercion. In the context of this study, I regard this point as demonstrated by the analysis of the exemplary problems sketched above.

It is perhaps worth emphasizing that the thesis of the two faces of social structure does not require a complete, or even partial, revision of the conceptual

[4]For purposes of clarity, I have deliberately chosen an example from a totalitarian state. But coercion is meant here in a very general sense, and the coercion model is applicable to all societies, independent of their specific political structure.

[5]This, it seems to me, is the only—if fundamental—legitimate criticism that can be raised against Parsons' work on this general level. In *The Social System*, Parsons repeatedly advances, for the integration theory of society, a claim that it is the nucleus of "the general" sociological theory—a claim which I regard as utterly unjustified. It is Lockwood's main concern also, in the essay quoted above, to reject this claim to universal validity.

apparatus that by now has become more or less generally accepted by sociologists in all countries. Categories like role, institution, norm, structure, even function are as useful in terms of the coercion model as they are for the analysis of social integration. In fact, the dichotomy of aspects can be carried through all levels of sociological analysis; that is, it can be shown that, like social structure itself, the notions of role and institution, integration and function, norm and substratum have two faces which may be expressed by two terms, but which may also in many cases be indicated by an extension of concepts already in use. "Interest and value," Radcliffe-Brown once remarked, "are correlative terms, which refer to the two sides of an asymmetrical relation".[6] The notions of interest and value indeed seem to describe very well the two faces of the normative superstructure of society: what appears as a consensus of values on the basis of the integration theory can be regarded as a conflict of interests in terms of the coercion theory. Similarly, what appears on the level of the factual substratum as integration from the point of view of the former model presents itself as coercion or constraint from the point of view of the latter. We shall presently have occasion to explore these two faces of societies and their elements rather more thoroughly with reference to the two categories of power and of role.

While logically feasible,[7] the solution of the dilemma of political thought which we have offered here for the more restricted field of sociological analysis nevertheless raises a number of serious prob-

lems. It is evidently virtually impossible to think of society in terms of either model without positing its opposite number at the same time. There can be no conflict, unless this conflict occurs within a context of meaning, i.e., some kind of coherent "system." No conflict is conceivable between French housewives and Chilean chess players, because these groups are not united by, or perhaps "integrated into," a common frame of reference. Analogously, the notion of integration makes little sense unless it presupposes the existence of different elements that are integrated. Even Rousseau derived his *volonte' ge'ne'rale* from a modified *bellum omnium contra omnes.* Using one or the other model is therefore a matter of emphasis rather than of fundamental difference; and there are, as we shall see, many points at which a theory of group conflict has to have recourse to the integration theory of social structure.

Inevitably, the question will be raised, also, whether a unified theory of society that includes the tenets of both the integration and the coercion models of society is not at least conceivable—for as to its desirability there can be little doubt. Is there, or can there be, a general point of view that synthesizes the unsolved dialectics of integration and coercion? So far as I can see, there is no such general model; as to its possibility, I have to reserve judgment. It seems at least conceivable that unification of theory is not feasible at a point which has puzzled thinkers ever since the beginning of Western philosophy.

---

[6] A. R. Radcliffe-Brown, "On social structure," in *Structure and Function in Primitive Society.* Glencoe, Ill.: Free Press, 1952, p. 199.

[7] As is demonstrated most clearly by the fact

that a similar situation can be encountered in physics with respect to the theory of light. Here, too, there are two seemingly incompatible theories which nevertheless exist side by side, and each of which has its proper realm of empirical phenomena: the wave theory and the quantum theory of light.

SOCIALIZATION PROCESSES

We may define *socialization* as "the processes by which individuals selectively acquire the skills, knowledge, attitudes, values, and motives current in the groups of which they are or will become members."[1] This specifically sociological conception has been gradually developing over the last half century, beginning with the writings of Cooley,[2] Simmel,[3] and Mead[4] and continuing down to the recent work of Parsons[5] and Brim.[6] (See Reading 13) More so than with the other processes to be examined, it is possible to say in the case of socialization that it is viewed by sociologists primarily as a morphostatic process. That is, socialization is viewed as the process by which social structure is able to endure even through changes in the occupants of social positions. People come and go, but the social positions and the relationships among positions persist. Brim has recently acknowledged this emphasis on social stability in the study of socialization:

There are two great traditions in the study of personality in relation to society. One is the interest in how individuals adjust to society and how in spite of the influence of society upon them they manage to be creative and gradually to transform the social order in which they have been born. The other is the interest in how society socializes the individual—how it transforms the raw material of biological man into a person suitable to perform the activities of society. The study of socialization falls into the latter tradition: its starting place is to ask the fundamental question of how it is possible for a society to endure and to continue to develop. The inquiry at all times is concerned with how society changes the natural man, not how man changes his society.[7]

In Reading 13, Brim clearly sets forth the major differences between the sociologist's view of socialization and its impact on individual personality as contrasted with that of the more traditional psychological perspective.

Mead's Conception of the Socialization Process   For the sociologist, the socialization process is a role-learning process that takes place in interaction with others. The chief architect of this perspective is the great philosopher and

---

[1]William H. Sewell, "Some recent developments in socialization theory and research," *Annals of the American Academy of Political and Social Science*, 349 (September, 1963), 163.

[2]Charles H. Cooley, *Human Nature and the Social Order*, Glencoe, Ill.: Free Press, 1956 (originally published 1909).

[3]Georg Simmel, *Conflict and The Web of Group Affiliation*, Glencoe, Ill.: Free Press, 1955, pp. 140-167 (originally published 1922).

[4]George H. Mead, *Mind, Self and Society*, Chicago: University of Chicago Press, 1934.

[5]Talcott Parsons, "Family structure and the socialization of the child," in Talcott Parsons and Robert F. Bales (eds.), *Family, Socialization and Interaction Process*, Glencoe, Ill.: Free Press, 1955, pp. 35–131.

[6]Orville G. Brim, Jr., "Socialization through the life cycle," in Orville G. Brim, Jr., and Stanton Wheeler, *Socialization After Childhood*, New York: Wiley, 1966, pp. 3-49.

[7]Brim, pp. 3-4.

social psychologist George Herbert Mead. In Mead's view, the biological individual becomes a social person only as he is exposed to the expectations of other persons who provide guides to his behavior. He is rewarded for behaviors that coincide with these prescriptions and is punished for behaviors that deviate from these prescriptions. Over time the individual comes to anticipate these expectations; he is able to *take the role of the other*—that is, he assumes the perspective of the role definers toward himself and in this manner comes to guide and evaluate his own behavior. The attitudes and expectations of others, internalized, become the basis for the individual's self-concept. As Mead explains, an individual "becomes a self in so far as he can take the attitude of another and act toward himself as others act."[8]

As might be guessed, this is a difficult area to study empirically, but we can briefly summarize one study whose results are consistent with Mead's conclusions. Miyamoto and Dornbusch asked 195 subjects in ten living groups to rate themselves and the other members of their groups on four characteristics: intelligence, self-confidence, physical attractiveness, and likableness.[9] In addition, each individual was asked to report on how he perceived he was rated by each of his fellows. The researchers found, as predicted, that the mean responses of other group members toward a given subject were higher for the members with a high self-rating than for those with a low self-rating on the various personality dimensions. Further, an individual's self-conception tended to be closer to the mean perceived response of others than to the mean of their actual responses. This study does not establish the causality between others' and self's attitudes—that is, one cannot determine from this type of data whether the individual's attitudes toward himself influenced the attitudes toward him held by other group members or, as seems more likely, whether the attitudes of other group members influenced those held by the individual member toward himself—but the results are not inconsistent with Mead's interpretation.

In this brief discussion, we cannot do full justice to the subtlety and brilliance of Mead's analysis of the emergence of self. He lays great stress, for example, on the role of language in this process, and he is also careful to note that all other group members do not play an equally important role—that some members are more *significant* others for the individual and have more to do with shaping his attitudes and his self-conception than do other group members. Also, Mead suggests that the individual does not keep separate the views and attitudes of each significant other with whom he interacts but that these become merged into a *generalized other*, allowing the individual to respond to a more coherent set of expectations and permitting him to develop a more integrated self-conception.

An important emphasis of the sociological view of socialization is that it is a process that is not restricted to childhood (primary socialization) but is one that continues throughout life (secondary socialization) . During the primary socialization period, the child learns to communicate with others by means of symbols having commonly shared meanings (language) ; and he learns to internalize the attitudes of others toward himself and to acquire self-consciousness. The child

[8]Mead, p. 171.

[9]S. Frank Miyamoto and Sanford M. Dornbusch, "A test of interactionist hypotheses of self-conception," *American Journal of Sociology*, 61 (March, 1956) , 399-403.

also learns to respond to the expectations (play the roles) that are directed at him. The child, however, does not learn the behavior and attitudes associated with a single set of positions that he then continues to play throughout his life, but, rather, he moves from one set of positions to another as long as he lives, learning the role behaviors associated with each set. In a very real sense, every new personal relationship entered and every group or organization joined, may be viewed as a socialization context, providing new roles to be played and new expectations to serve as guidelines for behavior and attitudes. And with each new role there is some modification—sometimes great and sometimes small—in the individual's self-concept.

An Oversocialized Conception of Man?   This discussion began with a recognition that the view of socialization just described is one-sided and, hence, leads to a somewhat distorted conception of both the process and the end-product. If followed too religiously, the view leads to what Wrong has described as an "over-socialized conception of man."[10] Wrong argues that sociologists have ignored the important insights of Freud, who emphasized the ever present tensions between the individual and society caused in part by man's biological nature. Wrong concludes:

"Socialization" may mean two quite distinct things; when they are confused, an oversocialized view of man is the result. On the one hand socialization means the "transmission of the culture," the particular culture of the society an individual enters at birth; on the other hand the term is used to mean the "process of becoming human," of acquiring uniquely human attributes from interaction with others. All men are socialized in the latter sense, but this does not mean that they have been completely molded by the particular norms and values of their culture. All cultures, as Freud contended, do violence to man's socialized bodily drives, but this in no sense means that men could possibly exist without culture or independently of society. From such a standpoint, man may properly be called, as Norman Brown has called him, the "neurotic" or the "discontented" animal and repression may be seen as the main characteristic of human nature as we have known it in history.[11]

In addition to Wrong's reminder that man is a biological as well as a social animal and that the regulation of behavior by external and internalized norms may exact a high cost on those so controlled, we should add some other brief comments to balance the view of socialization just sketched.

We should remember from our discussion of social roles that an individual cannot comply with the expectations of *all* others, since many of these expectations will be conflicting. There are certain individuals who do attempt to conform with even conflicting norms, who rapidly take on the colors of whatever group in which they are currently interacting. But such individuals are not very useful to anyone; they cannot be counted on to fulfill the social expectations of any group unless group members are physically present to enforce conformity. If such persons are not to be in the majority, socialization processes must include some mechanisms for teaching independence. Individuals must learn not only how to perceive and conform to social expectations directed at them; they must also be taught ways of *resisting* social influences and of maintaining some measure of independence in the face of social pressures to conform. It may be suggested

[10]See Dennis H. Wrong, "The oversocialized conception of man in modern sociology," *American Sociological Review*, 26 (April, 1961) , 183–193.
[11]Wrong, p. 192.

that one source of independence in our own culture is generalized societal values such as "individualism" and "freedom." Because such values are widely held, the individual who chooses to act independently under social pressure may gain the respect of a group even when he chooses not to comply with its demands.

Individuals can also be relatively impervious to the demands of a given social group because of their greater loyalty to another group. Just as all persons are not equally important to us, neither will the expectations of all persons be equally influential in guiding our behavior. Some persons and groups are sufficiently important to us that their expectations will determine our behavior even when we are in the presence of others whose beliefs are conflicting. For example, Newcomb carried out a study of the changes in political attitudes of students attending Bennington College.[12] With each year at college, a larger proportion of the student body shifted to politically liberal attitudes. However, some students were unaffected by the political climate of the student body. Intensive interviews with these students revealed that most of them failed to relate in any important way with the student body and that many of them continued to identify with and be oriented to their families. Groups importantly influencing the beliefs and attitudes of an individual have been termed *reference groups* by sociologists. Newcomb's study shows that all membership groups are not reference groups for a given individual.

We must also keep in mind that an individual often has some choice over the groups to which he belongs. A student with a strong religious background who goes to college is more likely to join a church-related group where he will feel comfortable in meeting the expectations of his associates than to join a young atheist league in which he would be likely to find his assigned role highly unsettling.

Finally, in the situations where membership is nonvoluntary, as the state, public school, or the army, control over the individual may be maintained only by the exercise of power. Individuals in such situations who are reluctant to adopt their assigned roles may retain some independence (and self-respect) by not internalizing the values and norms of their membership group but by responding only when forced to do so. Again we see, however, that social order may be a product of force as well as of socialization and internalization of norms. One should never overlook the importance of coercion as against conviction in human affairs.

[12]Theodore M. Newcomb, "Attitude development as a function of reference groups: The Bennington study," in Eleanor E. Maccoby, Theodore M. Newcomb, and Eugene L. Hartley (eds.), *Readings in Social Psychology*, New York: Holt, Rinehart and Winston, Inc., 1958, pp. 265–275.

13   Personality Development as Role-Learning

Orville G. Brim, Jr.

It is our contention that the traditional approaches to personality which either assume, or seek to find and measure, "general characteristics," "source traits," "genotypes," "life styles," "basic factors," and the rest have taken the wrong road to understanding the person, and are in error in their fundamental premise that there are such general styles, characteristics, or traits. In contrast to this is a general theory of personality development, presented here in outline, which draws heavily on sociological concepts.

This theory sets forth the view that personality differences consist of inter-individual differences in characteristics as expressed in social roles, and of little else. It holds that the proper explanatory variables include not only motivation, but also knowledge of the role demands and ability to perform. It maintains that variations in individual motivation, knowledge, and ability are produced not merely by cultural or idiosyncratic differences in background, but in addition by the types of social structure in which one has participated—the latter regulating, so to speak, which aspects of the culture one will learn.

A few observations are in order to clear the way. First, socialization is defined as a process of learning through which an individual is prepared, with varying degrees of success, to meet the requirements laid down by other members of society for his behavior in a variety of situations. These requirements are always attached to one or another of the recognized positions or statuses in this society such as husband, son, employee, and adult male. The behavior required of a person in a given position or status is considered to be his prescribed role, and the requirements themselves can be called role-prescriptions. In addition, the individual holding a given position has prescriptions concerning how people in other positions should behave toward him, as well as an understanding of what the others expect of him. Thus, between individuals in two social positions there are sets of reciprocal requirements or prescriptions, regulating the individuals' behavior towards each other.

If socialization is role-learning, it follows that socialization occurs throughout an individual's life. The new student, the army recruit, the young honeymooners—all become socialized as they enter their new statuses. It is fair to say that during the past decade probably the bulk of sociological research on socialization has not dealt with the process during childhood, but rather with entrance into roles during the adult period of life (2, 16). This work is often unrecognized by the persons engaged in it, or by students of personality development, as being systematically related to the study of socialization during childhood.

In any event, the concern in this essay is with personality development in children. That is, after all, the fundamental process. The socialization occurring during childhood correctly receives primary

Reprinted from Orville G. Brim, Jr., *Personality Development in Children*, Austin, Texas: University of Texas Press, 1960, pp. 127–157 (excerpts), by permission of the author and the publisher.

emphasis in research and theory. The potency and durability of the learning that occurs during this period is assumed on the basis of the frequency of learning situations, their primacy in the career of the organism, and the intensity of the rewards and punishments administered. Also, as McClelland (13) has argued, there is difficulty in extinguishing behavior learned in childhood because it was learned under conditions of partial reinforcement.

What is presented here builds upon the theories of personality presented by James (11), by the symbolic interactionists of an earlier day such as Cooley (6) and Mead (22), and by the latter-day protagonists of role-theories of personality such as Cottrell (7), Parsons (19; 20, Chap. 2), and Sullivan (17). However, in spite of the illustrious names associated with this approach to personality, at present it has yet to be explored in detail...

THE DEPENDENT VARIABLES

With these beginning observations complete, let us turn directly to the task of presenting the analysis of personality development as role-learning. The first step is to indicate the kinds of dependent variables with which the theory is concerned. These dependent variables involve differences between individuals in some characteristics, whether of motives, ideas, behavior, or effects of their actions. In this, traditional personality theory and the approach to personality through role-learning are identical. The critical difference, however, between the two is in the level of specificity at which such personality characteristics are to be studied.

Traditional personality theories deal with personal characteristics at a most general level; the analysis of the situation in which high or low amounts of a given trait will be displayed has received some

theoretical attention, of course, but the empirical work has dealt with the effects of electric shock, of simulated hostility in experimental small-group settings, and others, none of which remotely approach the degree of influence of the many different social-stimulus situations.

A next most specific level would be the specification of these traits within a role context, e.g., the person who is a dominant husband but a submissive storekeeper. A still more specific level follows from the fact that the behavior prescribed for a role may vary, depending on the person with whom one interacts. For example, the role of the salesgirl is quite different depending on whether she is interacting with her customer or with her floor manager. Gross and his colleagues have introduced the concept of role sector (9) to refer to the specific aspects of a role which pertain to interaction with other given persons, and Merton the concept of role set (15) to refer to those persons with whom the actor is concerned. However, even this does not lead us to the lowest important level of specification of personality traits. It may be that while behavior in a role is prescribed vis-a-vis specific others that there also are prescriptions regulating episodes within the ongoing interaction between persons. For example, are there not situations where it is expected by both the husband and the wife that he be angry towards her, and other occasions where it is expected that he be dependent, dominant, and so on?

One can argue that the "general trait" level, the "life style" approach to personality, has been unproductive; that it must necessarily be so; and that the study of personality must be more situationally specific. Whether an analysis in terms of roles, or even role sectors, is specific enough remains to be seen; i.e., research will indicate whether the gain in our predictive power is enough to warrant not moving down to an "episode" level. In any event, it is not necessary to take a position on the latter point in this essay, since the concepts advanced for the study of personality development involve learning in any normatively regulated social situation, whether roles or episodes.

What are some of the inadequacies of the traditional theories which conceive of the adult personality in terms of general characteristics? The common practice in these theories has been to conceptualize the personality in terms of settings on some of these traits; e.g., one is high, medium, or low on some of the many possible characteristics. Thus an individual may be introverted or extroverted; he may be anal-compulsive or not; he may be high or low in dependency, in aggression, in dominance, in nurturance and the rest. The more complicated theories include not one, but several, important traits and work toward the classification of adult personalities in terms of combinations of scores, or profiles, on this set of basic traits.

These general personality traits are viewed as abstractions from the individual's characteristic response pattern. Presumably they are discovered by studying the individual's behavior in all the important situations that he might meet, or by asking the individual to give verbal reports of his probable behavior in this sample of situations, and then striking an average. This approach leads to the idea of a consistent core of the personality, composed of a number of characteristics (e.g., "high dominance") with almost invariant settings. Research on personality development then looks at the socialization process to discover the antecedents of high or low scores for individuals on these various general traits.

This traditional approach, this search for general traits in the adult personality,

can be viewed as a romantic quest which intrigues one by the possibility of discovering major life styles in individuals, but one which cannot succeed because an individual is not the same in different aspects of his life. It is confronted with the same troubles which plague the efforts to formulate the single master ethical principle applicable to behavior in all conceivable situations, namely, that moral rules differ from one situation to the next; in contrast, the successful religions of the world have great numbers of moral rules (and often not consistent ones) to cover all situations. . . .

The actual lack of success of this traditional approach, entirely apart from other theoretical considerations to be advanced later, suggests the value of exploring a role-learning approach to personality development. This latter theory would view personality as composed of learned roles and role components, rather than of general traits descriptive of behavior across situations. It would be heartening to be able to refer to a large body of research, rather than the few studies (e.g., 8) that we have, showing how the characteristics of personality vary depending on the role one is in. But the work has not yet been done, and in lieu of it one must appeal to one's own familiar observations.

When one looks at what is actually going on around him, he finds striking the great variation in the individual's behavior from one situation to another during the course of the day: as the individual moves, for example, from his occupational role, to his various family roles, to his roles with the neighbors in the community, and so on. Recall the familiar example of the German adult male who is meek and subservient to his superiors in his occupational role, but who changes into a domineering, hostile, and aggressive father upon returning to his home. Consider the modern executive, who in his occupational role is autonomous, creative, and decisive but who upon going home and taking up his status as husband may become docile and dependent in family matters. What should capture the interest of the student of personality, therefore, is not the consistency of individual differences as he looks upon behavior. Rather it is the great adaptability, the truly impressive variation in response to situational demands, which characterizes man as he moves from one situation to another. The question becomes not "What is his life style?" but instead, "How can it be that his character is continually transformed to accord with the social demands of his life?"

The case could hardly be otherwise; obviously roles demand quite different responses from individuals at different times. The not-so-obvious conclusion that follows is that the function of the socialization process is not to produce for society something such as the "dominant" individual or "dependent" person; socialization instead is aimed at producing individuals equipped to meet the variety of demands placed upon them by life in a society. Socialization is successful to the extent that it prepares individuals to perform adequately the many roles that will be expected of them in the normal course of their careers throughout society. It does this by increasing a person's repertoire of behavior; extending the range and increasing the complexity of responses which he has at his command; freeing him from a limited series of stereotyped responses; providing him with a richer set of discriminations between various social situations; and proliferating the specific motives which can be switched into action by appropriate social stimuli.

Especially one sees that socialization must develop the individual's potential responses along the whole range of variation of some given characteristic; for example, given the fact that different social situations require varying degrees of dominance, from high dominance in one to extreme submission in another, it follows that the successfully socialized individual must have acquired the ability to make responses with all different degrees of dominance. Nor is this true alone of dominance. This applies to all dimensional characteristics of behavior, whether they be achievement, nurturance, hostility, or whatever. Here, also, socialization to be successful must equip the individual to respond, when appropriate, with any given amount of a characteristic. One has to know how to get ahead in life, as well as how to relax. One has to know how to be kind to people, and how to be demanding of them. One has to know how to get angry, as well as how to be friendly.

The fact that research is able to find any consistency at all in individual responses across situations reflects several things. First, it may be taken as an indication of the fact that the socialization process is not completely successful. Consistency in the behavior of some individuals in varied social situations probably reflects the degree to which their socialization was unsuccessful and left them unable to meet the contrasting role demands. Perhaps one has not had experience in dealing with certain kinds of interaction situations and therefore generalizes from his limited repertoire of roles. Or, he may have had little training in discriminating between different roles, so that he appears socially crude and clumsy in his behavior by treating everybody alike. Thus traditional personality theory might be viewed as studying the waste materials, so to speak, of the socialization process, rather than the standard product itself.

Consistency may indicate only that the situations in which it is found have similar prescriptions for the individual's behavior. The consistency comes not from some unyielding trait of the individual, but from just the opposite source, his ability to meet the similar demands of similar social situations.

Some traits may show more consistency than others. These would tend to be functionally unimportant characteristics, their greater consistency arising because the expression of these characteristics is less regulated by situational norms. This reduced regulation in turn arises because these traits are less important to the success of the interaction.

Finally, some individuals may show consistency in some characteristics but not in others. Here a straightforward process of generalization of response from one highly salient role to others would seem to be the explanation. For example, the business executive whose major rewards are derived from his occupational role, and the bulk of whose time is spent in this social situation, may find the responses acquired in this role to remain relatively high in his response hierarchy, and continually to spill over, as it were, in response to the stimulus conditions of other roles; e.g., he begins to treat his wife as if she were his secretary and needs to be reminded of the fact that he is no longer at the office.

We come then, finally, to our dependent variables in the theory. These dependent variables are interindividual differences in characteristics as expressed within situational contexts; the central problem becomes one of predicting such situationally specific individual differences. . . .

It is about this time that one might ask, "But what has become of the personality itself?" Many would say that to conceptualize the dependent variables in this way means that one is no longer studying personality, but only fragments of the individual's behavior that have little to do with his underlying character. The answer is that the learned repertoire of roles is the personality. There is nothing else. There is no "core" personality underneath the behavior and feelings; there is no "central" monolithic self which lies beneath its various external manifestations.

But, one says, what then of the self? The answer is that the "self" is a composite of many selves, each of them consisting of a set of self-perceptions which are specific to one or another major role, specific to the expectations of one or another significant reference group. The self-perceptions are of how one measures up to these expectations with respect to behaving adequately, possessing the right motives, producing the right results. The individual says, bringing together his many selves, "I am the person who is a husband, a father, a steam fitter, an Elk, a Democrat, and a Scout troop leader." The work by Kuhn and his associates at Iowa (12) shows that when a person is asked, "Who are you?" he responds by saying, "I am a Catholic, I am a student, I am a man," and so on. Note that he does not respond by saying, "I am strong," "I am dominant," "I am dependent." When these responses do occur in the Iowa data it is almost without exception after production of the status names which mark the role conceptions of the self.

But, one says, the fact remains that one is conscious of one's self, that one looks inward upon something which he views as his true self, or looks outward upon an expression of his self in some particular context. This does not mean that there exists some separate, fundamental self. Rather, this is to be understood very simply as the individual bringing together, however briefly, the various categories of his self-perceptions in a full, composite image; or in the latter case, as the individual viewing and appraising his performance with respect to one reference group from the vantage point of another.

Where one does in fact view his "self" as co-extensive with one particular role, then there has occurred the elevation of one particular segment of the self to a dominant position. To some extent this occurs with all persons. There will be roles in which the rewards and punishments to the individual are much greater than in others, and which demand his continuing concern with their performance. Thus, for one individual most of his waking thoughts may be concerned with his performance and achievement in his occupational role; it is himself in this particular role which he tends to think of as his "real" self. This elliptical manner of speaking, however, is misleading and it would be wiser to speak of the one or two selves of most significance to the individual.

It follows, too, that evaluation of the self as being good or bad must proceed in terms of evaluations of one's behavior along certain dimensions within specific roles; one says, "I am a person who is a good husband," "a sometimes too cross father," "a successful business man," and the like. Self-evaluation means that the individual compares his own performance in the role with the expectations he perceives others to hold for him, or which he holds for himself because of earlier learning of what his parents or others would have expected.

One's self-evaluation can be realistic or not, depending primarily on two factors. The first is whether one's own evaluation of his role-performance is similar to that made by other people. Another is the correctness of his appraisal of others' expectations of him so that his evaluation of his role-performance is made according to valid standards. In the first instance, the concepts of role-model and of reference group refer to the events wherein the individual stops to ask himself how a given person—perhaps someone he admires—would carry out this particular role, and then seeks to emulate his performance. In the second instance he seeks to orient his role-performance towards the expectations he perceives some given group to hold.

Quite clearly there are many other points on which a comparison of traditional trait-theories and of role-theories would be instructive. One thinks of topics such as conformity; of how new situations are handled by the individual; of the questions of personality change and creativity; of how the concepts of the unconscious and the defenses are handled.

THE INTERVENING VARIABLES

The problem has been defined as the explanation of individual differences in behavior in specific social situations. What intervening variables will be useful in explaining such individual differences?

The intervening variables must pertain to what has been learned, for differences between persons arise in greatest part from differences in the content of prior experiences, that is, their socialization. Two questions thus arise: how one learns, and how this learning is to be described. Regarding the first, we need not be concerned with detailed differences in learning theory. Many learning-theory issues are not pertinent to the level of inquiry of this kind of personality theory. It is necessary only to assume that the child learns from experience, and that the fundamental processes such as generalization and discrimination regulate this learning process.

The second appears as the critical question. The task of the intervening variables in this theory is to conceptualize what is learned. Here a role-theory of personality can make a contribution through its derivation from the more general analysis of conformity and deviance in role-performance.

The reference points for appraising the amount of individual variation are either the social norms (role-prescriptions) which regulate the social situation, or the median performance of persons in the role, which must reflect the social norms. Given this point of reference, then, in order to conform to such demands, an individual must know what is expected of him in a situation; he must have the ability to fulfill its demands upon him; and he must be motivated to do so. These three variables of awareness and knowledge of role demands, of ability to meet them, and of motivation to do so will serve in this theory as the intervening variables. They describe the learning that has accrued to the individual regarding a role. The major sources of variation between individuals in roles thus involve different degrees of ignorance of what is expected, different degrees of ability to learn and perform that which is expected, and different degrees of role-appropriate motivation.

This will be more familiar when one recognizes the contrast with traditional personality theory, where the major explanatory variable intervening between behavioral differences and prior learning has been that of motivation alone. There has been a pronounced tendency to view all learning as pertinent to the development of high or low strength of one or another motive, with the latter then carrying the burden of explanation of behavior variations. One possible contribution of a role-approach is to establish variations in ability to behave in certain

ways, and in conceptions of what is expected in a situation, as intervening variables worthy of research. . . .

THE INDEPENDENT VARIABLES

We have stated that it is the differences in learning related to knowledge, ability, and motivation which underlie the situationally specific differences in personality. The next question, therefore, must be that of how such differences in learning occur.

Consider that in the society where a child matures there are always a great number of discriminably different social situations, each with its own norms, its specification of motives and behavior. We have argued that the acquisition of knowledge, ability, and motivation is always situationally specific. With respect to knowledge, as one observes the course of the child's day one is impressed by the time and effort directed to identifying and discriminating new situations; to gaining understanding of the precise combination of responses which is called for; to exploring the degree to which this new situation is similar to ones previously identified and from which prior behavior might be generalized. Regarding ability, one sees him trying new responses; seeking to develop his abilities to discharge successfully his role in some given situation; appraising his performance after the fact and discovering those parts of his behavior which require improvement. Last, although not observable directly, one views the child acquiring situationally appropriate motives; learning that it is a desirable thing for him to behave in way x in situation y, in other words, developing the motive to perform x in situation y.

There are two major types of variation, two fundamental classes of events, which one can discern in this vast and complicated socialization of the child.

These two classes of events are the independent variables of the theory and serve to organize and describe systematically the sources of variation in learning that can accrue to children.

The first fundamental class of events pertains to the social-structural aspects of the child's environment, the network of related statuses in which he can be involved. The culture acquired by the child in socialization is associated with these specific interpersonal situations. The social structure through which he matures thus regulates in large degree which aspects of the culture the child will be exposed to and which he will learn. If certain statuses are not present in this social structure, it follows that the aspects of culture learned through interaction with individuals in such statuses are missed by the child, and that he remains deficient in learning in this respect, undeveloped in this potential aspect of his personality. Straightforward examples of these variations in social structure are the presence or absence of the father, the presence or absence of sibs of the same or opposite sex in the family, or the presence or absence of peers for the adolescent living upon the isolated farm. One can even conceive of differences in the overall "richness" of the social-structural environment of different children. Some children will grow up in a structure involving perhaps only one or both parents and themselves. Others will grow up in a crowded community with a large and extended family, where they are forced to differentiate between people in a complex social structure, and to acquire a wide response repertoire.

The importance of social-structure variation is based on several assumptions. One assumption is that what is learned in socialization is fairly large response units, involving interaction episodes or even larger segments of role behavior. Social interaction is not made up of bits and pieces, of tiny unit responses such as a smile, a posture, and the like, put together in a certain way upon this occasion. If this is attempted, role-performance becomes studied and false. Instead, it is something much more complex that is acquired all of a piece; consider the familiar example of the three-year-old suddenly playing the mother's role almost effortlessly.

A second assumption is that role-learning occurs from actual participation in interaction situations: the child must learn roles through interaction with individuals who are actually in the various positions, or ones quite similar to the positions, that he will encounter himself later on as an adult. This complicated learning process proceeds as the child moves from one experience to another during the course of the day, confronting in interaction a series of persons holding different statuses in the peer and adult world, who demand of him that he discriminate between them, that he behave in different ways towards them, and that he develop the desire to do so.

But these assumptions raise questions for which we have no answers. First, what of the implication that various roles or episodes cannot be learned vicariously, and cannot be taught by persons who are not actually in the position involved? One might say that this cannot be true: that always there is the ubiquitous parent, monitoring the child's actions as a representative of the larger society, overseeing and correcting behavior with respect to its appropriateness. The busy parent is concerned with the difficult tasks of teaching the child to be aggressive with his peer group, but not with his little sister; to be angry when he is insulted, but friendly when he is complimented; to be submissive to his adult superiors, but not necessarily so to his older siblings; to seek achievement in his school activities, but not in games with the family; to be dependent on his teacher in certain learning situations, but not upon his mother in other contexts. One sees that the function of these parental activities is to help the child to differentiate and understand the demands of the social structure. A parent's part in socialization often seems to be much more concerned with the child's behavior towards others than it is with the child's behavior toward the parent himself. Surely the child must learn something about interaction with others from listening to his parent's supervisory comments.

A second question is to what extent the parent can make up for the absence of important statuses in the social-structural environment of the child? At first it appears that the parent does little of this. Much of the parent's concern, described above, over the child's role behavior is directed to roles which the child actually has, rather than hypothetical roles which the child does not meet at all. Is not the parent's effort directed to teaching his son how to behave towards his younger brother, rather than teaching him how he should behave towards his sister, if in fact he had one? Although studies of the effects on children of the father's absence from the home have not had the same results, at least one (21) finds no large or durable effects. In this case the mother may be successful, either in acting the father's role or in training children in how they should act, if they had a father.

A third question is whether deficiencies in early life can be made up, so to speak, in adulthood through interaction with persons in statuses similar to those which were absent in earlier years. To what extent, or perhaps to what depth, is the socialization into adult roles, mentioned earlier, really successful? Does the person growing up without sisters and in relative isolation from age mates of the opposite sex readily overcome the effects of this deprivation of experience at a later time, for example, when he first gets into a co-educational environment at the college level? Or will he always be different because of this early deficiency of male-female peer interaction in his learning? Granted that certain people learn certain roles late in life, no one seems to know whether this is easier or harder, or simply makes no difference. A related matter is the use of role-playing as an educational and therapeutic procedure to overcome individual deficiencies in certain kinds of role-learning. The available evidence (14) leaves the question of its effects far from answered.

It is disappointing that there is an almost complete absence of research on the effects of social structure variation. There are a few studies on family size; a few on characteristics of siblings; a few on father absence; some impressionistic materials on the effects of grandparents, maids, and the like; but of the many thousands of research studies on child development there may be less than a hundred which relate variations in social structure to the developmental process and subsequent personality.

It may be that this research was not undertaken because it was hard to conceptualize the effects of social structure upon the personality. Or, it may be in part because this is viewed as lying within the sociological domain, and sociologists have only recently become active in number in the study of socialization. In any event, when variations in social structure are viewed as key circumstances which determine whether or not the child will be exposed to certain classes of learning, i.e., the learning related to certain kinds of roles, these variations can be dealt with systematically as experimental variables in studies of socialization. Out of this should come a better picture of the effects of the social structure on personality differences in later life.

The second fundamental class of events which regulates what is learned is the familiar one of cultural content. Because of its familiarity, only a brief review is warranted. We have stated above that the cultural content which the child learns in socialization is always attached to some specific interactional context, and that variations in the kinds of statuses he faces determine what is learned. Now, the second point is that the actual content associated with any particular role relationship—the characteristics of the interaction itself—will vary according to the particular culture or subculture in which it occurs. In different cultures, the conception of the desirable adult may differ and different ends may be sought in socialization. Or, there may be similarity in the values of different cultures, but disagreement on the means, i.e., on the ways children should be raised to produce the desired results. Thus in different cultures children interacting with some specific person in their social environment, for example, two boys interacting with their respective fathers, may be confronted with somewhat different experiences.

Another source of variation in the content of interaction is the expression of personal characteristics by the specific individuals actually occupying a given status with whom the child interacts. Every society allows individual variation in role-performance within certain prescribed limits. Thus there is always some amount of idiosyncratic difference in the experiences two boys will have in interacting with their fathers, even though the boys' cultural background is the same. The differences arise, of course, as each parent adapts his role (within the allowed range of variation) to better fit his own abilities and desires.

The differences become then personality differences attributable to the parents' own socialization experiences.

This fundamental class of independent variables, namely, cultural and idiosyncratic differences in the actual nature of the interaction engaged in by the child, traditionally is studied under the concept of child-rearing practices. Studies of basic personality structure or of national character have sought to relate differences between cultures in certain content, for example, that of the mother-and-infant interaction system, to variations in subsequent personality. This same approach, of course, has been taken with subcultural groups where one studies the effects of the varying child-rearing practices of religious, ethnic, social-class and other groups. Last, studies of the effects of within-culture, but between-parent, variation probably constitute the bulk of existing work on personality development which relates child-rearing content to later personality. Familiar here are the many studies describing differences between parents in their role-performance, e.g., in the degree of rejection, the mode of discipline, the demand for independence, and the effects of such differences upon the child.

SOME IMPLICATIONS FOR RESEARCH AND THEORY

What activities do these new concepts suggest? We have stressed that the proper study of personality requires that one focus on interindividual differences within roles. We have said that the conception of intervening variables should include such things as one's understanding of what is expected in a situation. We have stated the importance of the social structure that is characteristic of a given child's environment, which channels and regulates the culture learned.

The concepts presented in this essay suggest some different approaches to familiar problems. For example, the appraisal of child-rearing practices (probably the major source of variation in personality in later life) should give more attention to the ways in which parents teach children to be aware of different roles. What of the differences between parents in how they actually perceive the social structure, and in the discriminations which they pass on to the child? Which areas of differentiation do they see as the most important? Which ones do they insist that the child learn? Conversely, which are those areas of social structure that a particular set of parents fails to emphasize? Consider common cultural distinctions such as those between male and female and the possible differences among parental couples in their emphasis upon these. Certainly there are parents for whom the male-female role differentiation is substantially less than for other couples. The same is true of the differentiation of power and authority between generations. Parents must differ markedly in the degree to which they insist the child distinguish between various age levels as statuses. These degrees of insistence must have significant effects upon the child's ability to discriminate different role situations and also upon his ability to understand what is expected of him, and should take their rightful place beside modes of discipline and other child-rearing variables.

As another instance, consider the situation where a wife is described as acting toward her husband as if he were her father; that is, she treats him as a father figure. Rather than consider this characteristic to be the expression of unconscious motives on her part, why not explore the alternative hypothesis which is that her behavior is the only kind of intimate, female-to-male interaction pattern that she knows? Then one looks for causes of this deficiency in her repertoire of action both in the content of the child-rearing experiences which she

had and in the social-structural aspects of her early environment. Did she have the opportunity to interact, in a continuing and important relationship, with any man besides her father? Perhaps she never learned to discriminate between the different male-female status relations and never learned the behavior appropriate to each. A hypothesis is that wives who behave in this way come most frequently from families in which they were an only child; or, in any event, in which they had no brothers.

Something closely related to the preceding hypothesis is presented in an analysis (4) of a set of data originally collected by Helen Koch. These data consisted of teachers' ratings of children on many personality traits. All children had one sib. One finding was that boys with sisters had fewer masculine and more feminine traits than did boys with brothers. This was interpreted as the result of the necessary process of "taking the role of the other" in interaction, which in this case would lead to a dilution of the boy's own masculine responses. Now an additional and not incompatible interpretation is available with the concepts advanced here. Where the boy has only one sister, he learns peer level interaction patterns appropriate to a male-female relation. Certainly the expectations of his sister, and those of his parents for him toward her, include less aggression, less anger, and so on, than if another male (a brother) were involved. In the first-grade classroom he would tend, through generalization, to respond to his peers as he did to his sister, and hence would receive a lower rating on aggression and similar traits. As a firmer differentiation of male and female peers is learned, and the responses appropriate to interaction with both are acquired, these effects of sex of siblings should diminish.

What kind of research design is suggested by this view of personality? An example would be a study which obtained data on a number of children describing their behavior (e.g., the amounts of aggression and dependency) in several roles, such as with their sibs, with their teachers, with their male and female nonfamily peers, and their parents. The study would consider as antecedents of role-specific differences between children such variables as their knowledge of the other person's prescriptions for them in the roles involved, their ability to make the appropriate responses, and their motivation to do so. This would lead, in turn, to obtaining data on the structural aspects of each child's environment (e.g., who are the people with whom he has an opportunity to interact?), and to an appraisal of the nature of the interaction. . . .

In conclusion, this has all been a long excursion through some difficult terrain and one can ask if it has all been worth while. Yet it is fair to say that the issues raised are real, that people do vary considerably in the way they perform different roles; that this is a matter of both scientific and practical concern; and that a major source of such variation must be the kinds of experience acquired in specific role contexts during the socialization process. Somehow these matters must enter more fully into our theories of personality development and into our future research.

Bibliography

1. Baldwin, A. L. *Behavior and Development in Childhood*. New York: The Dryden Press, 1955.
2. Becker, H. S., and J. W. Carper. "The Development of Identification with an Occupation," *American Journal of Sociology*, LXI (January, 1956), 289-98.
3. Brim, O. G., Jr. "The Parent-Child Relation as a Social System: I. Parent and Child Roles," *Child Development*, XXVIII (September, 1957), 343-64.
4. Brim, O. G., Jr. "Family Structure and Sex Role Learning by Children: A Further Analysis of Helen Koch's Data,"

Sociometry, XXI (March, 1958), 1-16.
5. Cattell, R. B. *Personality and Motivation Structure and Measurement*. New York: World Book Co., 1957.
6. Cooley, C. H. *Human Nature and the Social Order*. New York: Charles Scribner's Sons, 1902.
7. Cottrell, L. S. "The Analysis of Situational Fields in Social Psychology," *American Sociological Review*, VII (June, 1942), 105-17.
8. Goffman, E. *The Presentation of Self in Everyday Life*. Edinburgh: University of Edinburgh Social Science Research Center, 1956.
9. Gross, N. C., W. S. Mason, and A. W. McEachern. *Explorations in Role Analysis: Studies of the School Superintendency Role*. New York: John Wiley & Sons, Inc., 1958.
10. Hall, C. S., and G. Lindzey. *Theories of Personality*. New York: John Wiley & Sons, Inc., 1957.
11. James, W. *Psychology*. New York: Henry Holt and Co., 1904.
12. Kuhn, M. H., and T. S. McPartland. "An Empirical Investigation of Self-Attitudes," *American Sociological Review*, XIX (January, 1954), 68-76.
13. McClelland, D. *Personality*. New York: The Dryden Press, 1951.
14. Mann, J. H. "Experimental Evaluations of Role Playing." *Psychological Bulletin*, LIII (May, 1956), 53, 227-34.
15. Merton, R. K. "The Role Set: Problems of Sociological Theory," *British Journal of Sociology*, VIII (June, 1957), 106-20.
16. Merton, R. K., G. G. Reader, and P. L. Kendall (eds.). *The Student Physician: Introductory Studies in the Sociology of Medical Education*. Cambridge: Harvard University Press, 1957.
17. Mullahy, P. (ed.). *The Contributions of Harry Stack Sullivan*. New York: Hermitage House, 1952.
18. Murray, H. A. *Explorations in Personality*. New York: Oxford University Press, 1938.
19. Parsons, T. *The Social System*. Glencoe: The Free Press, 1951. Chaps. 3, 6, 7.
20. Parsons, T. and R. F. Bales. *Family, Socialization and Interaction Process*. Glencoe: The Free Press, 1955.
21. Stolz, L. *Father Relations of War-Born Children*. Stanford: Stanford University Press, 1954.
22. Strauss, A. *The Social Psychology of George Herbert Mead*. Chicago: University of Chicago Press, 1956.

Section III

STATUS PROCESSES

In Part Two, we defined *social status* as "the evaluation of the characteristics of a given position relative to other positions with which it is compared." At that point our special concern was with the structural problem created when an individual simultaneously occupied two or more social positions with differently evaluated characteristics. Now, however, we wish to focus attention on social status viewed as process, specifically on the processes involved in the emergence of a status structure.

Clearly, the central process involved in the creation and perpetuation of a status structure is the evaluation process. But in order for this process to be carried out, other prior processes are required, including differentiation and ranking. Also, in order for the evaluation process to be meaningful to participants, something of value must be contingent on its outcome; in short, we must also be concerned with a reward process. Thus, to consider status as a process is to attempt to understand not one but four interrelated processes: differentiation, ranking, evaluation, and rewarding. This is the view of Tumin, who in Reading 14 provides us with a careful description of the operation and interrelation of these four status processes. Let us briefly examine this view of status as process and then consider in more detail some of the problems and issues that are associated with this perspective.

The Subprocesses of Social Status   We will view social status as a set of position characteristics that are differentiated, ranked, evaluated, and rewarded.[1] As previously noted, positions may be informally or formally defined. In the former case, positions are based on and coterminous with the characteristics attributed to a particular individual, so that it is impossible to separate position and individual; in the latter case, positions are defined independently of individual characteristics, and characteristics may be attributed to individuals because of their occupancy of a given position.[2]

Individuals possess, or may have attributed to them by others, certain *characteristics*, such as physical attributes, abilities, interests, or possessions. Status processes do not involve any and all such characteristics but involve only those that *differentiate* among individuals. Obviously, then, status processes do not operate on the characteristics that all persons share in common (for example,

---

[1]In addition to Tumin's views reprinted in this book, our conception of social status as process has been greatly influenced by the work of Bo Anderson, Joseph Berger, Bernard P. Cohen, and Morris Zelditch, Jr. See, for example, the series of articles by these authors on status processes in Berger, Zelditch, and Anderson (eds.), *Sociological Theories in Process*, Vol. 1, Boston: Houghton Mifflin, 1966.

[2]See pp. 65–66.

having two eyes) or on characteristics of a sort that no persons possess (for example, having green skin), although the latter often becomes the basis for imaginary status distinctions in science fiction novels. Of the great number of characteristics that differentiate among individuals, some are selected as a basis for the comparative *ranking* of individuals. As Tumin uses this term, ranking does not involve an evaluation of whether it is "good" or "bad" to have the characteristic but involves only an assessment of whether the person possesses the characteristic and, if so, to what extent. Some characteristics are such as to permit careful measurement and permit the making of elaborate distinctions (for example, an individual's height or his wealth); others permit only very rough comparisons among individuals (for example, how wise or fair or kind one person is in contrast with another).

Characteristics that are differentiated and ranked, however, do not become involved in status processes until they are *evaluated*. Individuals must believe that it is better to possess the characteristic than not to possess it (or vice versa if the characteristic is negatively evaluated) or that it is better to possess more rather than less of it, before the characteristic becomes a factor in a status process. Why do some differentiated characteristics give rise to differential evaluations? In general, we may say that evaluations of characteristics are based on differential expectations for the behavior of those possessing the characteristic. That is, beliefs about the goodness or badness of possessing a given characteristic are based on beliefs about how a person with this characteristic will behave in a given situation. Individuals possessing the valued characteristic (or more of the valued characteristic) will be expected by others to behave better or more adequately under given circumstances than persons lacking the valued characteristic. We will return in a moment to consider further the nature of these beliefs or expectations and the way in which they arise and to give some examples of this process at work. Let us first, however, comment briefly on the final subprocess.

We have said that associated with some differentiated characteristics are certain beliefs about how persons possessing these characteristics will behave and that these beliefs give rise to the differential evaluation of these characteristics. But there is another class of beliefs that comes to be associated with these characteristics: beliefs about how *rewards* should be distributed. Again, generally speaking, individuals will believe that a larger share of whatever rewards there are to distribute should go to the individuals possessing the valued characteristics or possessing more of the valued characteristics than to the individuals not possessing the characteristics or the individuals having less of them. We shall have more to say about status and the reward process in a later part of this book. (Reading 30)

Characteristics, Position Assignment, and Status Processes   To this point, our discussion of status processes has been quite general and abstract. We will attempt to make these ideas somewhat more comprehensible by relating this discussion to our earlier comments on positions and roles and by considering some examples of these processes at work.

In our discussion of the concepts position and role, an important issue was neglected; namely, how are individuals assigned to positions? We can now suggest that one important basis for position assignment are the characteristics an individual possesses or is believed to possess. Thus, a boy becomes a candidate for the position of king by being born at the right time in the right family; and a boy becomes a candidate for the position of medical doctor by going to the right kind of school and acquiring certain knowledge and skills that are certified by an examination. From these examples, it is clear that certain of these characteristics are *ascribed* in the sense that their existence is independent of the will or effort of the individual exhibiting them, for example, the sex, age, and race of an individual or the wealth of his parents. Other characteristics are *achieved* in that they represent accomplishments of the individual, things he has done or has gained, such as a college degree or the special skills necessary to practice some occupation. Still others represent combinations of ascribed and achieved characteristics. An individual's IQ, for example, appears to be a product of both his innate intellectual capacities and the kinds of experiences and training he has had.

But what precisely is the relationship between an individual's characteristics— whether achieved or ascribed—and his entry into a social position? Some individual characteristics are regarded as sufficiently important that they become the basis for the creation of a social position. Which characteristics these are varies somewhat from culture to culture, but most groups recognize race, sex, certain age ranges, and kinship as defining membership in discrete social positions[3] That is, the mere fact that a person is a male or that he is born to a certain family "locates him in a system of social relationships" and becomes the basis for certain expectations being directed at him by others that define what attributes he should have or how he is to behave. Other characteristics when considered in combination also define social positions. A particular combination of characteristics possessed by an individual that is recognized and defined as salient by his group determines his informal social position in that group. Formal positions are also usually defined by specific combinations of characteristics; for example, the position of physician may be defined as including such characteristics as a certain level of training, various technical skills and knowledge, certain attitudes held toward patients. These formal position characteristics serve as the basis for recruiting and selecting certain individuals— individuals believed to possess the appropriate characteristics—to fill the position.[4]

Even so, a question of enormous sociological interest is left unresolved by this discussion; namely, why do certain characteristics become the basis for position assignment rather than others? Why in this society, for example, do we place much greater emphasis on the age of a person than on his height, or on his skin color rather than the color of his eyes? Our answer must be general and incomplete, and it is hoped that the reader will not be completely satisfied with it. We would suggest that the association of certain individual characteristics with certain sets of expectations reflects beliefs learned by people in interaction over long periods of time. Thus, an individual observes that a

[3]See Kingsley Davis, *Human Society*, New York: Macmillan, 1949, pp. 97–113; and Talcott Parsons, "Age and sex in the social structure of the United States," *American Sociological Review*, 7 (1942), 604–614.
[4]This problem is also briefly discussed in Reading 6, pp. 67–68.

person possessing a certain characteristic behaves in a certain manner. If this correspondence is observed several times, the characteristic and the behavior become associated in the mind of the observer. Gradually, over time, what is observed becomes what is expected in the sense of anticipation, and what is anticipated becomes what is expected, now in a normative sense. Once such associations between characteristics and behavior have developed in the mind of the observer, he can, of course, communicate his beliefs to others who, if they accept his statements, will not bother to go through the same learning process on their own.

Such beliefs are *prejudices* in the strict meaning of that term—they are assessments made of an individual's characteristics and prejudgments as to how he will behave and, hence, how he is to be treated. (Recall in this connection Eliza Doolittle's pungent comment in Shaw's *Pygmalion* that "the difference between a lady and a flower girl is not how she behaves, but how she's treated."[5]) Such role expectations, once established, are very difficult to break down, as is so clearly illustrated in the case of expectations associated with racial characteristics. One important reason why these expectations are so stable is that they are self-fulfilling in character. We expect persons to behave in a certain way and, by assigning them to appropriate positions in the social structure, virtually guarantee that they will in fact behave in the expected manner. Some individuals in this society, for example, believe that Negroes are incapable of filling occupational positions that demand complex skills and intelligence. They assign Negroes to menial positions and prevent their access to training experiences and then point to the jobs that Negroes hold as evidence of their inferiority.[6]

This last illustration should make abundantly clear that we are dealing not simply with positions and roles but with statuses—not simply with expectations but also with evaluations. Characteristics provide cues that enable us to develop behavioral expectations; we react to these expectations and in so doing project our evaluation back onto the characteristics and the individual holding them.

We can carry our examination of this process one step further. We have already stressed in our earlier remarks on socialization the importance of others' expectations in this process. Because an individual, from his interactions with others, obtains an image of who he is and what his value is, expectations and evaluations directed at an individual by others over a period of time come to be internalized by the individual so that he tends to evaluate himself as others evaluate him. This process, too, can be illustrated by the situation of the American Negro.

A study conducted by Clark and Clark in the early 1940s asked 250 Negro children to describe and express their preference for white and black dolls.[7] The participating children were drawn from both the South and the North and

---

[5]George Bernard Shaw, *Pygmalion*, London: Constable, 1931, p. 269.

[6]This process by which behavior following from a set of beliefs causes behavior that in turn justifies the original beliefs is scrutinized by Robert K. Merton in his brilliant essay "The self-fulfilling prophecy," *Social Theory and Social Structure* (rev. ed.), Glencoe, Ill.: Free Press, 1957, pp. 421–436.

[7]Kenneth B. Clark and Mamie P. Clark, "Racial identification and preference in Negro children," in Eleanor E. Maccoby, Theodore M. Newcomb, and Eugene L. Hartley (eds.), *Readings in Social Psychology* (rev. ed.), New York: Holt, Rinehart and Winston, Inc., 1958, pp. 602–611.

ranged in age from three to seven years. A fairly high knowledge of racial differences was indicated by the fact that 94 percent of the subjects chose the correct doll when they were asked to give the experimenter the "white" doll, 93 percent chose correctly the "colored" doll, and 72 percent chose correctly the "Negro" doll. However, when asked to give the experimenter the doll that "looks like you," only 66 percent of the children identified themselves with the black doll. Further,

Approximately two-thirds of the subjects indicated . . . that they like the white doll "best," or that they would like to play with the white doll in preference to the colored doll, and that the white doll is a "nice" doll . . . . Fifty-nine percent of these children indicated that the colored doll "looks bad," while only 17 percent stated that the white doll "looks bad" . . . . Only 38 percent of the children thought that the brown doll was a "nice color," while 60 percent of them thought that the white doll was a "nice color". . . .[8]

There were no differences in knowledge of racial differences between Northern and Southern children; however, with respect to racial preferences a clear difference emerged:

. . . southern children in segretaged schools are less pronounced in their preference for the white doll, compared to the northern children's definite preference for this doll. Although still in a minority, a higher percentage of southern children, compared to northern, prefer to play with the colored doll or think that it is a "nice" doll.[9]

These regional differences in attitude provide considerable support for the view that an individual's attitude toward himself is influenced by the attitudes of others toward him. The argument is as follows:

1. An individual comes to share at least to some extent the attitudes that others hold toward him.

2. The most important others are those with whom the individual regularly interacts.

3. The attitudes of many whites toward Negroes are negative; and whites tend to see their own color as preferable.

4. The more Negroes interact with and are exposed to whites, the more they tend to share their attitudes—in particular, attitudes toward themselves.

5. Hence, Southern Negroes in segregated schools having less contact with whites are less likely to reflect the prejudices and color preferences of whites than are Northern Negroes who are exposed more to and interact more frequently with whites.

The view that much of the black man's burden and the current difficulties in the relations between the races in this country can be viewed as status problems—as problems in expectations associated with characteristics and the consequent evaluation of those characteristics—is carefully developed by Bernard P. Cohen in Reading 15. His discussion provides a concrete application of these concepts to a highly significant social problem area.

Cohen's discussion shows how the operation of status processes can unjustly determine the social fate of individual who possess negatively valued charac-

[8]Clark and Clark, p. 608.
[9]Clark and Clark, p. 610.

teristics. This is not to suggest, however, that we could or should do away with social expectations and with the assignment of individuals to positions. The fact that such expectations often lock certain kinds of individuals into certain kinds of positions is a problem that requires corrective actions, but a person must not too quickly conclude that the system should be demolished because it has some unfavorable consequences. For the simple truth is that social life as we know it would be impossible without the assignment of persons to positions and without the social expectations that become linked to those positions. Such expectations provide us with guides to the behavior of others with whom we must deal and, consequently, with guides for our own behavior in a multiplicity of social situations.

But if social categorization and position assignment is a necessity of social existence, what of invidious comparisons among these positions? Is inequality resulting from status processes also a requirement of social life? This question has been much debated in the social sciences, with no definitive answers forthcoming. In later discussions of status processes as they operate in small groups, organizations, and society at large, we will see that status distinctions do appear to play an important role in the functioning and maintenance of social units. But we should always keep in mind that it is inappropriate to argue that a given process is necessary because it performs certain important functions for a social unit unless we can demonstrate that no other element could conceivably perform the same functions. As might be supposed, it is exceedingly difficult to establish such an assertion. Hence, the argument rages with the defenders of status inequality pointing to the positive benefits of differential evaluations and differential rewards while the doubters ask whether these benefits could not be obtained in some less painful and costly manner.

14 Stratification Processes

Melvin M. Tumin

If systems of stratification are ancient, universal, and basically alike in their main features, there must be some common social processes that bring such systems into being, shape them, and maintain them. Four such processes can be identified: (1) differentiation, (2) ranking, (3) evaluation, and (4) rewarding.

THE PROCESS OF DIFFERENTIATION AND RANKING

Differentiation of Statuses

Status differentiation is the process by which social positions, such as father, mother, teacher, and employer, are defined and distinguished from one an-

Melvin M. Tumin, *Social Stratification: The Forms and Functions of Inequality*, pp. 19–42 (excerpts). © 1967 Reprinted by permission of the author and Prentice-Hall, Inc., Englewood Cliffs, N.J.

other by assigning to each a distinctive role—a set of rights and responsibilities. This process is indispensable to any society if it is to continue more than a generation, for to continue, a number of basic tasks must be performed satisfactorily, and hence in turn, responsibility for them must be assigned in such a way as to insure their completion. Among such tasks are the reproduction, care, and socialization of children. These three functions could each be assigned to a separate social unit; or each to several social units; or all to the same unit; and one could contrive many other combinations of these possibilities. But the tasks must be ascribed to *someone*, so that it is known who is responsible for what.

Status differentiation operates most effectively when (1) tasks are clearly defined; (2) lines of authority and responsibility for roles are clearly distinguished; (3) effective mechanisms exist for recruiting and training a sufficient number of persons to assume the statuses; and (4) adequate sanctions, including rewards and punishments, exist to motivate individuals to conscientious performance and to restrain them from indifference to or deviation from minimum standards of performance.

Most important social roles would probably not be performed, or at least not in the ways considered desirable and effective, if responsibilities were not formally assigned through the process of status differentiation. For roles are not in any sense simple or automatic responses. Rather, they are complex matters that involve a good deal of teaching, learning, motivating, and sanctioning. Thus, while it might be safely assumed that, in the absence of any conventions, men and women would engage indiscriminately in sexual relations, one could not safely assume that in the absence of such conventions men and women would enter into sustained and enduring relationships, keep newborn children alive, and

bear the costs and pains of raising them to maturity.

Even if one could be sure men and women would develop *some* pattern of family life and child rearing, one could not be confident that the desired pattern, whatever it may be, would be followed if there were no rules, procedures, and instructions. This is evident in the diversity of ways in which societies perform familial tasks throughout the world. Each of these ways of performing the familial tasks represents a "natural" choice by a human group from the range of possibilities; and presumably, if there were no deliberate efforts to foster one pattern against others, a random assortment of patterns would probably be found in each society.

Ranking of Statuses

Once statuses have been differentiated on the basis of their roles, it becomes possible to compare them. One special kind of comparison involves *ranking*. Statuses can be ranked on three criteria:

1. *Personal characteristics* such as intelligence, beauty, or strength that are believed to be required of anyone who is to play the role effectively.
2. *Trained skills and abilities* that are believed to be required to discharge a role efficiently, for example, manual dexterity, knowledge of the law, command over scholarly literature, or the ability to saw wood and hammer nails.
3. *Consequences or effects* upon others and upon society at large of the role, e.g., actors provide entertainment, judges ensure justice, policemen preserve order. These consequences are sometimes called the "social functions" of the role.

One major purpose of such ranking is to facilitate the search for the right people for the right positions. By specifying tasks in terms of levels of skill and talent required, amount of education necessary, or personal qualities desired, it becomes more possible to find and allocate manpower rationally and to train this manpower efficiently.

Though it is often technically difficult to measure accurately the extent to which persons possess certain qualities or skills and the extent that roles serve their intended functions, at least in theory it is possible to rank statuses on these kinds of criteria, even if only roughly in terms of more or less, or higher or lower.

Ranking does not involve an evaluative judgment of "better" or "worse." A role may be judged more difficult than another, may require more muscular dexterity, or may provide more entertainment without, however, implying any judgment of comparative "value." Such evaluation depends on what society regards as valuable. Though an actor may provide greater entertainment than a Supreme Court judge, the judge will be valued as more important when justice is considered more important than entertainment. Like differentiation then ranking is value-neutral and different from evaluation. It is concerned primarily with questions of "more and less" rather than "better and worse."

To be sure, ranking and evaluation often correlate in very similar ways in different societies, but these common patterns of correlation are due to the presence of common values. Thus, the *amount* of nobility in one's lineage significantly determines one's evaluation as superior and inferior in all those societies where nobility of descent is considered important. But there are two separate steps here: The first is a ranking of the *amount* of nobility in the lineage, and the second is the judgment of how much *value* is to be ascribed to such lineage. That there is nothing *inherently* valuable

about noble origins is quite evident from the fact that during popular democratic revolutions, such as in the United States and in France in the 18th century, or the Russian Revolution in the 20th century, proof of noble origins was sometimes a passport to ostracism, exile, or death.

Ranking is in two ways a selective process. First, of all the statuses that are differentiated in any society, only some are selected for comparative ranking; second, of all criteria on which statuses could be ranked, only some are actually employed in the ranking process. In the United States today, for example, there is much more concern and attention devoted to ranking occupational statuses than to ranking family background or religious affiliation. This is evidence that considerably greater importance is ascribed to economic than to family roles. In sharp contrast is the case of nonliterate societies, where considerably greater attention is usually given to kinship roles, whereas economic roles are more or less taken for granted.

One could contend that in any society greatest emphasis will be given to those social tasks which ought, in the judgment of those who have the power to determine such matters, to be emphasized. This assertion differs from that of Marx and Engels by not insisting that economic power is always the ultimate power, or that economic interests are always the ultimate interests at stake. This somewhat broader view makes it possible to argue, for instance, that an organized church in medieval Europe was responsible for keeping religion at the center of social organization, without suggesting that the church's primary interests in doing so were economic. The dominant emphases in any society, we argue, will tend to reflect the interests of the dominant power structure of the society; sometimes the economic bases and interests of such a power structure may be relatively unimportant.

The presence of dominant emphases in every society is an undeniable fact of social organization, and important consequences for status differentiation and ranking are entailed therein. For by comparison with unemphasized institutions, status differentiation in the emphasized institutions is distinctive in the following five ways:

1. It tends to be more complex, in the sense that there are usually a larger number and wider variety of statuses.
2. Roles tend to be more precisely specified.
3. The range of expectable performance in any given status tends to be narrower.
4. There are some acknowledged methods of measuring the adequacy of role performance, even if only roughly.
5. The sanctions of reward for expectable performance and punishment for deviation or failure tend to be more precisely formulated, uniformly understood and applied, and generally more ample or severe.

Compare, for instance, the spheres of occupation and of family life in modern industrial societies: In the former, the roles are more complex, the task expectations more specifically stated, the limits of acceptable performace narrower, the emphasis on measurement of performance greater, and the sanctions more specific and uniform. So, too, we find that under these circumstances there is considerable emphasis placed upon the importance of comparative ranking of jobs in terms of a number of criteria—educational prerequisites, requirements of intelligence and skill, difficulty of performance. By contrast, in the family sphere all roles are considered equally important and equally difficult to perform and are held to require equal, even if different kinds of intelligence and skill. No presumption is made that different skills,

such as those of mother and father, can be ranked higher or lower than one another. Indeed, comparisons of this kind are considered illegitimate and disruptive, whereas in the occupational sphere they are considered essential.

The explanation of why some criteria are selectively emphasized must be sought in the organizing values guiding the productive process. Where these values, as in industrial societies, are concerned primarily with efficiency, productivity, and profitability, there is an understandable emphasis upon fitting people to their appropriate tasks and upon standardizing functions. Hence, there is a clear-cut effort to minimize individual differences, and questions of educational adequacy, skill, and talent become the paramount criteria in job definitions and comparisons. Under other sets of organizing values the emphasis might be dominantly upon "meaningfulness of work" for the employee, and the criteria of ranking would then be substantially different.

THE PROCESS OF EVALUATION

The third process of stratification—evaluation—involves assigning to various statuses different places on a scale of value or worthiness. The gradation of this scale may also be described in terms such as superior to inferior, better to worse, more to less distinguished, or as evoking more to less favorable public opinion. These terms denote major types of judgments involved in evaluations. Another synonym for evaluation is *invidious distinction,* which means making distinctions "such as to bring odium, unpopularity, or envious dislike."

The Action Correlates
of Evaluation

The judgments of the relative worth or value of statuses must be distinguished from the actions to which the evaluations give rise. Such actions constitute the *operational meaning* of evaluations insofar as they represent the kinds of things that one individual, A, is likely to do to or with an individual, B, whom he judges to be superior or more worthy than another individual, C. In such a situation, A may give more honor to B; or will prefer to associate with B; or will prefer to *be* like B rather than like C; or will be inclined to defer more to the opinions and wishes of B; or will feel more honored if he is acknowledged as an equal by B; or will be more concerned about B's opinions of him; and, correlatively, A will be more ashamed if B thinks poorly of him than if C does and will more easily permit or be glad to have his children intimately associated with and marry those of B than those of C.

Two Dimensions of Evaluation: Prestige and Preferability

PRESTIGE   Several different kinds of evaluational judgments need to be distinguished. The first, *prestige*, refers primarily to honor, and involves deferential and respectful behavior. The effect of prestige can be seen most clearly in situations where there are well established hierarchies of status. Thus, a parishoner accords more honor to and is more respectful of a bishop or a cardinal than of a priest or a minister. So, too, a private or corporal is more respectful and deferential to a general than to a colonel, and more to a colonel than to a captain or a major. Comparably in a corporate structure, a junior executive will ascribe more honor and manifest more deference and respect to the president than to a vice-president or a bureau chief.

PREFERABILITY   The second type of evaluational judgment is *preferability*. The attitudes here are suggested by terms such as "I would like to be like him," "I

would like my children to be like him," "I would like to be friends with that kind of person," and so forth. In these cases judgments of worthiness are blended with considerations of realistic possibilities and social comfort. One must distinguish between the kinds of fantasy— preference to be a lord, a president, a king, or a pope, without regard to whether such preferences may become realized—from one's realistic preferences for being like, associating with, or being friends with those whom one considers his own equals, or superior to himself in some modest degree.

The preferability evaluation of a status may differ significantly from its prestige evaluation. One may assign high prestige to an occupation such as surgeon, which requires profound knowledge of anatomy, but at the same time express a very marked personal preference for an occupation that does not require such exacting skills. Preference and prestige are likely to coincide only at those points where the ranked criterion is in fact possessed by or is realistically attainable by the evaluator. The possible combinations of prestige and preferability are as follows:

	Prestige	Preference
1.	High	High
2.	High	Low
3.	Low	High
4.	Low	Low

The four possibilities indicated in the list above represent theoretical possibilities when only high-low levels are designated. One can always increase the number of such possibilities by distinguishing three or more levels of prestige and preferability rather than just two.

The Scope of Evaluation: Role-Specific Evaluation

It is important to distinguish between two major objects or foci of evaluation: one, a particular status or role, and two, generalized social standing. The distinction here is one of the scope of the focus of judgments.

In the first instance, the focus is a particular status and role, and the evaluation may therefore be termed role-specific. The criteria are precisely the same as those in the ranking of statuses: *personal qualities, trained skills* and *capacities*; and *functions, consequences,* or *effects* of the role on the society at large.

Role-specific evaluation includes assigning value, merit, or worth to a status because of the extent to which it manifests one or more of these criteria—skill, wisdom, or social service. In short, to the neutral judgment in ranking there is now added an assessment of the comparative value or worthiness of the rank.

Generalized Evaluation or the Judgment of Over-all Social Standing

The second major focus of evaluation is the *over-all social standing* of an individual. We refer here to an individual's place in a hierarchy of social worth based on some kind of *cumulative* assessment of all the statuses he occupies and the rewards they characteristically receive (i.e., property, power, and psychic gratifications). Sociological researchers have struggled for many years without much notable success to develop a satisfactory model of evaluation of over-all social standing. We persist in this effort, however, because we realize that in our social relationships we judge and evaluate each other and determine our respective acceptibilities, *not* in terms of occupation, income, or educational achievement alone, but rather in terms of a mixture of these and many other elements: sex, age, skin color, religion,

national origin, marital status, family background, and so on. We then add these up into some over-all score without, however, being certain of what factors we took into account, how much weight we assigned to each, why we included these and not other factors, and why we assigned the weights to each that we did.

Sociological research and theory have much to explore regarding the ways in which various factors contribute to over-all social evaluation. At the same time, enough is now known about how any given variable such as age, sex, or race is generally viewed in this society and in others to permit us to make admittedly rudimentary but significant assessments; for example, that in American society one is generally considered better, superior, or more worthy if he is

White rather than Negro
Male rather than Female
Protestant rather than Catholic or Jewish
Educated rather than Uneducated
Rich rather than Poor
White Collar rather than Blue Collar
Of Good Family Background rather than
   Undistinguished Family Origin
Young rather than Old
Urban or Suburban rather than Rural
   Dwelling
Of Anglo-Saxon National Origin rather
   than Any Other
Native-Born rather than of Foreign Descent
Employed rather than Unemployed
Married rather than Divorced

These choices or preferences are most easily made one pair at a time; any time we try to assess standing on the basis of more than one criterion, the complexities multiply horrendously. Moreover, there is considerable variability in the assessment of these criteria by different segments of the population. In general, members of any given group are likely to evaluate the distinguishing features of their group somewhat more highly than will others. Thus, though Negroes may be fully aware of the White man's low evaluation of "Negroness" as against "Whiteness," they do not publicly agree with such a low evaluation. This difference between the level of self-evaluation and one's evaluation by others probably applies for the entire list of criteria tabulated above. Enough has been said to indicate the complexity of both conceptualization and measurement of over-all social standing, a complexity due to the many different criteria involved, the different weights assigned to each, and the differences between evaluators. At the same time, since the judgment of over-all social standing is critically important in the determination of social relationships, life-chances, and life-styles, no student of social stratification can afford to ignore this level of evaluation. . . .

The Third Dimension of Evaluation

A distinction was made earlier in this chapter between two dimensions of evaluation, one called *prestige*, and the other, *preferability*. In considering occupational statuses in modern industrial societies, however, it is useful to distinguish still a third kind of evaluation that may be expressed by the term *popularity*. There are numerous occupations that enjoy considerable public attention, fame, or notoriety, but do not command real prestige or honor in the same sense that a Supreme Court judge does. These are hardly ever likely to be judged as preferable or desirable for oneself or one's children, simply because such occupations are either realistically seen as quite out of reach, or are considered undesirable.

The introduction of the dimension of popularity, and the increase therefore to a threefold distinction of dimensions of evaluation, has a number of important advantages. First, since we have no standard, acceptable procedures for adding these three types of values together—prestige, popularity, and preferability—nor any ways of computing the relative importance and weight of such diverse criteria as education, income, social importance, skill, attendance figures, sales records, and the like, the suggested distinction between prestige, popularity, and preferability is valuable to the degree in which we can thereby avoid engaging in these unjustifiable, social arithmetics.

An additional advantage of distinguishing three dimensions of evaluation lies in the fact that statuses often enjoy high quotients of honor and low quotients of property rewards, and vice versa. In the absence of a distinction between prestige and popularity, we tend to wonder how a movie star or an athlete may earn astronomically more than the President of the United States. Such asymmetry is sometimes interpreted as revealing internal contradictions in the value systems of the rewarding public. But these allocations of different rewards are disturbing only if we assume that rewards *ought* to be symmetrical or correlated with all forms of evaluation. If one recognizes, however, that property rewards can be and often are allocated in accordance with popularity or market value, rather than with honor, and that the scale of property rewards connected with honor may be much more modest than that connected with fame and popularity, then the sense of asymmetry disappears.

We see, too, with the aid of this distinction, that the determination of the level of property rewards is often a separate matter from the determination of popularity or prestige quotients. The salaries of government officials are determined in significantly different ways from those of crooners or boxers. The former are judged by criteria such as social importance and skills. The latter, by contrast, tend to be calculated on the basis of the returns to private employers, impresarios, or managers of the stars, predicated on the ability of the stars to command audiences or purchasers of their various products.

A final advantage of the threefold distinction of prestige, preferability, and popularity lies in the increased possibilities of sound measurement of evaluation. If we are concerned with prestige, our questions then center around the amount of honor, deference, and respect that respondents feel a status properly commands. If, by contrast, it is popularity we seek to measure, then we use various other means to estimate the kind and intensity of desire expressed by respondents to see or hear such persons perform their roles. Here we would find attendance figures and sales records most useful. Finally, if we are interested in the preferability dimension, we address our questions to the frequency and intensity with which respondents desire and seek the status, both for themselves and for their children. In each case, we measure a different attitude or orientation, and in each case we investigate the basis for the attitude. Social evaluation is obviously, then, a complex matter involving both different *kinds of value* and different *criteria* or grounds on which any value is assigned. . . .

THE PROCESS OF REWARDING

The fourth process involved in stratification is that of rewarding, whereby statuses which have been differentiated, ranked, and evaluated are allocated various amounts of the good things in life. In every society there are rules or norms that determine how rewards will be dis-

tributed. These rules can be very variable and operate so that large portions of a population experience extreme deprivation while others live in relative comfort or luxury. Or, they can call for relatively equal allocation to all. *Some* inequality in rewards is, of course, characteristic of every known society. Equality is approached most closely in those societies where the share of rewards that any individual receives is determined largely by his demonstrated *need*, rather than by other criteria. The greatest inequality, by contrast, is reached in societies where the elite in power and their ideology favor the notion of unrestricted competition, with minimal official control of the supply of goods and services; an individual's power determines the rewards he will receive, and the result is normally one of extreme inequality. The modern welfare state represents a middle point between the extremes of inequality and equality.

An important distinction must be made between scarce and abundant rewards. In theory, rewards like pleasure, love, respect, and freedom are abundant, if not limitless. The amount of these rewards that a person receives is not restricted or reduced in any way by the amount that another person attains. In general, these abundant rewards are spiritual or psychic rather than material, and are intrinsic rather than external in that they are secured *in the process* of performing roles. It has sometimes been argued that such abundant psychic gratifications are not useful as rewards since the desirability of a good or service increases in proportion to its scarcity. But as a rule this is patently untrue; some of the most valued things in life—love, happiness, and freedom—are in principle abundant almost without restriction. When, however, certain highly desired goods and services are also notably scarce, then their distribution becomes a serious problem. Social stratification becomes relevant in this area of desired, scarce rewards, for it is concerned precisely with the unequal distribution of desired rewards.

Rewards can be classified under three general headings: (1) *property*, or rights and responsibilities over goods and services; (2) *power*, or the ability to secure one's ends, even against opposition; (3) *psychic gratification*, any nonmaterial resource or response from others that brings contentment, well-being, or pleasure.

Property

Property is relatively easy to measure if we are willing to use standard money equivalents for its many different forms. In so doing we can compare the property rewards of various statuses, investigate their correlations with other factors, and analyze their range of consequences. Normally students of stratification simplify matters even further by using only some forms of property, such as current money income, as the unit of measurement and comparison. This has advantages, for it is relatively simple to collect reasonably accurate data on income and to use these incomes to compare general inequalities in property, even though we know that the wealthiest portions of a population possess much more property than is reflected in their salaried incomes alone.

A widely varying feature in different societies is the process by which property is distributed. In some societies a totally centralized authority determines the property rewards that any status can receive and insures uniformity of reward at the various ranks and levels. In other societies, such as those described by the terms free enterprise or laissez-faire, the amount of property reward any status receives tends to depend predominantly on mechanisms of the market, involving

some combination of the scarcity of, and the demand for, the services performed by the holder of a status.

Power is, of course, a crucial factor in determining the variations in rewards. Thus when workers, whether privately or publicly employed, have organized themselves into unions or associations, they are usually able to secure considerably higher wages than those paid to their unorganized peers. In fact, one may say that power is the single most important factor in any decision regarding property rewards; it may come from organization, from controlled scarcity of supply, from control over the instruments of production, from legislation, or from a variety of other sources. But in the last analysis, it is power that does determine what the level of reward is going to be.

Power

A second major type of reward in every society is *power*. There is no satisfactory way to measure how much power a status receives as reward, or how much an individual or group possesses. Power is not necessarily a more complex variable than property; at least the definitions of the terms do not suggest any greater complexity. Rather, those concerned with analyzing and measuring power have not been as willing to accept certain shorthand indices such as money, which serves in the measurement of property. The absence of a standard measure of power does not prevent us, however, from making certain important observations about this reward. It is first important to differentiate the power that a person requires to discharge his role responsibilities from the power he receives as a *reward* for discharging the role. The first type may be termed *role-specific* power, to distinguish it from the second, *reward*-power.

Inequalities in an individual's role-specific power may have either a great deal or virtually nothing to do with how much reward-power he also receives. All socialist societies, for example, insist in principle on dissociating these two types of power and on dissociating all role-specific characteristics from the reward system. Thus in the Israeli *kibbutz* there are great inequalities in role-specific power, but there is also a correlative insistence on equality of property and power *rewards*. The distinction here is between the inequalities inherent in the role-requirements and the inequalities in external rewards, whose justification may depend in part on role differences but often lies elsewhere.

A second important distinction is that between *personal* and *social* power. *Personal* power refers to our ability to shape our private life as we see fit. Such power includes the choice of working or not working, the allocation of our private and public time in accordance with our own preference, and the pursuit of a desired style of life or service, including leisure and luxuries. If most culturally sanctioned private life goals are purchasable with money, then in distributing property in unequal amounts a society is also distributing private power unequally.

Social power has two major dimensions. The first refers to our ability to realize our own ends in the network of statuses in which our own status is located. This may be a government bureaucracy, a community organization, or a corporate structure. Power in such networks depends primarily upon the amount of formal authority, i.e., role-specific power, to which our position entitles us, though it is characteristic of many bureaucracies that different persons in the same position exercise different amounts of power. The second dimension of social power is an individual's ability to shape the general social policy of his society in conformity with his personal beliefs and interests. Who in a society decides social policies and who

can implement these? Social scientists have investigated in considerable detail the role in decision-making of trade associations, trade unions, professional societies, special interest blocs, and the like, and they have made inquiries about the amount of influence that such groups wield over public policy.

Psychic Gratification

The third major type of reward allocated to statuses is *psychic gratification*. In this category are included all rewards not classifiable as property or power; while power and property can yield such psychic gratification, they are neither defined nor measured in terms of it. Sources of psychic gratification are numerous and varied and include such factors as honor, security, autonomy, freedom from schedules, creative satisfaction on the job, and the like. Some of these factors are admittedly more difficult to measure than others, but only because efforts to devise sound measurement of them have been late in developing.

The category of psychic gratification has a number of characteristics justifying its inclusion as one of the three major types of rewards. First, such gratifications often are as intensely desired and sought as the rewards of property and power. Second, inequalities in these rewards often are as consequential as inequalities in property and power. The absence of security, honor, or autonomy can have serious effects. Third, psychic gratifications exert an influence on the distribution of property and power, just as these in turn shape the distribution of psychic gratification. Thus the prestige of an occupation or the safety given by security and tenure can influence in diverse ways the property rewards of an occupation. Fourth, the intensity with which the rewards of psychic gratification are sought is as much a matter of cultural patterning as in the cases of property and power rewards. We learn to value different kinds of rewards; these rewards themselves do not have any inherent qualities that make them naturally more desirable than others. Fifth, if the role of psychic gratifications is as culturally patterned as the role of property or power, then it follows that these gratifications are as likely to vary in their significance and importance for different segments of the population, and from one society to another, as are the various components of property and power.

Having now specified five ways in which the dynamics of rewards in psychic gratification resemble those of property and power, it is important to recall one very significant difference, namely, that in the case of rewards such as honor, esteem, creative satisfaction, or "good" social relations, there is considerable room for subjective perceptions, so that an individual may to some extent define his own situation in accordance with his own wishes, or needs; he may avoid confronting the objective reality of his situation.

15   Status and Conflict: A Sociological Perspective on the Urban Race Problem

Bernard P. Cohen

One of the most serious problems confronting us today is the urban race problem. Sociologists are frequently called upon as experts on race relations or urban problems, but as a sociologist I am an expert in neither area. Indeed, I myself have never done research dealing directly with race relations or urban problems. Nevertheless, as a social scientist, part of my role is to apply general principles of sociology and social psychology to these major social problems. To me it is very clear that sociology has some important general principles that are applicable, and I want to present some of these principles and point out their implications.

Before getting into general principles, I want to make clear my view of what social science can and cannot do in dealing with the urban race problem. As the problems of our society intensify, the community looks more and more to the social sciences for solutions to these problems. They ask us for recipes and hope for panaceas. Society is somewhat impatient with us when we can provide neither, and social scientists often apologize defensively for their lack of answers by pointing to the youthfulness and immaturity of social science. I suggest that both the petitioners for answers and the social science apologists misunderstand the situation. Social science cannot now and will never be able to supply recipes or panaceas. The application of social science knowledge to social problems will always be an artistic activity requiring the social engineer to have mastery of the scientific principles as well

Reprinted from *Stanford Today*, Summer/Autumn 1968, Series I, No. 24, pp. 10–14, with the permission of the author and publishers, Stanford University. © 1968 by the Board of Trustees of the Leland Stanford Junior University.

as intimate clinical familiarity with the problem situation to which he is applying these principles.

My field of interest as a sociologist is the area known as expectation theory. Research in this area has generated principles that, I believe, have something to say to the urban race problem. What I want to do here, primarily, is to analyze the phenomenon of Black Power from the point of view of expectation theory, and draw out some consequences of this analysis, consequences which are not as easily seen from another point of view. Although I will draw some of the implications of expectation theory, I would hope that readers with practical experience in race relations or urban problems will be able to see many more applications than I can present in a short article.

I want to analyze the phenomenon of Black Power from the point of view of the beliefs of whites and blacks. I want to consider one particular kind of belief which I will call an expectation. This is a belief about how a person will behave, based solely on some characteristic of the person, such as his race. I will talk about white expectations for Negroes and black expectations for whites.

The terms "black and "Negro" immediately pose problems in our analysis. The man who regards himself as black has different beliefs about himself from the man who regards himself as Negro. Indeed, the ideology of "blackness" is an effort to change the system of beliefs that has been associated with Negroes. The ideology of "blackness" has achieved considerable success among some segments of society in changing these beliefs, but I suspect that the majority of whites and the majority of nonwhites still operate largely in terms of the beliefs associated with Negro. Hence, first, I want to consider the beliefs associated with Negro and then contrast the developing belief system of black.

I will often abbreviate, using the term "expectation for self" or "expectation for other." When I talk about Negro self expectation, I mean a Negro's belief about his own behavior. Furthermore, I will be concerned with the evaluations of "self" and "other" which these expectations imply. For example, if I expect you to be dirty, and you know I hold this expectation, then you will believe (quite correctly) that I have a negative evaluation of you.

There are several points to make about expectations:

1. Expectations are associated with status. This is an idea that occurred to sociologists very early in the game. Back in 1921, Robert E. Park pointed out that status conceptions organize the way people deal with one another. In our language today, this means that two persons, aware only of each other's status, form expectations about one another and these expectations govern in large measure how they behave toward one another.

2. The second and most crucial point about expectations is their relativity. Expectations are always relative to the particular others with whom one is interacting and to the particular situation in which one finds himself. I will return to this relativity later.

3. Status conceptions operate to give people who know nothing about each other a basis for predicting how each will act and how each should react. In other words, when you know a great deal about a person with whom you are working, you know how to predict his actions and you know how to react to him. But if you know very little about that person, you make use of his status attributes in forming your judgments about him. In fact, in the absence of prior experience with another person, status attributes become crucial in determining what your expectations are for him. Let me em-

phasize that again. In the absence of firsthand, direct interaction with another person, status conceptions operate like prior knowledge and prior experience in providing a basis for interaction. They are a substitute for this prior experience.

4. My final general point is that expectations associated with statuses are very stable and very resistant to change, and that efforts to change these expectations or to break the connection between the status attribute and the expectation will generate considerable conflict and tension.

Now, the idea of expectation as I am using it differs markedly from the notion of self image. That the Negro has a low self image is an old idea, well recognized in discussions of self hatred, apathy, low aspiration; and portrayed in James Baldwin's facelessness and Ralph Ellison's *Invisible Man.* Even the source of this self image has been noted frequently. The late Malcolm X wrote, "The worst crime the white man has committed has been to teach us to hate ourselves."

But the idea of self image can be misleading, because it looks at the problem either in personality terms or in historical terms. A self image is something an individual carries around with him. The hypothesis that the Negro self image is one of passivity, withdrawal, and low competence is likely to be supported by observing a Negro interacting with a white. But it will often be vigorously rejected observing that same Negro interacting with other Negroes.

The fact that self image changes dramatically, depending on those with whom you compare yourself, was documented in a study done some 28 years ago in which Negro college students in the South were asked to estimate how well they would do on an intelligence test. The study had three different treatments. In one treatment, the Negro students were told how well a group of white college students did on the test. In a second treatment, the students were told how well a group of college students at their own Negro college had done on the test. Finally, in the third treatment, the Negro college students were told how Negro students in general had done on the test. The Negro students had the lowest self expectation for performance on this intelligence test when the comparison group was the group of white college students. They had markedly higher expectation for how well they would perform when the comparison group was Negro college students.[1]

Believing that the self image is fixed and determined by long-term historical events, like 300 years of slavery, is a conception that is completely inconsistent with the results of studies such as the one I have described. Expectations, however, are relative to others in the interaction, and, hence, are situationally determined. An expectation theory has no problem in handling a result such as the one I commented upon. Expectation theory predicts that the same Negro will have high self expectation with respect to some other Negroes and low self expectation with respect to some whites.

Because of the relativity of expectations, our analysis must concern the whole system of expectations that govern an interaction situation. What do I mean by a system? In the case of Negro-white interaction, there are four elements which affect one another. These are: Negro expectations for self, Negro expectations for whites; white expectations for self, white expectations for Negroes. These elements form a system because you cannot alter one element without having repercussions for the other three.

[1]Preston, M. G. and J. A. Bayton, "Differential effect of a social variable upon three levels of aspiration," *Journal of Experimental Psychology*, 1941, 29, 351-69.

Up to this point, I have been developing some rudimentary tools for analysis. Now I would like to apply these tools. My fundamental theses are four:

1. To make significant progress in solving urban racial problems, we must change Negro self expectations, Negro expectations for whites; white self expectations, white expectations for Negroes.

2. Black Power as a phenomenon, although it means many different things and varies in rhetorical styles from Rap Brown to Whitney Young, can be viewed as an attempt to change Negro self expectations—to substitute black self expectations for Negro self expectations —to substitute positive evaluations of self for negative ones. This is the significance of "black is beautiful." Now this view of Black Power is certainly not the view of Black Power held by most whites, for certainly all but a small minority of whites would grant the necessity of Negroes having a better view of themselves. Why then is Black Power a fearful specter to much of the white community? In part it is because of the methods used by Black Power advocates, in part it is because of a lack of understanding of Black Power by the white community, and in part it is the result of the failure of the Black Power advocates to appreciate the consequences of their actions.

3. In order to break down or change the expectations based on status conceptions, we must create situations where all four of these expectations are operating and where experience can contradict status conceptions.

4. These contradictory experiences will generate considerable conflict and tension, and the tensions must be controlled. Otherwise the status conceptions will be reinforced because the actors in the situation are so defensive that experience cannot contradict their status conceptions.

Let us discuss each of these ideas. It is a fact that most whites expect Negroes to be inferior. The difference between the racist and the liberal is that the racist believes that this inferiority is hereditary and immutable, while the liberal attributes the inferiority to generations of cultural deprivation, impoverishment, and exploitation. Unfortunately, the liberal's expectations communicate themselves to Negroes in Lady-Bountiful, patronizing attempts to uplift the Negro. We all have many of these expectations. Let me take one belief that most of us hold: When a Negro family moves into a white neighborhood, property values decline because Negroes do not keep up the property and whites move out. Available evidence suggests that this belief is false: property values often increase and they decline only under special circumstances. Even when there is panic selling by whites, the decline in property values is only temporary. A first step toward any progress is to recognize these beliefs in ourselves.

Many Negroes are aware that whites expect them to be inferior, and this molds their own feelings of inferiority. The low self expectation of Negroes generates low aspiration ("If I am no good, I can't possibly get a good job."), low motivation ("So why try?"), and low performance. Low performance confirms the white's expectations for the Negro and the Negro's expectations for himself.

These expectations are changing. Not all Negroes have low self expectations in interaction with whites. The best illustration of these changes comes from the black militants themselves. At every opportunity they distinguish between black men and Negroes, looking with disdain on those Negroes who refuse to be black men. Without the rise of black expectations, Black Power and civil rights protests could not exist. But white expectations of Negroes' inferiority and Negro low self expectations are still sufficiently widespread to be a serious problem.

The interplay of white expectations for Negroes and Negro self expectations is well illustrated in a series of experiments by Irwin Katz and his associates.[2] In these studies, Katz investigates the behavior of teams composed of two Negroes and two whites (or one Negro and one white). These teams work for several hours on a series of tasks, ranging from those involving manual skills to those involving intellectual skills—solving puzzles and group discussions. Katz finds that Negroes behaved compliantly toward white partners. "Negroes made fewer suggestions than whites, readily accepted the latter's proposals, and tended to ignore one another. These features of Negro behavior occurred even when the men were told that they would receive extra pay if they worked well as a team, that they all had higher ability than men in other teams."[3] [The same phenomenon] also occurred . . . despite careful matching of Negro and white teammates on ability and the use of tasks where white and Negro performances were objectively similar. Negroes who actually did as well as white teammates perceived their own performances as inferior. As Katz writes, "If Negroes see themselves as incompetent in mixed groups, they may expect to be judged similarly by white partners. Hence, when disagree-

ments occur, they tend to assume that their opinions are probably wrong, and even if not wrong, are likely to be rejected by the whites."[4]

These studies illustrate a very general phenomenon: the association of highly generalized expectations with different positions in a status hierarchy. Katz notes that the behavior of his teams can be viewed as behavior of low status people interacting with high status people. Indeed, in our laboratory we are studying the same status phenomenon with a different status attribute. And we find the same generalized expectations—we use teams composed of one college student and one high school student, and the high school students in our groups behave like Katz's Negro team members—they are highly compliant to the college student even though all they know about him is that he is a college student.

My principal argument is that we have to operate on all of these expectation elements to produce any lasting changes. It is possible to produce short-run changes in Negro self expectations, for example, by the exercise of power through violence. There is a short-run gratification and feeling of competence that results from setting fire to a building, but that short-run gratification does not create self expectations of competence and control of one's own fate.

It is a basic tenet of sociology that one's self expectations are determined in large part by the conception that others hold of him. To produce feelings of competence and fate-control requires experiences of success, where the others with whom you interact acknowledge that success. The power to destroy is not a success experience that others will readily acknowledge as success. Without the total elimination of the white man, there

[2]Katz, Irwin, Judith Goldston, and Lawrence Benjamin, "Behavior and Productivity in Bi-Racial Work Groups," Human Relations, 1958, 11, pp. 123–41.

Katz, Irwin, and Lawrence Benjamin, "Effects of White Authoritarianism in Bi-Racial Work Groups," Journal of Abnormal Social Psychology, 1960, 61, pp. 448–56.

Katz, Irwin, and M. Cohen, "The Effects of Training Negroes upon Cooperative Problem Solving in Bi-Racial Teams," Journal of Abnormal Social Psychology, 1962, 64, pp. 319–25.

[3]Katz and Cohen, op. cit., p. 319.

[4]Ibid.

is no way to prevent white expectations from having an impact on Negro self expectations, except in the very short run.

My second thesis is that Black Power and the ideology of blackness operate primarily on Negro self expectations. The ideology does this quite consciously and deliberately. Black Power ignores the problems created by white expectations for Negroes. When I have pointed this out to black militants, their response is, "That's your problem, not ours." Now Black Power has had many striking successes. Young blacks walk with much more pride than young Negroes did a few years ago. There is a more widespread belief that they can control their own destiny. There is an effort to progress in the ghetto; but without an attack on white expectations of Negro inferiority, the gains to self expectations are likely to be consumed in disillusion.

While I agree that changing white expectations must be done by whites, I don't agree that it is solely the white man's problem. The actions of Black Power have consequences for white expectations of Negroes that are no less important because they are unrecognized. Although we do not have data dealing directly with the effects of Black Power on white expectations, we can reasonably ask, "In what ways does Black Power operate to reinforce negative white expectations of Negroes?" A component in these negative white expectations of Negroes is the view of the Negro as primitive, violent, and to be feared. How far does Black Power go in reinforcing this view? How far does it go in preventing whites from seeing genuine gains in Negro self pride by obscuring those gains in a haze of defensive fear?

Finally, what are the consequences of Black Power for Negro expectations of whites? Many Negroes hold as stereotyp-ical beliefs about whites as whites hold of Negroes. Many Negroes fear and mistrust *all* whites. Negroes are to be forgiven if they are skeptical of the public relations claim that white society takes its social responsibilities seriously. They are to be forgiven if they read special meanings into slogans like "law and order," "preserve the neighborhood school," and "protect property rights." If they interpret urban renewal to mean Negro removal, and if they don't believe the "equal opportunity" employment signs, it is understandable. After years of being the last hired for the most menial jobs, regardless of qualifications, and the first fired, is it any wonder that the slogan of "no preferential treatment" falls on deaf ears for those who have seen a wide range of preferential treatments, ranging from veterans' bonuses to farm subsidies? Even when programs are genuinely concerned with solving some of these problems, should we be surprised that Negroes look for ulterior motives and, if they don't question the motives, they do suspect that Lady Bountiful is about to ride again?

The Black Power attack on Whitey, while it may build racial pride, also reinforces the expectations of distrust and fear. How far does this go in preventing Negroes from discriminating between those whites who are "out to get them" and those whites with whom they can genuinely and successfully work? This lack of discrimination blinds many Negroes to the interracial situations in which power can be shared and success can be mutual, and in which the defensiveness that preserves expectations of superiority and inferiority does not occur.

This brings me to my third thesis, that changing the entire system of expectations requires situations where all four elements are operating; namely, interracial, integrated situations. As long as whites and Negroes do not interact,

status conceptions of one another operate. No experience occurs to contradict
these status conceptions. It is precisely
the ghetto dweller who, by his separation,
prevents these contradictory experiences
from occurring to him or to the whites
who live in the white noose surrounding
the ghetto. The ghetto dweller's image of
the white is that of Exploiter. The white's
image of the ghetto dweller is that of
Mugger and Stick-up Man. Just as the
vast majority of ghetto dwellers are law-
abiding, decent, and struggling human
beings, the majority of whites are not
exploiters. But our expectations make us
lose sight of both these facts.

Insofar as Black Power urges separat-
ism, it prevents the kinds of contradictory experience that I hold essential.
Insofar as Black Power attempts to
blackmail concessions from the white
power structure through fear and violence, it reinforces rather than contra-
dicts white expectations about the primitive and violent nature of Negroes. Insofar as the white power structure makes
concessions in the face of such blackmail, it reinforces Negro expectations
that whites will yield only to violence. In
the long run, these kinds of actions do
not contradict the expectations of whites
and Negroes. There is no recognition on
the part of whites of Negro competence
and success. There is no recognition on
the part of Negroes that at least some
whites are willing to share power and are
not exploiters.

It is only those situations where power
can be shared, along with success or
failure in coping with problems, that
contradictions of the expectations of superiority and inferiority will take place.
Black Power, in the sense of traditional
political power and power at the bargaining table, can create such situations.

How do we create integrated situations
where power can be shared and success
can be mutual? Let us briefly consider the
public school system as an example. The
problem of *de facto* school segregation
has received considerable attention in the
last few years. The analysis I have presented indicates that *de facto* segregated
schools deny the possibility of expectation change. Various plans for ending *de
facto* segregation have been proposed
including changing school boundaries or
bussing students, but even if we could
end *de facto* segregation immediately
with a snap of the fingers, we would not
necessarily provide the kind of interaction
situation that would deal with the problems we have described. Simply mixing
white and Negro students in the same
building will not change the expectations
whites hold for Negroes, the expectations
Negroes hold for themselves, nor the
expectations Negroes hold for whites.
How schools are integrated is more important than the fact of integration.
Integrating schools by working *with* the
black community rather than by working
for them, working to uplift them or, worse
still, working *on* them, is far more important than handing down from on high
some mechanical plan for mixing bodies.
Planning for ending *de facto* segregation
should mean that all members of the
community have a say in and a stake in
doing something to solve the problem.

Such interaction situations, where the
participants are not defensive, are by no
means easy to create. Another study of
Katz's is germane here.[5] In a second
experiment, Katz tried to change Negro
self expectations. He did so by giving his
Negro subjects what he called "assertion
training." It is interesting that this assertion training was also given in a biracial
situation. He found that the Negro subjects who were given assertion training
did raise their expectations higher than
Negro subjects who were not given the

[5]Katz and Cohen, *op. cit.*

training. Katz's result would be pretty remarkable if the Negro expectations *were* the enduring consequence of 300 years of slavery. But an even more significant result of this study had to do with the white team members—the whites were much more hostile to the Negroes who had assertion training than to the Negroes who did not have this training and who continued to behave passively. Studies such as Katz's show both the resistance to change that white expectations for Negroes have and also the tensions generated by attempts to change expectations.

We are a long way from knowing how to deal with these kinds of tensions and conflicts, let alone how to prevent them. Indeed research concerned with producing changes in expectation with minimal conflict and tension is currently in progress at the Stanford School of Education.[6] But we do know that defensiveness insulates individuals from expectation change. Conflict may be an essential part of expectation change, but what distinguishes useful conflict from conflict that produces defensive blindness is a major question.

The implications of expectation theory, then, can be briefly summarized.

[6]Studies are now being conducted by Professor Elizabeth Cohen in connection with her project, "A Generalization of Status Characteristic Theory."

First, expectations are changeable in the short run. We don't have to wait another 300 years.

Second, to produce lasting change we must work on the whole system of expectation: Negro self expectations, Negro expectations for whites; white self expectations, white expectations for Negroes.

Third, the proponents and leaders of Black Power must concern themselves not only with black pride but also with consequences of their actions on white expectations for Negroes and Negro expectations for whites.

Fourth, in order to change the system of expectations, we must create truly integrated situations where experience can contradict status conceptions of Negro and white.

In order to change the system of expectations, we must recognize that much of the responsibility rests with white society—in major part it is our problem—but that these changes require the working together of white, black militants, and Negroes and cannot be accomplished by any of these groups alone. It is this working together that will produce expectations which contradict the prevailing expectations.

Finally, we *must* learn to live with the conflict and tensions produced by these contradictory experiences.

Section IV

POWER PROCESSES

Many are the pages that have been filled with discussions of power, and many are the definitions of this phenomenon that have been proposed. One of the simplist and most satisfactory approaches to this topic is that taken by Emerson, who writes:

. . . it would appear that the power to control or influence the other resides in control over the things he values, which may range all the way from oil resources to ego-support, depending upon the relation in question. In short, *power resides implicitly in the other's dependency.*[1]

This approach emphasizes that power is not to be viewed as a characteristic possessed by an individual but, rather, as a property of a social relation. To say that a given person has power is vacuous unless we specify over whom he has power. One must take into account the characteristics of both the superordinate individual and the subordinate individual in describing a power relation.

Focusing first on the superordinate member, we can say that his power is based on his ability and willingness to *sanction* the other member—to provide or withhold rewards and penalties—but we must keep in mind that what constitutes a reward or a penalty is ultimately determined by the goals or values of the subordinate member to the relation. Thus, a gunman has no power over the individual who does not value his life, nor does a person with money have power over another who does not value money or the things it will buy.

Turning to the subordinate member, emphasis is placed on ascertaining what goals or values he holds. What factors determine the degree of dependence of one person on another? Emerson suggests two factors of importance: (1) how much value does the person place on the goals mediated by the other (the greater the value, the greater the dependence) and (2) to what extent are these goals available to the person in relationships other than the one in question (the greater the availability, the less the dependence on the other).[2]

Given this approach, we can see that power can have many bases. An individual's power is based on all the *resources*—money, skills, knowledge, strength, sex appeal—that he can employ to help or hinder another's attainment of his goals. But what constitutes a resource is always determined by the values of the subordinate member in the relation. Also, it should be clear that power relations may be reciprocal: one individual may hold resources of importance to another in one area but be dependent on the same person because of the resources the latter holds in some other area. Resources become sanctions when

[1]Richard M. Emerson, "Power-dependence relations," *American Sociological Review*, 27 (February, 1962), 32. Emphasis in original.
[2]Emerson, p. 32.

they are employed by one actor to reward or punish another, either as a means of inducing him to produce the desired behavior in the future or as a response to his behavior in the past. Sanctions applied to past behavior are intended to influence the future behavior of the other—the rewarding of one type of behavior is intended to motivate the person to repeat the same or a similar act in the future; the punishing of behavior is intended to extinguish it or make its performance less likely in future. Often sanctions directed at one person are not primarily intended to influence his future behavior but are intended to influence the behavior of others in the group who observe the application of sanctions. The person who is the object of the sanctioning behavior is held up as an example—positive or negative—to others.

Power has its origin in the dependency of one person on resources possessed or controlled by another, but *power* itself is best defined as a potential for influence. If he so chooses, a person with resources that another needs may make compliance with his demands a condition to employ his resources on the other's behalf. As Blau notes in Reading 16, "A person who commands services others need, and who is independent of any at their command, attains power over others by making the satisfaction of their need contingent on their compliance."

Blau's discourse on power relations is primarily concerned with the emergence of a differentiated power structure through the interactions of persons who begin as power equals. He emphasizes the importance of exchange processes in bringing about this transformation. Let us say a word here about *social exchange*, because several influential social scientists have emphasized the importance of this general social process and because we will be drawing on their insights throughout this volume.[3] Exchange theory focuses on the actions that are contingent on rewarding reactions from others and that cease when these expected reactions are not forthcoming. This perspective does postulate an underlying egoism in human behavior—an individual does the things he finds on balance rewarding—but it is an enlightened egoism, not simple selfishness, in that one basic reward people are assumed to seek in their behavior is the approval of others.

Blau sees the origin of power structures in unequal exchange relations that occur when some individuals become increasingly dependent on others for services required in reaching their objectives. A person lacking resources to repay the other for these services who is unwilling to do without them and unable to find them in other relations has but one alternative: "he must subordinate himself to the other and comply with his wishes, thereby rewarding the other with power over himself as an inducement for furnishing the needed help."

The emergence of power differences sets in motion other processes such as legitimation and opposition, as Blau notes, but we will reserve consideration of them to later portions of this volume. Blau's wide-ranging discussion nicely reinforces the central premise of this volume: that power processes operate within all social structures but that their forms vary from structure to structure.

[3]See John W. Thibaut and Harold H. Kelley, *The Social Psychology of Groups*, New York: Wiley, 1959; George C. Homans, *Social Behavior: Its Elementary Forms*, New York: Harcourt, 1961; and Peter M. Blau, *Exchange and Power in Social Life*, New York: Wiley, 1964.

16   Exchange and Power

Peter M. Blau

The basic social processes that govern associations among men have their roots in primitive psychological processes, such as those underlying the feelings of attraction between individuals and their desires for various kinds of rewards. These psychological tendencies are primitive only in respect to our subject matter, that is, they are taken as given without further inquiry into the motivating forces that produce them, for our concern is with the social forces that emanate from them.

The simpler social processes that can be observed in interpersonal associations and that rest directly on psychological dispositions give rise to the more complex social processes that govern structures of interconnected social associations, such as the social organization of a factory or the political relations in a community. New social forces emerge in the increasingly complex social structures that develop in societies, and these dynamic forces are quite removed from the ultimate psychological base of all social life. Although complex social systems have their foundation in simpler ones, they have their own dynamics with emergent properties. In this section, the basic processes of social associations will be presented in broad strokes, to be analyzed subsequently in greater detail, with special attention to their wider implications.

Social attraction is the force that induces human beings to establish social associations on their own initiative and to expand the scope of their associations once they have been formed. Reference here is to social relations into which men enter of their own free will rather than to either those into which they are born (such as kinship groups) or those imposed on them by forces beyond their control (such as the combat teams to which soldiers are assigned), although even in these involuntary relations the extent and intensity of the association depend on the degree of mutual attraction. An individual is attracted to another if he expects associating with him to be in some way rewarding for himself, and his interest in the expected social rewards draws him to the other. The psychological needs and dispositions of individuals determine which rewards are particularly salient for them and thus to whom they will be attracted. Whatever the specific motives, there is an important difference between the expectation that the association will be an intrinsically rewarding experience and the expectation that it will furnish extrinsic benefits, for example, advice. This difference calls attention to two distinct meanings of the term "attraction" and its derivatives. In its narrower sense, social attraction refers to liking another person *intrinsically* and having positive feelings toward him; in the broader sense, in which the term is now used, social attraction refers to being drawn to another person for any reason whatsoever. The customer is attracted in this broader sense to the merchant who sells goods of a given quality at the lowest price, but

Reprinted from Peter M. Blau, *Exchange and Power in Social Life*, New York: Wiley, 1964, pp. 19–25, by permission of the author and the publisher.

he has no intrinsic feelings of attraction for him, unless they happen to be friends.

A person who is attracted to others is interested in proving himself attractive to them, for his ability to associate with them and reap the benefits expected from the association is contingent on their finding him an attractive associate and thus wanting to interact with him. Their attraction to him, just as his to them, depends on the anticipation that the association will be rewarding. To arouse this anticipation, a person tries to impress others. Attempts to appear impressive are pervasive in the early stages of acquaintance and group formation. Impressive qualities make a person attractive and promise that associating with him will be rewarding. Mutual attraction prompts people to establish an association, and the rewards they provide each other in the course of their social interaction, unless their expectations are disappointed, maintain their mutual attraction and the continuing association.

Processes of social attraction, therefore, lead to processes of social exchange. The nature of the exchange in an association experienced as intrinsically rewarding, such as a love relationship, differs from that between associates primarily concerned with extrinsic benefits, such as neighbors who help one another with various chores, but exchanges do occur in either case. A person who furnishes needed assistance to associates, often at some cost to himself, obligates them to reciprocate his kindness. Whether reference is to instrumental services or to such intangibles as social approval, the benefits each supplies to the others are rewards that serve as inducements to continue to supply benefits, and the integrative bonds created in the process fortify the social relationship.

A situation frequently arises, however, in which one person needs something another has to offer, for example, help from the other in his work, but has nothing the other needs to reciprocate for the help. While the other may be sufficiently rewarded by expressions of gratitude to help him a few times, he can hardly be expected regularly to devote time and effort to providing help without receiving any return to compensate him for his troubles. (In the case of intrinsic attraction, the only return expected is the willingness to continue the association.) The person in need of recurrent services from an associate to whom he has nothing to offer has several alternatives. First, he may force the other to give him help. Second, he may obtain the help he needs from another source. Third, he may find ways to get along without such help.[1] If he is unable or unwilling to choose any of these alternatives, however, there is only one other course of action left for him; he must subordinate himself to the other and comply with his wishes, thereby rewarding the other with power over himself as an inducement for furnishing the needed help. Willingness to comply with another's demands is a generic social reward, since the power it gives him is a generalized means, parallel to money, which can be used to attain a variety of ends. The power to command compliance is equivalent to credit, which a man can draw on in the future to obtain various benefits at the disposal of those obligated to him.[2] The unilateral supply of important services establishes this kind of credit and thus is a source of power.

Exchange processes, then, give rise to

[1]The last two of these alternatives are noted by Parsons in his discussion of a person's reactions to having his expectations frustrated by another. See Talcott Parsons, *The Social System*, Glencoe, Ill.: Free Press, 1951, p. 252.

[2]See Talcott Parsons, "On the Concept of Influence," *Public Opinion Quarterly*, 27 (1963)·, 37-62, esp. pp. 59-60.

differentiation of power. A person who commands services others need, and who is independent of any at their command, attains power over others by making the satisfaction of their need contingent on their compliance. This principle is held to apply to the most intimate as well as the most distant social relations. The girl with whom a boy is in love has power over him, since his eagerness to spend much time with her prompts him to make their time together especially pleasant for her by acceding to her wishes. The employer can make workers comply with his directives because they are dependent on his wages. To be sure, the superior's power wanes if subordinates can resort to coercion, have equally good alternatives, or are able to do without the benefits at his disposal. But given these limiting conditions, unilateral services that meet basic needs are the penultimate source of power. Its ultimate source, of course, is physical coercion. While the power that rests on coercion is more absolute, however, it is also more limited in scope than the power that derives from met needs.

A person on whom others are dependent for vital benefits has the power to enforce his demands. He may make demands on them that they consider fair and just in relation to the benefits they receive for submitting to his power. On the other hand, he may lack such restraint and make demands that appear excessive to them, arousing feelings of exploitation for having to render more compliance than the rewards received justify. Social norms define the expectations of subordinates and their evaluations of the superior's demands. The fair exercise of power gives rise to approval of the superior, whereas unfair exploitation promotes disapproval. The greater the resources of a person on which his power rests, the easier it is for him to refrain from exploiting subordinates by making excessive demands, and consequently the better are the chances that subordinates will approve of the fairness of his rule rather than disapprove of its unfairness.

There are fundamental differences between the dynamics of power in a collective situation and the power of one individual over another. The weakness of the isolated subordinate limits the significance of his approval or disapproval of the superior. The agreement that emerges in a collectivity of subordinates concerning their judgment of the superior, on the other hand, has far-reaching implications for developments in the social structure.

Collective approval of power legitimates that power. People who consider that the advantages they gain from a superior's exercise of power outweigh the hardships that compliance with his demands imposes on them tend to communicate to each other their approval of the ruler and their feelings of obligation to him. The consensus that develops as the result of these communications finds expression in group pressures that promote compliance with the ruler's directives, thereby strengthening his power of control and legitimating his authority. "A feeling of obligation to obey the commands of the established public authority is found, varying in liveliness and effectiveness from one individual to another, among the members of any political society."[3] Legitimate authority is the basis of organization. It makes it possible to organize collective effort to further the achievement of various objectives, some of which could not be attained by individuals separately at all and others that can be attained more effectively by coordinating efforts. Although power that is not legitimated by the approval of subordinates can also be used to organize them, the stability of such an organization is highly precarious.

[3]Bertrand de Jouvenel, *Sovereignty*, University of Chicago Press, 1957, p. 87.

Collective disapproval of power engenders opposition. People who share the experience of being exploited by the unfair demands of those in positions of power, and by the insufficient rewards they receive for their contributions, are likely to communicate their feelings of anger, frustration, and aggression to each other. There tends to arise a wish to retaliate by striking down the existing powers. "As every man doth, so shall it be done to him, and retaliation seems to be the great law that is dictated to us by nature."[4] The social support the oppressed give each other in the course of discussing their common grievances and feelings of hostility justifies and reinforces their aggressive opposition against those in power. It is out of such shared discontent that opposition ideologies and movements develop—than men organize a union against their employer or a revolutionary party against their government.

In brief, differentiation of power in a collective situation evokes contrasting dynamic forces: legitimating processes that foster the organization of individuals and groups in common endeavors; and countervailing forces that deny legitimacy to existing powers and promote opposition and cleavage. Under the influence of these forces, the scope of legitimate organization expands to include ever larger collectivities, but opposition and conflict recurrently redivide these collectivities and stimulate reorganization along different lines.

The distinctive characteristic of complex social structures is that their constituent elements are also social structures. We may call these structures of interrelated groups "macrostructures" and those composed of interacting individuals "microstructures." There are some parallels between the social processes in mi-

[4] Adam Smith, *The Theory of Moral Sentiments* (2d ed.), London: A. Millar, 1761, p. 139.

crostructures and macrostructures. Processes of social attraction create integrative bonds between associates, and integrative processes also unite various groups in a community. Exchange processes between individuals give rise to differentiation among them, and intergroup exchanges further differentiation among groups. Individuals become incorporated in legitimate organizations, and these in turn become part of broader bodies of legitimate authority. Opposition and conflict occur not only within collectivities but also between them. These parallels, however, must not conceal the fundamental differences between the processes that govern the interpersonal associations in microstructures and the forces characteristic of the wider and more complex social relations in macrostructures.

First, value consensus is of crucial significance for social processes that pervade complex social structures, because standards commonly agreed upon serve as mediating links for social transactions between individuals and groups without any direct contact. Sharing basic values creates integrative bonds and social solidarity among millions of people in a society, most of whom have never met, and serves as functional equivalent for the feelings of personal attraction that unite pairs of associates and small groups. Common standards of valuation produce media of exchange—money being the prototype but not the only one—which alone make it possible to transcend personal transactions and develop complex networks of indirect exchange. Legitimating values expand the scope of centralized control far beyond the reach of personal influence, as exemplified by the authority of a legitimate government. Opposition ideals serve as rallying points to draw together strangers from widely dispersed places and unite them in a common cause. The study of these problems requires an analysis of the significance of social values and norms that must complement the analysis of exchange transactions and power relations but must not become a substitute for it.

A second emergent property of macrostructures is the complex interplay between the internal forces within substructures and the forces that connect the diverse substructures, some of which may be microstructures composed of individuals while others may themselves be macrostructures composed of subgroups. The processes of integration, differentiation, organization, and opposition formation in the various substructures, which often vary greatly among the substructures, and the corresponding processes in the macrostructure all have repercussions for each other. A systematic analysis of these intricate patterns . . . would have to constitute the core of a general theory of social structures.

Finally, enduring institutions typically develop in macrostructures. Established systems of legitimation raise the question of their perpetuation through time. The strong identification of men with the highest ideals and most sacred beliefs they share makes them desirous to preserve these basic values for succeeding generations. The investments made in establishing and expanding a legitimate organization create an interest in stabilizing it and assuring its survival in the face of opposition attacks. For this purpose, formalized procedures are instituted that make the organization independent of any individual member and permit it to persist beyond the life span or period of tenure of its members. Institutionalization refers to the emergence of social mechanisms through which social values and norms, organizing principles, and knowledge and skills are transmitted from generation to generation. A society's institutions constitute the social matrix in which individuals grow up and are socialized, with the result that some aspects of institutions are reflected in their own personalities, and others appear to them as the inevitable external conditions of human existence. Traditional institutions stabilize social life but also introduce rigidities that make adjustment to changing conditions difficult. Opposition movements may arise to promote such adjustment, yet these movments themselves tend to become institutionalized and rigid in the course of time, creating needs for fresh oppositions.

Section V

ADAPTIVE PROCESSES

To this point, we have acted as if the social unit under analysis were a closed system, a self-contained entity operating independently of its environment. This, of course, is not the case. All social units are *open systems*. And, as Buckley explains:

That a system is *open* means not simply that it engages in interchanges with the environment, but that this interchange is *an essential factor* underlying the system's viability, its reproductive ability or continuity, and its ability to change.[1]

That social units represent open systems is apparent when we consider the problem of defining the boundary of the social unit to be analyzed. Defining the boundaries of a social unit is always a difficult problem; and, in fact, boundaries drawn around social units are always somewhat arbitrary, being determined more by the nature of the problem to be analyzed than by the inherent characteristics of the social unit. We will consider in our discussion of small groups the problems of delimiting the boundaries of small informal groups. One may think that the task would be easier in the case of formal organizations, but consider the example of a business firm. We would probably want to consider as members all employees. But what about customers, suppliers, stockholders? In sum, social units do not come with clearly defined boundaries; the social investigator must draw and redraw the boundaries to fit the problems he wishes to explore. What is regarded as a social unit and what is regarded as environment is, hence, a problem confronting every social investigator.

Just as no investigator can hope to focus on all aspects of the social unit under analysis, neither can he take into account all aspects of the environment. Rather, certain features of the environment must be selected as most salient to the problem under investigation. Having said this, we may say that certain features of the environment of a given type of social unit are sufficiently powerful that the investigator ignores them at considerable peril. For example, for laboratory groups the type of task set for the group and the characteristics of the investigator and the study as perceived by the subjects typically have a powerful impact on the group. For business firms, the state of the technology and the condition of the market are typically factors of importance; and for voluntary associations and service groups, the relative hospitality of the larger community to the values served by the groups has an important bearing on the characteristics of the group. Communities are considerably affected by the beneficence of their natural environment, whether it be the richness of natural resources or the productivity of their hinterland regions and by the characteris-

[1]Walter Buckley, *Sociology and Modern Systems Theory*, Englewood Cliffs, N.J.: Prentice-Hall, 1967, p. 50. Emphasis in original.

200

tics of their population—age and sex ratios, level of skill, size. Societies, too, are affected by these factors, as well as by the security of their natural boundaries and the nature of their relations with neighboring states. These few examples are not meant to be in any sense definitive but are only to illustrate the range of important factors that may be subsumed under the concept of environment.

Hawley defines *adaptation* as "the securing and conserving of control over the environment." (See Reading 17) He distinguishes between two types of adaptation: individual and communal. As sociologists, we are, of course, more interested in communal than individual forms of adaptation. We shall be interested in determining what kinds of changes occur in collectivities that enable them to better survive in and meet the demands of their environments as well as what kinds of changes impede adjustment and survival. Communal adaptation depends upon the development of certain kinds of relationships among the several biological or social units struggling for survival, in particular, *symbiotic relations* (which denote a mutual dependence relation between unlike units) and *commensalistic relations* (which develop among similar units as they compete for survival). These relations emerge as the result of cooperative and competitive processes and result in the emergence of a differentiated structure. Symbiotic relations presume the existence of differentiated units, units that are dissimilar in the demands they make on their environment. Commensalistic relations also contribute to differentiation as a consequence of the working out of competitive processes. Hawley explains this development as follows:

That differentiation follows close upon the resolution of competition seems entirely probable. The deposed competitors may scatter to other areas which offer different opportunities and call forth different adaptations. The result is a territorial differentiation. Or they may remain in the home area and develop special abilities which will permit them to make oblique attacks on the supply. That is, they take up ancillary roles in which they become dependent on but noncompetitive with those who have gained command over the supply . . . . Competition differentiates and multiplies functions, thereby producing a more or less elaborate division of labor.[2]

Note the similarity between this statement and Blau's discussion (in Reading 16) of the emergence of a differentiated power structure. Competitive processes among specific units may become resolved over time as former competitors are differentiated and become exchange partners.

We are interested in differentiation here not for its own sake—as was the case when we were concerned with status and power processes—but because differentiation facilitates adaptation. It permits a group as a whole to improve its adaptation to the environment, thus allowing larger numbers of individual units to survive at a higher level. Extensive division of labor among the participating units eliminates wasteful duplication of effort and conflict and permits each unit to contribute according to its skills and resources. In the remainder of this book, we will find numerous examples of competition leading to differentiation and of differentiation promoting adaptation.

On the other hand, as Hawley notes, "Maladaptation is also common among human beings." The adjustment between a social unit and its environment is never perfect and often falls far short of what could conceivably be attained. As

[2]Amos Hawley, *Human Ecology*, New York: Ronald, 1950, p. 203.

we will have occasion to see later, leaders who are effective in one set of circumstances may become ineffective when the circumstances change and yet may retain their position to the detriment of the group's functioning.

We have already noted the advantages for the group in differentiation of structure. But although the group as a whole may be better off for having become differentiated, certain individuals may see themselves as disadvantaged by the division of labor established. For example, individuals who have lost out in the struggle for power and have reluctantly accepted lesser positions with less desirable duties may in this manner gain survival but not gain satisfaction. They may look at their more powerful exchange partners with envy and hostility and may compare their own meager returns with the bounty of former rivals. Those lower in the power hierarchy may band together to collectively better their situation, or they may individually search for weaknesses in the position of the dominant members which may be used to their advantage. There is no final resting place for the participants who must struggle to retain even their present level of adjustment, let alone to attempt to advance. Changing environmental conditions will mean new problems for some and new opportunities for others. Adaptation is a continuing process for all participants.

Finally, we must clear up a possible misconception of the concept adaptation. As conventionally employed, this term seems to suggest that it is the unit under analysis that adapts to the environment rather than vice versa. In fact, the process flows in both directions: influence is reciprocal. The environment does influence the characteristics of the individual unit in important ways, but it is no less true that the individual unit may have important effects on the environment and can result in its transformation. For example, an important part of the environment of any business organization is the market situation. A business organization, if it is to survive, must adapt to the conditions imposed by the larger market that consists of the cumulative effects of the actions of all buyers and sellers. But it is also true that the behavior of the business organization—or the combined behavior of several business organizations—can bring about a new set of market conditions. The organizations' actions may succeed in transforming the nature of the market so that a different environment is created for all—a new market situation to which they must adapt—and, in the process of adapting, they may bring about still further changes in the market.

In sum, in analyzing the process of adaptation we will not only be concerned with the manner in which a collectivity structures its actions so as to survive in its environment; we shall also want to keep one eye focused on changes that the collectivity by its actions may bring about in its environment. In this arena, as in others, the sociologist's working model must not be the analysis of action but the analysis of *inter*action.

17 Individual and Communal Adaptation

Amos H. Hawley

ADAPTATION   The central problem of life is adaptation to those external conditions which provide the materials for existence but which also impede and limit expansion. For every form of life there is an irreducible minimum of materials and conditions without which growth and reproduction are impossible. Light, temperature, humidity, food elements, etc., in varying degrees and combinations, are essential to all species. Variations in these qualities of the environment, together with the presence of competitors and predators, impose restrictions on the number of beings that may occupy an area. It is thus imperative that the organism gain control, through one device or another, over the factors that consititute its environment. Adaptation is the securing and conserving of control over the environment. . . .

The environment of any life form is a set of manifold external circumstances which influence, positively or negatively, the activities of the organism. Any attempt to enumerate the components of environment involves one in an endless task; for each species and type of life responds to a variety of stimuli in a way more or less peculiar to itself. It is possible for general purposes, however, to avoid the extreme multiplicity of factors included in the meaning of environment by reverting to the simple classification we have been using, namely: (1) inorganic; and (2) organic. In the former are included all the mechanical and nonliving conditions that surround the organism, such as light, air pressure, humidity, temperature, minerals, topography, etc. The latter, the organic environment, comprises all manifestations of life whose activities impinge upon the individual or group of individuals. This includes other members of the same species as well as representatives of different species present in the area. Thus man's organic environment is composed of the vegetation which impedes his movements, animals which prey upon him and upon which he preys, domesticated plants and animals, and, what is often most important, his fellowmen. The adaptive efforts of the individual organism, then, are directed toward both inorganic and organic phases of the environment.

We wish to make it clear that our use of the term adaptation does not imply perfection in the relationship between organism and environment. This might be possible were it not for the fact that both terms in the relationship are not only dynamic but differ in character and rate of change. It is obvious, however, that the organism must achieve some degree of harmony between its needs and the opportunities for their satisfaction, otherwise life would be impossible. Whether the harmony attained is ideal or perfect is a question for others to decide: we are interested in the extent to which it makes survival possible. As a process, adapta-

Reprinted from Amos H. Hawley, *Human Ecology: A Theory of Community Structure*, pp. 16–40 (excerpts) © 1950, The Ronald Press Company, New York.

tion means nothing more than a striving to establish a working relationship; as a state of being, adaptation is simply that which exists at the moment. . . .

TYPES OF ADAPTATION The almost infinite variety of ways in which organisms meet life problems may be classified in any manner appropriate to the problem at hand. For present purposes the distinction between individual and communal adaptations will serve. Since the individual organism is the common denominator of life and the manifest source of organic energy, adaptations are always observable in the actions of individuals. It is also true, however, that individuals are independent in but few respects; they inevitably live together and collaborate with their fellows in overcoming the resistances to life. To a large extent these two aspects of adaptation represent merely a difference in perspective. Individuals are simply abstractions of the totality of life; and the totality is merely an intellectual synthesis of individual units. We have no intention of trying to resolve this theoretical problem, except arbitrarily for the moment. It is convenient to proceed to an understanding of adaptation with the conception of individual and collective forms. The relationship of one type of adaptation to the other should become clear in the course of the following discussion.

Individual adaptations as they relate to these phases of the environment may be further subdivided into genetic and somatic types. That is to say, the responses of living forms to inorganic and organic factors may consist of either genetic or somatic changes. Genetic adaptations, although manifested by individuals, pertain to the morphology of the species; whereas somatic adaptations are characteristics peculiar to the individual. A brief survey of how these adaptations are exhibited by different organisms will enable us to grasp more fully the

meaning of adaptation and at the same time will reveal certain marked similarities in all forms of life.

GENETIC AND SOMATIC ADAPTATION The first and most elementary problem confronting the organism is that of acquiring a physiological equipment appropriate to its survival in a given environment. "The necessity for definite adaptations acts upon the (flora and) fauna like a sieve of definite mesh, allowing only more or less similar forms to pass."[1] That is to say, each habitat imposes basic requirements upon its occupants which must be fulfilled in the structures of the organisms. These we term genetic adaptations. Darwin emphasized this mode of adjustment in his explanation of the origin of species. Adaptations of the structural order are genetically produced; they result from hereditary variation and environmental selection. Every organism is unique to some degree in its genetic qualities. Those individuals whose genetic qualities enable them to live in a specific environment may establish themselves there; the rest perish or move to an environment in which they can survive.

Thus there tends to be "a definite correlation between the peculiarities of inhabitants and those of habitats."[2] . . .

Long-time changes in the environment are met by genetic adaptations . . . But at any given time for any given individual it is not sufficient that organic structure be fitted only to a particular set of external conditions. The organism must have within its structure a degree of plasticity which will enable it to accommodate itself to the cyclical variations as well as to other special conditions in the habitat. Somatic adaptation, observable in the

[1] R. Hesse, W. C. Allee, and K. P. Schmidt, *Ecological Animal Geography* (New York, 1937), 29. Parentheses are ours.
[2] H. G. Wells, J. S. Huxley, and G. P. Wells, *The Science of Life*, Vol. III, (Garden City, N.Y., 1936), 835.

bodily changes and forms of behavior that develop in the course of the individual's life cycle, is therefore of fundamental importance to the survival of the individual and indirectly of the species. The capacity for somatic adaptation is also genetically conditioned and may almost be considered a structural element. Plasticity is a general characteristic of all living forms, but is present in varying degrees in different species and in different individuals within a species. The somatic adaptations made by an organism reveal the inherent versatility of the organic structure in meeting local variations in the environment. Unlike genetic adaptations, however, adaptations of the somatic order are temporary; they exist in the life of an individual but are not passed on to succeeding generations.

A few illustrations will clarify what is meant by somatic adaptation. Members of the same species of plant manifest in different environments considerable variation in bodily form. Dandelions growing in short grass on a lawn hug the ground, and the blossom has a very short stem. But in deep grass a long stem raises the blossom to a position where sunlight may be had. . . .

The human organism is also capable of a considerable degree of somatic adaptation to food, climate, and other aspects of the environment. The digestive system though it suffers a disturbance upon a change of diet will generally become readjusted in a short time. Likewise when the body is exposed to the hot rays of the sun it will develop a protective shield, commonly referred to as skin tanning. Man's heart and lungs vary in size with the altitude at which he customarily lives, that is, with the atmospheric pressure and the proportion of oxygen in the air.[3] Somatic adaptations are also made to

many of the diseases that plague mankind. It is well known in medical science that persons who have been exposed for a long time to certain diseases develop a considerable degree of immunity. The practice of vaccination rests upon this principle. The extreme severity of measles, mumps, whooping cough, and chicken-pox among savage peoples has frequently been contrasted with the relative mildness of these diseases among civilized peoples. On the other hand, tropical peoples develop an effective immunity to malaria and often carry the germ for years without showing any marked evidence of debilitation.[4]. . .

The primary cause of man's extraordinary adaptability is his superior mental capacity. Other features of his unspecialized physiology, such as his erect bipedal posture, his opposable thumb, and his laryngeal apparatus, contribute to the relatively unrestricted functioning of this capacity. Whereas other animals depend largely on genetic changes for adaptation to environment, man's chief form of adjustment has been through agencies external to himself but largely of his own fashioning. Instead of developing claws, wings, hard shell coverings, horns, etc., man has constructed tools, clothing, weapons, and various other devices from the materials of his environment. More than any other organism he has relied upon the retention of past experience and constructive imagination to guide his adaptive efforts. This is not to say, however, as is sometimes implied, that there is a sharp demarcation between man and other animals in regard to the possession and exercise of mental capacity. Many other animals in adjusting to environment make use of agencies external to themselves. Monkeys use sticks to knock coconuts from trees, birds and insects construct nests, and beavers fell

[3]R. H. Whitbeck and O. J. Thomas, *The Geographic Factor* (New York, 1932), 48-49.

[4]G. H. L. Pitt-Rivers, *The Clash of Culture and the Contact of Races* (London, 1927), 75.

trees and build dams to refashion their natural habitats. The difference between man and other forms of life is a matter of degree rather than of kind, so far as present evidence permits generalization. . . .

Maladaptation is also common among human beings. For the most part it results from change in environment along with the persistence of habitual ways of acting. Thus . . . to the extent that individuals become cemented in a "cake of custom" they lose their ability to adapt to new conditions. This is one reason why many tribal peoples, such as the Tasmanians, become extinct when their territories are invaded by peoples with more efficient technologies. The specific maladaptations that appear in periods of transition are much the same whether the individuals are preliterate or civilized. The Chukchee, for example, who turned from sedentary coast-dwellers to pastoral nomads, carry with them heavy complicated shelters resembling their former permanent dwellings, instead of developing a simpler and more easily transportable type.[5] Likewise, people from northwestern Europe, notably Britain, who have sought to colonize the tropics have insisted on retaining food habits, manners of dress, and other inappropriate customs acquired in the mother country.[6] In every group may be found superstitions and customs that are no longer relevant to the conditions of life but which nevertheless are allowed to continue, creating confusion and interfering with efficient functioning. . . .

There is little agreement among scholars on standards by which a custom or set of customs may be classified as maladaptation. Such a classification is largely an ethical matter and standards vary with the observer and with the situation under observation. Who is able to assert authoritatively that maladaptation is revealed in the prevalence of exceptionally high frequencies of infanticide among certain primitive peoples, or in the destructive potlatch of the Kwakiutl Indians? How shall we regard the Hindu veneration of the cow which results in the keeping of millions of cattle at a cost of several times in excess of the total land revenue of India?[7] It might be argued that any practice which interferes with survival is maladaptation. This position has much to recommend it; but survival may take any of a number of different forms. Survival, in other words, is relative to the circumstances in which the organism lives. For this reason we have been content to define adaptation as the establishment of a working arrangement, the achievement of at least a partial equilibrium between contending forces.

COMMUNAL ADAPTATION   The discussion to this point has been centered principally upon the individual as the representative of a species. But one of the first lessons learned by the conscientious observer of life is that organisms do not live as discrete units, except, possibly, for brief periods of time. They do not, in other words, achieve their adaptation to environment alone and unaided. Nothing could be more erroneous than a conception of the organic world merely as a distribution of self-sufficient and disparate units of life. Living organisms are inevitably dependent upon their fellows in one way or another; and the organic world, viewed in its generality, is a multitude of partnerships and corporations that overlie and interpenetrate one another, thus constituting an intricate network of vital relationships.

[5]Franz Boas, *The Mind of Primitive Man* (New York, 1913), 162.

[6]A. Grenfell Price, *White Settlers in the Tropics* (New York, 1939), 217–27.

[7]G. Findlay Shirras, "Indian Agriculture and Indian Peasants," *Indian Journal of Economics,* IX (October, 1928), 120.

It has been pointed out that adaptations to both inorganic and organic phases of the environment are required of all life forms. These, as we have shown, are effected through genetic and somatic means. Of particular importance, though sometimes overlooked, is the fact that adaptation to one environmental phase is impossible without adaptation to the other. The complex character of the adaptation process derives in part from the inherent physical and mental limitations of the organism, but probably to a much greater extent from the rapid reproduction rate of which living creatures are capable with the resultant tendency to overcrowding the available life space. W. G. Sumner provides us with an apt, though somewhat oversimplified, explanation of the way in which organic and inorganic environments become interrelated. When an individual, he observes, is attempting to accomplish something in an area, the fact that other individuals are trying to do the same thing in the same area is for him a highly important condition. The individual organism may ignore the others and thus, by exposing itself to the risk of unnecessary interference and conflict, increase its chances of failure in the enterprise. Or it may adjust its activities to those of its co-inhabitants and thereby enhance the probability of success.[8] In other words, through cooperation energy is conserved and the effects of chance occurrences that threaten the life of the organism are minimized. Adaptation to the physical and mechanical conditions of the environment is facilitated, in fact is secured, through the mutual adaptation of organisms.

Students of life are in general agreement that the universal tendency is for organisms to confront the environment not as individuals but as units in a cooperative effort at adaptation. For ex-

ample, plants, the most independent of living forms, "do not ordinarily live alone like hermits but are found growing along with other plants in communities that usually consist of many individuals."[9] Concerning animals, Darwin wrote: "Although there is no evidence that any animal performs an action for the exclusive good of another species, yet each tries to take advantage of the instincts of the other, as each takes advantage of the weaker bodily structure of the other species."[10] Man is no exception to the general rule. Men everywhere live in association with other forms of life as well as with their fellowmen. Few instances of solitary human beings have come to light and, while information concerning these feral creatures is far from satisfactory, it appears that survival in every case was contingent upon the individual's adapting his activities to those of other species.[11]

Thus, it is evident that adaptation is a collective phenomenon, involving all the organisms occupying a given area. The exposition of this hypothesis is the subject of the following chapter, but it may be pointed out here that the adaptive efforts of individuals culminate in a community of interorganic relationships by means of which each organism maintains itself in the habitat. To this "higher physiology of organisms" we apply the term *communal adaptation* in order to convey the idea that adaptation to environment is a population rather than an individual problem.

Communal adaptation constitutes the distinctive subject matter of ecology which is a study not of individuals but of populations of living things. Individuals and their adaptations are of importance

[8]*Folkways* (New York, 1906), 16.

[9]W. B. McDougall, *Plant Ecology* (Philadelphia, 1931), 214.

[10]Charles Darwin, *Origin of Species* (New York, 1925), 6th ed., 186.

[11]Cf. R. E. Park and E. W. Burgess, *An Introduction to the Science of Sociology* (Chicago, 1921), 239-43.

to the ecologist only in that they serve as convenient units in the analysis of a community. Ecology concerns itself not with mere aggregations of individuals but with their organization and integration in a community. That the community is the essential adaptive mechanism may be taken as the distinctive hypothesis of ecology. . . .

INTERRELATEDNESS OF LIFE

Relationships among living creatures, however, are infinitely more complex than they appear on the surface. The oft repeated phrase "all flesh is grass and all fish is diatom" is more than a mere epigram; it is an accurate, if cryptic, expression of the subtle and highly ramified interconnectedness of life. Darwin was among the first to appreciate fully nature's intricate pattern which he described in the metaphor "web of life." This vivid concept has since become the point of departure for ecological study; it constitutes the frame of reference for an ecological, as against a physiological or psychological, analysis of life. We must, therefore, examine in some detail the meaning of this idea.

Darwin, in his description of the nexus between cats and next year's clover crop,[12] provided the now classic illustration of the network of vital linkages which bind different organisms together. Humble-bees alone, his observations disclosed, visit the red clover; other bees and insects cannot reach the nectar. But the number of humble-bees in an area depends in a great measure on the number of field-mice, since these latter invade the nests of humble-bees and rob

[12]*Origin of Species,* 59. According to J. Arthur Thomson, ". . . red clover imported to New Zealand did not bear fertile seeds until humble-bees were also imported." *Darwinism and Human Life* (New York, 1919), 53.

them of their food stores. Cats, in turn, are the natural enemies of mice and hence control their numbers. In areas adjacent to villages the nests of humble-bees were found to be more numerous than elsewhere, owing no doubt to the larger number of cats there. An increase in the cat population, it may be inferred, is followed by a decrease in the number of mice, thus permitting an increase of humble-bees and, consequently, a more widespread fertilization of red clover. Creatures that, to all outward appearances, are ". . . remote in the scale of nature . . ." are found to be linked together in a chain of relations. Much has been accomplished since Darwin stirred the intellectual world by the publication of his observations and theories and much new light has been shed on the correlations of organisms and their collective adjustment to the varying physical environment. Darwin and his colleagues sketched the principal outlines in nature's pattern and subsequent students have been rapidly filling in the details of the pattern with many valuable discoveries. The deeper the analysis of the "web of life" is pushed the more meaningless becomes such a word as "independent." . . .

SYMBIOSIS   Upon analysis of the web of life, we find that one of its most conspicuous and important components is the symbiotic relationship. The term *symbiosis* denotes a mutual dependence between unlike organisms. Because they make dissimilar demands on the environment members of different species may supplement the efforts of one another. The food-enemy relationship is of this order. The eater and the eaten are engaged in a vital cooperation, each contributing to and facilitating the circulation of life-giving matter. But their mutual assistance is also more direct. The food species produces a surplus population for the maintenance of a predator species. The latter, by its predation, exercises a control on the size of the food species population which, if it grew too large, would be exposed to extinction by contagion or by the exhaustion of its own food supply. "It is easy to see that what may be a one-sided harmful relation between individuals may be a tolerable or even beneficial relation between population."[13] There are, however, many less sanguinary expressions of symbiosis.

Nature is replete with instances of direct mutual helpfulness between unlike organisms. Much of the complexity of the web of life is due to the prevalence of this phenomenon. The association of leguminous plants and certain nitrogen-fixating bacteria is a typical example of symbiosis. Bacteria, existing in nodules on the roots of legumes, capture nitrogen from the air and transform it into substances that these plants can absorb; the plants in turn contribute materially to the sustenance of the bacteria. For this reason, legumes such as alfalfa and clover restore the fertility of soil in which they grow and are, therefore, of great importance to man in his agriculture. Another instance of symbiosis, which strikingly reveals the intimacy of the relationship, is represented in the heather of Britain.

It grows exuberantly on mountain and moorland where few other flowering plants can make a living. There is soil, but it is unready; there is water, but it is apt to be physiologically unavailable. How does the heather flourish so well? The answer is that it has entered into a very intimate partnership with a fungus, which penetrates through and through the heather, from root to stem, into every leaf, even into the flower and its seed. What an individual could not do, a firm achieves. The heather is a dual organism; it is like a flowering lichen! If it

stood alone it would be a remarkable curiosity, but it is only an instance of a kind of partnership that is now known to be common, between the highest plants and the lowest.[14]

The dependence of herbivora upon bacteria to assist in breaking down the cells of plants taken into the stomach as food; the cooperation between certain plants and animals by which the animals are provided with fruit and the plants have their seeds scattered widely over the environment; the entrance of the little plover into the mouth of the crocodile to pick the blood-sucking leeches from the gums of that huge amphibian; the exchange of hospitality by the ant for the milk of the aphid; the partnership between man and favored plants and animals—man providing an ideal habitat devoid of natural enemies and in return having his food supplied; these and numerous other occasions of symbiosis draw the threads of interrelationship in the living world into a tight and complex fabric.

Parasitism is sometimes distinguished as a unique relationship. Unlike the symbiont, one hears it said, the parasite does not pay its way; it draws its sustenance from another plant or animal without actually, or immediately, destroying the life of its host. But a note of caution must be introduced into this way of regarding organisms classed as parasites. The characterization appears to be valid only from the point of view of the individual host, not from that of the species. According to Elton, "the difference between the methods of a carnivore and a parasite is simply the difference between living upon capital and upon income . . ."[15] and this distinction

[13]A. E. Emerson, "The Biological Basis of Social Cooperation," *Illinois Academy of Science Transactions.* XXXIX (1946), 13.

[14]J. Arthur Thomson, *Concerning Evolution* (New Haven: Yale University Press, 1925), 104–105.

[15]Charles Elton, *Animal Ecology* (New York, 1927), 72.

involves an evaluation often difficult to make.[16] Realistically, the parasite is but a miniature herbivore or carnivore whose small size represents a structural adaptation that permits a most intensive utilization of environment. Parasitism is thus merely a special form of symbiosis.

Still other forms of interspecific relationship may be mentioned, such as helotism—or the enslavement of one species by another as practiced by termites; and predatism—another name for the food-enemy relationship but connoting the element of wanton destruction. Yet these, like parasitism, are merely special forms of symbiosis; their use as denotative terms depends largely upon the values carried in the mind of the observer. The one incontrovertible fact, to which all such terms point, is the mutualism of life. Diverse species associating together draw heavily or lightly on the special abilities of one another and the benefits returning to each may be immediate or delayed, direct or indirect; nevertheless each plays a necessary part in the ongoing drama of life. Symbiosis, then, appropriately describes all forms of living together of unlike organisms.[17] But symbiosis is not the only cohesive factor in the web of life.

COMMENSALISM Organisms relate themselves to one another on the basis of their likenesses as well as their differences. Hence a second and equally important relation in the web of life is that which arises between similar creatures—members of a given species or rather individuals that make similar demands on the environment. This is the relation of *commensalism* which, literally interpreted, means eating from the same table.[18]

The most elementary and yet salient expression of commenalism in nature is competition, the name given to the kind of interaction in which each individual affects the behavior of every other by its effect upon the common supply of sustenance materials. Wherever individuals with like demands crowd in upon limited resources there is competition. Competition is almost as general as are the phenomena of reproduction and aggregation. These processes, in fact, are the mainsprings of competition; they tend to bring about a situation in which the assembled organisms make demands for food and living space in excess of the available supply. The ensuing interaction may be exceedingly subtle, as in the competition of plants for light and nutri-

[16]"It is common to find parasites referred to as if they were in some way more morally oblique in their habits than other animals, as if they were taking some unfair and mean advantage of their hosts. If we once start working out such 'responsibilities' we find that the whole animal kingdom lives on the spare energy of other species or upon plants, while the latter depend upon the radiant energy of the sun. If parasites are to occupy a special place in this scheme we must, to be consistent, accuse cows of petty larceny against grass, and cactuses of cruelty to the sun." Charles Elton, *Animal Ecology,* p. 75. Published by The Macmillan Company and used with their permission.

[17]A narrower meaning is sometimes given to the term symbiosis in special studies where it is necessary to draw the distinction more finely. To Thomson and Geddes: "It means a mutually beneficial internal partnership between two organisms of different kinds." (J. A. Thomson and P. Geddes, *Life: Outlines of General Biology* (Lon-

don, 1931), 133.) This definition may be taken as representative of the more precise usage of the term and is illustrated in the relationship of the heather and the fungus. F. E. Clements declares: "The term symbiosis has sometimes been rendered meaningless or at least superfluous by being extended to include practically all the phenomena of association, but is here employed in its proper sense of a specialized coaction, involving some degree of mutuality." However, he continues: "This latter may fluctuate greatly from type to type, and in our present knowledge no hard and fast limits can be set." ("Social Origins and Processes Among Plants," *Handbook of Social Psychology,* ed. C. Murchison (Worcester, Mass., 1935), 31.) See also J. R. Carpenter, *An Ecological Glossary* (Norman, Okla., 1938), 268.

[18]"Le commensal est simplement un compagnon de table." (J. Braun-Blanquet, *Plant Sociology,* trans. George D. Fuller and Henry S. Conrad (New York, 1932), 9.)

ents, or frankly overt, as in the rivalry among chickens for food thrown into their pen. It may be indirect and unconscious, as the grazing of cattle in a fenced pastureland, or direct and conscious, as between business men seeking to outdo one another with their advertising.

Competition varies directly, as we have suggested, with the organism-resource ratio. The intensity of the relationship, however, depends not only upon the number of individuals in an area but also upon the degree of similarity existing among them. Thus, while competition is common between members of the same species, many different species possess requirements sufficiently alike to make them competitors. For example, seedlings of one species of tree compete with each other for space, water, light, and nutrients, as well as with seedlings of other species and also with the parent trees.[19] Animal competition pertains primarily to food and secondarily to space in which to breed and find shelter. To the extent that different species have different food habits competition is confined to each species. But there are numerous instances of interspecies competition: deer, rabbits, and mice compete for certain kinds of grass; and toads, garter snakes, salamanders, raccoons, birds and other carnivora compete for various forms of insect life.

The significance of competition is of-ten emphasized to the exclusion of the mutual support like organisms render one another. Organisms with similar requirements frequently combine their efforts to maintain favorable life conditions; an aggregate acting in concert can accomplish what a lone individual cannot. The number of individuals of a species banded together in an area, for instance, seems to be a factor of consequence for their survival. A large group of animals is more immune from attack by enemies than are individuals or small groups of twos and threes. This may partly account for the more pronounced herding tendency of herbivora than is exhibited by carnivora. Darling reports that "snow is less of a danger to a large mass of deer than it is to small groups...."[20] Allee showed experimenally that goldfish in large numbers are better able to overcome poisons in their habitat than when they encounter such conditions individually.[21] Illustrations of this very simple form of cooperation could be recited indefinitely, for it is a very commonplace phenomenon.[22]

Thus animate nature may be likened to a fabric ever in process of being woven upon the looms of the physical environment; the warp formed of symbiotic and the woof of commensalistic relations. There is no question as to which is the more important; both warp and woof are essential to the weaving.

---

[19]"Morosow counted on one hectare 1,048,660 ten-year old beeches. In a fifty-year old pure stand of the same area there were 4,460; in a stand one hundred and twenty years old only 509. The completely closed growth permitted, therefore, only 1 out of about 2,000 young beeches to come to maturity." (Braun-Blanquet, op. cit., 11–12.)

[20]A Herd of Red Deer (London, 1937), 97.

[21]The Social Life of Animals (New York, 1938), 53–57.

[22]P. Kropotkin, Mutual Aid; W. C. Allee, Animal Aggregations (Chicago, 1931); F. Alverdes, "The Behavior of Mammalian Herds and Packs," in A Handbook of Social Psychology, ed. C. Murchison, 194 ff.

PART FOUR

Social Processes in Small Groups

Although there were some like Charles Cooley[1] and Georg Simmel,[2] who early recognized the importance of the small group as "the cradle of human nature" and as a locus for studying elementary forms of social interaction, this area of study did not attract large numbers of students until the most recent decades of the 1950s and 1960s. Nevertheless, great progress has been made in this short period in our understanding of this important area. The small group has emerged as one of the most important settings within which sociologists work.

STRUCTURAL CHARACTERISTICS OF SMALL GROUPS

To begin, the small group is a subtype of a more general structural category: the *collectivity*. The collectivity is no more nor less than a specific instance of social organization—an identifiable "chunk" of the social order. The criteria for the existence of a collectivity are twofold: (1) a delimited social structure, that is, a bounded network of social relations, and (2) a normative order applicable to the participants linked by the relational network. The reader will recognize the two elements of social organization. The only additional notion contained in these criteria is that of some kind of boundary serving to distinguish one instance of social organization from another.

It is possible to suggest several specific indicators that may be helpful in establishing the boundaries that delimit a given collectivity. Interaction rates give one some clue to the boundaries of the social structure. Homans writes that group boundaries may be drawn where the web of interaction shows "certain

[1]Charles Horton Cooley, *Social Organization*, Glencoe, Ill.: Free Press, 1956 (originally published, New York: Scribner's, 1902).
[2]Georg Simmel, *The Sociology of Georg Simmel*, translated and edited by K. H. Wolff, Glencoe, Ill.: Free Press, 1950 (originally published 1908).

thin places."[3] Similarly, one may be able to examine the types of activities performed, as many groups perform distinctive kinds of activities. The researcher may also make use of such indicators as space and time in drawing group boundaries. Group activity always requires both space and time, and groups often take steps to establish spacial barriers (for example, doors and walls, guards and secretaries, and property laws) and temporal boundaries (for example, working hours, activity schedules, and meetings set at given intervals of specified duration). Finally, groups often have specified membership boundaries—social definitions of who is a member of the collectivity and hence subject to its normative order. Nonmembers may be excluded from group activities or if allowed to be present will be expected to behave and will be treated differently than members (for example, servants in a family group or visitors present in a meeting of a membership club). Among the many arrangements for defining membership boundaries in collectivities are initiation ceremonies, hiring contracts, occupational licenses, marriage ceremonies, and citizenship laws.

In sum, a collectivity is a network of bounded social relationships to which a normative structure is applicable. Individuals move into and out of these social relationships, with interactional, activity, spacial, temporal, and membership boundaries helping to specify who is and who is not included in the collectivity. A given collectivity may not be continuously operating but may be activated during only a relatively short time at periodic intervals. Thus, a bridge club may be in existence only one evening a month. Membership in the club may be acknowledged at any time, but the activation of the special set of relationships, the activities and interactions, and the application of the normative prescriptions are restricted to a particular time and place. It is almost as though a special magnet labeled "bridge club" drops from the sky every fourth Thursday of the month to select out and appropriately arrange the participants like iron filings in the proper patterns. At the end of the evening, other magnets perhaps labeled "family" pick up the participants, redistribute them with new partners, and specify new social relationships and normative codes to govern their behavior. In one sense, individuals pass sequentially from collectivity to collectivity, occasionally finding themselves caught between the conflicting demands of two or more groups. Focusing on collectivities rather than on individuals, however, most of them alternate between activation and existence and deactivation and temporary suspension of existence. Sociologists have paid too little attention to this alternating feature that characterizes most collectivities, although it undoubtedly has an important impact on the structural features and social processes of collectivities.

Having examined the generic concept of collectivity, we are now ready to define the small group. A *small group* is a collectivity of limited membership—of, perhaps, 2 to 20 members. Group size is important because of its potential effect on number and quality of social relationships in the group. Consider the matter of numbers first. The number of potential relationships in a group increases much faster than the number of members, as seen in the formula $\dfrac{N\ (N\text{-}1)}{2}$, where

[3]George C. Homans, *The Human Group*, New York: Harcourt, 1950, p. 85.

[4]See William M. Kephart, "A quantitative analysis of intragroup relationships," *American Journal of Sociology*, 55 (May, 1950), 544 549.

N is the number of group members.[4] Thus, the number of potential relationships in a group of size four is six[5] but increases to 21 potential relationships in a group of size seven.

The quality of social relationships is best considered by examining some of the common types of groups that have been identified.

Primary versus Secondary Groups   The distinction between the primary and the secondary group is based both on the nature of the relationships among members (the social structure) and on the nature of the normative structure. In the *primary group*, relationships are characterized by a warm intimacy, with close personal ties linking members. More precisely, social relations tend to be diffuse, involving many characteristics of the interacting parties and marked by positive affect. As for the normative structure, values emphasized by primary groups include much importance placed on the group as an end in itself. Simply the act of associating, of coming together, is positively valued by group members. The content of norms in primary groups may vary widely, but the norms are similar in form in that they are relatively particularistic; that is, they are adjusted to make allowance for the particular characteristics of the individual members. By contrast, relationships in *secondary groups* are more specific, being based on fewer characteristics of members; and affect among individuals is more highly controlled, so that relations are more emotionally neutral and detached. Members of secondary groups tend to view the group as primarily a means to some end rather than as an end in itself. Group members come together to do something and are more attracted by the group's purposes or activities than by the associations with other participants. Finally, norms in secondary groups are more likely to be universalistic in character, with few allowances being made for individual differences. Common examples of groups that are often primary in nature include families, close-knit neighborhood groups, and small work and play groups continuing over a considerable period of time. Secondary groups include such special-interest collectivities as bridge clubs and political parties and also include religious, educational, and occupational organizations. Obviously, any concrete group will represent some combination of these types. However, it is important to note that although a small group may be a primary group, a secondary group, or some combination of these, only a small group and never a large one can be a primary group. This points to the importance of size as a defining criterion of the small group. It appears that although the size of a group does not completely determine the quality of the relations among members, size does set some limits on what kinds of relations are possible.

In addition to the distinction between primary and secondary groups, there are two other closely related and widely employed bases for classifying small groups.

[5]A group with four members, John, Bill, Frank, and George, has the following potential relations: 1. John and Bill; 2. John and Frank; 3. John and George; 4. Bill and Frank; 5. Bill and George; 6. Frank and George. Of course, if one wishes to count individual-group relations (for example, John and the group), individual-subgroup relations (for example, John's relation with Frank, George, and Bill), or subgroup-subgroup relations (for example, John and Bill's relation with Frank and George), the number of potential relations in the group increases dramatically. There are 25 such relationships in a group of size 4 and 966 such relationships in a group of size 7. See Kephart. Such figures help explain how life even in a small group can get complicated!

Formal versus Informal Groups   The concepts formal and informal have been defined in our previous discussion of social positions, and the same definitions are applicable when these concepts are used to describe group structure. Thus, we speak of *formal groups* as groups in which the constituent social positions and the relations among them can be defined independently of the characteristics of persons occupying the positions. By contrast, in the *informal group* it is impossible to distinguish between the characteristics of social positions and the characteristics of persons occupying them. Like the distinction between primary and secondary groups, *formal-informal* describes a dimension along which a given group may vary. Hence, one may speak of groups that are more or less highly formalized.

Clearly, primary groups are more likely to have informal structures, and secondary groups to have formal structures, but there are important exceptions to this generalization. For example, the family, one of the types of groups most frequently exhibiting primary characteristics, is also likely to possess a considerable degree of formalization.

We regard formalization as an extremely important sociological variable, but we will postpone consideration of it here in order to devote a separate part to formal organizations. Our attention will be directed in this part to informal groups.

Task versus Nontask Groups   *Task groups,* also known as instrumental groups, are groups whose members can be said to be working toward some purpose apart from the goal of merely associating together. For *nontask* or expressive groups, it is impossible to distinguish a goal other than that of interaction for its own sake. This particular distinction obviously depends on the concept of group goal for its application, and the concept of group goal is not a very simple one. One source of confusion is that between motive and goal. An individual may join a church in order to meet a pretty girl, but his holding this motive does not make it a goal for the church group. The fact that a given motive is widely shared among members is also irrelevant so far as a determination of the group's goals are concerned. Rather, we can best think of a *group goal* in the sense of a goal held by individuals *for* the group. Most individuals can distinguish between what their group is attempting to do, on the one hand, and why they are willing to participate in and contribute to the group, on the other hand. It is certainly true, however, that groups vary in the extent to which their members agree on what the central goals are. Goals also vary in terms of clarity and specificity. Finally, we should not expect all members always to have an equal say in the setting of goals—goals may be set by democratic or authoritarian procedures. Keeping in mind these factors, it is usually possible to determine the extent to which a group is task-oriented. In sum, a task group comes together in order to do something; a nontask group does something in order to come together.

In reviewing these three typologies we have been able to comment on some of the more important structural variations that characterize the small group. In the remainder of this Part, as we take up the selected processes operating in small groups, we will be concerned with both primary and secondary groups, with informal rather than formal groups, and primarily with task-oriented groups rather than nontask-oriented groups, although we will have a few comments to make on the latter type.

INTEGRATIVE PROCESSES IN SMALL GROUPS

Because our approach must necessarily be selective, we will in this discussion focus exclusively on *normative* processes of integration in the small group. At the same time, however, we must always keep in mind that interdependence, power, and other social processes also operate to produce integration in most small groups. As will be recalled from our introductory remarks on this process, integration is concerned with the attainment of coherence and unity among the units (in this case, individuals) comprising the collectivity or group. In the past two decades some highly informative studies have been carried out concerning the influence that groups are able to exert on the perceptions, attitudes, and behavior of their members. Some of these studies have been conducted in laboratories and others have been carried out in natural settings, but the results of both types have tended to be consistent and cumulative.

Studies of the Emergence of Social Norms   The pioneer study in this tradition was carried out by Muzafer Sherif—the now classic "autokinetic effect" study.[1] In this research, subjects were asked to report their judgments as to the distance an apparently mobile but actually stationary point of light moved when it was flashed on in a totally darkened room. Sherif was able to show that the judgments of a given individual were influenced by those of others reacting to the same stimuli. More specifically, he was able to document the emergence of a normative standard that became the basis for the perceptual judgments of individuals. This study is summarized at greater length in the review chapter by Katz and Lazarsfeld (see Reading 19).

Sherif successfully showed that in an ambiguous situation individuals turned to their fellows for assistance in interpreting reality. Several years later, Asch determined to carry out a much more demanding test of the strength of a group by pitting its judgment *against* the perceptions of an individual subject. This study is reported in the book as Reading 18. Asch asked naive subjects to perform a simple task—to match the length of a given line with one of three unequal lines. The catch was that at the same time Asch instructed others who were ostensibly also subjects but who were, in fact, confederates of the researcher to report incorrect answers. Subjects were hence confronted by a conflict between the group's report of reality and their own observation of it. In this situation, approximately one third of all subjects' estimates on critical trials were distorted in the direction of the group's judgment.

Asch conducted several variations on his basic experiment to determine the conditions under which subjects were most likely to yield to group pressure or to act independently of it. Such factors as ambiguity of stimuli, size of group,

[1]Muzafer Sherif, *The Psychology of Social Norms*, New York: Harper & Row, 1936.

unanimity of group opinion, and certain personality characteristics were found to influence the level of conformity. For example, Asch discovered that the power the group was able to exert on an individual was greatly reduced if even one confederate deserted the majority opinion (by instruction) to report his perceptions accurately. Like the child in the fairy story who transformed the situation by calling out, "The Emperor has no clothes!" one individual "telling it like it is" could virtually destroy the power of the majority opinion in this situation. Further, the strength of the support provided by even one other person who departs from the majority opinion suggests one important reason why groups may react so strongly to deviance. On the other hand, the power that a unified majority opinion can exert on an individual suggests how important it is in a democracy to have norms supporting dissent and freedom of speech.

In spite of the impressive results obtained in the Sherif and the Asch experiments, it is important to point out that neither situation contained what by our definition is a full-fledged group. Participants in the experiments had no previous acquaintance with one another; there was no network of social relationships linking members. Further, in neither case was there a group goal: both tasks were defined as involving individual judgments. Both situations were "social" in the sense that other people were present and became objects of orientation for the participating individual who took account of their reported perceptions in describing his own. Out of these reports that each participant made and heard emerged certain standards or quasi-norms that participants used to evaluate and regulate their own judgments. These norms were not fully developed because there was no overt use of sanctions to control deviance. Indeed, Asch trained his confederates so they would not react in any way to the naive subject's judgment, whether it be conforming or independent. As would be expected, the changing of such factors as these in the direction of increasing the "group-like" quality of the situation increases pressures on individuals to conform. Thus, a study conducted by Deutsch and Gerard making use of the Asch situation with modifications found that conformity rates increased when (1) individuals were told they were working for a group reward that would be based on group score and (2) individuals were asked to report their judgments in the presence of others in contrast to being allowed to report their opinions anonymously.[2] In short, integrative processes can be expected to operate more effectively the more nearly a collection of individuals takes on the characteristics of a full-fledged task group.

The Sherif and the Asch studies are, of course, laboratory studies. The great advantage of the laboratory approach is that it allows the investigator to *control* many factors that affect the situation of interest, eliminating some of the factors (and in this way simplifying the situation) and regulating other factors so that they appear in the form and degree desired. Some have criticized laboratory studies of human behavior on the grounds that they are artificial or unnatural, but such criticisms reflect misunderstanding of the basic purpose of experiments, which is to simplify complex situations and thus to enable the scientist to focus on the relationships among a few selected variables. Social scientists have been

[2]Morton Deutsch and Harold B. Gerard, "A study of normative and informational social influences upon individual judgment," *Journal of Abnormal and Social Psychology*, 51 (1955), 629–636.

increasingly successful and ingenious in devising meaningful experimental situations, and these studies have contributed much to our knowledge of social
behavior. However, there is a very real problem associated with such studies:
one must use extreme care in generalizing findings from them to behavior
outside the laboratory. Generalizing from one setting to another is always a
problem for a scientist, but it is especially acute when moving from laboratory to
nonlaboratory, because factors arbitrarily eliminated from a laboratory study
may be of overriding importance when the phenomenon appears in its natural
state.[3]

Given the difficulties and dangers inherent in generalizing from laboratory
studies, we are fortunate not to have to rely exclusively on studies of this type in
our examination of integrative processes. A number of well-conducted field
studies—studies of natural groups—have been carried out, and the results of
these studies tend to reinforce those carried out in the laboratory. The best of
these studies—Newcomb's study of Bennington College;[4] Festinger, Schachter
and Back's study of the Westgate housing development;[5] and Merei's observations of children's play groups[6]—are all summarized in the chapter contributed
by Katz and Lazarsfeld (Reading 19).

The Katz and Lazarsfeld reading is important for reasons other than the
summaries it provides of these studies, for these authors go beyond providing a
descriptive summary to attempting an explanation of these integrative processes. Their explanation is at two levels: individual and group. At the individual level, they argue that individuals are disposed toward accepting attitudes,
opinions and perceptions similar to those held by their fellows because social
rewards are attached to such conformity (the *instrumental* function). Also,
individuals are often in need of "meanings for situations which do not explain
themselves," and opinions consensually held by group members furnish a definition of *social reality* in such cases. Shifting to the group level, groups *require*
conformity of attitude or opinion from their participants in those cases where
uniformity of opinion is a prerequisite for group action.

Katz and Lazarsfeld are here attempting to answer the question as to *why*
individuals conform to social norms. If they are correct, the factors they identify
should also help to account for variations among individuals in their tendency to
conform to norms. If some individuals conform for instrumental reasons, we
would expect individuals to conform more to the groups to which they are most
attracted. This appears to be the case, as has been demonstrated by several
studies.[7] In fact, an important generalization is that the more cohesive the

[3]Katz and Lazarsfeld provide a very informative discussion of the manner in which one might
attempt to generalize from the Sherif study. See Reading 19, pp. 235-236.

[4]Theodore M. Newcomb, "Attitude development as a function of reference groups: The
Bennington study," in Eleanor E. Maccoby, Theodore M. Newcomb, and Eugene L. Hartley
(eds.), *Readings in Social Psychology*, New York: Holt, Rinehart and Winston, Inc., 1958, pp.
265-275.

[5]Leon Festinger, Stanley Schachter, and Kurt Back, "The operation of group standards," in
Dorwin Cartwright and Alvin Zander (eds.), *Group Dynamics: Research and Theory*, Evanston, Ill.:
Row, Peterson & Company, 1953, pp. 204-222.

[6]Ferenc Merei, "Group leadership and institutionalization," in Maccoby, Newcomb, and Hartley,
pp. 522-532.

[7]See, for example, Festinger, Schachter, and Back; and H. H. Kelley and E. H. Volkart, "The
resistance to change of group-anchored attitudes," *American Sociological Review*, 17 (1952),
453-465.

group—that is, the more attractive it is to its participants—the higher the conformity to its norms. The importance of the group as a definer of social reality for its participants should vary with the ambiguity of the situation. That is, the individual should be more susceptible to group pressures in those situations in which there are few objective cues to guide action. This, of course, is precisely what the studies conducted by Asch show: the more ambiguous the physical stimuli presented to the subjects, the greater the individual subject's tendency to conform to group definitions of reality. Finally, we would expect group pressures toward conformity to be maximized in those areas of greatest importance to the functioning of the group. An experiment conducted by Schachter bears on this prediction.[8] Schachter constructed task groups including some individuals who, as confederates of the experimenter, deviated in specified ways from the norms of the group. Schachter reports that the more the deviant's behavior was relevant to the group's task activity, the more the deviant was likely to receive the censure of the group and to be rejected by them.

The three factors cited by Katz and Lazarsfeld can all be reduced to aspects of a more general exchange process. Thus, to conform for instrumental reasons is clearly to conform in order to obtain the social rewards attached to conformity. The social reality explanation suggests that finding oneself in agreement with others is a rewarding experience, whereas disagreements are often perceived as painful. Finally, groups see to it that certain behaviors of which they approve are positively reinforced—receive positive sanctions—while those of which they disapprove are punished.

Social Norms in Small Groups   As noted, Katz and Lazarsfeld focus on the question of why individuals conform to social norms. A different but equally important question to be asked is Why do norms develop in groups? The first question asks what advantages fall to members of groups who conform to group norms. The second question asks what advantages fall to groups that develop effective social norms.

Continuing with the exchange formulation, we may suggest that norms help to regulate and determine the distribution of rewards to group members. Many kinds of actions are aimed at obtaining a large variety of nonsocial rewards. The objective of group norms is to attach *social* rewards and penalties to certain behaviors in order to affect the probability that these behaviors will or will not occur. In particular, negative sanctions are attached to the behaviors by means of which an individual may gain personal advantage at the expense of his fellows. For example, norms develop in most student groups against cheating on examinations or against the "apple-polishing" of teachers that might bring rewards (high grades) to the individual but that would at the same time create problems for his fellow students (see Reading 7). On the other hand, positive sanctions are used to convert conduct that otherwise would be viewed by the individual as costly into rewarding behavior. Thus, an individual worker may be rewarded by his colleagues for restricting his production at a personal financial sacrifice to himself (see Readings 4 and 5).

[8]Stanley Schachter, "Deviation, rejection, and communication," *Journal of Abnormal and Social Psychology*, 46 (1951), 190–207.

From these general comments, we can go on to speculate as to the *type* of norms that may be likely to develop in task groups as compared to non-task groups. In task groups where members are oriented to the achievement of some goals other than the continued functioning of the group, norms are likely to develop that will encourage the development of consensus on objectives, promote cooperative action toward their achievement, insure dependability of task-related performances, and so on.

In nontask groups, which operate primarily to satisfy the socioemotional needs of members, we would expect to find norms that emphasize the obligation of each member to meet certain needs of other members, norms that encourage fair treatment, norms that discourage competition and aggression directed at members, and so on.

This discussion is intended to help explain why norms—and why different types of norms—emerge in small groups. We also have suggested a partial answer to the question as to what advantages fall to groups that develop effective social norms; namely, that social norms are one important mechanism available to groups by means of which they can regulate the conduct of their members so that group objectives will be attained. Later sections of this part will suggest that status and power processes also contribute to the regulation of member behavior. Hence, norms are one such mechanism of regulation, not the only one. However, after considering status and power processes in small groups, we will suggest that there are special advantages associated with the normative regulation of behavior.

18   Effects of Group Pressure upon the Modification and Distortion of Judgments

S. E. Asch

We shall here describe in summary form the conception and first findings of a program of investigation into the conditions of independence and submission to group pressure.[1]

Our immediate object was to study the social and personal conditions that induce individuals to resist or to yield to group pressures when the latter are perceived to be *contrary to fact*. The issues

[1]The earlier experiments out of which the present work developed and the theoretical issues which prompted it are discussed in S. E. Asch, *Social Psychology* (Englewood Cliffs, N.J.: Prentice-Hall, Inc., 1952), Ch. 16. A full account of the procedures and data on which the present report is based can be found in S. E. Asch, "Studies of independence and submission to group pressure: I. A minority of one against a unanimous majority." *Psychol. Monogr.*, 1956, 70.

Reprinted from Eleanor E. Maccoby, Theodore M. Newcomb, and Eugene L. Hartley (eds.), *Readings in Social Psychology* (3d ed.), New York: Holt, Rinehart and Winston: Inc., 1958, pp. 174–183. An earlier version appeared in *Groups, Leadership, and Men*, Harold Geutzkow (ed.), Pittsburgh: Carnegie Press, 1951. Some portions reprinted by permission of Carnegie Press.

which this problem raises are of obvious consequence for society; it can be of decisive importance whether or not a group will, under certain conditions, submit to existing pressures. Equally direct are the consequences for individuals and our understanding of them, since it is a decisive fact about a person whether he possesses the freedom to act independently, or whether he characteristically submits to group pressures.

The problem under investigation requires the direct observation of certain basic processes in the interaction between individuals, and between individuals and groups. To clarify these seems necessary if we are to make fundamental advances in the understanding of the formation and reorganization of attitudes, of the functioning of public opinion, and of the operation of propaganda. Today we do not possess an adequate theory of these central psycho-social processes. Empirical investigation has been predominantly controlled by general propositions concerning group influence which have as a rule been assumed but not tested. With few exceptions investigation has relied upon descriptive formulations concerning the operation of suggestion and prestige, the inadequacy of which is becoming increasingly obvious, and upon schematic applications of stimulus-response theory.

Basic to the current approach has been the axiom that group pressures characteristically induce psychological changes *arbitrarily*, in far-reaching disregard of the material properties of the given conditions. This mode of thinking has almost exclusively stressed the slavish submission of individuals to group forces, has neglected to inquire into their possibilities for independence and for productive relations with the human environment, and has virtually denied the capacity of men under certain conditions to rise above group passion and prejudice. It was our aim to contribute to a clarification of these questions, important both for theory and for their human implications, by means of direct observation of the effects of groups upon the decisions and evaluations of individuals.

THE EXPERIMENT AND FIRST RESULTS

To this end we developed an experimental technique which has served as the basis for the present series of studies. We employed the procedure of placing an individual in a relation of radical conflict with all the other members of a group, of measuring its effect upon him in quantitative terms, and of describing its psychological consequences. A group of eight individuals was instructed to judge a series of simple, clearly structured perceptual relations—to match the length of a given line with one of three unequal lines. Each member of the group announced his judgments publicly. In the midst of this monotonous "test" one individual found himself suddenly contradicted by the entire group, and this contradiction was repeated again and again in the course of the experiment. The group in question had, with the exception of one member, previously met with the experimenter and received instructions to respond at certain points with wrong—and unanimous—judgments. The errors of the majority were large (ranging between ½ and 1¾″) and of an order not encountered under control conditions. The outstanding person—the critical subject—whom we had placed in the position of a *minority of one* in the midst of a *unanimous majority*—was the object of investigation. He faced, possibly for the first time in his life, a situation in which a group unanimously contradicted the evidence of his senses.

This procedure was the starting point of the investigation and the point of departure for the study of further problems. Its main features were the follow-

TABLE 18–1 Lengths of Standard and Comparison Lines

Trial	Length of Standard Line (in Inches)	Comparison Lines (in Inches)			Correct Response	Group Response	Majority Error (in Inches)
		1	2	3			
1	10	8¾	10	8	2	2	—
2	2	2	1	1½	1	1	—
3	3	3¾	4¼	3	3	1°	+ ¾
4	5	5	4	6½	1	2°	− 1.0
5	4	3	5	4	3	3	
6	3	3¾	4¼	3	3	2°	1¼
7	8	6¼	8	6¾	2	3°	1¼
8	5	5	4	6½	1	3°	1½
9	8	6¼	8	6¾	2	1°	1¾
10	10	8¾	10	8	2	2	—
11	2	2	1	1½	1	1	—
12	3	3¾	4¼	3	3	1°	+ ¾
13	5	5	4	6½	1	2°	− 1.0
14	4	3	5	4	3	3	—
15	3	3¾	4¼	3	3	2°	+ 1¼
16	8	6¼	8	6¾	2	3°	− 1¼
17	5	5	4	6½	1	3°	+ 1½
18	8	6¼	8	6¾	2	1°	− 1¾

°Starred figures designate the erroneous estimates by the majority.

ing: (1) The critical subject was submitted to two contradictory and irreconcilable forces—the evidence of his own experience of a clearly perceived relation, and the unanimous evidence of a group of equals. (2) Both forces were part of the immediate situation; the majority was concretely present, surrounding the subject physically. (3) The critical subject, who was requested together with all others to state his judgments publicly, was obliged to declare himself and to take a definite stand vis-à-vis the group. (4) The situation possessed a self-contained character. The critical subject could not avoid or evade the dilemma by reference to conditions external to the experimental situation. (It may be mentioned at this point that the forces generated by the given conditions acted so quickly upon the critical subjects that

instances of suspicion were infrequent.)

The technique employed permitted a simple quantitative measure of the "majority effect" in terms of the frequency of errors in the direction of the distorted estimates of the majority. At the same time we were concerned to obtain evidence of the ways in which the subjects perceived the group, to establish whether they became doubtful, whether they were tempted to join the majority. Most important, it was our object to establish the grounds of the subject's independence or yielding—whether, for example, the yielding subject was aware of the effect of the majority upon him, whether he abandoned his judgment deliberately or compulsively. To this end we constructed a comprehensive set of questions which served as the basis of an individual interview immediately following the experimental period. Toward the conclusion of the interview each subject was informed fully of the purpose of the experiment, of his role and of that of the majority. The reactions to the disclosure of the purpose of the experiment became in fact an integral part of the procedure. The information derived from the interview became an indispensable source of evidence and insight into the psychological structure of the experimental situation, and in particular, of the nature of the individual differences. It should be added that it is not justified or advisable to allow the subject to leave without giving him a full explanation of the experimental conditions. The experimenter has a responsibility to the subject to clarify his doubts and to state the reasons for placing him in the experimental situation. When this is done most subjects react with interest, and some express gratification at having lived through a striking situation which has some bearing on them personally and on wider human issues.

Both the members of the majority and the critical subjects were male college students. We shall report the results for a total of fifty critical subjects in this experiment. In Table 18-1 we summarize the successive comparison trials and the majority estimates. The reader will note that on certain trials the majority responded correctly; these were the "neutral" trials. There were twelve critical trials on which the responses of the majority responded incorrectly.

The quantitative results are clear and unambiguous.

1. There was a marked movement toward the majority. One third of all the estimates in the critical group were errors identical with or in the direction of the distorted estimates of the majority. The significance of this finding

TABLE 18–2 Distribution of Errors in Experimental and Control Groups

Number of Critical Errors	Critical Group° (N = 50) F	Control Group (N = 37) F
0	13	35
1	4	1
2	5	1
3	6	
4	3	
5	4	
6	1	
7	2	
8	5	
9	3	
10	3	
11	1	
12	0	
Total	50	37
Mean	3.84	0.08

° All errors in the critical group were in the direction of the majority estimates.

becomes clear in the light of the virtual absence of errors in the control group, the members of which recorded their estimates in writing. The relevant data of the critical and control groups are summarized in Table 18-2.

2. At the same time the effect of the majority was far from complete. The preponderance of estimates in the critical group (68 percent) was correct despite the pressure of the majority.

3. We found evidence of extreme individual differences. There were in the critical group subjects who remained independent without exception, and there were those who went nearly all the time with the majority. (The maximum possible number of errors was 12, while the actual range of errors was 0-11.) One fourth of the critical

subjects was completely independent, at the other extreme, one third of the group displaced the estimates toward the majority in one half or more of the trials.

The differences between the critical subjects in their reactions to the given conditions were equally striking. There were subjects who remained completely confident throughout. At the other extreme were those who became disoriented, doubt-ridden, and experienced a powerful impulse not to appear different from the majority.

For purposes of illustration we include a brief description of one independent and one yielding subject.

Independent

After a few trials he appeared puzzled, hesitant. He announced all disagreeing answers in the form of "Three, sir; two, sir"; not so with the unanimous answers on the neutral trials. At Trial 4 he answered immediately after the first member of the group, shook his head, blinked, and whispered to his neighbor: "Can't help it, that's one." His later answers came in a whispered voice, accompanied by a deprecating smile. At one point he grinned embarrassedly, and whispered explosively to his neighbor: "I always disagree—darn it!" During the questioning, this subject's constant refrain was: "I called them as I saw them, sir." He insisted that his estimates were right without, however, committing himself as to whether the others were wrong, remarking that "that's the way I see them and that's the way they see them." If he had to make a practical decision under similar circumstances, he declared, "I would follow my own view, though part of my reason would tell me that I might be wrong." Immediately following the experiment the majority engaged this subject in a brief discussion. When they pressed him to say whether the entire group was wrong and he alone right, he turned upon them defiantly, exclaiming: "You're *probably* right, but you *may* be wrong!" To the disclosure of the experiment this subject reacted with the statement that he felt "exultant and relieved," adding, "I do not deny that at times I had the feeling: 'to heck with it, I'll go along with the rest.'"

Yielding

This subject went with the majority in 11 out of 12 trials. He appeared nervous and somewhat confused, but he did not attempt to evade discussion; on the contrary, he was helpful and tried to answer to the best of his ability. He opened the discussion with the statement: "If I'd been first I probably would have responded differently"; this was his way of stating that he had adopted the majority estimates. The primary factor in his case was loss of confidence. He perceived the majority as a decided group, acting without hesitation: "If they had been doubtful I probably would have changed, but they answered with such confidence." Certain of his errors, he explained, were due to the doubtful nature of the comparisons; in such instances he went with the majority. When the object of the experiment was explained, the subject volunteered: "I suspected about the middle—but tried to push it out of my mind." It is of interest that his suspicion did not restore his confidence or diminish the power of the majority. Equally striking is his report that he assumed the experiment to involve an "illusion" to which the others, but not he, were subject. This assumption too did not help to free him; on the contrary, he acted as if his divergence from the majority was a sign of defect. The principal impression this subject produced was of one so caught up by immediate difficulties that he lost clear reasons for his actions, and could make no reasonable decisions.

A FIRST ANALYSIS OF INDIVIDUAL DIFFERENCES

On the basis of the interview data described earlier, we undertook to differentiate and describe the major forms of reaction to the experimental situation, which we shall now briefly summarize.

Among the *independent* subjects we distinguished the following main categories:

1. Independence based on *confidence* in one's perception and experience. The most striking characteristic of these subjects is the vigor with which they withstand the group opposition. Though they are sensitive to the group, and experience the conflict, they show a resilience in coping with it, which is expressed in their continuing reliance on their perception and the effectiveness with which they shake off the oppressive group opposition.
2. Quite different are those subjects who are independent and *withdrawn*. These do not react in a spontaneously emotional way, but rather on the basis of explicit principles concerning the necessity of being an individual.
3. A third group of independent subjects manifests considerable tension and doubt, but adhere to their judgment on the basis of a felt necessity to deal adequately with the task.

The following were the main categories of reaction among the *yielding* subjects, or those who went with the majority during one half or more of the trials.

1. *Distortion of perception* under the stress of group pressure. In this category belong a very few subjects who yield completely, but are not aware that their estimates have been displaced or distorted by the majority. These subjects report that they came to perceive the majority estimates as correct.
2. *Distortion of judgment.* Most submitting subjects belong to this category. The factor of greatest importance in this group is a decision the subjects reach that their perceptions are inaccurate, and that those of the majority are correct. These subjects suffer from primary doubt and lack of confidence; on this basis they feel a strong tendency to join the majority.
3. *Distortion of action.* The subjects in this group do not suffer a modification of perception nor do they conclude that they are wrong. They yield because of an overmastering need not to appear different from or inferior to others, because of an inability to tolerate the appearance of defectiveness in the eyes of the group. These subjects suppress their observations and voice the majority position with awareness of what they are doing.

The results are sufficient to establish that independence and yielding are not psychologically homogeneous, that submission to group pressure and freedom from pressure can be the result of different psychological conditions. It should also be noted that the categories described above, being based exclusively on the subjects' reactions to the experimental conditions, are descriptive, not presuming to explain why a given individual responded in one way rather than another. The further exploration of the basis for the individual differences is a separate task.

EXPERIMENTAL VARIATIONS

The results described are clearly a joint function of two broadly different sets of conditions. They are determined first by the specific external conditions, by the particular character of the relation between social evidence and one's own experience. Second, the presence of pronounced individual differences points to the important role of personal factors or factors connected with the individual's character structure. We reasoned that there are group conditions which would produce independence in all subjects, and that there probably are group conditions which would induce intensified yielding in many, though not in all. Secondly, we deemed it reasonable to assume that behavior under the experimental social pressure is significantly related to certain characteristics of the individual. The present account will be limited to the effect of the surrounding conditions upon independence and submission. To this end we followed the procedure of experimental variation, systematically altering the quality of social evidence by means of systematic variation of the group conditions and of the task.

The Effect of Nonunanimous Majorities

Evidence obtained from the basic experiment suggested that the condition of being exposed *alone* to the opposition of a "compact majority" may have played a decisive role in determining the course and strength of the effects observed. Accordingly we undertook to investigate in a series of successive variations the effects of *nonunanimous* majorities. The technical problem of altering the uniformity of a majority is, in terms of our procedure, relatively simple. In most instances we merely directed one or more members of the instructed group to deviate from the majority in prescribed ways. It is obvious that we cannot hope to compare the performance of the same individual in two situations on the assumption that they remain independent of one another; at best we can investigate the effect of an earlier upon a later

experimental condition. The comparison of different experimental situations therefore requires the use of different but comparable groups of critical subjects. This is the procedure we have followed. In the variations to be described we have maintained the conditions of the basic experiment (e.g., the sex of the subjects, the size of the majority, the content of the task, and so on) save for the specific factor that was varied. The following were some of the variations studied:

1. *The presence of a "true partner."*
   (a) In the midst of the majority were *two* naïve, critical subjects. The subjects were separated spatially, being seated in the fourth and eighth positions, respectively. Each therefore heard his judgments confirmed by one other person (provided the other person remained independent), one prior to, the other after announcing his own judgment. In addition, each experienced a break in the unanimity of the majority. There were six pairs of critical subjects. (b) In a further variation the "partner" to the critical subject was a member of the group who had been instructed to respond correctly throughout. This procedure permits the exact control of the partner's responses. The partner was always seated in the fourth position; he therefore announced his estimates in each case before the critical subject.

The results clearly demonstrate that a disturbance of the unanimity of the majority markedly increased the independence of the critical subjects. The frequency of promajority errors dropped to 10.4 percent of the total number of estimates in variation (a), and to 5.5 percent in variation (b). These results are to be compared with the frequency of yielding to the unanimous majorities in the basic experiment, which was 32 percent of the total number of estimates. It is clear that the presence in the field of *one other* individual who responded correctly was sufficient to deplete the power of the majority, and in some cases to destroy it. This finding is all the more striking in the light of other variations which demonstrate the effect of even small minorities provided they are unanimous. Indeed, we have been able to show that a unanimous majority of 3 is, under the given conditions, far more effective than a majority of 8 containing 1 dissenter. That critical subjects will under these conditions free themselves of a majority of 7 and join forces with one other person in the minority is, we believe, a result significant for theory. It points to a fundamental psychological difference between the condition of being alone and having a minimum of human support. It further demonstrates that the effects obtained are not the result of a summation of influences proceeding from each member of the group; it is necessary to conceive the results as being relationally determined.

2. *Withdrawal of a "true partner."* What will be the effect of providing the critical subject with a partner who responds correctly and then withdrawing him? The critical subject started with a partner who responded correctly. The partner was a member of the majority who had been instructed to respond correctly and to "desert" to the majority in the middle of the experiment. This procedure permits the observation of the same subject in the course of the transition from one condition to another. The withdrawal of the partner produced a powerful and unexpected result. We had assumed that the critical subject, having gone through the experience of opposing the majority with a minimum of support, would maintain his independence when alone. Contrary

to this expectation, we found that the experience of having had and then lost a partner restored the majority effect to its full force, the proportion of errors rising to 28.5 percent of all judgments, in contrast to the preceding level of 5.5 percent. Further experimentation is needed to establish whether the critical subjects were responding to the sheer fact of being alone, or to the fact that the partner abandoned them.

3. *Late arrival of a "true partner."* The critical subject started as a minority of 1 in the midst of a unanimous majority. Toward the conclusion of the experiment one member of the majority "broke" away and began announcing correct estimates. This procedure, which reverses the order of conditions of the preceding experiment, permits the observation of the transition from being alone to being a member of a pair against a majority. It is obvious that those critical subjects who were independent when alone would continue to be so when joined by a partner. The variation is therefore of significance primarily for those subjects who yielded during the first phase of the experiment. The appearance of the late partner exerts a freeing effect, reducing the level of yielding to 8.7 percent. Those who had previously yielded also became markedly more independent, but not completely so, continuing to yield more than previously independent subjects. The reports of the subjects do not cast much light on the factors responsible for the result. It is our impression that some subjects, having once committed themselves to yielding, find it difficult to change their direction completely. To do so is tantamount to a public admission that they had not acted rightly. They

therefore follow to an extent the precarious course they had chosen in order to maintain an outward semblance of consistency and conviction.

4. *The presence of a "compromise partner."* The majority was consistently extremist, always matching the standard with the most unequal line. One instructed subject (who, as in the other variations, preceded the critical subject) also responded incorrectly, but his estimates were always intermediate between the truth and the majority position. The critical subject therefore faced an extremist majority whose unanimity was broken by one more moderately erring person. Under these conditions the frequency of errors was reduced but not significantly. However, the lack of unanimity determined in a strikingly consistent way the *direction* of the errors. The preponderance of the errors, 75.7 percent of the total, was moderate, whereas in a parallel experiment in which the majority was unanimously extremist (i.e., with the "compromise" partner excluded) , the incidence of moderate errors was 42 percent of the total. As might be expected, in a unanimously moderate majority, the errors of the critical subjects were without exception moderate.

The Role of Majority Size

To gain further understanding of the majority effect, we varied the size of the majority in several different variations. The majorities, which were in each case unanimous, consisted of 2, 3, 4, 8, and 10-15 persons, respectively. In addition, we studied the limiting case in which the critical subject was opposed by one instructed subject. Table 18–3 contains the mean and the range of errors under each condition.

With the opposition reduced to 1, the majority effect all but disappeared. When the opposition proceeded from a group of 2, it produced a measurable though small distortion, the errors being 12.8 percent of the total number of estimates. The effect appeared in full force with a majority of 3. Larger majorities did not produce effects greater than a majority of 3.

The effect of a majority is often silent, revealing little of its operation to the subject, and often hiding it from the experimenter. To examine the range of effects it is capable of inducing, decisive variations of conditions are necessary. An indication of one effect is furnished by the following variation in which the conditions of the basic experiment were simply reversed. Here the majority, consisting of a group of 16, was naive; in the midst of it we placed a single individual who responded wrongly according to instructions. Under these conditions the members of the naive majority reacted to the lone dissenter with amusement. Contagious laughter spread through the group at the droll minority of 1. Of significance is the fact that the members lacked awareness that they drew their strength from the majority, and that their reactions would change radically if they faced the dissenter individually. These observations demonstrate the role of social support as a source of power and stability, in contrast to the preceding investigations which stressed the effects of social opposition. Both aspects must be explicitly considered in a unified formulation of the effects of group conditions on the formation and change of judgments.

The Role of the Stimulus-Situation

It is obviously not possible to divorce the quality and course of the group forces which act upon the individual from the specific stimulus-conditions. Of necessity the structure of the situation molds the group forces and determines their direction as well as their strength. Indeed, this was the reason that we took pains in the investigations described above to center the issue between the individual and the group around an elementary matter of fact. And there can be no doubt that the resulting reactions were directly a function of the contradiction between the observed relations and the majority position. These general considerations are sufficient to establish the need to vary the stimulus-conditions and to observe their effect on the resulting group forces.

Accordingly we have studied the effect of increasing and decreasing the discrepancy between the correct relation and the position of the majority, going beyond the basic experiment which contained discrepancies of a relatively moderate order. Our technique permits the easy variation of this factor, since we can vary at will the deviation of the majority from the correct relation. At this point we can only summarize the trend of the results which is entirely clear. The degree of independence increases with the distance of the majority from correctness. However, even glaring discrepancies (of the order of 3-6″) did not produce independence in all. While independence increases with the magnitude of contradiction, a certain proportion of individuals continues to yield under extreme conditions.

We have also varied systmatically the structural clarity of the task, employing judgments based on mental standards. In agreement with other investigators, we find that the majority effect grows stronger as the situation diminishes in clarity. Concurrently, however the disturbance of the subjects and the conflict-quality of the situation decrease markedly. We consider it of significance that the majority achieves its most pronounced effect when it acts most painlessly.

SUMMARY

We have investigated the effects upon individuals of majority opinions when the latter were seen to be in a direction contrary to fact. By means of a simple technique we produced a radical divergence between a majority and a minority, and observed the ways in which individuals coped with the resulting difficulty. Despite the stress of the given conditions, a substantial proportion of individuals retained their independence throughout. At the same time a substantial minority yielded, modifying their judgments in accordance with the majority. Independence and yielding are a joint function of the following major factors: (1) The character of the stimulus situation. Variations in structural clarity have a decisive effect: with diminishing clarity of the stimulus-conditions the majority effect increases. (2) The character of the group forces. Individuals are highly sensitive to the structural qualities of group opposition. In particular, we demonstrated the great importance of the factor of unan-

TABLE 18–3 Errors of Critical Subjects with Unanimous Majorities of Different Size

Size of Majority	Control	1	2	3	4	8	10-15
N	37	10	15	10	10	50	12
Mean Number of Errors	0.08	0.33	1.53	4.0	4.20	3.84	3.75
Range of Errors	0-2	0-1	0-5	1-12	0-11	0-11	0-10

imity. Also, the majority effect is a function of the size of group opposition. (3) The character of the individual.

There were wide and, indeed, striking differences among individuals within the same experimental situation.

19   Norms and Small Groups: The Shared Character of Opinions and Attitudes

Elihu Katz and Paul F. Lazarsfeld

Our focus is the primary group. We are thinking specifically of families, friends, informal work teams, etc., as well as those relatively more formal groupings of clubs and organizations of all kinds within which individuals are likely to form what we might call sociometric connections, that is, mutual attractions for each other as personalities. Such groups are usually characterized by their small size, relative durability, informality, face-to-face contact and manifold, or more or less unspecialized, purpose.[1] We shall refer interchangeably to primary groups, small groups, intimate social ties, interpersonal relations or sometimes just to "others," with no attempt to be prematurely precise in our definitions. Our aim now is to see whether those who have studied such interpersonal relations can assist us in developing an idea of how to account for the role of *people* in the flow of mass media influence in modern society.

Our chief concern is with the hypothesis that such groups actively influence and support most of an individual's opinions, attitudes and actions. The evidence on this point is not yet very abundant, but what there is, is persuasive. We know, for example, from several studies that the members of a family are likely—except under certain conditions —to share similar attitudes on politics, religion, etc., and the same thing is true, we know, for most friendships.[2] We know from a set of pioneering studies (which

[1] From Cooley's (1909) classic definition. For the contrast of secondary groups, see Davis (1949), Chap. 11.

[2] Empirical evidence for the homogeneity of family opinion can be found in Newcomb and Svehla's (1937) study of parents' and children's attitudes, and in Lazarsfeld, Berelson and Gaudet (1948), pp. 140–145. Evidence for the homogeneity of friends' political opinions is reported by Berelson, Lazarsfeld and McPhee (1954). See also Fisher (1948) and the bibliography contained therein. While knowledge of the family as a primary group exceeds our knowledge of any other primary group, it is interesting that contemporary social scientists (unlike their more theoretically oriented predecessors) rarely attempt to generalize from the family to other intimate groups, though a recent, very notable exception is Homans (1950). Some parallels between the family and other primary groups will be implicit— though not spelled out—in this chapter. For example: it will be shown that there are mechanisms in every group for indoctrinating newcomers in the ways of the group, and bringing deviates back into line; it will be shown that individuals picture themselves much as others around them picture them; it will be shown that intimate groups of all kinds affect the opinions and attitudes of their members in spheres of thought and action that often go far beyond the group's immediate concerns. All these (and many more) are just what the family does.

Reprinted by permission of the author and The Macmillan Company from *Personal Influence: The Part Played by People in the Flow of Mass Communications* by Elihu Katz and Paul F. Lazarsfeld. Copyright 1955 by The Free Press, a Corporation, pp. 48-65 (excerpts).

now constitute the core of what is called "reference group theory") that individuals seem often to have particular groups "in mind" when reporting their opinions.[3] Here, then, is the suggestion that opinions are originated and maintained by an individual in common with specifiable others of his associates.

The fact that interacting individuals influence each other, or that an individual entering a new group is likely to adopt the thinking habits of that group is not an easy thing to prove because it almost always involves *disproving* the alternate hypothesis that individuals in a similar situation are each responding independently to the same external stimuli. Thus, even when it is demonstrated that Northern students attending Southern universities become increasingly prejudiced toward the Negro with each succeeding year at school (although never quite so prejudiced as the Southern students themselves), the authors cannot permit themselves to assert that the Northerners are adopting the attitude of their Southern classmates, because they must also show (and their data do not permit them to) that whatever it is that has caused prejudice in the Southerners is not also at work directly on the Northerners.[4]

But although we do not yet have a mass of statistical evidence to demonstrate the *fact* that opinions, attitudes, decisions and actions are rooted in relatively small groups, we can feel much surer than we ordinarily might because we know from careful case studies some of the *reasons why* we are warranted in our expectation that this is the case. Several reasons have been put forward quite convincingly.

THE INSTRUMENTAL FUNCTION: THE BENEFITS OF CONFORMITY

First of all, we might consider what can be called the *instrumental value*—the "benefits"—that can be derived from sharing the opinions and attitudes of those with whom an individual desires to be identified. We may cite here, as an illustration, Newcomb's well-known study of the political attitudes of a class of Bennington College girls.[5] By beginning his study in the freshman year and recording changes in attitudes over the four-year period of college, Newcomb was able to show that those students who were positively oriented toward the college community and who aspired to be accepted or to achieve leadership tended to assimilate the liberal attitudes and sentiments which prevailed on campus, despite the strongly conservative family background from which they had come. On the other hand, Newcomb demonstrates, a major factor associated with non-acceptance of the prevailing political climate was a strong positive identification with the family group. Thus, the family group, on the one hand, and the small college community, on the other— each serving as "positive" or "negative" reference points of varying intensity— seemed to be associated with the steadfast conservatism of some of the girls and the increasing non-conservatism of the majority. In Newcomb's own words,

In a membership group in which certain attitudes are approved (i.e., held by majorities, and conspicuously so by leaders) individuals acquire the approved attitudes to the extent that the membership group (particularly as symbolized by leaders and dominant subgroups) serves as a positive point of reference.[6]

In other words, to the extent that a group is attractive for an individual, and

---

[3]See the writings on reference group theory, notably Merton and Kitt (1950), and Newcomb (1952).
[4]Sims and Patrick (1947).

[5]Newcomb (1952).
[6]*Ibid.*, p. 420.

to the extent that he desires acceptance as a member of that group, he will be motivated—whether he is aware of it or not—to accept that group's outlook.

Another set of findings supports the implications of Newcomb's study very neatly. In *The American Soldier*,[7] Stouffer *et al*, compare the attitudes of those "green" soldiers (no combat experience) who had been sent as replacements to divisions composed of combat veterans, with the attitudes of equally "green" soldiers who were members of divisions composed only of others like themselves. Noting that 45% of the latter but only 28% of the former express attitudes reflecting a "readiness for combat," the authors indicate that this difference may derive from the two different social contexts in which these otherwise indistinguishable "green" troops were placed. It is suggested that those troops who found themselves in veterans' divisions were strongly influenced by the attitudes they encountered there since the combat veterans' own response to the same set of questions was overwhelmingly negative (only 15% indicated readiness for combat). The new men were seeking acceptance, it is argued, and they adjusted their opinions accordingly.

Conformity is not exacted from "new" members or potential members alone. Even long-time members who "deviate" too far from group opinion lose status, or may even lose membership in groups to which they already belong. Several recent experimental studies demonstrate this everyday fact quite well. In one study of a housing community by Festinger, Schachter and Back— (we shall refer repeatedly to this "Westgate" housing development study and to others by these

authors and their associates)—it was found that those who conformed least to the opinions of their immediate neighbors (as far as the particular item being studied was concerned) tended also to be the ones who were "underchosen" when people were asked in an interview to name their three best friends.[8] From another study by one of this same team of authors, we learn that when participants in clubs were asked, following their initial discussion periods, who among the participants they would like to see dropped from the club, those who had maintained extremely deviant opinions (these extremists were in the employ of the experimenter) were named most of all.[9]

Individuals conform, we have seen so far, and obtain acceptance and friendship in return. In order to become a *leader*, too, one must share prevailing opinions and attitudes. Merei demonstrates this very vividly in his study of leadership in children's group.[10]

Children were observed at play in a day nursery and those children who displayed leadership qualities were singled out and separated from the other children. The remaining children were formed into twelve groups, homogeneous as to age and sex, comprising three to six members each. Each of these twelve groups met separately over a period of several days and very soon each developed group "traditions" with regard to its activities, most of which centered about an experimentally prescribed task. The author reports that it took from three to six

---

[7]Stouffer *et al.* (1949) Vol. II, p. 244. See Shils' (1950) summary and analysis of this subject, and in the same volume, the treatment of the same subject by Merton and Kitt (1950).

[8]That is, they were not named as frequently as they named others. This is one of the standard sociometric procedures employed in Festinger, Schachter and Back (1950).

[9]Schachter (1951).

[10]Merei (1952). For confirmation, with case study illustrations, of the relationship between social status and degree of conformity to group norms, see Homans (1950) on "social ranking and norms."

meetings (35 to 40 minutes each) for the development of group "traditions" such as permanent seating arrangements, permanent division of objects (who plays with what) , a stable sequence of games, preference for certain activities rather than others, group jargon, etc. Then the original leaders, who had not been included in these twelve groups, were reintroduced. In every case, when an old leader attempted to assert authority which went contrary to a newly established "tradition" of the group, the group did not respond. Some of the leaders, as a matter of fact, never returned to power. Others, who were successful, did achieve leadership once more but only after they had completely identified with the new "tradition" and participated in it themselves.

In sum, all these studies seem to indicate that if an individual desires to attain, or maintain, an intimate relationship with others, or if he wants to "get somewhere" either within a group or via a group, he must identify himself with the opinions and values of these others. That does not necessarily mean that this identification is therefore rationally calculated. It may be quite unwitting. But conscious or not, the *consequences* of conformity or non-conformity which we have noted will remain the same.

Thus, from the "instrumental" point of view, we are led to expect that an individual's opinions will be substantially affected by the opinions of others whose company he keeps, or whose company he aspires to keep.[11]

---

[11]Warner and Lunt's (1941) "discovery" of the clique in Yankee City indicates that upward mobility in the social status system of a community involves being accepted by (and presumably, therefore, conforming with) small groups which personify each successive step on the status ladder. A whole series of such examples—cutting across traditionally rigid boundary lines in sociology—are provided by Merton and Kitt (1950) in their reference group paper. They begin with data from *The American Soldier* to indicate that army privates who at Time A have attitudes more closely

PROVIDING A SOCIAL REALITY

Let us now consider another of the reasons which may help explain our confidence in the assertion that individuals very largely share their opinions with other people who surround them. Here, we are thinking of the group not in instrumental terms (that is, not in terms of the "benefits" of conforming) but rather in terms of the function of the group as a provider of *meanings* for situations which do not explain themselves. Experimental social psychologists concerned with the impact of the group on perceptual processes,[12] and particularly the late Kurt Lewin and those who continue in his tradition, have studied this phenomenon. The Lewinians have named it "social reality" and they explain it as follows:

Experiments dealing with memory and group pressure on the individual show that what exists as "reality" for the individual is to a high degree determined by what is socially accepted as reality. This holds even in the field of physical fact: to the South Sea Islanders the world may be flat; to the European it is round. "Reality," therefore, is not an absolute. If differs with the group to which the individual belongs.[13]

---

resembling those of non-commissioned officers than other privates, are more likely at Time B to have attained a higher rank than other privates. Generalizing from this finding, they say: "An army private bucking for promotion may only in a narrow and theoretically superficial sense be regarded as engaging in behavior different from that of an immigrant assimilating the values of a native group, or of a lower-middle-class individual conforming to his conception of upper-middle-class patterns of behavior, or of a boy in a slum area orienting himself to the values of the street corner gang, or of a Bennington student abandoning the conservative beliefs of her parents to adopt the more liberal ideas of her college associates, or of a lower-class Catholic departing from the pattern of his in-group by casting a Republican vote, or of an eighteenth century French aristocrat aligning himself with a revolutionary group of the time."

[12]For an interesting formulation of the contributions of gestalt psychologists to the study of group processes as these influence perception, judgments, motivations, etc., see Katz, D. (1951) .

[13]Lewin and Grabbe (1945) . The notion of "social reality" has an important parallel in Harry Stack Sullivan's (1953) "consensual validation."

This concept provides an alternative or better, a supplementary, explanation for the soldiers' attitudes we reported above. Instead of attributing the attitude of the replacements (compared with their peers in all-"green" divisions) simply to their motivation to be accepted in the veterans' outfits, we might have suggested there, as we shall here, that the "reality" of the combat experience toward which attitudes were being expressed might well have been different for those who were in daily touch with combat veterans as compared with those who were not. The Westgate study makes this point very well:

The hypothesis may be advanced that the "social reality" upon which an opinion or an attitude rests for its justification is the degree to which the individual perceives that this opinion or attitude is shared by others. An opinion or attitude which is not reinforced by others of the same opinion will become unstable generally. There are not usually compelling facts which can unequivocally settle the question of which attitude is wrong and which is right in connection with social opinions and attitudes as there are in the case of what might be called "facts." If a person driving a car down a street is told by his companion that the street ends in a dead end, this piece of information may easily be checked against physical "reality." . . . The "reality" which settles the question in the case of social attitudes and opinions is the degree to which others with whom one is in communication are believed to share these opinions and attitudes.[14]

This is the way the stereotypes develop; and it is one of the reasons why ideas about what is real in religion or in politics vary from group to group. So many things in the world are inaccessible to direct empirical observation that individuals must continually rely on each other for making sense out of things. Several experimental studies illustrate this. For example, there is Sherif's now classic study which is perhaps the best single begin-

ning point for a review of the twenty or so years of attention in experimental social psychology to the role of the small group as an influence on opinions, attitudes and actions.[15] Sherif constructed experiments using the "autokinetic effect" which is the name given to the illusion of movement created by an actually stationary pinpoint of light when it is flashed on in a totally darkened room. He first tested each of his experimental subjects singly, asking them to make judgments about the number of inches the light "moved" each time it was lit. After each individual had developed a personal "norm"—that is, a modal number of inches—around which his judgments centered, Sherif brought his subjects together in groups of twos and threes, and asked them to repeat the experiment once more. Each of the subjects based his first few estimates on his previously established standard, but confronted, this time, with the dissenting judgments of the others each gave way somewhat until a new, group standard became established. Thus, knowing what each individual brought with him to the situation, Sherif was able to show how the effect of the judgments of others resulted in the convergence of substantially different private standards and the emergence of a shared norm. When the experiment was reversed—that is, when the group situation came first and the private situation second—individuals accepted the group standard as their own and carried it away with them into the private situation. The group norm thus became the norm of each group member. Interaction had given rise to a definition of "reality" which each participating individual retained.

Such laboratory experiments are sure to encounter a barrage of critical objections concerning the dangers of generalizing laboratory findings to "real life" situations. Often these warnings are

[14]Festinger, Schachter and Back (1950), p. 168.

[15]Sherif (1952).

very sound. Often, however, they are not more than pat pronouncements about the impossibility of studying human behavior in a laboratory. It may be interesting, then, to digress for a moment to consider some of the possible objections to the study we have just reported. Consider, for example, the arguments that (1) the situation was completely *unstructured* and therefore unreal, for, after all, nobody could know that the light did not move at all; (2) it was completely *without emotional affect* for the participating subjects—that is, they could not have cared much about the validity of their judgments; and (3) it was a situation where people were *forced* to make a decision in response to the artificial demands of the experimental situation. In short, these three objections taken together would imply that Sherif's experiment can be legitimately generalized only to situations where individuals are (1) forced to make decisions (2) about something they know nothing about and (3) about which they care not at all. The critic of laboratory experimentation too often retires at this point; but we shall continue. Let us suppose, now, that these objections are in fact valid and do limit the generalizability of Sherif's finding, as in fact they probably do. Still, that leaves us with a question: are there any real-life situations that resemble this laboratory one? And our answer happens to be—yes. Consider one: For very large numbers of people the presidential voting situation can be characterized as a situation where social pressures (1) force people to make a decision they would not otherwise make (2) between two candidates about whom they may know nothing and (3) about whom they may care not at all. In such a situation, for such people, we may expect informal groups to play a large part in defining the situation, and in influencing decisions. And let us add, that it would be wrong—in the case

of almost any of the complex issues on which people in our society are expected to have opinions—to overestimate the objective verifiability of any social situation.

INTERACTION: THE PROCESS OF CONVERGENCE

If we recall now that we are still engaged in the task of reasoning out the thesis that the opinions and attitudes of individuals are rooted in the social spheres to which they belong, we will find something more in the Sherif study. The Sherif study points out for us two basic ideas: first, that individuals turn to and depend on others, when they have to form opinions or make decisions in unclear situations—this we have called the "social reality" function of groups; and secondly, that individuals interacting with each other relative to a particular problem which concerns all, will develop a collective approach to that problem and thus create an opinion, an attitude, a decision, or an action which they then will grasp in common.

Here, then, is another "reason" why we can have confidence in the contention that opinions, attitudes and actions of individuals are likely to be connected with interpersonal relations. For, in Sherif's experiment, we find an early attempt to meet the problem of *the way in which* shared norms are created and we are offered the suggestion that when individuals interact with each other relative to a problem they have in common they begin to "see" things in the same way and consequently create a social norm. If the "benefits" of conformity and the "social reality" function of groups begin to answer the question *why* individual opinions and attitudes are so often anchored in groups, then the observation that norms arise from the interaction of individuals begins to answer the question *how*. We shall consider now the way in which individuals, interacting together, simultaneously *create* a shared way of looking at things or of doing them.[16]

The Westgate study presents an opportunity to watch norms arise in the "real-life" context of a newly-built housing community for married veterans who had come to study at a large Eastern university.[17]

The community was made up of residential courts, each court consisting of several buildings and each building of several apartments. Apartments were assigned at random and none of the residents seems to have known each other prior to moving in. Research began just as the project was completed and the residents arrived. The researchers opened their investigation by focusing on factors which were influencing the growth of friendships; and we are told that friendship ties—at least in this homogeneous population[18]—can be related directly to factors like physical proximity and functional proximity (where your daily route takes you by someone's door). Thus, the largest share of all friendships grew up among people living in the same court or the same building. "These ecological factors," say the authors, "determine not only specific friendships but the composition of groups as well." Stated otherwise, it is quite clear that contact—or interaction—was the basis for the formation of social groups. Now let us see about the rise of norms.

[16]In an essay on "Social-Psychological Theory," Newcomb (1951) remarks that it is "to Sherif's eternal credit that he . . . formulated the problems of social norms in terms of perceptual processes." "Norms," Newcomb says, "represent shared ways of perceiving things (or, more exactly, shared frames of reference in which things are perceived)."

[17]Festinger, Schachter and Back (1950).

[18]These were all young married couples, of about the same age and similar social and economic status. The husbands were all veterans of military service in World War II, and were all students at the university.

Friendships and informal groupings were mapped by means of a sociometric questionnaire which requested each member of the entire community to name the three people "whom you see most of socially." Then, some time following this sociometric questionnaire, an attitude questionnaire was administered in order to study the distribution of attitudes for and against a newly-formed Tenants' Council. In the majority of cases, the attitude of an individual was found to be identical with the prevailing attitude of the other members of the court in which he lived. And since we know that contact centered primarily around the residential court—and since the attitude toward the Tenants' Council varied from court to court—we may conclude, as the authors do, that the shared opinions of the members of each court arose out of their mutual contacts and interaction.

Variations in group "cohesion" from court to court were also examined by distinguishing the extent to which sociometric choices were confined to fellow court members by the residents of each court. They report that the greater the cohesiveness (and thus, the interaction) the greater the uniformity of attitudes. And furthermore, by studying the sociometric choices of those individuals who did *not* share the attitudes of their courts, the authors discovered that often these non-conformists were residents whose friends and social life were centered not only outside the court in which they lived but outside the housing community altogether.

What we learn is that individuals who were randomly assigned to apartments throughout a housing community quickly formed themselves into friendship groups and once formed, these groups of friends adopted shared ways of thinking and judging things to which their members adhered. Here are real-life groups and real-life evidence for our contention that ostensibly private opinions and attitudes are often, in fact, opinions and attitudes which are generated and maintained in interaction with small groups of other people.[19] . . .

INTERDEPENDENT INDIVIDUALS DEMAND CONFORMITY OF EACH OTHER

The instrumental value—the "benefits"—of conformity tells us that individuals will generally *desire* to adhere to the opinions, attitudes and habits of those with whom they are motivated to interact. The "social reality" aspect of group life tells us that individuals influence each other's perceptions, so that an individual's way of *"seeing"* things, may be limited to a large degree, by the extent of his social ties. Now, there is an aspect of interpersonal relations—the last one we shall discuss here—which is, in a sense, the obverse of these two, and it, too, contributes a "reason" for believing that interacting individuals will be homogeneous in their thinking and behaving. It is that groups *require* conformity of their members.

Some of the reasons why group members demand conformity of each other are worth looking into. First of all, individuals do not like to find their associates departing from a traditional way of "seeing" something. It is a very discomfiting experience for individuals to discover that one of their number proposes to "see" something in a new way. Consider, for example, the consequences of believing that witches do not exist, in the context of a witch-hunting Puritan community.

[19]In Chapter V, [of *Personal Influence*], some of the processes of interpersonal communication are explored in greater detail. Here, we are concerned with the fact that interpersonal communication—or interaction—seems, somehow, to lead to shared opinions and attitudes and with some of the reasons why we might expect this to be the case. The "how" of the case is also implicit, of course, but while it is touched on at various points in this chapter, it will be given more attention later.

Secondly, groups like to preserve their identities, and one of the chief ways a group can make its boundary lines clear is by the requirement of uniform behavior on the parts of its members.

Third, and most important perhaps, is the fact that groups, like individuals, have goals; and group goals often cannot be achieved without consensus. That is to say, uniformity of opinion may be a *pre-requisite* for group action. In this connection, Festinger observes that "pressures toward uniformity" of opinion or attitude among group members "may arise because such uniformity is desirable or necessary in order for the group to move toward some goal."[20] Clearly, if individuals cannot agree on "what should come next," they cannot take collective action.[21]

To this point, we have indicated a series of "reasons" which can be located in the literature of theory and research in the social sciences to account for the primarily social character of ostensibly individual opinions, attitudes and actions. We began, first of all, by pointing to the "benefits" for the individual of conformity to the opinions of others in terms of the satisfactions that come with accep-

[20]He calls this "group locomotion." In Festinger (1950).

[21]All this presupposes that an individual is motivated to retain his association with this group. Such motivation may be a purely voluntary matter or may, perhaps, be a consequence of the need for solidarity in a dangerous environment, or of the need to attain some goal which requires collective action. It should be clear, furthermore, that we are more concerned here with the "automatic" controls implicit in the aspects of group life we have been discussing than in coercion or any other "special" measures which groups may take to enforce conformity. Thus, in everyday life, individuals do not depart from group norms because they do not want to surrender the "benefits" of conformity (acceptance, friendship, leadership, attainment of private goals, etc.) ; because they do not like to threaten their own mental security by permitting themselves to "see" what others do not see; and the like. This is what we mean by "automatic." On this point, see Homans (1950) on "social control."

tance and achievement of desired status. Next, we spoke about the manner in which groups function as providers of standards and meanings for their members, and consequently the dependence of an individual on those about him for the definition of "social reality." In the course of our discussion we looked, too, at some fundamentals in the process of norm formation, and we saw how interaction among individuals operates to produce shared standards of judgment, opinions, and ways of behaving.[22] . . .

Thus, we have tried to make clear, primarily from the literature of small group research, why we are convinced that studying the relatively small groups of people to which an individual is attached, is a major key to understanding the content and the dynamics of individual opinions and actions. This is an appropriate point to hoist some warning signals for the reader, particularly relating to the oversimplifications we are employing.

SOME HASTY QUALIFICATIONS

We sometimes talk as if people belong to only one group; or we may imply, at other times, that only the groups to which an individual *belongs* influence his opinions, though we are fully aware that the study of "reference" groups is a primary focus of current research; and at still other times, we may talk as if we had established beyond doubt that individuals take their standards only from small groups of others with whom they are personally acquainted and never from people whom they don't know personally or from mass media. Sometimes, too, we talk as if no other structure except the informal group exists in the world and as

if no mechanisms of control or sanctions other than interpersonal influence and ostracism were operative. Very often, we sound as if all standards, judgments, values and ideas which govern an individual's thinking and acting *originate* within the small groups in which they are "anchored" (maintained and enforced).[23] For all these, we plead oversimplification.

And let it be noted, again, that we are aware of the sometimes misleading connotations of the word "group." It is the role that *other people* play in the communications process in which we are interested, and the use of the word "group" is often simply a shorthand device to connote the significant "others" with whom an individual associates. Which kinds of "others" are significant, is a problem we shall attempt to tackle from time to time, although not in a systematic way. For it still will not serve us well to tangle either with precise definitions of different kinds of groups or with complex speculations concerning the actual interplay of groups in the lives of actual individuals. Let us suggest only that at this point in our knowledge, precise definitions, learned speculations, or "answers" of any kind are all considerably less helpful than the kinds of questions which we have seen—and which we

[22]Of course, the *processes* of interpersonal influence and communication have barely been hinted at up to this point. Much more on this subject can be found in Chapter V [of *Personal Influence*] on "Interpersonal Networks."

[23]It is well worth noting here that reference group theory and research and small group theory and research have not yet been conceptually integrated. Merton and Kitt's (1950) analysis of the implications of data from *The American Soldier* for reference group theory suggests many points at which a knowledge of the small membership groups of the respondent is basic to the reference group concept. Some of the questions we raise at this point can be found in Merton and Kitt, e.g., do individuals relate themselves only to others whom they know personally or also to impersonal status categories such as, say, 'all draft-exempt war workers,' or 'high society.' If the latter is the case as well, then, our present interest immediately directs us to inquire into the mechanisms by which one establishes 'contact' with such anonymous others. Opinion leader research can make a major contribution at this point.

shall continue to see—emerge at every turn, for questions will point the way to empirical research.

Finally, a word about "conformity." Our discussion of the consequences of deviation and the "benefits" or conformity, etc., is on the level of agreement or divergence of opinion among intimately interacting individuals. Obviously, this is quite a different level from the one on which current political discussions concerning conformity and orthodoxy in American thought are taking place. The only implication in this text for the latter discussion is the following: A nonconformist on the level of the larger society is likely to be in close touch with another, like-minded non-conformist with whom he conforms.

References

Berelson, Bernard R., Paul F. Lazarsfeld, and William N. McPhee (1954), *Voting: A Study of Opinion Formation During a Presidential Campaign*, Chicago: University of Chicago Press.

Cooley, C. H. (1909), *Social Organization*, New York: Charles Scribner's Sons.

Davis, Kingsley (1949), *Human Society*, New York: Macmillan.

Festinger, Leon (1950), "Informal Social Communication," *Psychological Review*, Vol. 57, pp. 271–282.

Festinger, Leon, Stanley Schachter, and Kurt Back (1950), *Social Pressures in Informal Groups*, New York: Harper and Brothers. Excerpts in Cartwright and Zander (1953), *Group Dynamics*, Evanston, Ill.: Row, Peterson, Chaps. 8 and 16

Fisher, Sarah C. (1948), *Relationships in Attitudes, Opinions, and Values Among Family Members*, Berkeley, Calif.: University of California Press.

Homans, George C. (1950), *The Human Group*, New York: Harcourt, Brace.

Katz, Daniel (1951), "Social Psychology and Group Processes," *Annual Review of Psychology*, Vol. 2, pp. 137–172.

Lazarsfeld, Paul F., Bernard Berelson, and Hazel Gaudet (1948), *The People's Choice*, New York: Columbia University Press.

Lewin, Kurt and Paul Grabbe (1945),

"Conduct, Knowledge, and Acceptance of New Values," *Journal of Social Issues.* Vol. 1, No. 3, pp. 53–64.

Merei, Ferenc (1952), "Group Leadership and Institutionalization," in Swanson, Newcomb, and Hartley, eds., *Readings in Social Psychology*, New York: Henry Holt.

Merton, Robert K. and Alice Kitt (1950), "Contributions to the Theory of Reference Group Behavior," in Merton and Lazarsfeld, eds., *Continuities in Social Research*, Glencoe, Ill.: Free Press.

Newcomb, Theodore M. (1951), "Social Psychological Theory," in Rohrer and Sherif, eds., *Social Psychology at the Crossroads*, New York: Harper and Brothers.

Newcomb, Theodore M. (1952), "Attitude Development as a Function of Reference Groups: The Bennington Study," in Swanson, Newcomb, and Hartley, eds., *Readings in Social Psychology*, New York: Henry Holt.

Newcomb, Theodore M. and G. Svehla (1937), "Intra-family Relationships in Attitude," *Sociometry*, Vol. 1, pp. 180–205.

Schachter, Stanley (1951), "Deviation, Rejection, and Communication," *Journal of Abnormal and Social Psychology*, Vol. 46, pp. 190–207.

Sherif, Muzafer (1952), "Social Factors in Perception," in Swanson, Newcomb, and Hartley, eds., *Readings in Social Psychology*, New York: Henry Holt.

Shils, Edward A. (1950), "Primary Groups in the American Army," in Merton and Lazarsfeld, eds., *Studies in the Scope and Method of "The American Soldier,"* Glencoe, Ill.: Free Press.

Sims, Verner M. and James R. Patrick (1947), "Attitude Toward the Negro of Northern and Southern College Students," in Newcomb and Hartley, eds., *Readings in Social Psychology* (first edition), New York: Henry Holt.

Stouffer, Samuel A. *et al.* (1949), *The American Soldier: Studies in Social Psychology in World War II*, (Vols. 1 and 2), Princeton, N. J.: Princeton University Press.

Sullivan, Harry S. (1953), *The Interpersonal Theory of Psychiatry*, New York: Norton.

Warner, W. Lloyd and Paul S. Lunt (1941), *The Social Life of a Modern Community* (Vol. 1, Yankee City Series), New Haven, Conn.: Yale University Press.

SOCIALIZATION PROCESSES IN SMALL GROUPS

In Orville Brim's discussion of the socialization process (see Reading 13), great stress is placed on the characteristics of the specific situations in which socialization occurs. Brim writes:

Consider that in the society where a child matures there are always a great number of discriminably different social situations, each with its own norms, its specification of motives and behavior. We have argued that the acquisition of knowledge, ability, and motivation is always situationally specific.

In short, one must focus attention on the social context within which socialization occurs if one is to describe adequately the socialization process and if one is to understand the characteristics of the products of this process. These socialization contexts can be described in terms of the normative and social structures present at a given time and place. What positions are involved? What norms and values are held by those present? What roles are available to be learned? What are the characteristics of the existing system of behavior and interactions? Such examination of the characteristics of the socialization context should allow us to predict certain aspects of the personalities of those socialized in these settings.

In Reading 20, Stanley Elkins utilizes this approach in attempting to explain the creation of the "Sambo" personality type prevalent among American Negro slaves. Elkins begins his analysis by assuming that the Sambo personality is not simply a racist stereotype but a description of the actual characteristics found among many slaves socialized on the Southern plantations. The docility, irresponsibility, humility, and dependence of this personality type are viewed not as innate or inborn characteristics of the slave but as characteristics produced by a particular type of socialization context. In support of his thesis, Elkins shows that similar personality characteristics have been produced more recently under somewhat similar social arrangements, namely, the personalities of inmates in concentration camps in Nazi Germany.

Our selection from Elkins is only a portion of his discussion. In the original version, Elkins takes into account other data, such as the shock effect on the slave of being ripped from his original society, marched to the sea, and the long sea voyage itself; and he examines other types of theoretical explanations—such as the Freudian and interpersonal theories—that help to account for the resulting personality. The selection we have reprinted emphasizes the structural and cultural characteristics of the plantation and of the expectations defining the role of slave. Elkins effectively argues that the plantation as a system of roles, the plantation as a socialization context, the plantation as a small group, had an important impact on the personalities of those who grew up within its confines.

All socialization contexts do not have equally powerful effects on the personalities of individuals passing through them. What factors help determine the impact of a given context? A number of variables may be singled out, but Murray Straus argues for the importance of two in particular: power and affectivity.[1] Straus contends that previous research shows that the most profound socialization effects are realized under conditions of high power (a high degree of dominance or authority exerted by the socializing agent over the person being socialized) and high affectivity (a high degree of emotionality—either positive or negative—in the relation between the socializing agent and the person being socialized). The combination of high power and high affectivity are clearly present in the situations just described: antebellum plantations and concentration camps. In such situations, the affectivity component is high and usually negative, although Elkins discusses at length the complex emotions generated in the slave-master relation. High power and high affectivity also characterize another important context within which persons are socialized—the family. The family as a socialization context will be considered in a later section (see Reading 41). The important point here is that power and affectivity seem to be significant variables in determining the effectiveness of socialization contexts. High power combined with high affectivity appear to lead to the acquisition by the subject of relatively deep-seated motives and values. In later sections of this volume, we shall want to consider other variables that may be used to characterize socialization contexts and that may have an impact on the socialization process.

[1]Murray A. Straus, "Power and support structure of the family in relation to socialization," *Journal of Marriage and the Family*, 26 (August, 1964), 318–326.

20   Slavery and Personality

Stanley M. Elkins

The name "Sambo" has come to be synonymous with "race stereotype." Here is an automatic danger signal, warning that the analytical difficulties of asking questions about slave personality may not be nearly so great as the moral difficulties. The one inhibits the other; the morality of the matter has had a clogging effect on its theoretical development that may not be to the best interests of either.

And yet theory on group personality is still in a stage rudimentary enough that this particular body of material— potentially illuminating—ought not to remain morally impounded any longer.

Is it possible to deal with "Sambo" as a type? The characteristics that have been claimed for the type come principally from Southern lore. Sambo, the typical plantation slave, was docile but irresponsible, loyal but lazy, humble but chronically given to lying and stealing; his behavior was full of infantile silliness and his talk inflated with childish exaggeration. His relationship with his master was one of utter dependence and childlike attachment: it was indeed this childlike quality that was the very key to his being. Although the merest hint of Sambo's "manhood" might fill the Southern breast with scorn, the child, "in his place," could be both exasperating and lovable.

Was he real or unreal? What order of existence, what rank of legitimacy, should be accorded him? Is there a "scientific" way to talk about this problem? For most Southerners in 1860 it went without saying not only that Sambo was real—that he was a dominant plantation type—but also that his characteristics were the clear product of racial inheritance. That was one way to deal with Sambo, a way that persisted a good many years after 1860. But in recent times, the discrediting, as unscientific, of racial explanations for any feature of plantation slavery has tended in the case of Sambo to discredit not simply the explanation itself but also the thing it was supposed to explain. Sambo is a mere stereotype—"stereotype" is itself a bad word, insinuating racial inferiority and invidious discrimination.[1] This modern approach to Sambo had a strong coun-

terpart in the way Northern reformers thought about slavery in ante-bellum times: they thought that nothing could actually be said about the Negro's "true" nature because that nature was veiled by the institution of slavery. It could only be revealed by tearing away the veil.[2] In short, no order of reality could be given to assertions about slave character, because those assertions were illegitimately grounded on race, whereas their only basis was a corrupt and "unreal" institution. "To be sure," a recent writer concedes, "there were plenty of opportunists among the Negroes who played the role assigned to them, acted the clown, and curried the favor of their masters in order to win the maximum rewards within the system. . . ."[3] To impeach Sambo's legitimacy in this way is the next thing to talking him out of existence.

There ought, however, to be still a third way of dealing with the Sambo picture,

---

[1] The historian Samuel Eliot Morison was taken to task a few years ago by students of Queens College, Long Island, for his use of the name "Sambo" (in Volume I of his and H. S. Commager's text, The Growth of the American Republic) and for referring to the pre-Civil War Negroes as "a race with exasperating habits" and to the typical slave as "childlike, improvident, humorous, prevaricating, and superstitious." As a result, the use of the text at Queens was discontinued. See Time, February 26, 1951, pp. 48–49.
The following is from the "Concluding Summary" of one of the series of studies begun in the late 1930's under the inspiration of Gunnar Myrdal: "The description of the stereotypes held con-

cerning the American Negro indicates the widespread tendency to look upon the Negro as inferior, and to ascribe to him qualities of intellect and personality which mark him off with some definiteness from the surrounding white American population . . . [;] not all these alleged characteristics of the Negro are uncomplimentary, but even those which may be regarded as favorable have the flavor of inferiority about them. When the Negro is praised, he is praised for his childlike qualities of happiness and good nature or for his artistic and musical gifts. . . . Negro writers do express much more frequently, as one would expect, the belief that whites and Negroes have essentially equal potentialities, and that it is only the accidents of training and economic opportunity which have produced temporary differences; even among Negro writers, however, some have accepted the prevailing stereotype." Otto Klineberg (ed.), Characteristics of the American Negro (New York: Harper, 1944). Instead of proposing an actual program of inquiry, the intentions of this line of thought appear to be primarily moral and its objectives to be of a normative sort: desistance from the use of stereotypes.
[2] See [Slavery], Part IV, pp. 190–191.
[3] Kenneth Stampp, "The Historian and Southern Negro Slavery," American Historical Review, LVII (April, 1952), 617.

some formula for taking it seriously. The picture has far too many circumstantial details, its hues have been stroked in by too many different brushes, for it to be denounced as counterfeit. Too much folk-knowledge, too much plantation literature, too much of the Negro's own lore, have gone into its making to entitle one in good conscience to condemn it as "conspiracy." One searches in vain through the literature of the Latin-American slave systems for the "Sambo" of our tradition—the perpetual child incapable of maturity. How is this to be explained?[4] If Sambo is not a product of race (that "explanation" can be consigned to oblivion) and not simply a product of "slavery" in the abstract

(other societies have had slavery),[5] then he must be related to our own peculiar variety of it. And if Sambo is uniquely an American product, then his existence, and the reasons for his character, must be recognized in order to appreciate the very scope of our slave problem and its aftermath. The absoluteness with which such a personality ("real" or "unreal") had been stamped upon the plantation slave does much to make plausible the ante-bellum Southerner's difficulty in imagining that blacks anywhere could be anything but a degraded race—and it goes far to explain his failure to see any sense at all in abolitionism. It even casts light on the peculiar quality of abolitionism itself; it was so all-enveloping a problem in human

[4]There is such a word as "Zambo" in Latin America, but its meaning has no relation to our "Sambo." "A Zambo or Sambo (Spanish, *Zambo*, 'bandy-legged') is a cross between a *Negro* and an Amerindian (sometimes this name is given to the cross between a pure Negro and a mulatto, which the French called 'griffe')." Sir Harry Johnston, *The Negro in the New World* (London: Methuen, 1910), p. 3. I am not implying that racial stigma of some kind did not exist in South America (see above, pp. 77–78, n. 113); indeed, anthropological research has shown that the Latin-Americans were, and are, a good deal more conscious of "race" than such writers as Gilberto Freyre have been willing to admit. Even in Brazil, derogatory Negro stereotypes are common, and are apparently of long standing. On this point see Charles Wagley, *Race and Class in Rural Brazil* (Paris: UNESCO, 1952). On the other hand, it would be very difficult to find evidence in the literature of Brazil, or anywhere else in Latin America, of responsible men seriously maintaining that the Negro slave was constitutionally incapable of freedom. The views of a man like James H. Hammond, or for that matter the views of any average Southerner during the antebellum period, would have had little meaning in nineteenth-century Latin America. One is even inclined to think that these Latin-American stereotypes would compare more closely with the stereotypes of eastern and southern European immigrants that were held by certain classes in this country early in the twentieth century. See, e.g., Madison Grant's *Passing of the Great Race* (New York: Scribner, 1916). There are stereotypes and stereotypes: it would be quite safe to say that our "Sambo" far exceeds in tenacity and pervasiveness anything comparable in Latin America.

[5]It is, however, one thing to say that no longer are there any responsible men of science to be found advancing the racial argument, and quite another to assert that the argument is closed. In an odd sense we still find any number of statements indicating that the *other* side of the controversy is still being carried on, long after the bones of the enemy lie bleaching on the sands. For example, in the preface to a recent study on the American Negro by two distinguished psychologists, the authors define their "scientific position" by announcing that their book was "conceived and written on the premise that group characteristics are adaptive in nature and therefore not inborn, but acquired" and that "anyone who wishes to quote from [its] conclusions . . . to uphold any other thesis risks doing injustice to the material in the book, to the intentions of the authors, and to the Negro people." They then quote a kind of manifesto, signed by a group of prominent psychologists and social scientists, attesting that "as social scientists we know of no evidence that any ethnic group is inherently inferior." This is followed by a portion of the 1950 UNESCO "Statement on Race" which declares that "biological studies lend support to the ethic of universal brotherhood." From Abram Kardiner and Lionel Ovesey, *The Mark of Oppression: A Psychosocial Study of the American Negro* (New York: Norton, 1951), pp. v–vi. While these are sentiments which may (and must) be pronounced on any number of occasions among men of good will (the President regularly conceives it his duty to do this), their *scientific* content (which is the level at which they are here being offered) has long since ceased to be a matter of controversy.

personality that our abolitionists could literally not afford to recognize it. Virtually without exception, they met this dilemma either by sidetracking it altogether (they explicitly refused to advance plans for solving it, arguing that this would rob their message of its moral force) or by countering it with theories of infinite human perfectibility. The question of personality, therefore, becomes a crucial phase of the entire problem of slavery in the United States, having conceivably something to do with the difference— already alluded to—between an "open" and a "closed" system of slavery.

If it were taken for granted that a special type existed in significant numbers on American plantations, closer connections might be made with a growing literature on personality and character types, the investigation of which has become a widespread, respectable, and productive enterprise among our psychologists and social scientists.[6] Realizing that, it might then seem not quite so dangerous to add that the type corresponded in its major outlines to "Sambo."

Let the above, then, be a preface to the argument of the present essay. It will be assumed that there were elements in the very structure of the plantation system—its "closed" character—that could sustain infantilism as a normal feature of behavior. These elements, having less to do with "cruelty" per se than simply with the sanctions of authority, were effective and pervasive enough to require that such infantilism be characterized as something much more basic than mere "accommodation." It will be assumed that the sanctions of the system were in themselves sufficient to produce a recognizable personality type.[7]

It should be understood that to identify a social type in this sense is still to generalize on a fairly crude level—and to insist for a limited purpose on the legitimacy of such generalizing is by no means to deny that, on more refined levels, a great profusion of individual types might have been observed in slave society. Nor need it be claimed that the "Sambo" type, even in the relatively crude sense employed here, was a universal type. It was, however, a plantation type, and a plantation existence embraced well over half the slave population.[8] Two

[6] Among such studies are Robert K. Merton, "Bureaucratic Structure and Personality," *Social Forces*, XVIII (May, 1940), 560-68; Erich Fromm, *Man for Himself* (New York: Rinehart, 1947); David Riesman, *The Lonely Crowd* (New Haven: Yale University Press, 1950); and Theodore Adorno and Others, *The Authoritarian Personality* (New York: Harper, 1950)—a work which is itself subjected to examination in Richard Christie and Marie Jahoda (eds.), *Studies in the Scope and Method of "The Authoritarian Personality"* (Glencoe, Ill.: Free Press, 1954); and H. H. Gerth and C. Wright Mills, *Character and Social Structure: The Psychology of Social Institutions* (New York: Harcourt, Brace, 1953). For a consideration of this field in the broadest terms, see Alex Inkeles and Daniel J. Levinson, "National Character: The Study of Modal Personality and Sociocultural Systems," *Handbook of Social Psychology*, ed. Gardner Lindzey (Cambridge, Mass.: Addison-Wesley, 1954), II, 977–1020.

[7] The line between "accommodation" (as conscious hypocrisy) and behavior inextricable from basic personality, though the line certainly exists, is anything but a clear and simple matter of choice. There is reason to think that the one grades into the other, and vice versa, with considerable subtlety. In this connection, the most satisfactory theoretical mediating term between deliberate role playing and "natural" role-playing might be found in role-psychology. See below, pp. 131-33.

[8] Although the majority of Southern slaveholders were not planters, the majority of slaves were owned by a planter minority. "Considerably more than half of them lived on plantation units of more than twenty slaves, and one-fourth lived on units of more than fifty. That the majority of slaves belonged to members of the planter class, and not to those who operated small farms with a single slave family, is a fact of crucial importance concerning the nature of bondage in the antebellum South." Stampp, *The Peculiar Institution*, (New York: Knopf, 1956), p. 31.

kinds of material will be used in the effort to picture the mechanisms whereby this adjustment to absolute power—an adjustment whose end product included infantile features of behavior—may have been effected. One is drawn from the theoretical knowledge presently available in social psychology, and the other, in the form of an analogy, is derived from some of the data that have come out of the German concentration camps. . . .

ROLE THEORY OF PERSONALITY

Let us note certain of the leading terms.[9] A "social role" is definable in its simplest sense as the behavior expected of persons specifically located in specific social groups.[10] A distinction is kept between "expectations" and "behavior"; the expectations of a role (embodied in the "script") theoretically exist in advance and are defined by the organization, the institution, or by society at large. Behavior (the "performance") refers to the manner in which the role is played. Another distinction involves roles which are "pervasive" and those which are "limited." A pervasive role is extensive in scope ("female citizen") and not only influences but also sets bounds upon the other sorts of roles available to the individual ("mother," "nurse," but not "husband," "soldier"); a limited role ("purchaser," "patient") is transitory and intermittent. A further concept is that of "role clarity." Some roles are more specifically defined than others, their impact upon performance (and, indeed, upon the personality of the performer) depends on the clarity of their

definition. Finally, it is asserted that those roles which carry with them the clearest and most automatic rewards and punishments are those which will be (as it were) most "artistically" played.

What sorts of things might this explain? It might illuminate the process whereby the child develops his personality in terms not only of the roles which his parents offer him but of those which he "picks up" elsewhere and tries on. It could show how society, in its coercive character, lays down patterns of behavior with which it expects the individual to comply. It suggests the way in which society, now turning its benevolent face to the individual, tenders him alternatives and defines for him the style appropriate to their fulfilment. It provides us with a further term for the definition of personality itself: there appears an extent to which we can say that personality is actually made up of the roles which the individual plays.[11] And here, once more assuming "change" to be possible, we have in certain ways the least cumbersome terms for plotting its course.

The application of the model to the concentration camp should be simple and obvious. What was expected of the man entering the role of camp prisoner was laid down for him upon arrival:

"Here you are not in a penitentiary or prison but in a place of instruction. Order and discipline are here the highest law. If you ever want to see freedom again, you must submit to a severe training.

[11]"Personality development is not exclusively a matter of socialization. Rather, it represents the organism's more or less integrated way of adapting to *all* the influences that come its way—both inner and outer influences, both social and nonsocial ones. Social influences, however, are essential to human personality, and socialization accounts for a very great deal of personality development.

"From this point of view it would not be surprising to find that many personality disturbances represent some sort of breakdown or reversal of the socialization process." Theodore M. Newcomb, *Social Psychology* (New York: Dryden Press, 1950), p. 475.

[9]In this paragraph I duplicate and paraphrase material from Eugene and Ruth Hartley, *Fundamentals of Social Psychology* (New York: Knopf, 1952), chap. xvi. See also David C. McClelland, *Personality* (New York: Sloane, 1951), pp. 289–332. . . .

[10]Hartley, *Fundamentals of Social Psychology*, p. 485.

. . . But woe to those who do not obey our iron discipline. Our methods are thorough! Here there is no compromise and no mercy. The slightest resistance will be ruthlessly suppressed. Here we sweep with an iron broom!"[12]

Expectation and performance must coincide exactly; the lines were to be read literally; the missing of a single cue meant extinction. The role was pervasive; it vetoed any other role and smashed all prior ones. "Role clarity"—the clarity here was blinding; its definition was burned into the prisoner by every detail of his existence:

In normal life the adult enjoys a certain measure of independence; within the limits set by society he has a considerable measure of liberty. Nobody orders him when and what to eat, where to take up his residence or what to wear, neither to take his rest on Sunday nor when to have his bath, nor when to go to bed. He is not beaten during his work, he need not ask permission to go to the W.C., he is not continually kept on the run, he does not feel that the work he is doing is silly or childish, he is not confined behind barbed wire, he is not counted twice a day or more, he is not left unprotected against the actions of his fellow citizens, he looks after his family and the education of his children.

How altogether different was the life of the concentration-camp prisoner! What to do during each part of the day was arranged for him, and decisions were made about him from which there was no appeal. He was impotent and suffered from bedwetting, and because of his chronic diarrhea he soiled his underwear. . . . The dependence of the prisoner on the SS . . . may be compared to the dependence of children on their parents. . . .[13]

The impact of this role, coinciding as it does in a hundred ways with that of the child, has already been observed. Its rewards were brutally simple—life rather than death; its punishments were auto-

matic. By the survivors it was—it had to be—a role *well played*.

Nor was it simple, upon liberation, to shed the role. Many of the inmates, to be sure, did have prior roles which they could resume, former significant others to whom they might reorient themselves, a repressed superego which might once more be resurrected. To this extent they were not "lost souls." But to the extent that their entire personalities, their total selves, had been involved in this experience, to the extent that old arrangements had been disrupted, that society itself had been overturned while they had been away, a "return" was fraught with innumerable obstacles.[14]

[14]Theodore Newcomb is the only non-Freudian coming to my attention who has considered the concentration camp in the terms of social psychology. He draws analogies between the ex-inmates' problems of readjustment and those of returning prisoners of war. "With the return of large numbers of British prisoners of war . . . from German and Japanese camps, toward the end of World War II, it soon became apparent that thousands of them were having serious difficulties of readjustment. It was first assumed that they were victims of war neuroses. But this assumption had to be abandoned when it was discovered that their symptoms were in most cases not those of the commonly recognized neuroses. Most of the men having difficulty, moreover, did not have the kinds of personalities which would have predisposed them to neurotic disorders. Psychiatrists then began to wonder whether their disturbances represented only a temporary phase of the men's return to civilian life. But the difficulties were neither temporary nor 'self-correcting.' 'Even when men had been back for 18 months or even longer, serious and persistent difficulties were reported in something like one-third of the men.' . . . All in all . . . the authors were led to the conclusion that the returning war prisoner's troubles did not lie entirely within himself. They represented the strains and stresses of becoming *re*socialized in a culture which was not only different from what it had been but was radically different from that to which the men had become accustomed during their years of capture." "When a deliberate attempt is made to change the personality, as in psychotherapy, success brings with it changes in role patterns. When the role prescriptions are changed—as for . . . concentration-camp inmates—personality changes also occur. When forcible changes in role prescriptions are removed, the degree to which the previous personality is 're-

[12]Quoted in Leon Szalet, *Experiment "E"* (New York: Didier, 1945), p. 138.

[13]Cohen, *Human Behavior, in the Concentration Camp* (New York: Norton, 1953), pp. 173–74.

It is hoped that the very hideousness of a special example of slavery has not disqualified it as a test for certain features of a far milder and more benevolent form of slavery. But it should still be possible to say, with regard to the individuals who lived as slaves within the respective systems, that just as on one level there is every difference between a wretched childhood and a carefree one, there are, for other purposes, limited features which the one may be said to have shared with the other.

Both were closed systems from which all standards based on prior connections had been effectively detached. A working adjustment to either system required a childlike conformity, a limited choice of "significant others." Cruelty per se cannot be considered the primary key to this; of far greater importance was the simple "closedness" of the system, in which all lines of authority descended from the

master and in which alternative social bases that might have supported alternative standards were systematically suppressed.[15] The individual, consequently, for his very psychic security, had to picture his master in some way as the "good father,"[16] even when, as in the concentration camp, it made no sense at all.[17] But why should it not have made

[15]The experience of American prisoners taken by the Chinese during the Korean War seems to indicate that profound changes in behavior and values, if not in basic personality itself, can be effected without the use of physical torture or extreme deprivation. The Chinese were able to get large numbers of Americans to act as informers and to co-operate in numerous ways in the effort to indoctrinate all the prisoners with Communist propaganda. The technique contained two key elements. One was that all formal and informal authority structures within the group were systematically destroyed; this was done by isolating officers, non-commissioned officers, and any enlisted men who gave indications of leadership capacities. The other element involved the continual emphasizing of the captors' power and influence by judicious manipulation of petty rewards and punishments and by subtle hints of the greater rewards and more severe punishments (repatriation or non-repatriation) that rested with the pleasure of those in authority. See Edgar H. Schein, "Some Observations on Chinese Methods of Handling Prisoners of War," *Public Opinion Quarterly*, XX (Spring, 1956), 321-27.

[16]In a system as tightly closed as the plantation or the concentration camp, the slave's or prisoner's position of absolute dependency virtually compels him to see the authority-figure as somehow really "good." Indeed, all the evil in his life may flow from this man—but then so also must everything of any value. Here is the seat of the only "good" he knows, and to maintain his psychic balance he must persuade himself that the good is in some way dominant. A threat to this illusion is thus in a real sense a threat to his very existence. It is a common experience among social workers dealing with neglected and maltreated children to have a child desperately insist on his love for a cruel and brutal parent and beg that he be allowed to remain with that parent. The most dramatic feature of this situation is the cruelty which it involves, but the mechanism which inspires the devotion is not the cruelty of the parent but rather the abnormal dependency of the child. . . .

sumed' depends upon the degree to which the individual finds it possible to resume this earlier role patterns." Newcomb, *Social Psychology*, pp. 476–77, 482.

Social workers faced with the task of rehabilitating former concentration-camp prisoners rapidly discovered that sympathy and understanding were not enough. The normal superego values of many of the prisoners had been so throughly smashed that adult standards of behavior for them were quite out of the question. Their behavior, indeed, was often most childlike. They made extreme demands, based not on actual physical needs but rather on the fear that they might be left out, or that others might receive more than they. Those who regained their equilibrium most quickly were the ones who were able to begin new lives in social environments that provided clear limits, precise standards, steady goals, and specific roles to play. Adjustment was not easy, however, even for the most fortunate. On the collective farms of Israel, for example, it was understood that former concentration-camp inmates would be "unable to control their greed for food" for a number of months. During that time, concern for their neighbors' sensibilities was more than one could expect. Paul Friedman, "The Road Back for the DP's" *Commentary*, VI (December, 1948), 502-10; Eva Rosenfeld, "Institutional Change in Israeli Collectives" (Ph.D. diss., Columbia University, 1952), p. 278.

[17]Bruno Bettelheim tells us of the fantastic efforts of the old prisoners to believe in the benevolence of the officers of the SS. "They insisted that these officers [hid] behind their rough surface a feeling of justice and propriety; he, or

sense for many a simple plantation Negro whose master did exhibit, in all the ways that could be expected, the features of the good father who was really "good"? If the concentration camp could produce in two or three years the results that it did, one wonders how much more pervasive must have been those attitudes, expectations, and values which had, certainly, their benevolent side and which were accepted and transmitted over generations.

For the Negro child, in particular, the plantation offered no really satisfactory father-image other than the master. The "real" father was virtually without authority over his child, since discipline, parental responsibility, and control of rewards and punishments all rested in other hands; the slave father could not even protect the mother of his children except by appealing directly to the master. Indeed, the mother's own role loomed far larger for the slave child than did that of the father. She controlled those few activities—household care, preparation of food, and rearing of children—that were left to the slave family. For that matter, the very etiquette of plantation life removed even the honorific attributes of fatherhood from the Negro male, who was addressed as "boy"—until, when the vigorous years of his prime were past, he was allowed to assume the title of "uncle."

From the master's viewpoint, slaves had been defined in law as property, and the master's power over his property must be absolute. But then this property was still human property. These slaves might never be quite as human as *he* was, but still there were certain standards that could be laid down for their behavior: obedience, fidelity, humility, docility, cheerfulness, and so on. Industry and diligence would of course be demanded, but a final element in the master's situation would undoubtedly qualify that expectation. Absolute power for him meant absolute dependency for the slave—the dependency not of the developing child but of the perpetual child. For the master, the role most aptly fitting such a relationship would naturally be that of the father. As a father he could be either harsh or kind, as he chose, but as a *wise* father he would have, we may suspect, a sense of the limits of his situation. He must be ready to cope with *all* the qualities of the child, exasperating as well as ingratiating. He might conceivably have to expect in this child— besides his loyalty, docility, humility, cheerfulness, and (under supervision) his diligence—such additional qualities as irresponsibility, playfulness, silliness, laziness, and (quite possibly) tendencies to lying and stealing. Should the entire prediction prove accurate, the result would be something resembling "Sambo."

The social and psychological sanctions of role-playing may in the last analysis prove to be the most satisfactory of the several approaches to Sambo, for, without doubt, of all the roles in American life that of Sambo was by far the most pervasive. The outlines of the role might be sketched in by crude necessity, but what of the finer shades? The sanctions against overstepping it were bleak

---

they, were supposed to be genuinely interested in the prisoners and even trying, in a small way, to help them. Since nothing of these supposed feelings and efforts ever became apparent, it was explained that he hid them so effectively because otherwise he would not be able to help the prisoners. The eagerness of these prisoners to find reasons for their claims was pitiful. A whole legend was woven around the fact that of two officers inspecting a barrack one had cleaned his shoes from mud before entering. He probably did it automatically, but it was interpreted as a rebuff of the other officer and a clear demonstration of how he felt about the concentration camp." Bettelheim, "Individual and Mass Behavior in Extreme Situations," *Journal of Abnormal Psychology*, XXXVIII (Oct., 1943), p. 451.

enough,[18] but the rewards—the sweet applause, as it were, for performing it with sincerity and feeling—were something to be appreciated on quite another level. The law, untuned to the deeper harmonies, could command the player to be present for the occasion, and the whip might even warn against his missing the grosser cues, but could those things really insure the performance that melted all hearts? Yet there was many and many a performance, and the audiences (whose standards were high) appear to have been for the most part well pleased. They were actually viewing their own masterpiece. Much labor had been lavished upon this chef d'oeuvre, the most genial resources of Southern society had been available for the work; touch after touch had been applied throughout the years, and the result—embodied not in the unfeeling law but in the richest layers of Southern lore—had been the product of an exquisitely rounded collective creativity. And indeed, in a sense that somehow transcended the merely ironic, it was a labor of love. "I love the simple and unadulterated slave, with his geniality, his mirth, his swagger, and his nonsense," wrote Edward Pollard. "I love to look upon his countenance shining with content and grease; I love to study his affectionate heart; I love to mark that peculiarity in him, which beneath all his buffoonery exhibits him as a creature of the tenderest sensibilities, mingling his joys and his sorrows with those of his master's home.[19] Love, even on those terms, was surely no inconsequential reward.

But what were the terms? The Negro was to be a child forever. "The Negro . . .

in his true nature, is always a boy, let him be ever so old. . . ."[20] "He is . . . a dependent upon the white race; dependent for guidance and direction even to the procurement of his most indispensable necessaries. Apart from this protection he has the helplessness of a child—without foresight, without faculty of contrivance, without thrift of any kind."[21] Not only was he a child; he was a happy child. Few Southern writers failed to describe with obvious fondness the bubbling gaiety of a plantation holiday or the perpetual good humor that seemed to mark the Negro character, the good humor of an everlasting childhood.

The role, of course, must have been rather harder for the earliest generations of slaves to learn. "Accommodation," according to John Dollard, "involves the renunciation of protest or aggression against undesirable conditions of life and the organization of the character so that protest does not appear, but acceptance does. It may come to pass in the end that the unwelcome force is idealized, that one identifies with it and takes it into the personality; it sometimes even happens that what is at first resented and feared is finally loved."[22]

[20]Ibid., p. viii.
[21]John Pendleton Kennedy, Swallow Barn (Philadelphia: Carey & Lea, 1832).
[22]John Dollard, Caste and Class in a Southern Town (2d ed.; New York: Harper, 1949), p. 255. The lore of "accommodation," taken just in itself, is very rich and is, needless to say, morally very complex. It suggests a delicate psychological balance. On the one hand, as the Dollard citation above implies, accommodation is fraught with dangers for the personalities of those who engage in it. On the other hand, as Bruno Bettelheim has reminded me, this involves a principle that goes well beyond American Negro society and is to be found deeply imbedded in European traditions: the principle of how the powerless can manipulate the powerful through aggressive stupidity, literal-mindedness, servile fawning, and irresponsibility. In this sense the immovably stupid "Good Soldier Schweik" and the fawning Negro in Richard Wright's Black Boy who allowed the white man to kick him for a quarter partake of the same tradition. Each has a technique whereby he can in

[18]Professor Stampp, in a chapter called "To Make Them Stand in Fear," describes the planter's resources for dealing with a recalcitrant slave. Peculiar Institution, pp. 141-91.
[19]Edward A. Pollard, Black Diamonds Gathered in the Darkey Homes of the South (New York: Pudney & Russel, 1859), p. 58.

Might the process, on the other hand, be reversed? It is hard to imagine its being reversed overnight. The same role might still be played in the years after slavery—we are told that it was[23]—and yet it was played to more vulgar audi-

ences with cruder standards, who paid much less for what they saw. The lines might be repeated more and more mechanically, with less and less conviction; the incentives to perfection could become hazy and blurred, and the excellent old piece could degenerate over time into low farce. There could come a point, conceivably, with the old zest gone, that it was no longer worth the candle. The day might come at last when it dawned on a man's full waking consciousness that he had really grown up, that he was, after all, only playing a part.

---

a real sense exploit his powerful superiors, feel contempt for them, and suffer in the process no great damage to his own pride. Jewish lore, as is well known, teems with this sort of thing. There was much of it also in the traditional relationships between peasants and nobles in central Europe.

Still, all this required the existence of some sort of alternative forces for moral and psychological orientation. The problem of the Negro in slavery times involved the virtual absence of such forces. It was with the end of slavery, presumably, that they would first begin to present themselves in generally usable form—a man's neighbors, the Loyal Leagues, white politicians, and so on. It would be in these circumstances that the essentially intermediate technique of accommodation could be used as a protective device beneath which a more independent personality might develop.

[23]Even Negro officeholders during Reconstruction, according to Francis B. Simkins, "were known to observe carefully the etiquette of the Southern caste system." "New Viewpoints of Southern Reconstruction," *Journal of Southern History*, V (February, 1939), 52.

STATUS PROCESSES IN SMALL GROUPS

In our previous discussion of status processes (pp. 170–171) it was suggested that the processes are concerned with the differentiation and ranking of characteristics or positions, their evaluation, and the distribution of rewards based on these evaluations. Let us examine how these processes operate in two kinds of situations: (1) in small face-to-face groups in which the members are similar in many of their basic characteristics, for example, same sex, age, race, education, etc., and (2) in small face-to-face groups in which the members are differentiated with respect to some of their basic characteristics.

The Emergence of Status in Undifferentiated Groups   In order to best examine the manner in which status structures develop, it is advantageous to study behavior in newly formed groups whose members are basically similar in the characteristics they exhibit. Examples of such groups are newly formed bridge clubs composed of middle-class women, new factories whose work groups are composed of men of similar backgrounds and training, and college dormitories composed of freshmen. Robert Bales and his colleagues have studied many groups of this type in their laboratory as they bring together undergraduate men from Harvard who are similar in age, race, and school class level to work on discussion tasks. (See Reading 24)

Blau has already described for us in general terms the process of social attraction that governs the formation of such associations. As Blau notes (Reading 16, p. 196) :

A person who is attracted to others is interested in proving himself attractive to them, for his ability to associate with them and reap the benefits expected from the association is contingent on their finding him an attractive associate and thus wanting to interact with him. Their attraction to him, just as his to them, depends on the anticipation that the association will be rewarding.

There are, of course, innumerable ways of proving oneself to be attractive and of furnishing rewards to other persons, depending on the particular characteristics of the person and the nature of the group's activities. But there are also two general ways that are applicable to all types of persons and groups. The first is *conformity to norms*. One can conform to the group's norms as these shared expectations that govern participant's behavior begin to develop, as they do in all groups. As Homans writes:

To get any approval at all, a man must perform an activity valuable to others; and, as we have argued right along, others often find it valuable that the behavior of one of their companions should, like their own, conform to a norm.[1]

[1]George C. Homans, *Social Behavior: Its Elementary Forms,* New York: Harcourt, 1961, p. 146.

That is, a person will be positively evaluated by others for doing things that reward them, and conforming to norms is one way in which it is possible to reward others. This is not a new idea for us. Katz and Lazarsfeld in Reading 19 have already described what they refer to as the "instrumental benefits" accruing to the individual who conforms. Participants may differ in the extent to which they conform to group norms. Such differences will be evaluated and can lead to the emergence of a status ranking, as Homans suggests in an earlier work. Thus,

. . . the closer an individual or a subgroup comes to realizing in all activities the norms of the group as a whole, the higher will be the social rank of the individual or subgroup.[2]

Further study, however, has led Homans to argue that conformity to norms does not necessarily lead to the emergence of a status structure. This conclusion is based on the realization that although conformity is valuable to other members of the group, it may not result in differentiation, because it is possible for *all* members to conform to norms. As Homans suggests:

. . . what is important about conformity is not just that it is valuable but that it is in ample supply. Any old fool, so to speak, can conform, for many in fact do conform— including the very people that are giving approval in return.[3]

Since conformity is not necessarily scarce, the rewards that groups supply to members who conform should also not be scarce but, potentially, should be available to all. Both Homans and Blau suggest that the chief reward associated with conformity to group norms is approval or *acceptance*—recognition that one is a bona fide member of the group in good standing. It is true that acceptance is not automatic—that participants who fail to maintain a certain minimal level of conformity will be rejected and perhaps expelled from membership.[4] But it is also true that it is possible for all members of a given group to conform and hence for all members to receive acceptance from their associates. It appears that conformity to norms is not the most important criteria for differential evaluation leading to the emergence of a status structure.

The second technique for proving oneself attractive to one's associates is to *pursue or facilitate the pursuit of group values.* The content of group values varies enormously from one group to another. For a bridge group the chief values may be to win bridge games and to enjoy the company of one's companions. In such a group we would expect skill in playing bridge and perhaps social skills or skill in conversation to be valued by group members. For a basketball team, the chief value would probably be the winning of games, and the relevant valued skills would be those instrumental to the achievement of this value, for example, skills in ball handling, in shooting, and in defense. Although conformity is often plentiful, such skills as these are always scarce. They thus provide a basis for the differentiation of participants. Although all members of a basketball team may be fairly skillful ball handlers, a rank ordering of participants by this ability is usually possible; and not all team members can be the high scorer. Simply possessing the valued skills is not sufficient, however.

[2]George C. Homans, *The Human Group*, New York: Harcourt, 1950, p. 180.

[3]Homans, *Social Behavior*, p. 146.

[4]For an excellent experimental study of the process of rejection of deviant members in groups, see Stanley Schachter, "Deviation, rejection, and communication," *Journal of Abnormal and Social Psychology*, 46 (1951), 190-207.

The members who possess these relatively scarce skills must also be willing to use them on the group's behalf. They must be willing to apply their skills in the attainment of the group's goals.

The distribution and exercise of such skills provides a basis for the differentiation and ranking of group members. Group values supply the important criteria by which the characteristics (skills) of individual members are evaluated. Those possessing the valued characteristics, or more of them, are more highly evaluated by their peers than those not possessing the skills or those possessing less of them. And what kinds of rewards do all groups have at their disposal for the rewarding of such special talents? The answer is prestige or *esteem*, a recognition that these persons are in some sense on a higher level, are superior, are of higher status. Esteem is not only valuable; unlike acceptance, it is also scarce. Not all members of a group can enjoy equally high esteem. The very meaning of the term is that of differential recognition; it represents the end product of invidious comparisons of the merits of one person as against another.

Even where there are no group goals as such but there are only similar individual goals, as is the case in many work groups whose members are individually performing similar tasks, persons who use their skills to assist others to reach their goal may come to enjoy higher status as a reward for their efforts. Blau studied such a group of federal agents, each working individually on cases assigned to them. (This group is described and some of their interaction patterns are analyzed in Reading 9.) In a further analysis of this group, Blau examined the type of consultation patterns that developed among the agents, noting that the more competent agents were sought out more frequently for advice than those less competent and were held in high esteem by their colleagues. In discussing these consultations as a series of exchanges among the participants, Blau helps us to understand the process by which status differentiation occurs. Blau writes:

A consultation can be considered an exchange of values; both participants gain something, and both have to pay a price. The questioning agent is enabled to perform better than he could otherwise have done, without exposing his difficulties to the supervisor. By asking for advice, he implicitly pays his respect to the superior proficiency of his colleague. This acknowledgement of inferiority is the cost of receiving assistance. The consultant gains prestige, in return for which he is willing to devote some time to the consultation and permit it to disrupt his own work . . . .
The expert whose advice was often sought by colleagues obtained social evidence of his superior abilities.[5]

Briefly, then, the process by which a status structure emerges in an undifferentiated group may be described as follows. In early interaction, all members compete with one another to exhibit their superior characteristics. Some members, however, will have greater skills than other members that they may choose to employ in assisting other members or the entire group to realize their goals. Members with lesser skills will often be more interested in assuring the continued supply of these services than they will be in protecting their own standing in the group. They will therefore acknowledge the superiority of the other member and, hence, their own inferiority as a way of repaying the skillful member and assuring that he will continue to employ his skills on their behalf.

[5]Peter M. Blau, *The Dynamics of Bureaucracy*, Chicago: University of Chicago Press, 1955, p. 110.

The acknowledgement of status distinctions is one price paid by members of a group to secure the valued services of talented members. In this manner, competitive relations give way to exchange relations among socially differentiated partners, and a status structure has emerged.

The Activation of Status in Differentiated Groups

We turn now to the case in which participants who are not status equals assemble to form a group: status differences—for example, differences in sex, age, or occupation—are present at the outset of the group and are visible to participants. What effects do such pre-existing status differences have on the interaction of participants and on the creation of a status structure in the new situation? The study by Strodtbeck, James, and Hawkins (Reading 21) of interaction in mock juries throws considerable light on this problem.

As Strodtbeck and his colleagues note, the norms governing the operation of juries in this country support equality of participation and influence. Nevertheless, their studies reveal the development of a status order in which some types of members are more likely to be selected as jury foreman, have a higher rate of participation and influence, and are more likely to be perceived as fit for jury duty. These differential evaluations are strongly influenced by the pre-existing differences in status positions. Strodtbeck and his colleagues conclude:

Men, in contrast with women, and persons of higher in contrast with lower status, occupations have higher participation, influence, satisfaction, and perceived competence for the jury task.

Such members apparently enjoy high evaluations and are rewarded by receiving high esteem from their associates, as symbolized by their selection for foreman duty and their choice as competent jurors.

Why—and under what conditions—do status differences developed in and appropriate to one situation have an impact on the development of a status structure in a totally different situation? Berger, Cohen, and Zelditch have proposed a theory that attempts to account for these results.[6] Oversimplifying their approach, they first distinguish between what they call "specific status characteristics" and "diffuse status characteristics." Specific characteristics are those which are associated with a particular and limited set of expectations about how a person will perform in a given situation; for example, a person with high mathematical skills should perform mathematical problems better than a person with low mathematical skills. Diffuse characteristics are those associated with a generalized and unspecified set of expectations, suggesting that the person possessing the valued characteristic is in some general way superior or better than persons lacking the characteristic. Sex, race, and general occupational categories often function as diffuse status characteristics. Berger and his colleagues propose two sets of assumptions that they believe are sufficient to account for results such as those reported by Strodtbeck. The first describes the kind of situation in which diffuse status characteristics will be activated. They argue that activation will occur in any task situation (1) that is collective in the sense that the interaction of the participants is required if a solution is to be obtained, (2) where some outcomes are preferred over others (some outcomes

[6]Joseph Berger, Bernard P. Cohen, and Morris Zelditch, Jr., "Status characteristics and expectation states," in Joseph Berger, Morris Zelditch, Jr., and Bo Anderson (eds.), *Sociological Theories in Progress*, Vol. I, Boston: Houghton Mifflin, 1966. pp. 29-46.

are defined as successes and others as failures), and (3) where participants perceive the diffuse characteristic to be present and differentially distributed. The second assumption concerns the way in which expectations relating to ability to perform the task at hand are developed. This assumption is that in the absence of any knowledge concerning the skills of members with respect to the task at hand, and in the absence of any specific expectations linking the diffuse characteristic to the task at hand, the participants will presume that persons possessing the valued diffuse characteristic (or more of it) will be superior at the task at hand.[7] In short, under the conditions specified, persons who are perceived to be generally superior will be presumed to be superior at performing the task at hand, whatever the nature of that task. As Berger and his colleagues state, ". . . the external status characteristic operates not only when it is directly related to the task of the group, but often even when it has no obvious or direct bearing on the group's task."[8]

The Maintenance of Status in Differentiated Groups   We have considered how status structures emerge in formerly undifferentiated groups and how status structures developed in one context may be activated to function in different and novel situations. It remains for us to examine the processes by which status structures that have evolved in a group persist over time to govern the subsequent interaction of participants.

There are a number of factors that act to perpetuate a given status structure once it has emerged, even when the group undergoes changes in its situation or in the kinds of tasks in which it is engaged. Let us examine some of them. First, it may be the case that the characteristics that led a participant to be differentiated from his fellows, to be highly evaluated, and to be rewarded with their esteem will continue to be relevant in other situations and valued by the group. Verbal skills, for example, may be useful in a number of situations and hence be highly valued and serve as the basis for continued high status. And many basic athletic skills such as coordination and endurance may permit a member to be valuable to his associates through a variety of types of games and athletic contests.

Second, as we shall discuss later when we consider power processes, high status is often associated with high influence or high power in a small group. This suggests that persons with high status may have a stronger voice in determining the kinds of activities in which the group engages. The prudent member who wishes to retain his favored standing in the group will be motivated to push the group toward selecting an activity in which he can excel. Thus, an experimental study showed that groups whose leaders failed to influence choice of activities were less likely to remain leaders in later phases of group activities than those who were able to exert such influence.[9] It is very apparent from William Foote Whyte's description of the Norton Street gang that Doc, a successful leader enjoying high status in the group, was able to influence the group in its choice of activities.[10] (See Reading 22)

[7]Berger, Cohen, and Zelditch, pp. 34-39.
[8]Berger, Cohen, and Zelditch, pp. 30-31.
[9]See Elihu Katz et al., "Leadership stability and social change," *Sociometry*, 20 (1957), 36-50.
[10]William Foote Whyte, *Street Corner Society* (rev. ed.), Chicago: University of Chicago Press, 1955.

Third, we have already seen how status processes involve not only evaluations of present contributions but also expectations for future behavior. In an experiment involving two informal groups of adolescent boys that had already achieved a differentiated status structure, Harvey has shown the presence of such expectations.[11] The members were asked to predict how well they would do in a dart-throwing contest. Harvey's analysis shows that

The *higher* a member's standing in the group hierarchy, the *more* he will tend to overestimate his future performance on a meaningful task. Conversely, the *lower* an individual's relative standing in the group structure, the *less* will he tend to overestimate his future performance, even to the point of actual underestimation in some instances. Further . . . the *higher* the standing in the group hierarchy the *greater* are the expectations other group members hold of him. Thus the *higher* a subject's status the *more* his future performance was overestimated by lower ranking subjects. Conversely, the *lower* the standing in the group hierarchy of a given individual the *lower* were the expectations other group members tended to have for him, so much lower in fact that it was the tendency for high standing members to *underestimate* the performance of the lowest standing member.[12]

Those enjoying high status will expect themselves to do well and hence enjoy self-confidence; they will also be expected by others to do well and hence will enjoy group support. Whyte's analysis of bowling behavior shows the importance of both self-confidence and group support as factors affecting performance. (Reading 22)

Our first three factors indicate some of the ways in which the "deck may be stacked" in favor of the members already enjoying high status so as to allow them to retain their position. The fourth set of factors has to do with the performance itself. At some point our participants must perform. The situation may be biased in their favor because of their abilities, the type of task chosen, or the social support and personal confidence they possess because of the structuring of expectations. But is is still necessary for them to act and, in a sense, to lay their reputation on the line. Does their favored position help them when, in spite of these advantages, they perform badly? The apparent answer in many cases is that it does. Returning to the group situation examined by Harvey, a related study focused on the judgments of actual performance rather than expectations for performance.[13] For this study a ball (rather than darts) was thrown at the target to make observable performance somewhat ambiguous, although accuracy could be objectively evaluated by means of electronic gear attached to the target. The authors summarize their findings as follows:

. . . variations in judgment of performance are significantly related to status in the group. The performance of members of high status was overestimated; the performance of members of low status was underestimated, the extent of over- or under-estimation being positively related to status rankings.[14]

Such perceptual distortion of performance quality is more apt to occur, of course, where performance scores are somewhat ambiguous. The scores in a bowling contest would appear to be quite objective, and in Whyte's study of the Norton Street gang's contest we find no reference to such distortion. But other

[11]O. J. Harvey, "An experimental approach to the study of status relations in informal groups," *American Sociological Review*, 18 (August, 1953), 357–367.

[12]Harvey, p. 363. Emphasis in original.

[13]Muzafer Sherif, B. Jack White, and O. J. Harvey, "Status in experimentally produced groups," *American Journal of Sociology*, 60 (January, 1955), 370–379.

[14]Sherif, White, and Harvey, p. 379.

techniques are available, chief among which is simply discounting scores that do not coincide with one's expectations. They can be explained away as being due to "luck" or "chance" or "simply as a queer quirk of the game." It is by such simple and familiar techniques that a man's social standing can be insulated from occasional lapses and can be at least temporarily protected. And it is by such techniques that status structures are preserved, sometimes past the point where it is in the best interests of the group to maintain them.

21   Social Status in Jury Deliberations*

Fred L. Strodtbeck, Rita M. James, and Charles Hawkins

Occupational specialization has two distinguishable effects. First, it increases productivity and, second, it provides the basis for a status hierarchy. It is less commonplace to think of role differentiation in face to face groups as arising from a similar economic process and resulting in similar status differences. For groups to define and achieve their goals, they must control the use of their primary group resource, their common time together. Only one, or, at most, a few persons can talk at any given instant and be understood. Who talks and how much he talks is, within limits, determined by the reactions of the remainder of the group to the speaker. Acts that are perceived as relevant to the solution of the group's problems are generally fa-

vorably received and the responsible speaker is encouraged to continue. Over the long run participation tends to become differentiated with a small fraction of the group's members accounting for most of the participation.

For the purposes of the present study into the relationships between occupation and selected aspects of role differentiation, it is desirable that the focus of the small group discussion not be that narrowly circumscribed by status prerogatives. For example, a group of officers and enlisted men discussing military problems or a group of doctors and nurses discussing a medical problem would not provide the circumstance we require. A greater presumption of equality is desired.

In the jury situation there is not only the wide-spread norm that group members should act toward one another as equals but also the reinforcement of the presumption of equality by the requirement that the verdict be unanimous. Equal and responsible participation in the deliberation is an institutionalized expectation. Therefore, if there is evidence that the status differences of the larger com-

* A report of the experimental jury investigation conducted as part of the Law and Behavioral Science Project with funds granted by the Ford Foundation at the Law School, The University of Chicago.

Lee H. Hook and Kathleen Beaufait, current staff members, and Margaret R. McDonald, Leo Lynch, and Noreen Haygood, former staff members, are appreciatively acknowledged for their contribution toward the accumulation of the data on which this report is based.

Reprinted from Fred L. Strodtbeck, Rita M. James and Charles Hawkins, *American Sociological Review*, 22 (December, 1957), 713-719, by permission of the American Sociological Association and the author.

munity become manifest in the deliberation, then it may be expected that a similar generalization of status will be found in other interactional contexts where hierarchical considerations are more prominent.

It is essential for our study that wide background differences be present within the juror population. This is assured by the fact that in metropolitan areas such as Chicago, St. Louis, and Minneapolis where our experimental jury research has been conducted, jurors are selected by a random process from voting registration lists. The resultant jury pool population compares closely with the expected population computed from census reports, although there are several known sources of bias. Lawyers', doctors, teachers, policemen and other local and federal employees, including elected officials, are excused from jury service. Aliens, foreign visitors, recent migrants and persons under 21, who are not eligible to vote, do not appear on the jury lists. Finally, men who operate "one man" businesses and prospective jurors with pressing personal problems can ordinarily have their jury service deferred or cancelled. The net effect is that the professions and the very low education and occupation groups are slightly underrepresented.

Occupations are classified in four groups: proprietors, clerical, skilled and labor. "Proprietor" includes the census category[1] of Proprietors, Managers and Officials as well as professionals such as architects, accountants, and engineers who are not excluded from service. "Clerical" and "skilled" categories correspond to the census categories and "labor" subsumes the census categories semi-skilled workers, non-farm laborers and

servant classes. Farm owners and laborers are absent from our populations, and retired persons have been classified by their occupations prior to retirement. Women are classified by their stated occupations, except that housewives are classified by their husbands' occupations.

Previous studies indicate that power and participation in face to face situations are related to status. Caudill[2] observed the daily exchange of information at administrative conferences among the staff of a small psychiatric hospital and found that the relative participation by the director of the service, the residents, the head nurse, the nurses and the occupational therapist were ordered by their statuses in the hospital even though the lower status persons ordinarily spent more time with the patients. Torrance[3] used non-military problems but found that pilots, navigators, and gunners recognized a power hierarchy in the contrived situation which paralleled that ordinarily in effect in airship operation. Strodtbeck[4] demonstrated that the greater economic and religious power of Navaho in contrast with Mormon women was reflected in their greater power in husband-wife decision-making. More pertinent, perhaps, is a study[5] relating to the continuation in jury deliberations of a strong emphasis by women on expressive and integrative acts. The components that had been found descriptive of wom-

[1]Alba M. Edwards, *Bureau of the Census Alphabetical Index of Occupations by Industries and Social-Economic Groups*, Washington, D. C.: U. S. Department of Commerce, 1937.

[2]William Caudill, *The Psychiatric Hospital as a Small Society*, Cambridge: Harvard University Press, 1958.
[3]E. P. Torrance, "Some Consequences of Power Differences on Decision Making in Permanent and Temporary Three-Man Groups," *Research Studies*, Pullman: State College of Washington, 1954, 22, pp. 130–140.
[4]F. L. Strodtbeck, "Husband-Wife Interaction Over Revealed Differences," *American Sociological Review*, 16 (August, 1951), pp. 141–145.
[5]F. L. Strodtbeck and R. D. Mann, "Sex Role Differentiation in Jury Deliberations," *Sociometry*, 19 (March, 1956), pp. 3–11.

en's role in family interaction situations were found to characterize women's roles in jury deliberations.

It is important to stress that while the related studies are consistent insofar as they suggest a parallel between generalized status and status in face to face systems, they do not provide a firm basis for generalizing to the situation at hand, at least in terms of the measure of correspondence. In Torrance's experiment the pilots probably dominated to a lesser degree in the experimental situation than they would have when the airship was in operation. Thus, while the ordering was preserved, it was undoubtedly attenuated. In the present case, what differences are to be expected? Relations between roles like pilot-gunner and clerical worker-laborer are not equally clear in the interaction differences they imply. There is no compelling reason to believe that clerical workers and laborers will have had sufficient experience together to evolve a stable pecking order. Further, once jurors have completed their deliberations, there is no expectation of continued relations that would provide opportunity for external status differences to become manifest. If status differences are present in the jury room, it is almost certain that they arise in part because the varied requirements of the deliberation re-create within the jury the need for the differential experiences associated with status. Whether or not the determinants from the external system are great enough to become apparent in a one to two hour deliberation is the empirical question we seek to answer.

SOURCE OF DATA

Mock jury deliberations were conducted in which the participants were jurors drawn by lot from the regular jury pools of the Chicago and St. Louis courts.

The jurors listened to a recorded trial, deliberated, and returned their verdict—all under the customary discipline of bailiffs of the court. The jury deliberations were recorded, fully transcribed, and scored in terms of interaction process categories.

This paper is based primarily upon 49 deliberations for which interaction process analysis has been carried out. Although further work is in process on more than 100 additional deliberations which have been collected by the project during the past three years, the present report is final in that further interaction process analysis of the type here reported is not contemplated. Two civil trials were used as the basis for the deliberations. In the first (29 deliberations), the plaintiff, a secretary, seeks compensation for injuries incurred in a two-car collision, and in the second (20 deliberations), a young child seeks compensation for facial disfigurement incurred in a fire alleged to have been caused by a defective vaporizer. A total of 49 x 12, or 588 different jurors were involved. Data on 14 vaporizer cases and 28 recent experimental trials are utilized in other portions of the paper. In total, data from 91 juries are used in the examination of different status effects.

SELECTING A FOREMAN

After the jury listened to the case, they were told to select their foreman and begin their deliberation. In more than half of the deliberations, the foreman was nominated by one member and then quickly accepted by the remainder of the group. In about a third of the deliberations the man who opened the discussion and sought either to nominate another, or to focus the group's attention on their responsibility to select a foreman, was himself selected foreman. However, in all instances the selection of a foreman was

**TABLE 21–1 Occupational Status
of 49 Jury Foremen**

Occupation	Expected°	Observed	Index
Proprietor	9.73	18	185
Clerical	15.03	15	100
Skilled	9.56	8	84
Labor	14.68	8	54

°Computed under assumption that foremen will be proportional to portion of sample in the given occupation.

quickly and apparently casually accomplished. There was no instance in which mention of any socio-economic criteria was made, but this is not to say that socio-economic criteria were not involved. For example, Table 21–1 shows that some foremen were selected from all strata, but the incidence was three and a half times as great among proprietors as among laborers. In addition, although the details are not given in the table, tabulation shows that only one-fifth as many women were made foreman as would be expected by chance.

RELATIVE PARTICIPATION

The deliberations were recorded with two microphones to facilitate binaural identification of individual participants.

The protocols were fully transcribed, and from the protocol each speaker's contributions were unitized into discrete acts. These acts are roughly the equivalent of a simple declarative sentence. Identification of the speaker was checked with the original observer's notes and scoring was done by an assistant with the aid of the recording plus indications of non verbal gestures made by the original observer.

Since there are 12 persons in the jury, one-twelfth or 8 1/3 per cent, of the total acts is the pro rata percentage for each juror's acts. This provides the base-line against which the effects of external status may be appraised. The higher the average participation of an occupational group, the greater their relative share of the common resource of time. It may be seen in Table 21–2 that in all occupations males talked more than females and the amount of participation was sharply differentiated between higher than expected values for proprietors and clerical workers and lower than expected values for skilled and unskilled laborers.

While the moderately differing values in Table 21–2 are averages based upon the scores of more than 500 persons, within any particular deliberation, there was a very steep differentiation between the most and least-speaking jurors. For ex-

TABLE 21–2 Percentage Rates of Participation in Jury Deliberation by Occupation and Sex of Juror

Sex	Occupation				
	Proprietor	Clerical	Skilled	Laborer	Combined
Male	12.9	10.8	7.9	7.5	9.6
	(81)	(81)	(80)	(107)	(349)
Female	9.1	7.8	4.8	4.6	6.6
	(31)	(92)	(28)	(62)	(213)
Combined	11.8	9.2	7.1	6.4	8.5
	(112)	(173)	(108)	(169)	(562)°

°Numbers of jurors are shown in parentheses. Twenty-six of 588 jurors from the 49 juries used were not satisfactorily classified by occupation and are omitted.

ample, in 82 per cent of the juries the top three participators account for one-half or more of the total acts with the remainder distributed among the other nine members. It is to be emphasized that the averages of Table 21-2 are descriptive of the relative participation of the occupation and sex groups, but do not reflect the wide variation within a jury.

One of the sources of differences in participation within the jury may be attributed to the election of one member to play the role of foreman. The foreman was responsible for approximately one-fourth of the total acts, and as previously shown, was more frequently selected from the higher status groups, but when foreman scores were eliminated the average participation values were as follows: proprietor, 8.9; clerical, 7.0; skilled, 6.3; labor, 5.9. The gap between clerical and skilled workers is narrower but the rank order is unchanged.[6]

The latent premise in the study of participation is that high participation indicates greater ability to influence others in keeping with the actor's goals. Earlier research supports such an interpretation for *ad hoc* problem-solving groups and for families. Further evidence is available from the present research. Jurors were asked before the deliberation what, if anything, they would award the plaintiff. A detailed examination of pre-deliberation awards of the individual juror with the subsequent group awards in 29 deliberations reveals that the more active jurors shifted their pre-deliberation positions less than less active jurors in the process of agreeing with the group ver-

dict.[7] This interpretation of the relation between participation and influence or status level may be documented by comparing the average pre-deliberation award by occupational group with the jury verdict. The correlations are as follows: proprietor .50, (P < .05); clerical .11; skilled .29; labor .02. Members from the same occupational group sometimes initially favored different verdicts, and in this case not all the members of this group achieved their desired outcome. Nonetheless, the proprietors showed a significant correlation between their average and the jury verdicts. This result, which separates proprietors from other occupations, corresponds to the participation values after they have been corrected by eliminating the foreman. Since our content analyses clearly show that foremen were more neutral in the discussion of how much money to award the plaintiff than other high participating jurors, the corrected participation values are probably a more satisfactory measure of influence in the damage award discussion.

The meaning of levels of participation may be viewed from still another perspective. After the deliberation, the jurors were asked to answer a battery of questions reporting their personal satisfaction with the quality of the deliberation and the tone of interpersonal relations. The level of an individual's satisfaction was positively correlated with the level of his own participation (r=.52, P < .05). The involvement that high participation represents in the jury is not unlike the investment in the affairs of the larger community by higher status persons; both are instruments for group-derived satisfactions.

As a further commentary upon the

[6]A further check was made on the effects of being on a jury with differing numbers of one's own occupation group. For juries in which at least two of each occupational group are present, the values are quite similar to Table 21-2, and while there is some tendency for higher status persons to talk more when they are alone, or in a marked minority, further corrections have minor effects.

[7]Allen Barton, "Persuasion and Compromise in Damage Awards," December, 1956. Unpublished ms.

TABLE 21–3 Average Votes Received as Helpful Juror by Occupation and Sex

Sex	Occupation				
	Proprietor	Clerical	Skilled	Laborer	Combined
Male	6.8	4.2	3.9	2.7	4.3
	(113)	(108)	(115)	(143)	(479)
Female	3.2	2.7	2.0	1.5	2.3
	(34)	(116)	(36)	(76)	(262)
Combined	6.0	3.4	3.5	2.3	3.6
	(147)	(224)	(151)	(219)	(741) °

°This number includes 14 additional cases for which interaction process scores are not available.

interpretation of participation levels, responses to the post-deliberation question, "Who do you believe contributed most to helping your group reach its decision?" were tabulated by occupation of the target person. The average number of helpfulness votes received by occupation groups (see Table 21–3) closely parallels the participation by occupation groups (see Table 21–2). The correlation between votes received and participation is about .69 when sets of individual values are correlated. Male clerical workers get slightly fewer votes than their participation would appear to warrant and male skilled workers get slightly more, but the overwhelming impression is that votes received as a helpful juror, like participation, influence, and satisfaction parallels status differentiation in the larger society.

PERCEIVED FITNESS AS JURORS

Where is the quality of justice to be found? The Courts Martial reform, which permitted enlisted men to request other enlisted men for their trial panels, was largely nullified by their preference to leave their cases in the hands of officers. How do jurors react? A departure from random selection might tend toward overselection of the higher occupations as it

had in the helpfulness nominations, or, as one might predict in terms of class theory, departure from randomness might be in the direction of heightened choice for the chooser's own occupation. How these counter tendencies might be balanced is a question for which we have no theoretical answer and therefore must investigate empirically.

In an effort to probe deeper for evidence of class identifications, the following question was asked of 28 juries.

The jury pool is made up of people from all walks of life. However, if a member of your family were on trial and you had your choice, which of the following kinds of people would you prefer to make up the majority of the jurors who would hear your case?

(Business and professional people; clerical and white collar workers; skilled workers; unskilled workers.)

The expected values, determined by assuming that each status group is equally likely to be chosen, have been divided into the observed values and the resultant ratio multiplied by 100 to give the index numbers shown in Table 21-4. All groups, except laborers, would prefer to have a member of their family tried before a jury, the majority of whose members were proprietors. Like other groups, laborers were also upwardly ori-

**TABLE 21–4 Choice of Juror If Member of Respondent's Family Were on Trial,
Based upon Occupation Stereotypes (Pro Rata Expected is 100)°**

Respondent's Occupation	Preferred Occupation			
	Proprietor	Clerical	Skilled	Laborer
Proprietor (63)	241	95	51	13
Clerical (107)	206	112	71	11
Skilled (72)	172	55	139	33
Laborer (76)	126	42	147	84

°These data were collected from jurors in our 28 most recent experimental juries. See fn. 8.

ented in their preference rank but their first choice was skilled workers, then proprietors. Clerical and skilled workers chose persons from their own occupation group as their second choice. All groups except laborers ranked laborers last. Laborers placed themselves third and clerical persons last. It is to be stressed that Table 21-4 represents the choice of jurors in terms of occupational stereotypes. It is what a member of one occupational group perceives in terms of his generalized conception of his own and other occupational groups.

We also asked jurors to choose "four of your fellow jurors whom you would best like to have serve on a jury if you were on trial." This latter question asks jurors not for generalized conceptions of other occupational groups but for evaluations of particular persons. We wished to know if the selections when jurors chose on the basis of face to face contact were similar or different from stereotype choices.[8] If a prototype of a social system had grown during deliberation, jurors might come to regard one another more in terms of performance in the task at hand than in

[8]The stereotype juror preference question was not asked the juries in Table 21-5. The 28 juries of Table 21-4 are a wholly different set, so that the possible bias of face to face choices by the prior administration of the stereotype choices is avoided.

terms of general social status. It was also possible for the deliberation to reveal status-based ideologies that would open latent schisms. The data suggest that differences were ordinarily not magnified by the deliberation and the jurors came to be convinced that a just job had been done. The special thrust of the question "If a member of your family were on trial" could have sensitized jurors to think in terms of personal interests rather than abstract principles such as competence or justice. Heightened sensitivity of personal interests could have caused respondents to turn away from those who had been the arbiters of consensus in their deliberation.

Table 21–5 shows a preference for proprietors but at a somewhat lower level. More detailed effects of the face to face experience in contrast with the response to occupational categories may best be illustrated by subtracting Table 21-4 from 21-5. It is to be noted that while Tables 21-4 and 21–5 are based on different populations, the respondents in both cases are random samples from the population available in successive weeks in the jury pool.

When Table 21-4 is subtracted from Table 21–5 (see Table 21–6) a positive value in the matrix represents an increase in index value associated with the face to

TABLE 21–5 Choice of Juror If Respondent Were on Trial, Based upon Deliberation Experience (Pro Rata Expected is 100)°

Respondent's Occupation	Preferred Occupation			
	Proprietor	Clerical	Skilled	Laborer
Proprietor (78)	169	110	119	39
Clerical (129)	145	100	101	75
Skilled (74)	147	104	84	73
Laborer (130)	162	100	112	74

°The expected values used to form the index numbers have been determined by assuming that each person distributes his four choices under conditions that give an equal chance of each of the 11 fellow juror's being chosen. For example, for 2 proprietors, 4 clerical, 2 skilled, and 4 labor, the expected distribution of the 8 proprietor votes would be 2/11 (B), 8/11 (B), 4/11 (B) and 8/11 (B). It is assumed that no fellow juror can be chosen twice by the same subject. The expected and observed choices for individuals on one jury are combined by status groups and accumulated for the different juries. Only 6 randomly selected jurors in the 20 vaporizer cases were asked this form of the question, so the 411 responses come from a potential population of (29 x 12) + (20 x 6), or 468.

face experience. The boldface diagonal shows that "own group" choices were lower at each occupation level, particularly among proprietors and skilled laborers. That is, choices after the deliberation experience are not determined by a narrow "interest group." In addition, all values above the main diagonal are positive. That is, face to face experience caused lower status persons to be evaluated more highly. As shown below the main diagonal, proprietors were reduced in the evaluation of clerical and skilled workers and increased in the evaluation of laborers; clerical persons were rated more highly by both skilled workers and laborers; and laborers decreased their former preference for skilled workers. The lower range of index values in the face to face situation arises in part from the effects of forcing the distribution of 4 votes among the 11 jurors who were members of the respondent's particular jury. Notwithstanding this flattening effect, it still appears that the face to face experience (1) results in fewer proprietor and skilled worker "own group" choices; and (2) brings the choice gradients into

smoother conformity with the observed contribution of each status group to the deliberation.

DISCUSSION

Jury deliberations have been used to examine the intersection of occupational status and sex with the typically small group measures of participation, influence, satisfaction, and perceived competence. The null assumption that there is no relation between these modes of classification can be safely rejected. Men, in contrast with women, and persons of higher in contrast with lower status occupations have higher participation, influence, satisfaction and perceived competence for the jury task.

The present study does little to explain the cause of this differentiation. Insofar as selection of the foreman may be taken as a guide to more general expectations concerning desirable attributes for the jury task, it appears that the foreman is expected to be a male, preferably, a male of higher occupational status. Although we know of no empirical studies, we assume that the business discipline and

TABLE 21–6 Change in Index Value Associated with Deliberation Experience
(Value of Table 21–4 Subtracted from Table 21–5)

Respondent's Occupation	Preferred Occupation			
	Proprietor	Clerical	Skilled	Laborer
Proprietor	−72	15	68	26
Clerical	-61	−12	30	64
Skilled	−35	49	−55	40
Laborer	36	58	−35	−10

related experiences of higher status occupations involve both substantive knowledge and interactional skills that may be used during the deliberation. Hence, in the competition for the available deliberation time, higher status males may rise to prominence because their comments are perceived to have greater value. On the other hand, since the cues of status—dress, speech, and casual references to experiences—are easily read, the differentiation may in part be explained by these expectations instead of actual performance.

Jurors who used more of the group's scarce resource, their common time together, were perceived by respondents to be the jurors desired if they were on trial. This finding suggests that whatever the criteria used by the groups to regulate the contributions of their members, these criteria were broadly held. The differential distribution of speaking time was

achieved without serious violation of developing group norms. Further, face to face experience in contrast with occupational stereotypes, tended to smooth post-meeting choices into a gradient parallel to both activity rates and status. These findings and others reported constitute a preliminary clarification of the small group process within the deliberation.

While our data do little to illuminate *how* differentiation arises, the status gradients emerge clearly in as brief a time as the one or two hour discussions under study. Though careful study will be required to determine the degree to which one may generalize from status in the larger social system to a particular interaction context, the demonstration of the continuity of status in the present case should be noted in any theory directed to the description of the process of status affirmation and maintenance.

22 Bowling and Social Ranking

William Foote Whyte

One evening in October, 1937, Doc scheduled a bowling match against the Italian Community Club, which was composed largely of college men who held their meetings every two weeks in the Norton Street Settlement House. The club was designed to be an organization of well-educated and superior men, although Doc was a member, and Angelo, Lou, and Fred of the Nortons had been voted in upon his recommendation. The other Nortons felt that the club was "high-toned," and around the corner it was known as the "Boys' Junior League." They were a little flattered that members of their group could mix with such a club, but their opinion was formed largely from the personalities of Chick Morelli, the president, and Tony Cardio, another prominent member, both of whom they considered snobbish and conceited. Consequently, the Nortons took this match very seriously.

Doc was captain of the Nortons. He selected Long John, Frank, Joe, and Tommy for his team. Danny and Mike were not bowling in this period. Chick and Tony led the Community Club team.

Feeling ran high. The Nortons shouted at the club bowlers and made all sorts of noises to upset their concentration. The club members were in high spirits when they gained an early lead but had little to say as the Nortons pulled ahead to win by a wide margin.

After the match I asked Frank and Joe if there was any team that they would have been more eager to beat. They said that if they could pick out their favorite victims, they would choose Chick Morelli, Tony Cardio, Joe Cardio (Tony's brother), Mario Testa, and Hector Marto. These last three had all belonged to the Sunset Dramatic Club.

Frank and Joe said that they had nothing against the other three men on the Community Club team but that the boys had been anxious to beat that team in order to put Chick and Tony "in their places." Significantly, Frank and Joe did not select their favorite victims on the basis of bowling ability. The five were good bowlers, but that was not the deciding factor in the choice. It was their social positions and ambitions that were the objects of attack, and it was that which made victory over the Community Club so satisfying.

Lou Danaro and Fred Mackey had cheered for the club. Although they were club members, the boys felt that this did not excuse them. Danny said: "You're a couple of traitors—Benedict Arnolds. . . . . You're with the boys—and then you go against them. . . . . Go on, I don't want your support."

Fred and Lou fell between the two groups and therefore had to face this problem of divided allegiance. Doc's position on the corner was so definitely established that no one even considered the possibility of his choosing to bowl for the Community Club against the Nortons.

Reprinted from *Street Corner Society: The Social Structure of an Italian Slum* by William Foote Whyte by permission of The University of Chicago Press and the author. Copyright 1943 and 1955 by The University of Chicago, pp. 14–25.

This was the only match between the two teams that ever took place. The corner boys were satisfied with their victory, and the club did not seek a return match. Tony Cardio objected to the way in which the Nortons had tried to upset the concentration of his team and said it was no fun to bowl against such poor sports. There were, however, clashes with individual members of the club. One night in November, Doc, Frank Bonelli, Joe Dodge, and I were bowling when Chick Morelli and Lou Danaro came in together. We agreed to have two three-man teams, and Chick and Doc chose sides. Chick chose Lou and me. The match was fairly even at first, but Doc put his team far ahead with a brilliant third string. Toward the end of this string, Chick was sitting next to Joe Dodge and mumbling at him, "You're a lousy bum. . . . . You're a no-good bowler."

Joe said nothing until Chick had repeated his remarks several times. Then Joe got up and fired back at Chick, "You're a conceited———! I feel like taking a wallop at you. I never knew anybody was as conceited as you. . . . . You're a conceited———!"

Doc stood between them to prevent a fight. Chick said nothing, and Doc managed to get the six of us quietly into the elevator. Joe was not satisfied, and he said to me in a loud voice: "Somebody is going to straighten him out some day. Somebody will have to wallop him to knock some of that conceit out of him."

When we were outside the building, Lou walked away with Chick, and the rest of us went into Jennings' Cafeteria for "coffeeands." We discussed Chick:

Doc: It's lucky you didn't hit him. They'd be after you for manslaughter. You're too strong for the kid.

Joe: All right. But when somebody's too tough for me, I don't fool around. . . . . He shouldn't fool around me. . . . . If he's gonna say them things, he should smile when he says them. But I think he really meant it.

Doc: The poor guy, so many fellows want to wallop him—and he knows it.

Frank: I liked him all right until the other night. We went to the Metropolitan Ballroom. . . . . He didn't mingle in at all. He just lay down on a couch like he wanted to be petted. He wasn't sociable at all.

After driving Chick home, Lou joined us in Jennings'. He said that Chick felt very bad about the incident and didn't know what it was that made people want to hit him. Lou added: "I know he didn't mean it that way. He's really a swell kid when you get to know him. There's only one thing I don't like about him." Then he told about a time when Chick had started an argument with a dance-hall attendant on some technicality involved in regulations of the hall. Lou commented: "He was just trying to show how intelligent he was."

A few days later, when Joe's anger had subsided, Doc persuaded him to apologize.

Doc did not defend Chick for friendship's sake. Nor was it because they worked together in the Community Club. In the club Doc led a faction generally hostile to Chick, and he himself was often critical of the manner in which Chick sought to run the organization. But Doc had friends in both groups. He did not like to see the groups at odds with each other. Though friendship between the Nortons and Chick was impossible, it was Doc's function to see that diplomatic relations were maintained.

The Community Club match served to arouse enthusiasm for bowling among the Nortons. Previously the boys had bowled sporadically and often in other groups, but now for the first time bowling became a regular part of their social routine. Long John, Alec, Joe Dodge, and Frank Bonelli bowled several nights a week throughout the winter. Others bowled on frequent occasions, and all the bowlers appeared at the alleys at least one night a week.

A high score at candlepins requires

several spares or strikes. Since a strike rarely occurs except when the first ball hits the kingpin properly within a fraction of an inch, and none of the boys had such precise aim, strikes were considered matters of luck, although a good bowler was expected to score them more often than a poor one. A bowler was judged according to his ability to get spares, to "pick" the pins that remained on the alley after his first ball.

There are many mental hazards connected with bowling. In any sport there are critical moments when a player needs the steadiest nerves if he is to "come through"; but, in those that involve team play and fairly continuous action, the player can sometimes lose himself in the heat of the contest and get by the critical points before he has a chance to "tighten up." If he is competing on a five-man team, the bowler must wait a long time for his turn at the alleys, and he has plenty of time to brood over his mistakes. When a man is facing ten pins, he can throw the ball quite casually. But when only one pin remains standing, and his opponents are shouting, "He can't pick it," the pressure is on, and there is a tendency to "tighten up" and lose control.

When a bowler is confident that he can make a difficult shot, the chances are that he will make it or come exceedingly close. When he is not confident, he will miss. A bowler is confident because he has made similar shots in the past and is accustomed to making good scores. But that is not all. He is also confident because his fellows, whether for him or against him, believe that he can make the shot. If they do not believe in him, the bowler has their adverse opinion as well as his own uncertainty to fight against. When that is said, it becomes necessary to consider a man's relation to his fellows in examining his bowling record.

In the winter and spring of 1937–38 bowling was the most significant social activity for the Nortons. Saturday night's intraclique and individual matches became the climax of the week's events. During the week the boys discussed what had happened the previous Saturday night and what would happen on the coming Saturday night. A man's performance was subject to continual evaluation and criticism. There was, therefore, a close connection between a man's bowling and his position in the group.

The team used against the Community Club had consisted of two men (Doc and Long John) who ranked high and three men (Joe Dodge, Frank Bonelli, and Tommy) who had a low standing. When bowling became a fixed group activity, the Nortons' team evolved along different lines. Danny joined the Saturday-night crowd and rapidly made a place for himself. He performed very well and picked Doc as his favorite opponent. There was a good-natured rivalry between them. In individual competition Danny usually won, although his average in the group matches was no better than that of Doc's. After the Community Club match, when Doc selected a team to represent the Nortons against other corner gangs and clubs, he chose Danny, Long John, and himself, leaving two vacancies on the five-man team. At this time, Mike, who had never been a good bowler, was just beginning to bowl regularly and had not established his reputation. Significantly enough, the vacancies were not filled from the ranks of the clique. On Saturday nights the boys had been bowling with Chris Teludo, Nutsy's older cousin, and Mark Ciampa, a man who associated with them only at the bowling alleys. Both men were popular and were first-class bowlers. They were chosen by Doc, with the agreement of Danny and Long John, to bowl for the Nortons. It was only when a member of the regular team was absent that one of the followers in the clique was called in, and on such occasions he never distinguished himself.

The followers were not content with being substitutes. They claimed that they had not been given an opportunity to prove their ability. One Saturday night in February, 1938, Mike organized an intraclique match. His team was made up of Chris Teludo, Doc, Long John, himself, and me. Danny was sick at the time, and I was put in to substitute for him. Frank, Alec, Joe, Lou, and Tommy made up the other team. Interest in this match was more intense than in the ordinary "choose-up" matches, but the followers bowled poorly and never had a chance.

After this one encounter the followers were recognized as the second team and never again challenged the team of Doc, Danny, Long John, Mark, and Chris. Instead, they took to individual efforts to better their positions.

On his athletic ability alone, Frank should have been an excellent bowler. His ball-playing had won him positions on semiprofessional teams and a promise— though unfulfilled—of a job on a minor-league team. And it was not lack of practice that held him back, for, along with Alec and Joe Dodge, he bowled more frequently than Doc, Danny, or Mike. During the winter of 1937–38 Frank occupied a particularly subordinate position in the group. He spent his time with Alec in the pastry shop owned by Alec's uncle, and, since he had little employment throughout the winter, he became dependent upon Alec for a large part of the expenses of his participation in group activities. Frank fell to the bottom of the group. His financial dependence preyed upon his mind. While he sometimes bowled well, he was never a serious threat to break into the first team.

Some events of June, 1937, cast additional light upon Frank's position. Mike organized a baseball team of some of the Nortons to play against a younger group of Norton Street corner boys. On the basis of his record, Frank was considered the best player on either team, yet he made a miserable showing. He said to me: "I can't seem to play ball when I'm playing with fellows I know, like that bunch. I do much better when I'm playing for the Stanley A.C. against some team in Dexter, Westland, or out of town." Accustomed to filling an inferior position, Frank was unable to star even in his favorite sport when he was competing against members of his own group.

One evening I heard Alec boasting to Long John that the way he was bowling he could take on every man on the first team and lick them all. Long John dismissed the challenge with these words: "You think you could beat us, but, under pressure, you die!"

Alec objected vehemently, yet he recognized the prevailing group opinion of his bowling. He made the highest single score of the season, and he frequently excelled during the week when he bowled with Frank, Long John, Joe Dodge, and me, but on Saturday nights, when the group was all assembled, his performance was quite different. Shortly after this conversation Alec had several chances to prove himself, but each time it was "an off night," and he failed.

Carl, Joe, Lou, and Fred were never good enough to gain any recognition. Tommy was recognized as a first-class bowler, but he did most of his bowling with a younger group.

One of the best guides to the bowling standing of the members was furnished by a match held toward the end of April, 1938. Doc had an idea that we should climax the season with an individual competition among the members of the clique. He persuaded the owner of the alleys to contribute ten dollars in prize money to be divided among the three highest scorers. It was decided that only those who had bowled regularly should be eligible, and on this basis Lou, Fred, and Tommy were eliminated.

Interest in this contest ran high. The probable performances of the various bowlers were widely discussed. Doc, Danny, and Long John each listed his predictions. They were unanimous in conceding the first five places to themselves, Mark Ciampa, and Chris Teludo, although they differed in predicting the order among the first five. The next two positions were generally conceded to Mike and to me. All the ratings gave Joe Dodge last position, and Alec, Frank, and Carl were ranked close to the bottom.

The followers made no such lists, but Alec let it be known that he intended to show the boys something. Joe Dodge was annoyed to discover that he was the unanimous choice to finish last and argued that he was going to win.

When Chris Teludo did not appear for the match, the field was narrowed to ten. After the first four boxes, Alec was leading by several pins. He turned to Doc and said, "I'm out to get you boys tonight." But then he began to miss, and, as mistake followed mistake, he stopped trying. Between turns, he went out for drinks, so that he became flushed and unsteady on his feet. He threw the ball carelessly, pretending that he was not interested in the competition. His collapse was sudden and complete; in the space of a few boxes he dropped from first to last place.

The bowlers finished in the following order:

1. Whyte	6. Joe
2. Danny	7. Mark
3. Doc	8. Carl
4. Long John	9. Frank
5. Mike	10. Alec

There were only two upsets in the contest, according to the predictions made by Doc, Danny, and Long John: Mark bowled very poorly and I won. However, it is important to note that neither Mark nor I fitted neatly into either part of the clique. Mark associated with the boys only at the bowling alleys and had no recognized status in the group. Although I was on good terms with all the boys, I was closer to the leaders than to the followers, since Doc was my particular friend. If Mark and I are left out of consideration, the performances were almost exactly what the leaders expected and the followers feared they would be. Danny, Doc, Long John, and Mike were bunched together at the top. Joe Dodge did better than was expected of him, but even he could not break through the solid ranks of the leadership.

Several days later Doc and Long John discussed the match with me.

LONG JOHN: I only wanted to be sure that Alec or Joe Dodge didn't win. That wouldn't have been right.

DOC: That's right. We didn't want to make it tough for you, because we all liked you, and the other fellows did too. If somebody had tried to make it tough for you, we would have protected you. . . . . If Joe Dodge or Alec had been out in front, it would have been different. We would have talked them out of it. We would have made plenty of noise. We would have been really vicious. . . . .

I asked Doc what would have happened if Alec or Joe had won.

They wouldn't have known how to take it. That's why we were out to beat them. If they had won, there would have been a lot of noise. Plenty of arguments. We would have called it lucky—things like that. We would have tried to get them in another match and then ruin them. We would have to put them in their places.

Every corner boy expects to be heckled as he bowls, but the heckling can take various forms. While I had moved ahead as early as the end of the second string, I was subjected only to good-natured kidding. The leaders watched me with mingled surprise and amusement; in a very real sense, I was permitted to win.

Even so, my victory required certain adjustments. I was hailed jocularly as "the Champ" or even as "the Cheese Champ." Rather than accept this designation, I pressed my claim for recognition. Doc arranged to have me bowl a match against Long John. If I won, I should have the right to challenge Doc or Danny. The four of us went to the alleys together. Urged on by Doc and Danny, Long John won a decisive victory. I made no further challenges.

Alec was only temporarily crushed by his defeat. For a few days he was not seen on the corner, but then he returned and sought to re-establish himself. When the boys went bowling, he challenged Long John to an individual match and defeated him. Alec began to talk once more. Again he challenged Long John to a match, and again he defeated him. When bowling was resumed in the fall, Long John became Alec's favorite opponent, and for some time Alec nearly always came out ahead. He gloated. Long John explained: "He seems to have the Indian sign on me." And that is the way these incidents were interpreted by others—simply as a queer quirk of the game.

It is significant that, in making his challenge, Alec selected Long John instead of Doc, Danny, or Mike. It was not that Long John's bowling ability was uncertain. His average was about the same as that of Doc or Danny and better than that of Mike. As a member of the top group but not a leader in his own right, it was his social position that was vulnerable.

When Long John and Alec acted outside the group situation, it became possible for Alec to win. Long John was still considered the dependable man in a team match, and that was more impor-

tant in relation to a man's standing in the group. Nevertheless, the leaders felt that Alec should not be defeating Long John and tried to reverse the situation. As Doc told me:

Alec isn't so aggressive these days. I steamed up at the way he was going after Long John, and I blasted him. . . . . Then I talked to Long John. John is an introvert. He broods over· things, and sometimes he feels inferior. He can't be aggressive like Alec, and when Alec tells him how he can always beat him, Long John gets to think that Alec is the better bowler. . . . . I talked to him. I made him see that he should bowl better than Alec. I persuaded him that he was really the better bowler. . . . . Now you watch them the next time out. I'll bet Long John will ruin him.

The next time Long John did defeat Alec. He was not able to do it every time, but they became so evenly matched that Alec lost interest in such competition.

The records of the season 1937–38 show a very close correspondence between social position and bowling performance. This developed because bowling became the primary social activity of the group. It became the main vehicle whereby the individual could maintain, gain, or lose prestige.

Bowling scores did not fall automatically into this pattern. There were certain customary ways of behaving which exerted pressure upon the individuals. Chief among these were the manner of choosing sides and the verbal attacks the members directed against one another.

Generally, two men chose sides in order to divide the group into two five-man teams. The choosers were often, but not always, among the best bowlers. If they were evenly matched, two poor bowlers frequently did the choosing, but in all cases the process was essentially the same. Each one tried to select the best bowler among those who were still unchosen. When more than ten men were present, choice was limited to the first ten to arrive, so that even a poor bowler would be chosen if he came early. It was the order of choice which was important. Sides were chosen several times each Saturday night, and in this way a man was constantly reminded of the value placed upon his ability by his fellows and of the sort of performance expected of him.

Of course, personal preferences entered into the selection of bowlers, but if a man chose a team of poor bowlers just because they were his closest friends, he pleased no one, least of all his team mates. It was the custom among the Nortons to have the losing team pay for the string bowled by the winners. As a rule, this small stake did not play an important role in the bowling, but no one liked to pay without the compensating enjoyment of a closely contested string. For this reason the selections by good bowlers or by poor bowlers coincided very closely. It became generally understood which men should be among the first chosen in order to make for an interesting match.

When Doc, Danny, Long John, or Mike bowled on opposing sides, they kidded one another good-naturedly. Good scores were expected of them, and bad scores were accounted for by bad luck or temporary lapses of form. When a follower threatened to better his position, the remarks took quite a different form. The boys shouted at him that he was lucky, that he was "bowling over his head." The effort was made to persuade him that he should not be bowling as well as he was, that a good performance was abnormal for him. This type of verbal attack was very important in keeping the members "in their places." It was used particularly by the followers so that, in effect, they were trying to keep one another down. While Long John, one of the most frequent targets for such attacks, responded

in kind, Doc, Danny, and Mike seldom used this weapon. However, the leaders would have met a real threat on the part of Alec or Joe by such psychological pressures.

The origination of group action is another factor in the situation. The Community Club match really inaugurated bowling as a group activity, and that match was arranged by Doc. Group activities are originated by the men with highest standing in the group, and it is natural for a man to encourage an activity in which he excels and discourage one in which he does not excel. However, this cannot explain Mike's performance, for he had never bowled well before Saturday night at the alleys became a fixture for the Nortons.

The standing of the men in the eyes of other groups also contributed toward maintaining social differentiation within the group. In the season of 1938-39 Doc began keeping the scores of each man every Saturday night so that the Nortons' team could be selected strictly according to the averages of the bowlers, and there could be no accusation of favoritism. One afternoon when we were talking about bowling performances, I asked Doc and Danny what would happen if five members of the second team should make better averages than the first team bowlers. Would they then become the first team? Danny said:

Suppose they did beat us, and the San Marcos would come up and want a match with us. We'd tell them, those fellows are really the first team, but the San Marcos would say, "We don't want to bowl them, we want to bowl you." We would say, "All right, you want to bowl Doc's team?" and we would bowl them.

Doc added:

I want you to understand, Bill, we're conducting this according to democratic principles. It's the others who won't let us be democratic.

POWER PROCESSES IN SMALL GROUPS

We have already discussed the concept of power (see pp. 193–194), and Blau in Reading 16 has provided us with a good general description of the operation of power processes. Power-dependency relations in small informal groups are necessarily based on the personal characteristics or attributes that the individual members possess or are believed to possess. Certain characteristics, such as physical strength, intelligence, or wealth, may be used by one individual to mediate between another individual and the goals he desires. We may call such characteristics *resources*. Levinger in Reading 23 defines a resource as "any property of an individual which he makes available to persons in his environment as a means for their positive or negative need-satisfaction"—in our terms, as a means for mediating between a person and his goals or values. An individual using his resources in another's behalf may impose certain conditions on the recipient so that he comes to have influence or power over the other. That is, the resources may be used as sanctions—as a means of rewarding or punishing the other person for his compliance or deviance.

Blau has described the process by which power comes to be differentiated in a group, the greater power going to the individuals with the most highly valued and scarcest resources. The careful reader will have noted the similarity of the processes involved in bringing about differentiated power and status structures. High power and high status often go hand in hand, as do their opposites, but this is not invariably the case. In small informal groups, the two processes have a common origin in the personal characteristics (resources) differentially valued by participants. However, high status comes to the individual whose characteristics are highly and positively evaluated by group members and who uses these characteristics in behalf of individual group members or of the group as a whole. High power can result from this process, but it can also develop from a process that is virtually the opposite. A person possessing resources that others need may gain power over them by withholding the needed help or materials or by threatening to withhold them. Or a person may possess valued characteristics in the sense that they inspire fear and dread in others: they are highly but negatively evaluated characteristics. Thus, a person of great physical strength may obtain power by hurting or threatening to hurt others unless they conform with his wishes. He may obtain power in this manner, but not esteem. However, the same resource—physical strength—may win its possessor both power and esteem if he chooses to employ it in behalf of, rather than against, his fellows. In sum, the use of valued characteristics or resources to reward one's colleagues is likely to bring both power and esteem in its wake, whereas their use to browbeat or threaten one's colleagues is likely to bring power coupled with hostility and restraint.

Levinger's study of power processes provides an interesting experimental test of the notion that power is based on differential resources (Reading 23)

Levinger manipulated the perception of resources in two ways: first, by giving different initial information to his subjects about their competence at the task relative to their partners, and, second, by controlling the interaction in such a manner that the interacting pair demonstrated differing task competence (resources) or at least differing confidence in their own task competence. The results of the study indicate that the initial information on competence had some effect on power-relevant behaviors but not as great an effect as competence demonstrated during the course of the interaction. Levinger's study also shows that there tends to be less change in the subject's perception of his own power relative to that of his partner over time. This suggests that expectations concerning one's own behavior and the behavior of those with whom one interacts tend to become stabilized over time in the sense that they are more resistant to change.

23 The Development of Perceptions and Behavior in Newly Formed Social Power Relationships[1]

George Levinger

Empirical investigations of social power have been concerned for the most part with the description of power structures and with the sociological or psychological correlates of social power at some given point in time (6, 9, 10). Attention has been directed more toward persisting characteristics than toward changes. While this work has provided considerable understanding of the distribution of power and its consequences within different kinds of groups, relatively little is known about the ways in which power relations build up and maintain themselves or suffer modifications.

[1]This report is based on a doctor's dissertation submitted to the Doctoral Program in Social Psychology at the University of Michigan. I am grateful to Dr. Ronald Lippitt for his valuable help as chairman of the doctoral committee. I am also indebted to Drs. Dorwin Cartwright and Sidney Rosen for their constructive suggestions.

The research was supported in part under grant-in-aid (M-450 (C-2)) from the National Institute of Mental Health of the Public Health Service.

The present research deals with two questions concerning the development of power relations among members of informal groups: To what extent do different kinds of interpersonal information affect a group member's power perceptions? What is the relation between his perception of other members and his behavior toward them? Before phrasing these questions as specific hypotheses relevant to a particular behavioral setting, let us consider the concepts to be used.

THEORY AND HYPOTHESES

By *social power* we shall mean an individual's potentiality for influencing one or more other persons toward acting or changing in a given direction. According to this definition, social power is the ability to exert interpersonal influence. What, then, is the basis of interpersonal influence? Such influence is established by inducing other persons to perceive that acceptance or rejection of a given

Reprinted from Dorwin Cartwright (ed.), *Studies in Social Power*, Ann Arbor, Mich.: Research Center for Group Dynamics, Institute for Social Research, University of Michigan, 1959, pp. 83–98, by permission of the author and the publisher.

influence attempt will lead either to satisfying or depriving experiences for them.
In other words, interpersonal influence
implies the manipulation of valences in
another person's psychological environment.

In formally structured groups, the basis of such influence is grounded in the
established rules of organization. In informal groups, however, the members'
differing abilities to influence one another arise out of their continuing interaction. In a newly formed group of relative
strangers the prospective member has no
rank or status. In such a setting he brings
with him merely his individual properties such as his personal characteristics;
his knowledge, information, and skills;
his material possessions; and his social-
emotional capacities. If the prospective
member's properties are relevant to the
needs of other group members, these
properties may become resources which
he can use in his dealings with them. He
can satisfy or deprive other members to
the degree that his *intra*personal properties are convertible into *inter*personal
resources.

The concept "resource" requires
definition. A resource is any property of
an individual which he makes available to
persons in his environment as a means
for their positive or negative need-
satisfaction. This concept refers to the
actualization of properties for interpersonal consumption—a consumption
which may have either positive or negative utility for the consumer. In other
words, a resource refers to some definite
act, past or present, which has the effect
of either facilitating or hindering the
locomotion of other persons or the group
as a whole.[2]

One other concept is important for this
research. Let us use the term "resource

[2]The concepts "resource" and "property" also
have been used by Bales (2) in his theoretical
discussion of group interaction. However, Bales
does not distinguish between these terms and uses
them in a less general sense.

potential" to mean those properties of
the individual which are perceived by
other members of the group as relevant
to their goalward locomotion, but which
have not as yet been demonstrated by his
behavior. Thus, resource potential refers
to properties which are convertible into
resources at some future time.

It is proposed here that in an informal
group the bases of a member's power lie
in his capacity for making available and
for withholding resources which are important for the need-satisfaction of other
members. This proposition derives from
the assumption of an underlying exchange process by which group members
attain satisfaction and avoid deprivation
of their needs. The more a member is
perceived as controlling resources which
will satisfy or deprive others' needs, the
more he will be able to influence other
persons' behavior. His power in the group
will be enhanced particularly when his
resources have relevance for furthering
the group's progress toward its goal.

In order that an individual's power may
become established in a group setting,
then, other group members must perceive
his ability to make available and to
withhold resources. This may occur
through their receiving information about
his potential resources or through their
seeing a behavioral demonstration of his
actual resources.

During the establishment of a group,
how do group members come to relate to
one another in terms of resources? If we
consider the hypothetical individual as he
enters a new group, we may assume the
following process. As he begins his contact with other members he receives
some initial information about them,
which leads him to form his first perceptions of his relationship with them. These
perceptions will determine his first action
toward the others, and this action is likely
to modify their perceptions of him. Their
behavior in turn will be shaped according
to their modified perceptions and will

probably induce a readjustment in the individual's initial perceptions. In short, it is conceived that interpersonal perceptions and behavior develop as the products of the circular process of interaction, and that the individual continually generates and is fed back information concerning his own and others' social resources.

The feedback process outlined here has implications for the growth of interpersonal relations in the group. It would appear that information fed into the circuit may lead to effects which will persist much longer than the immediate instant. If such information affects the recipient's actions, it is likely to alter the consequent perceptions and behavior of the other members and thus may have an observable impact on the pattern of interaction. It is evident that not all information will have such persisting effects. First, the saliency of such information will determine its ability to modify a relationship. The less its saliency for a given dimension of social interaction, the less it will affect the relationship. Second, the consistency of the information with other available information will affect its impact. The more it is contradicted by other relevant information, the less will be its effect. Third, its priority over later information is important. During the stages of group development, the later that information is introduced, the less will be its effect.

The present study was influenced by the above theoretical considerations. We were confronted with a choice among the many possible determinants of power in developing social relationships. It seemed worth while to consider the effects of information concerning both actual and potential resources. The following two determinants were chosen: (1) the initial information concerning the individual's resource potential relative to others in the group, (2) the information received during the group's interaction concerning the relative amount of actual resources of the members. Five hypotheses were stated.

Hypothesis 1. The individual's perceptions of the magnitude of his power will be positively associated with the favorableness of the initial information concerning his relative resource potential in the group.

This hypothesis is derived from the assertions that power is founded on resources and that relevant information will have a persistent impact over the course of the group's interaction.

Hypothesis 2. The individual's perceptions of the magnitude of his power will be positively associated with the relative amount of the resources he demonstrates in comparison with others during the group's interaction.

This hypothesis has the same derivation as Hypothesis 1. Also, there should be a far stronger effect on the individual's perceptions from the information about actual than about potential resources.

Hypothesis 3. Changes in the amount of the individual's power-relevant behavior will vary positively with changes in his perception of the magnitude of his power.

Studies by Lippitt, Polansky, Redl, and Rosen (9) and by French and Snyder (see *Studies in Social Power*, Chapter 8) have demonstrated in field settings that a person's social power is positively related to the success, the frequency, and the directiveness of his attempts to influence other persons. This hypothesis states that a person's power perception and power-relevant behavior—e.g., number of influence attempts—are sufficiently interdependent that when one is changed the other also is changed.

Hypothesis 4. The individual's power-relevant behavior will be positively associated with the favorableness of the initial information concerning his relative resource potential in the group.

Hypothesis 4 is derivable from Hypotheses 1 and 3. If the initial information has measurable effects on perception, it ought to have similar effects on behavior.

Hypothesis 5. Changes in the individual's perception of his power during the first half will exceed those during the second half of the interaction period.

Although there are likely to be continual readjustments in an individual's perceptions during social interaction, if the situation remains relatively stable these readjustments will tend to become progressively less. This hypothesis is in accordance with statements by Asch (1) and Bruner (3) that early impressions or early hypotheses tend to become resistant to change.

PROCEDURE

An experiment to test these hypotheses was designed in the following manner. The subjects were sixty-four male underclassmen at the University of Michigan who participated as members of two-person groups. Each subject was paired with a paid participant in a series of twenty-four joint decision-making trials, during which the two partners were required to reach decisions concerning a number of city planning problems. The subject was led to perceive his partner as merely another subject, who had also volunteered to help the experimenter "develop a new version of a city planning aptitude test." In reality, the partner had been trained by the experimenter, his behavior was controlled, and each trial outcome was carefully prearranged. Subjects were assigned randomly to the various experimental conditions.

INSTRUCTIONS   The essence of the experimental instructions was as follows—for the full instructions see (8):

A national foundation, which had developed a test for city planning aptitude, has found that the test needs revision because in its original form it neglected social factors. The foundation has given a contract to the Research Center for Group Dynamics for building the missing social factors into the test. The two group members are helping therefore to standardize a task in which the following three factors are important: "the knack of knowing where good building sites are; the ability to maintain effective discussions with other persons; and the accuracy for understanding one's relationship with other persons."

The two partners were told that they would be presented the plans of twenty-four different small towns, one after another. In each instance they would choose the "best building site" from among three possible sites for some given construction—such as a school, a fire station, or a supermarket. They were informed that in each case they would have fifteen seconds to look at the town, to indicate their preferred site on a slip of paper, and to pass the slip to the experimenter. This was "to indicate their aptitude for choosing good sites." Then they would have one-and-a-half minutes to discuss their choice with their partner and to come to a joint decision (failure to agree on a common site would penalize the group score). This part of the task was "to indicate their ability to maintain effective discussions." Finally, before each new trial, each person would estimate his relative influence as a group member and indicate this as a percentage (from 0 per cent to 100 per cent) on a slip of paper. This was "to indicate their accuracy for understanding their relationship with the other person."

MANIPULATIONS   The manipulation of the independent variables was accomplished in the following manner. The first manipulation involved differences in subjects' initial information about their partners. Half the subjects received indications that the partner had somewhat less experience relevant to the task than they (Superior information) and the other half that he had more experience (Inferior information). That is, after the instructions, and before the start of the task, the experimenter questioned the subject and the partner concerning their college major, their acquaintance with city planning, their performance in social studies and art in high school, and their degree of confidence about doing well at this task. The subject always replied first. Where the subject was made to feel "superior," the partner said he was majoring in English, that he had never even heard of city planning before, that he had been uninterested in social studies and had done poorly at art, and that he had little confidence. In the "inferior" variation, the partner said he was majoring in architecture, that in one course he had taken up city planning for several weeks, that he had done well in social studies and art, and that he was pretty confident about this task.

The second manipulation involved two different behavior patterns on the part of the partner, the "Accept" and the "Reject" patterns. It was arranged in both patterns that during the twenty-four trials the partner would *agree* in his initial choice of site exactly eight times. As for the remaining sixteen initial disagreements, in the Accept pattern the partner would bow to the subject on fourteen trials; whereas in the Reject pattern he would find suitable arguments for maintaining his initial choice in the same fourteen trials, so that on such trials the subject either had to concede or he had

to *disagree* at the end of the minute-and-a-half. Thus for any given trial there were four possible outcomes: Agree, Bow, Concede, and Disagree. In the Accept pattern there were always 8 Agrees, 14 Bows, and 2 Concedes. In the Reject pattern there were always 8 Agrees, 2 Bows, and some combination of 14 Concedes and Disagrees.

In order to determine the adequacy of the second experimental manipulation, a check was made of the partner's behavior. It was found that *within* either the Accept or the Reject condition there were no significant differences in his behavior toward the subjects. However, *between* these two conditions, he made more influence attempts and he was more assertive toward subjects in the Reject condition ($p < .001$). Thus, except for the intentional difference between the Accept and Reject conditions, it appears that the partner's behavior was satisfactorily controlled.[3]

[3]In addition to the two experimental manipulations reported here, a third manipulation was introduced which will not be treated in this report. At the halfway mark, between the twelfth and thirteenth trials, subjects were given differential information about their previous performance. Some subjects were informed they had done very well, others that they had done very poorly, and still others were told nothing about their performance.

This third manipulation had no essential effect on the results to be reported here. The effects of this third manipulation were briefly as follows: The half-time information significantly influenced subject's perceptions of their power. It also had a similar effect on their behavior, but not when it was contradicted by the partner's behavior (second manipulation).

TABLE 23–1 Effects of Initial Superior and Inferior Information on Subjects'
Average Perceived Relative Power (48 Reject Subjects)

Initial Information	*Average Perceived Power*			
	Hi	*Med Hi*	*Med Lo*	*Lo*
Superior	10	6	5	3
Inferior	2	6	7	9
	Chi² $= 8.69$; $p < .02$			

MEASURES   The dependent variables were the subjects' perceptions of own power and their behavior during the course of the interaction period. The former was indicated by the twenty-five estimates of their relative influence, which subjects reported before each trial and after the last one in the series.

Three separate indices were used for describing the subjects' power-relevant behavior: (1) influence attempts—the number of attempts the subject made to influence his partner to his own point of view; (2) resistances—the number of times he refused to concede when his partner maintained until the end his initial choice of site; (3) assertiveness—the degree of confidence he expressed when he spoke to his partner about his choice of site. In reliability checks, it was found that "number of influence attempts" was coded with an average r of .84, and "assertiveness" had an average r of .72. The index of resistance had perfect reliability, since it was always clear whether the subject had conceded or retained his initial position at the end of a trial. These reliabilities were considered sufficiently high to justify the use of a single observer for the behavior coding. Correlations among these three behavioral indices ranged from .60 to .62 $(p < .01)$.

Of the sixty-four subjects, sixteen were exposed to the Accept pattern and forty-eight to the Reject pattern. In each pattern, half the subjects received Superior information initially and the other half Inferior information.

Because of the difference between the partner's behavior toward the Accept subjects and the Reject subjects as mentioned above, it was found that these two groups differed significantly in their experimental experience. According to responses on a post-experimental questionnaire, Accept subjects tended to see their partners as "yielding" and "unsure of himself," whereas the Reject subjects perceived their partners as "resistant" and "strong." On the basis of these differences, one would be disposed to test a number of hypotheses separately for the two groups. Yet for demonstrating statistical significance, the number of Accept subjects is too small for making comparisons within that group. Therefore, while Hypotheses 2 and 5 are tested by the data on all sixty-four subjects, the results concerning Hypotheses 1, 3, and 4 are confined to the data from the forty-eight Reject subjects.

RESULTS

Figure 23-1 illustrates the contrasting effects of the two experimental manipulations on the subjects' perceptions of their power during the course of the interaction period. Both the variation in the initial information and in the partner's behavior exerted noticeable effects on these perceptions, but the Accept-Reject variation had clearly the greater influence.

TABLE 23–2 Effects of Partner's Accept or Reject Behavior on Subjects' Perceptions of Relative Power (64 Subjects)

Partner's Behavior	Subject's Perceived Power (at end of task)		
	Greater than Partner	Equal to Partner	Less than Partner
Accept	16	0	0
Reject	2	5	41

$$Chi^2 = 54.51; \ p < .001$$

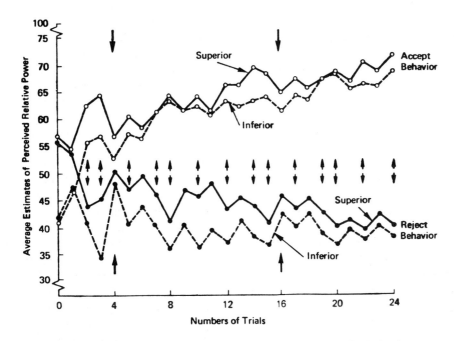

FIGURE 23-1. Effects of initial information and partner's behavior on subjects' perceptions of their relative power (64 subjects). (The fourteen arrows pointing up for the Accept and down for the Reject condition, refer to those trials where the partner's prearranged acceptances or rejections occurred. Two other arrows, for each condition, indicate where the partner reversed his predominant behavior.)

Hypothesis 1. Table 23-1 shows that the initial information had a significant effect on subjects' perceptions of their relative power.[4] Those subjects who were given to understand that their potentiality was superior estimated their power as higher than did those who heard it was inferior. Although the differential effects of the initial information tended to diminish over time (cf. Figure 23-1), these effects were still present to some degree at the end of the period.

[4]All *p*-values refer to one-tailed tests of significance, since the direction of the expected relationships was specified in the hypotheses.

TABLE 23-3 Relation between Changes in Perceived Power and Behavioral Power (Number of Influence Attempts Initiated) (48 Reject Subjects)

Changes in Number of Influence Attempts	Changes in Perceived Power (from 2nd to 4th quarter)		
	Increase ($N=17$)	No Change ($N=7$)	Decrease ($N=24$)
Increase ($N=21$)	10	3	8
No Change ($N=6$)	4	1	1
Decrease ($N=21$)	3	3	15

$$Chi^2 = 8.91; \ p < .035$$

Hypothesis 2. Table 23-2 indicates that the two variations in the partner's behavior had strikingly different effects. All sixteen subjects whose partners demonstrated much acceptance of their ideas and suggestions developed perceptions that their power was greater than their partners'. On the other hand, those subjects whose partners showed much initiative and resisted their contributions developed perceptions that their power was less than their partners'.

Hypothesis 3. It was found in this study that subjects' perceived relative power correlated .55 with their number of influence attempts, .48 with their number of resistances, and .51 with their degree of assertiveness—all significant beyond the .01 level of confidence. These correlations between perceived power and indices of behavioral power corroborate findings by earlier investigators (9). However, in order to test Hypothesis 3, we need to compare subjects' *changes* in perceptions with their *changes* in behavior from one time to another. We must ask the question, Do perceptions and behavior show corresponding shifts from one part of the period to another?

Table 23-3 shows some of the data concerning subjects' changes in their perceptions and behavior from the second to the fourth quarter of the experimental period.[5] It is evident that there was a correspondence in direction between subjects' changes in their perceived power and their number of influence attempts from one part to another part of the period, at beyond the .035 level of confidence. This finding was even stronger for the other two indices of behavioral power. Changes in number of resistances were associated with per-

---

[5]It should be noted that the second and fourth quarters were identical with respect to the partner's behavior pattern. The first and third quarters were not used for the analysis, because of the probable confounding by the impact of the experimental information.

ceptual changes at the .025 level (Chi^2=10.12; $d.f.$=4); and changes in subjects' assertiveness were related at the .001 level (Chi^2=20.06; $d.f.$=4).

The results for this hypothesis demonstrate that, comparing succeeding twelve-minute time units, over a continuous period of interaction there was a definite correspondence between persons' readjustments in their interpersonal perceptions and their interpersonal behavior.

The feedback orientation toward the process of social interaction also led to the examination of the more microscopic fluctuations of perceptions and behavior from one trial to the next. It was possible to break into the circuit and to look at the immediate effects of perceptual changes upon the immediately following behavioral changes between any given pair of successive trials, or look at the parallel effects of behavioral on perceptual changes. In this analysis it was found, contrary to expectation, that trial-to-trial changes in perceived power *did not* significantly determine parallel trial-to-trial changes in number of influence attempts or degree of assertiveness. On the other hand, trial-to-trial fluctuations in such behavior *were reflected* significantly ($p < .01$) in subjects' immediately following estimates of their perceived power. This finding seems to indicate that subjects' periodic estimates of their perceived power responded rather sensitively to their own immediately previous performance; while, on the other hand, their behavior was affected mostly by a fairly global perceptual restructuring of the situation and by the particular impact of each social episode.

Hypothesis 4. All three indices of subjects' power-relevant behavior were significantly affected by the initial manipulation concerning the relative expertness of the partner. Table 23-4 gives the data regarding subjects' number of influence attempts initiated toward their

**TABLE 23–4 Effects of Initial Information on Power-Relevant Behavior
(Number of Influence Attempts Initiated) (48 Reject Subjects)**

	Number of Influence Attempts Initiated			
Initial Information	Hi	Med Hi	Med Lo	Lo
Superior	10	5	5	4
Inferior	2	7	7	8

$$Chi^2 = 7.33; \ p < .035$$

partners, showing that the initial information about the partners' relative resource potential was an effective determinant of this kind of behavior. The other two indices were similarly affected: number of resistances ($Chi^2 = 7.19$) and degree of assertiveness ($Chi^2 = 7.33$) both at the .035 level of confidence with three degrees of freedom.

Hypothesis 5. We may observe in Table 23-5 that, in accordance with this hypothesis, there was a significant decrease from the early to the late stages in subjects' trial-to-trial changes in their estimates of their relative power. This finding confirms that the experimental task provided a rather constant situation for the subjects. Thus, the more they became acquainted with their partners, the less they found it necessary to make revisions in their perceptions of the relationship.

In this experimental setting, one member of the pair was a trained participant whose behavior was influenced rather little by the subject's actions. Outside this laboratory situation, a stable rela-

tionship would probably be reached sooner and to a greater degree. In that case, *both* partners would be sensitive to the social feed-back and mutually would govern their behavior in order to reinforce the relationship. On the other hand, such increasing stability in social perceptions over time probably is limited to settings where a minimum of new information is introduced into the interpersonal relationship.

DISCUSSION

It was found that both experimental manipulations were significant determinants of the interaction throughout the session. Even the information introduced at the very start still had a measurable effect on the subjects at the end of the session.

It will be remembered that the first kind of information was provided by the experimental partner, who varied the amount of task-relevant properties which he attributed to himself. This initial information was given to the subject before

TABLE 23–5 Mean Number of Changes in Subjects' Perceived Relative Power

First Half	Second Half	Difference between Means	t	N	p
7.4	5.9	1.5	2.59	64	.01

he had any behavioral contact with his partner.

The literature on social perception abounds with studies treating of the formation of impressions concerning other people—see the review by Bruner and Tagiuri (4). All but one of these studies, however, have been confined to the impressions that individuals form after having had contact only with photographs or with verbal descriptions of other people. The one published study directed at the formation of impressions during personal contact is that by Kelley (7). Kelley informed half of his subjects that the instructor they were to meet was "warm," and the other half that he was "cold." After listening to a lecture by this instructor the two groups of subjects differed considerably in their impression of him.

The results of the present experiment give support to Kelley's findings. These subjects had considerably more opportunity for interacting with the stimulus figure than did Kelley's subjects. Even so, we find that the initial information exerted a persisting effect upon their structuring of the relationship, despite the objectively identical behavior of their partner.

However, Kelley's findings also must be qualified in an important respect. The effects of the initial information were small when compared to the effects of the second kind of information which the subject received. Regardless of whether the subject initially received "superior" or "inferior" information, the actual behavior of his partner became more important for determining his perceptions. Depending on whether his partner accepted or rejected his ideas, the average subject's perceptions of his power moved steadily up or down. In terms of our earlier discussion concerning potential versus actual resources, we may consider

that the first type of information referred to the group member's comparative potential resources, whereas the second type of information gave comparative evidence about the member's actual resources. The continuous and recurring feedback of the second type of information was certainly effective in overriding the impact of the first type.

Let us now turn to the correspondence between the perceptual and the behavioral indices of the subjects' social power. Beyond the confirmation of findings in previous field studies (5, 9, 10) of the correlation between average perceived power and average behavioral output, it was demonstrated that shifts in subjects' power perceptions were related to corresponding shifts in their power-relevant behavior. This finding lends support to a general feedback assumption concerning the mutual modification and readjustment of perception and behavior during the process of social interaction.

One point of possible theoretical significance concerns the marked intercorrelations among the three behavioral indices of power. Number of influence attempts, number of resistances, and degree of assertiveness toward the partner correlated with one another in the .60's. Whereas previous studies have pointed to the positive relation between the initiation of influence attempts and the initiator's directiveness, the present indication that resistances also may betoken power warrants some comment. The explanation is simple. Usually, power is defined in terms of ability to get others to do things. This experimental setting, however, involved a somewhat competitive situation where power was measured on a relative basis. Thus, in order to enhance his own power, the individual to some extent had to resist the influence of his partner. It is probable that in situations which are less competitive, or which involve a larger number of possible areas of influence, the frequency of resistances would be a less important indicator of social power.

Finally, it was established that subjects' perceptual estimates of their power fluctuated more during the first than during the second half of the experimental session. This result is in accordance with those of other studies of social perception, notably those of Asch (1); and it is explained in terms of Bruner's assertion (3) that an individual's hypotheses become more resistant to revision the longer they are held. This finding implies that as a power relationship develops over a period of time—in an otherwise stable setting—it requires a progressively stronger input of contradictory information in order to revise the growing perceptions of the persons involved.

References

1. Asch, S. E. *Social psychology.* New York: Prentice-Hall, 1952.
2. Bales, R. F. *Interaction process analysis.* Cambridge: Addison-Wesley, 1950.
3. Bruner, J. S. Personality dynamics and the process of perceiving. In R. R. Blake & B. V. Ramsey (Eds.), *Perception: an approach to personality.* New York: Ronald Press, 1951.
4. Bruner, J. S., & Tagiuri, R. The perception of people. In G. Lindzey (Ed.), *Handbook of social psychology.* Cambridge: Addison-Wesley, 1954.
5. Cartwright, D., & Zander, A. (Eds.). *Group dynamics: research and theory.* Evanston: Row, Peterson, 1953.
6. Hurwitz, J. I., Zander, A., & Hymovitch, B. Some effects of power on the relations among group members. In D. Cartwright & A. Zander (Eds.). *Group dynamics: research and theory.* Evanston: Row, Peterson, 1953.
7. Kelley, H. H. The warm-cold variable in first impressions of persons. *J. Pers.,* 1950, 18, 431-439.
8. Levinger, G. Perceptions and behavior in the development of social power relationships. Unpublished doctor's dissertation, University of Michigan, 1955.
9. Lippitt, R., Polansky, N., Redl, F., & Rosen, S. The dynamics of power. In D. Cartwright & A. Zander (Eds.), *Group dynamics: research and theory.* Evanston: Row, Peterson, 1953.
10. Polansky, N., Lippitt, R., & Redl, F. An investigation of behavioral contagion in groups, *Hum. Relat.,* 1950, 3, 319-348.

ADAPTIVE PROCESSES IN SMALL GROUPS

All collectivities exist in some kind of environment with which they must come to terms. The most salient aspects of the environment of a gang of delinquents may include the physical and social characteristics of the immediate neighborhood in which they carry on their activities, the vigilance and attitude of the local police force, and the strength of rival gangs. The environment for a bridge club may include the rules of the game (set by an external authority), the physical circumstances under which the group meets, and competing demands on the members' time. And the environment for a work group in a factory will include the physical layout of the work, the technical facilities provided, and the managerial controls exercised over the members. In all these cases, the physical, technical, and social environment exerts certain constraints on the collectivity. It sets limits on the behavior of the group; it constitutes a set of conditions within which and to which the group must adapt.

We have previously discussed the process by which groups become differentiated along the lines of power and status. And, in our general discussion of adaptation, we noted that differentiation contributes to the adaptation of the group. Now we attempt to make this connection between differentiation and adaptation somewhat more clear. We stated that status processes were based on the differential evaluation of characteristics possessed by individuals. And we stated that power processes were based on the differential possession by individuals of valued resources. But what determines the value placed on individual characteristics and resources? Certainly one extremely important determining factor is the environment. The demands made by the environment on the collectivity help determine the value placed on individual characteristics and resources. For example, if the environment is a desert island on which a group of individuals are stranded, high value is apt to be placed on such individual characteristics and resources as physical stamina, inventiveness, and courage. But if the environment is a British drawing room, high value is more likely to be placed on inherited wealth and on social gentility.[1] Status and power differences result as some members become dependent upon and obligated to other members who have the capacity to do things that the group wants done. And one of the most important things the group wants to do is survive, and, if possible, thrive in its environment. As Bales states: "The price of accomplishment is differentiated status."[2]

[1]James M. Barrie has dramatically illustrated the relation between the evaluation of characteristics and the demands of the environment in his amusing but highly convincing play *The Admirable Crichton*. He describes the shifts in power and status positions resulting when an upper class British family is shipwrecked on a desert island and then returned safely to England. The servant, Crichton, becomes master on the island but returns to his former station when the family is rescued.

[2]Robert F. Bales, "The equilibrium problem in small groups," in Talcott Parsons, Robert F. Bales, and Edward A. Shils (eds.), *Working Papers in the Theory of Action*, Glencoe, Ill.: Free Press, 1953, p. 133.

Over a period of several years, Robert F. Bales has intensively studied the process by which small groups adapt to their environment. (See Reading 24) Bales has worked with groups of undergraduates who are brought together in a laboratory so that their interaction together may be observed and recorded. For the Bales groups, the most salient feature of the environment is the demand made upon the group by the experimenter that they reach a collective solution to the task presented to them. The participants are expected to exchange information and opinions concerning the problem at hand and to arrive at some kind of agreement on a proposed solution. The participants begin their discussion as presumed status equals—all are male Harvard undergraduates. All expect and are expected to contribute, but time is scarce: everyone cannot talk as much or as long as he wants to. There is, then, competition for participation time—time to show that one can contribute to the creation of an intelligent solution to the group's task. Some members make what are considered to be good suggestions, and the responses they receive encourage them to continue their contributions; others make less-acceptable comments and are discouraged by the responses their ideas receive. Over time, as the members continue to interact, some individuals tend to dominate the discussion, whereas other individuals become more passive. The group has begun to differentiate itself into leaders and followers. Members who are regarded as contributing most to the group's task—meeting the demands of the group's environment—are allowed a disproportionate share of the group's time and attention. Bales' data show that persons who were highest in total amount of participation were most likely to be selected by others as contributing the "best ideas" and furnishing the "most guidance" to the group as it searched for a task solution.

Adaptation and Integration Processes   We have argued that the demands of the environment on a group provide one important set of criteria for determining the value to be placed on individual characteristics and resources. The process of power differentiation is under way as members begin to acknowledge their dependence on selected individuals who are then in a position to exercise control over them. The adaptation capabilities of the group are strengthened as members are selected for leadership roles in terms of their ability to make contributions to the solution of task problems. However, in Bales' view, as the group structures itself for dealing with its task environment, a new set of problems emerges. The differentiation of the group along power and status lines impares the group's integration—its cohesion and sense of unity. Bales regards this as a general problem confronting all social collectivities. He argues:

Looking at large scale systems in a very abstract way, one can form an idea of two 'chains of events' or 'series of strains' starting from opposite poles and proceeding in opposite directions, tending to cancel each other out, and each in its terminal effects tending to set off the opposite chain of events. One chain of events has its starting point in the *necessities of adaptation* to the outer situation and proceeds in its series of strains through changes in the division of labor, changes in the distribution of property, authority, and status and has its malintegrative terminal effects in the disturbance of the existing state of solidarity. The other chain of events has its starting point in the *necessities of integration* or reintegration of the social system itself and proceeds in its series of strains through a reactive (or perhaps aboriginal) emphasis on solidarity which exerts a dissolving, undermining, equalizing, or curbing effect on the differential distribution of status, or differences in authority, differences in distribution of property, and differences in functional roles in the division of labor, with an ultimate terminal effect that may be maladaptive. The social system in its organization, we postulate, tends to swing or falter indeterminately back and forth between these two theoretical poles: optimum adaptation to the outer situation at the cost of internal malintegration, or optimum internal integration at the cost of maladaptation to the outer situation.[3]

In short, Bales suggests that a group's attempts to adapt itself to its task environment interferes with its attempts to achieve integration; and a group's attempts to achieve internal harmony and cohesion interfere with its efforts at adaptation. Why is this the case? Simply put, actions required for task leadership are somewhat contradictory to those required for furnishing socioemotional support to group members. The task leader must assert himself over other members: he must propose and defend his opinions, evaluate the task contributions of others, and attempt to exert control over others. His support of the efforts of other members working on task solutions is conditional on the quality of their efforts. By contrast, integrative processes are advanced by the acceptance of all members, irrespective of their task contributions—by the dampening of competitive pressures and the de-emphasizing of status and power differences.[4]

This dilemma in which adaptive efforts interfere with integrative efforts and vice versa is what Bales calls the "equilibrium problem." Bales writes:

The problem of equilibrium is essentially the problem of establishing arrangements (or an "orbit of activity") whereby the system goes through a repetitive cycle, within which all of the disturbances created in one phase are reduced in some other. The dilemma of all action systems is that no one disturbance can be reduced without creating another.[5]

In order to examine this and related problems, Bales developed a set of 12 categories for recording the type and sequence of interaction as it occurred in problem-solving groups. As is shown in Figure 24-1 in Reading 24, the 12 categories are divided into two areas—the task area and the socioemotional area—and each of these areas is further subdivided: the task area into questions and attempted answers, the socioemotional area into positive and negative reactions. The unit of behavior scored in terms of these categories is "the smallest discriminable segment of verbal or non-verbal behavior to which the observer . . . can assign a classification under conditions of continuous serial scoring."[6] Following is an example of the coding of an interaction sequence:

Member 1: I wonder if we have the same facts about the problem? [Asks for opinion.] Perhaps we should take some time in the beginning to find out. [Gives suggestion.]
Member 2: Yes. [Agrees.] We may be able to fill in some gaps in our information. [Gives opinion.] Let's go around the table and each tell what the report said in his case. [Gives suggestion.]

[3]Robert F. Bales, "Adaptive and integrative changes as sources of strain in social systems," in A. Paul Hare, Edgar F. Borgatta, and Robert F. Bales (eds.), *Small Groups: Studies in Social Interaction*, New York: Knopf, 1955, pp. 127–128.
[4]See Robert F. Bales and Philip E. Slater, "Role differentiation in small decision-making groups," in Talcott Parsons and Robert F. Bales (eds.), *Family: Socialization and Interaction Process*, Glencoe, Ill.: Free Press, 1955, p. 294. The relevant results of this study are summarized in Verba's discussion in Reading 25. Verba's chapter also briefly restates much of the present argument.
[5]Bales, "The equilibrium problem," p. 123.
[6]Robert F. Bales, *Interaction Process Analysis*, Reading, Mass.: Addison-Wesley, 1950, p. 37.

Member 3: Oh, let's get going. [Shows antagonism.] We've all got the same facts. [Gives opinion.]

Member 2: (Blushes). [Shows tension.][7]

Groups attempt to resolve their equilibrium problems in a variety of ways, two of which are described in the reading from Bales. The first, which Bales labels "phase movements," is concerned with the differentiation of the group's *time*, early portions of the meeting being given over to task-oriented activities and later portions of the meeting allowing more time for socioemotional responses. The second entails *role* differentiation: the emergence of a division of labor among participants. One member comes to specialize in the task area—the "task leader" or the "idea man"—while a second member specializes in affective responses—the "socioemotional leader" or the "best-liked man."

What is the evidence for role differentiation in the small discussion groups observed by Bales? We have already reported Bales' finding that individuals who participated most were more likely to be regarded as providing task leadership by other members. But these same individuals are not typically the most popular members of the group. As Figure 24-2 shows, they did not receive the highest number of "like" choices from other members and were the recipients of the highest number of "dislike" choices. Instead, in many groups, another person emerges as the most popular member of the group—often the person who is second highest in rate of participation. Also, analysis in terms of the interaction categories reveals important differences in the *nature* of their participation. As Slater reports, the task leader or "idea man" is more likely to

. . . initiate interaction more heavily in Area B (Problem Solving Attempts) and the Best-liked man in Area A (Positive Reactions). The Idea man also seems to disagree somewhat more, and shows a little more antagonism, while the Best-liked asks more questions and shows more tension. On the receiving end, the situation is largely reversed, with the Idea man receiving more agreement, questions, and negative reactions, while the Best-liked man receives more problem solving attempts, and more solidarity and tension release. The general picture is thus one of specialization and complementarity, with the Idea man concentrating on the task and playing a more aggressive role, while the Best-liked man concentrates more on social-emotional problems, giving rewards and playing a more passive role.[8]

Thus, this body of research suggests that to solve the adaptation problem a group differentiates into leaders concentrating on task solutions and followers; and to solve the problems of integration thus created, a further differentiation may occur within the leadership circle with one individual continuing to concentrate on the task while another focuses on the socioemotional problems generated in the course of pursuing task solutions.

Is this second type of differentiation a universal tendency in all social groups? Do all groups tend to develop a bifurcated leadership structure with one person serving as a task master and another as a morale booster and group therapist? Some sociologists have supported this view, but others, including Sidney Verba, question this generalization. (Reading 25) Verba reminds us that we must

[7]Robert F. Bales, "Task roles and social roles in problem-solving groups," in Eleanor E. Maccoby, Theodore M. Newcomb, and Eugene L. Hartley (eds.), *Readings in Social Psychology* (3d ed.), New York: Holt, Rinehart and Winston, Inc., 1958, p. 439. Rules for coding and many examples of coding decisions are discussed by Bales in *Interaction Process Analysis*, pp. 85–99, 177–195.

[8]Philip E. Slater, "Role differentiation in small groups," *American Sociological Review*, 20 (June, 1955), 304–305.

examine not only the reported findings or generalizations resulting from sociological research but also *the conditions under which they were observed to occur.*
Groups such as those studied by Bales exhibit certain special characteristics that
all groups do not share. These include (1) participants who enter the interaction as presumed status equals, (2) the absence of an appointed or recognized
leader, and (3) the absence of strong commitment to the group goal. All these
factors operate to hinder the task leader's acceptance by group members. The
first and second factors encourage competition by all members for leadership
positions, and such struggles may create hard feelings among the losers. The
third factor takes away from the task leader an important resource. The leader
cannot reward group members by helping them attain the group goal if they do
not value that goal. When the leader's actions do not provide rewards to
members, his exercise of power over them is less likely to be viewed as
legitimate. Recall in this connection Blau's discussion of power processes (Reading 16, p. 197):

Collective approval of power legitimates that power. People who consider that the
advantages they gain from a superior's exercise of power outweigh the hardships that
compliance with his demands imposes on them tend to communicate to each other their
approval of the ruler and their feelings of obligation to him.

In short, legitimation of the power structure may serve as an alternative to the
emergence of a differentiated leadership structure in stabilizing the leadership
structure. As Verba suggests:

In on-going groups and organizations, it is the development of a legitimate leadership
structure rather than the development of a dual leadership structure that constitutes
the major way in which the conflict between affective and instrumental leadership is
resolved.

Social processes shape and are shaped by distinctive social structures.

We shall have more to say about the legitimation process—leading to the
emergence of an authority structure—when we discuss power processes in
formal organizations.

24   The Equilibrium Problem in Small Groups[1]
Robert F. Bales

The purpose of this paper is to present
certain empirical findings from the program of observation of small groups at the
Harvard Laboratory of Social Relations

and to discuss their relevance to the
theory of equilibrium developed elsewhere.

[1]The research reported in this paper was facilitated by the Laboratory of Social Relations, Harvard University. The funds for the observation
project now in progress are provided by the
RAND Corporation, Santa Monica, California. I
am indebted to Philip E. Slater, Research Assistant
in the Laboratory of Social Relations, especially for
work on the latter parts of this paper on problems

of role specialization, and more generally for the
many stimulating discussions we have had on the
research as a whole. Similarly, I owe much to
Christoph Heinicke, Social Science Research
Council Fellow, for initial insights on the nature of
the status struggle as it appears through the series
of meetings of our groups. This phenomenon will
be described in later papers.

Reprinted with permission of the author and The Macmillan Company from *Working Papers in the
Theory of Action* by Talcott Parsons, Robert F. Bales and Edward A. Shils. Copyright 1953 by the Free
Press, a Corporation, pp. 111–117, 140–150.

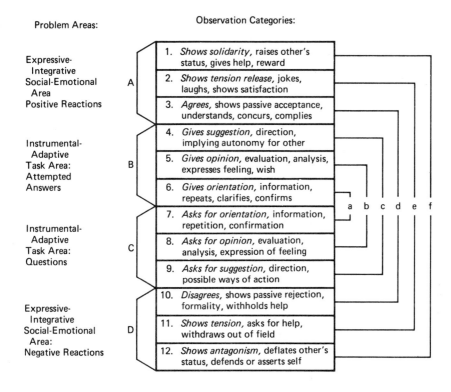

Problem Areas:

Observation Categories:

A sub-classification of system problems to
which each pair of categories is most relevant:

a. Problems of orientation
b. Problems of evaluation
c. Problems of control

d. Problems of decision
e. Problems of tension-management
f. Problems of integration

FIGURE 24-1. Set of categories used for direct observation of the interaction process.

METHOD

Some of these findings have been published previously, and the reader is referred to these earlier articles for details omitted here.[2] It will also be assumed that the reader is familiar with the method of observation, recording, and analysis used in the direct study of the interaction process as it takes place in our small laboratory groups.[3] The observation categories are shown in Figure 24-1. . . .

CONDITIONS OF OBSERVATION

A number of different types of groups have been observed, in natural as well as laboratory settings, and some of the generalizations to be discussed were obtained before the present observational

[2]Bales, Robert F., "A Set of Categories for the Analysis of Small Group Interaction", *American Sociological Review*, Vol. XV, No. 2, April, 1950, pp. 257–263.

Bales, Robert F., and Strodtbeck, Fred L., "Phases in Group Problem Solving", *Journal of Abnormal and Social Psychology*, Vol. 46, No. 4, October, 1951, pp. 485-495.

Bales, Robert F., Strodtbeck, Fred L., Mills, Theodore M., and Roseborough, Mary, "Channels of Communication in Small Groups". *American Sociological Review*, Vol. 16, No. 4, August 1951, pp. 461-468.

Bales, Robert F., "Some Statistical Problems of Small Group Research", *Journal of the American Statistical Association*, Vol. 46, No. 255, September 1951, pp. 311- 322.

[3]Bales, Robert F., *Interaction Process Analysis, A Method for the Study of Small Groups*, Reading, Mass., Addison-Wesley, 1950.

series was begun. For purposes of exposition, however, it will be simpler to confine the description of the conditions under which the generalizations hold best to the series of groups now under observation since these groups were specifically set up to epitomize the appropriate conditions.

Groups of sizes two through ten are under observation in the present series. Data for sizes three through six have been gathered. The groups are experimental discussion groups, each group meeting for four meetings. The subjects are all males, Harvard undergraduates, who are obtained through the Harvard employment service and typically do not know each other prior to the first meeting. In each of its four meetings, the group examines and discusses a "human relations case." A different case is used for each of the four meetings. Each case is a summary of facts, five pages in length, about a person in an administrative setting who is having some kind of difficulty with the men under him, and has some superior putting pressure on him to get some technically important job done. The summaries for a given case discussion are distributed separately to the subjects. After each member has read his summary the actual typed copy of the case is collected from each by the experimenter. The manner of presentation is such that the subjects are made specifically uncertain as to whether or not they possess exactly the same facts, but are assured that each does possess an accurate, though perhaps incomplete, factual summary.

The subjects are asked to consider themselves as members of the administrative staff of the central person in the case. He has asked them to meet and consider the case. He wishes an answer to two questions: (1) why are the persons in the case behaving as they do, and (2) what should he do about it. The members of the discussion group are asked to come to their decision in forty minutes. No leader is appointed. The host experimenter leaves the room. The discussion is observed through a one-way mirror and sound recorded. The interaction is observed and recorded in the categories shown on Table 24–1. After the meeting the members fill out a questionnaire asking certain questions about their reactions, their satisfaction, their relations to each other, and their opinions about their discussion group.

This particular concrete task has certain abstract characteristics which are important in eliciting a range of diversified behavior. The problems of *orientation*, *evaluation*, and *control* are each to a major degree unsolved at the beginning of observation. More specifically:

(a) With regard to *orientation*, members of the group have some degree of ignorance and uncertainty about the relevant facts, but individually possess facts relevant to decision. Their problem of arriving at a common cognitive orientation or definition of the situation must be solved, if at all, through interaction.

(b) With regard to problems of *evaluation*, the members of the group ordinarily possess somewhat different values or interests and the task is such that it involves several different values and interests as criteria by which the facts of the situation and the proposed course of action are to be judged. The problem of arriving at common value judgments necessary to a concrete plan must be solved, again, if at all, through interaction.

(c) With regard to problems of *control*, (that is, attempts of the members to influence directly the action of each other and arrive at a concrete plan) the acceptance of the task sets up in most instances a moderately strong pressure for group decision, with the expectation that the excellence of the decision can and will be evaluated by each of them as well as by the experimenter, so that the decision will affect their status. There are a number of possible alternative decisions or solutions, with uncertain degrees of potential frustration or satisfaction associated with various choices.

These abstract conditions, with emphasis varying according to circumstances, are met in very much this form and emphasis in a great many group conferences, work groups, committees, and the like. When group problems or tasks lack or greatly minimize any of the three abstract characteristics described above (a, b, c) we speak of them as being "truncated." When these three characteristics are all present and marked, we speak of the problem as "full-fledged." We have felt that full-fledged problems give us a better opportunity to explore the range and interconnections of various sorts of social behavior, and so have begun to develop empirical norms and a body of theory around this particular set of conditions as a standard diagnostic task. Once this baseline has been estab-

lished, other sets of conditions expected to have different results can be described as modifications or accentuations or reversals of the laboratory conditions. The more we learn about the typical effects of the particular diagnostic *task* we employ, the more we are able to use discrepancies from our typical base-line patterns of observed interaction as diagnostic indicators of the *personalities*, *culture*, and *role organization* of the participants, since these are all sets of conditions which influence the way interaction actually goes.

Under each mode of analysis discussed below some of the main uniformities of behavior we have found will be compactly stated. Space does not permit the presentation of the evidence in detail. In general, the patterns described and illustrated can be understood to refer to approximate or average uniformities in aggregates of large numbers of group meetings under randomly varying exter-

TABLE 24–1 Profile of a "Satisfied" and a "Dissatisfied" Group on Case Discussion Task

| Type of Act: | Meeting Profiles in Percentage Rates | | | |
	Satisfied°	Dissatisfied°°	Ave. of the Two	Ave. Rates by Sections
1. Shows Solidarity	.7	.8	.7	
2. Shows Tension Release	7.9	6.8	7.3	25.0
3. Agrees	24.9	9.6	17.0	
4. Gives Suggestion	8.2	3.6	5.9	
5. Gives Opinion	26.7	30.5	28.7	56.7
6. Gives Orientation	22.4	21.9	22.1	
7. Asks for Orientation	1.7	5.7	3.8	
8. Asks for Opinion	1.7	2.2	2.0	6.9
9. Asks for Suggestion	.5	1.6	1.1	
10. Disagrees	4.0	12.4	8.3	
11. Shows Tension	1.0	2.6	1.8	11.4
12. Shows Antagonism	.3	2.2	1.3	
Percentage Total	100.0	100.0	100.0	100.0
Raw Score Total	719	767	1486	

° The highest of sixteen groups. The members rated their own satisfaction with their solution after the meeting at an average of 10.4 on a scale running from 0 to a highest possible rating of 12.

°° The lowest of sixteen groups. Comparable satisfaction rating in this group was 2.6.

nal conditions, and in addition, they can be understood to hold more uniformly and in particular under the full-fledged conditions of the standard diagnosis task described above.

THE PROFILE OF ACTIVITY AND THE EQUILIBRIUM PROBLEM

One of the interesting characteristics of interaction is the distribution of total number of acts among the twelve categories, according to quality. A distribution of this kind in percentage rates based on the total is called a profile. An illustrative comparison of group profiles of two five-man groups working on the standard diagnostic task is shown in Table 24-1.

In the present illustration the "satisfied" group attained a higher rate of suggestions, more often followed by positive reactions and less often by negative reactions and questions than did the "dissatisfied" group.

The profiles produced by groups, however, are not completely and radically different from each other. The profile produced by the average of these two illustrative groups is more or less typical of averages of larger aggregates under laboratory standard conditions. Attempted Answers, that is, giving orientation, opinion, and suggestion, are always more numerous than their cognate Questions, that is, asking for orientation, opinion, or suggestion. Similarly, Positive Reactions, that is agreement, showing tension release, and solidarity, are usually more numerous than Negative Reactions, i.e., showing disagreement, tension, and antagonism. Intuitively one would feel that the process would surely be self-defeating and self-limiting if there were more questions than answers and more negative reactions than positive.

On the average, for groups we have examined, the relations of amounts by Sections are about as they are in the illustration. The relations between the amounts can be viewed as the final result of a repetitive series of cycles, each of which consists of: (1) an initial disturbance of the system (precipitated by the introduction of a new idea, or opinion, or suggestion into the group) followed by (2) a "dwindling series of feedbacks" and corrections as the disturbance is terminated, equilibrated, or assimilated by other parts or members of the system. Attempted Answers, or as one might call them for the moment, "Initial Acts," account for a little over half (or 57 percent) of the total activity, with Positive and Negative Reactions and Questions accounting for the other half, roughly.

Looking at the *Reaction* side alone, and assuming it to be 50 percent of the total, about half the reactions (or 25 percent of the total) are Positive and presumably terminate the disturbance introduced by the initial action. The other half of the time the Reaction fails to terminate the disturbance. Of this non-terminating portion again, about half (or 12 percent of the total) are Negative Reactions, which typically precipitate another Attempted Answer, thus beginning a repetition of the cycle. Of the remaining hypothetical 13 percent or so, about half (or 7 percent) are Questions, which also typically precipitate another Attempted Answer. If about 7 percent of Attempted Answers are in direct response to Questions, these might well be called "Reactions," thus leaving the relation of "Initial Acts" to "Reactions" about 50-50, as assumed above. One might say that quantitatively (as well as qualitatively, by definition) interaction is a process consisting of action followed by reaction. The balance of action with reaction is one of the equilibrium problems of the system. . . .

PHASE MOVEMENT AND THE PROBLEM OF EQUILIBRIUM

Changes in quality of activity as groups move through time in attempting to solve their problems may be called phase patterns. The pattern of phases differs in detail under different conditions. However, these changes in quality seem to be subject to system-influences which produce similarities from group to group. An increase of task-oriented activities in the early parts of a meeting, that is, Questions and Attempted Answers, seems to constitute a disturbance of a system equilibrium which is later redressed by an increase in social-emotional activities, that is, both Positive and Negative Reactions.

Part of our observations prior to the development of the standard diagnostic task were kept by time sequence. Each available meeting was divided into three equal parts, and the amount of each type of activity in each part of each meeting was determined. The meetings were divided into two kinds: those which were dealing with full-fledged problems (essentially problems of analysis and planning with the goal of group decision as described for the standard diagnostic task), and those dealing with more truncated or specialized types of problems. Those groups dealing with full-fledged problems tended to show a typical phase movement through the meeting: the process tended to move qualitatively from a *relative* emphasis on attempts to solve problems of *orientation* ("what is it") to attempts to solve problems of *evaluation* ("how do we feel about it") and subsequently to attempts to solve problems of *control* ("what shall we do about it"). Concurrent with these transitions, the relative frequencies of both *negative reactions* (disagreement, tension, and antagonism), and *positive reactions* (agreement, tension release, and showing solidarity), tend to increase. Figure 24–2 presents the summary data for all group sessions examined in the phase study.

The underlying theory as to why the phase movement just described is characteristic of full-fledged conditions is again a system-equilibrium rationale. An individual may be cognitively oriented to a situation and speak of it to others in cognitive terms without committing himself, or the other when he agrees, either to evaluation of it, or an attempt to control it. But in speaking to the other in evaluative terms he attempts to commit both himself and the other to some assumed previous orientation, and further, if he suggests a way to control the situation by joint cooperative action, he assumes both previous orientation and evaluation. When the problems of arriving at a common orientation and evaluation of the situation have not been substantially solved by the group members, attempts at control will meet with resistance on the part of the others and frustration on the part of the person attempting to exercise the control. Probably generally, unless there are contrary cultural, personality, or group organizational factors, the interacting persons tend to avoid or retreat from this frustration-producing type of interaction by "back-tracking" toward orientation and evaluative analysis until the prior problems are solved.

In addition to their task problems, the members of any cooperating group have problems of their social and emotional relationships to each other to solve and keep solved. Efforts to solve problems of orientation, evaluation, and control as involved in the task tend to lead to differentiation of the roles of the participants, both as to the functions they perform and their gross amounts of participation. . . . Both qualitative and quantitative types of differentiation tend to carry status implications which may threaten or disturb the existing order or balance of status relations among members. Disagreement and an attempt to change existing ideas and values instrumentally may be necessary in the effort to solve the task problem but may lead,

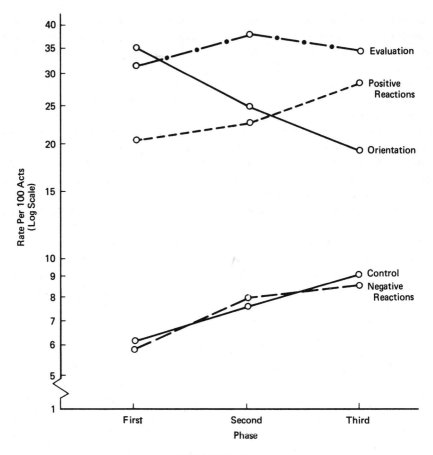

FIGURE 24 -2.

nevertheless, to personalized anxieties or antagonisms and impair the basic solidarity of the group.

This impairment, or the threat of it, we may assume, tends to grow more marked as the group passes from emphasis on the less demanding and more easily resolved problems of cognitive orientation on to problems of evaluation, and still more acute as it passes on to its heaviest emphasis on problems of control. . . . The assumption seems to be a more generalized way of stating the findings of certain other studies. For example, Lippitt[4] found negative reactions to autocratic control or leadership in boys' clubs under certain conditions, while Rogers[5] and his associates tend to find a minimization of negative reactions on the part of clients when the counselor confines himself to nondirective (or, in our categories, orienting rather than evaluating or controlling) types of activity. The present assumption may be regarded as a generalization of this connection between degree of control and negative reactions, so that it is viewed as applying to different points in the process of the same group, not simply to differences between groups. Thus, a series of changes. in the social-emotional relationships of the members tend to be set in motion by pressures arising initially from the

[4]Lippitt, R., "An Experimental Study of Authoritarian and Democratic Group Atmospheres". *Stud. Topolog. Vector Psychol.*, No. 1, Univ. Ia. Stud. Child Welf., 1950, 16.

[5]Rogers, C. R., *Counselling and Psychotherapy: New Concepts in Practice*, Boston, Houghton Mifflin, 1942.

demands of the external task or outer situation. These social emotional problems tend to be expressed in overt interaction as they grow more acute—hence the increasing rate of negative reactions.

However, at the extreme end of the final period, assuming that the members' attempts at control over the outer situation and over each other are successful and a final decision is reached, the rates in Categories 1, 2, and 3 also rise to their peak. In other words, one might expect the successfully recovering group to confirm its agreement and to release the tensions built up in its prior task-efforts, repairing the damage done to its state of consensus and social integration. We note joking and laughter so frequently at the end of meetings that they might almost be taken as a signal that the group has completed what it considers to be a task effort, and is ready for disbandment or a new problem. This last-minute activity completes a cycle of operations involving a successful solution both of the task problems and social-emotional problems confronting the group. The apparent incongruity of predicting a peak for both negative and positive reactions in the third phase is thus explained. Negative reactions tend to give way to positive reactions in the final part of the crudely defined third phase.

CHANGES IN ROLE STRUCTURE AND THE EQUILIBRIUM PROBLEM

We now consider a series of role changes which take place on "the next rung up" the ladder of microscopic-to-macroscopic contexts in which the general theory of action systems can be applied. Changes in quality of act from one act to the next are on a very microscopic level as to time span involved. Changes in rates of acts of various types through the course of a single meeting are on a more macroscop-

ic level. As we have seen, very much the same sort of general system theory can be applied to both, with proper allowance for changes in conditions which will surely be characteristic of any shift up or down on the microscopic-macroscopic ladder. We now proceed up another rung of the ladder to consider changes that take place from meeting to meeting in a time span of four meetings. And for the present analysis, we shift from a primary emphasis on consideration of interaction rates to a consideration of more "generalized" or partially "structured" roles as reflected in post-meeting ratings and choices of members by each other. Much more detailed treatment of changes within the four meeting time span, using interaction rates as well as post-meeting measures will be given in later publications.

The essential rationale for the ratings and choices we ask members to make at the end of meetings is rooted back in the four types of system problems, the "dimensions" along which system change takes place—the instrumental, adaptive, integrative, and expressive. For present purposes we link the instrumental and adaptive dimensions together to obtain one "pole" of specialization: the instrumental-adaptive pole. On the other side we link the integrative and expressive dimensions together to obtain the integrative-expressive pole.

Toward the instrumental-adaptive pole we distinguish two types of roles: The first is a role emphasizing specifically task-oriented achievement addressed to the problems of the external situation confronting the group. In terms of the type of task we give our groups, this role appears to be fairly well defined operationally by answers to the question: "Who contributed the best ideas for solving the problem? Please rank the members in order. . . . Include yourself." The second type of instrumental-adaptive role we distinguish is one which emphasizes regulation or management of the group process in the service of task oriented achievement—a role approximating that of "chairman" or perhaps in a more general sense that of "executive," (as contrasted with that of "technical specialist" which is the first type of role above). We attempt to get at the second type of role by the question: "Who did the most to guide the discussion and keep it moving effectively? Please rank the members in order. . . . Include yourself."

Toward the integrative-expressive pole we also distinguish two subtypes of roles, but this time according to a "positive-negative" distinction rather than according to an "external-internal" distinction as above. The questions we ask here are fairly orthodox sociometric choice questions—essentially "Who do you like in rank order" and "Who do you dislike in rank order," although we ask them in a somewhat more complicated way that would take unnecessarily long to describe here. Detailed description of scoring methods will also be omitted—by inverting ranks it is possible to obtain high scores for top ranking men and low scores for low ranking men. This is done for greater intuitive ease in grasping the meaning of the data. I shall refer to high ranking men as "receiving the most votes," sacrificing accuracy a bit to convenience.

Now, according to the line of thought embodied in the sample statistical model for reproducing the matrix, and its "rationalization," one might make the following sorts of inferences: Since a man may receive agreement for advancing ideas which appeal to other members, or for making neutral suggestions with procedural content rather than task content, or simply because people like him emotionally, and since agreement tends to encourage a man to go ahead and talk more, we might suppose that such men would tend to have high rates of participation. Conversely, since disagreement tends to discourage a man from talking, and since disagreement is often a manifestation of dislike, we might suppose that dislikes would tend to center around men with low rates of participation. And since the model makes no assumptions about the incompatibilities of these various roles (excepting the incompatibility of Liking and Disliking) we might suppose that the same man— "The Leader"—might receive the most votes on all three roles—Best Ideas, Guidance, and Best Liked, and that another man— "The Scapegoat"—at the bottom of the heap might receive the fewest votes on all three of these virtuous roles, but the most on Dislikes. The simplest assumption is that the votes on each of these roles will grade according to Basic Initiating Rank—the rank on total amounts of participation given out. Such a group we might call a "simply organized group," meaning that no matter what criterion of status were chosen, it would place the men in the same rank order of relative status. Now those who are acutely aware of the lack of such perfect integration of various criteria of status in larger social systems will be likely to suspect that small groups will not be so "simply organized" either. Nevertheless, we had evidence of some appreciable degree of positive correlation of these various status criteria with Basic Initiating Rank, and the hypothesis of the "simply organized group" was adopted as a working hypothesis for the first ordering and examination of the data.

Our first major insight with regard to what we now regard as a basic problem of role structure was obtained from a tabulation of data from twelve meetings of five-man groups (twelve instead of sixteen because of absences in four meetings). No distinction was made as to which meetings in the series of four were represented. The identity of men was not preserved from meeting to meeting. We simply took each meeting, listed the men in rank order of total amounts of participation given out, and recorded "the number of votes received" on each role.

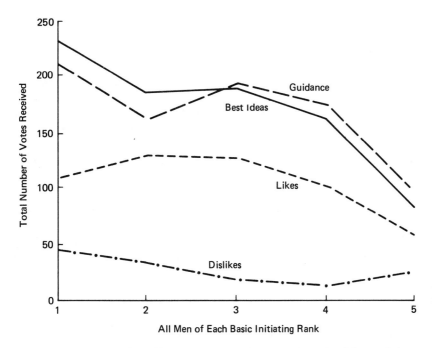

FIGURE 24–3. "Total number of votes received" on each of four roles, pooled for men of each basic initiating rank as of each meeting. (Data from twelve assorted meetings of four five-man groups.)

Then the data for all rank one men on total acts initiated were pooled, and so for all rank two men, and so on for the five. The fact that Joe Smith might have been rank one man in the first meeting, rank two man in the second, and so on, was ignored. The data are represented in Figure 24-3.

First it may be noted that there is a general gradation of votes on Best Ideas and Guidance by Basic Initiating Rank as expected by the working hypothesis. Second, note that these two curves are very close together and move in the same way, indicating the relative lack of segregation of these roles from each other. But there is a departure from the prediction of the working hypothesis: on both curves the second man is unaccountably low.

But a more serious departure from the prediction is in terms of the curve on Likes. There the top man is unaccountably low, and the second man is highest in the group—by an insignificant margin, but still enough to give birth to the

idea: can there be any connection between the fact that the second man, who is unaccountably low on Best Ideas and Guidance, is also Best Liked? Can it be that he is avoiding too heavy participation in the instrumental-adaptive area? Can it be that the man who is participating most heavily and is receiving the most votes on Best Ideas and Guidance is provoking dislikes and losing likes? Here we note the Dislike curve. Contrary to the prediction of the working hypothesis, the top man receives *most* Dislikes, and they grade down by rank—until we come to the bottom man, and here the curve shows an upturn. The upturn is consistent with the scapegoat hypothesis.[6] Looking again at the Like curve, we note that although the second man is receiving more likes than the top man, actually both are depressed in terms of an expec-

[6]Similar curves are found in 3 and 4-man groups. The 6-man groups introduce a special complication at a level of subtlety which is inappropriate to these preliminary generalizations.

tation of an evenly graded curve. The new hypothesis is strengthened: there must be something about high participation and specialization in the technical and executive directions which tends to provoke hostility.

Here I think it can be seen that we are dealing with the same equilibrium problem encountered before in attempting to understand the uniformities of the profile, the matrix, and the phase movement. Movement in the instrumental-adaptive direction tends to upset the equilibrium of the system, and recovery mechanisms must be worked out if the system is to turn full cycle and regain equilibrium. The more "directive" and "constricting" the quality of activity, the more likely it is to arouse negative reactions. If a man begins to specialize noticeably in this direction, the negative reactions tend to be centered on him. The displacement of hostilities on a scapegoat at the bottom of the status structure is one mechanism, apparently, by which the ambivalent attitudes toward the instrumental-adaptive specialist—the "top man"—can be diverted and drained off. The centering of positive affect on a secondary man is another mechanism by which the solidarity of the group—its integration as a collectivity of persons—can be re-established. Such a man can be warm, receptive, responsive, and rewarding, can "conciliate" and "bind up the wounds," without diverting the movement of the system too far from the kind of movement in the instrumental-adaptive direction which is also felt to be necessary. He can do this because he does not assume the "responsibility" for the movement of the system in these directions, but leaves this to the technical or executive specialist.

But suppose the best liked man is not willing to do this? Suppose that his perceptions of the likes of others "goes to his head" and encourages him to begin

to "take over" from the technical or executive specialist? He is in a position to command considerable support, and the "top man" is in a vulnerable position because of the latent or overt hostility centered on him. Or suppose, on the other hand, that the top man is emotionally unable to stand the hostility, or is unable to tolerate the fact that not he, but another, is best liked? The top man is under strains, we might suppose, to try to "undercut" his nearest rival. Here are the seeds of a fundamental status struggle, exceedingly damaging, in potentiality, both   for   the   instrumental-adaptive achievement of the group, and for its effective integration. This, as I see it now, is the core of the status struggle we see our groups go through in the course of their four meetings. The first meeting is typically rather cautious and tentative, and such "simply organized groups" as we do find, tend to be found at the end of this meeting. With the second meeting, the role structure which has crystallized, if at all, in the first meeting, is challenged in a status struggle which may result in either confirmation of the first structure, or an exchange of status positions between the top two or three men. If the original structure "holds up," the group may begin to "level out," and the status struggle slacks off. If a new man comes to the top, the *new* structure is challenged in the third meeting. Some groups apparently arrive at a fairly stable differentiated structure, others never do. Things go "from bad to worse," with a last meeting that breaks records for disagreement, antagonism, tension, perhaps tension release, and other signs of serious strains and an inability to achieve an equilibrated role structure. However, the stable structure is never, in our data, a "simply organized" one. It is rather one in which differentiated roles have appeared, in which one specialist "undoes" the disturbance to equilibrium created by another, and in turn is dependent upon another to remove the strains he himself creates—the total constellation of specialists being one which allows or aids the system to establish a full orbit in its dimensions of necessary movement.

Furthermore, there are probably "typical" solutions which tend to be found with considerable frequency, and may in older and more permanent types of groups, give rise to cultural arrangements and supporting symbol constellations including explicit ritual. Three constellations which are exceedingly ubiquitous, in a cross-cultural sense, come to mind as possibly significant in this connection. They are incest taboos, totem taboos and rituals, and scapegoat patterns. In the experimental small-group setting, of course, nothing concretely resembling these exceedingly complicated and elaborate cultural complexes appears, but certain functional equivalents may be possible.

There is some reason to believe that one possible arrangement by which the status struggle between the top instrumental-adaptive leader and the best liked man can be prevented or stabilized is the formation of a kind of "coalition" between them, such that the two tacitly agree, as it were, not to undercut each other, which is to say, not to be "seduced" into attempting to form a coalition with lower status members in order to displace each other. If such a coalition can be formed, it becomes quite difficult for lower status members to revolt, unseat the top men, or develop the norms of the group in any different direction.

Does this bear any resemblance, in functional terms, to the incest taboo as a cognate mechanism in the nuclear family? Is the incest taboo, at least in certain of its aspects, a kind of coalition between the father (in some family systems comparable to the senior technical and executive specialist) and the mother (similarly often the first major target of positive affect) ? Such a coalition could be a powerful mechanism for forcing the socialization of the child, by putting him in a position where he must accept the authority and values of the father in order to obtain gratification, rather than allowing him to retain and overdevelop an affectively gratifying relation to the mother which would leave him insufficient incentive to acquire the skills, values, and other characteristics of the adult role. It may well be, I think, that the ubiquity of the incest taboo as it applies in the nuclear family, is simply another case of the much more general equilibrium problem.

Similarly with totem taboos and rituals. This is not the place for an adequate attempt to examine the problem, but the killing of the totem on certain ritual occasions is certainly suggestive of a ritual display of aggression against the principal authority figures, and the eating of the totem can be viewed as an "undoing"—a reacceptance of the target of aggression after all. In some cases, as Frazier documents at length, the king himself is killed—the king becomes the scapegoat. In many other cases, as we know, some low status person or group is victimized. These facts are well known, and on one level, fairly well understood. The only new emphasis here, if any, is the suggestion that these patterns, culturally elaborated and various in form, can be viewed as particular cases of mechanisms relevant to the much more general problem of equilibrium, which has cognates on every level, from the most microscopic to the most macroscopic.

25   Leadership: Affective and Instrumental

Sidney Verba

CONFLICTING EXPECTATIONS: THEIR RESOLUTION IN SMALL GROUPS

THE TWO LEADERS   To shed some light upon the way in which the conflict between instrumental and affective leadership is resolved, we turn first to the small group experimental literature. The resolution of the conflict in these small groups will then be compared with the resolution in larger, on-going social systems. In the small groups studied by Bales and his associates, the conflict between instrumental and affective leadership is resolved by a differentiation within the leadership role. In these groups different individuals tend to specialize in the instrumental leadership role and in the socio-emotional leadership role. . . . those members highly selected by the group by an affective criterion were not likely to be selected by the group as having contributed to the instrumental task, nor were they likely to be active in giving the group direction toward the accomplishment of that task. On the other hand, the individual selected by the group as contributing the most to the external task (Best Ideas) was also highly selected as contributing most to the instrumental aspect of the internal group task (Best Guidance). High choice by one criterion was closely correlated with high choice by the other, and the individual rated lowest by one was likely to be lowest by the other. The findings by Bales and his associates that the leadership role tends to be split between a task-oriented instrumental leader and a "so-

ciometric star" is supported by small group studies of other authors. Both Gibb and Olmstead found that affective choice did not correlate highly with choice by an instrumental criterion. And Cattell and Stice in a factor analysis of leader characteristics found that different characteristics are associated with leadership defined in "syntality" terms (i.e., in terms of contribution to changes in group productivity) and leadership defined by an affective sociometric criterion.[1]

ACTIVITIES OF THE TWO LEADERS   The fact that group leadership tends to be split between two individuals is reflected not only in the fact that group members

[1] Bales, in Talcott Parsons, Robert F. Bales and Edward Shils, *Working Papers in the Theory of Action*, Glencoe, Ill.: Free Press, 1953, p. 147; Michael S. Olmstead, "Orientation and Role in the Small Group," *Am. Soc. Rev.*, 19 (1959), pp. 741 51; and Raymond B. Cattell and G. F. Stice, "Four Formulae for Selecting Leaders on the Basis of Personality," *Hum. Rel.*, 7 (1954). It should be pointed out that role differentiation of this sort is a tendency in small groups, not something that happens in every small group—even in experimental situations. See Robert F. Bales and Philip E. Slater, "Notes on 'Role Differentiation in Small Experimental Groups': Reply to Dr. Wheeler," *Sociometry*, 20 (1957), pp. 152–55. However, Parsons and Bales (*Family Socialization and Interaction process*, by Talcott Parsons and Robert F. Bales, Glencoe, Ill.: Free Press, 1960, chap. 7) suggest that this role differentiation has a high level of generality. Morris Zelditch (*ibid.*, chap. 6) presents evidence for such a role differentiation within the nuclear family between the father (the instrumental leader) and the mother (the affective leader). We shall, however, look at the development of leadership bifurcation as an hypothesis to be tested in different situations. As we shall see, in some social situations there are mechanisms that lower the level of functional necessity of this role differentiation.

choose different individuals by socio-emotional and instrumental criteria, but also in the fact that the behavior patterns of the individuals thus selected differ. When one looks at the interaction rates of the group members most highly selected on the basis of the socio-emotional and the instrumental (Best Ideas) criteria, one finds significant differences. The socio-emotional leader tends to initiate and receive more interactions in the socio-emotional categories of interaction than does the task specialist. He gives and receives more solidarity and tension-release interactions. The task specialist, on the other hand, is more active in giving opinions and suggestions; and he receives larger amounts of agreement, questions, and negative reactions. The difference between the behavior of the two leaders is best described by Slater: "The most salient general difference between the rates of interaction of the two types of leaders is the tendency for the Idea man to initiate interactions more heavily in Area B (Problem Solving Attempts) and the Best-liked man in Area A (Positive reactions). . . . On the Receiving end, the situation is largely reversed, with the Idea man receiving more agreement, questions and negative reactions, while the Best-liked man receives more problem solving attempts, and more solidarity and tension release. The general picture is thus one of specialization and complementarity, with the Idea man concentrating on the task and playing a more aggressive role, while the Best-liked man concentrates more on social emotional problems, giving rewards, and playing a more passive role."[2] The qualitative ratings given the two leaders by the group members are thus

reflected in their quantitative interaction rates.

The difference between the two specialists extends to the attitudes of these two group members. Not only do they specialize in certain areas of the group activity, but they receive their satisfactions from those areas. The instrumental leader, it has already been suggested, is relatively less motivated to receive positive affective responses from the group. His personal satisfactions derive not from the affective responses of the group members, but from the instrumental task directly. For the "sociometric star," on the other hand, ". . . *primary* satisfaction derives from his success in his role as promoter of solidarity and provider of opportunities for tension release. . . ."[3] The socio-emotional leader also tends to be more accepting of the other group members, while the task specialist differentiates among the other members in the degree to which he accepts them. On the sociometric question in which the group members were asked to rate the other members on the degree to which they liked them, 42 per cent of the socio-

[2]Slater, in A. Paul Hare, Edgar F. Borgatta and Robert F. Bales, eds., *Small Groups*, New York: Alfred A. Knopf, 1955, p. 507. See Bales and Slater, in Parsons and Bales, *Family, Socialization and Interaction Process*, p. 279, table 6, for the rates of interaction of the two specialists; and *ibid.*, pp. 280 83, for the tests of significance that have been applied to the data.

[3]Bales, in Parsons, Bales, and Shils, *Working Papers in the Theory of Action*, p. 250. The distinction between the two types of leaders based upon the source of their satisfaction from participation in the group is similar to the distinction between various organizational clientele made by Chester I. Barnard, *The Functions of the Executive* (Cambridge, Mass.: Harvard University Press, 1938), chaps. 11 and 16; and Herbert Simon, *Administrative Behavior*, 2nd ed. (New York: Macmillan, 1957), chap. 6.

It bears a close resemblance as well to the distinction drawn by Harold Lasswell (based on quite different psychological evidence) between the two political types—administrator and agitator. "The essential mark of the agitator is the high value he places upon the emotional response of the public" (Harold Lasswell, "Psychopathology and Politics," in *The Political Writings of Harold Lasswell*, Glencoe, Ill.: Free Press, 1951, p. 78). Administrators, on the other hand, ". . . are distinguished by the values they place upon coordinated effort in continuing activity." Whereas agitators are emotionally involved with the people with whom they deal politically, the administrators ". . . display an impersonal interest in the task of the organization itself. . . ." (*ibid.*, p. 263).

emotional leaders did not differentiate among the members (they said, in effect, "I like everybody") while only 20 per cent of the task leaders did not so differentiate.[4]

RELATIONS BETWEEN THE TWO LEADERS The balance between affective tone and instrumental accomplishment is maintained in these groups, then, by the development of two leaders. The disturbance in the expressive area caused by the instrumental directives of the task leader is countered by positive affective reactions from the socio-emotional leader. In understanding this process, it is important to note the relations between the two leaders. Bales and Slater found that the two had close relations, one with the other. The task and socio-emotional leaders tended to interact more frequently with each other than did any other pair of members; and, what is equally significant, tended to agree more frequently with each other.[5] In this way, it may be suggested, the task leader receives indirectly through the socio-emotional leader the expressive support that he could not directly obtain because of his instrumental role. That such a coalition between the two group leaders is important for the effective functioning of the group is suggested by a comparison made by Bales and Slater between High Status Consensus groups and Low Status Consensus groups.[6] In the former type of group—in which, as was pointed out earlier, task accomplishment and member satisfaction are both higher—the relationships between the two leaders are statistically significant. In the Low Consensus groups, though there is a tendency for the two leaders to interact with

each other, the pattern is neither as consistent nor as strong.[7]

CONFLICTING EXPECTATIONS: THEIR RESOLUTION IN ON-GOING SYSTEMS

The conflict in expectations placed upon leaders has now been spelled out. In small experimental groups we have found that this conflict is resolved by the development of two leaders—an affective and a task leader—accompanied by an implicit coalition between the two men. On-going social systems, including political systems, must also deal with instrumental and affective relationships. Political systems, as well as small groups, depend upon inputs from their members of both instrumental activities (contributions of resources, services, etc.) and affect (loyalty, respect, etc.). And these systems maintain the adherence of their members by outputs in both these areas: specific services as well as affective rewards for participation in the system.[8]

[4]Bales and Slater, in Parsons and Bales, *Family, Socialization and Interaction Process*, p. 294. The difference is significant at the .06 level using a Chi-square test.

[5]*Ibid.*, pp. 282-84.

[6]For a definition of these types of groups, see *ibid.*, pp. 274-77.

[7]*Ibid.*, pp. 283-84. The discovery of the dual functions of leaders and the fact that these functions tend to be split between two different group members suggest one reason why low correlations have been found between various measures of influence. We may define influence, as does March, in terms of its effect on the recipient of the influence attempt—i.e., ". . . if the individual deviates from the predicted path of behavior, influence has occurred. . . ." (J. G. March, "An Introduction to the Theory and Measurement of Influence," *Am. Pol. Sci. Rev.*, 49 [1955], p. 435.) Under this definition, influence may have a single result: changing the behavior of the recipient of the influence attempt. But several behaviors may be required of the influential to accomplish this. An influence act may, for instance, have an instrumental and affective component. And, as the studies cited in the text indicate, the two components of such an act may be divided between two individuals. Studies that find a low correlation among measures of influence may not be demonstrating the weakness of these measures, but may reflect the complexity of the influence act and the fact that a single influence act may be performed by several influentials at once.

[8]This analysis of political systems is suggested by David Easton, "An Approach to the Analysis of Political Systems," *World Politics*, 9 (1957), pp. 383-400.

The model suggested by the studies of experimental groups suggests that the conflict between the affective and the instrumental aspects might best be resolved by a bifurcation of the leadership function. Faced with this conflict, does the on-going social system develop such a differentiated leadership structure, or are other mechanisms available to it to resolve this conflict? Clearly we can give no final answer to such a broad question. But a preliminary attempt to explore the resolution of this conflict in on-going social systems will be rewarding both in heightening our understanding of these systems and, what is more important in terms of this present study, in helping us to specify some of the differences between processes in experimental and non-experimental systems. An understanding of these differences is essential if we are to attempt to apply the results of experimental studies to nonexperimental systems.

SPECIAL CHARACTERISTICS OF SMALL GROUP LEADERSHIP

When one attempts to compare the way in which the conflict between the two group tasks is handled in experimental and non-experimental systems, one is struck by certain special characteristics of the culture of the experimental laboratory—characteristics that tend systematically to affect the nature of the relations between the two tasks. The situation in the experimental groups is such as to raise the level of conflict between instrumental control and affective acceptance above that which one would expect in non-experimental situations. This heightened conflict derives from the external culture of these groups as well as from the internal structure.

The experimental groups discussed by Bales and his associates and by Gibb commence their interaction with a leaderless internal structure. No leader has been appointed or sanctioned by the experimenter. The object of these experiments is to see the way in which leadership structures develop in response to the group task. But the behavior of the leader with no external support who must emerge from a group differs significantly from the behavior of a leader who has some external sanction for his leadership position. In a series of experiments, Launor Carter found that group leaders who had been appointed by the experimenter were less active in expressing opinions, in arguing, and in defending their positions from attack than were group leaders who emerged on their own. "It appears that in the appointed situation, the leader may conceive of his role as that of a coordinator of activity or as an agent through which the group can accomplish its goal. In the emergent group, on the other hand, the person who becomes the leader may take over the leadership by energetic action and by trying to get the other members to accept his leadership."[9] The emergent leader, it would seem, is engaged in a struggle for power in the group. His directive acts are not supported by the sanction of the experimenter's appointment and are not expected by the group members. If his directives are to be accepted he must exert his direction more vigorously than must an appointed leader. And increased vigor leads to increased resistance.

This position is supported by studies of leaders who have developed high status in a group over time. As their status becomes more secure, they can afford to "let up" and lower their amount of directive acts without risking their position. Thus Heinicke and Bales found that in later meetings of a group in which a high-status individual had emerged, the high-status person performed fewer di-

[9]Launor J. Carter, *et al.*, in "The Behavior of Leaders and Other Group Members" by Dorwin Cartwright and Alvin Zander, eds., *Group Dynamics*, Evanston, Ill.: Row, Peterson, 1953, p. 557.

rective acts than he had performed in the group meetings that preceded his achievement of high status.[10] March suggests a similar tendency for leaders, selected as such on a post-session sociometric test, to reduce their overt attempts to influence other group members in those cases where such overt behavior does not seem to be necessary.[11] Moreover, leaders in on-going groups with diffuse and long-term relations are able to delegate their leadership in particular instrumental areas without risking their overall position. Whyte's description of the street corner gang leader is instructive in this connection: "It is my observation that interaction can be patterned and still have no resemblance to the stereotype of autocratic leadership. Take for example, Doc in the Nortons gang as described in my *Street Corner Society*. Doc gave the impression of being very unaggressive in that he did not often come out with ideas for action for the group. On the contrary there were many occasions when members of the group would suggest actions that the group subsequently carried out. But note this important point. The suggestions were always made to Doc and were not acted upon positively unless Doc gave at least his acquiescence. I observed that activity involving the whole group would be initiated either through the acceptance by Doc of suggestions presented by others or by proposals directed from Doc to the group."[12]

This description of leadership in an

on-going group with a history of interactions suggests that experimental groups with no previous experience together differ in a systematic way from such systems. Insofar as members are similar in age, insofar as they are similar in status in the external culture of the group, and insofar as the experimenter supplies no sanction for any particular leadership structure, any directive attempt by a group member will be looked upon as a challenge to the other members. With no status consensus among the group members at the beginning of interaction and no status guides, would-be leaders in the new experimental groups are placed in a clear power struggle. The increased vigor necessary to control the group increases the negative reaction to the leader and heightens the conflict between acceptance and instrumental control.

The nature of the task in the small

---

[10]C. Heinicke and Robert F. Bales, "Developmental Trends in the Structure of Small Groups," *Sociometry*, 16 (1953), pp. 35-37.

[11]James G. March, "Influence Measurement in Experimental and Semi-experimental Groups," *Sociometry*, 19 (1956), 260-271.

[12]William Foote Whyte, unpublished paper, quoted in Heinicke and Bales, "Developmental Trends in the Structure of Small Groups," p. 36.

That longer-lived groups are not beset by such a sharp split between instrumental and affective aspects of leadership suggests that, as experimental groups continue their interaction over time, the division between the two leaders should diminish.

One would expect that the split between the two forms of leadership would be quite sharp during the first few group sessions before any leadership structure had been developed, but that as a consistent leader emerged whose control attempts came to be expected by the members, the negative affect in response to his control attempts would diminish. The experimental evidence on this point is mixed. Slater found that as the meetings of his experimental groups progressed, the percentage of times in which the same member held the highest position on Best Ideas and Best-liked fell considerably—from 56.6 per cent of the time in the first meeting to 8.8 per cent of the time in the fourth. (Significant by Chi square at the .01 level. See Slater in Hare, Borgatta, and Bales, eds., *Small Groups*, p. 504, table 4.) Gibb, on the other hand, reports a tendency for the split between affective choice and instrumental leadership to diminish over time (*ibid.*, p. 536, table 3). It is in any case doubtful whether the groups used by Slater or by Gibb had sufficient time together to test the hypothesis that the leadership split will diminish over time. (There were four sessions in the Slater experiment, and three in the experiment by Gibb.)

Furthermore, our hypothesis states that as the group progresses over time, instrumental controls will receive less negative affect. This does not mean they will necessarily receive positive affect. As a stable group structure develops, group members may begin to differentiate themselves more from the group leader and direct their positive affect toward peers in the group rather than toward the higher-status leader.

experimental groups also tends to heighten the conflict between the affective and instrumental aspects of the leadership function. Insofar as the accomplishment of the group task is important to the group members, those leaders who contribute to the accomplishment of that task will be rewarded with positive affect from the group members. But in the experimental groups considered above, the group task is assigned to the group by the experimenter and is not one toward which the members are highly motivated. The members may recognize that a particular individual contributed more to the accomplishment of the task, but they will not like that group member any more because of this.[13] Furthermore the use of college students of similar age may well create groups that negatively value the exertion of direct interpersonal influence. The evidence from the experiment by Hemphill cited above suggests a reluctance to use interpersonal influence in these groups. Similarly, Beatrice Shriver found that there were definite cultural limits beyond which group members selected as leaders by the experimenter would not go in exerting influence in the group. Thus the group leaders balked at selecting certain group members to receive higher rewards for their participation in the group. When it was suggested that they give bonuses to the most effective group members, the leaders either refused to make such a selection or did so by some random means (flipping coins, throwing darts) .[14]

[13]In a replication of the Bales experiment, Philp and Dunphy increased the motivation of the experimental subjects to accomplish the task set for them. The subjects were told that group performance would be taken into consideration in deciding upon class grades. Under this situation of heightened motivation to accomplish the task, affective-instrumental conflict was not as strong as in the work of Bales. See Hugh Philp and Dexter Dunphy, "Developmental Trends in Small Groups," *Sociometry*, 22 (1959), pp. 162-74. A similar finding is reported by March, *ibid.*, 19 (1956), pp. 260 61.

[14]B. Shriver, unpublished Ph.D. dissertation,

In the experiments, therefore, individuals who do not value highly interpersonal control by others are brought together in groups where the exercise of such control has no external backing from some extra-group hierarchy. The members are unknown to each other and have no apparent status differences such that one member would be expected to exert more influence in the group than another. Under these circumstances it is no wonder that the most active group member, even if he contributes the most to group performance, will tend to be rejected by the group on socio-emotional criteria. His control attempts are viewed as arbitrary and as direct personal challenges. And such directives are likely to arouse negative reactions. As Frank has put it, "Resistance to an activity is readily aroused if it involves submitting to an arbitrary personal demand of someone else, and it is thereby equivalent to a personal defeat."[15]

LEGITIMATE LEADERSHIP   Such arbitrary interpersonal influence exists when the recipient of the influence attempt does not consider that attempt legitimate—i.e., when the recipient does not feel that the leader *should* perform the acts he does perform. In cases where there is a nonlegitimate use of interpersonal influence, followers may accept the directives of leaders because the leader controls certain sanctions or because of a desire to see the group task accomplished, but such influence relationships are likely to cause resistance and to be unstable. On the other hand, if the recipient of the directive believes that directive to be right and proper, resistance will not develop. Where, as in the experimental work by Carter described above, the ap-

cited in Launor Carter, *Annual Status Report*, Office of Navel Research, Contract Nbonr-241, Task Order V, Feb. 1, 1952.

[15]J. D. Frank, "Experimental Studies of Personal Pressure and Resistance," *J. General Psychology*, 30 (1944), pp. 23-56.

pointed leader had his position legitimized by the experimenter, he was not
rejected by the group nor did he have to
engage in as much overt influence. A
more striking example of the difference
between legitimate leadership that is expected and nonlegitimate leadership is
found in the contrasting reaction to the
directives of the emergent leader and
the directives of the experimenter himself. One often forgets that there is an
authority figure in the leaderless experimental groups—the experimenter. He is
usually older and of higher status. Above
all, by entering the experimental situation the group members expect his directives and accept them as legitimate.
Consequently, unlike their rejection of
the emergent leader, experimental subjects follow the directives of the experimenter without complaint or resistance.
In fact, Frank reports the failure of an
experiment to measure resistance to unpleasant tasks because subjects could not
be induced to resist any task assigned
them by the experimenter.[16]

In on-going groups and organizations,
it is the development of a *legitimate*
leadership structure rather than the development of a dual leadership structure
that constitutes the major way in which
the conflict between affective and instrumental leadership is resolved. In a study
of 72 on-going chaired committees in
business and government, Berkowitz
found that when the chairman who was
expected to control the group did so, the
satisfaction of the group members increased. Negative reactions developed
only when he failed to perform as expected. Furthermore, and this is significant, when the chairman performed as
expected and controlled the group, control attempts initiated by other group
members led to the rejection of those
members by the group—just as the
control attempts of the non-legitimized
leaders in the experimental groups led to

negative reactions. But where the chairman did not perform as expected, the
group member who attempted to fill the
gap was not rejected by the group.[17] In
groups in which there is an expected
leadership pattern, negative affect will be
engendered not by the control attempts

[17]Leonard Berkowitz, "Sharing Leadership in
Small Decision Making Groups," *J. Abnorm. Soc.
Psych.*, 48 (1953), 231-38; reprinted in Hare,
Borgatta, and Bales, eds. *Small Groups.* Several
other studies support this point. Heyns compared
two sets of experimental groups. In one set a
high-status leader performed the leadership acts
expected of him. In the other set of groups, the
leader did not so perform. In the first case, where
the control of the leader was expected and the
leader did in fact exercise such control, attempts
to lead the group by other members resulted in their
rejection on a sociometric test after the group
session. In the groups where the leader did not
perform as expected, control attempts by other
members resulted in their receiving higher
rankings on a post-session sociometric test. (R. W.
Heyns, "Effects of Variations in Leadership on
Participant Behavior in Discussion Groups," unpublished Ph.D. dissertation, University of Michigan, 1948.) Similar findings are reported by
Walter H. Crockett, "Emergent Leadership in
Small Decision Making Groups," *J. Abnorm. Soc.
Psych.*, 51 (1955), 378-83.

That the group member from whom the other
group members expect control attempts will be
rejected not for these attempts but for violating the
group's expectation that he will exercise such
control is supported by a finding in the classic
Lippitt and White experiments. They found that
of the three leader styles they used—the democratic, the authoritarian, and the laissez-faire—the style
least liked by the children in the groups was the
laissez-faire. Since the group leaders were adults
appointed as leaders of the children's clubs, it is
likely that the rejection of the laissez-faire leader,
whose instructions were to keep his activity down
to a minimum, resulted from his violations of the
children's expectations that he would lead. See
Ralph White and Ronald Lippitt, "Leader Behavior and Member Reaction in Three 'Social Climates'", pp. 585-611 in Cartwright and Zander,
eds. *Group Dynamics.*

Informal leadership, it would seem, arises in
general as a gap-filler when formal leadership
does not perform as expected. Kahn and Katz, for
instance, point out that in production groups led
by supervisors who did not perform differentiated
leadership functions, an informal leader who spoke
for the group was more likely to arise than in those
groups where the supervisor performed the differentiated leadership functions expected of him.
Robert L. Kahn and Daniel Katz, "Leadership
Practices in Relation to Productivity and Morale"
pp. 612-628, *ibid.*

[16]*Ibid.*

of the legitimate leader, but by a failure of that leader to perform as expected; or if he performs as expected, by individuals who challenge his leadership.

The negative reactions to leader non-performance suggest that the model developed by Bales and his associates must be modified when the instrumental control attempts come from a legitimate leader. When control attempts are initiated by someone who is expected to initiate them, the disequilibrating force is not the control attempt, but any opposition that may develop to that control. Violation of the directive, not the directive itself, disturbs the smooth functioning of the group. In this case, the equilibrating mechanism is the sanction that the leader or the other group members employ to enforce acceptance of the directive.

Further Reading

It is possible to view the small group as a particular type of collectivity with its own distinctive structural features and social processes, as we have done. It is also possible to treat the small group simply as a convenient research setting within which a large range of psychological, social-psychological, and sociological phenomena may be explored. Both approaches are widely employed, and hence the literature on this subject is vast.

The most influential pioneering works are those of Charles H. Cooley, who formulated the distinction between primary and secondary groups in *Social Organization*, Glencoe, Ill.: Free Press, 1956 (originally published 1902); and Georg Simmel, whose concern was the analysis of the forms of social interaction, in his work, *The Sociology of Georg Simmel*, Glencoe, Ill.: Free Press, 1950 (a collection of writings originally published between 1902 and 1917).

Major attempts to provide theoretical integration to this field of study are those of George C. Homans, *The Human Group*, New York: Harcourt, 1950; and his *Social Behavior: Its Elementary Forms*, New York: Harcourt, 1961; Robert F. Bales, *Interaction Process Analysis: A Method for the Study of Small Groups*, Reading, Mass.: Addison-Wesley, 1950 (provides both a theoretical rationale and an empirical method for the analysis of small group interactions). Other theoretical approaches emphasizing the social-psychological dimensions of group behavior are John W. Thibaut and Harold H. Kelley, *The Social Psychology of Groups*, New York: Wiley, 1959; and Fritz Heider, *The Psychology of Interpersonal Relations*, New York: Wiley, 1958. Albert K. Cohen develops a theory of the emergence and persistence of deviant groups in his book *Delinquent Boys: The Culture of the Gang*, Glencoe, Ill.: Free Press, 1955. Two brief but useful introductions to the study of small groups are available in paperback: Michael S. Olmsted, *The Small Group*, New York: Random House, 1959; and Theodore M. Mills, *The Sociology of Small Groups*, Englewood Cliffs, N.J.: Prentice-Hall, 1967.

By far the most oft-cited study of a small group operating in its natural setting is William Foote Whyte, *Street Corner Society* (2d ed.), Chicago: University of Chicago Press, 1955. This study of a small group of Italian men in a Boston slum focuses on the relation of the leader to his group, intergroup behavior, and the relation between the gang and larger elements of the social structure, including racketeering and politics. A recent highly readable study by Elliot Liebow, *Tally's Corner*, Boston: Little, Brown, 1967, compares and contrasts the social structure of Whyte's group with that of a group of Negro street-corner men in Washington, D.C.

Three collections of research articles are available that provide a good overview of empirical work in this area, particularly laboratory studies of small group behavior. These are Dorwin Cartwright and Alvin Zander (eds.), *Group Dynamics: Research and Theory* (2d ed.), New York: Harper & Row, 1960; Eleanor Maccoby, Theodore M. Newcomb, and Eugene L. Hartley (eds.), *Readings in Social Psychology*, (3d ed.), New York: Holt, Rinehart and Winston, Inc., 1958; and A. Paul Hare, Edgar F. Borgatta, and Robert F. Bales (eds.), *Small Groups: Studies in Social Interaction* (2d ed.), New York: Knopf,

1965. In addition, A. Paul Hare has compiled an extensive summary of the findings of small groups research together with a comprehensive bibliography in his *Handbook of Small Group Research*, New York: Free Press, 1962.

Several research monographs have treated one or another aspect of small group functioning and have had a significant impact on the development of this research tradition. Among these studies are Leon Festinger, Stanley Schachter, and Karl Back, *Social Pressures in Informal Groups: A Study of Human Factors in Housing*, New York: Harper & Row, 1950, a study of the formation of group norms in student housing groups; Theodore M. Newcomb, *Personality and Social Change: Attitude Formation in a Student Community*, New York: Holt, Rinehart and Winston, Inc., 1943, an examination of attitude change as related to membership and reference group orientations; Muzafer Sherif *et al., Intergroup Conflict and Cooperation: The Robbers Cave Experiment*, Norman, Okla.: University Book Exchange, 1961, a study of conflict between two experimentally created small groups of boys in a camp setting; Ralph White and Ronald Lippitt, *Autocracy and Democracy*, New York: Harper & Row, 1960, an examination of the morale and productivity of groups under differing types of leaders; James F. Short, Jr., and Fred L. Strodtbeck, *Group Process and Gang Delinquency*, Chicago: University of Chicago Press, 1965, an empirical study of a large number of delinquent gangs; and Philip E. Slater, *Microcosm: Structural, Psychological, and Religious Evolution in Groups*, New York: Wiley, 1966, a detailed study of group behavior, relying heavily on psychoanalytic theory.

Finally, many of the better textbooks on social psychology contain extensive discussions of small groups phenomena. Representative works include Solomon Asch, *Social Psychology*, Englewood Cliffs, N.J.: Prentice-Hall, 1952; Theodore Newcomb, *Social Psychology*, New York: Holt, Rinehart and Winston, Inc., 1950; Paul F. Secord and Carl W. Backman, *Social Psychology*, New York: McGraw-Hill, 1964; and Roger Brown, *Social Psychology*, New York: Free Press, 1965.

PART FIVE

Social Processes in Formal Organizations

In turning to formally organized structures, we will not completely leave behind the small informal group or informal group processes. The small group is an important building block for larger and more complex social arrangements including organizations, communities, and institutions. And informal group processes are present in all these structural contexts, filling them out, supporting them, undermining them, and changing them. Indeed, this is one reason why these structures are more complex: they encompass the kinds of informal group processes with which we have been concerned, and in addition, they contain other kinds of processes.

Modern industrialized societies like our own are often described as "organizational societies." Large, complex organizations are a prominent if not the dominant characteristic of modern society. As Wolin notes:

> Everywhere there is organization, everywhere bureaucratization; like the world of feudalism, the modern world is broken up into areas dominated by castles, but not the castles of *les chansons de gueste*, but the castles of Kafka.[1]

Consider for a moment the organizations with which you come into contact in a single day. Do you go to school, ride a bus, mail a letter, buy groceries, eat at a restaurant, go to the movies or a bowling alley? These are but a few of the many ways in which all of us come into contact with organizations every day. As Parsons has stated:

> . . . the development of organizations is the principal mechanism by which, in a highly differentiated society, it is possible to "get things done," to achieve goals beyond the reach of the individual and under conditions which provide a relative maximization of effectiveness. . . .[2]

---

[1]Sheldon S. Wolin, *Politics and Vision*, Boston: Little, Brown, 1960, p. 354.
[2]Talcott Parsons, "A sociological approach to the theory of organizations," *Structure and Process in Modern Societies*, Glencoe, Ill.: Free Press, 1960. p. 41.

STRUCTURAL CHARACTERISTICS OF FORMAL ORGANIZATIONS

Formal organizations, like small groups, are collectivities, but they are characterized by two additional features. First, participants are organized for the pursuit of relatively specific objectives; second, their social structure exhibits a relatively high degree of formalization. We will discuss these features and their significance after we introduce a further complication. Sociologists studying organizations are of two minds in approaching their subject. One group places emphasis on the characteristics that distinguish organizations from other types of collectivities; that is, they emphasize the importance of goal specificity and formalization in shaping the structure and functioning of organizations. For reasons that will become clear later, we will refer to this as the "rational system" approach. The other group chooses to focus not on the distinguishing characteristics exhibited by organizations but instead on the characteristics that organizations share with all other collectivities. We will refer to this as the "social system" approach.[3] From time to time in this part we will concentrate on one or the other of these perspectives, but it should be clear from the outset that both perspectives are valid and both are necessary if we are to develop a complete understanding of organizational structures and processes.

Let us turn now to examine the distinguishing characteristics of formal organizations.

Goal Specificity   From the rational system point of view, organizations are, fundamentally, instruments for attaining goals. How blunt or fine an instrument they in fact are depends on many factors that are summarized by the concept *rationality* of structure. In this context, *rationality* is defined as the extent to which a series of actions is organized so that it leads to a previously defined goal. Goal specificity is of great importance for rationality of structure, because the more clearly defined and precise the definition of the goal that is to be pursued, the more possible it is to design a rational structure. In short, specific goals supply the criteria to be employed in making decisions about the structuring of the organization. What tasks are to be performed? What kinds of personnel are to be hired? How are resources and tasks to be allocated among participants? How are power and status to be distributed among positions? Who is to be paid and how much? These are the kinds of decisions that are more easily made if the goals to be pursued are clearly specified. After all, if one does not know where he wants to go, any road will take him there!

It must be recognized that goal specificity is a variable: some organizations pursue much more specific goals than other organizations. The goals pursued by a university, for example, are much less well defined than those pursued by a retail store. As we would predict, because universities cannot fully agree on the definition of their goal—what constitutes a "good" education, for example—they suffer much difficulty in attempting to rationalize their structure. Questions such as the type of student to be admitted, the requirements for graduation, and the distribution of scarce resources among departments are not easily resolved in

---

[3]For more complete descriptions of these competing points of view in organizational analysis, see Alvin W. Gouldner, "Organizational analysis," in Robert K. Merton, Leonard Broom, and Leonard S. Cottrell, Jr. (eds.), *Sociology Today*, New York: Basic Books, 1959, pp. 400–428; and W. Richard Scott, "Theory of Organizations," in Robert E. L. Faris (ed.), *Handbook of Modern Sociology*, Chicago: Rand McNally, 1964, pp. 485–529.

most universities. Even though the goals of organizations such as universities are not highly specific, they are, nevertheless, relatively so if compared with the goals of other social units, such as families or communities. Hence, universities are included within the category of "formal organization" while families and communities are usually excluded.

Sociologists approaching organizations from the social system point of view are unimpressed by the importance of goal specificity. They argue that regardless of what specific goals the organization happens to be pursuing, it, like all collectivities, places more importance on a general goal: to survive. They note that organizations often give up pursuit of their professed objectives and change directions if their survival is at stake. "The important point about organizations," according to Philip Selznick, an apostle of the social system view, "is that, though they are tools, each nevertheless has a life of its own."[4] Social system analysts argue that much of the behavior of organizational participants will be incomprehensible unless it is realized that much effort is directed toward merely continuing to exist as a collectivity. In reality, of course, most formal organizations are concerned with both specific goal attainment and survival, though in varying combinations.

Formalization   We have already defined the concept "formal" as referring to structures in which the constituent social positions and the relations among them are specified independently of the characteristics of the persons occupying the position. (See pp. 65-66) The term *formalization* refers to this same phenomenon but reminds us, first, that it may be treated as a process—as a series of changes that a given structure may undergo over time—and, second, that it should be treated as a variable—that a given structure may exhibit a higher or lower degree of formality at a given point in time.

Beginning again with the view of the rational system analyst, the degree of formalization is seen to have important implications for rationality of structure. Formalization objectifies structure, making it more explicit and more visible. It is possible to draw diagrams of a formal structure—to hold it up and look at it. Hence, it is possible to design it and to redesign it, attempting to make it a more effective instrument for goal attainment. Also, a formal structure is less dependent on personal relationships and the individual qualities of participants for effective operation. This means that functioning of the organization is not made dependent on the sociometric structure. As Merton notes: ". . . formality facilitates the interaction of occupants of offices despite their (possibly hostile) private attitudes toward one another."[5] This also means that it is not as essential to recruit visibly superior people to fill leadership positions in the organization, because it is the office that commands, not the occupant. In this connection, Robert MacIver has written:

The man who commands may be no wiser, no abler, may be in some sense no better than the average of his fellows; sometimes, by any intrinsic standard he is inferior to them. Here is the magic of government.[6]

---

[4]Philip Selznick, *TVA and the Grass Roots*, Berkeley, Calif.: University of California Press, 1949, p. 10.

[5]Robert K. Merton, "Bureaucratic structure and personality," *Social Theory and Social Structure* (rev. ed.), Glencoe, Ill.: Free Press, 1957, p. 195.

[6]R. M. MacIver, *The Web of Government*, New York: Macmillan, 1947, p. 13.

More generally, here is the magic of the formalization of any kind of organizational structure. Finally, the formalized structure is less dependent on the
participation of any particular individual. Individuals can come and go, whereas
the structure remains unimpared. The process of *succession*—the movement of
persons into and out of offices—is routinized so that individuals are promoted
according to explicit rules and are trained in advance to occupy the positions in
which they are placed, and no man is indispensable. In short, in the well-
designed formal structure, rationality resides in the structure—in the rules of
operation that specify the division of labor and the lines of responsibility and
authority, and in the rules of controlling recruitment and promotion and all
other matters affecting the operation of the organization—not in the participants.

The manner in which formalization can contribute to rationality of functioning may perhaps best be illustrated by analogy—the analogy of a machine. Ward
describes a machine in the following manner:

> A well-designed machine is an instance of total organization, that is, a series of
> interrelated means contrived to achieve a single end. The machine consists always of
> particular parts that have no meaning and no function separate from the organized
> entity to which they contribute. A machine consists of a coherent bringing together of
> all parts toward the highest possible efficiency of the functioning whole, of interrela-
> tionships marshalled wholly toward a given result. In the ideal machine, there can be
> no extraneous part, no extraneous movement; all is set, part for part, motion for motion,
> toward the functioning of the whole. The machine is, then, a perfect instance of total
> rationalization of a field of action and of total organization. This is perhaps even more
> quickly evident in that larger machine, the assembly line.[7]

Here we have a graphic statement of the aims of formalization: to design each
position in the organization, to specify the activities of its occupant and the ways
in which he relates to those in other positions, so that it plays its part in the
functioning of the larger structure. This is the contribution that formalization
can make to rationality of structure.

Note, however, that to say that formalization contributes to rationality of
operations specifies nothing about precisely what form is to be used. It states
that positions are to be precisely defined, but it does not indicate *how* they are
to be determined. The great German sociologist Max Weber attempted to
supply some content by specifying a set of structural characteristics that he
believed would collectively promote rationality of administrative activity.[8]
Weber enumerated many specific structural characteristics but most important
among them are the following:

> The organization is guided by a set of explicit and specific purposes from which a
> system of rules and regulations is derived that governs the operations of officials.
> The activities required to accomplish the purposes are distributed among offices so
> that each incumbent has a specified sphere of competence.
> The offices are arranged in a hierarchical authority structure, each official exercising
> and being subject to authority only in his capacity as office-holder and within the limits
> established by the rules.
> Officials are personally free, being bound to their offices by a contractual relationship
> and contributing their services in return for compensation, normally, a salary.

[7]John William Ward, "The ideal of individualism and the reality of organization," in Earl F.
Cheit (ed.), *The Business Establishment*, New York: Wiley, 1964, p. 62.
[8]See Max Weber, *The Theory of Social and Economic Organization*, Glencoe, Ill.: Free Press,
1947, pp. 329–336 (originally published 1925).

Candidates for positions are selected on the basis of their technical competence, being appointed rather than elected.

Officials carry out their functions in an impersonal manner.

Weber's characteristics are assumed by some to constitute a definition of a rational administrative arrangement, but such an assumption is misguided. They should instead be considered a set of propositions or hypotheses to be investigated, not taken for granted, because this set or any set of characteristics may promote rationality under some conditions but may lead to irrationality under other conditions.

Analysts using the social system approach to organizations point to the problems associated with formalization and also argue that its importance has been overstated. They note that formalization places a great burden on those who would attempt to design the structure. Planners are not omniscient so that they know all the possible contingencies that are going to confront various position occupants in the structure. The environment within which the organization operates and the environment for any particular position is sufficiently unstable and unpredictable that it is dangerous to program in advance the behaviors of participants. In a highly formalized structure, participants are not expected to exercise personal discretion but only to conform to their performance program—to carry out their assigned duties in the specified manner. Such programing, if misguided, can result in a high order of inefficiency and ineffectiveness—the "trained incapacity" for which some organizations are notorious.

Assuming that the formal structure is well designed, an even more critical problem is stressed by the social system analyst. Positions are filled by persons, and although some of their activities may be determined by the role expectations associated with the positions they occupy, all their behavior will not be so determined. Individuals participate in the organization as whole people; a man may fill the position of welder with some of his task activities regulated by his job definition, but he comes into the organization with all his characteristics, sentiments, needs, and motives. Such characteristics and their associated behavior furnish the basis for the emergence within the formal organization of an *informal structure*. The same processes we considered in the last Part operate within the formal organization. Sometimes they undermine and oppose the formal arrangements; sometimes they support and complement them; and sometimes their operation is largely irrelevant to the operations carried on within the formal structure. In general, sociologists have given more attention to the informal structure within formal organizations—the sociometric structure, the informal power and status structure, the cohesiveness of work groups, the personal characteristics of supervisors—than to the formal structures themselves. While the informal dimensions of the organizational structure are sometimes important, we would argue that the formal structures are also worthy of study, and we will concentrate attention on them in this Part.

INTEGRATIVE PROCESSES IN FORMAL ORGANIZATIONS

Many sociologists approaching organizations from the perspective of the social system analyst have emphasized the integrative functions performed by the informal organization and the personal relationships that develop among participants. Work groups have been observed to develop norms that support and regulate the conduct of their members (see Reading 5), sociometric ties develop among members as friendships develop, and feelings of loyalty and identification with the common enterprise are often an important source of motivation and morale. Important and, perhaps, indispensable as such developments are for the smooth functioning of organizations, no formal organization depends exclusively on such informal processes to achieve integration. Because we have already discussed informal integration processes, we shall concentrate in this section on the more formally established processes that operate in formal organizations.

Formalization   We have already discussed the process of formalization, but we would like to emphasize here its important contributions to the attainment of coherence and unity among the units (individuals, work groups, departments) comprising the organization. The attempt to specify as precisely as possible the several positions comprising the organizations in terms of the activities to be performed by their occupants and the kinds of relationships that are to develop is one way to build integration into the very structure of the organization. For example, by carefully specifying the activities to be performed by the several groups of workers, one can more readily assure that the products produced by one group will mesh with those produced by others. Or, to specify that several specific departmental managers are to report to one general manager whose job it is to plan, oversee, and coordinate their activities is another way in which integration of effort can be attained.

One important aspect of formalization is the development of rules governing the behavior of participants. As Aiken and Hage note, "A high degree of formalization implies not only a preponderance of rules defining jobs and specifying what is to be done, but also the enforcement of those rules."[1] In his chapter on the functions of bureaucratic rules, reprinted in this book (Reading 26), Alvin Gouldner points out that "the informal group and its norms . . . constituted a functional equivalent for bureaucratic rules . . . ." We would make here, however, precisely the opposite point: namely, that bureaucratic rules may

[1]Michael Aiken and Jerald Hage, "Organizational alienation: A comparative analysis," *American Sociological Review*, 31 (August, 1966), 499.

317

be viewed as a functional equivalent for informal group norms. That is, just as norms contribute to the integration of informal groups, rules promote the coherence and unity of formal organizations.

Gouldner's discussion also describes how the use of formal rules may solve some of the integrative problems raised by interactions that occur among persons who are not status or power equals. (Recall in this connection Bales' analysis of the ways in which efforts directed at task solutions, which entail attempts by some participants to influence and control others, created problems of integration for the group—see Reading 24.) Gouldner argues that because the rules appear to be impersonal in the sense that they control both superiors and subordinates, they act to "obscure the existence of power disparities" present in the organization.

Gouldner points to the variety of ways in which rules contribute to the coherence and unity of behavior in the organization but also notes some disadvantages associated with their use. In particular, rules specify the "*minimum* level of acceptable performance" and, hence, often maintain worker apathy rather than provide encouragement for exceptional performance. Formal rules may bring about minimal conformity and integration of worker behaviors but cannot of themselves inspire high motivation and commitment among workers. Such motivations are typically only produced by informal structures and personal relations: by work group solidarity and high morale and by imaginative and inspiring leadership exercised by *persons* in superior positions.[2]

Bureaucratization   Formalization is an attempt to substitute explicit rules of behavior for implicit and informal norms and understandings. As Gouldner notes, its focus is on the integration of the behavior of participants rather than on their beliefs or values. Another organizational process that contributes to the attainment of integration is that of bureaucratization. *Bureaucratization* refers to the creation and development of a specialized administrative staff whose task it is to control and coordinate the activities of other participants. In simple organizations, such work is performed by the owner-manager, but as organizations grow in size and complexity one person can no longer handle the job. As Bendix notes:

Seen historically, bureaucratization may be interpreted as the increasing subdivision of the functions which the owner-managers of the early enterprises had performed personally in the course of their daily routine. These functions may be divided into labor management, technical staff work, administrative management, and mercantile functions of purchasing, sales, and finance.[3]

Reflecting the increasing complexity of modern organizations, the size of this administrative component in most industrial organizations has increased rapidly over the last half century, as data complied by Melman makes clear (See Reading 27) .

Our definition of bureaucratization makes it sound as if this process were primarily concerned with task management and power processes, not inte-

[2]For elaboration of this argument, see Peter M. Blau and W. Richard Scott, *Formal Organizations: A Comparative Approach*, San Francisco: Chandler Publishing Company, 1962, pp. 140-141.
[3]Reinhard Bendix, *Work and Authority in Industry*, New York: Wiley, 1956, pp. 211-226.

gration. Although these matters are indeed involved, bureaucratization also contributes importantly to integration. As Blau and I note:

The term "bureaucratic organization," . . . calls attention to the fact that organizations generally posses some sort of administrative machinery. In an organization that has been formally established, a specialized administrative staff usually exists *that is responsible for maintaining the organization as a going concern and for coordinating the activities of its members*.[4]

Hence, one way of conceiving of the bureaucratic staff is to view it as a group of officials whose major efforts are devoted to maintenance of the organization qua organization. It is the task of this group to formulate the rules regulating the activities of other participants, to chart the lines of authority and responsibility, to design and maintain the communication channels, to determine the distribution of sanctions, to recruit workers, and to plan and oversee their training and socialization. It is this group that assumes responsibility for the daily and the long-term operation of the organization and, hence, for identifying and solving the integrative problems that arise.

Weber attempted to specify the characteristics of the bureaucratic staff positions that would best fulfill these responsibilities. He attempted to identify the structural characteristics that would together provide routine, efficient administration. As noted in our earlier discussion, one should not take Weber's description of administrative characteristics as inevitably leading to greater rationality of operations, but it is nevertheless true that many existing organizations adhere to his model of bureaucratic administration and that still others are moving in directions indicated by his model. Bendix describes this process of bureaucratization as it is currently developing in industrial concerns (see Reading 27). As is clear from his discussion, the process of bureaucratization is also one of formalization as positions and relationships among position-occupants become more clearly and explicitly defined over time.

Ideology   Bendix also examines the interesting problem of how managers attempt to justify to themselves and to others the status and power distinctions separating them from workers. He suggests that various ideologies are developed " (1) to demonstrate that the authority and power of the industrial leader is legitimate and (2) to aid the specific job of managerial coordination." These ideologies, which change over time with changing circumstances, are in effect an attempt on the part of managers to invoke a set of norms that will serve to legitimate their special role and status in the organization. The acceptance by both workers and managers of a common ideology of success—whether it be the Puritan virtues or the new ethic of human relations—helps to explain why some are more successful than others and at the same time provides a set of techniques believed useful for career advancement. This acceptance constitutes an important basis for integration within formal organizations.

In summary, organizations, like all collectivities, are faced by problems of achieving and maintaining some degree of integration. Rather than relying primarily on informal processes of normative regulation or on the sociometric structure among the persons involved, organizations tend to develop specialized

---

[4] Blau and Scott, p. 7. Emphasis ours.

mechanisms of control and coordination. These include formalization (the process by which roles and role relationships are explicitly defined), bureaucratization (the process by which a specialized adminstrative staff emerges whose primary responsibilities include the preservation of the organization as an integrated, functioning entity), and ideology (the development of normative systems that support and provide stability to existing structural arrangements). Because integration is, in a sense, forced on members as a condition of their participation in the organization, it relates primarily to the activities of participants rather than to their inner convictions. It is designed to achieve outward conformity of behavior rather than inner consistency of values, norms, or beliefs. No organization, however, relies exclusively on such external, formal mechanisms of integration and control. All organizations attempt to cultivate a belief in the legitimacy of their structures, in part by the creation and inculcation of ideological beliefs on the part of participants. Further, in all organizations, informal processes operate to support or undermine existing arrangements and to create new ones. Wise managers attempt to utilize these processes to strengthen and supplement the formal structures.

26   About the Functions of Bureaucratic Rules*

Alvin W. Gouldner

First, it can be noted that the rules comprise a functional equivalent for direct, personally given orders. Like direct orders, rules specify the obligations of the worker, enjoining him to do particular things in definite ways. Usually, however, rules are given, or are believed to be given, more deliberation than orders, and thus the statement of obligations they explicate can be taken to be definitive.

*This chapter is taken from a larger work in which Gouldner reports empirical materials concerning the bureaucratization of a gypsum factory. Comparisons are made throughout the work between the mining sector and the "surface" (processing) sector of the factory, the former being more resistant to bureaucratic trends. There are occasional references in this excerpt to a man named Peele. Peele was the new plant manager, who was intent on improving plant operations and, as a consequence, was instrumental in enlarging the bureaucratic apparatus within the plant.

Since the rules are also more carefully expressed, the obligations they impose may be less ambiguous than a hastily worded personal command.[1] Looked at in

[1]Mill also saw the function of rules as a definitive statement of explicit obligations. He insisted that the successful conduct of a business required two things, "fidelity and zeal." Fidelity, easier to obtain than zeal, could be partly ensured when "work admits of being reduced to a *definite set of rules;* the violation of which conscience cannot easily blind itself, and on which responsibility may be enforced by the loss of employment." Nevertheless, he conceded, many things needed for business success cannot be reduced to "distinct and positive obligations." Finally, in this connection, he adds "the universal neglect by domestic servants of their employer's interest, wherever these are not protected by some fixed rule, is a matter of common remark . . . " John Stuart Mill, *Principles of Political Economy*. London and New York: Longmans, Green, and Co., Ltd., 1926, p. 139.

this light, rules are a form of *communication* to those who are seen as desirous of evading responsibilities, of avoiding commitments, and of withholding proper and full performance of obligations. Comprising in one facet an explicit body of obligations, the rules serve to draw a worker's *attention* to managerial expectations and to dissolve the residues of diffuseness which may allow the worker to "hedge." Thus, on the one hand, the rules explicate the worker's task while on the other, they shape and specify his relationships to his superior. Stated in the language of the political scientist, the rules serve to narrow the subordinate's "area of discretion." The subordinates now have fewer options concerning what they *may* or *may not* do, and the area of "privilege" is crowded out by the growing area of "obligation."

It might be asked, why were work obligations comparatively diffuse in the mine, but much more explicit on the surface? An illustration previously used was the situation in which a group of workers were standing around, waiting for the mine head to assign them. He stepped out of his office and said, "One of you, clean out the rock crusher."

How was a *specific* individual chosen for this "dirty" job? This was the question asked a worker who had been through the situation. "It's simple," he replied. "We all just turn around and *look* at the newest guy in the group and he goes and does it." In other words, there existed an *informal* norm among miners to the effect that *new* workers got the dirty jobs; it was a norm to which the men were so sensitive that a mere "look" could bring the expected results. The informal group among miners spontaneously and with solidarity acted to enforce its norms. The informal group and its norms, then, constituted a functional equivalent for bureaucratic rules to the degree, at least, that it served to allocate concrete work responsibilities and to specify individual duties. It would appear, therefore, that the explication of obligations provided by bureaucratic rules is particularly necessary where there is no other instrumentality, specifically an effective informal group, which does this.[2]

THE SCREENING FUNCTIONS OF RULES

A second, less obvious, function of bureaucratic rules can be observed if we notice that, in part, they provide a substitute for the personal repetition of orders by a supervisor. Once an obligation was incorporated into a rule, the worker could not excuse himself by claiming that the supervisor had failed to tell him to do a specific thing. To take one example: The worker who operated a machine without using the safety guard could not "pass the buck" by saying that the supervisor neglected to mention this when he gave him a task. Since there existed a standing rule that "safety guards should always be used," the supervisor need not warn the worker of this every time he instructed him to use a machine.

Once standing rules have been installed, there are fewer things that a supervisor has to direct a worker to do; thus the frequency and duration of worker-

[2] This situation is in seeming contrast to one described by William Foote Whyte in his perceptive, *Human Relations in the Restaurant Industry*, McGraw-Hill Book Co., New York, 1948. Whyte recounts an incident in which a supervisor gave an order to two women, without specifying which one was to carry it out. Whyte remarks, "For effective action, orders and directions must be definite and clear as to what must be done, *how* and *when* it is to be done, and *who is to do it.*" (Ibid., p. 261.) Our own formulations are not necessarily in contradiction to Whyte's practical strictures. From our viewpoint, however, Whyte's conclusions should be limited to situations in which informal cohesion among workers has deteriorated so that they are unable to apply pressure to get the work done themselves, or if they are *unwilling* to do so. Our earlier point, about the tensions generated by close supervision, leads us to suspect that Whyte's prescriptions of detailed orders signify the presence of a motivational problem which may only be further exacerbated by the remedy he proposes.

foreman interaction in their *official* capacities is somewhat lessened. Moreover, even if the super does intervene in his capacity as a superior, he need not appear to be doing so on his own account; he is not so apt to be seen as "throwing his weight around." He can say, as one foreman said about the no-absenteeism rule: "I can't help laying them off if they're absent. *It's not my idea.* I've got to go along with the rules *like everyone else.* What *I* want has nothing to do with it." In other words, the rules provide the foreman with an impersonal crutch for his authority, screening the superiority of his power which might otherwise violate the norm of equality. Instead, equality presumably prevails because, "like everyone else," he, too, is bound by the rules which the plant manager has sanctioned.

Differences in power which are not justifiable in terms of the group's norms, or which violate them, seem to establish a situation requiring the utilization of impersonal control techniques. Impersonal and general rules serve in part to obscure the existence of power disparities which are not legitimate in terms of the group's norms.[3] The screening function of the rules would seem, therefore, to work in two directions at once. First, it impersonally bolsters a supervisor's claim to authority without compelling him to employ an embarrassing and debatable legitimation in terms of his personal superiority. Conversely, it permits *workers* to accept managerial claims to deference without committing them to a merely personal submission to the supervisor that would betray their self-image as "any man's equal."

THE "REMOTE CONTROL" FUNCTION OF RULES

It would be a mistake, however, to continue assuming that management instituted rules only when it perceived workers as unmotivated. For top management was often as much concerned with the low motivation of those in the lower echelons of its own ranks, i.e., middle management, as it was with workers'. This was quite evident in Peele's feeling that foreman and supervisors were "shirking." It was also a pattern that was more generally evident. Thus, for example, if all supervisors could be "counted on" to enforce safety regulations there would have been no need for the main office to employ a "safety engineer" to check upon safety conditions in the local plants.[4]

The problem of handling the "enemy within" was sometimes more difficult than

[3]William F. Whyte has made an observation in his restaurant studies which, if reconceptualized, in effect constitutes an interesting example of this pattern. Whyte points out that tension arises between the waitresses and the pantry help who fill their orders, under several conditions: when the waitresses are *younger* than the pantry people— even though both groups are women; or when those in the pantry are *men*. It would seem that these tensions emerge because *traditional* criteria of authority in our society are being violated. That is, younger people are initiating action for older people, while our cultural prescriptions prefer that power be vested in older folk. Again, women are initiating action for men, while the culture prescribes that men should wield the power. In an acute analysis, Whyte makes the following interpretation of the "insignificant-looking spindle" on which the waitresses place their orders, and from which the pantry people take them. "Wherever the people on the receiving end of the orders are related to the order givers as males vs. females, or older vs. younger, then it is important for the pantry help to have some *impersonal* barrier to block the pressure from themselves." (Ibid., p. 75.) In other words, instead of having the waitresses orally inform the pantry help of what they want, the waitresses can now write it out and place their order on the spindle. The pantry personnel can pick the order off the spindle without coming into direct interaction with the waitresses and without seeming to take orders from those culturally prescribed as inferiors. The spindle thus masks the existence of a relationship which violates internalized cultural prescriptions.

[4]Safety rules are discussed more fully in Chapter X. Alvin W. Gouldner, *Patterns of Industrial Bureaucracy.* Glencoe, Ill.: Free Press.

that of coping with those in the "out-group." For at least on the factory level, in-group and out-group could stand face to face and might sniff watchfully at each other, and could place their confidence for a while in "close supervision." But what could the safety engineer, for example, do to control some twenty-five plants? How could he control the supervision of safety work throughout the entire Company by means of "close supervision" alone? (Notice that the safety engineer's problem was only an extreme case of a common problem; it was not qualitatively different from that experienced by many of the plant's middle managers.)

In some way the safety engineer had to utilize a "spot check" system. That is, he made occasional visits to a plant, spending a little while there, and then moved on to another factory. If, however, each plant was to operate on a unique basis, each having its own distinctive techniques for handling safety, it would be difficult for the safety engineer to make his *own* judgment about plant conditions. He would be forced to place greater reliance on local management, which was precisely what he wanted to avoid. Insofar as he had established certain general rules applying to all plants, he could go to each one and "see for himself." He could "tell at a glance" whether the rules concerning machine guards or debris on the floor were being followed. In part, then, the existence of general rules was a necessary adjunct to a "spot check" system; they facilitated "control from a distance" by those in the higher and more remote reaches of the organization.[5]

There was another aspect of the rules which was also helpful to control from a distance. This was their *public* character. Because the rules were publicly known, an "enemy" could be used to control an "ally." For example, when the safety engineer inspected a plant he was not averse to speaking to workers whom he himself characterized as "troublemakers." The safety engineer told of a plant tour which he had made while in the company of a "troublemaker." This worker showed the engineer that there was a pile of debris in front of the blacksmith's bench, and took him to another spot and showed him how a machine had had its guard removed. He could only do this because the rules were public knowledge, and like everyone else, the "troublemaker" knew what they were. On the basis of these observations the safety engineer could then apply pressure to the supervisors. In sum, the *public* character of the rules enabled deviance to be detected by the *out-group*. This enlarged the information channels open to the heads of the in-group, in turn enabling them to keep their own junior officers in line.

---

[5]Some further implications of this, in the context of labor relations problems, may be seen from the comments of Frederick H. Harbison and Robert Dubin about the General Motors Company: "A rigid grievance procedure has made it easier for the corporation to control the decisions and actions of management's rank and file. Thousands of plant managers, department superintendents and foremen have been dealing with union representatives on a day-to-day basis. Many of them have been inexperienced in labor relations, and some were bound to make mistakes. *The existence of a system of rules has made it easier for top company officials to locate quickly those spots where local management has been 'off base.'*" (Our emphasis—A. W. G.) *Patterns of Union-Management Relations*, Science Research Associates, Chicago, 1947, pp. 83-84. The remote control function of bureaucratic measures has also been noted by Franz Neumann and Julian Franklin. For example, Franklin writes: "Rigid hierarchy and a precisely articulated framework of offices and functions make it possible for discretionary policy to be set at *one point* outside the bureaucracy and then to be administered automatically at all levels of the hierarchy." "The Democratic Approach to Bureaucracy," *Readings in Culture, Personality and Society*, Columbia College, N. Y., n. d., p. 3.

These considerations lead us to expect that bureaucratic rules flourish, other things being equal, when the senior officers of a group are impressed with the recalcitrance of those to whom they have delegated a measure of command. In other words, bureaucratic patterns are particularly useful to the degree that distrust and suspicion concerning role performance has become diffuse and directed to members of the "in-group," as well as to those on the outside; and when, as the Old Testament puts it, "A man's enemies are the men of his own house."

THE PUNISHMENT LEGITIMATING FUNCTIONS OF RULES

Faced with subordinates who were only reluctantly performing their roles, or at least, who were seen in this way, management was experiencing a status-threatening and hence aggression-provoking situation. The supervisor wanted to eliminate these threats when they arose and to prevent their recurrence. These were the supervisor's needs which emerged from his relations with workers when the latter began to behave apathetically ("goldbricking") or disobediently ("talking back"). On another level, the personality plane, the supervisor was beginning to "burn up" and was getting set to "blow his top." He was, in brief, accumulating a cargo of aggression with which he had to do something.

Why didn't the supervisor express his aggression and "tell the worker off"? Why didn't he *punish* the worker, thereby killing two birds with one stone; namely, unburdening himself of hostile feelings and compelling the worker to conform to his expectations? After all, punishment, or the infliction of "pain, failure, or ego-degradation"[6] upon the worker might help to bolster the supervisor's threatened status and salve his wounded ego.

There was one important drawback. Among surface workers in particular, and for the Company as a whole, supervisors were expressly forbidden, formally, to express aggression. As seen when contrasting miners with the more bureaucratized surface workers, the overt expression of aggression was taboo among the latter. Moreover the Company "labor relations manual" asserted that "A *friendly* attitude toward . . . all employees will provide the basis for sound Company-employee relations in each plant." The manual also insisted that one of the characteristics of every good employee was an "ability to *control emotion*." In the face of these proscriptions, it was difficult to express aggression openly.

In our society, moreover, it is not permissible to inflict a punishment under any and all conditions. There seems to be a deep-grooved inscription in our culture which asserts that punishment is permissible only on the condition that the offender could know *in advance* that certain of his behaviors are forbidden.[7] This is one of the sentiments which underlies the rejection of *ex post facto* laws in our legal structure. If it has become a formally announced legal principle that "ignorance of the law is no excuse," this has, in part, been necessary because traditional folkways informally insist that ignorance of the law constitutes an extenuating circumstance.

[6]Norman F. Maier, *Frustration*, McGraw-Hill Book Co., 1949, p. 194.

[7]Here, again, there is evidence suggesting that we are dealing with a culturally induced sentiment rather than one peculiar to this factory or to industrial phenomena alone. On the basis of their wartime studies of the U. S. Armed Forces, the authors of *The American Soldier* suggest that punishment is more likely to be effective if "the men are given specific *advance* warning about the consequences of an occurrence of the offense, since *most men consider fair warning as a condition for fair punishment*." Ibid., p. 425. (Our emphasis—A. W. G.)

Within the plant, orientation to this traditional norm was expressed in several ways. First, the frequent claim that so-and-so was a good foreman because he gave his workers a "second chance," a factor in the "indulgency pattern," implied that such a foreman did *not* take the first opportunity that presented itself to inflict a punishment. Instead he used this first deviation as an occasion to *warn* the worker that future infractions would meet with punishment.

That punishments which were not preceded by warnings were only doubtfully legitimate, in the eyes of plant personnel, can be inferred from the introduction of the formal warning notice. One of the functions of the *worker's signature* on the warning notice was to forestall a claim that he had not been warned and could not, therefore, be punished. Day, the old personnel manager, complained precisely of this point after he had been demoted, saying, "Why didn't Peele tell me about it long before now, instead of just replacing me?"

Bureaucratic rules, then, serve to legitimate the utilization of punishments. They do so because the rules constitute statements in advance of expectations. As such, they comprise explicit or implicit *warnings* concerning the kind of behavior which will provoke punishment.

In actuality, the establishment of a rule explicating an obligation is frequently accompanied by a specific statement of the punishment, i.e., another rule specifying the punishment which will result if the first rule is violated. Two things, rather than one, have thus been clarified: (1) what is expected of the man and (2) what will happen to him if he does *not* fulfill these expectations. For example, the no-absenteeism rule did not merely state that the worker must not be absent without cause; it also specifically provided that he was to be laid off a like number of days for those which he took.

In brief, when rules explicate obligations, they are producing consequences recognized and intended by most participants in the situation. When rules explicate a punishment, however, they are legitimating the use of punishments, a consequence sometimes not at the center of the group's intention or awareness. The relationship between the explicational and the punishment functions of rules is like the relation between the locomotive and the trains which it pulls. Attention can all too readily be diverted to the noisy, smoking locomotive in the vanguard, while the attached trains carrying the pay load are easily neglected.

An example of the punishment function of the rules occurred in the dehydrating section of the mill: There were a number of large vats, used to heat and dehydrate the gypsum into powder, which occasionally needed to be cleaned out. A rule specified that the man who went down into one of these vats must wear a harness with a rope leading up to the top; there was also supposed to be someone at the top holding onto the rope and watching the man inside. These precautions stemmed from the fear that a man at the bottom of a vat could be killed by fumes or smothered by a cave-in of the "cake" covering the inside of the vat.

One day a main office executive passed through the plant on an inspection tour and noticed a rope leading down into a vat. He looked over the side and saw a worker cleaning it out, but there was no one around at the top watching the man and guarding the rope. Immediately the executive looked for the man's foreman, who was not to be seen. After a search, however, he discovered the foreman doing exactly the same thing, cleaning out a vat without having someone watch him. The executive then "raised hell" with the foreman and took it to higher plant authorities.

In short, the first thing the executive did when he discovered the infraction of vat-cleaning rules, was to look for some-one to punish and blame. Instead of calling the man up from the vat, he left him down there. Instead of doing something to forestall an accident, the manifest function of this rule, he exploited the situation as an opportunity to inflict a punishment.

The rules thus channel aggression, providing permissible avenues for its expression and legitimating the utilization of punishments. To the extent that possible objects of punishment and aggression are members of the "in-group," as suggested in our discussion of the "remote control" function of rules, it becomes all the more necessary to legitimate meticulously the use of these control measures. For, by and large, aggression and punishments directed toward in-group members are not preferred patterns of behavior in our culture and require especially unambiguous justification. Bureaucratic rules are thereby particularly functional in a context in which reliance upon the in-group has been shaken.

THE "LEEWAY" FUNCTION OF RULES

Another commonplace pattern observable in management's[8] application of bureaucratic rules, which is related to their punishment function, was the curious rhythmic quality with which rules were *enforced*. Sometimes demands for rigorous conformance to a rule would be made, but would later lapse into periods of disinterest when the rules were ignored or only fitfully observed. For example, occasionally the plant guard would carefully examine packages which workers brought out of the plant, while at other times these would be given only cursory

[8]Later chapters will emphasize that these functions of bureaucratic rules were not peculiar to management, but apply also to workers.

inspection. Sometimes punctual "punching in" would be rigorously enforced; at other times lateness would be given only casual comment. What was the significance of these periodic alternations? A clue to part of their meaning may be found in the *contexts* in which enforcement or relaxation of rules occurred.

Usually, it was noted that a fever of enforcement occurred when small tensions between workers and their supervisors began to coalesce into more definite rifts. A case in point was the "no-floating around" rule which specified that workers must stay at their work-place, except to go to the washroom or to eat. When foremen felt that things were going smoothly in their group, that their men were "doing a day's work" and were friendly and "cooperative," they would allow their workers to "sneak off" for a smoke, and they would make no caustic comments if they wandered over to talk to a friend. If, however, a man or the group as a whole was felt to be "goofing off," or was becoming "snotty," foremen were then more likely to invoke the "no-floating" rule.

By a strange paradox, *formal* rules gave supervisors something with which they could "bargain" in order to secure *informal* cooperation from workers. The rules were the "chips" to which the Company staked the supervisors and which they could use to play the game; they carved out a "right" which, should supervisors wish to, they could "stand upon." In effect, then, formal bureaucratic rules served as a control device not merely because they provided a legitimating framework for the *allocation* of punishments, but also because they established a punishment which could be *withheld*. By installing a rule, management provided itself with an instrument which was valuable even if it was not used; the rules were serviceable because they created something which could be *given up* as well as *given use.*[9]

THE APATHY-PRESERVING FUNCTION OF BUREAUCRATIC RULES

Nor is this the last of paradoxes. For though bureaucratic rules were fostered by situations involving worker apathy, or its semblance, the rules actually contributed to the preservation of work apathy. Just as the rules facilitated punishment, so, too, did they define the behavior which could permit punishment to be *escaped.* The discussion of the "leeway" function of rules has considered the importance of this from the supervisor's standpoint, but it was also significant for the worker as well. The rules served as a specification of a *minimum* level of acceptable performance. It was therefore possible for the worker to *remain* apathetic, for he now knew just how *little* he could do and still remain secure.

For example, after Peele had ruled that workers could not "punch in early" and

accumulate a little overtime in that way, one mill worker said acidly:

"Well, if that's the way he wants it, that's the way he wants it. But I'll be damned if I put in any overtime when things get rough and they'd like us to."

Said another worker:

"O.K. I'll punch in just so, and I'll punch out on the nose. But you know you can lead a horse to water and you can lead him away, but it's awful hard to tell just how much water he drinks while he's at it."

This, of course, is the stuff of which "bureaucratic sabotage" is made. "Bureaucratic sabotage" is deliberate apathy fused with resentment, in which, by the very act of conforming to the letter of the rule, its intention is "conscientiously" violated. The worker's feeling and attitudes toward his work were thus essentially left untouched by the bureaucratic rules. The worker could, as it were, take any attitude toward his work that he wished, so long as he conformed to the rules. The rules did little to modify *attitudes* toward work, but were significant primarily as guidelines for *behavior.* In the last analysis, it would seem that proliferation of bureaucratic rules signifies that management has, in effect if not intention, surrendered in the battle for

---

[9]This is an aspect of the functioning of bureaucratic rules which tends to be neglected by those who, like Julian Franklin, emphasize the discretion-narrowing role of bureaucratic measures. Thus Franklin writes: ". . . the aim in organizing a bureaucratic structure is to narrow the area of discretion and, as far as possible, to reduce the process of administration to a series of routine actions." Julian Franklin, "The Democratic Approach to Bureaucracy," *Readings in Culture, Personality and Society.* New York: Columbia College, p. 3.

Our comments are not necessarily in contradiction to Franklin's, since he is here, I presume, speaking of the manifest functions of bureaucratic techniques with which we ourselves concur (as indicated by the discussion of the "explicational functions" of the rules): in examining the "leeway function," however, we have been talking of their latent functions—the unrecognized and unintended consequences. Here, as in our discussion of the apathy-preserving functions of the rules, we are talking about unanticipated consequences generated by distinctively bureaucratic characteristics. This is a rather different direction than the one taken by Philip Selznick in his study of the TVA,

where the "existential" dilemmas of organization—the universal ills to which the organizational flesh is presumably heir—are painstakingly examined. Our focus is on the ills specific to bureaucracy, whose universality we more than doubt. Selznick's study, more generally, can be conceived of as concerned with the reverse side of the penny. He is largely attending to the forces that generate discretionary drives and that subvert the formal ends and organization to "narrower" interests. He finds these, however, not in peculiar bureaucratic traits, but in the above mentioned existential dilemmas. For our part, we have been focusing, in the main, on forces that sustain formal ends and bureaucratic patterns. Where we note tensions which subvert them, we are concerned, in particular, with their origin in distinctive patterns peculiar to bureaucracy. See Philip Selznick, *TVA and the Grass Roots.* Berkeley and Los Angeles: University of California, 1949.

the worker's motivation. In his study of *Social Organization*, Charles Horton Cooley came to much the same conclusion:

"Underlying all formalism, indeed, is the fact that it is psychically cheap; it substitutes the outer for the inner as more tangible, more capable of being held before the mind *without fresh expense of thought and feeling.*"[10]

And again:

". . . the merely formal institution does not enlist and discipline the soul of the individual, but takes him by the outside, his soul being left to torpor or to irreverent and riotous activity."[11]

Thus bureaucratic rules may be functional for subordinates, as well as for superiors; they permit "activity" without "participation;" they enable an employee to work without being emotionally committed to it.

This function of bureaucratic rules is of peculiar importance since it suggests one of the inherent sources of bureaucratic

[10]C. H. Cooley, *Social Organization*, Chas. Scribner's Sons, 1919, p. 349. (Our emphasis—A. W. G.)

[11]Ibid., p. 343.

rules' instability; for the rules do not seem to *resolve* the very problem, worker apathy, from which they most directly spring. Insofar as formal rules merely "wall in," rather than resolve, worker apathy, it may be expected that other mechanisms more competent to muster motivations will challenge and compete with them.[12]

[12]It may well be that this is one of the organic contradictions of bureaucratic organization that make it susceptible to infiltration and displacement by "charismatic" elements, which involves loyalty to leadership based on belief in the leader's unusual *personal* qualities. Weber vaguely explained the vulnerability of bureaucracy as a breakdown of its efficiency in the face of new problems and accumulating tensions. He did little to analyze the specific nature of these tensions and tended to focus on their origins in the environment, neglecting their inner-organizational sources. We are suggesting, in effect, that bureaucratic authority is supplanted by charismatic when it is no longer possible to bypass the question of motivation. Charismatic leadership, it has been widely noted, has an ability to arouse new enthusiasms and to ignite irrational sources of motivation inaccessible to the bureaucrat. Indeed, some observers have insisted that this is one of the distinctive characteristics of modern totalitarianism. Thus George Orwell, in his *1984*, brings this novel to its climax when his hero is being tortured not merely to confess, nor to conform—but to *believe*.

27   Bureaucratization in Industry

Reinhard Bendix

The bureaucratization of modern industry has increased over the last half century. At the same time the changes of industrial organization which have accompanied this development have contributed to industrial peace. The following essay is designed to explore some background

factors which tend to support these two propositions. It seeks to establish that industrial entrepreneurs considered as a class have undergone major changes since the beginning of the 19th century. These changes have culminated in the development of an industrial bureaucracy. The consequences of this bureaucratization may be observed in the changing system of supervision as well as in the transformation of the prevailing ideology of industrial managers.

INTRODUCTION

Webster's Collegiate Dictionary defines "bureaucracy" as routine procedure in administration, as a system of carrying on the business of government by means of bureaus, each controlled by a chief. This definition reflects the fact that it has not been customary to speak of bureaucracy in industry. Traditionally, the term has been applied to the activities of government; it has been broadened to include large-scale organizations generally only in recent years.[1]

The polemic implications of the term bureaucracy obscure its use in a descriptive sense, and yet it is important to use it in that sense. "A system of carrying on the business of industry and government by means of bureaus" is a definition of "administration" as well as of bureaucracy. Yet the two terms are not synonymous. Bureaucracy suggests in addition that the number of bureaus has increased, that their functions have become specialized as well as routinized, and that increasing use is made of technical apparatus in the performance of these specialized functions, which is in

turn related to the increasing use of expert, technical knowledge. The use of technical knowledge in the administration of industry implies the employment of specialists, whose work presupposes the completion of a course of professional training. The work of these specialists entails the subdivision and consequent elaboration of the managerial functions of planning, production organization, personnel selection, and supervision.

These developments have many ramifications. They depend, on the one side, on the growth of training facilities in many fields of applied science. They make possible a centralization of authority in industrial management, which can be made effective only by a simultaneous delegation of circumscribed authority to specialized bureaus or departments. This encourages the substitution of deliberately planned methods of procedure for rule-of-thumb "methods," and this in turn promotes the utilization of mechanical devices. But the adoption of rational procedures achieves greater operating efficiency than is possible in less elaborated organizational structures at the constant risk of more bureaucracy, in the negative sense.

These remarks give an idea of the complexity of the process called "bureaucratization." Little is gained, however, by adopting a concise definition of this term. It is rather intended as the common denominator of many related tendencies of administrative procedure which have characterized government and industry in recent decades. But while the term itself remains vague, its component elements do not.

The following aspects of bureaucratization will be considered in this essay. In the first section it is shown that industrial entrepreneurs as a group have been transformed since the inception of modern industry at the beginning of the 19th century. This has resulted in the elabora-

[1]Bureaucracy in government has been analyzed in great detail, frequently with the implication that waste and indolence were widespread. Many of these studies received their impetus from the scientific-management movement. Cf. Dwight Waldo, *The Administrative State*, New York, Ronald, 1948, pp. 47-61. The conventional term for industrial bureaucracy is "business administration." The implication of this terminology is obviously that waste and indolence are absent from business, that productivity is synonymous with efficiency, and that business administration involves technical know-how which the businessman has to keep secret in order to retain his competitive advantage. The semantics of this controversy have not been analyzed to my knowledge.

tion of managerial functions in industry. In the second section an attempt is made to sketch the changes of managerial ideology which have accompanied bureaucratization. The first section characterizes the development of industrial bureaucracy. In the second section certain ideological consequences are analyzed which are especially relevant for an understanding of peace and conflict in industrial relations.

CHANGES IN MANAGERIAL FUNCTIONS

The growing bureaucratization of industry may be analyzed in a variety of ways. The role of the employer has changed fundamentally since the rise of modern industry. The manager or owner of old, who knew and directed every detail of his enterprise, has become the modern industrialist who is above all else a specialist in business administration. Evidence for this transformation of the entrepreneur may be reviewed briefly.

In a report for 1792 Robert Owen states that it took him 6 weeks of careful observation to become thoroughly familiar with every detail of an enterprise employing 500 men.[2] An enterprise employing 500 men could be comprehended and managed at one time by a man of talent and experience. It is improbable that the same could be done today. A manager of a plant with 500 employees cannot be in daily touch with the details of the manufacturing process as Owen was. He will have various subordinates to supervise this process for him; also, this manager has lost most or all of his personal contacts with the workers in the plant. And although labor may be as efficient as it had been before this depersonalization of the employment relationship, this same efficiency is now obtained

"at an increased cost in supervisory staff, complicated accounting methods, precise wage systems, liberal welfare provisions, checks and balances, scheduling and routine."[3] The point to emphasize is that bureaucratization of industry is not simply synonymous with the increasing size of the enterprise but with the growing complexity of its operation.

The bureaucratization of industry is, therefore, not simply the outcome of a recent development. In his analysis of the Boulton and Watt factory in 1775–1805 Erich Roll has described an elaborate system of keeping records, which was used as a basis of wage-determination, of cost-calculation, and of planning new methods of production. It is probable that this system was introduced when the firm passed from the original founders, who were in close contact with every operation of their enterprise, into the hands of the younger generation, who were not in touch with every operation and who, therefore, needed such a system of control.[4] At that time few firms were organized as efficiently as Boulton and Watt, but the case illustrates the fact that the bureaucratization of industry is not synonymous with the recent growth in the size of the large enterprises.

Corroborative evidence on this point is also contained in a study of American business leaders in the railroads and in the steel and textile industries, in the decade 1901–1910. The careers of 185 prominent industrialists were classified in terms of whether they had made their way in business by their own efforts exclusively, whether they had made their way in a family-owned enterprise, or

---

[2]G. D. H. Cole, *The Life of Robert Owen*, London, Macmillan & Co., 1930, p. 70.

[3]P. Sargant Florence, *The Logic of Industrial Organization*, London, Kegan Paul, Trench, Trubner & Co., 1933, pp. 159–160.

[4]Erich Roll, *An Early Experiment in Industrial Organization, Being a History of the Firm of Boulton and Watt*, 1775–1805, New York, Longmans, 1930, pp. 250–251.

TABLE 27-1 American Business Leaders, by Type of Career and Date of Birth°

Type of career	Before 1841 %	1841–1850 %	1851–1860 %	After 1860 %
Independent	26	19	11	8
Family	22	24	42	36
Bureaucratic	52	57	47	56
Total cases (=100%)	23	59	55	25

°William Miller, "The Business Elite in Business Bureaucracies," in William Miller (ed.), *Men in Business*, Cambridge, Mass., Harvard University Press, 1952, p. 291. Reprinted by permission.

whether they had risen through the ranks of an industrial bureaucracy; the results of the classification are shown in Table 27-1. These data make it apparent that prominent industrialists have had a bureaucratic career pattern at a relatively early time.[5]

Occupational statistics reflect this decline of the independent enterpriser and the increase of the "industrial bureaucrat," especially in the heavy industries. In the period 1910–1940 the number of independent industrial enterprisers declined from about 425,000 in 1910 to 390,000 in 1930 and 257,000 in 1940, in manufacturing, construction, and mining. In the same industries the number of managerial employees increased from 375,976 in 1910 to 769,749 in 1930 and 802,734 in 1940.[6]

The bureaucratization of industry has also profoundly altered the job environment of the lowest rung on the managerial ladder.[7] Until about a generation or two ago the foreman occupied a position of real importance in industry, especially with regard to the management of labor.

In the majority of cases the foreman would recruit workers, he would train them on the job, he would supervise and discipline them, which included such handling of grievances as was permitted, and he would pay their wages on a time basis.[8]

Today the foreman performs the functions of the immediate supervisor of the workers, who is in effect the executive agent of various supervisory departments. And it is increasingly a matter of discretion for these departments whether or not they decide to consult the foreman. The following summary based on a study of 100 companies which were sampled for the purpose of analyzing the *best* practices in American industry, illustrates this point clearly:

Hiring. In two-thirds of the companies replying, the personnel department interviews and selects new employees, while the foreman has final say; but in one-third the foreman has no voice in hiring.

Discharge. Foremen have some say in discharge, but only in one-tenth of all cases can they discharge without any consultation.

Pay Increases and Promotion. These must almost always be approved by other authorities.

[5]See William Miller, "The Business Elite in Business Bureaucracies," in William Miller (ed.), *Men in Business*, Cambridge, Mass., Harvard University Press, 1952, pp. 286–305.
[6]See Lewis Corey, "The Middle Class," *Antioch Review*, Spring, 1945, pp. 73, 77.
[7]See Chap. 13 [in *Industrial Conflict*], by Melville Dalton, for a detailed discussion of the foreman's modern role in industry.

[8]See the detailed analysis of the rights and duties of subcontractors and foremen in England during the 19th century in William T. Delaney, "The Spirit and Structure of Labor Management in England, 1840–1940," Master's thesis, University of California (Berkeley), Chap. 3.

TABLE 27-2 All Manufacturing Industries: Composition of Work Force in Administration and Production Categories, 1899-1947 (In Thousands)*

Personnel	1899	1909	1923	1929	1937	1947
Administration	457	886	1,345	1,562	1,567	2,672
Production	4,605	6,392	8,261	8,427	8,602	12,010
Administration personnel, as per cent of production personnel	9.9%	13.9%	16.3%	18.5%	18.2%	22.2%

*Seymour Melman, "The Rise of Administrative Overhead in the Manufacturing Industries of the United States 1899–1947," *Oxford Economic Papers,* Vol. 3, No. 1 (January, 1951), p. 66. Reprinted by permission.

Discipline. In only one-tenth of all cases do foremen have complete charge of discipline.

Grievances. Discussion with the foreman is generally the first step in the grievance procedure, but the extent to which he settles grievances is not clear. A small sample in the automotive-aircraft industries shows that this may range from 45 to 80%.

Policy-making. Only 20% of the companies replying held policy meetings with foremen.[9]

These findings make it apparent that the "average" foreman's responsibilities have remained, while his authority has been parceled out among the various supervisory departments. It is not surprising that this bureaucratization of supervisory functions has entailed inescapable tensions between the various departments performing these functions as well as tensions between these departments and the foremen. The latter have had to surrender their authority to the supervisory departments, but their responsibility for the execution of decisions has remained.

The changes in managerial functions which have grown out of the increasing division of labor within the plant and which are evident in the changing activities and career patterns of business exec-

[9]Ernest Dale, *The Development of Foremen in Management,* American Management Association Research Report 7, 1945, p. 9.

utives and foremen are reflected also in the rise of "administrative overhead." A recent study of the rise of administrative personnel in American manufacturing industries since 1899 makes it clear that this rise has occurred throughout the economy (Table 27-2).

A detailed examination reveals that this over-all increase in the ratio of administrative and production personnel is *not* systematically related to any one factor except size. Melman finds, somewhat paradoxically, that administrative cost as a proportion of production cost is lower in large than in small firms, despite the general upward trend in administrative personnel. His explanation is that all firms have shown an absolute increase in administrative overhead but that at any one time large firms as a group have a proportionately lower administrative overhead than small firms. This relative advantage of the larger firms is attributed to skill in organization. In the long run, however, all firms must anticipate an increase in administrative cost.

It should be added that a comparative study of administrative personnel in the manufacturing industries of other countries reveals similar trends, though it is noteworthy that the ratio of administrative as compared with productive personnel has increased more in the United States than in France, Germany, or Eng-

TABLE 27–3 Sampled Manufacturing Industries: Administration and Production Personnel, 1899–1937[*]

Industry	Administration personnel as per cent of production personnel				
	1899	1909	1923	1929	1937
Agricultural implements	22.1	18.6	19.8	18.3	20.6
Boots and shoes	6.2	8.1	10.8	11.0	8.5
Boxes, paper	6.3	9.1	13.6	14.4	16.1
Cash registers and business machines	15.9	23.8	23.2	36.9	37.7
Drugs and medicines	45.7	69.2	51.3	61.5	58.1
Electrical machinery	12.5	20.7	31.4	24.6	26.7
Explosives	17.3	12.3	33.6	38.2	44.4
Glass	4.5	5.3	8.6	9.7	11.5
Lighting equipment	12.8	20.1	22.9	20.6	19.2
Locomotives, not built in railroad shops	3.9	13.6	9.5	20.9	29.8
Meat packing, wholesale	15.3	20.1	24.8	22.8	29.2
Motor vehicles	13.1	13.3	11.5	14.8	16.9
Petroleum refining	10.0	19.3	24.1	35.6	45.3

[*]Seymour Melman, "The Rise of Administrative Overhead in the Manufacturing Industries of the United States 1899–1947," *Oxford Economic Papers*, 3 (January, 1951),p. 66. Reprinted by permission.

land.[10] Melman's summary figures for a nationwide sample of manufacturing industries do not reveal the striking differences between industries and it may therefore be helpful to cite a few sample figures from his data (Table 27–3). These figures make it apparent that the over-all upward trend of administrative overhead covers a great diversity of particular developments. Although it is true that the average proportion of administration to production personnel has increased, there are significant differences between industries, and important fluctuations of this ratio have also occurred within an industry over time.

It may be useful to enumerate, in addition, some of the factors which are relevant for the interpretation of these statistics. Economically, it makes a great difference whether administrative personnel in industry increases together with a rapidly or a slowly expanding work force. That is to say, increasing administrative expenditures can be easily sustained in a rapidly expanding industry. Also, the increases of personnel in administration are accompanied by capital investments. Today, a given number of clerks can do a great deal more work than formerly, with the aid of various computing and multigraphing machines. As a group they also do a greater variety of

[10]This comparative study cannot be reported here for reasons of space. But it should be mentioned that the economic meaning of this ratio depends in large part on the rate of capital investment. Industries which have a rate of increase in administrative overhead similar to that of the industries of the United States without, however, a similar increase in capital investment are obviously suffering from industrial bureaucratization far more than this country.

work, owing to specialization and partial mechanization. However, neither the greater complexity of administrative work nor the various efforts at standardization and routinization can be measured by the number of clerks employed. The increase of administrative personnel is, therefore, only a proximate measure of bureaucratization.

MANAGERIAL IDEOLOGY AND BUREAU-CRACY

The general trend is in the direction of an increase in the complexity of managerial tasks. To assess the problems created by this trend, it is not sufficient, for example, to describe how the functions of hiring and discharge, of administering an equitable wage structure, and of processing grievances and disciplining workers have become the special tasks of separate departments. In order to understand the modern problems of management, we must realize that this separation of functions has created for all ranks of management an ambiguity which is in many respects similar to, though it is not so intense as, that of the foreman. The over-all managerial problem has become more complex because each group of management specialists will tend to view the "interests of the enterprise" in terms which are compatible with the survival and the increase of its special function. That is, each group will have a trained capacity for its own function and a "trained incapacity" to see its relation to the whole.

The problem of industrial management is to subdivide, as well as to coordinate, the tasks of administration and production and then to maximize the efficiency of each operation. In so doing it employs specialists, and each group of specialists must exercise considerable discretion in order to get the work done. That is to say, with each step toward specialization the centrifugal tendencies and, hence, the

coordinating tasks of central management increase. Bureaucratization has accompanied the whole development of industry, but it has increased more rapidly since the inception of scientific management in the 1890's. The major development of trade-unions has occurred during the same period. If we consider these parallel changes it becomes apparent that the greater complexity of the managerial task has consisted in the need for intramanagerial coordination at a time when managerial leadership was challenged by the organizing drives of trade-unions as well as by the ideological attacks of the muckrakers. Hence the ideology of business leaders, their justification of the authority they exercise and of the power they hold, has gradually assumed a double function: (1) to demonstrate that the authority and power of the industrial leader is legitimate and (2) to aid the specific job of managerial coordination.

Until recently the ideologies of the industrial leaders did not serve this double function. In the past their leadership was justified by a reiteration of time-tested shibboleths which would make clear what was already self-evident to all but the most die-hard radicals. Success is virtue, poverty is sin, and both result from the effort or indolence of the individual. Together with this belief went the idea that every use made of property was beneficial to the social welfare, as long as it resulted in an increase of wealth. These ideas, which justified the authority and power of the industrial leaders, established a goal in life for everyone. The tacit assumption was that in the prevailing economic order the chances of each "to get to the top" were the same. Hence the success of the industrial leader was itself the token of his proved superiority in a struggle between equals. To question this was to bar the way of those who would succeed after him.

These ideas have never really died; there is much contemporary evidence to show that the beliefs of industrial leaders have remained essentially the same. Successful industrialists as a group have always tended to express views which ranged from the belief that their virtue had been proved by their works and that their responsibilities were commensurate with their wealth to the assertion that their eminence was self-evident and that their privileges could not be questioned. They would speak with Andrew Carnegie of the "trusteeship of wealth" and point to their benevolent relations to their employees, their philanthropic activities, and their great contributions to the nation's wealth as evidence of their worth. Others would think of themselves as "Christian men to whom God in his infinite wisdom has given the control of the property interests of the country." Nor can we dismiss the possibility that some of these industrial giants would say the first and think the second.

Fifty years later the same opinions are expressed, albeit in modern dress. Alfred P. Sloan[11] writes:

> . . . those charged with great industrial responsibility must become industrial statesmen. . . . Industrial management must expand its horizon of responsibility. It must recognize that it can no longer confine its activities to the mere production of goods and services. It must consider the impact of its operations on the economy as a whole in relation to the social and economic welfare of the entire community.

On the other hand, Tom Girdler[12] has written of his role in the company town which he had helped to develop:

> In fact I suppose I was a sort of political boss. Certainly I had considerable power in politics without responsibility to "the people." But who were the people in question?

An overwhelming majority of them were the men for whom the company aspired to make Woodlawn the best steel town in the world. . . What did it matter if the taxes were soundly spent? What did it matter if Woodlawn had just about the best school system in Pennsylvania? What did it matter if there were no slums, no graft, no patronage, no gambling houses, no brothels? What did it matter if it was a clean town?

If all these wonderful things were done by the company for the people of Woodlawn, what did it matter that the company and its managers were not responsible to the people? As an Episcopalian vestry man, Girdler could also speak of Christian men who, by the grace of God, controlled the property interests of the community on behalf of the people.

Businessmen express themselves with the intention of demonstrating statesmanship and intransigeance, then as now.[13] Yet even the celebration of the industrial leader has had to accommodate, albeit tardily, the Puritan virtues of hard work, frugality, and unremitting effort to the qualities useful in a bureaucratic career. As the size and bureaucratization of business increased, this ideological accommodation could no longer be accomplished on the model of the Horatio Alger story. Of course, the idea of success as a reward of virtue is as much in evidence today as it was 100 years ago. But the celebration of the industrial leader can no longer suffice; it is accompanied today by a celebration of the organization and of the opportunities it has to offer. When A. P. Sloan writes that "the corporation [is] a pyramid of oppor-

---

[11]Alfred P. Sloan, *Adventures of a White-collar Man*, New York, Doubleday, 1941, p. 145.

[12]Tom Girdler, *Boot Straps*, New York, Scribner, 1943, p. 177.

[13]The belief in progress and individual success through effort has not changed basically for the last century and a half, though it is possible to note a gradual secularization. There is little evidence of God in the praise of "work and still more work [by which] we capitalize our unlimited opportunities . . ." (Alfred P. Sloan). This secularization of the Puritan ideology of individual success has been traced by A. W. Griswold, "The American Gospel of Success," Doctor's dissertation, Yale University, 1933.

tunities from the bottom to the top with thousands of chances for advancement" he refers to the promise of a bureaucratic career not to the earlier image of the individual enterpriser. And when he adds that "only capacity limited any worker's chance to improve his own position,"[14] he simply ignores the fact that the methods of promotion themselves are bureaucratized, that they are regarded as a legitimate object of collective-bargaining strategies between union and management, and that under these circumstances minimum rather than maximum capacity is often a sufficient basis for promotion. At any rate, the idea of thousands of chances for promotion is different from the idea of individual success. Outstanding industrial leaders of today will reflect this difference in their attempts to define the image of success in an era of bureaucratization.

It is important to recognize that today managerial ideology performs a second function. While it is still designed to inspire confidence in the leaders of industry, it should also aid modern managers to achieve effective coordination within their enterprises, which is today a far more difficult task than it was formerly. There is a literature of advice to the ambitious young man which has accompanied the development of industry. In this literature the hero cult of the industrial leader has been abandoned gradually, and advice well suited to the industrial bureaucrat has taken its place.[15]

Hero cult and advice to the industrial bureaucrat involve partly incompatible themes. The qualities of ruthlessness and competitive drive, while appropriate for the "tycoon," are ill suited for his managerial employees. This does not mean that these qualities are no longer useful but that they no longer provide a workable rationale for the majority of industrial managers.[16]

It may be useful to put formulations of these two themes side by side. The classic text of the individual enterpriser is *Self-help with Illustrations of Character, Conduct and Perseverance,* written by Samuel Smiles in 1859 and copied interminably ever since. Its purpose was,

. . . to re-inculcate these old-fashioned but wholesome lessons . . . that youth must work in order to enjoy—that nothing creditable can be accomplished without application and diligence—that the student must not be daunted by difficulties, but conquer them by patience and perseverance—and that, above all, he must seek elevation of character, without which capacity is worthless and worldly success is naught.[17]

The classic text of the industrial bureaucrat is *Public Speaking and Influencing Men in Business,* written by Dale Carnegie

---

[14]Sloan, *op. cit.,* p. 153.

[15]We speak here of intellectual trends and do not imply that such trends occur by design. On the other hand, the problems of large-scale industry are real problems, and any intellectualized concern with them will have meaning in the context of these problems, even if they are deliberately ignored. If, for example, industrial leaders are praised today in the same manner as they were in the 1870's, it would indicate an ideological distortion of the present situation, when the opportunities for social mobility consist, for the most part, in climbing the bureaucratic ladder in industry.

[16]And it is possible that the ideology of the industrial bureaucrats, which was well summed up in Dale Carnegie's title *How to Win Friends and Influence People,* has affected the tycoon to the extent of changing his manners. See the suggestive comments on this point in David Riesman, *The Lonely Crowd,* New Haven, Conn., Yale University Press, 1950, esp. pp. 166–174, 236–239. Riesman posits a major change in character from the "inner-directed" personality of the "captains of industry" to the "other-directed" personality of the industrial bureaucrat, but I question whether one is warranted in inferring changes in "social character" from ideological and institutional trends. I question in particular whether white-collar workers of 1870 were inner-directed or whether industrial leaders of today are other-directed compared with their respective opposite numbers.

[17]Samuel Smiles, *Self-help* . . . , Chicago, Belford, Clarke and Co., 1881, p. vii (from the preface to the second edition, in which Smiles restated his major purpose, as he saw it, in response to the criticism which the book had received) .

in 1926 and used as the "official text" by such organizations as the New York Telephone Company, the American Institute of Banking, the YMCA schools, the National Institute of Credit, and others.[18] Though there is no single statement of purpose which can be cited, the following summary statement will suffice: "We have only four contacts with people. We are evaluated and classified by four things: by what we do, by how we look, by what we say, and how we say it."[19] In his foreword to this book Lowell Thomas[20] has written a testimonial to Dale Carnegie which gives the gist of this and many similar books with admirable clarity:

Carnegie started at first to conduct merely a course in public speaking: but the students who came were businessmen. Many of them hadn't seen the inside of a class room in thirty years. Most of them were paying their tuition on the installment plan. They wanted results; and they wanted them quick—results that they could use the next day in business interviews and in speaking before groups.

So he was forced to be swift and practi-

[18]A new version of this book was published in 1936 under the title *How to Win Friends and Influence People*. It has sold a total of 4 million copies.

[19]Dale Carnegie, *Public Speaking and Influencing Men in Business*, New York, Association Press, 1938, p. 509. Carnegie writes as follows: "I once asked a group of American businessmen in Paris to talk on *How to Succeed*. Most of them praised the homely virtues, preached at, lectured to, and bored their hearers. . . . So I halted this class and said something like this: 'We don't want to be lectured to. No one enjoys that. Remember you must be entertaining or we will pay no attention whatever to what you are saying. Also remember that one of the most interesting things in the world is sublimated, glorified gossip. So tell us the stories of two men you have known. Tell why one succeeded and why the other failed. We will gladly listen to that, remember it and possibly profit by it.' " *Ibid.*, p. 429. The shift from the praise of virtue to the description of "how to succeed" is well illustrated here, and if this passage is taken together with the one quoted in the text, it becomes clear that the techniques of "human relations" have superseded the idea of an emulation of virtues.

[20]Lowell Thomas, "Introduction," in Carnegie, *op. cit.*, p. x.

cal. Consequently, he has developed a system of training that is unique—a striking combination of Public Speaking, Salesmanship, Human Relationship, Personality Development and Applied Psychology. . . . Dale Carnegie . . . has created one of the most significant movements in adult education.

This new ideology of personality salesmanship appeared to put within reach of the average person the means by which to climb the ladder to success. No doubt this accounts for its popularity. But it should be added that its public acceptance implied a prior disillusion with the more old-fashioned methods of achieving success. The bureaucratization of modern industry has obviously increased the number of steps from the bottom to the top at the same time that it has made the Puritan virtues largely obsolete. It is probable, then, that the techniques of personality salesmanship became popular when the ideal of individual entrepreneurship ceased to be synonymous with success, while the image of a career of promotions from lower to higher positions became of greater significance. From the standpoint of the individual these techniques became a means of career advancement; from the standpoint of management they seemed to facilitate the coordination of a growing and increasingly specialized staff. In the context of American society this new ideology reflected the increasing importance of the service trades as well as the growing demand for skill in personnel relations.[21]

These considerations place the human-relations approach to the problems

[21]In this context it would appear as if the "New Thought" movement, which Griswold has analyzed, is *not* the lineal descendant of the "gospel of success," which may be identified with the Puritan tradition and the Darwinian creed of the Gilded Age. The outstanding difference between New Thought and "self-improvement" as well as the personality cult is that the first remained a cultist belief, while the second called for action and promised success if the lessons had been learned well.

of labor management in a historical perspective. Attention to human relations has arisen out of the managerial problems incident to the bureaucratization of industry. It has also arisen out of the discrepancy between a people's continued desire for success and the increasing disutility of the Puritan virtues or of the tenets of Darwinian morality. But whatever their origins, the "personality cult" as well as the more sophisticated philosophies of personnel management have helped to make more ambiguous the position of the industrial manager. In giving orders to his subordinates in the past, the manager could claim to derive his authority from the rights of ownership conferred on him. For a long time the managerial employee had represented the "heroic entrepreneur," and he had justified his own actions by the right which success had bestowed upon him. But with the dispersion of ownership this justification became increasingly tenuous. Strictly speaking, the old ideology of success no longer applied to the managers since theirs was a bureaucratic, not an entrepreneurial, success. As the human-relations approach is extended downward from the office staff to the work force, managers come to attenuate their tough-minded conception of authority. But in so doing they are never single-minded. Their careers are often inspired by the older belief in the self-made man, though this belief is more and more at variance with their own experience in industry. In asserting their authority over subordinates as if they were the successful entrepreneurs of old, they come into conflict with the bureaucratic reality of their own careers. Yet if they adjust their beliefs to that reality, then they are faced with the dilemma of exercising authority while they deny the traditional claims which had hitherto justified this authority.[22]

[22]This ideological ambiguity is not confined to the managers of industry. In so far as salaried

It is at this point that managers are divided today in their attitudes toward their employees and toward their own exercise of authority. Many continue to believe in the heroic entrepreneur whose success is justification in itself, and they consequently resist the "tender-minded" approach to human relations in industry. They also resist recognition of the fact that the industrial environment has changed. Others have begun to reformulate the older statements of "business statesmanship" and "business responsibility" in keeping with the realities of industry in an era of bureaucratization. But in their attempts to do so they have had to demonstrate the self-evident truths once more that the economy provides ample opportunities, given drive and talent, and that those who succeed deserve to do so and provide a model to be followed. To develop an ideology along these lines by advertising the techniques of personality salesmanship and by celebrating the career opportunities of an industrial bureaucracy implies an interest in industrial peace, for these techniques and opportunities are beside the point under conditions of conflict. The new ideology is less combative than the old; but it is also insufficient because its appeals are more readily applicable to the salaried employee than to the industrial worker. The idea that all employees are members of "one big happy family" is a case in point, for the efforts to make this idea meaningful to the workers frequently

employees continue to believe in the free-enterprise system, they will tend to ignore their own dependent status and bureaucratic careers, which are the reverse of both freedom and enterprise (in the conventional economic meaning of these terms). Ideas are not abandoned readily under the pressure of circumstances. Indeed, there is some evidence to show that modifications of the ideal of individual success survive today among groups whose chances of individual success are minimal. Cf. Reinhard Bendix, "A Study of Managerial Ideologies, as It Bears on Drucker's Thesis," paper read before the American Sociological Society, Atlantic City, N.J., Sept. 3, 1952.

take the form of personalizing an impersonal employment relationship. Perhaps this is appropriate for the managerial and ideological coordination of the salaried employees. It is, moreover, not surprising that the idea of the "family of employers and employees" often becomes the fighting creed of hard-pressed executives who seek to solidify their enterprises against the competing appeals of the trade-unions. But there is an element of cant in this approach which does not make it a promising foundation for a new ideology as long as democratic institutions prevail. Perhaps Horatio Alger is so reluctant to pass into limbo because his image implied an idealistic message. Perhaps it is the absence of such a message which makes the appeal to employees as members of a family so questionable. The ideological rationale of an economic order should have a positive meaning for everyone. The fact is that in this era of bureaucratization the industrialist does not have a fighting creed.

Section II

SOCIALIZATION PROCESSES IN FORMAL ORGANIZATIONS

In most societies, the socialization of children takes place in small groups rather than in formal organizations. The family and neighborhood play groups are obvious examples of such primary socialization contexts. There are some exceptions. The Soviet *yazli* and the Israeli *Kibbutz* represent contemporary attempts to collectivize in more complex organizations the care and socialization of young children.[1] Generally speaking, however, the socialization which takes place in an organizational context is primarily *secondary* socialization concerned with the further training or the retraining of adults.

Brim argues in Selection 13 that all socialization is concerned with the acquisition of motivation, knowledge and abilities needed to play social roles. In a later essay, Brim adds the further familiar distinction between behavior and values to produce the following combinations (the letter in each cell is merely for simplicity of reference) [2]:

	Behavior	*Values*
Knowledge	A	B
Ability	C	D
Motivation	E	F

According to Brim:

The highest priority in childhood socialization is represented by Cell F, namely, to take the basic drives of the infant and transform them over time into desires for recognition and approval and finally to the pursuit of more specific cultural values. Early-life socialization thus emphasizes the control of primary drives, while socialization in later stages deals with secondary or learned motives generated by the expectations of significant others.

The usual concern of adult socialization is represented by Cell A. Society assumes that the adult knows the values to be pursued in different roles, that he wants to pursue them with the socially appropriate means, and that all that may remain to be done is to teach him what to do.[3]

In addition to emphasizing the acquisition of knowledge, organizations may also attempt to affect the ability levels of their participants (Cell C) and to persuade them that they should be willing to employ their knowledge and ability in

---

[1] See R. Schlesinger (ed.), *The Family in the U.S.S.R.*, London: Routledge and Kegan Paul, 1949; and M. E. Spiro, *Children of the Kibbutz*, Cambridge, Mass.: Harvard University Press, 1958.

[2] Orville G. Brim, Jr., "Socialization through the life cycle," in Orville G. Brim, Jr., and Stanton Wheeler, *Socialization after Childhood*, New York: Wiley, 1966, p. 25.

[3] Brim, p. 26.

carrying out their new role (Cell E). Only rarely do secondary socializing institutions attempt to tackle more fundamental deficiencies in the backgrounds of their participants by attempting to alter their fundamental values. As Brim comments:

In general, then, socialization after childhood deals primarily with overt behavior in the role and makes little attempt to influence motivation of a fundamental kind or to influence basic values.[4]

All organizations socialize their participants to at least some extent, but in most organizations the training function is not the primary goal of the organization and is only carried out to assure an adequate supply of trained personnel. Some organizations operate special training units where newcomers stay until they have acquired the basic skills, or, if the skills demanded are not great, workers may be trained on-the-job. Organizations that require highly-trained personnel such as scientists or physicians typically must rely on other agencies— universities or professional schools—for their supply of participants, since they cannot bear the cost of elaborate and extended training programs. All such organizations assume the presence of adequate levels of motivation on the part of their participants. They typically are content to attempt to influence to some degree the behavior of their participants and do not attempt to alter their fundamental values.

A smaller set of organizations, however, do have as their primary goal the socialization of their participants. Secondary schools, colleges and universities, and professional and technical schools have as a primary objective advancing the motivation, abilities and knowledge of their clients—they seek to continue the socialization process begun by primary agencies such as the family. Other organizations such as prisons, reform schools, and mental hospitals have as a primary objective the re-socialization of their inmates—they attempt to completely re-socialize them or to correct certain deficiencies in the past socialization experiences of their participants. All or most of these types of organizations are concerned with influencing the values as well as the behaviors of their participants; the socializing they attempt is secondary only in the sense that it comes later in the life cycle of their participants.

Organizations that socialize may be broadly classified as *homogenizing* or *differentiating* contexts.[5] Homogenizing settings attempt to strip their participants of their previous identifying characteristics so that all may be treated as equal, isolate them from contacts and influences external to the organization, establish a gradation of statuses through which the trainees move from less to more valued positions and, in the end, turn out "graduates" who are basically similar in values, attitudes, knowledge and abilities. Dornbusch's discussion of the military academy provides a good description of this type of socializing institution. (See Reading 28)

Differentiating settings, by contrast, allow for more individuality in the treatment of recruits and more flexibility in the definition as to what constitutes a successful completion of the program. Universities, for example, allow for some

---

[5]See Stanton Wheeler, "The structure of formally organized socialization settings," in Brim and Wheeler, p. 78.

flexibility in the programs pursued by students, permit the student to participate in setting the goals of his training program, and often take into account previous training and experience. Differentiating as compared to homogenizing organizations require a higher ratio of socializers to trainees if students are to receive individualized attention. Since individualized training is costly in terms of number of staff per trainee, most differentiating settings are only partially successful in giving individualized training, and many organizations with differentiating goals—such as therapeutic mental hospitals—often in fact operate as homogenizing settings because of inadequate staffing.

Selected Context Variables   In our discussion of socialization in small groups, two variables characterizing context were described—power and affectivity. It was argued then that where power and affectivity are high, more profound socialization effects are produced. Generally speaking, because secondary socialization deals with relations between adults rather than between adults and children, power and affectivity tend to be lower in secondary than in primary socialization contexts. In agencies that concentrate on adult socialization or re-socialization, such as prisons, mental hospitals, and general and professional schools, socializers have some degree of power over those being socialized and there may be some degree of affectivity in the relation between the two groups, but these variables seldom reach the levels found in primary settings such as families.[6] It is partly for this reason that basic changes in attitudes and values are seldom produced in such settings. For example, studies reviewed by Jacob and by Newcomb and Feldman show little evidence of profound value changes in students as a result of attending college.[7]

Another variable of importance in dealing with adult socialization contexts is the size and disposition of the group being socialized. In the typical case, persons are not trained as individuals in socializing organizations, but as members of a group. The group of persons being socialized often becomes informally organized in order to gain some control in the situation. Studies in settings as diverse as medical schools[8] and prisons[9] indicate the relatively powerful role that informal ties among those being socialized play in determining the outcome of the socialization process. In some circumstances, such as those described by Dornbusch in Reading 28, the type of organization which develops among the trainees serves primarily to support and strengthen the efforts of the official socializers. In other situations, such as prisons, the informal structure which develops among those being socialized is such as to frustrate and defeat the aims of the official program. In both kinds of situations it is often the case that persons being socialized learn as much from each other as they do from their official trainers.

---

[6]A possible exception is the psychiatric relation in which one adult may have considerable power over another and in which strong affective ties (transference) may develop. Such relationships may, of course, produce relatively profound changes in the personality of the patient.

[7]Philip Jacob, *Changing Values in College*, New York: Harper & Row, 1957; and Theodore Newcomb and Kenneth Feldman, *The Impact of Colleges upon Their Students*, New York: Carnegie Foundation, 1968.

[8]See Howard S. Becker *et al.*, *Boys in White: Student Culture in the Medical School*, Chicago: University of Chicago Press, 1961.

[9]See D. R. Cressey (ed.), *The Prison*, New York: Holt, Rinehart and Winston, Inc., 1961.

28   The Military Academy as an Assimilating Institution

Sanford M. Dornbusch*

The function of a military academy is to make officers out of civilians or enlisted men. The objective is accomplished by a twofold process of transmitting technical knowledge and of instilling in the candidates an outlook considered appropriate for members of the profession. This paper is concerned with the latter of these processes, the assimilating function of the military academy. Assimilation is viewed as "a process of interpenetration and fusion in which persons and groups acquire the memories, sentiments, and attitudes of other persons and groups, and, by sharing their experience and history, are incorporated with them in a common cultural life. . . . The unity thus achieved is not necessarily or even normally like-mindedness; it is rather a unity of experience and of orientation, out of which may develop a community of purpose and action."[1]

Data for this study consist almost entirely of retrospective material, based on ten months spent as a cadet at the United States Coast Guard Academy. The selective nature of memory obviously may introduce serious deficiencies in the present formulation. Unfortunately, it is unlikely that more objective evidence on life within the Academy will be forthcoming. Cadets cannot keep diaries, are formally forbidden to utter a word of criticism of the Academy to an outsider, and are informally limited in the matters which are to be discussed in letters or conversations. The lack of objective data is regrettable, but the process of assimilation is present here in an extreme form. Insight into this process can better be developed by the study of such an explicit, overt case of assimilation.

The Coast Guard Academy, like West Point and Annapolis, provides four years of training for a career as a regular officer. Unlike the other service academies, however, its cadet corps is small, seldom exceeding 350 cadets. This disparity in size probably produces comparable differences in the methods of informal social control. Therefore, all the findings reported here may not be applicable to the other academies. It is believed, however, that many of the mechanisms through which this military academy fulfills its assimilating function will be found in a wide variety of social institutions.

THE SUPPRESSION OF PRE-EXISTING STATUSES

The new cadet, or "swab," is the lowest of the low. The assignment of low status is useful in producing a correspondingly high evaluation of successfully completing the steps in an Academy

*The writer is indebted to Harold McDowell, Frank Miyamoto, Charles Bowerman, and Howard S. Becker for their constructive criticism of this paper.
[1]Robert E. Park and Ernest W. Burgess, *Introduction to the Science of Sociology* (Chicago: University of Chicago Press, 1921), pp. 735, 737.

Reprinted from Sanford M. Dornbusch, "The military academy as an assimilating institution" *Social Forces*, 33, No. 4 (May, 1955), 316–321, by permission of the University of North Carolina Press and the author.

career and requires that there be a loss of identity in terms of pre-existing statuses. This clean break with the past must be achieved in a relatively short period. For two months, therefore, the swab is not allowed to leave the base or to engage in social intercourse with non-cadets. This complete isolation helps to produce a unified group of swabs, rather than a heterogeneous collection of persons of high and low status. Uniforms are issued on the first day, and discussions of wealth and family background are taboo. Although the pay of the cadet is very low, he is not permitted to receive money from home. The role of the cadet must supersede other roles the individual has been accustomed to play. There are few clues left which will reveal social status in the outside world.[2]

It is clear that the existence of minority-group status on the part of some cadets would tend to break down this desired equality. The sole minority group present was the Jews, who, with a few exceptions, had been informally excluded before 1944. At that time 18 Jews were admitted in a class of 162. Their status as Jews made them objects of scrutiny by the upper classmen, so that their violations of rules were more often noted. Except for this "spotlight," however, the Jews reported no discrimination against them—they, too, were treated as swabs.

LEARNING NEW RULES AND ADJUSTMENT TO CONFLICTS BETWEEN RULES

There are two organized structures of rules which regulate the cadet's behavior. The first of these is the body of regulations of the Academy, considered by the public to be the primary source of con-

trol. These regulations are similar to the code of ethics of any profession. They serve in part as propaganda to influence outsiders. An additional function is to provide negative sanctions which are applied to violations of the second set of expectations, the informal rules. Offenses against the informal rules are merely labeled as breaches of the formal code, and the appropriate punishment according to the regulations is then imposed. This punitive system conceals the existence of the informal set of controls.

The informal traditions of the Academy are more functionally related to the existing set of circumstances than are the regulations, for although these traditions are fairly rigid, they are more easily forgotten or changed than are the formal regulations. Unlike other informal codes, the Academy code of traditions is in part written, appearing in a manual for entering cadets.

In case of conflict between the regulations and tradition, the regulations are superseded. For example, it is against the regulations to have candy in one's room. A first classman orders a swab to bring him candy. Caught en route by an officer, the swab offers no excuse and is given 15 demerits. First classmen are then informally told by the classmate involved that they are to withhold demerits for this swab until he has been excused for offenses totaling 15 demerits. Experience at an Academy teaches future officers that regulations are not considered of paramount importance when they conflict with informal codes—a principle noted by other observers.[3]

Sometimes situations arise in which the application of either form of control is circumvented by the commanding officer.

[2]Cf. Arnold Van Gennep, *Les Rites de Passage* (Paris: Emile Nourry, 1909). Translated by Everett C. Hughes in *Anthropology-Sociology 240, Special Readings* (Chicago: University of Chicago Bookstore, 1948), Pt. II, p. 9.

[3]Ralph H. Turner, "The Navy Disbursing Officer As a Bureaucrat," *American Sociological Review*, XII (June 1946), 344 and 348; Arnold Rose, "The Social Structure of the Army," *American Journal of Sociology*, LI (March 1946), 361.

The following case is an example. Cadets cannot drink, cannot smoke in public, can never go above the first floor in a hotel. It would seem quite clear, therefore, that the possessor of a venereal disease would be summarily dismissed. Cadets at the Academy believed that two upper-class cadets had contracted a venereal disease, were cured, and given no punishment. One of the cadets was an outstanding athlete, brilliant student, and popular classmate. Cadets were told that a direct appeal by the commanding officer to the Commandant of the Coast Guard resulted in the decision to hush up the entire affair, with the second cadet getting the same treatment as his more popular colleague. The event indicated the possibility of individualization of treatment when rules are violated by officers.

THE DEVELOPMENT OF SOLIDARITY

The control system operated through the class hierarchy. The first class, consisting of cadets in their third or fourth year at the Academy, are only nominally under the control of the officers of the Academy. Only one or two officers attempt to check on the activities of the first classmen, who are able to break most of the minor regulations with impunity. The first class is given almost complete control over the rest of the cadet corps. Informally, certain leading cadets are even called in to advise the officers on important disciplinary matters. There are one or two classes between the first classmen and the swabs, depending on the existence of a three- or four-year course. These middle classes haze the swabs. Hazing is forbidden by the regulations, but the practice is a hallowed tradition of the Academy. The first class demands that this hazing take place, and, since they have the power to give demerits, all members of the middle classes are compelled to haze the new cadets.

As a consequence of undergoing this very unpleasant experience together, the swab class develops remarkable unity. For example, if a cadet cannot answer an oral question addressed to him by his teacher, no other member of his class will answer. All reply, "I can't say, sir," leaving the teacher without a clue to the state of knowledge of this student compared to the rest of the class. This group cohesion persists throughout the Academy period, with first classmen refusing to give demerits to their classmates unless an officer directly orders them to do so.

The honor system, demanding that offenses by classmates be reported, is not part of the Coast Guard Academy tradition. It seems probable that the honor system, if enforced, would tend to break down the social solidarity which the hazing develops within each class.

The basis for interclass solidarity, the development of group feeling on the part of the entire cadet corps, is not so obvious. It occurs through informal contacts between the upper classmen and swabs, a type of fraternization which occurs despite the fact it traditionally is discouraged. The men who haze the swab and order him hazed live in the same wing of the dormitory that he does. Coming from an outside world which disapproves of authoritarian punishment and aggressiveness, they are ashamed of their behavior. They are eager to convince the swab that they are good fellows. They visit his room to explain why they are being so harsh this week or to tell of a mistake he is making. Close friendships sometimes arise through such behavior. These friendships must be concealed. One first classman often ordered his room cleaned by the writer as a "punishment," then settled down for an uninterrupted chat. Such informal contacts serve to unite the classes and spread a "we-feeling" through the Academy.

In addition, the knowledge of common interests and a common destiny serves as a unifying force that binds together all Academy graduates. This is expressed in the identification of the interest of the individual with the interest of the Coast Guard. A large appropriation or an increase in the size of the Coast Guard will speed the rate of promotion for all, whether ensign or captain. A winning football team at the Academy may familiarize more civilians with the name of their common alma mater. Good publicity for the Coast Guard raises the status of the Coast Guard officer.

The Coast Guard regulars are united in their disdain for the reserves. There are few reserve officers during peacetime, but in wartime the reserve officers soon outnumber the regulars. The reserves do not achieve the higher ranks, but they are a threat to the cadets and recent graduates of the Academy. The reserves receive in a few months the rank that the regulars reach only after four grueling years. The Academy men therefore protectively stigmatize the reserves as incompetents. If a cadet falters on the parade ground, he is told, "You're marching like a reserve." Swabs are told to square their shoulders while on liberty, "or else how will people know you are not a reserve?" Myths spring up—stories of reserve commanders who must call on regular ensigns for advice. The net effect is reassurance that although the interlopers may have the same rank, they do not have equal status.

Another out-group is constituted by the enlisted men, who are considered to be of inferior ability and eager for leadership. Segregation of cadets and enlisted men enables this view to be propagated. Moreover, such segregation helps to keep associations within higher status social groups. There is only one leak in this insulating dike. The pharmacist mates at sick bay have direct contact with the cadets, and are the only enlisted personnel whom cadets meet on an equal basis. The pharmacist mates take pleasure in reviling the Academy, labeling it "the p---k factory." Some of the cadets without military experience are puzzled by such an attitude, which is inconsistent with their acquired respect for the Academy.

THE DEVELOPMENT OF A BUREAUCRATIC SPIRIT

The military services provide an excellent example of a bureaucratic structure. The emphasis is upon the office with its sets of rights and duties, rather than on the man. It is a system of rules with little regard for the individual case. The method of promotion within the Coast Guard perfectly illustrates this bureaucratic character. Unlike the Army or Navy, promotions in the Coast Guard up to the rank of lieutenant-commander do not even depend on the evaluation of superior officers. Promotion comes solely according to seniority, which is based on class standing at the Academy. The 50th man in the 1947 class will be lieutenant-commander before the 51st man, and the latter will be promoted before the 1st man in the 1948 class.

The hazing system contributes directly to acceptance of the bureaucratic structure of the Coast Guard, for the system is always viewed by its participants as not involving the personal character of the swab or upper classman. One is not being hazed because the upper classman is a sadist, but because one is at the time in a junior status. Those who haze do not pretend to be superior to those who are being hazed. Since some of those who haze you will also try to teach you how to stay out of trouble, it becomes impossible to attribute evil characteristics to those who injure you. The swab knows he will have his turn at hazing others. At most, individual idiosyncrasies will just affect the type of hazing done.[4]

This emphasis on the relativity of status is explicitly made on the traditional Gizmo Day, on which the swabs and their hazers reverse roles. The swabs-for-a-day take their licking without flinching and do not seek revenge later, for they are aware that they are under the surveillance of the first classmen. After the saturnalia, the swabs are increasingly conscious of their inability to blame particular persons for their troubles.

Upper classmen show the same resentment against the stringent restrictions upon their lives, and the manner in which they express themselves indicates a feeling of being ruled by impersonal forces. They say, "You can't buck the System." As one writer puts it, "The best attitude the new cadet can have is one of unquestioning acceptance of tradition and custom."

There is a complete absence of charismatic veneration of the Coast Guard heroes of the past and present. Stirring events are recalled, not as examples of the genius of a particular leader, but as part of the history of the great organization which they will serve. A captain is a cadet thirty years older and wiser. Such views prepare these men for their roles in the bureaucracy.

NEW SATISFACTIONS IN INTERACTION

A bureaucratic structure requires a stable set of mutual expectations among the occupants of offices. The Academy develops this ability to view the behavior of others in terms of a pre-ordained set of

[4]Compare this viewpoint with that expressed in Hugh Mullan, "The Regular Service Myth," *American Journal of Sociology*, LIII (January 1948), 280, where hazing is viewed as the expression of "pent-up sadism." Such individualistic interpretations do not take into account the existence of an institutional structure, or else they give psychological interpretations to social processes.

standards. In addition to preparing the cadet for later service as an officer, the predictability of the behavior of his fellows enables the cadet to achieve a high degree of internal stability. Although he engages in a continual bustle of activity, he always knows his place in the system and the degree to which he is fulfilling the expectations of his role.

Sharing common symbols and objects, the cadets interact with an ease of communication seldom found in everyday life. The cadet is told what is right and wrong, and, if he disagrees, there are few opportunities to translate mental reservations into action. The "generalized other" speaks with a unitary voice which is uncommon in modern societies. To illustrate, an upper classman ordered a swab to pick up some pieces of paper on the floor of a washroom. The latter refused and walked away. There were no repercussions. The swab knew that, if he refused, the upper classman would be startled by the choice of such an unconventional way of getting expelled from the Academy. Wondering what was happening, the upper classman would redefine his own behavior, seeing it as an attack on the high status of the cadet. Picking up litter in a washroom is "dirty work," fit only for enlisted men. The swab was sure that the upper classman shared this common universe of discourse and never considered the possibility that he would not agree on the definition of the situation.

Interaction with classmates can proceed on a level of confidence that only intimate friends achieve in the outside world. These men are in a union of sympathy, sharing the same troubles, never confiding secrets to upper classmen, never criticizing one another to outsiders. Each is close to only a few but is friendly with most of the men in his class.

When interacting with an upper classman in private, a different orientation is useful. The swab does not guess the reason why he is being addressed, but instead assumes a formal air of deference. If the upper classman says, "Aw cut it out," the swab relaxes. In this manner the role of the upper classman is explicitly denoted in each situation.

In addition to providing predictability of the behavior of others, the Academy provides a second set of satisfactions in the self-process. An increase in the cadet's self-esteem develops in conjunction with identification in his new role. Told that they are members of an elite group respected by the community, most cadets begin to feel at ease in a superordinate role. One may be a low-ranking cadet, but cadets as a group have high status. When cadets visit home for the first time, there is a conflict between the lofty role that they wish to play and the role to which their parents are accustomed. Upon return to the Academy, much conversation is concerned with the way things at home have changed.

This feeling of superiority helps to develop self-confidence in those cadets who previously had a low evaluation of themselves. It directly enters into relationships with girls, with whom many boys lack self-confidence. It soon becomes apparent that any cadet can get a date whenever he wishes, and he even begins to feel that he is a good "catch." The cadet's conception of himself is directly influenced by this new way of viewing the behavior of himself and others. As one cadet put it, "I used to be shy. Now I'm reserved."

SOCIAL MOBILITY

A desire for vertical social mobility on the part of many cadets serves as one means of legitimizing the traditional practices of the Academy. The cadets are told that they will be members of the social elite during the later stages of their career. The obstacles that they meet at the Academy are then viewed as the usual barriers to social mobility in the United States, a challenge to be surmounted.

Various practices at the Academy reinforce the cadets' feeling that they are learning how to enter the upper classes. There is a strong emphasis on etiquette, from calling cards to table manners. The Tactics Officer has been known to give long lectures on such topics as the manner of drinking soup from an almost empty bowl. The cadet must submit for approval the name of the girl he intends to take to the monthly formal dance. Girls attending the upper-class college in the vicinity are automatically acceptable, but some cadets claim that their dates have been rejected because they are in a low status occupation such as waitress.

Another Academy tradition actively, though informally, encourages contact with higher status girls. After the swabs have been completely isolated for two months, they are invited to a dance at which all the girls are relatives or friends of Coast Guard officers. A week later the girls at the nearby college have a dance for the swabs. The next week end finds the swab compelled to invite an acceptable girl to a formal reception. He must necessarily choose from the only girls in the area whom he knows, those that he met during the recent hours of social intercourse.

JUSTIFICATION OF INSTITUTIONAL PRACTICES

In addition to the social mobility theme which views the rigors of Academy life as obstacles to upward mobility, there is a more open method of justifying traditionally legitimated ways of doing things. The phrase, "separating the men from the boys" is used to meet objections to practices which seem inefficient or foolish. Traditional standards are thus redefined as further tests of ability to take punishment. Harsh practices are defended as methods by which the insincere, incompetent, or undisciplined cadets are weeded out. Cadets who rebel and resign are merely showing lack of character.[5]

Almost all cadets accept to some extent this traditional view of resignations as admissions of defeat. Of the 162 entering cadets in 1944, only 52 graduated in 1948. Most of the 110 resignations were entirely voluntary without pressure from the Academy authorities. Most of these resignations came at a time when the hazing was comparatively moderate. Cadets who wish to resign do not leave at a time when the hazing might be considered the cause of their departure. One cadet's history illustrates this desire to have the resignation appear completely voluntary. Asked to resign because of his lack of physical coordination, he spent an entire year building up his physique, returned to the Academy, finished his swab year, and then joyously quit. "It took me three years, but I showed them."

Every cadet who voluntarily resigns is a threat to the morale of the cadet corps, since he has rejected the values of the Academy. Although cadets have enlisted for seven years and could theoretically be forced to remain at the Academy, the usual procedure is to isolate them from the swabs and rush acceptance of their resignation. During the period before the acceptance is final, the cadets who have resigned are freed from the usual duties of their classmates, which action effectively isolates them from cadets who

might be affected by their contagious disenchantment.

REALITY SHOCK

Everett C. Hughes has developed the concept of "reality shock," the sudden realization of the disparity between the way a job is envisaged before beginning work and the actual work situation.[6] In the course of its 75-year history the Coast Guard Academy has wittingly or unwittingly developed certain measures to lessen reality shock in the new ensign. The first classmen, soon to be officers, are aided in lessening the conflict between the internalized rules of the Academy world and the standards for officer conduct.

On a formal level the first classmen are often reminded that they are about to experience a relative decline in status. On their first ship they will be given the most disagreeable duties. The first classmen accept this and joke about how their attitudes will change under a harsh captain. On a more concrete level, first classmen are given week-end leaves during the last six months of their stay at the Academy. These leaves allow them to escape from the restrictive atmosphere of the nearby area. It is believed wise to let them engage in orgiastic behavior while still cadets, rather than suddenly release all controls upon graduation.

Rumors at the Academy also help to prepare the cadets for their jobs as officers. Several of the instructors at the Academy were supposed to have been transferred from sea duty because of their incompetence. Such tales protect the cadets from developing a romantic conception of the qualities of Coast Guard officers, as well as providing a graphic illustration of how securely the

---

[5]"At each step of the ceremonies he feels that he is brought a little closer, until at last he can feel himself a man among men." A. R. Radcliffe-Brown, *The Andaman Islanders* (Glencoe, Illinois: The Free Press, 1948), p. 279.

[6]Miriam Wagenschein, Reality Shock. Unpublished M.A. thesis, Department of Sociology, University of Chicago, 1950.

bureaucratic structure protects officers from their own derelictions. In addition, many stories were told about a junior officer whose career at the Academy had been singularly brilliant. He had completely failed in his handling of enlisted men because he had carried over the high standards of the Academy. The cadets were thus oriented to a different conception of discipline when dealing with enlisted personnel.

CONCLUSION

The United States Coast Guard Academy performs an assimilating func-tion. It isolates cadets from the outside world, helps them to identify themselves with a new role, and thus changes their self-conception. The manner in which the institution inculcates a bureaucratic spirit and prevents reality shock is also considered in this analysis.

The present investigation is admittedly fragmentary. Much of the most relevant material is simply not available. It is also clear that one cannot assume that this analysis applies completely to any other military academy. However, as an extreme example of an assimilating institution, there is considerable material which can be related to other institutions in a comparative framework.

STATUS PROCESSES IN FORMAL ORGANIZATIONS

In our introduction to status processes,[1] we talked of characteristics that are differentiated, ranked, evaluated, and rewarded. In the case of informal group processes, the characteristics of interest are those possessed by or attributed to individuals. In the case of formal organizations, however, we can speak of characteristics possessed by or attributed to positions—positions that are occupied by individuals but that can be described and analyzed independently of the characteristics of any particular occupant. Let us first consider the formal stratification system and focus only on position characteristics and their evaluation.

The Formal Stratification System   Although power and status processes are analytically distinct, they are often found to be closely associated in the empirical world. Thus, a prominent feature of virtually all formal organizations is the hierarchy of positions or, as they are sometimes called, offices. We speak of the existence of a *hierarchy* to the extent that the positions are arranged in such a manner that one position is clearly superordinate to another and is itself subordinate to a third, and so on, so that a continuous chain of positions is formed. A given position A is superordinate to B in the sense that A is superior to B in power and is expected to exercise control over B. In addition to the characteristic of higher power, superordinate positions are defined as having greater responsibility for the operation of the enterprise than subordinate positions.

Contrasting lower positions with higher positions, then, we see a differentiation of characteristics—greater power and more responsibility attributed to higher positions than to lower positions. We know that these characteristics, when differentiated, are likely to be evaluated, with higher value placed on possession than on nonpossession (or possession of more as opposed to less). Also, with differential evaluation is likely to go differential rewards. At any rate, these are the ways such positions are likely to be designed. A hierarchy of positions is established, with the higher offices holding more power and responsibility. In order to motivate persons to seek such offices, the higher positions are associated with greater rewards—high salaries, more luxurious offices, more important sounding titles. Interestingly enough, the exercise of power is both a characteristic associated with high rewards and also a reward in itself. (Recall Tumin's distinction between role-specific power and reward power in Reading 14.)

[1]See pp. 170–171.

Chester Barnard has noted in a classic paper some of the advantages associated with formal status systems for the functioning of the organization.[2] He argues that the insignia of formal status helps to structure social expectations appropriately in that

they create a presumption with respect to the character, ability, and specific skills or functions of individuals. They are not conclusive, of course, but as preliminaries, as introductions, they save time and prevent awkwardness and embarrassment. The general's stars indicate at a glance the nature of his responsibilities and the probably relative reliability of his utterances in certain fields.[3]

One can hardly imagine the coordination of efforts among large numbers of people in the absence of formal status categories that allow members to readily distinguish among various types of functionaries. Formal titles play an important part in introductions when strangers meet and are immediately expected to relate appropriately to one another: "This is Dr. Smith of our Radiology Department." "I'd like you to meet Jones, our chief chemist." "White, your foreman, will show you the ropes." These are examples of the way in which formal statuses are employed every day to establish the appropriate set of expectations.

Barnard also points out the advantages of formal distinctions in allowing persons of differing abilities to work effectively together. He notes:

Much experience demonstrates that those who are unequal cannot work well for long as equals. But experience also demonstrates that where differences of status are recognized formally, men of very unequal abilities and importance can and do work together well for long periods.[4]

The formal acknowledgement of differences allows a group to avoid the sorts of status struggles described by Bales in Reading 24. When members are presumed to be status equals, would-be leaders must compete to prove themselves, and those left behind in the competition offer only grudging recognition of services received.

Finally, Barnard suggests that formal status systems provide essential incentives to cooperative effort, not only by motivating participants to seek higher offices and the attached perquisites but also by encouraging those who occupy these positions to behave responsibly. Barnard argues:

The desire for improvement of status and especially the desire to protect status appears to be the basis of the sense of general responsibility. Responsibility is established and enforced by specific penalties for specific failures and by limitation of status or by loss of a particular status for failure in general . . . . In view of the extreme importance of dependable behavior, the function of status in creating and maintaining dependable behavior is probably indispensable.[5]

Positions and Persons   Having briefly considered the formal system of stratification and some of its contributions to the organization, we should give equal time to the social system analyst who reminds us that organizational positions are filled by persons. The relation of person and position is a complex topic and we shall attempt here to explore only one of its facets, namely, the ability of an occupant.

[2]Chester I. Barnard, "Functions and pathology of status systems in formal organizations," in William Foote Whyte (ed.), *Industry and Society*, New York: McGraw-Hill, 1946, pp. 46–83.
[3]Barnard, pp. 56–57.
[4]Barnard, p. 62.
[5]Barnard, p. 69.

To begin with Barnard's earlier comment, occupancy of a high office creates certain presumptions about the capabilities of its incumbent. It is typically presumed that he possesses high abilities. Thompson comments on the basis for such expectations:

Since a person's hierarchical position is a matter of definition, of defined rights and duties, it should be clear at the outset that any special deference paid to the incumbent may constitute a confusion of person and role. That is to say, a person may be entitled to deference by virtue of one or more of his qualities, but his role is not one of his qualities. However, a person is perceived by others through his roles, his public or perceived personality being the sum of his various roles . . . . People impute superior abilities to persons of higher status, and this imputed superior ability is generalized into a halo of superiority . . . .

Cognitive stability is promoted if one's superior by definition is perceived as one's superior in abilities. The subordinate's self-image is protected by the same mechanism. The superordinate position and the person who occupies it are perceptually merged.[6]

The generation of such expectations concerning the abilities of position occupants is a part of the "magic" of organizations associated with the formalization process.[7] The importance of these expectation processes for the stability and functioning of the organization should not be overlooked. At the same time, the problems associated with the expectations should not be overlooked: if magic is involved it may be, at least partially, "black magic."

Paul Torrance has conducted an experiment in which he demonstrates both the differential expectations associated with occupancy of a formal position and also the negative consequences for the group created by acting on these expectations.[8] Torrance formed three-man work groups composed of a pilot, a navigator, and a gunner from B-29 crews and gave them a series of problems to solve collectively. As expected, pilots, the superior status, were more likely to influence the group decision, navigators, second in status, were next most likely, and gunners, lowest in status, were the least likely. Torrance also ascertained who had the correct solution prior to allowing discussion to arrive at a joint solution. These data allowed Torrance to observe the following significant results:

In the permanent crews, 31 percent of the pilots, 50 percent of the navigators and 19 percent of the gunners had the correct answer . . . the pilots are most successful and the gunners least successful in influencing the crew to accept their correct solutions. Only 6 percent of the pilots compared with 20 percent of the navigators and 37 percent of the gunners, failed to influence the crew to accept their solutions when they had the correct answer. . . .[9]

In short, higher status persons were more likely to be able to persuade the group to accept their own position than were lower status persons, even when this position was incorrect. Such are the negative consequences of status. Barnard is also aware of this pathological aspect of status. He writes:

[6]Victor A. Thompson, *Modern Organization*, New York: Knopf, 1961, pp. 66–67, 69.

[7]See pp. 313–314.

[8]E. Paul Torrance, "Some consequences of power differences on decision making in permanent and temporary three-man groups," *Research Studies*, Pullman, Wash.: State College of Washington, 1954, pp. 130–140. Torrance utilized both "permanent" and "temporary" bomber crews for these studies, the permanent crews composed of men who normally worked together as part of the same crew and the temporary crews composed of men who did not normally work together. In general, the effects of status were less pronounced in the temporary than in the permanent crews.

[9]Torrance, p. 133. These data describe one of four problems on which the groups worked. Results on the other three tests were in general consistent with these findings.

. . . we find that the rating of the individual by the role he occupies and emphasis upon the importance to the organization of immediate local abilities of positions leads to under- and overevaluation of individuals artificaly, i.e., in terms of status as an end instead of as an intermediate means.[10]

In today's complex world, if organizations are to function effectively, *real* competence is required, not simply presumed competence. As the technical demands on organizations grow, Thompson argues, there is an increasing separation of the right to command from the ability to command and of the right to make complex decisions from the ability to do so.[11] One popular "solution" to this organizational dilemma is to leave intact the organizational hierarchy with its right to command as the *line* organization but to supplement it with the addition of a *staff* organization—technical specialists who serve in an advisory capacity, providing the necessary expertise to inform the decisions of the persons in the line who retain ultimate responsibility. Although this approach is now widely used by many types of organizations, Dalton's analysis suggests that it is fraught with problems (see Reading 29). Line officers feel threatened by the technical competence of their "subordinates," and staff officials are discontent with their relative status and power in the organization, given their training and abilities. In short, the line-staff pattern may help to solve some of the adaptive problems of the organization but creates profound disturbances in the status structure because it attacks traditional beliefs concerning the relation that should obtain among ability, hierarchical position, and rewards.

Evaluation and Rewards   In our earlier discussion of status processes,[12] we noted that two kinds of beliefs are involved in the generation of a status system. First, there are beliefs about the relation between characteristics and future behavior that give rise to the evaluation of these characteristics. We have devoted considerable attention to such expectations throughout the course of this book. Second, there are beliefs about how rewards should be distributed. Up to this point, such beliefs have not received systematic treatment, but Adams' discussion of inequity is devoted to this topic (see Reading 30). Adams approaches this problem from the perspective of Festinger's theory of cognitive dissonance.[13] This theory deals with the relations among various cognitive elements.

By the term *cognitive element* is meant any knowledge, opinion, or belief about the environment, about oneself, or about one's behavior. The term *dissonance* is introduced to represent an inconsistency between two or more cognitive elements. Two cognitive elements are in a dissonant relation if, considering these two alone, *the obverse of one element would follow from the other.*[14]

The theory predicts that when two or more cognitive elements are regarded as relevant to one another and are in a state of dissonance, the individual will be uncomfortable and will engage in behaviors designed to reduce the dissonance and to achieve consonance.

[10]Barnard, p. 77.
[11]Thompson, pp. 73-80.
[12]See p. 171.
[13]For a full discussion of this approach, see Leon Festinger, *A Theory of Cognitive Dissonance,* Evanston, Ill.: Row, Peterson & Company, 1957.
[14]Paul F. Secord and Carl W. Backman, *Social Psychology,* New York: McGraw-Hill, 1964, p. 115. Emphasis in original.

The cognitive elements that Adams considers are beliefs an individual holds about his abilities, his background, or his training and beliefs about rewards he should receive based on his characteristics. Criteria for determining which of an individual's characteristics are relevant—that is, should be taken into account in determining the rewards one should receive—and standards for determining what constitutes a "fair" or "equitable" reward are obtained from one's membership or reference groups. As the theory predicts, and as data reported by Adams demonstrates, dissonance can result from imbalances due to overrewarding as well as underrewarding.[15]

A formulation such as that proposed by Adams is enormously useful for beginning to understanding the relation between evaluated characteristics and social rewards. However, the difficulties associated with research in this area should not be minimized. First, individuals will vary in their definition as to what constitutes a reward and in the relative importance they ascribe to different types of rewards. Second, individuals will vary in the evaluations that they place on various sorts of characteristics. For example, racial background is a salient characteristic for some persons but not for others, whereas a college degree may be highly valued by some individuals but given lesser value by others. Third, individuals possess not one but numerous characteristics, and it is quite possible for them to enjoy a high rank on some and a low rank on others, that is, to have low status crystallization (see Reading 8). When status crystallization is low and the individual presents characteristics that receive both high and low evaluations, it is difficult to ascertain what set of rewards is appropriate or equitable. Research has shown that individuals tend to overevaluate the importance of the characteristics on which their rank is high, so that, for example, an individual with high seniority will believe that seniority is an important characteristic to take into account in determining the distribution of rewards.

Fourth, as Adams notes, individuals refer to various groups in obtaining and reaffirming their notions concerning the relevance of characteristics and the standards of fairness. However, an individual can be satisfied or dissatisfied with his situation, depending on the groups with which he chooses to compare himself and on which characteristics he emphasizes in making the comparison. For example, a Negro college graduate who holds the position of bank teller may decide that relative to other Negroes he is well situated, or he may decide that relative to other college graduates he is the victim of discrimination. Although it is true that choice of reference groups may lead to satisfaction or dissatisfaction with one's situation, it is no less true that satisfaction and dissatisfaction may cause a person to seek out those reference groups in order to make comparisons that will justify his sentiments. Finally, although individuals seek equity, organizations typically attempt to husband their resources, giving participants not what they "deserve" but only rewards sufficient to keep them in the system. Thus, a high prestige university may pay lower salaries than a low prestige school. When a faculty member points out the disparity between his characteristics and income in comparison with that of a faculty member in the

[15]For a related discussion of the relation between individual characteristics and social rewards based on balance theory that also treats the problem of status classes in organizations, see B. Anderson et al., "Status classes in organizations," Administrative Science Quarterly, 11 (September, 1966), 264-283.

low prestige school, university officials may point out that the faculty member is free to move to the low prestige school, banking on the presumption that he will be unwilling to move to the weaker institution. Such considerations as these suggest that justice or equity can be an illusive commodity.

29   Conflicts between Staff and Line Managerial Officers

Melville Dalton

In its concentration on union-management relations, industrial sociology has tended to neglect the study of processes inside the ranks of industrial management. Obviously the doors to this research area are more closely guarded than the entry to industrial processes through the avenue of production workers, but an industrial sociology worthy of the name must sooner or later extend its inquiries to include the activities of all industrial personnel.

The present paper is the result of an attempt to study processes among industrial managers. It is specifically a report on the functioning interaction between the two major vertical groupings of industrial management: (1) the *staff* organization, the functions of which are research and advisory; and (2) the *line* organization, which has exclusive authority over production processes.

Industrial staff organizations are relatively new. Their appearance is a response to many complex interrelated forces, such as economic competition, scientific advance, industrial expansion, growth of the labor movement, and so on. During the last four or five decades these rapid changes and resulting unstable conditions have caused top industrial officials more and more to call in "specialists" to aid them toward the goal of

greater production and efficiency. These specialists are of many kinds including chemists, statisticians, public and industrial relations officers, personnel officers, accountants, and a great variety of engineers, such as mechanical, drafting, electrical, chemical, fuel, lubricating, and industrial engineers. In industry these individuals are usually known as "staff people." Their functions, again, for the most part are to increase and apply their specialized knowledge in problem areas, and to advise those officers who make up the "line" organization and have authority[1] over production processes.

This theoretically satisfying industrial structure of specialized experts advising busy administrators has in a number of significant cases failed to function as expected. The assumptions that (a) the staff specialists would be reasonably content to function without a measure of formal authority[2] over production, and that (b) their suggestions regarding improvement of processes and techniques for control over personnel and production would be welcomed by line officers and be applied, require closer examination. In

[1] *Inside* their particular staff organization, staff officers also may have authority over their subordinates, but not over production personnel.

[2] To the extent that staff officers influence line policy they do, of course, have a certain *informal* authority.

Reprinted from Melville Dalton, "Conflicts between staff and line managerial officers," *American Sociological Review*, 15 (June, 1950), 342–351, by permission of the author and the publisher, The American Sociological Association.

practice there is often much conflict between industrial staff and line organizations and in varying degrees the members of these organizations oppose each other.[3]

The aim of this paper is, therefore, to present and analyze data dealing with staff-line tensions.

Data were drawn from three industrial plants[4] in which the writer had been either a participating member of one or both of the groups or was intimate with reliable informants among the officers who were.

Approached sociologically, relations among members of management in the plants could be viewed as a general conflict system caused and perpetuated chiefly by (1) power struggles in the organization stemming in the main from competition among departments to maintain low operating costs; (2) drives by numerous members to increase their status in the hierarchy; (3) conflict between union and management; and (4) the staff-line friction which is the subject of this paper.[5] The milieu of tensions was not only unaccounted for by the blue-print organizations of the plants, but was often contradictory to, and even destructive of, the organizations' formal aims. All members of management, especially in the middle and lower ranks,[6] were caught up in this conflict system. Even though they might wish to escape, the obligation of at least appearing to carry out formal functions compelled individuals to take sides in order to protect themselves against the aggressions of others. And the intensity of the conflict was aggravated by the fact that it was formally unacceptable and had to be hidden.

For analytical convenience, staff-line

[3]Some social scientists have noted the possibility of staff-line friction, and industrial executives themselves have expressed strong feelings on the matter. See Burleigh B. Gardner, *Human Relations in Industry* (Chicago: Richard D. Irwin, Inc., 1945) and H. E. Dimock, *The Executive in Action* (New York: Harper & Brothers, 1945). Dimock believes that we are too "staff-minded" and that we should become more "executive-minded" (p. 241). A high line officer in a large corporation denounced staff organizations to the writer on the ground of their "costing more than they're worth," and that "They stir up too much trouble and are too theoretical." He felt that their function (excepting that of accountants, chemists, and "a few mechanical engineers") could be better carried out by replacing them with "highly-select front-line foremen [the lowest placed line officers] who are really the backbone of management, and pay them ten or twelve thousand dollars a year."

[4]These plants were in related industries and ranged in size from 4,500 to 20,000 employees, with the managerial groups numbering from 200 to nearly 1,000. Details concerning the plants and their location are confidential. Methodological details concerning an intensive study embracing staff-line relations and several other areas of behavior in one of the plants are given in the writer's unpublished doctoral thesis, "A Study of Informal Organization Among the Managers of an Industrial Plant," (Department of Sociology, University of Chicago, 1949).

[5]Because these conflict areas were interrelated and continually shifting and reorganizing, discussion of any one of them separately—as in the case of staff-line relations—will, of course, be unrealistic to some extent.

[6]From bottom to top, the line hierarchy consisted of the following strata of officers: (1) first-line foremen, who were directly in charge of production workmen; (2) general foremen; (3) departmental superintendents; (4) divisional superintendents; (5) assistant plant manager; (6) plant manager. In the preceding strata there were often "assistants," such as "assistant general foreman," "assistant superintendent," etc., in which case the total strata of the line hierarchy could be almost double that indicated here.

In the staff organizations the order from bottom to top was: (1) supervisor (equivalent to the first-line foreman); (2) general supervisor (equivalent to the general foreman); (3) staff head—sometimes "superintendent" (equivalent to departmental superintendent in the line organization). Occasionally there were strata of assistant supervisors and assistant staff heads.

The term "upper line" will refer to all strata above the departmental superintendent. "Middle line" will include the departmental superintendent and assistants. "Lower line" will refer to general and first-line foremen and their assistants.

"Lower," "middle," and "upper" staff will refer respectively to the supervisor, general supervisor and staff head.

"Top management" will refer to the upper line and the few staff heads with whom upper line officers were especially intimate on matters of policy.

friction may be examined apart from the reciprocal effects of the general conflict system. Regarded in this way, the data indicated that three conditions were basic to staff-line struggles: (1) the conspicuous ambition and "individualistic" behavior among staff officers; (2) the complication arising from staff efforts to justify its existence and get acceptance of its contributions; and, related to point two, (3) the fact that incumbency of the higher staff offices was dependent on line approval. The significance of these conditions will be discussed in order.

MOBILE BEHAVIOR OF STAFF PERSONNEL

As a group, staff personnel in the three plants were markedly ambitious, restless, and individualistic. There was much concern to win rapid promotion, to make the "right impressions," and to receive individual recognition. Data showed that the desire among staff members for personal distinctions often over-rode their sentiments of group consciousness and caused intra-staff tensions.[7]

The relatively high turnover of staff personnel[8] quite possibly reflected the

dissatisfactions and frustrations of members over inability to achieve the distinction and status they hoped for. Several factors appeared to be of importance in this restlessness of staff personnel. Among these were age and social differences between line and staff officers, structural differences in the hierarchy of the two groups, and the staff group's lack of authority over production.

With respect to age, the staff officers were significantly younger than line officers.[9] This would account to some extent for their restlessness. Being presumably less well-established in life in terms of material accumulations, occupational status, and security, while having greater expectations (see below), and more energy, as well as more life ahead in which to make new starts elsewhere if necessary, the staff groups were understandably more dynamic and driving.[10]

---

[7]In a typical case in one of the plants, a young staff officer developed a plan for increasing the life of certain equipment in the plant. He carried the plan directly to the superintendent of the department in which he hoped to introduce it, but was rebuffed by the superintendent who privately acknowledged the merit of the scheme but resented the staff officer's "trying to lord it over" him. The staff organization condemned the behavior of its member and felt that he should have allowed the plan to appear as a contribution of the staff group rather than as one of its members. The officer himself declared that "By G—it's my idea and I want credit. There's not a damn one of you guys [the staff group] that wouldn't make the same squawk if you were in my place!"

[8]During the period between 1944 and 1950 turnover of staff personnel in these plants was between two and four times as great as that of line personnel. This grouping included all the nonmanagerial members of staff and line and all the hourly-paid (non-salaried) members of management (about 60 assistant first-line foremen). Turnover was determined by dividing the average number of employees for a given year (in line or

staff) into the accessions or separations, whichever was the smaller.

[9]Complete age data were available in one of the larger plants. Here the 36 staff heads, staff specialists, and assistants had a mean age of 42.9 years. This value would have been less than 40 years, except for the inclusion of several older former line officers, but even a mean of 42.9 years was significantly less (C.R. 2.8) than that of the 35 line superintendents in the plant who had a mean age of 48.7 years. The age difference was even more significant when the staff heads were compared with the 61 general foremen who had a mean age of 50.0 years. And between the 93 salaried first-line foremen (mean age of 48.5 years) and the 270 salaried nonsupervisory staff personnel (mean age of 31.0 years) the difference was still greater.

[10]One might also hypothesize that the drive of staff officers was reflected in the fact that the staff heads and specialists gained their positions (those held when the data were collected) in less time than did members of the line groups, e.g., the 36 staff officers discussed above had spent a median of 10 years attaining their positions, as against a median of 11 years for the first-line foremen, 17 years for the general foremen, and 19 years for the superintendents. But one must consider that some of the staff groups were relatively new (13–15 years old) and had grown rapidly, which probably accelerated their rate of promotions as compared with that of the older line organization.

Age-conflict[11] was also significant in staff-line antagonisms. The incident just noted of the young staff officer seeking to get direct acceptance by the line of his contribution failed in part—judging from the strong sentiments later expressed by the line superintendent—because of an age antipathy. The older line officers disliked receiving what they regarded as instruction from men so much younger than themselves, and staff personnel clearly were conscious of this attitude among line officers.[12] In staff-line meetings staff officers frequently had their ideas slighted or even treated with amusement by line incumbents. Whether such treatment was warranted or not, the effects were disillusioning to the younger, less experienced staff officers. Often selected by the organization because of their outstanding academic records, they had entered industry with the belief that they had much to contribute, and that their efforts would win early recognition and rapid advancement. Certainly they had no thought that their contributions would be in any degree unwelcome. This naivete[13] was appar-

ently due to lack of earlier first-hand experience in industry (or acquaintance with those who had such experience), and to omission of realistic instruction in the social sciences from their academic training. The unsophisticated staff officer's initial contacts with the shifting, covert, expedient arrangements between members of staff and line usually gave him a severe shock. He had entered industry prepared to engage in logical, well-formulated relations with members of the managerial hierarchy, and to carry out precise, methodical functions for which his training had equipped him. Now he learned that (1) his freedom to function was snared in a web of informal commitments; (2) his academic specialty (on which he leaned for support in his new position) was often not relevant[14] for carrying out his formal assignments; and that (3) the important thing to do was to learn who the informally powerful line officers were and what ideas they would welcome which at the same time would be acceptable to his superiors.

Usually the staff officer's reaction to these conditions is to look elsewhere for a job or make an accommodation in the direction of protecting himself and finding a niche where he can make his existence in the plant tolerable and safe. If he chooses the latter course, he is likely

---

[11]E. A. Ross in *Principles of Sociology* (New York: D. Appleton-Century Co., 1938) pp. 238–48, has some pertinent comments on age conflict.

[12]Explaining the relatively few cases in which his staff had succeeded in "selling ideas" to the line, an assistant staff head remarked: "We're always in hot water with these old guys on the line. You can't tell them a damn thing. They're bull-headed as hell! Most of the time we offer a suggestion it's either laughed at or not considered at all. The same idea in the mouth of some old codger on the line'd get a round of applause. They treat us like kids."
Line officers in these plants often referred to staff personnel (especially members of the auditing, production planning, industrial engineering, and industrial relations staffs) as "college punks," "slide-rules," "crackpots," "pretty boys," and "chairwarmers."

[13]John Mills, a research engineer retired from the telephone industry, has noted the worldly naiveté of research engineers in that field in his *The Engineer in Society* (New York: D. Van Nostrand Co., 1946).

[14]Among the staff heads and assistants referred to earlier, only 50 per cent of those with college training (32 of the 36 officers) were occupied with duties related to their specialized training. E.g., the head of the industrial relations staff had a B.S. degree in aeronautical engineering; his assistant had a similar degree in chemical engineering. Considering that staff officers are assumed to be specialists trained to aid and advise management in a particular function, the condition presented here raises a question as to what the criteria of selection were. (As will be shown in a separate paper, the answer appeared to be that personal—as well as impersonal—criteria were used.) Among the college-trained of 190 line officers in the same plant, the gap between training and function was still greater, with 61 per cent in positions not related to the specialized part of their college work.

to be less concerned with creative effort for his employer than with attempts to develop reliable social relations that will aid his personal advancement. The staff officer's recourse to this behavior and his use of other status-increasing devices will be discussed below in another connection.

The formal structure, or hierarchy of statuses, of the two larger plants from which data were drawn, offered a frustration to the ambitious staff officer. That is, in these plants the strata, or levels of authority, in the staff organizations ranged from three to five as against from five to ten in the line organization. Consequently there were fewer possible positions for exercise of authority into which staff personnel could move. This condition may have been an irritant to expansion among the staff groups. Unable to move vertically to the degree possible in the line organization, the ambitious staff officer could enlarge his area of authority in a given position only by lateral expansion—by increasing his personnel. Whether or not aspiring staff incumbents revolted against the relatively low hierarchy through which they could move, the fact remains that (1) they appeared eager to increase the number of personnel under their authority,[15] (2) the

personnel of staff groups *did* increase disproportionately to those of the line,[16] and (3) there was a trend of personnel movement from staff to line,[17] rather than the reverse, presumably (reflecting the drive and ambition of staff members) because there were more positions of authority, as well as more authority to be exercised, more prestige, and usually more income in the line.

Behavior in the plants indicated that line and staff personnel belonged to dif-

---

[15]This was suggested by unnecessary references among some staff officers to "the number of men under me," and by their somewhat fanciful excuses for increase of personnel. These excuses included statements of needing more personnel to (1) carry on research, (2) control new processes, (3) keep records and reports up-to-date. These statements often did not square with (1) the excessive concern among staff people about their "privileges" (such as arriving on the job late, leaving early, leaving the plant for long periods during working hours, having a radio in the office during the World Series, etc.) ; (2) the great amount of time (relative to that of line officers) spent by lower staff personnel in social activities on the job, and (3) the constantly recurring (but not always provoked) claims among staff personnel of their functional importance for production. The duties of middle and lower staff personnel allowed them sufficient time

to argue a great deal over their respective functions (as well as many irrelevant topics) and to challenge the relative merit of one another's contributions or "ideas." In some of the staffs these discussions could go on intermittently for hours and develop into highly theoretical jousts and wit battles. Where staff people regarded such behavior as a privilege of their status, line officers considered it as a threat to themselves. This lax control (in terms of line discipline) was in part a tacit reward from staff heads to their subordinates. The reward was expected because staff superiors (especially in the industrial relations, industrial engineering, and planning staffs) often overlooked and/or perverted the work of subordinates (which was resented) in response to pressures from the line. This behavior will be noted later.

[16]In one of the larger plants, where exact data were available, the total staff personnel had by 1945 exceeded that of the line. At that time the staff included 400 members as against 317 line personnel composed of managerial officers and their clerical workers, but not production workers. By 1948 the staff had increased to 517 as compared with 387 for the line (during this period *total* plant personnel declined over 400). The staff had grown from 20.8 per cent larger than the line in 1945 to 33.6 per cent larger in 1948, and had itself increased by 29.3 per cent during the three years as against a growth in the line of 22.1 per cent. Assuming the conditions essential for use of probability theory, the increase in staff personnel could have resulted from chance about 1.5 times in a hundred. Possibly post-war and other factors of social change were also at work but, if so, their force was not readily assessable.

[17]This movement from staff to line can disorganize the formal managerial structure, especially when (1) the transferring staff personnel have had little or no supervisory experience in the staff but have an academic background which causes them to regard human beings as mechanisms that will respond as expected; (2) older, experienced line officers have hoped—for years in some cases—to occupy the newly vacated (or created) positions.

ferent social status groups and that line and staff antipathies were at least in part related to these social distinctions. For example, with respect to the item of formal education, the staff group stood on a higher level than members of the line. In the plant from which the age data were taken, the 36 staff officers had a mean of 14.6 years of schooling as compared with 13.1 years for 35 line superintendents, 11.2 years for 60 general foremen, and 10.5 years for 93 first-line foremen. The difference between the mean education of the staff group and that of the highest line group (14.6–13.1) was statistically significant at better than the one per cent level. The 270 non-supervisory staff personnel had a mean of 13.1 years—the same as that of the line superintendents. Consciousness of this difference probably contributed to a feeling of superiority among staff members, while the sentiment of line officers toward staff personnel was reflected in the name-calling noted earlier.

Staff members were also much concerned about their dress, a daily shave, and a weekly hair-cut. On the other hand line officers, especially below the level of departmental superintendent, were relatively indifferent to such matters. Usually they were in such intimate contact with production processes that dirt and grime prevented the concern with meticulous dress shown by staff members. The latter also used better English in speaking and in writing reports, and were more suave and poised in social intercourse. These factors, and the recreational preferences of staff officers for night clubs and "hot parties," assisted in raising a barrier between them and most line officers.

The social antipathies of the two groups and the status concern of staff officers were indicated by the behavior of each toward the established practice of dining together in the cafeterias reserved for management in the two larger plants. Theoretically, all managerial officers upward from the level of general foremen in the line, and general supervisors in the staff, were eligible to eat in these cafeterias. However, in practice the mere taking of one of these offices did not automatically assure the incumbent the privilege of eating in the cafeteria. One had first to be invited to "join the association." Staff officers were very eager to "get in" and did considerable fantasying on the impressions, with respect to dress and behavior, that were believed essential for an invitation. One such staff officer, a cost supervisor, dropped the following remarks:

> There seems to be a committee that passes on you. I've had my application in for three years, but no soap. Harry [his superior] had his in for over three years before he made it. You have to have something, because if a man who's in moves up to another position the man who replaces him doesn't get it because of the position—and he might not get it at all. I think I'm about due.

Many line officers who were officially members of the association avoided the cafeteria, however, and had to be *ordered* by the assistant plant manager to attend. One of these officers made the following statement, which expressed more pointedly the many similar spontaneous utterances of resentment and dislike made by other line officers:

> There's a lot of good discussion in the cafeteria. I'd like to get in on more of it but I don't like to go there—sometimes I have to go. Most of the white collar people [staff officers] that eat there are stuck-up. I've been introduced three time to Svendsen [engineer], yet when I meet him he pretends to not even know me. When he meets me on the street he always manages to be looking someplace else. G—d—such people as that! They don't go in the cafeteria to eat and relax while they talk over their problems. They go in there to look around and see how somebody is dressed or to talk over the hot party they had last night. Well, that kind of damn stuff don't go with me. I

haven't any time to put on airs and make out I'm something that I'm not.

COMPLICATIONS OF STAFF NEED TO PROVE ITS WORTH

To the thinking of many line officers, the staff functioned as an agent on trial rather than as a managerial division that might be of equal importance with the line organization in achieving production goals. Staff members were very conscious of this sentiment toward them and of their need to prove themselves. They strained to develop new techniques and to get them accepted by the line. But in doing this they frequently became impatient, and gave already suspicious line officers the impression of reaching for authority over production.

Since the line officer regards his authority over production as something sacred, and resents the implication that after many years in the line he needs the guidance of a newcomer who lacks such experience, an obstacle to staff-line cooperation develops the moment this sore spot is touched. On the other hand, the staff officer's ideology of his function leads him to precipitate a power struggle with the line organization. By and large he considers himself as an agent of top management. He feels bound to contribute something significant in the form of research or ideas helpful to management. By virtue of his greater education and intimacy with the latest theories of production, he regards himself as a managerial consultant and an expert, and feels that he must be, or appear to be, almost infallible once he has committed himself to top management on some point. With this orientation, he is usually disposed to approach middle and lower line with an attitude of condescension that often reveals itself in the heat of discussion. Consequently, many staff officers involve themselves in trouble and report their failures as due to "ignorance" and "bullheadedness" among these line officers.

On this point, relations between staff and line in all three of the plants were further irritated by a rift inside the line organization. First-line foremen were inclined to feel that top management had brought in the production planning, industrial relations, and industrial engineering staffs as clubs with which to control the lower line. Hence they frequently regarded the projects of staff personnel and manipulative devices, and reacted by cooperating with production workers and/or general foremen (whichever course was the more expedient) in order to defeat insistent and uncompromising members of the staff. Also, on occasion (see below), the lower line could cooperate evasively with lower staff personnel who were in trouble with staff superiors.

EFFECT OF LINE AUTHORITY OVER STAFF PROMOTION

The fact that entry to the higher staff offices in the three plants was dependent on approval of top line officers had a profound effect on the behavior of staff personnel. Every member of the staff knew that if he aspired to higher office he must make a record for himself, a good part of which would be a reputation among upper line officers of ability to "understand" their informal problems without being told. This knowledge worked in varying degrees to pervert the theory of staff-line relations. Ideally the two organizations cooperate to improve existing methods of output, to introduce new methods, to plan the work, and to solve problems of production and the scheduling of orders that might arise. But when the line offers resistance to the findings and recommendations of the staff, the latter is reduced to evasive practices of getting some degree of acceptance of its programs, and at the same time of convincing top management that "good relations" exist with officers down the line. This necessity becomes even more acute when the staff officer aspires (for some of the reasons given above) to move over to the line organization, for then he must convince powerful line officers that he is worthy. In building a convincing record, however, he may compromise with line demands and bring charges from his staff colleagues that he is "selling out," so that after moving into the line organization he will then have to live with enemies he made in the staff. In any case, the need among staff incumbents of pleasing line officers in order to perfect their careers called for accommodation in three major areas:[18] (1) the observance of staff rules, (2) the introduction of new techniques, and (3) the use of appropriations for staff research and experiment.

With respect to point one, staff personnel, particularly in the middle and lower levels, carried on expedient relations with the line that daily evaded formal rules. Even those officers most devoted to rules found that, in order not to arouse enmity in the line on a scale sufficient to be communicated *up* the line, compromising devices were frequently helpful and sometimes almost unavoidable both for organizational and career aims. The usual practice was to tolerate minor breaking of staff rules by line personnel, or even to cooperate with the line in evading rules,[19] and in ex-

change lay a claim on the line for cooperation on critical issues. In some cases line aid was enlisted to conceal lower staff blunders from the upper staff and the upper line.[20]

Concerning point two, while the staff organizations gave much time to developing new techniques, they were simultaneously thinking about how their plans would be received by the line. They knew from experience that middle and lower line officers could always give a "black eye" to staff contributions by deliberate malpractices. Repeatedly top management had approved, and incorporated, staff proposals that had been verbally accepted down the line. Often the latter officers had privately opposed the chang-

---

[18]The relative importance of one or more of these areas would vary with the function of a given staff.

[19]In a processing department in one of the plants the chemical solution in a series of vats was supposed to have a specific strength and temperature, and a fixed rate of inflow and outflow. Chemists (members of the chemical staff) twice daily checked these properties of the solution and submitted reports showing that all points met the laboratory ideal. Actually, the solution was usually nearly triple the standard strength, the temperature was about ten degrees Centigrade higher than standard, and the rate of flow was in excess of double the standard. There are, of course, varying discrepancies between laboratory theory and plant practice, but the condition described here resulted from production pressures that forced line foremen into behavior upsetting the conditions expected by chemical theory. The chemists were sympathetic with the hard-pressed foremen, who compensated by (1) notifying the chemists (rather than their superior, the chief chemist) if anything "went wrong" for which the laboratory was responsible and thus sparing them criticism; and by (2) cooperating with the chemists to reduce the number of analyses which the chemists would ordinarily have to make.

[20]Failure of middle and lower staff personnel to "cooperate" with line officers might cause the latter to "stand pat" in observance of line rules at a time when the pressures of a dynamic situation would make the former eager to welcome line cooperation in rule-breaking. For example, a staff officer was confronted with the combined effect of (1) a delay in production on the line that was due to an indefensible staff error; (2) pressure on the line superintendent—with whom he was working—to hurry a special order; and (3) the presence in his force of new inexperienced staff personnel who were (a) irritating to line officers, and (b) by their inexperience constituted an invitation to line aggression. Without aid from the line superintendent (which could have been withheld by observance of formal rules) in covering up the staff error and in controlling line personnel, the staff officer might have put himself in permanent disfavor with all his superiors.

es, but had feared that saying so would incur the resentment of powerful superiors who could informally hurt them. Later they would seek to discredit the change by deliberate malpractice and hope to bring a return to the former arrangement. For this reason there was a tendency for staff members to withhold improved production schemes or other plans when they knew that an attempt to introduce them might fail or even bring personal disrepute.

Line officers fear staff innovations for a number of reasons. In view of their longer experience, presumably intimate knowledge of the work, and their greater remuneration, they fear[21] being "shown up" before their line superiors for not having thought of the processual refinements themselves. They fear that changes in methods may bring personnel changes which will threaten the break-up of cliques and existing informal arrangements and quite possibly reduce their area of authority. Finally, changes in techniques may expose forbidden practices and departmental inefficiency. In some cases these fears have stimulated line officers to compromise staff men to the point where the latter will agree to postpone the initiation of new practices for specific periods.

In one such case an assistant staff head agreed with a line superintendent to delay the application of a bonus plan for nearly three months so that the superintendent could live up to the expedient agreement he had made earlier with his grievance committeeman to avoid a "wildcat" strike by a group of production workmen.[22] The lower engineers who had devised the plan were suspicious of the formal reasons given to them for withholding it, so the assistant staff head prevented them (by means of "busy work") from attending staff-line meetings lest they inadvertently reveal to top management that the plan was ready.

The third area of staff-line accommodations growing out of authority relations revolved around staff use of funds granted it by top management. Middle and lower line charged that staff research and experimentation was little more than "money wasted on blunders," and that various departments of the line could have "accomplished much more with less money." According to staff officers, those of their plans that failed usually did so because line personnel "sabotaged" them and refused to "cooperate." Specific costs of "crack-pot experimentation" in certain staff groups were pointed to by line officers. Whatever the truth of the charges and counter-charges, evidence indicated (confidants in both groups supported this) that pressures from the line organization (below the top level) forced some of the staff groups to "kick over" parts of the funds appropriated for staff use[23] by top management. These compromises were of course hidden from top management, but the relations described were carried on to such an extent that by means of them— and line pressures for manipulation of accounts in the presumably impersonal auditing departments—certain line officers were able to show impressively low

---

[21]Though there was little evidence that top management expected line officers to refine production techniques, the fear of such an expectation existed nevertheless. As noted earlier, however, some of the top executives *were* thinking that development of a "higher type" of first-line foreman might enable most of the staff groups to be eliminated.

[22]This case indicates the over-lapping of conflict areas referred to earlier. A later paper will deal with the area of informal union-management relations.

[23]In two of the plants a somewhat similar relation, rising from different causes, existed *inside* the line organization with the *operating* branch of the line successfully applying pressures for a share in funds assigned to the *maintenance* division of the line.

operating costs and thus win favor[24] with top management that would relieve pressures and be useful in personal advancement. In their turn the staff officers involved would receive more "cooperation" from the line and/or recommendation for transfer to the line. The data indicated that in a few such cases men from accounting and auditing staffs were given general foremanships (without previous line experience) as a reward for their understanding behavior.

SUMMARY

Research in three industrial plants showed conflict between the managerial staff and line groups that hindered the attainment of organizational goals. Privately expressed attitudes among some of the higher line executives revealed their hope that greater control of staff groups could be achieved, or that the groups might be eliminated and their functions taken over in great part by carefully selected and highly remunerated lower-line officers. On their side, staff members wanted more recognition and a greater voice in control of the plants.

All of the various functioning groups of the plants were caught up in a general conflict system; but apart from the effects of involvement in this complex, the struggles between line and staff organizations were attributable mainly to (1) functional differences between the two groups; (2) differentials in the ages, formal education, potential occupational ceilings, and status group affiliations of members of the two groups (the staff officers being younger, having more education but lower occupational potential, and forming a prestige-oriented group with distinctive dress and recreational tastes); (3) need of the staff groups to justify their existence; (4) fear in the line that staff bodies by their expansion, and well-financed research activities, would undermine line authority; and (5) the fact that aspirants to higher staff offices could gain promotion only through approval of influential line executives.

If further research should prove that staff-line behavior of the character presented here is widespread in industry, and *if* top management should realize how such behavior affects its cost and production goals—and be concerned to improve the condition—then remedial measures could be considered. For example, a corrective approach might move in the direction of (1) creating a separate body[25] whose sole function would be the coordination of staff and line efforts; (2) increasing the gradations of awards and promotions in staff organizations (without increase of staff personnel); (3) granting of more nearly equal pay to staff officers, but with increased responsibility (without authority over line processes or personnel) for the practical working of their projects; (4) requiring that staff personnel have a minimum supervisory experience and have shared repeatedly in successful collaborative staff-line projects before transferring to the line; (5) steps by top management to remove the fear of veiled personal reprisal felt by officers in most levels of both staff and line hierarchies (This fear—rising

---

[24]The reader must appreciate the fact that constant demands are made by top management to maintain low operating costs.

[25]This body, or "Board of Coordination," would be empowered to enforce its decisions. Membership would consist of staff and line men who had had wide experience in the plant over a period of years. The Board would (a) serve as an arbiter between staff and line; (b) review, screen, and approve individual recommendations submitted; and (c) evaluate contributions after a trial period. Such a body would incidentally be another high status goal for seasoned, capable, and ambitious officers who too often are trapped by the converging walls of the pyramidal hierarchy.

from a disbelief in the possibility of bureaucratic impersonality—is probably the greatest obstacle to communication inside the ranks of management) ;

(6) more emphasis in colleges and universities on realistic instruction in the social sciences for students preparing for industrial careers.

30　Toward an Understanding of Inequity[1]

J. Stacy Adams

Equity, or more precisely, inequity, is a pervasive concern of industry, labor, and government. Yet its psychological basis is probably not fully understood. Evidence suggests that equity is not merely a matter of getting "a fair day's pay for a fair day's work," nor is inequity simply a matter of being underpaid. The fairness of an exchange between employee and employer is not usually perceived by the former purely and simply as an economic matter. There is an element of relative justice involved that supervenes economics and underlies perceptions of equity or inequity (Homans, 1961; Jaques, 1956, 1961a, 1961b; Patchen, 1961; Stouffer, Suchman, DeVinney, Star, & Williams, 1949; Zaleznik, Christensen, & Roethlisberger, 1958) .

The purpose of this paper is to present a theory of inequity, leading toward an understanding of the phenomenon and, hopefully, resulting in its control. Whether one wishes to promote social justice or merely to reduce economically disadvantageous industrial unrest, an understanding of inequity is important. In developing the theory of inequity, which is based upon Festinger's (1957) theory of cognitive dissonance and is, therefore, a special case of it, we shall describe major variables involved in an employee-employer exchange, before we proceed to define inequity formally. Having defined it, we shall analyze its effects. Finally, such evidence as is available will be presented in support of the theory. Throughout we shall emphasize some of the simpler aspects of inequity and try to refrain from speculating about many of the engaging, often complex, relationships between inequity and other phenomena, and about what might be termed "higher order" inequities. In the exposition that follows we shall also refer principally to wage inequities, in part because of their importance and in part because of the availability of methods to measure the marginal utility of wages

[1]This paper and some of the experimental work reported in it are part of a program of theory development and research on wages and productivity undertaken by the author at the Behavioral Research Service, General Electric Company. The author wishes to acknowledge his indebtedness to Leon Festinger for his work on cognitive dissonance and to George C. Homans for his ideas on distributive justice, which stimulated much of the present essay. He is also grateful to A. J. Arrowood, W. B. Rosenbaum, F. Tweed, and Patricia Jacobsen for assistance in conducting experiments.

From J. Stacy Adams, "Toward an Understanding of Inequity," *Journal of Abnormal and Social Psychology*, Vol. 67, 1963, pp. 422-436. Copyright 1963 by the American Psychological Association, and reproduced by permission from the publisher and the author.

(Adams, 1961; Jeffrey & Jones, 1961). It should be evident, however, that the theoretical notions advanced are relevant to any social situation in which an exchange takes place, whether the exchange be of the type taking place between man and wife, between football teammates, between teacher and student, or even, between Man and his God.

Whenever two individuals exchange anything, there is the possibility that one or both of them will feel that the exchange was inequitable. Such is frequently the case when a man exchanges his services for pay. On the man's side of the exchange are his education, intelligence, experience, training, skill, seniority, age, sex, ethnic background, social status, and, very importantly, the effort he expends on the job. Under special circumstances other attributes will be relevant: personal appearance or attractiveness, health, possession of an automobile, the characteristics of one's spouse, and so on. They are what he perceives are his contributions to the exchange, for which he expects a just return. Homans (1961) calls them "investments." These variables are brought by him to the job. Henceforth they will be referred to as his *inputs*. These inputs, let us emphasize, are *as perceived by their contributor* and are not necessarily isomorphic with those of the other party to the exchange. This suggests two conceptually distinct characteristics of inputs, *recognition* and *relevance*.

The possessor of an attribute, or the other party to the exchange, or both, may recognize the existence of the attribute in the possessor. If either the possessor or both members of the exchange recognize its existence, the attribute has the potentiality of being an input. If only the nonpossessor recog-

nizes its existence it cannot be considered psychologically an input so far as the possessor is concerned. Whether or not an attribute having the potential of being an input is an input, is contingent upon the possessor's perception of its relevance to the exchange. If he perceives it to be relevant, if he expects a just return for it, it is an input. Problems of inequity arise if only the possessor of the attribute considers it relevant in the exchange. Crozier[2] relates an observation that is apropos. Paris-born bank clerks worked side by side with other clerks who did identical work and earned identical wages, but were born in the Provinces. The Parisians were dissatisfied with their wages, for they considered that Parisian breeding was an input deserving monetary compensation. The bank management, while recognizing that place of birth distinguished the two groups, did not, of course, consider birthplace relevant in the exchange of services for pay.

The principal inputs listed earlier vary in type and in their degree of relationship to one another. Some variables, such as age, are clearly continuous; others, such as sex and ethnicity, are not. Some are intercorrelated, seniority and age, for example; sex, on the other hand, is largely independent of the other variables, with the possible exception of education and some kinds of effort. Although these intercorrelations, or the lack of them, exist in a state of nature, it is probable that the individual cognitively treats all input variables as independent. Thus, for example, if he were assessing the sum of his inputs, he might well "score" age and seniority separately.

On the other side of the exchange

---

[2] M. Crozier, personal communication, 1960.

are the rewards received by an individual for his services. These *outcomes*, as they will be termed, include pay, rewards intrinsic to the job, seniority benefits, fringe benefits, job status and status symbols, and a variety of formally and informally sanctioned perquisites. An example of the latter is the right of higher status persons to park their cars in privileged locations, or the right to have a walnut rather than a metal desk. Seniority, mentioned as an input variable, has associated with it a number of benefits such as job security, "bumping" privileges, greater fringe benefits, and so on. These benefits are outcomes and are distinguished from the temporal aspects of seniority (that is, longevity), which are properly inputs. As in the case of job inputs, job outcomes are often intercorrelated. For example, greater pay and higher job status are likely to go hand in hand.

In a manner analogous to inputs, outcomes are *as perceived*, and, again, we should characterize them in terms of recognition and relevance. If the recipient or both the recipient and giver of an outcome in an exchange recognize its existence, it has the potentiality of being an outcome psychologically. If the recipient considers it relevant to the exchange and it has some marginal utility for him, it *is* an outcome. Not infrequently the giver or "buyer," to use economic terms, may give or yield something which, perhaps at some cost to him, is either irrelevant or of no marginal utility to the recipient. An employer may give an employee a carpet for his office in lieu, say, of a salary increment and find that the employee is dissatisfied, perhaps because in the subculture of that office a rug has no meaning, no psychological utility. Conversely, a salary increment may be inadequate, if formalized status recognition was what was wanted and was what had greater utility.

In classifying some variables as inputs and others as outcomes, it is not implied that they are independent, except conceptually. Job inputs and outcomes are, in fact, intercorrelated, but imperfectly so. Indeed, it is because they are imperfectly correlated that we need at all be concerned with job inequity. There exist normative expectations of what constitute "fair" correlations between inputs and outcomes. The bases of the expectations are the correlations obtaining for a reference person or group—a co-worker or colleague, a relative or neighbor, a group of co-workers, a craft group, an industry-wide pattern. A blank clerk, for example, may determine whether her inputs and outcomes are fairly correlated—in balance, so to speak—by comparing them with the relationship between the inputs and outcomes of other female clerks in her section. The sole punch press operator in a manufacturing plant may base his judgment on what he believes are the inputs and outcomes of other operators in the community or region. For a particular physicist the relevant reference person may be an organic chemist of the same academic "vintage." While it is clearly important to be able to specify the appropriate reference person or group, it represents a distinct theoretical area in which work has begun (Merton & Kitt, 1950; Patchen, 1961; Stouffer et al., 1949) but which would take this paper too far afield. For the purposes of this paper, it will be assumed that the reference person or group will be one comparable to the comparer on one or more attributes, usually a co-worker.[3]

When the normative expectations of the person making social comparisons

---

[3]This assumption follows Festinger (1954), who states: "Given a range of possible persons for comparison, someone close to one's own ability or opinion will be chosen for comparison [p. 121]." Generally, co-workers will more nearly fit this criterion than will other persons.

are violated—when he finds his inputs and outcomes are not in balance in relation to those of others—feelings of inequity result.

INEQUITY DEFINED

Although it has been suggested how inequity arises, a rigorous definition must be formulated. But we introduce first two references terms, Person and Other. Person is any individual for whom equity or inequity exists. Other is any individual or group used by Person as a referent when he makes social comparisons of his inputs and outcomes. Other is usually a different individual, but may be Person in another job, or even in another social role. Thus, for example, Other might be Person in the job he held 6 months earlier, in which case he might compare his present and past inputs and outcomes. Or, as Patchen (1961) has suggested, Other might be Person in a future job to which he aspires. In such an instance he would make a comparison of his present inputs and outcomes to his estimates of those in the future. The terms Person and Other may also refer to groups rather than to individuals, as for example when a class of jobs (for example, toolmakers) is out of line with another class (for example, maintenance men). In such cases, it is convenient to deal with the class as a whole rather than with individual members of the class. This is essentially what is done when the relative ranking of jobs is evaluated in the process of devising an equitable wage or salary structure.

Using the theoretical model introduced by Festinger (1957), inequity is defined as follows: Inequity exists for Person whenever his perceived job inputs and/or outcomes stand psychologically in an obverse relation to what he perceives are the inputs and/or outcomes of Other. The first point to note about the definition is that it is the perception by Person

of his and Other's inputs and outcomes that must be dealt with, not necessarily the actual inputs and outcomes. The point is important, for, while perception and reality may be and often are in close accord, wage administrators are likely to assume an identity of the two. Second, if we let A designate Person's inputs and outcomes and let B designate Other's, by "obverse relation" we mean that not A follows from B. But we emphasize that the relation necessary for inequity to exist is psychological in character, not logical. Thus, there is no logical obversion in male Person's being subordinate to female Other, but, as Clark (1958) has observed, the inputs of Person and Other in such a situation may be dissonant, with the consequence that inequity is felt by Person.

As was previously suggested, the dissonant relation of an individual's inputs and outcomes in comparison to another's is historically and culturally determined. This is why we insist that the incongruity is primarily psychological, even though it might, in addition, have a logical character. Each individual has a different history of learning, but to the extent that he learns from people sharing similar values, social norms, and language, that is, the extent to which he shares the same culture, his psychological reactions will be similar to theirs. The larger the cultural group, the greater will be the number of individuals who perceive similarly and react similarly to a given set of relations between input and outcomes. In the United States there is a strong, but perhaps weakening, predilection for the belief that effort and reward must be positively correlated. Considering the population at large, this belief has the status of a cultural norm and partially explains rather uniform reactions toward certain kinds of inequity—toward "featherbedding," for example.

It is interesting to note that the American attitude toward work and reward is

TABLE 30-1 Amount of Inequity for Person as a Result of Different Inputs and Outcomes for Person and Other

| Person | Inputs-Outcomes | | | |
| | Other | | | |
	Low-High	High-Low	Low-Low	High-High
Low-High	0	2	1	1
High-Low	2	0	1	1
Low-Low	1	1	0	0
High-High	1	1	0	0

Note.—The first member of the pair indicates inputs and the second member, outcomes.

by no means universal. In highly industrialized Japan, for example, there is little relationship between the kind and amount of work an employee does and the monetary reward he receives. Pay is largely determined by age, education, length of service, and family size, and very little, if at all, by productivity. In his study of Japanese factories, Abegglen (1958) states:

It is not at all difficult to find situations where workers doing identical work at an identical pace receive markedly different salaries, or where a skilled workman is paid at a rate below that of a sweeper or doorman. The position occupied and the amount produced do not determine the reward provided [p. 68].

This, of course, is not to suggest that inequity is nonexistent for Japanese workers. They and their employers enter into an exchange just as Americans, but the terms of the exchange are quite different. Hence, the basis for inequity is different.

In order to predict when an individual will experience inequity under given conditions of inputs and outcomes, it is necessary to know something of the values and norms to which he subscribes—with what culture or subculture he is associated. Granted this knowledge, it is then possible to specify what constitutes an obverse relation of inputs and outcomes for Person. In a given society, even ours, there is usually enough invariance in fundamental beliefs and attitudes to make reasonably accurate, general predictions.

It is shown in Table 30–1 how inequity results whenever the inputs or outcomes, or both, of Person stand in an obverse relation to either the inputs or outcomes, or both, of Other. Though inputs and outcomes may in most cases be measured continuously (ethnicity and sex are obvious exceptions), we have dichotomized them into "high" and "low" for the purpose of simplicity. The entries in the table are relative rather than absolute quantities. Thus, 1 indicates more felt inequity than 0, and 2 indicates more felt inequity than 1. But before pursuing the implications of Table 1 and of the definition of inequity, let us agree to use amount of effort as an instance of inputs and pay as an instance of outcomes. Any other input and outcome would do as well; we wish merely to use constant instances for the illustrations that will follow.

The first important consequence to observe from the definition is that inequity results for Person not only when he is relatively underpaid, but also when he is relatively overpaid. Person will, for example, feel inequity exists not only when his effort is high and his pay low, while Other's effort and pay are high, but also when his effort is low and his pay high, while Other's effort and pay are low.

Although there is no direct, reliable evidence on this point, it is probable that the thresholds for inequity are different (in absolute terms from a base of equity) in cases of under- and overcompensation. The threshold would be greater presumably in cases of overcompensation, for a certain amount of incongruity in these cases can be acceptably rationalized as "good fortune." In his work on pay differentials Jaques (1961a) notes that in instances of undercompensation British workers paid 10% less than the equitable level show

an active sense of grievance, complaints or the desire to complain, and, if no redress is given, an active desire to change jobs, or to take action . . . [p. 26].

In cases of overcompensation, he observes that at the 10 15% level above equity

there is a strong sense of receiving preferential treatment, which may harden into bravado, with underlying feelings of unease . . . [p. 26].

He states further:

The results suggest that it is not necessarily the case that each one is simply out to get as much as he can for his work. There appear to be equally strong desires that each one should earn the right amount—a fair and reasonable amount relative to others [p. 26].

While Jaques' conceptualization of inequity is quite different from that advanced in this paper, his observations lend credence to the hypothesis that overcompensation results in feelings of inequity and that the threshold for these feelings is higher than in the case of undercompensation.

From the definition and Table 30-1, we may observe as a second consequence that when Person's and Other's inputs and outcomes are analogous, equity is assumed to exist, and that when their inputs and outcomes are discrepant in any way inequity will exist. We assume that it is not the absolute magnitude of perceived inputs and outcomes that results in inequity, but rather the relative magnitudes pertaining to Person and Other. For example, there will be no inequity if both Person and Other expend much effort in their jobs and both obtain low pay. The 0 entries in the main diagonal of Table 30-1 reflect the fact that when the inputs and outcomes of Person and Other are matched, no inequity exists. It is further assumed, and shown in Table 30-1, that no inequity will result if both the inputs and outcomes of Person are matched and those of Other are matched, but are different for Person and for Other. To illustrate: if Person expends low effort and receives low pay, while Other expends high effort and receives high pay, equity rather than inequity will result. The converse also holds true.

With regard to the amount of inequity that exists, we have assumed that greater inequity results when both inputs and outcomes are discrepant than when only inputs or outcomes are discrepant. This signifies, for example, that Person will experience more inequity when his effort is high and pay low, while Other's effort is low and pay high, than when Person's effort is high and pay low, while Other's effort and pay are both high. In Table 30-1 only three relative magnitudes of inequity, ranging from 0 to 2, are shown. In reality, of course, many more degrees could be distinguished, especially with variables such as effort and pay which are theoretically continuous. The point to be emphasized is that equity-inequity is not an all-or-none phenomenon.

It will be noted that in the definition of inequity and in Table 30-1, inputs have not been differentiated, nor have outcomes. There are two reasons for this.

First, the processes that govern inequity are applicable irrespective of the specific inputs and outcomes obtaining in a particular situation. For example, inequity may result whether low inputs are in the form of low effort or of poor education, or whether high outcomes stem from high pay or from great rewards intrinsic to the job. Second, there is a degree of interchangeability between different inputs and between different outcomes; furthermore inputs are additive, as are outcomes. It is implied, therefore, that a given total of Person's inputs may be achieved by increasing or decreasing any one or more separate inputs; similarly, a given total of Person's outcomes may result from increasing or decreasing one or more separate outcomes. For example, if Person found it necessary to increase his inputs in order to reduce inequity, he could do so not only by increasing his effort, but also by acquiring additional training or education. If, on the other hand, greater outcomes were required to achieve equity, obtaining new status symbols might be equivalent to an increase in compensation, or a combination of improved job environment and increased discretionary content of the job might be.

The question of the interchangeability and additivity of different inputs on the one hand, and of different outcomes on the other is an important one. Does a man evaluating his job inputs give the same weight to formal education as he does to on-the-job experience? If he has completed high school and has held his job 2 years, and a co-worker, whom he uses as a comparison person, completed the ninth grade only and has been on the job 4 years, will he judge their inputs as equivalent or not? Is the frequently used practice of giving a man a prestigeful title an effective substitute for greater monetary outcomes? Definitive answers to such questions await research. However,

this much may be hypothesized: Within certain limits of inequity there will be a tendency on the part of Person to manipulate and weight cognitively his own inputs and outcomes and those of Other in such a manner as to minimize the degree of felt inequity. Beyond these limits of inequity the tendency will be to manipulate and weight inputs and outcomes so as to maximize the inequity, because as will be discussed later, this will increase the motivation to adopt behavior that will eliminate the inequity entirely.[4] In both processes it is assumed that normal men are limited by reality in the amount of cognitive manipulation and weighting of inputs and outcomes they can perform. Except, perhaps, in the case of very small degrees of inequity such manipulation and weighting could not serve by themselves to achieve equity.

In discussing inequity, the focus has been exclusively on Person. In so doing, however, we have failed to consider that whenever inequity exists for Person, it will also exist for Other, provided their perceptions of inputs and outcomes are isomorphic or nearly so. A glance at Table 30-1 will make this apparent, and we may predict from the table the inequity for Other as well as for Person. Only when the perceptions of Person and Other do not agree, would the inequity be different for each. In such a case, one would enter Table 30-1 twice, once for Person and once for Other. It is sufficient at this point merely to note that inequity is bilateral or multilateral, and symmetric under some conditions. Later we shall consider the implications of this in greater detail.

[4]This process is analogous to that postulated by Festinger (1957) when he discusses the relation of magnitude of cognitive dissonance to seeking information that will increase dissonance. He hypothesizes that at high levels of dissonance increasing information may be sought, with the result that the person will change his opinion and thus reduce dissonance.

EFFECTS OF INEQUITY

Having defined inequity and specified its antecedents, we may next attend to its effects. First, two general postulates, closely following dissonance theory (Festinger, 1957): (a) The presence of inequity in Person creates tension in him. The tension is proportional to the magnitude of inequity present. (b) The tension created in Person will drive him to reduce it. The strength of the drive is proportional to the tension created; *ergo*, it is proportional to the magnitude of inequity present. In short, the presence of inequity will motivate Person to achieve equity or reduce inequity, and the strength of motivation to do so will vary directly with the amount of inequity. The question, then, is *how* may Person reduce inequity? The following actions enumerate and illustrate the means available to Person when reducing inequity.

1. Person may increase his inputs if they are low relative to Other's inputs and to his own outcomes. If, for example, Person's effort were low compared to Other's and to his own pay, he could reduce inequity by increasing his effort on the job. This might take the form of Person's increasing his productivity, as will be shown in experiments described later, or enhancing the quality of his work. If inputs other than effort were involved, he could increase his training or education. Some inputs cannot, of course, be altered easily—sex and ethnicity, for instance. When such inputs are involved, other means of reducing inequity must be adopted.

2. Person may decrease his inputs if they are high relative to Other's inputs and to his own outcomes. If Person's effort were high compared to Other's and to his own pay, he might reduce his effort and productivity, as is illustrated later in a study of grocery clerks. It is interesting to note that effort is the principal input

susceptible to reduction; education, training, experience, intelligence, skill, seniority, age, sex, ethnicity, and so on are not readily decreased or devalued realistically, though they may be distorted psychologically within limits. They are givens; their acquisition is not reversible. The implication is that when inequity results from inputs being too high, decreases in productivity are especially likely to be observed. One may speculate that restrictive production practices often observed are in fact attempts at reducing inequity.

There exists in industry a tendency to select and hire personnel with education, intellect, and training which are often greater than that required by the job in which they are placed. Since it is likely that in many instances the comparison persons for these individuals will have lesser inputs and, perhaps, greater outcomes, it is evident that some of the newly hired will experience feelings of inequity. In consequence, education, intellect, and training not being readily modified, lowered productivity may be predicted.

3. Person may increase his outcomes if they are low relative to Other's outcomes and to his own inputs. When Person's pay is low compared to Other's and to his expended effort, he may reduce inequity by obtaining a wage increase. Evidence of this is given later in a study of clerical workers. He could also, if appropriate, acquire additional benefits, perquisites, or status. An increase in status, however, might create new problems, for the acquisition of higher status without higher pay would of itself create dissonance, particularly if the new status of Person placed him in a superordinate position vis-à-vis Other.

4. Person may decrease his outcomes if they are high relative to Other's outcomes and to his own inputs. This might take the form of Person's lowering his

pay. Though an improbable mode of reducing inequity, it is nevertheless theoretically possible. Although it is usually assumed that persons with very high personal incomes are motivated by tax laws to donate much to charitable and educational institutions, it is not improbable that this behavior on the part of some is motivated as well by feelings of inequity.

5. Person may "leave the field" when he experiences inequity of any type. This may take the form of quitting his job or obtaining a transfer or reassignment, or of absenteeism. In a study by Patchen (1959) it was observed that men who said their pay should be higher had more absences than men who said the pay for their jobs was fair. Although the author did not conceptualize "fair pay" as in the present paper, it is clear at least that "fair" was defined by respondents in relational terms, for he states:

The data show also that the actual amount of a man's pay has, in itself, little effect on how often he is absent. The important question, regardless of how much he is getting, is whether he thinks the rate is fair [p. 12].

Leaving the field is perhaps a more radical means of coping with inequity, and its adoption will vary not only with the magnitude of inequity present, but also with Person's tolerance of inequity and his ability to cope with it flexibly. Though it has not been demonstrated, there are probably individual differences in tolerance and flexibility.

6. Person may psychologically distort his inputs and outcomes, increasing or decreasing them as required. Since most individuals are heavily influenced by reality, distortion is generally difficult. It is pretty difficult to distort to oneself that one has a BA degree, that one has been an accountant for 7 years, and that one's salary is $500 per month, for example. However, it is possible to alter the utility

of these. For example, State College is a small, backwoods school with no reputation, or, conversely, State College has one of the best Business Schools in the state and the Dean is an adviser to the Bureau of the Budget. Or, one can consider the fact that $500 per month will buy all of the essential things of life and quite a few luxuries, or, conversely, that it will never permit one to purchase period furniture or a power cruiser.

7. Person may increase, decrease, or distort the inputs and outcomes of Others, or force Other to leave the field. Basically, these means are the same as discussed above, but applied to Other. The direction of change in inputs and outcomes would, however, be precisely opposite to changes effected in Person. Thus, for example, if Person's effort were too low compared to Other's and to his own pay, he might induce Other to decrease his effort instead of increasing his own effort. Or, if he were comparatively poorly qualified for his job, he might try to have his better qualified colleague fired or transferred.

8. Person may change his referent Other when inequity exists. If Person were a draftsman working harder, doing better quality work, and being paid less than Other at the next board, he might eschew further comparisons with Other and pick someone with more nearly the same capability and pay. The ease of doing this would vary considerably with the ubiquity of Other and with the availability of a substitute having some attributes in common with Person.

Not all the means of reducing inequity that have been listed will be equally satisfactory, and the adoption of some may result in very unsteady states. The nature of the input and outcome discrepancies and environmental circumstances may render some means more available than others, as may personality characteristics of Person and Other. To illustrate this we may consider a Person whose effort is high and whose pay is low, and an Other whose effort and pay are low. If Person acts to increase his pay and is successful, he will effectively reduce the inequity; but if he is unsuccessful, as well he might be, given rigid job and wage structures, inequity will continue. Person might, on the other hand, try to reduce his productivity. This, however, might be quite risky if minimal production standards were maintained and unsatisfactory productivity were penalized. There is the further consideration that if Person and Other are both on the same production line, a decrease in effort by Person might affect Other's production and pay, with the result that Other would object to Person's behavior. Another means for Person to reduce his inequity is to try to have Other increase his effort. If Other perceives his and Person's inputs and outcomes in the same way as Person, he might, indeed, accede to this influence and raise his effort. If, to the contrary, he perceives no discrepancy between his and Person's inputs, he may be expected to resist Person strongly. Alternatively, Person could resort to leaving the field, or to distortion, as discussed earlier. If distortion is unilateral on Person's part, it may resolve his inequity, though not Other's. This leads into another interesting aspect of inequity.

Person and Other may or may not constitute a social system, that is, Person may be to Other what Other is to Person, so that they are referents for one another. Or, Other's referent may be someone other than Person, say, an individual X, who is quite irrelevant to Person's social comparisons. When Person and Other do not form a social system, the way in which Person reduces his inequity will have no effect on Other and there will,

therefore, be no feedback effects upon Person. When the two do constitute a social system, the interaction that may take place is of considerable interest. Considering only those instances when Person and Other have identical perceptions of their inputs and outcomes it is a truism that when inequity exists for Person it also exists for Other (though probably not in the same amount since one will be overpaid and the other underpaid). Hence, both will be motivated to reduce the inequity; but it does not follow that they will adopt compatible means. If compatible means are adopted, both will achieve equity. For example, if Person expended little effort and received high pay, while Other's effort and pay were both high, a state of equity could be achieved by Person's increasing his effort somewhat and by Other's reducing his a bit. Or, the two could agree that the easiest solution was for Other to reduce his effort to Person's level. However, this solution might prove inadequate, for other reasons; for example, this might endanger their jobs by reducing production to an economically unprofitable level.

Many possibilities of incompatible solutions exist for Person and Other. Continuing with the preceding example, Person could increase his effort and Other could decrease his. From the point of view of each considered alone, these actions should reduce inequity. When considered simultaneously, however, it is apparent that now Person's effort and pay will be high, whereas Other will expend low effort and receive high pay. A new state of inequity has been created! As a further example, if Person's effort were high and his pay low, while Other's effort were low and his pay high, Person might reduce his own effort while Other was trying to induce the supervisor to increase Person's salary. If Other were unsuccessful in his attempt, a new, but reduced, state of inequity would result. If, on the other hand, Other were successful in obtaining a raise for Person, equity might be established, but a new situation, hardly more comfortable than inequity, would result: Person would have received a pay increment for a decrement in effort.

Private, psychological distortion of one's inputs and outcomes is especially likely to result in unsuccessful reduction of inequity, if done by only one party. For instance, if Person is overcompensated and manages to convince himself that he is not, it will be extremely difficult for Other to convince him, say, that he should work harder. Or, if Other were to convince himself that he was working just as hard as Person, Person could not effectively convince Other to increase his productivity or to take a cut in pay. The very fact that one of the parties is operating at a private, covert level makes it nearly impossible to communicate. The perceptions of the two parties being now different, the fundamental premises that must underlie joint action cannot be agreed upon. Distortion by one party in effect breaks the social system that had previously existed.

SUPPORTING EVIDENCE

The evidence in direct support of the theory of inequity will now be considered. The data that are available may be divided grossly into two types, observational and experimental. Directly supporting evidence is, on the whole, somewhat meager for the reason that little research has been focused on the specific question of job inequity. The work of Zaleznik et al. (1958), Homans (1953, 1961), and Patchen (1959, 1961) has dealt with significant aspects of the problem, but, with the exception of Homans' (1953)

study of clerical employees, the data collected by these researchers are difficult to relate to the present theory.

A Case of Pay Inequity among Clerical Workers (Homans, 1953)

Rather than dealing with two individuals, we are here concerned with two groups of female clerical workers, cash posters and ledger clerks, in one division of a utilities company. Both groups worked in the same large room. Cash posting consisted of recording daily the amounts customers paid on their bills, and management insisted that posting be precisely up to date. It required that cash posters pull customer cards from the many files and make appropriate entries on them. The job, therefore, was highly repetitive and comparatively monotonous, and required little thought but a good deal of physical mobility. Ledger clerks, in contrast, performed a variety of tasks on customer accounts, such as recording address changes, making breakdowns of over- and underpayments, and supplying information on accounts to customers or company people on the telephone. In addition, toward the end of the day, they were required by their supervisor to assist with "cleaning up" cash posting in order that it be current. Compared to the cash posters, "ledger clerks had to do a number of nonrepetitive clerical jobs . . . requiring some thought but little physical mobility." They had a more responsible job.

Ledger clerks were considered to be of higher status than cash posters, since promotion took place from cash poster to ledger clerk. Their weekly pay, however, was identical. In comparison to cash posters, ledger clerks were older and had more seniority and experience.

These are the facts of the situation. In terms of the theory, the following may be stated:

1. The cash posters had lower inputs than the ledger clerks: They were younger, had less seniority and experience, and had less responsible jobs. Their outcomes were in some respects lower than the ledger clerks': Their job had less variety, was more monotonous, required greater physical effort, and had less intrinsic interest. Very importantly, however, their pay was equal to the ledger clerks'.

2. The ledger clerks had higher inputs than the cash posters: They were older, had more seniority and experience, and had more responsible positions. Their outcomes were higher on several counts: Their status was higher, their job had greater variety and interest, and physical effort required was low. Their pay, nonetheless, was the same as the cash posters'. The requirement that they help "clean up" (note the connotation) posting each day introduced ambiguity in their inputs and outcomes. On the one hand, this required greater inputs—that is, having to know two jobs—and, on the other hand, lowered their outcomes by having to do "dirty work" and deflating their self-esteem.

It is clear from the discrepancies between inputs and outcomes that inequities existed. In capsule form, the outcomes of ledger clerks were too low compared to their own inputs and to the inputs and outcomes of cash posters. The evidence is strong that the ledger clerks, at least, felt the inequity. They felt that they ought to get a few dollars more per week to show that their job was more important —in our terms, their greater inputs ought to be paralleled by greater outcomes. On the whole, these clerks did not do much to reduce inequity, though a few complained to their union representative, with, apparently, little effect. However, the workers in this division voted to abandon their independent union for the CIO, and Homans (1953)

intimates that the reason may have been the independent union's inability to force a resolution of the inequity. He further implies that had management perceived and resolved the inequity, the representative function of a union would have been quite superfluous.

A Case of Status Inequity in Supermarkets (Clark, 1958)

We shall be concerned here with the checkout counters in a chain of supermarkets, which are manned by a "ringer" and a "bundler." Ringers are the cashiers who add on the register the sum due from the customer, take his payment, and make change. Bundlers take goods out of the cart and put them in bags to be taken out. Under normal conditions, ringing was a higher status, better paid job, handled by a permanent, full-time employee. Bundling was of lower status and lower pay, and was usually done by part-time employees, frequently youngsters. Furthermore, psychologically, bundlers were perceived as working *for* ringers.

Because customer flow in supermarkets varies markedly from day to day, a preponderance of employees were part-timers. This same fact required that many employees be assigned to checkout counters during rush hours. When this occurred, many ringer-bundler teams were formed, and it is this that resulted in the creation of status inequity, for employees differed considerably in a number of input variables, notably sex, age, and education. Not infrequently, then, a bundler would be directed to work for a ringer whose status (determined by sex, age, education, etc.) was lower. For example, a college male 21 years of age would be ordered to work for a high school girl ringer of 17. Or a college girl would be assigned as a bundler for an older woman with only a grade school education. The resulting status inequities may be described as follows in our theoretical terms: A bundler with higher inputs than a ringer had lower outcomes.

When interviewed by the investigator, the store employees were quite explicit about the inequities that existed. Furthermore, this was true of ringers, as well as bundlers, showing that inequities were felt bilaterally in these cooperative jobs. To restore equity it would have been necessary to form teams such that inputs and outcomes were matched. Clark (1958) has stated the principle in the following manner:

A person's job status (which is determined by the amount of pay, responsibility, variety and absence from interference his job has) should be in line with his social status (which is determined by his sex, age, education, and seniority) [p. 128].

That store employees attempted to reduce existing inequities is evident from the data. The principal means of doing so appeared to be by the bundlers reducing their work speed—that is, by reducing their inputs, which would have effectively decreased inequity since some of their other inputs were too high relative to their own outcomes and to the inputs of the ringers. One girl explicitly stated to the investigator that when she was ordered to bundle for a ringer of lower social status than hers, she deliberately slowed up bundling.

Interestingly, this behavior is nicely reflected in the financial operation of the stores. A substantial part of the total labor cost of operating a supermarket is the cost of manning checkout counters. It follows, therefore, that one should be able to observe a correlation between the incidence of inequities among ringer-bundler teams and the cost of store operations, since the inequity reduction took the form of lowered productivity.

This is indeed what was found. When the eight supermarkets were ranked on labor efficiency[5] and "social ease,"[6] the two measures correlated almost perfectly—that is, the greater the inequity, the greater the cost of operating the stores. To give an example, one of the two stores studied most intensively ranked high in inequity and had a cost of 3.85 man-hours per $100 of sales, whereas the other which ranked low in inequity, had a cost of only 3.04 per $100 of sales. Thus, it cost approximately 27% more to operate the store in which inequities were higher.

A further finding of Clark's is worth reporting, for it gives one confidence that the relative inefficiency of the one store was indeed due to the presence of relatively more inequity. This store went through a period of considerable labor turnover (perhaps as a result of employees leaving the field to reduce inequity), and associated with this was an increase in labor efficiency and an increase in the social ease index. There is, therefore, quasi-experimental evidence that when inequities are reduced, individual productivity increases, with the result that operating costs decrease.

Experiment I (Adams & Rosenbaum, 1962)

One of the more interesting hypotheses derivable from the theory of inequity is that when Person is overpaid in relation to Other, he may reduce the inequity by increasing his inputs. Therefore, an experiment was designed in which one group of subjects was overcompensated

[5]As an index of labor efficiency, Clark (1958) used the number of man-hours per $100 of sales.

[6]"Social ease" is a complex index, devised by Clark (1958), the value of which is basically the number of pairs of part-time employees, out of all possible pairs, whose inputs and outcomes were "in line," according to the definition given in the quotation from Clark.

and one was equitably compensated— that is, one group in which outcomes were too great and one in which outcomes were equitable, given certain inputs, relative to some generalized Other.

The task chosen was a one page controlled association public opinion interview (for example, "Which of these five automobiles do you associate with a rising young junior executive?"), which subjects were to administer in equal numbers to male and female members of the general public. The subjects were under the impression that they were being hired for a real task and that their employment would continue for several months. In actuality, however, they conducted interviews for 2.5 hours only, after which time they were told about the experiment and were paid for their participation.

Two groups of 11 male university students, hired through the college employment office, were used as subjects. Each was paid $3.50 per hour—an amount large enough so that a feeling of overcompensation could be induced, but not so large that it could not also be made to appear equitable. In one group (E), subjects were made to feel quite unqualified to earn $3.50 per hour, because of lack of interviewer training and experience. The other group of subjects (C) were made to feel fully qualified to earn $3.50 per hour, by being informed that they were far better educated than census takers and that education and intelligence were the prime requisites of interviewing. It may be noted that the referent Others for all subjects were trained interviewers at large, not a specific, known person. The complete instructions to the groups were, of course, much more elaborate, but details need not be given here. The critical point is that the E group felt overcompensated, whereas the C group felt fairly paid.

From the theory, it was predicted that the E group would attempt to increase their inputs so as to bring them in line with their outcomes and with the alleged inputs of trained interviewers. Since there was little they could do to increase their training and experience, this left productivity as the principal means of altering inputs. Theoretically, E group subjects could also have tried to reduce their outcomes; this, however, was impossible since the pay was fixed. In sum, then, it was predicted that the E group would obtain more interviews per unit time than the C group. This is what the results demonstrated. Whereas the C group obtained an average of only .1899 interviews per minute, the E group obtained a significantly greater average of .2694, or an average of 42% more $(\chi^2 = 4.55, df = 1, p < .05)$.

Results comparable to these have been obtained by Day (1961) in a laboratory experiment with children who were given training trials in which they pushed a plunger mechanism to obtain M&M candies. The number of candies received varied between 1 and 6 and was directly dependent upon the magnitude of pressure exerted on the plunger. After responses had stabilized, 25 M&Ms were received by each subject on each of five trials regardless of the pressure exerted. Day's data show that a significant number of subjects respond to the increased reward by increased pressure on the overrewarded trials. In terms of our theoretical model, the children in Day's study are comparing their inputs (pressure) and outcomes (M&Ms) during the overrewarded trials with those during the training trials. The latter trials establish a base upon which to determine what constitutes "equity." The "overpayment" of 25 M&M candies results in inequity, which may be reduced by increasing pressure inputs.

TABLE 30–2 Production Scores of Subjects in Experiment II

	Public	Private
Overpaid	67.20	52.43
Equitably paid	59.33	41.50

Experiment II (Arrowood, 1961)

If it is reasonable to suppose that the results of the previously described experiment by Adams and Rosenbaum (1962) were a result of the E subjects' working harder to protect their jobs because they were insecure in the face of their "employer's" low regard for their qualifications, it is reasonable to suppose that the same results would not obtain if subjects were convinced that their "employer" would have no knowledge of their productivity. Conversely, if the theory we have offered is valid, overpaid subjects should produce more than controls, whether they thought the "employer" knew the results of their work or whether they thought he did not.

Following this reasoning, Arrowood (1961) designed a factorial experiment in which subjects from Minneapolis were either overpaid or equitably paid and performed their work under either public or private conditions. The first two conditions were similar to those in Experiment I: Subjects were hired at $3.50 per hour to conduct interviews and were made to feel unqualified or qualified for the job. The public-private distinction was achieved by having subjects either submit their work to the "employer" (the experimenter) or mail it in preaddressed envelopes to New York. In the latter case, subjects were under the impression that the experimenter would never see their work.

The results, shown in Table 30-2, validate the hypothesis tested in Experiment I and permit one to reject the alternative hypothesis. In both the Public and Private conditions, overpaid subjects produced significantly more than equitably paid subjects. The fact that mean production in the Public conditions was significantly greater than in the Private conditions is irrelevant to the hypothesis since there was no significant interaction between the inequity-equity and public-private dimensions.

Experiment III (Adams & Rosenbaum, 1962)

Since the results of the two previous experiments strongly corroborated a derivation from the theory, it was decided to test a further, but related, derivation. The hypothesis was that whereas subjects overpaid *by the hour* would produce more than equitably paid controls, subjects overpaid *on a piecework basis* would produce less than equitably paid controls. The rationale for the latter half of the hypothesis was that because inequity was associated with each *unit* produced, inequity would increase as work proceeded; hence, subjects would strive not so much to *reduce* inequity as to *avoid* increasing it. In other words, because inequity would mount as more units were produced, overpaid piecework subjects would tend to restrict production.

Nine subjects were assigned to each of the following groups: Overpaid $3.50 per hour (H_e), equitably paid $3.50 per hour (H_c), overpaid $.30 per unit (P_e), equitably paid $.30 per unit (P_c). In all major respects, the task and instructions were identical to those in Experiment I.

As may be seen in Table 30-3, the hypothesis received unequivocal support. Overpaid hourly subjects produced more than their controls and overpaid piecework subjects produced less than their controls. The interaction between the inequity-equity and hourly-piecework dimensions is highly significant $(x^2 = 7.11, df = 1, p < .01)$.

TABLE 30–3 Mean Productivity and Median Distribution of Hourly and Piecework Experimental and Control Subjects in Experiment III

	Condition			
	H_e	H_c	P_e	P_c
Mean productivity	.2723	.2275	.1493	.1961
Cases above median	8	4	1	5
Cases below median	1	5	8	4

Experiment IV (Adams, 1963)

The prediction that piecework subjects experiencing wage inequity would have a lower productivity than subjects perceiving their wages as fair was supported by the previous experiment. The rationale for the prediction was that because dissonance is linked with units of production, dissonance would increase as more units were produced, and, consequently, subjects would attempt to avoid increasing dissonance by restricting production. There is, however, an alternative explanation that would account for the same manifest behavior. It is entirely possible for subjects to *reduce* dissonance by increasing their effort on the production of each unit, for example, by increasing the quality of their work, which would have the effect of increasing the production time per unit and, therefore, have the consequence of reducing productivity. In terms of the theoretical framework presented earlier, this explanation assumes that pieceworkers would reduce their dissonance by increasing their inputs, very much as the hourly workers. Only the mode of increasing inputs varies: Whereas hourly workers increase inputs on a *quantitative* dimension, pieceworkers increase them on a *qualitative* dimension.

Unfortunately, the task used in Experiment III did not lend itself to measuring quality of work. In the present experiment the work performed by subjects was so designed as to permit measurement of both amount of work and quality of work. The specific hypothesis tested is: Pieceworkers who perceive that they are inequitably overpaid will perform better quality work and have lower productivity than pieceworkers who are paid the same rate and perceive they are equitably paid.

The interviewing task used in the previous experiments was modified so as to permit the measurement of quality. The modification consisted of making the three principal questions open-end questions. As an example, one question was "Does a man who owns a shelter have the moral right to exclude others from it, if they have no shelter?" (Yes or No), which was followed by, "What are your reasons for feeling that way?" The subjects task was to obtain as much information as possible from a respondent on the latter part of the question. The measure of work quality thus was the amount of recorded information elicited from respondents. More specifically, the dependent measure of quality was the number of words per interview recorded in the blank spaces following the three open-end questions. As before, the measure of productivity was the number of interviews obtained per minute during a total period of approximately 2 hours.

Twenty-eight subjects were used, half randomly assigned to a condition in which they were made to feel overpaid, half to a condition in which the identical piecework rate was made to appear equitable. The results supported the hypotheses. First, as in the previous experiment, the productivity of subjects in whom feelings of inequitable overpayment were induced was significantly lower than that of control subjects. Productivity rates for these groups were .0976 and .1506, respectively ($t = 1.82$, $p < .05$, one-tailed test). Second, work quality was significantly higher among overpaid subjects than among controls (69.7 versus 45.3, $t = 2.48$, $p < .02$, two-tailed test).

These quality and productivity data support the hypothesis that under piecework conditions subjects who perceive that they are overpaid will tend to reduce dissonance by increasing their inputs on each *unit* so as to improve its quality and, as a result, will decrease their productivity. Thus, the alternative explanation for the results obtained with pieceworkers in Experiment III has some validity. This is not to say that the dissonance avoiding hypothesis originally offered is invalid, for if a job does not permit an increase of work input *per unit produced*, dissonance avoidance may well occur. This, however, remains to be demonstrated; the fact that we were unable to measure quality of work in Experiment III does not mean that subjects did not reduce dissonance by some means, including the improvement of quality, on each unit produced.

CONCLUSION

We have offered a general theory of inequity, reviewed its implications, and presented evidence in support of it. Although the support given the theory is gratifying, additional data are required to test particular aspects of it. In addition, research is needed to determine what variables guide the choice of comparison persons. While this is a theoretical and research endeavor in its own right, it would contribute much to the understanding of inequity.

The analysis of inequity in terms of discrepancies between a man's job inputs and job outcomes, and the behavior that may result from these discrepancies, should result in a better understanding of one aspect of social conflict and should increase the degree of control that may be exercised over it. In moving toward an understanding of inequity, we increase our knowledge of our most basic productive resource, the human organism.

References

Abegglen, J. G. *The Japanese factory*. Glencoe, Ill.: Free Press, 1958.

Adams, J. S. The measurement of perceived equity in pay differentials. Unpublished manuscript, General Electric Company, Behavioral Research Service, 1961.

Adams, J. S. Productivity and work quality as a function of wage inequities. *Industr. Relat., Berkeley*, 1963.

Adams, J. S., & Rosenbaum, W. B. The relationship of worker productivity to cognitive dissonance about wage inequities. *J. appl. Psychol.*, 1962, 46, 161–164.

Arrowood, A. J. Some effects on productivity of justified and unjustified levels of reward under public and private conditions. Unpublished doctoral dissertation, University of Minnesota, Department of Psychology, 1961.

Clark, J. V. A preliminary investigation of some unconscious assumptions affecting labor efficiency in eight supermarkets. Unpublished doctoral dissertation, Harvard Graduate School of Business Administration, 1958.

Day, C. R. Some consequences of increased reward following establishment of output-reward expectation level. Unpublished master's thesis, Duke University, 1961.

Festinger, L. A theory of social comparison processes. *Hum. Relat.*, 1954, 7, 117–140.

Festinger, L. *A theory of cognitive dissonance*. Evanston, Ill.: Row, Peterson, 1957.

Homans, G. C. Status among clerical workers. *Hum. Organiz.*, 1953, 12, 5–10.

Homans, G. C. *Social behavior: Its elementary forms.* New York: Harcourt, Brace, & World, 1961.

Jaques, E. *Measurement of responsibility.* London: Tavistock, 1956.

Jaques, E. *Equitable payment.* New York: Wiley, 1961. (a)

Jaques, E. An objective approach to pay differentials. *Time motion Stud.*, 1961, 10, 25–28. (b)

Jeffrey, T. E., & Jones, L. V. *Compensation-plan preferences: An application of psychometric scaling.* Chapel Hill: University of North Carolina, Psychometric Laboratory, 1961.

Merton, R. K., & Kitt, Alice S. Contributions to the theory of reference group behavior. In R. K. Merton & P. F. Lazarsfeld (Eds.), *Studies in the scope and method of "The American Soldier."* Glencoe, Ill.: Free Press, 1950. Pp. 40–105.

Patchen, M. *Study of work and life satisfaction: Report II. Absences and attitudes toward work experiences.* Ann Arbor: Institute for Social Research, 1959.

Patchen, M. *The choice of wage comparisons.* Englewood Cliffs, N. J.: Prentice-Hall, 1961.

Stouffer, S. A., Suchman, E. A., DeVinney, L. C., Star, Shirley A., & Williams, R. M., Jr. *The American soldier: Adjustment during Army life.* Princeton: Princeton Univer. Press, 1949.

Zaleznik, A., Christensen, C. R., & Roethlisberger, F. J. *The motivation, productivity and satisfaction of workers.* Boston: Harvard University, Graduate School of Business Administration, 1958.

POWER PROCESSES IN FORMAL ORGANIZATIONS

Power has been defined as potential for influence that is based on one person's ability and willingness to sanction another person by manipulating rewards and punishments important to the other person. Power is based on resources that allow one person to mediate between another person and the attainment of his goals.[1] As noted, power in informal groups is based upon the characteristics of individuals, individual differences that can function as resources to be used in sanctioning others. It is the differential distribution and use of such characteristics-resources that give rise in informal groups to a power structure, as the readings by Blau (16), Levinger (23), and Bales (24) have described.

By contrast, power in formal groups is at least in part determined by design—by the way in which formal positions are defined. Most organizations are designed in such a manner that a hierarchy of positions is created: one position is defined as having the power to control another. A supervisory position, for example, is defined as being more powerful than that of a worker; and, in accordance with this definition, sanctioning powers are attached to the position. A supervisor, for example, may be allowed to evaluate the work of his subordinates, determining by these evaluations who receives what rate of pay and who is to be recommended for promotion. He may also be allowed to determine which workers take which shifts and to determine their vacation and holiday schedule. Such powers are attached to the position; they are available to any person who occupies the position, regardless of his personal qualities. Men who design organizations and who are concerned with creating a rational structure attempt to create structures in which power is allocated to positions in such a manner that each position occupant will have power sufficient to carry out his responsibilities. An organizational hierarchy presumes a graded distribution of power from lower to higher officials, with power increasing as scope of responsibility is enlarged.

No organization ever succeeds, however, in completely controlling all sources of power or rationally allocating power among its positions. There are two reasons why this is the case. First, in the organization's allocation of resources to positions, some members inevitably obtain access to resources that can be used in ways not intended by the organizational designers. For example, access to information is an important resource that can become the basis for sanctioning and controlling others. A position such as secretary may give its occupant access to important information that she may attempt to use in ways not intended by the persons who planned the formal distribution of power and responsibility.

[1]See pp. 193–194.

Second, we come again to the chief thesis of the social system analyst, who reminds us that positions are filled by persons and that persons possess diverse and variable characteristics, some of which may become the basis for informal power differences in formal organizations. Differences among individuals in intelligence, training, skills, attractiveness, and other respects can serve as resources that sometimes supplement and sometimes contradict the formal distribution of power and privilege.[2]

Authority   Max Weber has pointed out that in his experience no organization

. . . voluntarily limits itself to the appeal to material or affectual motives as a basis for guaranteeing its continuance. In addition, every such system attempts to establish and to cultivate the belief in its "legitimacy."

In other words, no organization is likely to be content with establishing a power structure; in addition, it attempts to create an authority structure. *Authority* is defined as legitimate power. *Legitimacy* has to do with the existence of a set of social norms that defines situations or behaviors as correct or appropriate. Thus, to speak of legitimate power is to speak of (1) a set of persons or positions linked by power relations and (2) a set of norms or rules governing the distribution and exercise of power and the response to it.

In informal groups, we refer to the exercise of power as legitimate to the extent that there emerges a set of norms and beliefs among the members subordinate to the power that the distribution and exercise of power is acceptable to them and is regarded as appropriate. The emergence of such norms significantly alters the control structure, as Blau and I have noted:

Given the development of social norms that certain orders of superiors ought to be obeyed, the members of the group will enforce compliance with these orders as part of their enforcement of conformity to group norms. The group's demand that orders of the superior be obeyed makes obedience partly independent of his coercive power or persuasive influence over individual subordinates and thus transforms these other kinds of social control into authority.[3]

In short, a set of dyadic power relations between the superior and each of his subordinates is transformed by the emergence of legitimacy norms into a multiperson control structure, with each subordinate now participating in the control of each of his colleagues. Another way of describing these important developments is to say that a stable role structure has emerged that guides the expectations of participants, making it possible for leaders to lead and for followers to follow, without the generation of disruptive emotional responses. Further, the emergence of legitimacy norms helps to render power relations more impersonal and reduces the tensions associated with the exercise of interpersonal power. As Thibaut and Kelley suggest, in an authority structure, in contrast with a power structure,

Nonadherence is met with the use of power to attempt to produce conformity, but the influence appeal is to a supra-individual value ("Do it for the group" or "Do it because

[2]See, for example, David Mechanic, "Sources of power of lower participants in complex organization," *Administrative Science Quarterly*, 7 (December, 1962) , 349–362.

[3]Peter M. Blau and W. Richard Scott, *Formal Organizations: A Comparative Approach*, San Francisco: Chandler Publishing Company, 1962, p. 29.

it's good") rather than to personal interests ("Do it for me" or "Do it and I'll do something for you") .[4]

For all these reasons—involvement of subordinate participants in the control system, development of differentiated expectations among participants, impersonalization of power processes with consequent reduction of interpersonal tensions—authority structures tend to be much more stable and effective control systems than power structures.

But there is another equally important consequence of the legitimation process. The emergence of social norms not only allows a greater measure of control of subordinates by the power wielder but also operates to regulate and circumscribe the exercise of power by the power wielder. Emerson has noted that the emergence of legitimacy norms among subordinates allows them to act as a coalition vis-à-vis the power wielder, defining the arena within which he can appropriately exercise his power.[5] That is, legitimacy norms specify the orders to which subordinates are expected to comply—hence, supporting his exercise of power—but also specify the demands that the power wielder cannot appropriately make of subordinates—hence, limiting his exercise of power. As Thibaut and Kelley note:

Norms are, in the first place, rules about behavior. They tell each person what is expected of him in certain situations, and in so doing they indirectly indicate requests that others may not properly make of him. In this way he is protected from subjugation to another's whimsically exercised power.[6]

In sum, the legitimacy norms cut both ways: they permit greater control of subordinates within certain areas defined as appropriate areas of control, and they limit and regulate the exercise of power to this specified arena. We may conclude that authority is legitimate power and that legitimate power is normatively regulated power.

Two Types of Authority: Endorsed Power and Authorized Power   At this point, a critical question must be raised. We have said that social norms regulating power relations provide the basis for legitimate control structures. But whose norms—norms defined and enforced by what group of participants—are we to focus on? In most informal groups, there is only one possible source of social norms: the set of participants who are subject to and hence subordinates of the power wielder. But an important characteristic of formal organizations is the presence of persons superordinate to as well as subordinate to a given power wielder. Norms may be developed and/or enforced by persons *superior* to the power wielder in a formal organization. In fact, this is the significance of the existence of a hierarchy of offices. As Weber states:

The principles of office hierarchy and of levels of graded authority mean a firmly ordered system of super- and subordination in which *there is a supervision of the lower offices by the higher ones.*[7]

To distinguish these two types of authority, we may refer to authority legiti-

[4]John W. Thibaut and Harold H. Kelley, *The Social Psychology of Groups*, New York: Wiley, 1959, p. 129.

[5]Richard M. Emerson, "Power-dependence relations," *American Sociological Review*, 27 (February, 1962) , 37–39.

[6]Thibaut and Kelley, p. 134.

[7]Max Weber, *From Max Weber: Essays in Sociology*, edited by Hans H. Gerth and C. Wright Mills, New York: Oxford, 1946, p. 197. Emphasis ours.

mated by social norms enforced by persons subordinate to the power wielder as *endorsed power* and to authority legitimated by social norms enforced by persons superior to the power wielder as *authorized power.*

In the article "Organizational evaluation and authority" my colleagues, Dornbusch, Busching, and Laing, and I develop a conception of authority as authorized power based on an analysis of the evaluation process in formal organization. (See Reading 31) The basic premise underlying our conception is that if power is to be employed to control the behavior of others, evaluation, however crudely carried out, is necessary. Someone must in some manner tell a person what he is expected to do; someone must determine the extent to which he has conformed with these demands and must reward or punish him accordingly. Since evaluation is the crucial process involved in the act of attempting to control the behavior of others, authority can be defined in terms of the right (authorized power) to activate one or another component of the evaluation process. The components identified in our discussion are *allocation* (telling a person what he is expected to do); *criteria setting* (determining what standards are to be employed in evaluating his behavior); *sampling* (deciding what aspects of his behavior or which products of his behavior to inspect); and *appraising* (comparing his behavior with the standard to arrive at an evaluation). These components of the evaluation process may be exercised by one person, or, as often happens in complex organizations, each component may be assigned to a different person.

As noted in this discussion, authorized power may or may not be endorsed by the norms of the persons subordinate to the power wielder. In some cases, the norms of subordinate participants will support the authorized exercise of power; in other cases they will not. Because authorized power and endorsed power refer to the existence of norms enforced by participants in differing locations with respect to the power wielder, it seems reasonable to argue that authorized systems that are also endorsed enjoy greater legitimacy than power systems that are only endorsed or power systems that are only authorized. Most students of power in formal organizations have dealt exclusively with what we have called endorsed power. However, to do so is, in our opinion, to neglect an important structural feature that helps distinguish formal from informal power structures, namely, the presence of a hierarchy of officials, with senior members regulating the exercise of power by persons below them in the hierarchy. Authorized power is not always *formal*, as we have defined this term, but it frequently is formal, because organizational superiors are more likely to support positional rights as against personal rights in the interests of preserving the integrity of hierarchical arrangements.

The alert reader will have noticed that we are again talking about the importance of evaluation as a social process. We have already described the significant role this process plays in status phenomena, and now we are concerned with its operation in systems of control. It is important to note, however, that although the process is the same in both cases, the objects of evaluation may be different. In the case of status processes, personal or positional characteristics are the object of evaluation. Characteristics are viewed as important, as we have noted, because of their presumed relation to behavior; but it is characteristics, not behavior, that are evaluated. As Chester Barnard has written:

It is the presumption of capacities and limitations without necessary regard to the immediate concrete activities of the individual that is the essential feature of systematic status. The emphasis is on the potentialities of behavior, not necessarily upon the immediately observable behavior.[8]

There is no question that much of the evaluation and sanctioning behavior in organizations is related to the status characteristics of participants. Purely on the basis of their high education, their advanced seniority, or their preferred ethnic background, some participants receive high evaluations and their attendant rewards. It is presumed that because of their valued characteristics they are making valued contributions to the organization. Such behavior on the part of the organization's evaluators both creates and perpetuates status differentials among participants. These presumptions on the part of organizational evaluators are not necessarily ill-founded. We noted in our earlier discussion of status processes in organizations that the rewards attached to high status not only motivate persons to seek higher levels in the organization but also encourage those who occupy these positions to behave responsibly for fear of losing their advantaged position.[9] Status systems are a source of control no less than power systems.

Returning to the authority processes, the object of evaluation described in Reading 31 is not the characteristics of individuals but is their behavior or task performance. It is apparent that most formal organizations in industrialized societies are unwilling to base evaluations and the distributions of sanctions exclusively on the status characteristics displayed by participants. Such evaluations are at best indirect evaluations of performance. Most organizations seek more direct performance measures. Indeed, it is within formal organizations that the art of performance evaluation—the precision with which task allocations are made, the care with which standards are set, the concern for reliability of sampling, and the accuracy of making appraisals—has reached its highest development.

Professionals in Organizations   Increasingly professional people no longer function as solo practitioners, but are employed by organizations. Physicians join clinics and spend more of their time dispensing care in hospitals: scientists no longer work in a basement laboratory but are employed by industrial and research organizations; and although a good many lawyers still hang out their shingles and establish private practice, an increasing number find their niche in government departments, law departments of corporations, and large law firms. Generally speaking, a *professional* person is one who has undergone considerable advanced training to prepare himself to carry out nonroutine, socially valued tasks. The nature of his work is such that he is expected to exercise discretion. Therefore, he demands and usually receives considerable autonomy. His work is sufficiently technical that he prefers to be evaluated only by persons who have had comparable training—in short, by his professional colleagues.[10]

[8]Chester I. Barnard, "Functions and pathology of status systems in formal organizations," in William Foote Whyte (ed.), *Industry and Society*, New York: McGraw-Hill, 1946.

[9]See p. 352.

[10]These brief comments on the type of work performed by professionals and appropriate work arrangements for them are elaborated in Reading 33.

In fact, one of the chief objectives of professional associations is to organize practitioners for self-regulation and, in so doing, attempt to protect individual practitioners from inappropriate "lay" (nonprofessional) evaluations.[11]

Because of the nature of the work that they do and because through their professional organizations they have achieved sufficient power to in large measure determine the nature of the conditions under which they work, professionals create authority problems for the organizations within which they work. One attempt to devise appropriate organizational arrangements for accommodating the demands and needs of professionals is the staff-line structure, previously described in Reading 29. The staff-line solution—if such it can be called, given Dalton's description of the problems associated with its operation—is, however, only appropriate when professional employees are seen as supplemental to rather than directly responsible for performing the major organizational tasks. In organizations where professionals are directly involved in achieving the primary goals of the organization—as are professors in universities, scientists in research organizations, and physicians in clinics—other arrangements are necessary. Burton Clark in Reading 32 provides a general description and analysis of emerging control systems in American universities. Universities should not be viewed as necessarily typical of other professional organizations, and the arrangements which Clark describes do not exhaust organizational designs for accommodating their professional employees, but his discussion does illuminate the problems associated with the evaluation and control of highly specialized professional employees and provides a lucid description of the complex authority arrangements developing in this one important type of organization.

Oligarchical Processes in Organizations   There is a tendency within all formal organizations toward *oligarchy*—that is, the concentration of power in the hands of a small minority of the participants. These tendencies prevail in large part because of the structural arrangements which develop within organizations. In the interests of effectiveness and efficiency, there occurs a differentiation of functions such that certain positions are allowed to make policy decisions, determine rules and operating procedures, and control and coordinate activities, while other positions are excluded from these activities. The superior positions inevitably gain control over the communication channels, so that they can determine the content of information flowing through the system. Individuals who occupy these positions soon come to enjoy a greater knowledge of the functioning of the organization, and their technical expertise tends to make them indispensable. Also, because status prerogatives tend to go hand in hand with power, officials occupying these superordinate positions are reluctant to relinquish them and to "step down" from their high offices. Conversely, individuals who are excluded from the upper positions and, hence, from participation in the policy, planning, and control functions tend to become relatively ignorant of the organization's operations over time and generally apathetic or indifferent to its functioning.

[11]See William J. Goode, "Community within a community: The professions," *American Sociological Review*, 22 (April, 1957), pp. 194–200.

Such considerations as these led the German sociologist Robert Michels to formulate "the iron law of oligarchy" in the following terms:

It is organization which gives birth to the dominion of the elected over the electors, of the mandataries over the mandators, of the delegates over the delegators. Who says organization, says oligarchy.[12]

Oligarchical tendencies constitute more of a problem for some types of organizations than for others. In the case of many business and commercial organizations, it is expected that a small subset of participants will have primary responsibility for determining the goals of the organization; other persons contribute their services in return for incentives—for example, wages and salaries—unrelated to these goals. However, other types of organizations such as political parties, unions, and professional associations come into existence in order to serve the interests of their members. The egalitarian ideology and objectives of these organizations would lead one to expect them to be democratically governed by their membership. Indeed, most such organizations develop democratic mechanisms by which the will of the majority can be expressed in the setting of the organization's goals. Nevertheless, even within this latter type of organization, an oligarchy tends to arise. The need for efficient administration to insure success in bargaining for unions or in elections for political parties encourages the development of a bureaucratic machinery with effective control of the organization centralized in the hands of a small elite.

Michels argues that it is not simply democratic procedures which are endangered by oligarchical processes but the original goals which the organization was created to pursue. In his own study of the Social Democratic Party in pre-World War I Germany, Michels noted that the radical programs of the party became increasingly modified and conservative once bureaucratic hierarchies had developed. Such changes transpired because the leaders, interested in preserving and increasing the organization's strength—which was the basis of their own power—abandoned radical objectives in favor of more moderate ones that did not threaten the organization's survival in a society hostile to the original objectives. Disagreements and dissent were stifled in the interests of preserving party strength and harmony. In this manner, a preoccupation with means results in a transformation of ends. Michels provides a classic statement of the central tenet of the social-system analysts of organizations in the following summary:

Thus, from a means, organization becomes an end. To the institutions and qualities which at the outset were destined simply to ensure the good working of the party machine (subordination, the harmonious cooperation of individual members, hierarchical relationships, discretion, propriety of conduct), a greater importance comes ultimately to be attached than to the productivity of the machine. Henceforward, the sole preoccupation is to avoid anything which may clog the machinery.[13]

Michels thus poses the following dilemma: a party or a union must build a strong organization and assure its survival to achieve its objectives, yet preoccupation with such organizational problems leads to the surrender of these very objectives. Experience since Michels' time generally tends to validate his pessimistic conclusions. Most unions, most professional associations and other types of voluntary associations, and most political parties tend to exhibit oligarchical

---

[12]Robert Michels, *Political Parties* (tr. by Edan and Cedar Paul), Glencoe, Ill.: Free Press, 1949, p. 418. (Originally published in 1915.)
[13]Michels, p. 390.

leadership structures with the democratic machinery established to prevent such arrangements functioning primarily as a feeble device allowing rank-and-file participants to ratify ("rubber stamp") executive decisions and "elect" slates of nominees running unopposed for office.[14]

On the other hand, there is some little evidence which suggests that Michels may have overstated his conclusions. First, the tendencies which he described as characteristic of *all* organizations are particularly applicable to only a subset of organizations. An important condition for the operation of the processes described by Michels is the presence of a hostile environment—that is, an environment within which the organization cannot pursue its stated objectives without endangering its own survival. Such an environment was clearly present for the German Social Democratic Party analyzed by Michels, since their original objectives were revolutionary and hence not acceptable to the traditional power structures of German society. Labor unions in their early days were also confronted by much opposition—from employers, from the state and federal governments, and from the public in general—but unions are now an accepted part of the industrial scene, and such wholesale opposition is no longer a fact of their existence. With reduction in levels of opposition to a given organization, some of the pressures toward oligarchical developments should be reduced—for example, leaders should not be able to argue that the organization's very survival depends on their presenting a united front to the "enemy" with consequent need for suppression of dissent.

Other types of pressures toward oligarchical tendencies are also sometimes mitigated in particular circumstances. For example, it sometimes happens in high status occupations such as printing, university teaching, and professional acting that no particular prestige is associated with the holding of office. Officers are willing and sometimes eager to step down from leadership positions after serving their terms.[15] Also, in the case of one union, the International Typographical Union, special conditions analyzed in detail by Lipset and his colleagues have created an occupational community among printers which acts to support participation in political activity among rank-and-file members, helps to keep them informed about current issues, and serves as an important channel of communication among members unregulated by the leadership groups. These and other factors have helped to create and maintain a two-party democratic system for choosing leaders in contested elections and for expressing membership sentiment on important issues in this union.[16] This all suggests that tendencies toward oligarchy in organizations originally designed to serve the interests of members, though prevalent, are not inevitable.

[14]See, for example, Editors of *The Yale Law Journal*, "The American Medical Association: Power, purpose, and politics in organized medicine," *The Yale Law Journal*, 63 (May, 1954), 938-1022; John R. Coleman, "The compulsive pressures of democracy in unionism," *American Journal of Sociology*, 61 (May, 1956), 519-526; and Bernard Barber, "Participation and mass apathy in associations," in Alvin W. Gouldner (ed.), *Studies in Leadership*, New York: Harpers, 1950, pp. 477-504.

[15]Seymour Martin Lipset, "The political process in trade unions: A theoretical statement," in Walter Galenson and Seymour Martin Lipset (eds.), *Labor and Trade Unionism: An Interdisciplinary Reader*, New York: Wiley, 1960, pp. 216-242; and Leonard I. Pearlin and Henry E. Richards, "Equity: A Study of Union Democracy," in Galenson and Lipset, pp. 265-281.

[16]Seymour Martin Lipset. Martin A. Trow, and James S. Colemen, *Union Democracy*, Glencoe, Ill.: Free Press, 1956. See also, Alice Cook, *Union Democracy: Practice and Ideal*, Ithaca, N.Y.: Cornell University Press, 1963; and David Edelstein, "An organizational theory of union democracy," *American Sociological Review*, 32 (February, 1967), 19-31.

Finally, Michels and his followers may have let their own pessimistic outlook color their entire analysis of these issues. As Gouldner suggests:

> When . . . Michels spoke of the "iron law of oligarchy," he attended solely to the ways in which organizational needs inhibit democratic possibilities. But the very same evidence to which he called attention could enable us to formulate the very opposite theorem—the "iron law of democracy." Even as Michels himself saw, if oligarchical waves repeatedly wash away the bridges of democracy, this eternal recurrence can happen only because men doggedly rebuild them after each inundation. Michels chose to dwell on only one aspect of this process, neglecting to consider this other side. There cannot be an iron law of oligarchy, however, unless there is an iron law of democracy.[17]

[17]Alvin W. Gouldner, "Metaphysical pathos and the theory of bureaucracy," *American Political Science Review*, 49 (June, 1955) , 506.

31   Organizational Evaluation and Authority

W. Richard Scott, Sanford M. Dornbusch, Bruce C. Busching, and James D. Laing

This paper presents a conception of authority and authority systems, and a theory predicting the instability of certain kinds of authority systems.[*] Empirical studies designed to explore the utility of the conception and to test hypotheses derived from the theory are presently under way in a number of organizations. In a forthcoming monograph and later papers, we shall discuss the operationalization of our concepts and report empirical findings.[1]

[*]Only the first half of this paper concerned with the development of a conception of authority is reprinted here. [Ed.]

[1]This research project is supported by National Science Foundation Grant G23990. Collaborators on the project are Joseph Berger, Santo F. Camilleri, Bernard P. Cohen, and Morris Zelditch, Jr. We are indebted for suggestions to Kathryn U. Barchas, Patricia Barchas, Marjorie J. Seashore, James C. Moore, and Thomas R. Burns.

An early version of this paper, "Evaluation Processes and Authority Structures," was read at the Annual Meetings of the American Sociological Association in Chicago, September, 1965.

The conception of authority presented here is based on the process by which performance evaluations of organizational participants are made. The conception is believed to be useful as a descriptive and analytic tool, independent of the theory. Our intent has been to develop a formulation which is sufficiently abstract to be applicable to a wide variety of concrete systems in many types of organizations and specific enough to be useful in guiding the collection of empirical data.

The theory locates certain inconsistencies and deficiencies in the evaluation of the performance of an organizational participant that make the authority system incompatible with the participant's achievement of his personal goals. This incompatibility is predicted to be a sufficient condition for internal pressures for change in the authority system; i.e., for instability of the system.

Reprinted from W. Richard Scott, Sanford M. Dornbusch, Bruce C. Busching, and James D. Laing, "Organizational evaluation and authority," *Administrative Science Quarterly*, 12 (June, 1967) , 93–105, by permission of the *Administrative Science Quarterly* and the authors.

Both conception and theory are limited in scope by the following conditions:

1. Organizational sanctions are distributed, at least in part, on the basis of evaluations made of participants.

2. Evaluators who influence the distribution of organizational sanctions attempt to base their evaluations, at least in part, on the performance of organizational tasks by participants.

3. Participants place some value on the evaluations of their task performance made by these evaluators.

The first and second conditions delimit the kind of organizations to which this conception of authority applies. The first condition excludes organizations in which sanctions are distributed independently of any evaluation of participants. (For example, where all rewards are distributed equally among participants.) The second condition excludes organizations in which, although sanctions may be distributed on the basis of evaluations, no attempt is made to base these evaluations even in part on how well or how poorly participants perform in organizational tasks. Thus, this condition excludes organizations in which evaluations are based entirely on status characteristics (such as ethnicity or seniority) or on other nonperformance criteria, even though in some cases these criteria may be related to performance. These conditions exclude very few organizations, however, at least in industrialized societies.

The third condition insures that the motivational basis of the theory is present by further delimiting the scope of the theory to those participants within the organization who place some value on the organizational sanctions themselves. It does require that they value the *performance evaluations* made of them by those who influence these sanctions. If performance evaluations were of no consequence to participants, they could ignore negative evaluations and could

hardly be expected to become concerned about inadequacies in the way performance evaluations are made. (A rich boy working as a lark.) This condition, like the first two, is not very limiting. In an organizational context, most participants value their performance evaluations because at least some of the attendant sanctions are important to them. Furthermore, performance evaluations often possess symbolic value of their own, in part because of their importance to the development and maintenance of one's self-conception.[2]

Although based on the work of many predecessors, the conception described here has some elements of novelty. Comparisons with previous perspectives are made after defining the concept, and then the theory is presented.

AUTHORITY AND AUTHORITY SYSTEMS

Authority as Authorized Control

In this paper the concept of authority is defined in terms of authorization to engage in certain attempts at control. One participant has authority over another to the extent that his control attempts are "authorized"; i.e., would be supported by superiors in the organization. A participant who is authorized to exercise a given control attempt over another is said to have an *authority right* over the other with regard to that attempt. Four different kinds of control attempts can be identified; when authorized, these constitute authority rights.

The process by which the performance of organizational participants is evaluated plays two major roles in this concept of authority. First, its importance is seen in the types of control attempts identified.

[2]S. F. Miyamoto and Sanford M. Dornbusch, A Test of Interactionist Hypotheses in Self-Conception, *American Journal of Sociology*, 61 (1956), 399–403; L. G. Reeder, G. A. Donohue, and A. Biblarz, Conceptions of Self and Others, *American Journal of Sociology*, 66 (1960), 153–159.

These control attempts, and therefore the authority rights themselves, are chosen to embody the main components of the evaluation process: allocating, criteria setting, sampling, and appraising. These rights are identified in part because they are often assigned in various combinations to different participants. (The superintendent may allocate the job, engineers may set the criteria for acceptable tolerance limits, foremen may select the sample to be evaluated, and inspectors may be the appraisers.) Also, each of these rights can become a locus of problems in the authority system. Although other rights can be constructed within the general definition of an authority right, this set is sufficient for the analysis of most authority systems.

Second, the evaluation process is basic to this concept of authority since authorization stems from *significant evaluators*—those whose evaluations influence the distribution of organizational sanctions. By definition, A is said to be authorized to exercise a given control attempt over B with respect to a given task to the extent that:

1. the significant evaluators of A, if aware that A was attempting this kind of control over B, would not negatively evaluate A for making the attempt, and

2. the significant evaluators of all participants whose compliance is necessary for the success of A's attempt to control B, if aware of noncompliance to the attempt, would negatively evaluate those not complying.

Note that this general definition allows for varying degrees of authorization. A's authorization is incomplete if, for example, some evaluators require, while others prohibit, compliance with A's control attempts. Problems arising from incomplete authorization are considered later.

Authority Rights

The four authority rights can now be defined by applying the general definition

to each of the kinds of control attempts. The first criterion in this general definition of an authority right applies consistently to A for each of the authority rights. Under the second criterion, the participants whose compliance is necessary for the success of A's control attempts vary according to the specific authority right under consideration and must be specified in defining each right. In these definitions, and throughout the rest of the paper, "evaluator" and "evaluation" refer only to *significant* evaluators and evaluations.

To assign a goal is simply to give an individual the task of attempting to achieve that goal. An *allocating right* is the right to assign an organizational goal to a participant. (For example, an employer assigns a typist the task of typing a manuscript.) A has the right to allocate to B to the extent that: (1) A would not be negatively evaluated for allocating, and (2) B would be negatively evaluated for noncompliance with A's allocation.

Allocations vary in the amount of discretion they permit the recipient in performing the task. To facilitate the discussion, two polar types on this continuum are identified:

1. *Directive*, in which the particular operations to be performed are specified, leaving the performer minimal discretion in determining how to proceed. (For example, a typist is told to type a letter from dictation.)

2. *Delegation*, in which only the characteristics of the desired end result are specified, with the performer allowed to make the decisions on how to proceed. (For example, a typist is told to answer a letter.)

It is quite possible for occupants of a given position to have the right to allocate a given task only by directive or only by delegation. (Private physicians may be authorized to allocate to resident physicians in a hospital only by delegation, while the residents are authorized to allocate certain medical routines to clinical clerks only by directive.) Approximations of these two types of allocations can usually be distinguished empirically, but rarely are they perfectly represented. Directives cannot be detailed enough to specify all operations of the performance to be carried out; some decisions are always left to the performer. Thus, even the typist told to follow a standard format in the preparation of letters may still be allowed to determine which sheet of paper to use and the order in which the letters are to be prepared. Likewise, delegations do not usually allow the performer complete discretion, although, if genuine, they will allow him considerable latitude. Many allocations appear to be delegations to a naive observer, but because they occur in the context of an understood set of standard operating procedures, they are actually directives. For example, when an intern is told by a resident to "Bring this patient's fever down," he may know from past experience that he is to carry out a set of established procedures. Misunderstandings among participants can occur when directives are mistaken for delegations and vice versa, and can cause problems in the evaluation of performances.

A *criteria-setting right* is the right to specify those performance properties to be considered, their weights or relative importance, and the standards to be used in determining a performance evaluation. Those holding this right, therefore, are authorized to determine which properties of the performance of another will be considered and what evaluation is merited by any given level of performance. (For evaluating a manuscript typist, the criteria-setter may decide that, with no errors, a speed of at least forty words per minute is necessary for an evaluation of "good," and a minimum of sixty words per minute is required for "excellent.") A has the right to set criteria for B to the extent that: (1) A would not be nega-

tively evaluated for setting criteria, and (2) B's appraiser would be negatively evaluated by his own evaluator for failure to use A's criteria in evaluating B.

The *outcome* of a task performance is the actual end result of a performance, in contrast to the desired end result, defined by the goal. A performance evaluation may be based on assessment of the characteristics of the performance of the task operations or on assessment of the characteristics of the task outcome. In either case, information on the actual performance or the outcome must be obtained. A *sampling right* is the right to select aspects of performances or outcomes that will be observed to provide information for an evaluation. (For sampling a manuscript typist's work, the sampler decides to inspect every fourth page.) A has the right to sample B's performance to the extent that: (1) A would not be negatively evaluated for sampling, (2.1) B would be negatively evaluated for not allowing the observations specified by A, and (2.2) the appraiser would be negatively evaluated if he did not use information from the sample specified by A in evaluating B.

An *appraising right* is the right to decide how the level of performance is to be inferred from the sample and to apply the criteria to arrive at a performance evaluation. (The appraiser judges the manuscript typist's work to be excellent on the basis of number of completed pages, a count of errors in the sample, and the criteria that accuracy is a primary and speed a secondary criterion of performance.) Since, as noted earlier, only significant evaluations are considered, participants holding the appraising right are authorized to make performance evaluations which are considered in the distribution of organizational sanctions. For this particular right, only the first criterion is applicable. A has the right to appraise B's performance of a given task to the extent that: A would not himself be negatively evaluated for appraising *B*'s performance.

Authority Systems

An authority right that is regularly exercised by one participant over another is termed an *authority link* between the two. The sum of all authority links connecting two participants constitutes, by definition, an *authority relationship* between the two. The constellation of all authority relationships of a participant, both with others over whom he exercises rights and with those who exercise rights over him, with respect to a given task constitutes his *authority system* for that task. (The following relationships may constitute the authority system of a resident physician in a teaching hospital with respect to diagnoses of patients assigned to his service: his chief resident exercises the rights of allocating patients to him and of sampling and appraising his diagnostic performance; certain faculty members exercise their rights to set criteria, sample and appraise him; and the resident himself exercises all four rights over the interns, and also exercises the right to allocate tasks necessary to his diagnoses to nurses and laboratory technicians.)

The resident physician's authority system is a fairly complex one. Complexity of authority systems is a function of the total number of right holders and the extent to which there is differentiation among them. One source of differentiation involves the number of rights per right holder: in one system, one person may hold all four rights; in another, the four rights may be distributed among four or more individuals. Another kind of differentiation occurs when right holders only decide how their respective rights are to be exercised but do not themselves implement their decisions. For example, the person holding the right to decide

how *B*'s performance is to be sampled does not himself take the sample but directs another individual to do so.

In addition to examining an individual participant and his relevant authority system, authority can be analyzed as it is associated with positions. A *position* is a location within an organization whose occupants share a common organizational title and are members of the same organizational context. (Occupants of the position of quarterback on the first string of the varsity football team; nurses aides on the pediatrics ward, for example.)

An authority link is *structural* at a given position if the link is associated with the position itself, rather than with a particular occupant of the position. There need not be a complete correspondence between the relationships associated with a position and those associated with a particular occupant of that position. The exceptional competence, stupidity, or charm of a given occupant may produce discrepancies between his authority system and the system usually associated with the position. (A particular quarterback may not be authorized to allocate plays because of his inability to detect weaknesses in the opposition's defense, although other quarterbacks are not so restricted.) Authority relationships and systems are structural at a given position to the extent that the authority links comprising them are structural at that position. The set of structural links for a given position, i.e., that portion of occupants' authority systems which is structural, constitutes the *authority structure* at that position. Although more inclusive units of analysis can be constructed from these concepts, in this paper systems and structures are defined from the perspective of a focal position and task.[3]

[3]This conception has characteristics that can readily be modified for other analytic purposes: (*1*) As we have indicated, other authority

COMPARISONS WITH PREVIOUS CONCEPTIONS

At this point it is appropriate to compare the concept of authority developed in this paper with some previous conceptions. Since for an authority right to exist those subordinate to its exercise are subject to negative evaluations, ultimately, negative sanctions for noncompliance, some may argue that we are studying power rather than authority. But our approach exphasizes the extent to which a participant is allowed by others in the organization to exercise control. A is authorized to exercise specified control attempts over B to the extent that significant evaluators permit him to attempt the control and require the compliance of others with the attempt. This definition makes it clear that we are concerned only with a particular kind of power: that which is authorized by other organizational participants. Authorized power, reflecting the interests of interdependent organizational members, tends to be circumscribed in its domain and regulated in its exercise. In short, we propose to study authority systems as the distribution of authorized power across persons or positions in organizations.

This view of authority can be compared with those of two influential organizational theorists, Max Weber and Chester I. Barnard. Weber[4] focused attention on the motivations of the subordinate group in his definition of an authority system as a legitimate power system: a system in which differences in power between A and B are justified by a set of beliefs that define the exercise of control by A and its acceptance by B as appropriate. Weber showed in his well-known typology how different systems of beliefs—traditional, charismatic, or legal—provide the bases for different kinds of authority structures. [Since this perspective emphasizes the norms enforced by subordinates we shall refer to it as *endorsed power* to distinguish it from *authorized power* where the norms are enforced by those in positions superior to the power wielder. Power may be legitimated by authorization or by endorsement or by both.] . . .

In some respects, our concept of authority is similar to that developed by Barnard.[5] Barnard's view that authority resides in the authenticated "authorized communications" from an office appears to be consistent with our approach. Barnard recognizes the importance of sanctions to participants through his emphasis on orders being acceptable to subordinates only if they are consonant with their personal interests. We would only add that if the distribution of sanctions is perceived to be affected by the evaluation process, then this is an important reason why evaluations themselves can become important to participants. Barnard's view of authority differs from our approach, however, in that it contains elements of [endorsement] that supplement his concern with authorization; his "zone of indifference" argument places emphasis on what orders subordinates will accept automatically. The two approaches are also put to a different use. Barnard uses the distribution of sanctions (incentives, in his terms) in order to explain the continued participation of members in the organization. We

rights can be identified (e.g., the right to select personnel for occupancy of a given position). (2) A similar authority system model could be based upon evaluators whose significance is defined in terms of perceived importance of their evaluations to participants, whatever their influence in the distribution of organizational sanctions. (3) Finally, more inclusive authority systems and structures can be identified across positions or tasks.

[4]Max Weber, *The Theory of Social and Economic Organization*, trans. A. M. Henderson and Talcott Parsons (Glencoe, Ill.: Free Press, 1947).

[5]Chester I. Barnard, *The Functions of the Executive* (Cambridge, Mass.: Harvard University, 1938).

also focus on the distribution of sanctions, as determined by the evaluation process. However, rather than emphasizing exclusively the decision to participate, we wish to account for one source of instability of authority systems which regulate the day-to-day behavior of participants.

An important feature of our view of authority, which differentiates it from previous conceptions, is its emphasis on the extent to which authority rights may be task-specific. *A*'s authority rights over *B* may be limited to a specific task. In complex organizations, it is possible for an individual to participate in a large number of authority systems. For example, the authority system in which an intern in a teaching hospital participates for the task of developing a therapeutic plan may depend on how the patient was admitted to the ward. For some patients, the intern reports to the patient's private physician; for others, he reports to an attending physician assigned to the ward. For other tasks, such as the clinical instruction of medical students, the intern may participate in still another authority system under the chief resident, and so forth. Concepts of authority which fail to recognize that authority may be limited in domain to a specific task encourage the investigator to over-simplify authority systems which are actually very complex.

The close relationship between the evaluation process and authority has been implicitly recognized by many students of organizations, although it has not been systematically examined. Some investigators have described evaluation systems designed to improve managerial control and have detailed how such systems can fail.[6] Others have examined the difficulty of establishing valid and reliable criteria for the evaluation of professionals. Vollmer[7] has investigated the difficulty in evaluating the performance of research and development personnel; and Freidson and Rhea[8] have studied problems in the evaluation of clinic physicians by their peers and the consequent difficulties in control by the professional group. Also of interest is the work of Jaques[9] who has empirically explored the idea that responsibility can be measured by the length of time between successive evaluations by a superior. These studies, together with many others, indicate that we are not alone in recognizing the importance of the evaluation process for the study of organizational behavior. . . .

[6]See Joseph S. Berliner, *Factory and Manager in the USSR* (Cambridge, Mass.: Harvard University, 1957); Peter M. Blau, *The Dynamics of Bureaucracy* (Chicago: University of Chicago, 1955); and Melville Dalton, *Men Who Manage* (New York: John Wiley, 1959).

[7]Howard M. Vollmer, *Applications of the Behavioral Sciences to Research Management: An Initial Study in the Office of Aerospace Research* (Menlo Park, Calif.: Stanford Research Institute, November, 1964). Mimeo.

[8]Eliot Freidson and Buford Rhea, Processes of Control in a Company of Equals, *Social Problems*, 11 (1963), 119-131.

[9]Elliot Jaques, *The Measurement of Responsibility* (Cambridge, Mass.: Harvard University, 1956).

32 Faculty Organization and Authority

Burton R. Clark

As we participate in or study various faculties in American higher education, we observe decisions being made through informal interaction among a group of peers and through collective action of the faculty as a whole. Formal hierarchy plays little part, and we have reason to characterize the faculty as a collegium.[1] At the same time we sense that what we now observe is not a counterpart of the collegiality of the days of old. The modern faculty in the United States is not a body to be likened to the guilds of the medieval European university,[2] or to the self-government of a dozen dons in a residential college at Oxford or Cambridge,[3] or to the meagre self-rule that was allowed the faculty in the small liberal arts college that dominated American higher education until the end of the last century.[4] The old-time collegium has

modern reflections, as in the Fellowships of the colleges at Yale, but for the most part it is no longer winningly with us, and the kind of collegiality we now find needs different conceptualization. We also observe on the modern campus that information is communicated through formal channels, responsibility is fixed in formally-designated positions, interaction is arranged in relations between superiors and subordinates, and decisions are based on written rules. Thus we have reason to characterize the campus as a bureaucracy. But, at the same time, we sense that this characterization overlooks so much that it becomes misleading. Though the elements of bureaucracy are strong, they do not dominate the campus; and though they grow, their growth does not mean future dominance if other forms of organization and authority are expanding more rapidly.

The major form of organization and authority found in the faculties of the larger American colleges and universities, and toward which many small campuses are now moving, is now neither predominantly collegial nor bureaucratic. Difficult to characterize, it may be seen as largely "professional," but professional in a way that is critically different from the authority of professional men in other organizations such as the business corporation, the government agency, and the hospital. To approach this unusual pattern, we will first discuss trends in the organization and culture of the campus as a whole and then turn to the related

[1] A major type of collegiality is that involving collegial decision: "In such cases an administrative act is only legitimate when it has been produced by the cooperation of a plurality of people according to the principle of unanimity or of majority." Max Weber, *The Theory of Social and Economic Organization*, A. M. Henderson and Talcott Parsons, (trans.) Glencoe, Ill.: Free Press, 1947, p. 400.

[2] Hastings Rashdall, *The Universities in Europe in the Middle Ages*, T. M. Powicke and A. B. Emden (eds.) (Oxford: Clarendon Press, 1936), three vols.

[3] C. P. Snow, *The Masters* (New York: The Macmillan Company, 1951).

[4] Richard Hofstadter and Walter P. Metzger, *The Development of Academic Freedom in the United States* (New York: Columbia University Press, 1955); George P. Schmidt, *The Liberal Arts College* (New Brunswick, New Jersey: Rutgers University Press, 1957).

Reprinted from Terry F. Lunsford (ed.), *The Study of Academic Administration*, Boulder, Colo.: Western Interstate Commission for Higher Education, 1963, pp. 37–51, by permission of the author and the publisher.

trends in the organization and authority of the faculty.

We begin with broad changes in the nature of the campus because they condition the structure of authority. Authority is conditioned, for example, by the nature of work, the technology of an organization. The mass assembly of automobiles does not allow much personal discretion on the part of the worker; surgery in the hospital operating room requires on-the-spot judgment and autonomous decision by the surgeon and one or two colleagues. To understand faculty authority, we need some comprehension of what academic work has in common with work in other settings and how it differs from work elsewhere. Authority is also conditioned by patterns of status. Status comes in part from formal assignment, hence men called deans usually have much of it, but status is also derived in academia from one's standing in a discipline, and this important source of status is independent of the official scheme.[5] Authority is also conditioned by traditional sentiments. Legends and ideologies have a force of their own. Conceptions of what should be are formed by what has been or by ideals handed down through the generations. The stirring ideologies of community of scholars and academic freedom are forces to be reckoned with when one is dealing with faculties and in understanding their organization. Thus, the work itself, the status system, the traditional sentiments, all affect authority.

TRENDS IN THE SOCIAL ORGANIZATION OF THE CAMPUS

Four trends in the campus, closely related, are as follows: unitary to composite or federal structure; single to

[5]Logan Wilson, *The Academic Man* (New York: Oxford University Press, 1942); Theodore Caplow and Reece J. McGee, *The Academic Marketplace* (New York: Basic Books, Inc., 1958).

multiple value systems; nonprofessional to professional work; consensus to bureaucratic coordination.

Unitary to Federal Structure

The history of American higher education is a history of movement from unitary liberal arts colleges to multistructured colleges and universities. The American college of 1840 contained a half dozen professors and fifty to a hundred students;[6] in 1870, average size was still less than 10 faculty and 100 students. All students in a college took the same curriculum, a "program of classical-mathematical studies inherited from Renaissance education."[7] There was no need for subunits such as division and department; this truly was a unitary structure. In comparison, the modern university and college is multi-structured. The University of California at Berkeley in 1962–63, with over 23,000 students and 1,600 "officers of instruction," was divided into some 15 colleges or schools (e.g., College of Engineering, School of Public Health); over 50 institutes, centers, and laboratories; and some 75 departments (including Poultry Husbandry, Romance Philology, Food Technology, and Naval Architecture). In three departments and three schools, the subunit itself contained over 50 faculty members. Such complexity is not only characteristic of the university: a large California state college contains 40 or so disciplines, grouped in a number of divisions; and even a small liberal arts college today may have 20 departments and three or four divisions.

The multiplication of subunits stems in part from increasing size. The large college cannot remain as unitary as the small one, since authority must be extensively delegated and subsidiary units formed around the many centers of au-

[6]Hofstadter and Metzger, *op. cit.*, pp. 222–223.
[7]*Ibid.*, p. 226.

thority. The subunits also stem from plurality of purpose; we have moved from single- to multi-purpose colleges. Goals are not only more numerous but also broadly defined and ambiguous. Those who would define the goals of the modern university speak in such terms as "preserving truth, creating new knowledge, and serving the needs of man through truth and knowledge."[8] The service goal has a serviceable ambiguity that covers anything from home economics for marriage to research and development for space. A tightly integrated structure could not be established around these goals. Organizational structure accommodates to the multiplicity of goals by dividing into segments with different primary functions, such as liberal arts and professional training, scientific research and humanistic education. The structure accommodates to ambiguity of goals with its own ambiguity, overlap, and discontinuity. We find some liberal arts disciplines scattered all over the campus (e.g., statistics, psychology), residing as components of professional schools and of "other" departments as well as in the appropriately-named department. No neat consistent structure is possible; the multiple units form and reform around functions in a catch-as-catch-can fashion. Needless to say, with a multiplicity of ambiguous goals and a variety of subunits, authority is extensively decentralized. The structure is federal rather than unitary, and even takes on some likeness to a loosely-joined federation.

Single to Multiple Value Systems

Most colleges before the turn of the century and perhaps as late as the 1920's possessed a unified culture that extended across the campus,[9] and this condition still obtains in some small

colleges of today. But the number of colleges so characterized continues to decline and the long-run trend is clear: the campus-wide culture splits into subcultures located in a variety of social groups and organizational units. As we opened the doors of American higher education, we admitted more orientations to college—college as fun, college as marriage, college as preparation for graduate school, college as certificate to go to work tomorrow, college as place to rebel against the Establishment, and even college as a place to think. These orientations have diverse social locations on campus, from fraternity house to cafe espresso shop to Mrs. Murphy's desegregated rooming house. The value systems of the students are numerous.

The faculty is equally if not more prone to diversity in orientation, as men cleave to their specialized lines of work and their different perspectives and vocabularies. Faculty orientations differ between those who commit themselves primarily to the local campus and those who commit themselves primarily to their farflung discipline or profession; between those who are scientists and those who are humanists; between those who think of themselves as pure researchers or pure scholars and those who engage in a professional practice and train recruits. The value systems of the faculty particularly cluster around the individual disciplines and hence at one level of analysis there are as many value systems as there are departments.

Nonprofessional to Professional Work

Intense specialization characterizes the modern campus; academic man has moved from general to specific knowledge. The old-time teacher—Mr. Chips—was a generalist. He covered a wide range of subject-matter, with less intensity in any one area than would be true today, and he was engaged in pure transmission

[8]Clark Kerr, *The Uses of the University*, The Godkin Lectures, Harvard University, 1963.
[9]Hofstadter and Metzger, *op. cit.*; Schmidt, *op. cit.*

of knowledge. In the American college of a century ago, the college teacher had only a bachelor's degree (in the fixed classical curriculum), plus "a modest amount of more advanced training, perhaps in theology . . ."[10] There was no system of graduate education, no reward for distinction in scholarship, and the professor settled down into the groove of classroom recitation and the monitoring of student conduct. We have moved from this kind of professor, the teacher generalist, to the teacher of physics, of engineering, of microbiology, of abnormal psychology, and to the professor as researcher, as consultant, as professional-school demonstrator. We have moved from transmission of knowledge to innovation in knowledge, which has meant specialization in research. Taking the long view, perhaps *the* great change in the role of academic man is the ascendance of research and scholarship—the rise of the commitment to create knowledge. This change in the academic role interacts with rapid social change: research causes change, as in the case of change in technology and industrial processes; and such changes, in turn, encourage the research attitude, as in the case of competition between industrial firms, competition between nations, competition between universities. In short, the research component of the academic role is intimately related to major modern social trends.

In his specialism, modern academic man is a case of professional man. We define "profession" to mean a specialized competence with a high degree of intellectual content, a specialty heavily based on or involved with knowledge. Specialized competence based on involvement in knowledge is the hallmark of the modern professor. He is pre-eminently an expert. Having special knowledge at

his command, the professional worker needs and seeks a large degree of autonomy from lay control and normal organizational control. Who is the best judge of surgical procedure—laymen, hospital administrators, or surgeons? Who is the best judge of theories in chemistry—laymen, university administrators, or professors of chemistry? As work becomes professionalized—specialized around esoteric knowledge and technique—the organization of work must create room for expert judgment, and autonomy of decision making and practice becomes a hallmark of the advanced profession.

Not all professional groups need the same degree of autonomy, however. Professionals who largely give advice or follow the guidelines of a received body of knowledge require extensive but not great autonomy for the individual and the group. They need sufficient leeway to give an honest expert opinion or to apply the canons of judgment of their field. Those requiring great autonomy are those who wish to crawl along the frontiers of knowledge, with flashlight or floodlight in hand, searching for the new—the new scientific finding, the new reinterpretation of history, the new criticism in literature or art. Academic man is a special kind of professional man, a type characterized by a particularly high need for autonomy. To be innovative, to be critical of established ways, these are the commitments of the academy and the impulses of scientific and scholarly roles that press for unusual autonomy.

Consensual to Bureaucratic Coordination

As the campus has moved from unitary to composite structure, from single to multiple systems of values, from general to specialized work, it has moved away from the characteristics of community, away from "community of scholars." A

[10]Hofstadter and Metzger, *op. cit.*, p. 230.

faculty member does not interact with most other members of the faculty. In the largest places, he may know less than a fifth, less than a tenth. Paths do not cross. The faculty lounge is no more, but is replaced by coffee pots in dozens of locations. The professor retains a few interests in common with all others, such as higher salaries, but he has an increasing number of interests that diverge. Even salary is a matter on which interests may diverge, as men bargain for themselves, as departments compete for funds, as scientists are paid more, through various devices, than the men of the humanities.

In short, looking at the total faculty, interaction is down, commonality of interest is down, commonality of sentiments is down. With this, coordination of work and policy within the faculty is not so much now as in the past achieved by easy interaction of community members, by the informal give-and-take that characterizes the true community—the community of the small town where everyone knows nearly every one else, or the community of the old small college where the professors saw much of everyone else in the group. The modern campus can no longer be coordinated across its length and breadth by informal interaction and by the coming together of the whole. Informal consulting back and forth is still important; the administration and the faculty still use the lunch table for important business. But campus-wide coordination increasingly moves toward the means normal to the large-scale organization, to bureaucratic means. We appoint specialists to various areas of administration, give them authority, and they write rules to apply across the system. They communicate by correspondence, they attempt to make decisions fairly and impartially by judging the case before them against the criteria of the rulebook. Thus we move toward bureaucratic coordination, as the admis-

sions officer decides on admissions, the registrar decides on the recording of grades, the business officer decides proper purchasing procedures, and various faculty committees decide on a wide range of matters, from tenure to travel funds to the rules of order for meetings of an academic senate.

In sum: the campus tends toward composite structure, toward a multiplicity of subcultures, toward intense professionalism, and toward some bureaucratic coordination.

CHANGE IN FACULTY ORGANIZATION AND AUTHORITY

The organization and authority of the faculty accommodate to these trends in at least three ways: by segmentation, by a federated professionalism, and by the growth of individual power centers.

Segmentation

As campuses increase in size, complexity, and internal specialization, there is less chance that the faculty will be able to operate effectively as a total faculty in college affairs, less as the governmental body we have in mind when we speak of a community of scholars. The decision-making power and influence of the faculty is now more segmented—segmented by subcollege, by division, and particularly by department. Since the interests of the faculty cluster around the departments, faculty participation in government tends to move out to these centers of commitment. Who selects personnel, decides on courses, and judges students? The faculty as a whole cannot, any more than the administration. Indeed, as departments and professional schools grow in size and complexity, even they often do not; it is a wing of the department or a part of the professional school that has most influence. A liberal arts department that numbers 40 to 80 faculty members may contain six or eight or a dozen specialties. The day has arrived when a department chairman may not even know the name, let alone the face and the person, of the new instructors in "his" department.

What happens to the governmental organs designed for the faculty as a whole? They move in form from Town Hall to representative government, with men elected from the various "states" coming together in a federal center to legislate general rules, which are then executed by the administration or the faculty committees that constitute an administrative component of the faculty. With the move to representative government, there is greater differentiation in participation: a few "actives" participate a great deal; a considerably larger group constitutes an alert and informed public and participates a modest amount; the largest group consists of those who are not very interested or informed and who participate very little. The structure of participation parallels that found in the larger democratic society, and apparently is normal to a representative mass democracy. The situation is, of course, vexing to those who care about faculty government.

Professionalization

The authority of the faculty which flows out toward the departments and other units of the campus becomes located in the hands of highly specialized experts; and, as suggested earlier, takes on some characteristics of professional authority. Almost everywhere in modern large-scale organizations, we find a tug-of-war going on between administrative and professional orientations. In the hospital, the basic conflict in authority lies between the control of the non-medical hospital administrator and the authority of the

doctors. In industry, a fascinating clash is occurring between management and the scientist in the research and development laboratory.[11] The fantastic expansion of research and development has brought over 400,000 scientists and engineers into industry, there to be committed to innovation and to the development of new inventions to the point of practical utility. Many of these technologists have a high degree of expertise, a strong interest in research— often "pure" research—and they press for a large degree of freedom. Their fondest wish is to be left alone; they make the point that in scientific work it seems rational to do just that, that basic discoveries stem not from managerial direction but from the scientist following up his own initial hunches and the leads he develops as he proceeds. Management has found such men difficult to deal with; their morale suffers easily from traditional forms of management, and they present unusual demands on management to change and accommodate. In this situation, professional authority and bureaucratic authority are both necessary, for each performs an essential function: professional authority protects the exercise of the special expertise of the technologist, allowing his judgment to be pre-eminent in many matters. Bureaucratic authority functions to provide coordination of the work of the technologists with the other major elements of the firm. Bureaucratic direction is not capable of providing certain expert judgments; professional direction is not capable of providing the over-all coordination. The problem presented by the scientist in industry is how to serve simultaneously the requirements of autonomy and the

[11]See William Kornhauser, *Scientists in Industry: Conflict and Accommodation* (Berkeley: University of California Press, 1962); and Simon Marcson, *The Scientist in American Industry* (New York: Harper & Row, Publishers, 1960.

requirements of coordination, and how to accommodate the authority of the professional man and his group of peers to the authority of management and vice versa.[12]

The professional-in-the-organization presents everywhere this special kind of problem. He gains authority, compared to most employees, by virtue to his special knowledge and skills; he loses authority, compared to a man working on his own, by virtue of the fact that organizations locate much authority in administrative positions. The problem of allocation of authority between professionals and bureaucrats does, however, vary in intensity and form in different kinds of organizations. As mentioned earlier, advisers and practitioners need a modest degree of authority, while scientists and academics have perhaps the highest requirements for autonomy to engage in research, in unfettered teaching, and in scholarship that follows the rules of consistency and proof that develop within a discipline.

The segmentation of the faculty into clusters of experts gives professional authority a special form in academic organizations. In other situations, there usually are one or two major professional groups within the organization who, if they are influential, substitute professional control for administrative control. This occurs in the case of medical personnel in the hospital who often dominate decision making. The internal controls of the medical profession are strong and are substituted for those of the organization. But in the college or university this situation does not obtain; there are 12, 25, or 50 clusters of experts. The experts are prone to identify with their own disciplines, and the "academic profession" over-all comes off a poor second. We have wheels within wheels, many professions within a profession. No one of

[12]Kornhauser, *op. cit.*

the disciplines on a campus is likely to dominate the others; at a minimum, it usually takes an alliance of disciplines, such as "the natural sciences" or "the humanities," to put together a bloc that might dominate others. The point is that with a variety of experts—chemists, educationists, linguists, professors of marketing—the collective control of the professionals over one another will not be strong. The campus is not a closely-knit group of professionals who see the world from one perspective. As a collection of professionals, it is decentralized, loose, and flabby.

The principle is this: where professional influence is high and there is one dominant professional group, the organization will be integrated by the imposition of professional standards. Where professional influence is high and there are a number of professional groups, the organization will be split by professionalism. The university and the large college are fractured by expertness, not unified by it. The sheer variety of the experts supports the tendency for authority to diffuse toward quasi-autonomous clusters. Thus, faculty authority has in common with professional authority in other places the protection of individual and group autonomy. It is different from professional authority in other places in the extremity of the need for autonomy and in the fragmentation of authority around the interests of a large variety of groups of roughly equal status and power. The campus is a holding company for professional groups rather than a single association of professionals.

Individualization

When we speak of professional authority we often lump together the authority that resides with the individual expert and the authority that resides with a collegial group of experts. Both the individual and the group gain influence at the expense of laymen and the general administrator. But what is the division of authority between the individual and the group? Sometimes group controls can be very tight and quite hierarchical, informally if not formally, as young doctors learn in many hospitals, and as assistant professors learn in many departments. The personal authority of the expert varies widely with the kind of establishment, and often with rank and seniority. The campus is a place where strong forces cause the growth of some individuals into centers of power. We will review several of these sources of personal authority.

First, we have noted the expertise of the modern academy. The intense specialization alone makes many a man into king of a sector in which few others are able to exercise much judgment. Thus, *within* a department, men increasingly feel unable to judge the merits of men in specialties they know nothing about. The technical nature of the specialized lines of work of most academic men, then, is a source of personal authority. If we want to provide a course on Thomas Hardy, we are likely to defer on its content to the judgment of the man in the English Department who has been knee-deep in Hardy for a decade. The idea of such a course would really have been his in the first place; Hardy falls within his domain within the English Department, and his judgment on the need for the course will weigh more than the judgment of others.

Second, some professorial experts now have their personal authority greatly enhanced by money. Despite his location within an organization, the professor in our time is becoming an entrepreneur. It used to be that the college president was the only one on campus, other than an enterprising and dedicated member of the board of trustees, who was capable of being an entrepreneur. Many of the great

presidents were great because they were great at coming home with the loot—adventurers who conquered the hearts and pocketbooks of captains of industry and then with money in hand raided wholesale the faculties of other institutions. Presidents who can raise money and steal faculty are still with us, but they have been joined by professors. Kerr has suggested that the power of the individual faculty member is going up while the power of the collective faculty is going down because the individual as researcher, as scholar, and as consultant relates increasingly to the grant-giving agencies of the Federal government and to the foundation.[13] He has direct ties to these major sources of funds and influence; indeed, he participates in their awarding of grants and even has problems of conflict of interest. A professor-entrepreneur, by correspondence and telephone and airplane trips, lines up money for projects. He sometimes arranges for the financing of an entire laboratory; occasionally he even brings back a new building. Even when the professor does little of the arranging, it is *his* presence that attracts these resources. He represents competence, and the grant-givers pursue competence.

The entrepreneurial activity and resources-gaining influence of professors, which extends down to assistant professors in the social as well as the natural sciences, has had remarkable growth since World War II, and the personal autonomy and power thus achieved in relation to others in the university is considerable. A professor does not have to beg postage stamps from a departmental secretary nor a two hundred dollar raise from the department chairman nor travel money to go to a meeting from a dean or a committee if he has monies assigned to him to the tune of $37,000,

[13]Kerr, *op. cit.*

or $175,000, or $400,000. His funds from outside sources may be called "soft" funds, in the jargon of finance, but they are hard enough to hire additional faculty members and assistants, to cover summer salaries, and to provide for travel to distant, delightful places.

The following principle obtains: a *direct* relation of faculty members to external sources of support affects the distribution of influence within the campus, redistributing influence from those who do not have such contacts to those who do, and moving power from the faculty as a whole and as smaller collectivities to individual professors. In the university of old, members of the faculty achieved a high degree of influence by occupying the few professorial positions available in a structure that narrowed at the top. Their source of influence was structural and internal. The source of great influence in the modern American university is less internal and less tied to particular positions; it is more external and more tied to national and international prestige in a discipline, and to contact with the sources of support for research and scholarship that are multiplying and growing so rapidly.

The individualization in faculty organization and authority excites impulses in the faculty and the administration to establish some collective control, for much is at stake in the balance of the curriculum, the equality of rewards in the faculty, and even the character of the institution. But the efforts at control do not have easy going. Collective bodies of the faculty and the administration are hardly in a position, or inclined, to tell the faculty member he can have this contract but not that one, since the faculty member will define the projects as part of his pursuit of his own scholarly interests. When the faculty member feels that this sensitive right is infringed, he will run up the banners of academic freedom and

inquiry, or he will fret and become a festering sore in the body politic of the campus, or he will retreat to apathy and his country house, or he will make it known in other and greener pastures that he will listen to the siren call of a good offer.

Third, personal authority of the professorial expert is increased in our time by the competitiveness of the job market. The expansion of higher education means a high demand for professors, and the job market runs very much in the professor's favor in bargaining with the administration. His favorable position *in* the market enhances his position *on* campus. He can demand more and get it; he can even become courageous. In the world of work, having another job to go to is perhaps the most important source of courage.

To recapitulate: faculty organization and authority tends in modern times to become more segmented, more professional in character, and somewhat more individualized. We are witnessing a strong trend toward a federated structure in colleges and especially in universities— with the campus more like an United Nations and less like a small town—and this trend affects faculty authority by weakening the faculty as a whole and strengthening the faculty in its many parts. Faculty authority becomes less of a case of self-government by a total collegium, and more of a case of authority exercised department by department, sub-college by sub-college. The *role* of faculty authority is shifting from protecting the rights of the entire guild, the rights of the collective faculty, to protecting the autonomy of the separate disciplines and the autonomy of the individual faculty member.

Faculty authority in our time tends to become professional authority in a federated form. We have a loose alliance of professional men. The combination of professional authority and loosely-joined structure has the imposing function of protecting the autonomy of the work of experts amidst extensive divergence of interests and commitments. The qualities of federation are important here. The federation is a structure that gives reign to the quasi-autonomous, simultaneous development of the interests of a variety of groups. Within an academic federation, a number of departments, divisions, colleges, professional schools, institutes, and the like can coexist, each pushing its own interests and going its own way to a rather considerable extent. Professional authority structured as a federation is a form of authority particularly adaptive to a need for a high degree of autonomous judgment by individuals and subgroups.

This trend toward a federation of professionals is only part of the story. To hold the separate components of the campus together, we have a superimposed coordination by the administration, and, as Kerr has suggested, this coordination increasingly takes on the attributes of mediation.[14] The administration attempts to keep the peace and to inch the entire enterprise another foot ahead. The faculty, too, in its own organization, also counters this divisive trend with a machinery of coordination. The very fact of a diffusion of authority makes the faculty politician more necessary than ever, for the skills of politics and diplomacy are needed. There must be faculty mediators; men who serve on central committees, men with cast iron stomachs for lunch table discussions and cocktail parties, men who know how to get things done that must be done for the faculty as a whole or for part of the faculty. There must be machinery for setting rules and carrying them out impartially across the faculty. The modern campus is, or is becoming, too large and complicated for collegial or professional arrangements to provide the over-all coordination, and

[14]*Ibid.*

coordination is performed largely by bureaucratic arrangements—e.g., the rulebook, and definite administrative domains.

Federated professionalism within an organization, like many other trends, thus promotes counter-trends. Specialization and individualization seriously weaken the integration of the whole. The weakness of collegiality or professionalism in the large organization, as suggested earlier in the case of industry, is that it cannot handle the problem of order, it cannot provide sufficient integration. Thus the above trends in faculty organization and authority open the door to bureaucracy—more bureaucracy in the administration, more within the faculty itself. The modern large faculty, therefore, combines professionalism, federated structure, and bureaucracy—perhaps in a mixture never before evidenced in human history.

This combination of what seem contradictory forms of organization perplexes observers of academia. Is the faculty collegial? Yes, somewhat. Is it split into fragments? Yes, somewhat. It is professional? Yes, somewhat. Is it unitary? Yes, somewhat. Is it bureaucratic? Yes, somewhat. Different features of the faculty strike us according to the occurrences of the week or the events we chance to observe. The evermounting paperwork firmly convinces us that the campus is doomed to bureaucratic stagnation. The fact that the president often gets what the president wants convinces us that he really has all the authority. The inability of a campus to change a department that is twenty years behind in its field convinces us that departmental autonomy has run amok and the campus is lacking in leadership and in capacity to keep up with the times. One observer will see the campus as a tight ship, the next will speak of the same campus as a lawless place where power lies around loose. No wonder we are confused and no wonder that outsiders are so often even more confused or more irrelevant in giving advice.

But in the combination of forms of organization and forms of authority that we find today within the campus and within the faculty itself, there are certain trends that are stronger than others and certain features that tend toward dominance. The society at large is tending to become a society of experts, and the campus has already arrived at this state. Expertise is a dominant characteristic of the campus, and organization and authority cluster around it. Because of its expertness, together with its ever-growing size, the faculty moves away from community, moves away from collegiality of the whole. The faculty moves toward decentralized or federated structure, and authority moves toward clusters of experts and the individual expert. Thus professional authority tends to become the dominant form of authority, and collegial and bureaucratic features fall into a subsidiary place. In short, when we say college, we say expert. When we say expert, we say professional authority.

ADAPTIVE PROCESSES IN FORMAL ORGANIZATIONS

More so than is the case with most types of collectivities, organizations come into being in order to accomplish something other than merely to provide satisfactions to their participants. Explicit goals are usually specified, and persons are assembled and organized to pursue them. Officials in charge of organizations worry a good deal about the effectiveness of their operation (whether they are in fact accomplishing these stated purposes) and the efficiency of their efforts (whether they are achieving their goals at the least possible cost). There is cause for worry because, unlike many other types of collectivities, organizations that are ineffective or inefficient are liable to cease to exist. It is commonly recognized that business concerns must compete successfully if they are to survive (the average life expectancy of an American business is six years), but we are less apt to think of other organizations as subject to similar demands. But even the least secular of organizations, the church, finds itself in competition for its parishioners with other churches and such unlikely competitors as the golf course and the professional football game. Churches must also be concerned about the quality of services rendered to members and the larger community, and about the efficient use of their own resources. Hospitals, universities, and even government agencies must devote much attention to the problem of surviving in their respective environments.

Talcott Parsons has suggested one useful way of viewing the relation between an organization and its environment. He suggests:

An organization is a system which, as the attainment of its goal, "produces" an identifiable something which can be utilized in some way by another system; that is, the output of the organization is, for some other system, an input. . . .

What from the point of view of the organization in question is its specified goal is, from the point of view of the larger system of which it is a differentiated part or sub-system, a specialized or differentiated function. This relationship is the primary link between an organization and the larger system of which it is a part. . . .[1]

Thus, all organizations produce something: automobile factories produce cars; insurance companies produce economic security for their clients; mental hospitals produce rehabilitated and resocialized persons; and universities produce educated individuals, persons with a high degree of technical training, and new knowledge. The production of this "something" is, from the organization's point of view, its goal. But from the point of view of the larger system—the community or the society, perhaps—this "something" is the "function" of the organization. Organizations enjoy differing amounts of support and acceptance from their

---

[1]Talcott Parsons, "A sociological approach to the theory of organizations," *Structure and Process in Modern Societies*, New York: Free Press, 1960, pp. 17, 19.

environment, depending on the extent to which their functions are highly valued by those who utilize or depend upon their outputs.

There are two separable aspects to the problem of organization adaptation. The first has to do with how the organization arrives at a definition of the goals it will pursue and how it structures itself to accomplishing its tasks effectively and efficiently. The second has to do with how the organization relates to its environment—to its potential buyers and sellers, to its competitors, and to the public at large.

In Reading 33, I consider the first set of problems. This article was written originally to focus on medical care organizations, so that most of the illustrations used concern this type of organization, but the discussion is applicable to all types of organizations. This reading describes the processes by which goals are set in organizations and describes various arrangements for accomplishing the tasks set by the adoption of a particular set of goals. The type of task performed and the conceptions of these tasks are seen to have important implications for the types of structures designed to effectively and efficiently accomplish them.

The second problem—relating to the larger environment—is the subject of the discussion by James D. Thompson in Reading 34. Employing the useful concept of *domain*, Thompson analyzes selected aspects of organizational environment relations. As all analysts must, he confronts the problem of what aspects of the environment to take into account and decides to focus primarily on the task environment of organizations. In his analysis of interorganizational relations, we see again the important role played by power processes as they define dependency relations among the several competing and cooperating units.

The boundaries separating an organization from its environment can never exclude all external influences, because organizations are open systems depending on their environments for various vital inputs (personnel, raw materials, knowledge) and for markets for their outputs. However, if organizations are to function as rational systems, they must enjoy at least a modicum of autonomy from their environment. Recall that rationality requires that organizations deploy their personnel and resources in ways that they deem appropriate for the efficient attainment of goals. Hence, if rationality of operation is to be attained, the persons in charge of organizations must be free to decide such matters as what types of personnel are to be hired, how labor is to be divided among them, and how resources are to be distributed throughout the organization.

Some organizations have special structures to help insulate them from various aspects of their environment. For example,

boards of trustees for educational and eleemosynary institutions and boards of directors for corporate concerns must see to it that the organization's existence and activities are accorded legitimacy in the community, and they must marshall broad sources of support—moral, economic, and political. They also function as a buffer between the organization and its environment, protecting organizational officials from outside criticism and attempts to influence.[2]

When organizations do not enjoy such autonomy, rationality is apt to suffer. For example, Udy carried out a study of 34 production organizations in nonindustrial societies. In some of the societies, the organizations were able to exercise control over the criteria by which workers were recruited into the organizations,

---

[2]W. Richard Scott, "Theory of Organizations," in Robert E. L. Faris (ed.), *Handbook of Modern Sociology*, Skokie, Ill.: Rand McNally, 1964, p. 522.

and in some of the societies the organizations had little control over hiring criteria (for example, membership might be determined by kinship criteria). Udy reports that organizations having control over recruitment criteria were more likely than organizations lacking such control to exhibit such rational characteristics as specific job assignment, the presence of specialization, and emphasis on performance as the basis for distributing sanctions to partici- pants.[3]

A measure of autonomy is necessary if organizations are to attempt to structure themselves rationally for the pursuit of objectives. However, because every organization "in virtue of the services it performs, the areas it regulates, the interests between which it mediates, and its own structure and organization, develops into a centre of power which may become independent and unregu- lated"[4] limits must be set on this autonomy. As organizations grow in size and influence, the larger community of which they are a part has reason to be increasingly concerned with what these organizations do and how they go about doing it. Corporate decisions can affect the lives of thousands or even hundreds of thousands of persons, both within and outside the formal boundaries of the organization. Some organizational managers are showing signs of becoming increasingly aware of their social responsibilities and attempting to consider the interests of the larger public in making their decisions. But external controls are also necessary and are exercised, at least to some extent, by government agencies in behalf of the public. Whether or not these controls can keep pace with the growing scale and power of modern organizations is a question of vital importance to all of us. (See Readings 39 and 45)

[3]Stanley H. Udy, Jr., "Administrative rationality, social setting, and organizational develop- ment," *American Journal of Sociology*, 68 (November, 1962), 299–308.
[4]S. N. Eisenstadt, "Bureaucracy and bureaucratization," *Current Sociology*, 7 (1958), 102.

33   Organizational Goals and Tasks*

W. Richard Scott

Organizations are social units consisting of a network of relations which ori- ents and regulates the behavior among a specific set of individuals in the pursuit of relatively specific goals. An organiza- tion is said to be *formal* to the extent that positions are identified and defined and relations with other positions specified irrespective of the characteristics of the individuals occupying the positions.[1]

°*Portions of the section on Organizational Tasks are based on work done in connection with a study of "Authority Structures and Evaluations" under a grant from the National Science Founda- tion (G 23990). My major collaborators in this research are Sanford M. Dornbusch, Bruce C. Busching and James D. Laing.*

[1]Important advantages, as well as some disad- vantages, are associated with formalization from the standpoint of rationality of operation. *See* Scott, W. Richard, Theory of Organizations, *in* Faris, Robert E. (Editor), HANDBOOK OF MOD- ERN SOCIOLOGY, Chicago, Rand McNally & Co., 1964, pp. 491–492.

Reprinted from W. Richard Scott, "Some implications of organization theory for research on health services" (original title), *The Milbank Memorial Fund Quarterly;* Health Services Research II, Vol. XLIV, No. 4, Oct. 1966, part 2, pp. 35–64 (excerpts), by permission of the Milbank Memorial Fund.

Formal organizations contain many idiosyncratic and "informal" elements, but so much stress has been put on the latter by other analysts that the present discussion will concentrate on the formal system. Although all organizations are subsystems of larger social units, such as communities and societies, this discussion will center on the internal structure of organizations rather than on their external relations.

ORGANIZATIONAL GOALS

Goals perform a variety of functions for an organization. They assist in the task of carving out a specified arena of activity and in mobilizing legitimacy and support from the environment; they frequently serve as a source of identification and motivation for participants. This paper, however, will focus on the way in which goals are established and on some of the problems met in assuring that the established goals are those which guide the behavior of participants.

Goal Setting

Debate continues over whether the term "organizational goal" is appropriate and accurate. Some insist that such a concept involves reification—that this concept should be forgotten. The behavior of participants could more accurately be termed goal-directed. However, the concept has meaning if carefully employed to refer to the desired ends toward which participants are expected to direct their behavior.

A much neglected question in organizational analysis is who sets the goals toward which participants are expected to direct their activities?[2] One answer to this question is the so-called *entrepreneurial*

solution. The organization's goals are accepted as what the owners and/or the managers of the enterprise say they are. This view assumes that the managers actually succeed in managing and directing the performances of participants. While this state of affairs may prevail in some types of organizations, it describes few medical organizations, where administrators with such views are unlikely to retain their positions for extended periods. Another answer is that organizational goals are those shared in common by all participants in the system—goals are assumed to be *consensually* defined.[3] If this view is taken, however, most medical organizations would appear to be in trouble, for little consensus exists among their members as to the primary organizational objectives. At least, this is what Wessen found when he asked 75 respondents in various positions within a general hospital to list the basic aims of the institution.[4]

Perhaps for the majority of medical organizations the most satisfactory answer to the question of who sets goals is that goals emerge from a continual *bargaining process* among shifting coalitions of the more powerful participants.[5] Coalitions are formed and reformed through the use of side-payments, one group backing another and, in turn, receiving support for its own demands. A group successful in getting its demands accepted as policy commitments contrib-

[2]This question goes begging in part because one of the major approaches to organizations—the "rational instrument" view championed by Weber and his intellectual disciples—takes the goals as given.

[3]This solution is proposed by Barnard, who did, however, differentiate between the organizational purpose—agreements among participants as to the aims of the organization—and the personal motives of participants which lead them to contribute their efforts. *See* Barnard, Chester I., THE FUNCTIONS OF THE EXECUTIVE, Cambridge, Massachusetts, Harvard University Press, 1938, pp. 86-89.

[4]Wessen, Albert F., Hospital Ideology and Communication between Ward Personnel, *in* Jaco, E. Gartley (Editor), PATIENTS, PHYSICIANS AND ILLNESS, Glencoe, Illinois, Free Press, 1958, p. 459.

[5]Cyert, Richard M. and March, James G., A BEHAVIORAL THEORY OF THE FIRM, Englewood Cliffs, New Jersey, Prentice-Hall, Inc., 1963, pp. 26-32.

utes to goal setting just as does a group which succeeds in obtaining binding agreements as to the side-payments it will receive. Both involve the allocation of scarce resources which adds new goals and puts contraints upon the attainment of goals set by earlier agreements. Much theoretically significant and useful research on medical organizations could be conducted from this perspective. Careful descriptions are called for as well as attempts to specify the conditions under which various kinds of groups will coalesce and be more or less successful in promoting their demands.

Two recent papers analyzing medical situations are consistent with this bargaining perspective. Perrow's historical analysis of shifts in the goals of a general hospital as related to shifts in the relative power positions of trustees, physicians, and administrators is a study of changes in the relative bargaining position of these three groups over a period of time.[6] Bucher and Strauss' depiction of the segmented medical specialties acting as "social movements" to defend and extend their position vis-a-vis other competing groups provides rich descriptive data of the sort necessary to carry forward this type of analysis.[7]

The fierceness with which coalitions bargain is clearly affected by the state of the organization as a whole. If times are good and the organization is fat with resources, the several groups can afford to be generous in the bargains they strike; competing and even conflicting goals may be simultaneously pursued. However, in those lean times when the organization is forced to struggle for its very survival, hard bargaining takes place with the result that the desires of weaker groups are sacrificed.[8]

Subgoal Formation

A vexing problem is faced by organizations insofar as they parcel general goals into subgoals and delegate these subgoals to particular individuals or departments. In such cases—and they are very frequent in most organizations—what is delegated as a goal or end to the department is for the organization only a means for attaining a more general objective.[9] For example, within a hospital, a goal for the radiology department— processing and interpreting x-rays—is only a means to attain a more general objective—arriving at a definitive diagnosis. Certain cognitive and motivational factors conduce participants to pursue their particular subgoals in ways which are not always consistent with the goal attainment efforts of related departments or of the organization as a whole. Thus, March and Simon note that a given participant assigned a subgoal will, because of the processes of selective perception and rationalization, focus exclusively on attaining this objective without regard to the possibly negative consequences for the larger system to which his actions are supposed to contribute. These individual tendencies are reinforced both by the content of ingroup communications and by the selective exposure of his department to stimuli from the larger organizational environment.[10]; In addition to these cognitive processes, both Selznick and Dalton have emphasized the motivational factors supporting such actions, an individual being encouraged by self-

[6]Perrow, Charles, The Analysis of Goals in Complex Organizations, *American Sociological Review*, 26, 854–866, December, 1961.

[7]Bucher, Rue and Strauss, Anselm, Professions in Process, *American Journal of Sociology*, 66, 325–334, January, 1961.

[8]Cyert and March, *op. cit.*, pp. 36–38.

[9]Simon, Herbert A., ADMINISTRATIVE BEHAVIOR, (Second edition), New York, The Macmillan Company, 1957.

[10]March, James G. and Simon, Herbert A., ORGANIZATIONS, New York, John Wiley & Sons, Inc., 1958, pp. 151–154.

interests, by identification with his work group or department,[11] or by his "commitment" to particular skills, arrangements or other vested interests generated in the course of action,[12] to pursue his own limited objectives even at the expense of interfering with the attainment of more general goals.

One characteristic of medical organizations encourages subgoal formation while another mitigates its negative consequences. The feature conducive to subgoal formation is the plethora of specialty groups brought together under a single organizational canopy. Such skilled occupational groups have a "trained incapacity"—to use Veblen's happily descriptive phrase—to see situations in which they are involved from any perspective other than their own. They tend to exaggerate the importance of their own endeavors and see their own skills and standards as applicable to virtually every circumstance encountered. In short, organizations staffed by specialty professional and technical workers are particularly vulnerable to the processes of subgoal formation. The organizational characteristic which helps to neutralize the negative consequences of subgoal formation is the type of departmental specialization which tends to predominate in medical organizations: most departments exhibit "parallel" rather than "interdependent" specializations.[13] Parallel departments perform specialized but relatively independent functions; e.g., the departments of pediatrics and geriatrics. Interdependent departments perform specialized and interrelated functions; e.g., the departments of medicine and radiology or pathology. To the degree that departments are organized to function relatively autonomously of the rest of the organization, the negative effects of subgoal formation among departments (albeit not within departments) will be minimized. However, as medical technology becomes more complex and medical specialty groups more specialized, parallel departmental organization is giving way to a more interdependent structure. The more pronounced these changes, the more deleterious the consequences of subgoal formation for the achievement of general organizational goals.

Goal Specificity

Formal organizations are, fundamentally, instruments for attaining goals. How blunt or fine an instrument depends on many factors which are summarized by the concept "rationality" of structure. Rationality has in this context a specific and limited meaning, referring to the extent to which " a series of actions is organized in such a way that it leads to a previously defined goal."[14] Specific goals supply criteria by means of which the organization's structure may be rationally designed: they specify what tasks are to be performed, what kinds of personnel are to be hired, how resources are to be allocated among participants. Goals determine the basis for compensation of members—the degree to which each contributes to goal attainment— and stipulate the prerogatives of status and authority according to position. That virtually every organization theorist insists on the importance of specific goals as a defining criterion of organizations is not surprising.

Although organizations as a category

[11]Dalton, Melville, MEN WHO MANAGE, New York, John Wiley & Sons, Inc., 1959.

[12]Selznick, Philip, TVA AND THE GRASS ROOTS, Berkeley, University of California Press, 1949, pp. 253-259.

[13]Blau, Peter M. and Scott, W. Richard, FORMAL ORGANIZATIONS, San Francisco, Chandler Publishing Co., 1962, pp. 183-184.

[14]Mannheim, Karl, MAN AND SOCIETY IN AN AGE OF RECONSTRUCTION, New York, Harcourt, Brace & World, Inc., 1950, p. 53.

define their goals more precisely than do other collectivities, organizations still vary greatly in the specificity of their objectives. The goals of a governmental bureau or a small private firm typically exhibit a relatively high degree of specificity, but the goals of most professional organizations, such as medical institutions or universities, are lamentably lacking in precision. Universities are supposedly geared to the production of educated men, but the definitions of precisely what constitutes an education vary widely both within and outside the academic community. Similarly, most medical institutions are concerned with promoting health and preventing illness, but who has yet satisfactorily defined these states? As Thompson and Bates point out, in universities and hospitals as compared with factories or commercial establishments, "the general goal of the organization specifies an area of activity instead of a specific activity and therefore is subject to wide differences in specific interpretations."[15] If the previous argument is correct, lack of specificity of objectives will reverberate throughout the structure as disagreements over choosing tasks to be performed, personnel to be hired, resources to be allocated, members to be compensated and status and authority to be distributed.

One solution to these problems, the "strong man" approach in which one individual or group decrees the organization's objectives, and forces conformity in accordance with this definition, is comparatively rare for medical organizations in this country. The extra-organizational power wielded by medical groups makes them impervious to the coercive pressures of administrators. Also, lack of agreement on goals and too few common

[15]Thompson, James D. and Bates, Frederick L., Technology, Organization, and Administration, *Administrative Science Quarterly*, 2, 329, December, 1957.

interests hinder the medical staff as a body in arbitrarily specifying the objectives to pursue. The other solution for the problems created by lack of goal specificity is to decentralize the structure as much as possible, allowing considerable autonomy for individuals and groups to pursue self-defined objectives. In this approach the administrator's tasks are to represent the interests of the "organization as a whole" in those instances where such interests are involved and can be identified, serve as mediator when conflicts erupt between powerful departments, and plea the cause of weaker groups. In short, hospital administrators and medical managers have their work cut out for them, and committees, standing and *ad hoc*, will meet far into the night.

ORGANIZATIONAL TASKS

Goals are only conceptions of desired ends. If they are to have consequences for the behavior of organizational participants—and all professed goals do not have such consequences, as numerous investigators have noted—they must become operative: that is, they must be translated into specific tasks which are allocated to participants. A *task* is simply a set of activities performed to achieve some goal. The end product of performing a task is an *outcome*—the actual result achieved by carrying out the activities. Of course, an outcome may or may not correspond closely with the original goal—the desired result.

Carrying out a set of task activities always entails overcoming some kind of "resistance." For example, the inertia of an object which is to be moved, the opposition of a competitor, or the complexity presented by a problem to be solved. For present purposes, the amount of resistance to be overcome is not so critical as its variability. Thus, two polar types of tasks may be distinguished. *Inert* tasks consist of those activities performed against resistance which is relatively constant across performances. *Active* tasks are those activities performed against resistance which is relatively variable across performances.[16] In the case of inert tasks, because resistance is constant, it is predictable; for active tasks, the amount of resistance to be encountered at any given time is less likely to be known.[17] These task characteristics have important implications both for designing efficient work arrangements and for evaluating and controlling task performances.

Nature of Task and Work Arrangements

ROUTINE TASK ACTIVITIES   Inert tasks are more likely to call forth routine task activities. That is, when the resistance confronted is constant and known, the appropriate task activities to be performed may be specified in advance. In March and Simon's terms, "performance programs" can be devised.[18] Developing efficient work arrangements for inert tasks requires economy in centralizing decisions concerning appropriate task activities and assigning specific sequences of standard activities to individual, subordinate participants. Inert tasks lend themselves to subdivision and thereby permit the efficiencies associated with specialization: short training periods, replaceability of participants, increased skills through frequent repetition of activities,

ease of control, etc. Costs are also associated with extreme specialization, including the fatigue associated with repetitive activities, lowered worker satisfaction and work group morale, and job insecurity. A large administrative staff is required to design the performance programs, recruit, train and supervise the work force, handle unusual problems, direct the flow of materials, and coordinate the contributions of the various participants. In short, bureaucratic[19] arrangements seem to be ideally suited for carrying out activities in the performance of inert tasks. Innumerable examples may be found of bureaucratic structures dealing with inert tasks. To name but a few, automobile production assembly lines, the Bureau of Internal Revenue, post offices, and housekeeping, cafeteria, and laboratory facilities in hospitals.

Of course, the bureaucratized arrangements just outlined may be used to process active tasks. In such cases organization participants must behave as if the resistance offered by the objects being processed were constant. This assumption can only be made at a cost. Because the standard prescribed activities may be inappropriate to meet the particular amount of resistance encountered at a given time, standard approaches to active tasks will entail a high proportion of errors or failures. Such a situation is exemplified, at least to a

---

[16]Scott, W. Richard, Sanford M. Dornbusch, Bruce C. Busching, and James D. Laing, Organizational Evaluation and Authority, *Administrative Science Quarterly*, 12, 109, June, 1967.

[17]It is possible to distinguish between active tasks in terms of whether or not the resistance encountered is patterned. If the resistance exhibits regularity its strength is more likely to be predictable, and to the extent that it is, patterned active tasks may be organized in a manner comparable to inert tasks.

[18]March and Simon, *op. cit.*, pp. 141–150.

[19]A bureaucratic organization is characterized by the existence of particular structural features, the most critical of which is a specialized administrative staff. Also involved, in varying degrees, are elaborate procedural rules, an advanced division of labor, impersonal relations between hierarchical levels and an emphasis on technical criteria of recruitment and advancement. See Weber, Max, THE THEORY OF SOCIAL AND ECONOMIC ORGANIZATION, Glencoe, Illinois, Free Press, 1947, pp. 328–341. Since these several features do not necessarily exhibit concomitant variation, measures of the degree of bureaucratization exhibited by a given organization will vary depending on choice of indicator.

considerable degree, by the operation of public welfare agencies in this country. Here, over the protests of the professional social work community, a very diverse client group is "processed" in large measure by the performance of standardized sets of activities.[20]

NONROUTINE TASK ACTIVITIES   The proportion of errors associated with performing active task can be reduced by allowing individual performers to assess the amount of resistance with which they are confronted at a given time and to adjust their activities accordingly. To the extent that individual workers are permitted to exercise discretion in handling tasks, the subdivision of such tasks is not feasible. A performer usually carries out the entire sequence of activities, making adjustments in later activities in accordance with the responses to his earlier efforts. The greater discretion permitted workers must usually be coupled with greater individual competence—requiring longer training periods—if the discretion granted them is to be effectively employed in guiding the selection and sequencing of task activities. A smaller administrative overhead usually results since less planning, supervision and coordination are required. But, generally speaking, processing task activities by large numbers of skilled practitioners is a more costly organizational arrangement than the one previously described.

Obviously, the arrangement just outlined, in which individual performers are delegated discretion over their own task performances, has many of the earmarks of a professional system. The most important missing element is one which is likely to develop in these circumstances; namely, the formation of coalitions

among practitioners to establish and maintain performance standards and to prevent undue interference from "outsiders"—those not possessing similar skills.[21] As noted, professional arrangements are more expensive than bureaucratic ones. They do, however, facilitate the effective handling of active tasks. Hence, in situations where persons are concerned about the quality of outcomes—where they are unwilling to allow a high proportion of errors—these increased costs are accepted and borne. Such is the case for physicians' tasks in clinics and hospitals, for scientific tasks in research enterprises, and for scientific and, to a lesser degree, teaching tasks in most colleges and universities.

To summarize, tasks aimed at surmounting constant resistance can be effectively organized by means of bureaucratic arrangements. Tasks aimed at overcoming variable resistance are usually better organized in a "professional" manner since skilled, nonroutine responses are better calculated to meet unpredictable resistance with a minimum of errors. The nature of the resistance to be overcome in task performance is certainly not the only factor to be taken into account in developing appropriate organizational arrangements. It does, however, appear to be a factor of considerable consequence.[22]

TASK CONCEPTIONS   Whether a given task is active or inert can usually be determined by empirical investigation. However, occupational groups tend to develop collective conceptions of the

---

[20]*See* Scott, W. Richard, Professional Employees in a Bureaucratic Structure: Social Work, *in* Etzioni, Amitai (editor), *The Semi-Professions and Their Organization*, New York: Free Press, 1969, 82–140.

[21]For a discussion of professional groups placing heavy emphasis on the organization of practitioners for self-regulation, *see* Goode, William J., Community within a Community: The Professions, *American Sociological Review*, 22, 194–200, April, 1957.

[22]For a related discussion of routine-nonroutine task activities and associated organizational arrangements, *see* Litwak, Eugene, Models of Bureaucracy which Permit Conflict, *American Journal of Sociology*, 67, 177–184, September, 1961.

nature of the tasks they perform. For example, all tasks performed by professional persons, such as physicians, are not active in nature, but professionals often define them as such, demanding the right to exercise discretion, free from bureaucratic controls, with respect to all of their tasks. In short, task conceptions may in some circumstances reflect ideological claims rather than empirical realities as occupational groups seek justification to support preferred work arrangements.

Conceptions of tasks can have rather far-reaching implications for occupational groups. Nursing groups, for example, have never reached agreement as to the basic nature of their primary tasks. Some, such as the British advocates of the "Nightingale approach," see nurses performing largely routine tasks under the direction of physicians and the matron. Strict discipline and conformity are emphasized and apprenticeship to ward nurses is perferred as the principle training method over theoretical or didactic instruction. Others, such as the United States advocates of the "professional approach," believe that nurses should exercise discretion in meeting the nursing needs of individual patients and emphasize the importance of theoretical training.[23] Advocates of the professional approach in this country have been fairly successful in inculcating students with their views, but have been less successful in transforming hospital arrangements within which nurses must work, with the result that large numbers of professionally trained nurses refuse to work in a hospital setting.[24]

To conclude, the nature and the conceptions of the tasks to be performed are important determinants of organizational structures. The distinction which has been proposed between active and inert tasks is admittedly crude and will require much refinement. However, researchers must concern themselves with the actual work that is done by participants in organizations if they are to understand the structural arrangements which allocate and control this work. This distinction may be of some use in obtaining a preliminary focus on these matters.

[23]Glaser, William A., Nursing Leadership and Policy: Some Cross-national Comparisons, in Davis, Fred (Editor), THE NURSING PROFESSION: FIVE SOCIOLOGICAL ESSAYS, New York, John Wiley & Sons, Inc., 1966, pp. 4–30.

[24]Davis, Fred, Olesen, Virginia L. and Whittaker, Elvi W., Problems and Issues in Collegiate Nursing Education," in Davis, op. cit., pp. 162–167.

34   Domains of Organized Action

James D. Thompson

In accounting for the produced automobile, we ultimately must take into consideration the mining of ore and the production of steel, the extraction and refining of petroleum, and the production of rubber or synthetic rubber, all of which are essential (within current technology) if an automobile is to roll from a factory. Along the way the firm may also receive contributions from others who make fabricating machinery and conveyor belts, or build factories, and still others who generate and distribute power and credit. Some automobile manufacturers include within their boundaries a larger proportion or different array of these essential activities than other such firms, but none is self-sufficient.

Consider the technology of treating medical ills. A fairly routine hospital case may now rely on a series of complex organizations which perform research, make pharmaceuticals, ship, store, and prepare medications. It involves use of the products of medical schools and nursing schools (which may be incorporated within the hospital), and of factories which construct x-ray apparatus or weave cloth to make sheets. Hospitals vary in the extent to which they include or exclude certain essential activities, but none is self-sufficient.

The overall technology of producing steel products involves the discovery and extraction of ore, its transportation to points where furnaces and power are concentrated, and the processing of ores into steel. Ultimately it includes the fabrication of steel into items for final consumption. An organization within the steel industry must establish some niche and some boundaries around that part of the total effort for which the organization takes initiative. For reasons to be discussed later, firms involved in extraction, ore transport, and the basic processing of steel seldom undertake the ultimate conversion of steel into products for final use. In any event, the steel firm is dependent on others along the way.

The essential point is that all organizations must establish what Levine and White (1961) have termed a "domain." In their study of relationships among health agencies in a community, domain consists of "claims which an organization stakes out for itself in terms of (1) diseases covered, (2) population served, and (3) services rendered." With appro-

priate modifications in the specifics of the definition—for example, substituting "range of products" for "diseases covered"—the concept of domain appears useful for the analysis of all types of complex organizations. Thus universities are universities, but their domains may range considerably; some offer astronomy courses, others do not; some serve local populations, others are international; some offer student housing and graduate education, others do not. No two firms in the oil industry are identical in terms of domain. Some refine petroleum, and market gasoline and other derivatives; others buy and market gasoline and oil Some operate in a regional territory; others are national or international. Some provide credit cards; others are cash and carry. Prisons may be prisons at one level of analysis, but the concept of domain may prevent us from making inappropriate comparisons of prisons with very different domains.

Domain, Dependence, and Environment

In the final analysis the results of organizational action rest not on a single technology but upon a technological matrix. A complicated technology incorporates the products or results of still other technologies. Although a particular organization may operate several core technologies, its domain always falls short of the total matrix. Hence the organization's domain identifies the points at which the organization is dependent on inputs from the environment. The composition of that environment, the location within it of capacities, in turn determines upon whom the organization is dependent.

The organization may find that there is only one possible source for a particular kind of support needed, whereas for another there may be many alternatives; the capacity of the environment to provide the needed support may be dispersed or concentrated. Similarly, demand for that capacity may be concentrated or dispersed; there may or may not be competition for it. If the organization's need is unique or nearly so, we can say that demand for the input is concentrated; if many others have similar needs, we can say that the demand is dispersed.

Similar distinctions can be made on the output side of the organization. Its environment may contain one or many potential customers or clients, and the organization may be alone in serving them or it may be one of many competitors approaching the client or clients.

The extent to which the sources of input and output support coincide may also be important to the organization. The general hospital in a major metropolitan area may draw its financial support from one sector of the environment, its personnel inputs from another, and its clientele from still a different one; and there may be no interaction among these elements except via the hospital. The general hospital in a small community, however, may find that the necessary parties are functionally interdependent and interact regularly with respect to religious, economic, recreational, and governmental matters.

The public school usually finds its clientele and financial supporters concentrated, and the two interconnected. The municipal university may be in a similar situation, whereas the private university may collect financial inputs, students, faculty, and research data from quite varied and separated sources.

Task Environments

But the notion of environment turns out to be a residual one; it refers to "everything else." To simplify our analysis, we can adopt the concept of *task environment* used by Dill (1958) to denote those parts of the environment which are "relevant or potentially relevant to goal setting and goal attainment." Dill found the task environments of two Norwegian firms to be composed of four major sectors: (1) customers (both distributors and users); (2) suppliers of materials, labor, capital, equipment, and work space; (3) competitors for both markets and resources; and (4) regulatory groups, including governmental agencies, unions, and interfirm associations. With appropriate modifications of the specific referrents—for example, substituting "clients" for "customers" in some cases—we have a useful concept to work with, and one much more delimited in scope than environment. We are now working with those organizations in the environment which make a difference to the organization in question; Evan (1966) employs the term "organization set" for this purpose.

[The remaining environment can be set aside for a while, but we cannot discard it for two reasons: (1) patterns of culture can and do influence organizations in important ways, and (2) the environment beyond the task environment may constitute a field into which an organization may enter at some point in the future. We will consider both of these aspects later.]

Just as no two domains are identical, no two task environments are identical. Which individuals, which other organizations, which aggregates constitute the task environment for a particular organization is determined by the requirements of the technology, the boundaries of the domain, and the composition of the larger environment.

Task Environments and Domain Consensus

The establishment of domain cannot be an arbitrary, unilateral action. Only if the organization's claims to domain are recognized by those who can provide the necessary support, by the task environment, can a domain be operational. The relationship between an organization and its task environment is essentially one of exchange, and unless the organization is judged by those in contact with it as offering something desirable, it will not receive the inputs necessary for survival. The elements typically exchanged by the health organizations studied by Levine and White fall into three main categories: (1) referral of cases, clients, or patients; (2) giving or receiving of labor services encompassing the use of volunteers, lent personnel, and offering of instruction to personnel of other organizations; and (3) sending or receiving of resources other than labor services, including funds, equipment, case and technical information. The specific categories of exchange vary from one type of organization to another, but in each case, as they note, exchange agreements rest upon *prior consensus regarding domain.*

The concept of domain consensus has some special advantages for our analysis of organizations in action, for it enables us to deal with operational goals (Perrow, 1961a) without imputing to the organization the human quality of motivation and without assuming a "group mind," two grounds on which the notion of organizational goals has been challenged.

Domain consensus defines a set of expectations both for members of an organization and for others with whom they interact, about what the organization will and will not do. It provides, although imperfectly, an image of the organization's role in a larger system, which in turn serves as a guide for the ordering of action in certain directions and not in others. Using the concept of domain consensus, we need not assume that the formal statement of goals found in charters, articles of incorporation, or institutional advertising is in fact the criterion upon which rationality is judged and choices of action alternatives are made. Nor need we accept such ideologies as that which insists that profit is

the goal of the firm. The concept of domain consensus can be clearly separated from individual goals or motives. Regardless of these, members of hospitals somehow conceive of their organizations as oriented around medical care, and this conception is reinforced by those with whom the members interact. Members of regulatory agencies likewise conceive of a jurisdiction for their organizations, and members of automobile manufacturing firms conceive of production and distribution of certain kinds of vehicles as the organization's excuse for existence.

MANAGEMENT OF INTERDEPENDENCE

Task environments of complex organizations turn out to be multifaceted or pluralistic, composed of several or many distinguishable others potentially relevant in establishing domain consensus. This appears to be true even of organizations embedded in totalitarian politico-economic systems, since for any specific organization there appears to be alternative sources of some inputs; the several kinds of inputs required come under the jurisdictions of different state agencies; and there are alternative forms of output or places for disposal of output (Berliner, 1957; Granick, 1959; Richman, 1963). The evidence is inescapable that elaborate state planning and decrees do not fully settle for specific industrial organizations in the Soviet Union the questions of domain and domain consensus.

This pluralism of task environments is significant for complex organizations because it means that an organization must exchange with not one but several elements, each of which is itself involved in a network of interdependence, with its own domain and task environment. In the process of working out solutions to its problems, an element of the task environment may find it necessary or desirable to discontinue support to an organization. Thus task environments pose contingencies for organizations.

Task environments also impose constraints. The capacities of supporting organizations and the absence of feasible alternatives may fix absolute limits to the support which may be available to an organization at a given time. The most dramatic example of constraints, perhaps, arises in the case of governmental organizations which are captives of a particular population. The public school system treated badly by its mandatory population may lose some of its members, but the organization as such cannot move to another community; it must stay home and fight the "in-law" battle. The foreign office of a world power cannot elect to negotiate in another, rosier world. The captive organization exists in the business world, as well, in the form of the satellite or subsidiary firm, or the firm which produces for a single buyer, as in the missile business during the 1950s. Carlson (1951) notes that some organizations have no control over selection of clientele, and that the clientele likewise lacks an option. He refers to these as "domesticated" because they are not compelled to attend to all of their needs, society guaranteeing their existence.

Since the dependence of an organization on its task environment introduces not only constraints but also contingencies, both of which interfere with the attainment of rationality, we would expect organizations subject to norms of rationality to attempt to manage dependency.

Power and Dependence

Building on a conception advanced by Richard Emerson (1962), we can say that an organization is dependent on some element of its task environment (1) in proportion to the organization's need for resources or performances which that element can provide and (2) in inverse proportion to the ability of other elements to provide the same resource or performance. Thus a manufacturing firm is dependent on a financial organization to the extent that the firm needs financial resources, and financial resources are not available from other sources. The hospital is dependent on physicians in the community to the extent that the hospital needs patients and that physicians monopolize the capacity to refer patients to hospitals.

Emerson points out that dependence can be seen as the obverse of power. Thus an organization has power, relative to an element of its task environment, to the extent that the organization has capacity to satisfy needs of that element and to the extent that the organization monopolizes that capacity.

This approach to dependence and power has several advantages for our analysis of complex organizations and their domains. It frees us from the necessity of viewing power as some generalized attribute of the organization, and leads us to consider net power as resulting from a set of relationships between the organization and the several elements of its pluralistic task environment. Thus an organization may be relatively powerful in relation to those who supply its inputs and relatively powerless in relation to those who receive its outputs, or vice versa. Or an organization may be relatively powerful in relation to both input and output sectors, a situation which may generate "countervailing power" (Galbraith, 1958) in the form, for example, of new or strengthened regulatory agencies which become part of its task environment (Palamountain, 1955).

An organization may be relatively powerless on all sectors of its task environment, as Burton Clark (1956) has shown in his study of an adult education organization. This organization rested on "precarious values," in the sense that none of the important elements of its environment was fully committed to adult education as a high-priority activity. The organization therefore had to cater to whatever fleeting interests of an unstable population it could activate at a particular time, had to scrounge for resources, and could not develop a sustained domain consensus which would have facilitated planning for efficiency.

An organization may have power with respect to competitors if it has ability to act without regard for their actions; i.e., if competitors do not pose contingency factors for the organization. In the business sphere this is illustrated by the phenomenon of "price leadership," where it appears that no matter what action the price leader takes, it will be copied by followers. This situation also illustrates that an organization may be powerful in its task environment whether this is advantageous or not; for instance, being the price leader may be embarrassing in an environment which suspects collusion in such situations, and which contains regulatory agencies to penalize collusion. One of the advantages of the definition of power we have chosen is that it does not rest on any assumptions of intent or usage.

Finally, the power-dependence concept advanced here provides an important escape from the "zero-sum" concept of power (Emerson, 1962; Parsons, 1960), which assumes that in a system composed of A and B, the power of A is power at the expense of B. By considering power in the context of interdependence, we admit the possibility of A and B becoming increasingly powerful with regard to each other—the possibility that increasing interdependence may result in increased net power. It is this possibility on which coalitions rest.

The hospital, for example, may be quite dependent on referring physicians who control the supply of patients, and

we would say that physicians are powerful with respect to the hospital. At the same time, if the hospital is the only one available or is sufficiently superior to others, physicians may be highly dependent on the hospital, and we would say that the hospital was powerful with respect to physicians. Thus the conception of power as rooted in dependence permits us to consider power in non-zero-sum terms.

The Competitive Strategy

We noted earlier that the task environment is defined by the dependence of the organization. Since dependence introduces constraints or contingencies, the problem for the organization is to avoid becoming subservient to elements of the task environment.

Proposition 3.1: Under norms of rationality, organizations seek to minimize the power of task-environment elements over them by maintaining alternatives.

To the extent that the needed capacity is dispersed through the task environment, the organization may develop alternative sources. By scattering its dependence, it prevents the concentration of power over it. It need not concede power to a single element of the task environment. (This maneuver sometimes encourages the several suppliers to coalesce into a united front, thus gaining power through its concentration. Cartels are an example.) We might expect, for example, that under favorable conditions the organization would practice exchanging with each of its several possible sources, thus establishing with each a precedent for support if conditions become less favorable (Kriesberg, 1955).

Now if the task environment contains not only many elements with the needed capacity but also many elements requiring such capacity, we are at or near the point which economists describe as perfect competition, when sufficient numbers of suppliers and demanders make the actions of any one insignificant. We would expect organizations to elect to compete under such conditions, for the organization knows that support will be available when needed and that it can maintain its freedom from commitment by negotiating an exchange each and every time a need occurs.

In reality, however, conditions of perfect competition are infrequent and highly unstable over time; and even if the organization faces perfect competition in one sector—for example, in disposing of its output—it may face imperfect competition in other sectors—for example, the recruitment of personnel. Competition in an imperfect market introduces considerable contingency, for it forces the relevant elements of the task environment to seek alternative sources of exchange, and thereby raises the possibility of losing out on any particular negotiation to such "third parties." Each time the organization needs a particular kind of support, it offers something in exchange; but if the elements of the task environment which control that support have better offers, the organization may be without a source of supply. Buffering capacity may reduce the severity of this problem (Prop. 2.2), but does not eliminate it.[1]

If the organization engaged in competing for its needs must assume imperfect competition, in which the actions of (large) elements in the market can make significant differences, it becomes advisable to skew the imbalance in the organization's favor.

Proposition 3.2: Organizations subject to rationality norms and competing for support seek prestige.

Acquiring prestige is the "cheapest" way of acquiring power. To the extent that an environmental element finds it prestigeful to exchange with an organization, the organization has gained a measure of power over that element without making any commitments; i.e., it has gained power without yielding power. The importance of prestige is underscored in the study of a voluntary general hospital by Perrow (1961b), who sees the creation and maintenance of a "favorable image of the organization in its salient publics" as an important way of controlling dependency. Perrow concludes that if an organization and its products are well regarded, it may more easily attract personnel, influence relevant legislation, wield informal power in the community, and ensure adequate numbers of clients, customers, donors, or investors. Litwak and Hylton (1962) found that welfare organizations which could establish distinctive bases for raising funds could reduce their dependency on the other agencies in the community and thereby resist efforts to incorporate them into Community Chest programs.

The fostering of prestigeful images is widely evident among business firms, universities, and government agencies.

Proposition 3.3: When support capacity is concentrated in one or a few elements of the task environment, organizations under norms of rationality seek power relative to those on whom they are dependent.

We are not asserting that organizations with power will necessarily exercise or flaunt it, nor that the desire for power

---

[1] "Buffering" is a set of techniques by which the organization attempts to absorb fluctuations in the environment. For example, on the input side, the organization may stockpile materials and supplies acquired in an irregular market so that they may be inserted into the production process in a steady fashion. On the output side, buffering may take the form of maintaining warehouse inventories which allow for production of items at a constant rate but for distribution to fluctuate with market conditions. [*Ed.*] See Thompson, *Organizations in Action*, pp. 20-21.

provides personal motives for individuals holding responsibilities at the institutional level of the organization. The proposition does assume, however, that power is a way of handling what would otherwise be serious contingencies, and that rationality is not achieved by completely powerless (dependent) organizations. We would expect, therefore, that organizations subject to rationality norms and constrained by monopolized or nearly monopolized capacity for support, will maneuver toward achieving power to offset their dependence. The question is how to achieve such power.

THE ACQUISITION OF POWER

Complex organizations "acquire" dependence when they establish domains, but the acquisition of power is not so easy. Organizations may, however, trade on the fact that other organizations in their task environments also have problems of domain and face constraints and contingencies. In the management of this interdependence, organizations employ cooperative strategies (Thompson and McEwen, 1958). As Cyert and March (1963) conclude, organizations avoid having to anticipate environmental action by arranging negotiated environments.

Cooperative Strategies

Using cooperation to gain power with respect to some element of the task environment, the organization must demonstrate its *capacity to reduce uncertainty* for that element and *must make a commitment* to exchange that capacity.

Thus an agreement between A and B, specifying that A will supply and B will purchase, reduces uncertainty for both. A knows more about its output targets, and B knows more about its inputs. Likewise, the affiliation of a medical practitioner

with a hospital reduces uncertainty for both. The medical practitioner has increased assurance that his patients will have bed and related facilities, and the hospital has increased assurance that its facilities will be used.

Convincing an environmental element of the organization's capacity to satisfy future needs is enhanced by historical evidence; prior satisfactory performance tends to suggest satisfactory performance in the future, and we might expect the organization to prefer to maintain an on-going relationship rather than establish a new one for the same purpose.

Under cooperative strategies, the effective achievement of power rests on the exchange of commitments, the reduction of potential uncertainty for both parties. But commitments are obtained by giving commitments and uncertainty, reduced for the organization through its reduction of uncertainty for others. Commitment thus is a double-edged sword, and management of interdependence presents organizations with dilemmas. Contracting, coopting, and coalescing represent different degrees of cooperation and commitment, and present organizations with alternatives.

Contracting refers here to the negotiation of an agreement for the exchange of performances in the future. Our usage is not restricted to those agreements which legal bodies would recognize. It includes agreements formally achieved between labor and industrial management via collective bargaining, but it also includes the understanding between a police department and minor criminals to forego prosecution in exchange for information about more important criminal activities. It also covers the understanding between a university and a donor involving, for example, the naming of buildings or the awarding of honorary degrees. Contractual agreements thus may rest on faith and the belief that the other will perform in order to maintain a reputation or prestige (Prop. 3.2), or they may depend on institutional patterns whereby third parties can be depended upon to evaluate fulfillment of obligations and assess penalties for failure (Macaulay, 1963).

Coopting has been defined (Selznick, 1949) as the process of absorbing new elements into the leadership or policy-determining structure of an organization as a means of averting threats to its stability or existence. Cooptation increases the certainty of future support by the organization coopted. The acceptance on the corporation's board of directors of representatives of financial institutions, for example, increases the likelihood of access to financial resources for the duration of the cooptive arrangement. But coopting is a more constraining form of cooperation than contracting, for to the extent that cooptation is effective it places an element of the environment in a position to raise questions and perhaps exert influence on other aspects of the organization.

Coalescing refers to a combination or joint venture with another organization or organizations in the environment. A coalition may be unstable, or may have a stated terminal point; but to the extent that it is operative, the organizations involved act as one with respect to certain operational goals. Coalition not only provides a basis for exchange but also requires a commitment to future joint decision making. It is therefore a more constraining form of cooperation than coopting.

Proposition 3.3 said that when support capacity is concentrated within few elements in the task environment, organizations under norms of rationality seek power relative to those on whom they are dependent. We can refine that proposition somewhat, using the distinctions just introduced relative to degrees of cooperation and commitment.

Proposition 3.3a: When support capacity is concentrated *and balanced against concentrated demands* the organizations involved will attempt to handle their dependence through contracting.

Proposition 3.3b: When support capacity is concentrated *but demand dispersed,* the weaker organization will attempt to handle its dependence through coopting.

Proposition 3.3c: When support capacity is concentrated and balanced against concentrated demands, but the power achieved through contracting is inadequate, the organizations involved will attempt to coalesce.

DEFENSE OF DOMAIN

The attainment of a viable domain is, in essence, a political problem. It requires finding and holding a position which can be recognized by all of the necessary "sovereign" organizations as more worthwhile than available alternatives. It requires establishing a position in which diverse organizations in diverse situations find overlapping interests. The management of interorganizational relations is just as political as the management of a political party or of international relationships. It can also be just as dynamic, as environments change and propel some elements out of and new elements into a task environment.

And just as political parties and world powers move toward their objectives through compromise, complex purposive organizations find compromise inevitable. The problem is to find the optimum point between the realities of interdependence with the environment and the norms of rationality.

Proposition 3.4: The more sectors in which the organization subject to rationality norms is constrained, the more power the organization will seek over remaining sectors of its task environment.

The public school, for example, which is constrained to accept virtually all students of a specified age, under conditions of population growth has urgent need for power with respect to those in the task environment who control financial and other inputs. If the task environment imposes mandatory loads, the school must seek power with respect to resources. The private school, on the other hand, may be able to treat both student load and inputs as variables, and seek their mutual adjustment.

The business firm constrained by an impoverished market, as during a recession, finds it urgent to have power to curtail the rate and price of inputs provided by supply elements of the task environment. To the extent that it has power, it may renegotiate contractual arrangements. If the firm is also constrained by large fixed costs, as in heavy industries, our proposition would predict that the organization will seek power to curtail the flow of labor inputs. It is in such industries that wage payments typically are in hourly or piece rates, and the firms are not committed to fixed salaries or guaranteed annual wages. By contrast, in the university, where variations in student load occur primarily at only one time of the year, wage payments are in annual terms.

Proposition 3.5: The organization facing many constraints and unable to achieve power in other sectors of its task environment will seek to enlarge the task environment.

Captive organizations frequently find themselves boxed in on several sides, to the point where norms of rationality are threatened or overwhelmed. It is at this point that captive organizations often join forces to establish noncaptive, evaluating organizations which develop yardsticks of rationality and set standards for accreditation. Community hospitals, prisons, city governments, and public schools all exhibit this device of creating new elements in the task environment to offset other constraints within it. To the extent that

the new element has power to confer or withhold prestige, it can loosen the constraints operating on the organization (Prop. 3.2). The nonaccredited school or hospital, for example, may be threatened with irreplaceable loss of personnel, to the point where those who control financial inputs are forced to increase their support.

RECAPITULATION

The domain claimed by an organization and recognized by its environment determines the points at which the organization is dependent, facing both constraints and contingencies. To attain any significant measure of self-control, the organization must manage its dependency. Under norms of rationality, therefore (Prop. 3.1), organizations seek to minimize the power of task-environment elements over them by maintaining alternatives. When competing for support (Prop. 3.2), organizations seek prestige, which is a way of gaining power without increasing dependency.

Often, however, the environment does not offer many alternative sources of support. When support capacity is concentrated in the task environment (Prop. 3.3), organizations seek power relative to those on whom they are dependent. Subject to the nature of the interdependence, the organizations may resort to contracting, coopting, or coalescing.

The more an organization is constrained in some sectors of its task environment (Prop. 3.4), the more power it will seek over remaining elements of its task environment. When the organization is unable to achieve such a balance (Prop. 3.5), it will seek to enlarge its task environment.

From the point of view of a rational model of organizations, the compromises and meaneuvering in defense of domains are disruptive and costly. We would therefore expect organizations subject to norms of rationality to seek to design themselves so as to minimize the necessity of maneuvering and compromise. . .

References

Berliner, Joseph S. (1957), *Factory and Manager in the USSR*, Cambridge, Mass.: Harvard University Press.

Carlson, Sune (1951), *Executive Behavior*, Stockholm: Strömberg Aktiebolag.

Clark, Burton R. (1956), *Adult Education in Transition*, Berkeley, Calif.: University of California Press.

Cyert, Richard M and James G. March (1963), *A Behavioral Theory of the Firm*, Englewood Cliffs, N.J.: Prentice-Hall.

Dill, William R. (1958), "Environment as an Influence on Managerial Autonomy," *Administrative Science Quarterly*, Vol. 2, March, pp. 409-443.

Emerson, Richard M. (1962), "Power-Dependence Relations," *American Sociological Review*, Vol. 27, February, pp. 31-40.

Evan, William M. (1966), "The Organization-Set: Toward a Theory of Interorganizational Relations," in James D. Thompson, ed., *Approaches to Organizational Design*, Pittsburgh, Pa.: The University of Pittsburgh Press.

Galbraith, John K. (1958), *American Capitalism: The Concept of Countervailing Power*, Boston: Houghton Mifflin Company.

Granick, David (1959), *Management of the Industrial Firm in the USSR*, New York: Columbia University Press.

Kriesberg, Louis (1955), "Occupational Controls Among Steel Distributors,"

American Journal of Sociology, Vol. 61, November, pp. 203-212.

Levine, Sol, and Paul E. White (1961), "Exchange as a Conceptual Framework for the Study of Interorganizational Relationships," *Administrative Science Quarterly*, Vol. 5, March, pp. 583-601.

Litwak, Eugene and Lydia F. Hylton (1962), "Inter-Organizational Analysis," *Administrative Science Quarterly*, Vol. 6, March, pp. 395-420.

Macaulay, Stewart (1963), "Non-Contractual Relations in Business: A Preliminary Study," *American Sociological Review*, Vol. 28, February, pp. 55-67.

Palamountain, Joseph C., Jr. (1955), *The Politics of Distribution*, Cambridge, Mass.: Harvard University Press.

Parsons, Talcott (1960), *Structure and Process in Modern Societies*, New York: The Free Press of Glencoe.

Perrow, Charles (1961a), "The Analysis of Goals in Complex Organizations," *American Sociological Review*, Vol. 26, December, pp. 854-866.

Perrow, Charles (1961b), "Organizational Prestige: Some Functions and Dysfunctions," *American Journal of Sociology*, Vol. 66, January, pp. 335-341.

Richman, Barry M. (1963), "Managerial Motivation in Soviet and Czechoslovak Industries: A Comparison," *Academy of Management Journal*, Vol. 6, June, pp. 107-128.

Selznick, Philip (1949), *TVA and the Grass Roots*, Berkeley, Calif.: University of California Press.

Thompson, James D. and William J. McEwen (1958), "Organizational Goals and Environment: Goal-setting as an Interaction Process," *American Sociological Review*, Vol. 23, February, pp. 23-31.

Further Reading

Several recent textbooks provide an introduction to the sociology of organizations. These include two short introductions in paperback: Peter M. Blau, *Bureaucracy in Modern Society*, New York: Random House, Inc., 1956; and Amitai Etzioni, *Modern Organizations*, Englewood Cliffs, N.J.: Prentice-Hall, 1964. Other widely used texts are Peter M. Blau and W. Richard Scott, *Formal Organizations*, San Francisco: Chandler Publishing Company, 1962; Daniel Katz and Robert Kahn, *The Social Psychology of Organizations*, New York: Wiley; and James D. Thompson, *Organizations in Action*, New York: McGraw-Hill, 1967.

The two individuals who have done most to shape the sociological conception of organizations are undoubtedly Weber and Barnard. Their major works are Max

Weber, *The Theory of Social and Economic Organization*, Glencoe, Ill.: Free Press, 1947; and Chester I. Barnard, *The Functions of the Executive*, Cambridge, Mass.: Harvard University Press, 1938.

There have been many empirical monographs devoted to the study of a variety of organizations, particularly in the last fifteen years. Influential studies are those of Philip Selznick, *TVA and the Grass Roots*, Berkeley, Calif.: University of California Press, 1949, a study of environmental pressures that forced the Tennessee Valley Authority to revise some of its goals; Alvin W. Gouldner, *Patterns of Industrial Bureaucracy*, Glencoe, Ill.: Free Press, 1954, an examination of bureaucratization processes occurring in a gypsum mine and factory; Peter M. Blau, *Dynamics of Bureaucracy*, Chicago: University of Chicago Press, 1955, a study of informal work groups in a state and federal agency; and Seymour Martin Lipset, Martin Trow, and James S. Coleman, *Union Democracy*, Glencoe, Ill.: Free Press, 1956, an attempt to determine why the International Typographers Union has been able to resist tendencies toward oligarchy affecting most unions and to successfully maintain a two-party democratic structure.

Finally, there are available several good readers and a collection of original review articles on organizations. Readers include Robert K. Merton *et al.* (eds.), *Reader in Bureaucracy*, Glencoe, Ill.: Free Press, 1952; Amitai Etzioni, *Complex Organizations: A Sociological Reader*, New York: Holt, Rinehart and Winston, Inc., 1961; and Joseph A. Litterer, *Organizations: Structure and Behavior*, New York: Wiley, 1963. A collection of original articles in which a number of specialists review current developments on selected topics is James G. March (ed.), *Handbook of Organizations*, Skokie, Ill.: Rand McNally, 1965.

PART SIX

Social Processes in Communities

The term *community* is employed by both the general public and by sociologists to refer to a distressingly large and disparate group of phenomena. It is used to refer to cities of every size range, to occupational groups (for example, one frequently hears reference to "the professional community" or to "the blue-collar community"), and, indeed, to groups of almost any kind, ranging from nation states, as in "the Atlantic community," to individuals sharing certain characteristics or attitudes, as in "the radical community." The term *community* has been applied by some sociologists to the organizations, such as prisons and mental hospitals, that encompass the full life, at least for a time, of their inmates. The term is also employed to refer to a particular type of relationship characterized by social intimacy, similarity of values, and cohesion, a type of relation that is said to no longer exist in the urban situation.[1] All this can be confusing in that we have the absence of community (by one definition) in the midst of community (by another definition).

In the interests of terminological clarity, we prefer to restrict the definition of *community* to social units having a territorial basis. This would exclude many of the above usages, such as application to occupational or other types of special interest groups. Communities can be distinguished from organizations by the absence of explicit and specific objectives. Further, as Moe notes:

The community is not structurally and functionally centralized in the same sense as a formal organization. The great range and diversity of the needs, interests, goals and activities of people of the community are met through a variety of separate institutions and groups—no one of which holds a completely dominant position in relation to the others.[2]

[1]See, for example, Maurice R. Stein, *The Eclipse of Community*, Princeton, N.J.: Princeton University Press, 1960.

[2]Edward O. Moe, "Consulting with a community system: A case study," *Journal of Social Issues*, 15, No. 2 (1959), 29. Emphasis in original.

431

Finally, we do not want to prejudge the quality of the social relationships among the participants by restricting the concept of community to the relationships characterized by a high degree of intimacy and affect.

STRUCTURAL CHARACTERISTICS OF COMMUNITIES

Our view of community is strongly influenced by the work of Albert J. Reiss, Jr.[3] Reiss defines community as follows:

We shall say that *a community arises through sharing a limited territorial space for residence and for sustenance and functions to meet common needs generated in sharing this space by establishing characteristic forms of social action.*[4]

As was the case with organizations, sociologists have developed two somewhat distinct approaches to the study of communities. Each approach emphasizes somewhat different aspects of the phenomenon; hence, they are in one sense competing definitions but in a larger sense complementary perspectives. Reiss labels the first approach *ecological* and the second the *social organization* approach. Let us examine each in turn. The ecological approach—like the rational approach of the formal organization theorists—tends to emphasize the structures and processes that distinguish the community from other types of social phenomena, whereas the social organization approach—like the social system perspective on organizations—is more likely to focus on the aspects of community that are shared with other types of collectivities.

The Ecological Approach to the Study of Communities   Amos Hawley is the chief framer and advocate of the ecological view of community organization. In developing his theory of community structure, Hawley proposes that

From a spatial standpoint, the community may be defined as comprising that area the resident population of which is interrelated and integrated with reference to its daily requirements, whether contacts be direct or indirect. Arbitrary as this definition may seem, it is consistent with common usage. Participation in a daily rhythm of collective life is the factor which distinguishes and gives unity to the population of a locality.[5]

Hawley proposes to concentrate on the aspects of community structure that result from the working through of symbiotic and commensalistic relations among the members of the resident population (see Reading 17). The emphasis on "daily" interaction incorporates time as well as space into the proposed perspective. As Reiss notes, research conducted within this framework has tended to focus on the internal structure of communities or sets of communities integrated into a larger metropolitan community rather than on relations among community subunits. Within communities, the major research emphases have been on the relations of production units within a community and on the residential structure of communities.[6]

The ecological perspective is incomplete in that it omits from consideration concern with the possible "community of interests" that may develop among elements of the population. Hawley is aware of these concerns, and notes:

[3]Albert J. Reiss, Jr., "The sociological study of communities," *Rural Sociology*, 24 (June, 1959), 118–130.

[4]Reiss, p. 118. Emphasis in original.

[5]Amos H. Hawley, *Human Ecology: A Theory of Community Structure*, New York: Ronald, 1950, pp. 257–258.

[6]Reiss, pp. 122–125.

The human community, of course, is more than just an organization of symbiotic relationships and to that extent there are limitations to the scope of human ecology. Man's collective life involves, in greater or less degree, a psychological and a moral as well as a symbiotic integration. But these, so far as they are distinguishable, should be regarded as complementing aspects of the same thing rather than as separate phases or segments of the community.[7]

As Schnore concludes,

The ecologist, then, does not deny the existence or importance of the psychological aspect of community life. He simply prefers to regard it as a separate facet of the object under investigation, and to leave its study to others.[8]

The Social Organization Approach to the Study of Communities   This approach encompasses two subschools of thought concerning the appropriate subject matter and approach to the study of communities. The first of these two approaches is the most obvious and, theoretically, the least interesting. Reiss describes this perspective as follows:

The conventional treatment of communities, particularly omnibus community studies, presents the community as a microcosm of the larger social macrocosm—as the smallest territorial system which encompasses the major features of society. A community is usually seen then as possessing a system of stratification, a power structure, characteristic institutions such as educational, religious, and economic ones, and so on, depending upon the "complexity" of its organization.[9]

The difficulty with this approach is that one is not able to analytically separate the subject matter of study from the setting in which it is studied. As Reiss comments, "A typical study of 'community stratification' fails to show that there is variation in stratification which can be shown to be a property of communities."[10]

A number of community theorists have proposed a basically similar strategy for overcoming this deficiency. Their approach, the second to the study of the social organization of the community, may be identified as the *interaction-space* perspective. First suggested in an article by E. T. Hiller,[11] this approach "takes as its major focus that the *community involves collective action toward the realization of common goals, arising in a residence-sustenance locality*."[12] This perspective has been further elaborated by Harold Kaufman, who argues that "the community field consists of an organization of actions carried on by persons working through various associations and groups."[13] But how is this complex of actions and interactions to be distinguished from other systems of interaction occurring in the community setting but not necessarily relevant to the community itself? To confront this problem, Kaufman suggests that "the community may be seen as a network of interrelated associations, formal and informal, whose major function is problem solving for the local society."[14] More specifically Kaufman suggests a series of dimensions that can be used for differentiating

[7]Amos H. Hawley, "Ecology and human ecology," *Social Forces*, 22 (May, 1944), 404.

[8]Leo F. Schnore, "Community," in Neil J. Smelser (ed.), *Sociology: An Introduction*, New York: Wiley, 1967, p. 86.

[9]Reiss, p. 125.

[10]Reiss, p. 125.

[11]E. T. Hiller, "The community as a social group," *American Sociological Review*, 6 (April, 1941), 189-202.

[12]Reiss, p. 126. Emphasis in original.

[13]Harold F. Kaufman, "Toward an interactional conception of community," *Social Forces*, 38 (October, 1959), 9-17.

[14]Kaufman, p. 12.

community action from the actions not appropriate to the community field. The dimensions are

1. The degree of comprehensiveness of interests pursued and needs met (the wider the range, the more likely the action is to be community oriented).

2. The degree to which the action is identified with the locality (many activities carried on in the community are chiefly relevant either to a special interest group or to the larger society of which the community is a part).

3. The relative number, status, and degrees of involvement of local residents (however, care must be taken to avoid biasing the analysis in favor of smaller communities, where a higher proportion of "important" participants may be involved in a given issue than is the case in larger communities).

4. The relative number and significance of local associations involved (but see reservations in entry 3).

5. The degree to which the action maintains or changes the local community (community action may be directed toward maintenance of the status quo, toward maintaining community spirit in a world with many forces acting to destroy locality group identity, and toward changes in the institutional structure of community life).

6. The extent of organization of the action (unrelated activities of individuals do not themselves constitute the interactional community; a degree of coordination, integration, and unity is essential both at the group interaction level and at the normative level with a sharing of values and objectives).[15]

In summary, what are we to make of these varying perspectives? First, the ecological substructure emphasized by many community analysts is clearly an important area of study. The ecological perspective is essential to a full understanding of the concept of community when the perspective addresses itself to the fundamental problem of how a population organizes to survive in a particular locality and how it distributes itself in space and time as it goes about the business of getting a living. This perspective, however, requires supplementation if we are to comprehend the full significance of locality for social life. The development of special interests, values, and norms that add social-psychological flesh to the ecological skeleton is an equally important aspect of community life. Focusing on those particular interactions that have primary relevance to the maintenance and change of the social organization of a locality-based group provides a means of distinguishing community organization from other aspects of social life that occur in, but are not of, the community.

TYPES OF COMMUNITIES

Communities, whether viewed as ecosystems or as one basis for social organization, are complex entities characterized by a multitude of variables, and it is very difficult to determine which variable or set of variables is of primary importance. Attempts to classify various types of communities have made use of many variables; in this volume we will take note of some of the more widely accepted attempts.

Population Variables   Among the most oft-used variables in distinguishing among types of communities are those describing characteristics of the population. Such variables as size, density, and social heterogeneity have been widely

[15]Kaufman, pp. 12–16.

employed. Using these three particular variables, Louis Wirth has argued that a host of others can be deduced that help to account for rural-urban differences.[16] As an example, consider some of Wirth's deductions from the single variable of increasing population size.

Large numbers involve, as has been pointed out, a greater range of individual variation. Furthermore, the greater the number of individuals participating in a process of interaction, the greater is the *potential* differentiation between them. The personal traits, the occupations, the cultural life, and the ideas of the members of an urban community may, therefore, be expected to range between more widely separated poles than those of rural inhabitants.

That such variations should give rise to the spatial segregation of individuals according to color, ethnic heritage, economic and social status, tastes and preferences, may readily be inferred. The bonds of kinship, of neighborliness, and the sentiments arising out of living together for generations under a common folk tradition are likely to be absent, or, at best, relatively weak in an aggregate the members of which have such diverse origins and backgrounds. Under such circumstances competition and formal control mechanisms furnish the substitutes for the bonds of solidarity that are relied upon to hold a folk society together.[17]

Without attempting to summarize adequately what has become a lively debate among students of the community, we should note that many students have questioned Wirth's conclusions. Some students point out that many of the relevant characteristics cited by Wirth do not in fact vary closely with population size,[18] other students point out "some rural-urban differences appear to be valid only for specific types of societies—e.g., for either industrial or pre-industrial," but not both types,[19] and still other students point out that it is not meaningful to show that selected population variables are related to other sociological variables without specifying the reasons for these interconnections, without explaining why and how, for example, population size affects social differentiation.[20]

Dependency as a Variable   Amos Hawley[21] has suggested that one important basis for distinguishing between types of communities is "the extent to which they are truly 'localized,' that is, the degree to which they are *independent* of, or *dependent* upon, close ties with other communities."[22] Hawley defines these community types as follows, noting other important variables that tend to be associated with them:

As the name indicates, the *independent community* is a self-sufficient entity, that is, it produces most of the goods and services it consumes. Associated with this characteristic are a number of other distinctive attributes including isolation, small population, simple technology, and marked stability. Community independence is a consequence of the interconnected effects of these several attributes.[23]

[16]Louis Wirth, "Urbanism as a way of life," *American Journal of Sociology*, 44 (July, 1938), 1–24.

[17]Wirth, p. 11.

[18]See, for example, Otis Dudley Duncan, "Community size and the rural-urban continuum," in Paul K. Hatt and Albert J. Reiss, Jr. (eds.), *Cities and Society*, (rev. ed.), Glencoe, Ill.: Free Press, 1957.

[19]Gidion Sjoberg, "Comparative urban sociology," in Robert K. Merton, Leonard Broom, and Leonard S. Cottrell, Jr. (eds.), *Sociology Today: Problems and Prospects*, New York: Basic Books, 1959, p. 342.

[20]See Leonard Reissman, *The Urban Process*, New York: Free Press, 1964, pp. 139–144.

[21]Hawley, *Human Ecology*, pp. 222–347.

[22]Schnore, p. 97. Emphasis in original.

[23]Hawley, *Human Ecology*, p. 223. Emphasis ours.

The *dependent community,* by definition, is not self-sufficient. It obtains its sustenance materials through exchange with other communities. What it has to offer in exchange is usually gained through intensive specialization in extractive, manufacturing, or service industry. Isolation is obviously contrary to the requisites for exchange. . . . Dependence exposes the community to the effects of events that occur anywhere within the scope of intercommunity relations. The probability that change will occur is therefore vastly greater than in the independent community.[24]

Hawley also argues that certain groupings that make up the internal structure of communities vary with the amount of dependency. He proposes that all groups within the community may be classified as either corporate or categoric groups. *Corporate groups* are groups based on symbiotic relations, with groups internally differentiated and symbiotically integrated, such as the family, economic firms, schools, and churches. *Categoric groups* are based on commensalistic relations, with groups composed of similar and functionally homogeneous individuals. Examples include age grades, sex groupings, castes, classes, races, and occupational groups. Communities are comprised of a number of corporate and categoric groups, together with the relations between and among such groupings. For the independent community, the number and variety of corporate and categoric groups is relatively small. The principal type of corporate group to be found is the family or household; representative categoric groups include ones formed on the basis of age and sex distinctions. By contrast, the structure of the dependent community is formed of a large variety and number of both corporate and categoric groups.[25]

Other Variables   In his influential book on the community, Warren proposes four dimensions along which communities may vary with important implications for their structure and functioning.[26] The first dimension, *autonomy,* is similar to Hawley's distinction between independent and dependent communities. The second dimension is the *coincidence of service areas,* that is, "the extent to which the service areas of local units (stores, churches, schools, and so on) coincide or fail to coincide."[27] The extent to which residents have a *psychological identification* with a common locality serves as the third dimension along which communities may vary. Residents in some communities have a strong attachment to the area and to other residents, whereas in other communities inhabitants have little sense of relationship to one another. Finally, communities vary in the extent to which the community's horizontal pattern is strong or weak. Warren defines the *horizontal pattern* as "the structural and functional relation of the various units (individuals and social systems) to each other."[28] These relations are composed of the sentimental or emotional attachments of individuals within the locality for one another and composed of certain formal organizations, such as the chamber of commerce, that perform coordinating functions for the various subunits of the community.

The discerning reader will have noted that the three sets of variables just described (population, dependency, and others) all relate fundamentally to the

[24]Hawley, *Human Ecology,* p. 225. Emphasis ours.
[25]See Hawley, *Human Ecology,* pp. 209-233.
[26]Roland L. Warren, *The Community in America,* Skokie, Ill. Rand McNally, 1963.
[27]Warren, p. 13.
[28]Warren, p. 13.

hoary distinction between rural and urban communities. Generally speaking, urban centers are high on population size, density, and social heterogeneity; rural communities are low on these population variables. Urban communities are relatively dependent on other communities; rural communities are more likely to be independent. And urban centers are low on autonomy, service areas tend to differ, psychological identification with the locality is weak, and the horizontal pattern is weak; whereas rural communities are likely to be high on autonomy, possess service areas that tend to coincide, have residents with strong psychological attachment, and have subunits exhibiting a strong horizontal pattern. To suggest that the underlying framework for these schemata is the rural-urban dichotomy is not to criticize them. Each is an attempt to make more explicit the number and kinds of variables that are incorporated in the broader distinction.

Another basis for differentiating among types of communities—the functional typologies—will be described when we take up the subject of adaptation processes in communities.

There is, of course, no single correct variable or set of variables to use in classifying communities. Different investigators focus on differing bases, depending on their divergent analytical purposes. A particular typology is useful insofar as it helps to order certain categories of dependent variables. This is why we stated earlier that a typology is the beginning, not the end product, of an investigation. In a sense, however, all such typologies are useful in that they serve as constant reminders of the diversity of phenomena encompassed by a simple-sounding concept such as "community."

As we turn to a consideration of social processes operating at the community level, we shall concentrate our attention on the urban, and especially on the metropolitan community, because this is the predominant form of community life in our type of society.

INTEGRATIVE PROCESSES IN COMMUNITIES

In discussing small groups, emphasis was placed on integrative processes flowing from commonly held norms and sentiments, although we might well have given more attention to the integration produced by the mutual interdependence that is associated with role differentiation: In considering formal organizations, we emphasized the role of formalization in bringing about integration—in relying on formal rules instead of on informal norms and in transforming informal status and power structures into formal bureaucratic hierarchies. Both rules and administrative hierarchies aim to produce coherence and consistency in the behavior of participants. In short, both are attempts to produce integration.

Types of structural arrangements promoting integration similar to those found in small groups and organizations can be found in communities. Take the case of informal norms. The role that these commonly held beliefs and sentiments have in providing normative integration to community life has been much emphasized in discussions of small town life, as in such fictional works as Thornton Wilder's *Our Town* and in such nonfictional community studies as the Lynds' studies of Middletown[1] and West's study of Plainville.[2] Sociologists writing early in the twentieth century were struck by the relative coherence and tranquility of the small rural community in contrast with the tensions and conflicts of urban life. Thus, in his famous essay "Urbanism as a Way of Life," Louis Wirth concluded:

The distinctive features of the urban mode of life have often been described sociologically as consisting of the substitution of secondary for primary contacts, the weakening of bonds of kinship, and the declining social significance of the family, the disappearance of the neighborhood, and the undermining of the traditional basis of social solidarity. All of these phenomena can be substantially verified through objective indices.[3]

As it turned out, Wirth and the many others who described the city in such somber tones overstated the case. Later sociologists have noted that Wirth tended to contrast the worst of the urban situation (conditions in the inner city) with the best of the small community (an idealized view of small town life) and that he overlooked the social structures and cultural arrangements that the new urban dweller "either brought to the city, or developed by living in it."[4] In fact,

[1]Robert S. Lynd and Helen M. Lynd, *Middletown: A Study in Contemporary American Culture*, New York: Harcourt, 1929; and *Middletown in Transition: A Study in Cultural Conflicts*, New York: Harcourt, 1937.

[2]James West, *Plainville, USA*, New York: Columbia University Press, 1945.

[3]Louis Wirth, "Urbanism as a way of life," *American Journal of Sociology*, 44 (July, 1938), 20–21.

[4]Herbert J. Gans, "Urbanism and suburbanism as ways of life: A reevaluation of definitions," in Arnold M. Rose (ed.), *Human Behavior and Social Processes*, Boston: Houghton Mifflin, p. 629.

informal norms supported by face-to-face relations continue to operate in urban areas, albeit at somewhat reduced levels, as many empirical studies have demonstrated.[5]

The failure of the early urban sociologists to take account of primary group behavior in urban settings can be used to illustrate a more general point: scientists often become the captives of their concepts. In our introduction to this book, we noted that concepts provide a way of selecting certain aspects of reality for attention—they help us to focus on certain aspects of a phenomenon, but they also prevent us from seeing other aspects. In the case of urban sociologists, most approached their subject armed with a set of dichotomous concepts: perhaps Durkheim's distinction between "mechanical" and "organic" solidarity,[6] or Tönnies' *Gemeinschaft und Gessellschaft,*[7] or Redfield's "folk" versus "urban,"[8] or the more conventional distinction between "rural" and "urban." Using such dichotomies, sociologists tended to emphasize the distinctive features of the situations they wished to contrast and to overlook the possibility that some elements were common to both types of situations. Because of the blindness of one generation of sociologists to certain phenomena, it became necessary for later generations to "rediscover" the importance of the primary group in various aspects of mass society—in industry, in mass communications, and in the city.[9]

Formal rules, such as laws and city ordinances, and administrative hierarchies also contribute to the integration of communities. Most communities have governing bodies and regulatory agencies that assure a certain degree of order and coherence in community affairs. However, the importance of such political and bureaucratic structures in regulating community life should not be overemphasized. As Long comments:

. . . even in a city where the municipal corporation provides an apparent over-all government, the appearance is deceptive. The politicians who hold the offices do not regard themselves as governors of the municipal territory. . . . Their roles, as they conceive them, do not approach those of the directors of a TVA developing a territory. The ideology of local government is a highly limited affair in which the office-holders respond to demands and mediate conflicts. They play politics, and politics is vastly different from government if the latter is conceived as the rational, responsible ordering of the community. In part, this is due to the general belief that little government is necessary. . . . In part, the separation of economics from politics eviscerates the formal theory of government of most of the substance of social action.[10]

[5]See, for example, Wendell Bell and Marion D. Boat, "Urban neighborhoods and informal social relations," *American Journal of Sociology,* 62 (January, 1957), 391–398; Scott Greer, "Urbanism reconsidered: A comparative study of local areas in a metropolis," *American Sociological Review,* 21 (February, 1956), 19–25; Joel Smith, William H. Form, and Gregory P. Stone, "Local intimacy in a middle-sized city," *American Journal of Sociology,* 60 (November, 1954), 276–284.

[6]Emile Durkheim, *The Division of Labor in Society,* Glencoe, Ill.: Free Press, 1947 (first published 1893).

[7]Ferdinand Tönnies, *Fundamental Concepts in Sociology,* New York: American Book, 1940 (first published 1887).

[8]Robert Redfield, *The Folk Culture of Yucatan,* Chicago: University of Chicago Press, 1941. For a discussion of Redfield's concepts and the critics of his approach, see Leonard Reissman, *The Urban Process,* New York: Free Press, 1964, pp. 126–138.

[9]See Elihu Katz and Paul F. Lazarsfeld, *Personal Influence,* Glencoe, Ill.: Free Press, 1955, pp. 34–42.

[10]Norton E. Long, "The local community as an ecology of games," *American Journal of Sociology,* 64 (November, 1958), 255.

If informal norms are weakened and local government is not particularly effective, what then is the source of whatever order and coherence is displayed by our communities? We will propose that much of the structural integration of communities is produced by the operation of certain ecological processes.

Ecological Processes in the Local Community   Long has written:

Observation of certain local communities makes it appear that inclusive over-all organization for many general purposes is weak or non-existent. Much of what occurs seems to just happen with accidental trends becoming cumulative over time and producing results intended by nobody. A great deal of the communities' activities consist of undirected co-operation of particular social structures, each seeking particular goals and, in so doing, meshing with others.[11]

Long may be correct that the unintentional result of the combination of "accidental trends" is cooperation, but the major impetus for such trends is competition, as Reading 35 by Jessie Bernard makes clear. Bernard suggests that the structure of most American communities was created by "autonomous competition operating under a laissez-faire policy," which in large measure reflected economic values. Since the 1950s, however, other values are beginning to be emphasized as more and more cities begin to recognize the need for long-range planning and redevelopment. Integration, which has been left to chance and to the "natural" play of ecological processes, is increasingly a problem to be worked at by planning boards and redevelopment commissions.

Ecological Processes in the Metropolitan Community   Bernard limits her discussion to the ecological processes that operate within the confines of the boundaries of a particular community. However, with improved transportation, men are less dependent upon the economic condition in their own immediate environment; instead, they become dependent upon a more complex system of production and exchange extending over a wider area. A new type of ecological unit has emerged whose boundaries extend far beyond those of a single town or city to encompass whole sets of cities and their surrounding environs. We have the development of the *metropolitan community*.

The ecologist McKenzie was among the first to recognize and describe this new phenomenon:

By reducing the scale of local distance, the motor vehicle extended the horizon of the community and introduced a territorial division of labor among local institutions and neighboring centers which is unique in the history of settlement. The large center has been able to extend the radius of its influence; its population and many of its institutions, freed from the dominance of rail transportation, have become widely dispersed throughout surrounding territory. Moreover, formerly independent towns and villages and also rural territory have become part of this enlarged city complex. This new type of super community organized around a dominant focal point and comprising a multitude of differentiated centers of activity differs from the metropolitanism established by rail transportation in the complexity of its institutional division of labor and the mobility of its population. Its territorial scope is defined in terms of motor transportation and competition with other regions. Nor is this new type of metropolitan community confined to the great cities. It has become the communal unit of local relations throughout the entire nation.[12]

[11]Long, p. 252.
[12]R. D. McKenzie, *The Metropolitan Community*, New York: McGraw-Hill, 1933, p. 7. An even earlier statement is to be found in S. S. B. Gras, *Introduction to Economic History*, New York: Harper & Row, 1922.

McKenzie collected considerable data in support of his proposition that the metropolitan center is the dominant form among existing community types, but the definitive study of metropolitan dominance was carried out by Bogue some years later. Dominance has a special meaning to the ecologist. For Bogue, *dominance* "is a special kind of control over a community of interfunctioning units." Further, "a dominant in nature exercises its control not by ordering and forbidding, not by virtue of any authority or right to command, but *by controlling the conditions of life.*"[13] In his study of metropolitan dominance, Bogue compared metropolitan centers and hinterland zones with respect to levels of production or activity in manufactures, trade, and service industries. These data reflected patterns consistent with his hypothesis of metropolitan dominance. His conclusions are summarized in the following definitions and propositions:

1. A *dominant city* is a city which controls many of the conditions of life of all the communities lying within a broad area surrounding it. This control arises from a higher than average degree of specialization in such functions as services and wholesaling, and from an ability to foster industrial development in its immediate vicinity by provision of favorable combinations of the factors of production. Other communities must accept these conditions of life by specializing in other activities and by becoming dependent upon the central city for those goods and services which their residents require but which they cannot provide locally. The metropolitan market center mediates a complex inter-community exchange, and thereby integrates the activities of outlying communities with each other and with the activities of the metropolis. . . .

2. A *subdominant city* is a city which adapts to the condition of general dependence upon the center and which functions, through specialization in one or more of the sustenance activities, as an intermediary between the metropolis and the outlying areas. . . .

3. A *metropolitan community* is an organization of many subdominant, influent, and subinfluent communities, distributed in a definite pattern about a dominant city, and bound together in a territorial division of labor through a dependence upon the activities of the dominant city . . . .

4. The metropolitan community has come to be a characteristic pattern by which at least one urbanized commercial-industrial society, the United States, is organized. This pattern reflects an underlying set of interrelationships which are based on interdependency and on a division of labor. In making use of new techniques of production, transportation, distribution, and exchange, the population of the nation appears to have arranged itself by a pattern which is repeated, with individual variations, many times.[14]

With the case of the metropolitan community, we have, perhaps, one of the clearest examples of a social unit integrated by dominance or power rather than by the presence of common values or by the existence of a legitimate hierarchy of authority. Only gradually, long after the fact of their economic interdependency and integration, are some of these supercommunities slowly becoming organized as political communities. Indeed, one study of political arrangements in our largest metropolitan community, the New York City area, is aptly titled *1400 Governments!*[15]

Two final comments concerning the dominance of the central city within the metropolitan community should be made. First, dominance, like all forms of power, exists because of interdependence and is hence not completely one-

[13]Donald J. Bogue, *The Structure of the Metropolitan Community*, Ann Arbor, Mich.: Horace H. Rackham School of Graduate Studies, University of Michigan, 1949, pp. 10–11.

[14]Bogue, pp. 61–63.

[15]Robert C. Wood, *1400 Governments: The Political Economy of the New York Metropolitan Region*, Cambridge, Mass.: Harvard University Press, 1961.

sided. The central community is dependent upon its satellites and hinterland for certain necessary supplies and inputs (raw materials, labor, specialized manufacturing products, foodstuffs) as well as for its markets. The dominance of the central city is, then, a matter of degree. Second, the dominance of a metropolitan center may not be restricted to its immediate hinterland but, for certain functions, may extend to encompass national and even international markets. As was noted by a study conducted in the 1930s,

Metropoli are geographically of two kinds—regional foci and supraregional creations. In other words, some large cities are created by the regions which contain them and for which they are in many respects centers of integration, but many other cities are not products of regional forces. These instead are created by larger factors in the total national economy. Most of the million-cities are probably of this latter type.[16]

This suggests that, at least for industrialized nations, some measure of integration may be provided for the entire society by the dominance exerted by overlapping and interpenetrating systems or networks of metropolitan communities. Vance and Smith have attempted to describe such a system of metropolitan dominance for the South,[17] and Duncan and his colleagues give some indication of how this structure may look for the United States as a whole.[18]

[16]United States National Resources Committee, *Regional Factors in National Planning*, Washington, D.C.: Government Printing Office, 1935, p. 159.

[17]Rupert B. Vance and Sara Smith, "Metropolitan dominance and integration," in Rupert B. Vance and Nicholas J. Demerath (eds.), *The Urban South*, Chapel Hill, N.C.: The University of North Carolina Press, pp. 114–134.

[18]Otis Dudley Duncan *et al.*, *Metropolis and Region*, Baltimore: The Johns Hopkins Press, 1960, pp. 248–275.

35   Ecological Competition within Communities and Its Institutionalization

Jessie Bernard

INSTITUTIONAL FRAMEWORK IN CYCLE ONE

[The ecological structure of the community refers] . . . to its functional structure in terms of land use. This ecological structure . . . is inextricably related to the demographic and institutional structure, both as cause and as effect. That is, the demographic structure and the institutional structure influence the ecological structure and it, in turn, reacts to influence them. A heavy concentration of ethnic or racial groups will reflect itself in the ecological structure; and so will cus-

toms and laws. But an existing ecological structure will itself have profound repercussions on the relationships among groups and hence, indirectly, also on the demographic structure. It will also have reverberations on institutional norms.

The ecological structure is the result of basic processes which allocate space to the different uses to which land can be put. These processes are competition, segregation, invasion, and succession.[1] In

[1]Other ecological processes, not pertinent here, include centralization, decentralization, and dominance. See Amos Hawley, *Human Ecology* (New

From *American Community Behavior* by Jessie Bernard, pp. 117–128. Copyright 1949, ©1962 by Holt, Rinehart and Winston, Inc. Reprinted by permission of Holt, Rinehart and Winston, Inc., and the author.

the so-called First Cycle[2] of development of American communities, that is, up to the middle of the twentieth century, the processes were primarily autonomous and the institutional framework was one of modified laissez-faire, with only relatively minor tinkering in the form of zoning regulations, or of "planning" which sought to impose other than strictly economic tests on the competitive process. It was not, however, until the beginning of the Second Cycle that the idea of radical rethinking of urban communities began to take hold.

To say that the institutional framework within which ecological processes operated in the First Cycle was one of laissez-faire does not mean that American communities permitted land to be allocated in an institutional vacuum. The settlers brought with them traditional ways of using land, imposing them on the competitive process. Thus, for example, the basic plan of the New England village came, according to one anthropologist, from the open-field village of the North European plain by way of the manorial village of the English Midlands.

By way of contrast, the distribution of land use of the southern community, according to the same analyst, was an American counterpart of the Iberian *municipio*, the French *commune*, or the German *Gemeinde;* it was a rural version of the baroque capital or city of palace and parade. It reflected and accommodated a two-class community.

The distinctive community form of the South was and is the county. Dispersed a day's ride in and out around the county seat, that community assembled planter and field- or house-hand from the fat plantations, free white or Negro from the lean hills and swamps, for the pageantry and the drama of Saturdays around the courthouse, when the courthouse, the jail, the registry of deeds, and the courthouse square of shops and lawyers' row made a physical center of the far-flung community. . . . It is a mistake to treat this county and county seat for its separate parts and to try to find the community in the Old South at any other level. The poor white or Negro hamlets about a country church, set in hill or swamp retreat, the plantation, however large and proud and populous, the county seat as town . . . were and are none of them complete communities. The county itself was the unit of dispersal and assemblage, and it was a two-class community from its inception in the gathering-in of nobles into the king's palace and capital along with *noblesse de robe* and rich *bourgeois*. Formed from the coming together of landowner and *peon*, its pattern of dispersal was a double one, with estates covering the good land, and little men, now clients, now runaways, taking up the leavings in the bad.[3]

This type of land use spread all across the country to California.

The basic plan for allocating land use which characterizes the middle-western community, according to the same author, derives from West Britain, Scotland, and Scandinavia; it reflects a community resulting from the accretion of individual families rather than a planned settlement. "Their first communities were mere crossroads where scattered neighbors met. Their schools and churches and stores, like their camp meetings and their fairs, were set haphazardly in the open country or where roads met, with no ordered clustering and no fixed membership."[4] They were open-country neighborhoods.

The coming of industrialization in the nineteenth century created a characteristic pattern of relationships and the ecological structure of the mill town or factory city reflected it. Play and park

York: Ronald, 1950) ; James A. Quinn, *Human Ecology* (Englewood Cliffs, N. J.: Prentice-Hall, 1950) ; D. J. Bogue, *The Structure of the Metropolitan Community: A Study of Dominance and Subdominance* (Ann Arbor: Michigan, 1949) .

[2]Philip Hauser, interviewed in *U. S. News and World Report*, Nov. 28, 1958, p. 81.

[3]Conrad M. Arensberg, "American Communities," in Morton H. Fried, ed., *Readings in Anthropology*. Vol. II. Cultural Anthropology (Crowell, 1959) , p. 361. Original publication in *American Anthropologist*, 57 (1955) , pp. 1143–1162.

[4]*Ibid.*, p. 365.

space disappeared; work and leisure were separated.

The major emphasis here is on the fact that although modern American cities tended to permit competitive processes to allocate land uses during Cycle One, these processes operated within a traditional framework. When industrialization introduced a new set of forces, the competitive process registered a new set of values. Economic efficiency was the value tested. The ecological structure of American cities thus expresses their values in the allocation of space. In Cycle Two values other than strict economic efficiency are increasingly taken into consideration and the competition tends to become judgmental rather than autonomous. The implementation of new values does not proceed without opposition; indeed some of the most basic values in American society are fought over in this area.

Competition, in brief, may be viewed as a process by which land use comes to respond to community values. The ecological processes have widely ramifying effects on the relationships among groups and classes, as well as themselves reflecting these relationships.

ECOLOGICAL PROCESSES IN CYCLE ONE

The ecological structures of communities vary widely. They vary according to the function served by the community . . . ; they vary according to the age of the community; and they vary according to the size of the community. In general, however, certain basic processes tend to operate, namely, competition, segregation, invasion, and succession.

Segregation

In any community there may be many uses to which land can be put: it may be used for factories, mills, foundries; for

wholesale warehouses or retail stores; for office buildings or banks; for theatres and amusement centers; for housing Negroes and foreigners or native-born whites, poor people or wealthy people. These several uses can be reduced to three main types: heavy industrial; business or commercial and light industrial; and residential.

Some of these uses of land profit from being in proximity to one another. Thus, for example, "retail districts benefit from grouping which increases the concentration of potential customers and makes possible comparison shopping. Financial and office-building districts depend upon facility of communication among offices."[5] High-grade residential use benefits from use for parks and boulevards.

Other combinations of land use, however, are detrimental to one another. "The antagonism between factory development and high-class development is well known. The heavy concentrations of pedestrians, automobiles, and streetcars in the retail district are antagonistic both to the railroad facilities and the street loading required in the wholesale district and to the rail facilities and space needed by large industrial districts, and vice versa."[6]

As a result of these congenial and antagonistic relationships in land use, there tends to develop a pattern of segregated land use—retail districts, wholesale districts, financial districts, residential districts, and so on. What is more to the point is that they are in competition with one another for desirable areas. For not all land uses are equally capable of paying for desirable sites. "Certain activities are unable to afford the high rents of the most desirable sites. . . . Examples are bulk

[5] Chauncey D. Harris and Edward L. Ullman, "The Nature of Cities," *Annals Amer. Acad. Pol. & Soc. Sci.*, 242 (November, 1945) , p. 14.
[6] *Ibid.*

wholesaling and storage activities requiring much room, or low-class housing unable to afford the luxury of high land with a view."[7] In the first cycle of community growth in the United States the allocation of land use rested basically on autonomous competition, and ability to pay was the value tested. The use that was most profitable won out.

In all American communities there resulted a definite segregation of land use, sometimes simple, sometimes complex. These segregations were sometimes spoken of as "natural areas." There was a business district, which was further segregated into a wholesale and warehouse area, into areas for retail stores, theatres and amusements, specialty shops, banks, and the like, according to the functional principles cited above. The physical structure of the community reflected this fairly stable segregation of land use.

Invasion

But the competitive process which sorted out these several natural areas, alloting space to the different functional uses was a continuing one. No segregation was fixed or final. Land which was desirable for industrial use at one stage of development later became undesirable. Areas which were desirable for residential purposes ceased to be so. There was a tendency for those who could afford it to move farther and farther away from the grime and dirt of the city, out into the suburbs. The mansions of the rich were deserted as the business district expanded. By what real estate men call the "trickling down" process, these houses in time were taken over by the poorest. Thus competition for the use of land was always blurring the original natural areas or segregation of land uses by a process known as invasion. Middle-class people

[7]*Ibid.*, p. 15.

invaded upper-class areas or Negroes invaded white areas. As a result, one group was displaced by another; a succession of groups moved through the same area.

Succession

In New York City in recent decades Harlem and the Bronx illustrate the process of succession of groups. Between the two world wars, "Harlem shifted from a moderately populated community of well-to-do, middle-class and working-class Jews, Italians, Irish, Germans and Greeks into a tightly packed, predominantly low-income region, inhabited largely by Negroes. . . ."[8] In the Bronx a similar process has taken place:

Historically, the upper Bronx has been the top of an escalator on which successive waves of population rode from bargain-basement living in teeming lower Manhattan in quest of "a nicer neighborhood" and "a better life." First came the Irish and German, then Italian immigrants and Poles and Slavs and Jews, displacing and leap-frogging each other, hop-scotching from the lower East Side to Harlem to the lower Bronx to the upper Bronx. And the escalator kept moving, latterly bringing up Negroes and Puerto Ricans.[9]

ECOLOGICAL PATTERNS IN CYCLE ONE

At least three types of community structure in the first cycle of development of American cities have been distinguished by students of community growth, namely: (1) the concentric-circle pattern, (2) the sector or axial pattern, and (3) the multiple-nuclear pattern.

The concentric-circle theory, developed

[8]Raymond Robinson, Jr., "Our Changing City: Harlem Now on the Upswing," *New York Times*, July 8, 1955. The phenomenon known as "tipping" in this invasion-succession process will be discussed in greater detail in a later chapter.

[9]Richard Amper, "Our Changing City: Conflicts in the Upper Bronx," *Ibid.*, July 15, 1955.

by sociologists at the University of Chicago and based on studies of that city, asserted that communities tended to grow out from a center along radii, evolving five concentric circles around this center. The zones, out from the center were: (1) the central business district, "the focus of commercial, social, and civic life and of transportation. In it is the downtown retail district with its department stores, smart shops, office buildings, clubs, banks, hotels, theaters, museums, and organization headquarters. Encircling the downtown retail district is the wholesale business district."[10]

The second zone, which surrounded the first, was called the zone in transition. It was a "zone of residential deterioration. Business and light manufacturing encroached on residential areas, characterized particularly by rooming houses. In this zone were the principal slums, ,with their submerged regions of poverty, degradation, and disease, and their underworlds of vice. In many American cities it had been inhabited largely by colonies of recent immigrants."[11] This was the area of the city where newcomers from rural areas also tended to live because rents were cheap. The landowners in this zone were holding their property in anticipation of increased value from higher-rent-paying land uses. The hope was that business would expand and invade the area, finally displacing the residential use entirely. In the past, while American cities were growing rapidly this was a fairly safe gamble. When Cycle One

came to an end, however, at midcentury, holding for an anticipated rise in value was not so likely to be rewarded.

The community paid for such deteriorated areas not only in the high price for police, fire, and sanitary protection but also in the blighting effect such areas had on human personality. Extensive studies in Chicago showed that juvenile delinquency, gangsterism, vice, mental illness, physical illness—particularly contagious diseases—and family disorganization tended to characterize them. They did not constitute a suitable environment for human beings. In small communities the undesirable areas might be known as "the other side of the tracks."

The third zone which developed under the competitive conditions in Cycle One was one of independent workingmen's homes, inhabited by industrial workers who had escaped from the zone in transition but who wanted to live within easy access to their work. In many cities second-generation immigrants were important segments of the population in this area. This zone was usually thought of as lower middle class. It may have appeared bleak to outsiders, but it often signified an improvement for those who lived there and they took pride in it.

The fourth zone consisted of better residences, usually single-family houses, or of exclusive restricted districts, and also of high-class apartment buildings.

There was, finally, the commuters' zone. This included both suburban areas and satellite cities, as well as spotty developments of high-class residences along lines of rapid travel, primarily railroads. But it may also have included slums. Sometimes a so-called urban fringe was already present, neither part of the city nor yet suburban. It might contain heavy industry or residences of low quality.

This concentric-zone theory of city development did not apply without mod-

[10]Harris and Ullman, op. cit., p. 12. A more detailed and technical description of the five areas may be found in Ernest W. Burgess, "The Growth of the City," in The City, edited by R. E. Park, E. W. Burgess, and R. D. McKenzie (Chicago: University of Chicago, 1925), pp. 47–62; also in "Urban Areas," in Chicago, An Experiment in Social Science Research, edited by T. V. Smith and L. D. White (Chicago: University of Chicago, 1929), pp. 113–138.

[11]Harris and Ullman, op. cit., pp. 12–13.

ification. It was supposed to represent what would have tended to be the typical situation if no interference were present, much as the law of falling bodies represents the rate at which bodies fall at sea level in a vacuum. Many factors served to distort the picture. The presence of water, hills, rivers, railroad tracks, arterial highways, or other natural or technological features may have distorted the pattern. Nevertheless, it was a useful concept in illustrating the basic structure of a community as determined by competition for the use of land when the quality being tested was primarily economic and the policy in force one of laissez-faire.

The sector theory of community structure, propounded by Homer Hoyt, was also based on competition. But it held that cities tended to grow along main transportation lines, or axes, or along lines of least resistance, forming a star-shaped pattern. The important feature was that growth along any one axis tended to consist of similar land uses.

The entire city is considered as a circle and the various areas as sectors radiating out from the center of that circle; similar types of land use originate near the center of that circle and migrate outward toward the periphery. Thus a high-rent residential area in the eastern quadrant of the city would tend to migrate outward, keeping always in the eastern quadrant. A low-quality housing area, if located in the southern quadrant, would tend to extend outward to the very margin of the city in that sector. The migration of upper-class residential areas outward along established lines of travel is particularly pronounced on high ground, toward open country, to homes of community leaders, along lines of fastest transportation, and to existing nuclei of buildings or trading centers.[12]

[12]Harris and Ullman, *op. cit.*, pp. 13-14. For a more technical statement, see Homer Hoyt, "City Growth and Mortgage Risk," *Insured Mortgage Portfolio*, Vol. 1, Nos. 6-10 (December, 1936-April, 1937), *passim;* and Homer Hoyt, *The Structure and Growth of Residential Neighborhoods in American Cities* (United States Federal Housing Administration, 1939), *passim.*

A third, so-called multinuclear, theory described cities which consisted of six types of nuclei, namely: (1) the central business district, (2) the wholesale and light manufacturing district, (3) the heavy industry district, (4) the residential district, (5) minor nuclei such as parks, outlying and small industrial centers, and universities, and (6) suburban and satellite nuclei. (The satellite was farther away than the suburb and its residents practiced less commuting, although its economy was closely geared to that of the main center.) Certain activities required specialized facilities; thus, for example, retail activities must be accessible to the whole community, ports must, of course, be on water fronts, manufacturing must be near transportation facilities. This fact, together with the compatibility and incompatibility of different uses already commented on, and the fact that certain activities were unable to afford the high rents of the most desirable sites determined the relationships among the several nuclei.

WHAT VALUES WERE BEING TESTED?

What was this autonomous competition in Cycle One testing? What values did the resulting structures register? What policies guided it? Obviously it was testing ability to pay rent which, by implication, reflected economic productivity. If that was the value the community wished to register, the Cycle One competitive processes were fair, whatever the result.

Even in Cycle One, however, the necessity for some kind of control had been recognized. Zoning restrictions were one of the first attempts made to regulate competition for the use of land. It was based, essentially, on a recognition of the different uses to which land could be put and the relationships among them. It had to begin with the structure as it was; it could not begin from scratch. But it did attempt to protect certain areas from the competition of more profitable uses. Commercial and industrial establishments were forbidden to invade residential areas, and so on. But often it became impossible to enforce the zoning regulations in the face of concerted opposition. It was, at best, a stopgap solution.

Increasingly, however, people began to question whether the values which competitive processes registered were really the values the community wanted registered. Water fronts illustrate the point. Europeans often commented on the fact that in so many American communities river, lake, and ocean fronts, which in such cities as Paris or London were reserved for nonindustrial uses that do not contaminate and destroy the beauty of the setting, were laced with railroad tracks and given over to heavy industry. So that what could have been the loveliest location, enjoyed by all, was shrouded in smoke and grime. Would the river land transformed into a public park be less productive? In Cycle One the answer was an unqualified Yes. But by midcentury many thoughtful people began to think it would not.

It began to be clear also that although competition was quite natural, it was not mechanical nor was it necessarily blind. It was a neutral engine that could be put to use for one purpose as well as for another. For a long time it had been assumed that this impersonal way of distributing land use through ecological processes, whatever they were testing, desirable or undesirable, was inevitable, "natural," inviolable. People may have deplored the results, but they took a shoulder-shrugging, laissez-faire attitude.

Increasingly, however, students of community life—planners, engineers, economists, sociologists, political scientists, and even the more advanced real estate specialists—came to see that the old way of deciding how land should be

used—autonomous competition operating under a laissez-faire policy—was uneconomical on the basis of almost any standard of value. Slums and blighted areas cost more than they yielded in taxes. The smoke, grime, fumes, and other by-products of heavy industry cost citizens more in cleaning bills, ill health, and discomfort than the economy effected by the location of the factory. It was found that proper planning could house more people on less land and do it more healthfully and attractively than the old method.

By and large, then, those who went into the subject most completely opposed autonomous competition in assigning land to its several uses. True, there would always have to be some choice made among alternative uses, so that competition might be inevitable. But increasingly it was felt that it should be judgmental and designed to test other than merely economic values. Planning boards and authorities, on the basis of a consideration of many community values, tended to become the judges of land use.

THE END OF CYCLE ONE

Whether or not this was a perfect solution to the problem was beside the point. By midcentury Cycle One had ground, or was in process of grinding, to a halt. The processes which characterized it had reduced it to an absurdity. Not only heavy industry, but also retail establishments—the so-called shopping centers—had leapfrogged out of the central business districts into low-rent areas outside of the city limits where parking facilities were available. Light industry which now needed one-story, space-consuming areas, also with parking facilities, moved out. Drive-in movies sprang up in open fields. More to the point, residents were moving out of the cities into the suburbs. Indeed, the flight to the suburbs became almost a rout. Central cities could not compete with suburbs in holding people. It was estimated in 1959, for example, that by 1975 central cities would have 12,000,000 more people but the suburban ring would have 54,000,000 more. Of these, 32,000,000 would go to open country or unincorporated areas known as exurbia or interurbia; the other 21,000,000 would go into incorporated areas in the suburban ring.[13] For those who could afford it . . . suburban life seemed far more attractive than city life.[14]

The autonomous competitive processes of Cycle One—testing ability to pay, guided by laissez-faire policy—had been allowed to defeat their own purposes. The plight of American cities had become "the great unspoken, overlooked, underplayed problem of our time."[15]

The processes that produced this situation were not new; they were the same as those that had been operating for decades. Sociologists had been analyzing them for many years. What was new was automobile transportation on an unheard-of scale, making it possible to expand the suburban area in all directions, independently of railroad facilities. New also were the architectural requirements of factories, space-consuming both in layout and in parking needs. New also were machines and organizations that could build scores of houses quickly and cheaply.

As in the case of the national community the competitive processes which ceaselessly locate and relocate people in local communities would be of only incidental interest to sociologists if they did not reflect values and if they did not have profound effects on the relationships between and among groups of people. The flight of middle-class families from central cities to the suburbs deprived the cities of leadership; it left less privileged—not, of course, innately inferior—people in its wake, poorer and hence less good customers, poorer sources of tax revenues, less able to meet the challenges posed by modern urban community living. It became clear, finally, that the autonomous competitive processes had almost destroyed the city as a functioning unit. Something had to be done if it were to be salvaged. Zoning, slum clearance, and housing projects were not enough. The concept of urban renewal or rehabilitation developed and became embodied in the Federal Housing Acts of 1949 and 1961.

CYCLE TWO: THE SALVAGING OF CITIES

The characteristic approach to community development in Cycle Two is one of salvaging the city, to redevelop it, to rehabilitate it, to try to win back people who can furnish leadership—as well, of course, as pay taxes—and to make the city functional once more by making traffic more efficient and parking space more available.

Such urban renewal implies a great deal more than a mere tinkering with existing patterns and the processes that produced them. It is not merely a negative undoing of past errors; it is, rather, a positive working toward new goals, the implementing of new values.

Urban renewal . . . encompasses not just clearing away slums, but building something better in their place; not just ridding a city of slums but preventing their onset. Urban renewal embraces the act of continuously revitalizing the urban core; keeping cities, towns and neighborhoods fresh and growing, giving people better places to live, in areas adjacent and convenient of access to school, park, shops, church, health center or meeting hall.[16]

[13]*New York Times*, Dec. 1, 1959.
[14]See William Dobriner, ed., *The Suburban Community* (New York: Putnam, 1958) for an excellent summary of sociological research in suburbs.
[15]Then Senator John Kennedy. *Ibid.*

[16]Thomas P. Coogan, "You—and Urban Renewal," in "Can We House Our Exploding Population?" in the *New York Times*, Oct. 11, 1959.

The process remains one of competition, but the values being tested have been expanded. In the first cycle, for example, the competitive tests were applied lot by lot. That is, each individual plot of land had to prove itself more profitable for one use rather than for another. But in the end this proved to be a wrong way to apply competitive tests. The sum of the individual "profits" added up to a loss for the whole community. It became evident that land use could not be allocated tiny parcel by tiny parcel; it had to be allocated in large units. It was found, for example, that when larger units were used more people could be housed in the same space, more comfortably, and with room to spare for yards, play areas, and lawns.

Even more radical is the proposal offered by some students to plan for deliberate diversity in neighborhoods, so that there will not be a segregation of low-income from high-income families. The feeling is that high-income families should not be shielded from contact with low-income families, and that low-income families should not be deprived of leadership from high-income families. It will doubtless be a long time before this set of values is reflected in the ecological structure of communities, if it ever is.

In addition to making cities more attractive in luring people back, other appeals are such things as freedom from the care of property, time saved in transportation, privacy, diversity, cultural opportunities—having them available seems to offer satisfaction whether or not they are taken advantage of—and more time with the family for the head.

One study of "returnees" from the suburbs found the largest number to consist of upper-income people whose children had grown up and married. But these were not the major sources to be tapped. People with long and irregular working hours, people with relatively

short assignments in certain cities, say only two or three years, widows, divorcees, spinsters, bachelors, young unmarried people, childless couples, academic people—these were among the people it has been suggested cities should compete for. It is not supposed that the city can successfully compete with the suburbs for young middle-class families with children; but even for this class there may be more attraction when the cities have become rehabilitated.[17]

URBAN SPRAWL AND MEGOLOPOLIS

There is an old cliché to the effect that generals are always planning to fight the last war rather than the next one. While it is true that cities in Cycle Two are beginning to restructure and rehabilitate themselves to implement new values, larger units are developing which include areas even beyond the suburbs and they are being shaped as much without guidance as cities themselves were in Cycle One.

With modern transportation, suburban developments spring up anywhere and everywhere. The result has been called urban sprawl. There is no planned use of the land, its development being left almost completely in the hands of speculative builders. Again the sum of individual "profit" often adds up to community loss. It has been said that it takes five acres to do the work that one acre could do better and, in addition, the result of present trends is, aesthetically, a mess.[18]

Because of this uneconomic use of land, suburbs, or at least settlements and developments, tend to spread out until

[17]The above discussion is based on William H. Whyte, Jr., "Are Cities Un-American?" in *The Exploding Metropolis, A Study of the Assault on Urbanism and How Our Cities Can Resist It*, by the editors of Fortune. Anchor (New York: Doubleday, 1958), pp. 1–18.

[18]*Ibid.*, p. 116.

they meet. Thus metropolitan areas become great agglomerations to which the name megolopolis, or strip cities, has been given. Filling in the countryside would, it has been estimated, result by 1975 in a series of such megolopolises in different parts of the country. There would be a Great-Lakes-opolis around Chicago, stretching from Milwaukee at the north to Chicago to South Bend at the south. There would be a Gulf-opolis from Houston to Galveston to New Orleans, in addition to Tex-opolis extending from Fort Worth and Dallas to Houston and Galveston. There would be also Pacific-opolis (San Francisco to San Diego), Puget-opolis (Everett-Seattle-Tacoma down through Portland and Salem), Florid-opolis (Miami to Jacksonville, Fort Myers to Jacksonville), and Atlantic-opolis (Boston to Baltimore and Washington).[19]

Whatever the size and structure of communities may be in Cycle Two of American city development, they will certainly result from the operation of competitive processes, however institutionalized, and they will register the values the communities wish to have tested.

[19]Philip Hauser, interviewed in *U. S. News and World Report*, Nov. 28, 1958, p. 84.

SOCIALIZATION PROCESSES IN COMMUNITIES

We speak of *socialization* when we focus on the process by which individuals acquire the knowledge, skills, and motivation required to perform social roles. However, we speak of *acculturation* when we consider the process by which one group takes on certain elements of the knowledge, skills, and motivations of another group. Acculturation is the important process to be studied at the community level as we examine the ways in which groups with varying cultures come together, selecting and rejecting elements from the cultural store of each, and often creating a new cultural pattern in the process.

Although we focus in this discussion on acculturation, it should be clear that, from the standpoint of an individual member of one of these groups, the process of concern remains socialization. But it is socialization under very special and complex circumstances. In a sense, two or more sets of socialization agents are vying for an individual's attention and acceptance. One set of socializers (perhaps his family) proposes one set of norms and behavior patterns as appropriate, while another set (perhaps his teachers) may propose a different set. An individual in such a situation is clearly subject to role conflict, on the one hand finding it impossible to fulfill the expectations of his parents as their son and on the other hand meeting the demands placed on him by his teachers as their student. Very often, the individual under these circumstances becomes a *marginal man*, no longer accepted by his previous associates and not yet fully accepted by his new associates.[1] In short, the socialization contexts with which we are now concerned are troubled and conflicting, placing the individual being socialized under great cross-pressures.

It need hardly be said that the meeting of two or more groups with differing cultures sets in motion a complex series of forces. The consequences for each group are influenced by many variables, including size of group (Is one group clearly dominant and another clearly subordinate in the situation?), the extent to which the groups are similar in culture and racial characteristics, and the values or goals held by the groups that indicate the preferred outcome of the encounter. For a long time in the United States it was presumed that the desirable outcome of encounters between groups would be the complete *assimilation* of the minority by the dominant culture. This "melting pot" ideology assumed that, over two or three generations, minority group members would become indistinguishable from the majority. Total assimilation of minority groups is only one possible goal, and other goals may come to take precedence, as we will see.

The Old and New Immigrants   All told, some 42 million immigrants have settled in this country since 1820, the first year in which accurate records were kept. This flow of people across an ocean is unprecedented in the history

[1]See Robert E. Park, "Human migration and the marginal man," *American Journal of Sociology*, 33 (1927–1928), 881–893.

of mankind, making the American experience unique. The policy of assimilation was somewhat self-consciously followed from the foundation of this country up to the late nineteenth century, during which time the primary source of immigrants was Northwestern Europe. (The policy, of course, was not meant to apply to the hundreds of thousands of slaves brought to this country prior to 1808, when the slave trade was outlawed.)

As the "Old Immigrants" from Northwestern Europe were gradually replaced by "New Immigrants" from Southern and Eastern Europe, whose ethnic characteristics were less like those of the dominant population (Nordic versus Mediterranean, Protestant versus Catholic), the desirability and inevitability of assimilation of the new minorities began to be questioned by the majority group. *Nativism* developed as dominant groups became determined to protect their majority culture from assaults and inroads by minority groups. Efforts were devoted to regulating the number of immigrants and to setting up certain qualitative restrictions applying to broadly defined nationality groups. In the last quarter of the nineteenth century, legislation was passed restricting and finally prohibiting Chinese immigration. And, in 1882, Congress passed the first law regulating general immigration, excluding certain classes of persons such as convicts, "lunatics," "idiots," and persons likely to become a public charge. Additional specific categories of persons were excluded by succeeding legislation, but it was not until 1924 that Congress passed an immigration bill greatly limiting the number of immigrants to this country and establishing an annual quota system: European immigration was limited to 2 percent of the number of foreign-born of each nationality residing in the United States at the time of the 1880 census.

Advocates of immigration restriction made much of the presumed differences between the social characteristics of the early and the later immigrants. There were indeed changes in the national origin of the old (prior to 1880) and the new (after 1880) immigrants, but even more important were the changed economic conditions in this country that greeted those arriving after 1880. As Petersen points out:

The shift in the main source of immigration from Northwestern to Southern and Eastern Europe also coincided with a transformation of the American economy. The German or Swedish peasant who immigrated during the years right after the Civil War took advantage of the Homestead Act and became a farmer; but when the Italian or Polish peasant arrived, this entry into the economy was closed, and burgeoning American industry was calling for more and more unskilled labor. . . .

The New Immigrants, therefore, had simultaneously to undergo two processes of adjustment: from their native cultures to the American one and from a rural to an urban way of life. In many respects, the second adaptation was the more difficult. The social ills attributed to the innate inadequacies of the New Immigrants were the result basically of the extremely rapid, haphazard development of an urban-industrial society, a process of which the New Immigrants were the most conspicuous victims.[2]

The circumstances confronting the newer immigrants to this country were, at best, difficult. Most of them poured into the slums of the big cities. Knowing little or no English and lacking skills useful in an urban environment, they typically entered the labor market at the bottom.[3] Many immigrant groups,

[2]William Petersen, *Population*, New York: Macmillan, 1961, pp. 98–99.
[3]For a graphic description of the hardships endured and types of adjustment made by immigrants to this country, see Oscar Handlin, *The Uprooted: The Epic Story of the Great Migrations That Made the American People*, New York: Grosset & Dunlap, 1951.

faced with hostility and prejudice from native groups, developed their own brand of nativism as a protective measure. Petersen comments:

> In many cases it was only after they had left it that immigrants learned to identify themselves with "their" country. They were taught this first of all by native Americans, who demanded a simple, understandable answer to the question, "What are you?" Having learned that they belonged to a nation, some of the immigrants became nationalists. They submerged their provincialisms into a broader patriotism, their local dialects into languages . . . . The nativism of such groups was often one facet of their acculturation, paradoxical as this may seem.[4]

Some nationality groups banded together for mutual help and protection, founding their own clubs, churches, welfare organizations, and burial societies. Others, like the Southern Italian group described by Herbert Gans in Reading 36, retained the intense familial structure imported from their homeland. The reading from Gans is taken from his book describing the social structure developed by a group of native-born Americans of Italian parentage (second-generation Italian-Americans) living in an inner-city Boston neighborhood called the West End. In the reprinted reading, Gans begins by describing the social structure of Southern Italian society—the social structure immigrants brought with them to America and that they attempted to recreate in their new homeland. Then the process of acculturation is described as the second- and third-generation Italian-Americans begin to take on some of the characteristics of the majority culture. The primary socializing agent in this acculturation process is the public school; also important are the peer group and the development of occupational opportunities drawing young adults away from the influence of family and neighborhood.

For many minority groups, acculturation to the majority culture over the generations is inevitable. However, the precise stages of this process and the speed with which it occurs vary from group to group. Gans, for example, discusses at length some of the factors that make the experiences of the Italian-American group somewhat unique.

Nor should we assume that the acculturation process is in any sense complete in this country. Most great metropolitan cities are composed of many ethnic groups that are still to some extent identifiable. The groups tend to be stratified, but, unlike geological strata, the newest layer is added to the bottom. For example, in New York City, English and Scottish immigrants were among the first to arrive, followed in the 1840s by Irish and Germans, in the 1880s by the Jews and Italians, with the Negroes beginning to arrive after World War II. These groups retain to a greater or lesser degree their separate identities: members are linked by recognizable names, a common past, the ties of family and friendships, common interests, and special organizations.[5]

Further, as Petersen notes, although newly arriving groups typically begin at the bottom of the social structure, the nature of that bottom rung differs over time, and so various groups tend to begin their climb in distinctive occupations. They and their children move up from different starting points and along different routes. This description applies not only to legitimate but also to deviant occupations, as Daniel Bell has pointed out:

[4]Petersen, pp. 130–131.

[5]See Nathan Glazer and Daniel Patrick Moynihan, *Beyond the Melting Pot: The Negroes, Puerto Ricans, Jews, Italians and Irish of New York City*, Cambridge, Mass.: M.I.T. Press, 1963.

The Italian community has achieved wealth and political influence much later and in a harder way than previous immigrant groups. Early Jewish wealth, that of the German Jews of the late nineteenth century, was built in the garment trades, though with some involvement with the Jewish gangster, who was typically an industrial racketeer. . . . Irish immigrant wealth in the northern urban centers, concentrated largely in construction, trucking, and the waterfront, has, to a substantial extent, been wealth accumulated in and through political alliance, e.g., favoritism in city contracts. . . .

The Italians found the more obvious big-city paths from rags to riches pre-empted. In part this was due to the character of the early Italian immigrant. Most of them were unskilled and from rural stock. . . . The children of the immigrants, the second and third generation, became wise in the ways of the urban slums. Excluded from the political ladder—in the early thirties there were almost no Italians on the city payroll in top jobs, nor in books of the period can one find discussion of Italian political leaders—and finding few open routes to wealth, some turned to illicit ways.[6]

As noted in previous parts of this book (see Reading 11), we see again the extent to which deviance is socially structured, in this case by the blocking of legitimate opportunities to move up in the social structure. Such data as these suggest one important limitation to the melting-pot thesis, for, as Petersen concludes, "Total assimilation by ethnic background is possible only if nationalities are randomly distributed among all occupations; for to the degree that the contrary is the case, variation by ethnic background tends to persist in the form of class differences."[7]

A final factor perhaps helping to perpetuate cultural differences among ethnic groups is a new ideological emphasis in this country on *pluralism:* a recognition that differing cultural traditions add color and interest to social life, that we can learn much of value from minority groups, and that these divergent traditions are worth preserving.

The Black Migrants Not all the significant movement of population is across national boundaries; profound shifts occur as well within the borders of a nation. By far the most significant shift of population within the United States during this century has been the movement of Negroes from the rural South to the urban North. The movement of the black man from South to North began as a trickle following the Civil War. It increased at the turn of the century in response to repressive measures and to Jim Crow legislation in the South. But the major flow began during World War I in response to labor shortages in Northern industries.

With labor the scarce factor of production even before American entry into the war, Northern industries began sending labor agents into the rural South, recruiting Negroes just as they had recruited white workers in Ireland and Italy during the nineteenth century . . . emigration from the eleven states of the Old Confederacy jumped from 207,000 in 1900–1910 to 478,000 in 1910–1920.[8]

Following the wartime boom, the flow continued as the agrarian revolution began in the South and farmers, both white and black, moved off the soil. But while the majority of the rural whites settled in Southern cities, the bulk of

[6]Daniel Bell, "Crime as an American way of life," *The End of Ideology*, Glencoe, Ill.: Free Press, 1960, pp. 128–129.

[7]Petersen, p. 137.

[8]Charles E. Silberman, *Crisis in Black and White*, New York: Vintage Books, a Division of Random House, 1964, p. 26.

Negroes headed North. In a very real sense, blacks were the unanticipated beneficiaries of the new immigration laws of the 1920s, for they moved into jobs formerly taken by new immigrants. And the movement North has continued, stimulated anew by the war economy of the 1940s and by the economic expansion of the 1950s and 1960s. Altogether, 2.75 million Negroes left the South between 1940 and 1960.

Note that the vast majority of Negroes have moved North since 1910 and by far the largest movement has occurred since 1940. Just as the Southern and Eastern European migrants arriving after 1890 found different economic circumstances confronting them than did the Northwestern European migrants arriving prior to 1890, so the Negro migrants moving North in this century have been faced with different economic conditions than the conditions met by the second stream of European migrants. Southern and Eastern Europeans at least could participate in the economy by moving into unskilled positions. This route is to an increasing extent closed to Negroes. The number of positions for unskilled workers has been rapidly decreasing as mechanization eliminates these jobs. Hence, for many blacks the choice is all too often between taking an extremely menial job that does not pay a living wage and does not lead anywhere in terms of potential mobility, or not working at all.[9] The implications of long-term unemployment of Negro men for their position as head of a household are all too obvious. To the extent that they cannot provide adequate financial support for their families, their position as husband and father is severely jeopardized. Many Negro fathers find that the only course open to them is desertion. The consequence of this action for the socialization of Negro children—being reared in a mother-dominated family—has yet to be fully explored but is undoubtedly of extreme importance.[10]

"Most of the Negroes moving North have crowded into the slums of the twelve largest cities, which in 1960 held 60 percent of the Negroes living outside the Deep South."[11] To a much greater extent than with any previous ethnic group, the movement of large numbers of blacks to Northern cities has resulted in *segregation*. This occurs in spite of the fact that the newcomers share with the older residents the same national origin, the same language, and the same religion. Nevertheless, the degree of segregation of Negroes is universally high in all American cities:

. . . systematic study of the block-by-block patterns of residential segregation reveals little difference among cities. A high degree of racial residential segregation is universal in American cities. Whether a city is a metropolitan center or a suburb; whether it is in the North or South; whether the Negro population is large or small—in every case, white and Negro households are highly segregated from each other.[12]

In support of the above generalization, Taeuber and Taeuber used 1960 census data for city blocks to calculate segregation indexes for 207 American cities. The index values ranged from a low of 60.4 to a high of 98.1, but only

[9]See Elliot Liebow, *Tally's Corner*, Boston: Little, Brown, 1967, pp. 29–71.

[10]See E. Franklin Frazier, *The Negro Family in the United States*, Chicago: University of Chicago Press, 1939; Liebow, pp. 72–136; and U.S. Department of Labor, Office of Policy Planning and Research, *The Negro Family: The Case for National Action* (The Moynihan Report), March, 1965.

[11]Silberman, p. 30.

[12]Karl E. Taeuber and Alma F. Taeuber, *Negroes in Cities*, Chicago: Aldine, 1965, p. 2.

eight cities had values below 70 and half the cities had values above 87.8.[13] Further, the degree of segregation appears to be on the increase: the data from the 1940 and 1950 censuses calculated for 109 cities indicated that 83 of these cities exhibited a higher index for 1950 than for 1940.[14]

The high degree of segregation between Negroes and whites in our society is both a cause and a result of the majority culture's failure to assimilate them. Many blacks in urban ghettos have little contact with white society, and the contacts they have are not conducive to improving their relative situation. In earlier portions of this volume we have attempted to explain some of the factors inhibiting the type of interaction that could lead to full equality for black citizens. Blacks have waited so long to be fully integrated in American society that some of them have come to reject the goal of assimilation and are now impatiently demanding complete separation of the races, perhaps an intense form of the nativism that has been observed among some European minority groups. The hard questions raised by the Negro experience are posed for us by Tilly:

Has there been a standard process of assimilation into an American mainstream via the big city, one that is still working today for Negroes and other racial minorities? Or have the mechanisms broken down, has the economic situation changed too much, has the system of exclusion become too efficient, are the groups now seeking inclusion too different in character? Or is the notion of assimilation into the mainstream itself based on a misunderstanding of how American life works?

If the standard process of assimilation is still working, then designers of American public policy could reasonably seek ways to speed up an established pattern of change. If the process is not working, then they would have to envisage changes in the very structure of American society.[15]

We do not have the answers to these questions now, but they are among the questions that increasingly are finding their way to the top of this nation's agenda for solution and for appropriate action.

[13]Taeuber and Taeuber, pp. 31–34. The segregation index is an index of dissimilarity that may be interpreted to represent the percentage of nonwhites that would have to shift from one block to another to effect an even, unsegregated distribution.

[14]Taeuber and Taeuber, pp. 37–38.

[15]Charles Tilly, "Race and Migration to the American City," in James Q. Wilson (ed.), *The Metropolitan Enigma*, Cambridge, Mass.: Harvard University Press, 1968, p. 152.

36 The Peer Group Society in Process

Herbert J. Gans

Although the antecedents of the present West Enders can be studied in several ways, perhaps the best approach would have been to consult their parents and other immigrants who were still living in the West End. This would have required a

Reprinted with permission of the author and the Macmillan Company: from *The Urban Villagers: Group and Class in the Life of Italian-Americans* by Herbert J. Gans. © The Free Press of Glencoe, a Division of The Macmillan Company, 1962, pp. 197-226.

knowledge of Italian—and of regional dialects—which I did not have. It also might have created a picture distorted by faulty memories and nostalgia for the past. There are also two other possible approaches: to discover what West Enders themselves report about their parents and the generations in Italy; and to consult existing sociological studies of Italian immigrants and of Italian society before the exodus to America. Such studies also can be backed up by research in present day Italian communities.

Both approaches are fraught with considerable danger. The West Enders know the past only from their experience, most of which was collected in childhood.[1] The use of other sociological studies, on the other hand, requires the assumption that the ancestors of the West Enders are like the people in the Italian communities where the research took place. Moreover, the attempt to describe people by generations assumes that generations are cultural units, and that Italian, immigrant, and second-generation groups in one place and time will be roughly similar to those of another place and time. But the society and culture of any generation are affected and altered by the social and economic conditions within which they exist.

As it turns out, however, the studies made among immigrants and of Italian society at the time of the major exodus, as well as those made recently in Southern Italy, have reported many similar findings. Moreover, these findings do not diverge significantly from the picture which I have drawn of the West Enders. It would seem, therefore, that not only are Italians much the same everywhere, but that there is a clearly identifiable Italian social structure that has changed remarkably little in the passage of time and place from Italy to America. This stability can be traced largely to the uniformity in social and economic conditions under which the several generations have lived.

From the types of change that have taken place between the immigrant and the second generation, and from behavioral patterns visible among the more mobile West Enders and their children, it is possible to project some of the changes that will be likely to take place when the third generation reaches adulthood. Observations about the West Enders' resistance to change, and especially to the middle class, would suggest, however, that the family circle and the other institutions basic to the peer group society will continue to exist in the third generation. Thus, the children of the West Enders will neither move—nor be swept —into the institutions of middle-class American society nor adopt its value premises.[2]

THE SOUTHERN ITALIAN SOCIETY

Southern Italian society—that is, the provinces below Rome and in Sicily—was agrarian, feudal, and static when the exodus to America began at the turn of the century. Most of the land was owned by a relatively small number of large absentee landowners—some of them of the nobility—who either leased their land to peasants, or had it farmed by landless day laborers under the supervision of resident managers. The local community consisted typically of four major social strata, each rigidly separated from the other: the "galantuomini," or gentry, including the nobility, other large landowners, the professionals, and the clergy; the "artigiano," or artisans, including craftsmen and small shopkeepers; the "contadini," or peasants, who owned or leased tiny plots of land; and the "giornalieri," or day laborers who looked each day for work on the estates, and who

[1]Consequently, their comments about the past will be used only sparingly.

[2]It must be remembered of course that the West Enders are not entirely representative of all second-generation Italian-Americans. See Chapter 2 of *The Urban Villagers*.

were rarely employed more than a third of the year. The vast majority of the people were either peasants or farm laborers, who lived in a chronic state of poverty and deprivation. The farm laborers were poorest, but in many communities the peasants controlled so little land that they were economically no better off, even though landownership did give them a somewhat higher status.[3]

Recent studies of Southern Italian communities have made it clear that relatively little change has occurred in the over-all economy and social structure, and that the conditions which existed at the turn of the century still hold today.[4] Consequently, it is possible to draw on studies made just before the immigration to America,[5] as well as on those conducted in contemporary communities.[6] Since most of the Southern Italians who went to America came from the ranks of the day laborers and peasants, information about the ancestors of the West Enders can be taken from data about these two strata in past and present studies.

These data suggest strongly that the society and culture of the West Enders are quite similar to those of the Southern Italians, past and present. In Italy, as in the West End, households consisted of nuclear or expanded families.[7] Husband-wife relationships were segregated, and family life was adult-centered.[8] Children were reared by reward and punishment,[9] and parents had little interest in them as individuals, except to show them off.[10] Because of the poverty, children were expected to work as soon as they were old enough. Moreover, since the available work was unskilled, they had learnt all of the adult skills between the ages of seven and ten.[11]

The two studies of present-day Southern Italy found no evidence of an extended family, noting that the land was too poor to justify several family members working on it jointly.[12] Covello reported that among the Sicilians whom he studied the extended family had existed around the turn of the century.[13] It then had provided mutual aid and companionship under the leadership of a family head, who was chosen informally from among the adult men, and who maintained the family honor, supervised disputes, and administered interhousehold aid.[14] Functioning as a social rather than an economic unit, it seems to have been only a more cohesive and slightly more structured form of the family circle which has been reported in all of the studies, past and present.

Social life was centered almost exclusively around the family circle of relatives, and people outside it were conceived to be strangers.[15] Friendship as

[3]For a convenient summary of Southern Italian life, see R. A. Schermerhorn, *These Our Children*, Boston: D. C. Heath, 1949, Chap. 11.

[4]See, for example, Edward C. Banfield, *The Moral Basis of a Backward Society*, New York: The Free Press of Glencoe, 1958; and Donald Pitkin, "Land Tenure and Farm Organization in an Italian Village," unpublished Ph.D. Dissertation, Harvard University, 1954. For a detailed analysis of the poverty of Sicily, see Danilo Dolci, *Report from Palermo*, New York: Orion Press, 1959.

[5]These are based largely on interviews with immigrants in America. Cf. Phyllis H. Williams, *Southern Italian Folkways in Europe and America*, New Haven: Yale University Press, 1938; or on interviews in America combined with informal research in Italy, cf. Leonard Covello, "The Social Background of the Italo-American School Child," unpublished Ph.D. Dissertation, New York University, 1944; and Walter H. Sangree, "Mel Hyblaeum: A Study of the People of Middletown of Sicilian Extraction . . . ," unpublished M.A. Thesis, Wesleyan University, 1952. My account here rests heavily on the detailed description in Covello's study.

[6]Most of my observations are drawn from Pitkin, *op. cit.*, and Banfield, *op. cit.*

[7]Covello, *op. cit.*, p. 237; Pitkin, *op. cit.*, p. 114.

[8]Covello, *op. cit.*, pp. 562–563.

[9]Banfield, *op. cit.*, pp. 154 ff.

[10]Pitkin, *op. cit.*, pp. 219–220.

[11]Covello, *op. cit.*, pp. 364 ff.

[12]Banfield, *op. cit.*, p. 10; Pitkin, *op. cit.*, pp. 114, 245.

[13]Covello, *op. cit.*, pp. 238 ff.

[14]*Ibid.*, pp. 236–241.

[15]*Ibid.*, pp. 271–275.

we know it was rare, and people who did become friends were adopted into the family through god-parentship.[16] Only relatives were invited into the home.[17]

Although the available studies provide no data on the existence of peer groups among adults, Pitkin has noted that boys and girls did separate themselves into age-graded groups.[18] Moreover, there was little respect for old people,[19] and Covello reported that a family head was replaced quickly if he became too old, or was senile.[20] These data suggest that the relationship between the generations, as in the West End, was less important than that within the generations. Relatives of similar age associated with each other, and the men competed for the leadership of the family circle. Covello noted that this provided the primary opportunity for individualism in Southern Italian society.[21]

Southern Italians, like West Enders, were only marginally attached to the community. Although people were expected to attend church, there was little involvement in the church itself.[22] As the priests generally supported the landowners, a strong anticlericalism developed among the peasants and farm laborers, especially among the men.[23] The Southern Italian attitude was summarized, as follows, by one of Sangree's respondents: "Fatalism is our religion; the church just supplies the pageantry of life."[24] In addition, there was widespread belief in animistic superstitions such as the evil eye, a malevolent spirit that caused illness and other disasters.

The rejection of the outside world was more intense than in the West End, and its boundaries began immediately outside the family circle. People from other communities, even nearby ones, were characterized as criminals.[25] The government and the police, run from Rome, were rejected with the traditional hostility felt toward Northern Italy. Within the community itself, the higher classes were treated as part of the outside world because they exploited the peasants and farm laborers, and denied them any opportunity to improve their lot.[26] Individual peasants or laborers who did manage to move to a higher social stratum were treated as renegades.[27]

Work patterns and attitudes in Southern Italy are not comparable to those of the West Enders because work was so desperately needed, so hard to find, and strenuously competed for when it was available. Children were put to work at an early age, for their help was needed to keep the family going.[28] Southern Italian parents saw little need for education once the child was old enough to work. They could neither have afforded to keep him in school, nor would the education he received have helped him to get a better job. Moreover, education was thought to remove the children from parental influence, and to question parental authority.[29] Indeed, in many towns, the schools were run largely for the children of the higher classes, and the children of peasants and laborers were neither expected nor encouraged to attend.[30]

Caretaking agencies were generally ignored, for they were thought to be for

[16]*Ibid.*, pp. 294 ff.
[17]*Ibid.*, pp. 140, 290.
[18]Pitkin, *op. cit.*, pp. 184–185.
[19]*Ibid.*, p. 224.
[20]Covello, *op. cit.*, pp. 245, 306.
[21]*Ibid.*, p. 244.
[22]*Ibid.*, pp. 208 ff.; Banfield, *op. cit.*, p. 17.
[23]Covello, *op. cit.*, p. 223; Banfield, *op. cit.*, p. 17.
[24]Sangree, *op. cit.*, p. 87.

[25]Jerre Mangione, *Mount Allegro*, Boston: Houghton Miflin, 1942, p. 6.
[26]Pitkin, *op. cit.*, pp. 155 ff.; Banfield, *op. cit.* Chap. 4.
[27]Covello, *op. cit.*, pp. 137 ff.
[28]*Ibid.*, pp. 398 ff.; Banfield, *op. cit.*, pp. 20–23.
[29]Covello, *op. cit.*, pp. 407 ff.
[30]*Ibid.*, pp. 394, 404.

families who could not fall back on their families for help.[31] At the turn of the century, hospitals were run on a charity basis which the peasants and laborers were too proud to accept.[32] Furthermore, as most of the caretaking agencies were organized by people from Northern Italy, they were doubly suspect.[33]

Banfield's study, which dealt specifically with the lack of community organization and civic activity in a Southern Italian village, emphasized the total bifurcation between the immediate family and the rest of society:

. . . the extreme poverty and backwardness . . . is to be explained largely but not entirely by the inability of the villagers to act together for their common good, or indeed for any end transcending the immediate material interest of the nuclear family. This inability . . . arises from an ethos . . . of *amoral familism*, which has been produced by three factors acting in combination: a high death rate, certain land tenure conditions, and the absence of the institution of the extended family. . . .[34]

The hypothesis [of amoral familism] is that the [villagers] act as if they were following this rule: Maximize the material, short-run advantage of the nuclear family; assume that all others will do likewise.[35]

Banfield's description of the local patterns of political participation suggests that they are similar to those in the West End. He noted that, "In a society of amoral familism, only officials will concern themselves with public affairs, for only they are paid to do so. For a private citizen to take a serious interest in a public problem will be regarded as abnormal or even improper."[36] He found extreme suspicion of the politician, and indicated that, "Whether an office holder takes bribes or not, it will be assumed by

the society of amoral familism that he does."[37] Likewise, "The claim of any person or institution to be inspired by zeal for public rather than private advantage will be regarded as a fraud."[38] He quotes a respondent: "If ever anyone wants to do anything, the question always is: what is he after?"[39]

Moreover, "In a society of amoral familists, there will be no leaders and no followers. No one will take the initiative in outlining a course of action and persuading others to embark on it—except as it may be to his private advantage to do so—and if one did offer leadership, the group would refuse it out of distrust."[40] Even attitudes toward voting are similar:

The voter will place little confidence in the promise of the parties. He will be apt to use his ballot to pay for favors already received, rather than for favors which are merely promised. Moreover . . . it will be assumed that whatever group is in power is self-serving and corrupt. Hardly will an election be over before the voters will conclude that the new officials are enriching themselves at their expense and that they will have no intention of keeping the promises they have made.[41]

FROM IMMIGRANT TO SECOND GENERATION

The Southern Italians who migrated to America came to better themselves; many had intended to remain only long enough to earn money so that they could purchase land in their home village, and become small landowners. Some were successful—especially among the early arrivals. But as the Italian immigration increased in number, the large majority either were unable to save enough to return home, or relinquished the original

[31]Williams, *op. cit.*, p. 75.
[32]*Ibid.*, pp. 171–172.
[33]*Ibid.*; Covello, *op. cit.*, p. 387.
[34]Banfield, *op. cit.*, p. 10.
[35]*Ibid.*, p. 85.
[36]*Ibid.*, p. 87.

[37]*Ibid.*, p. 94.
[38]*Ibid.*, p. 98.
[39]*Ibid.*, p. 98.
[40]*Ibid.*, pp. 99–100.
[41]*Ibid.*, p. 102. See also Sangree, *op. cit.*, pp. 78–79.

dream, and brought their families to America.[42]

The studies of the immigrant generation would suggest that the move to America resulted in little change in the pattern of adult life.[43] The social structure which the immigrants brought with them from Italy served them in the new country as well. Those who moved to the cities, for example, settled in Italian neighborhoods, where relatives often lived side by side, and in the midst of people from the same Italian town. Under these conditions, the family circle was maintained much as it had existed in Southern Italy.

The outside world continued to be a source of deprivation and exploitation. The immigrants worked in factories and on construction gangs, but while work was more plentiful than in Italy, people had to strive as hard as ever to support their families. Situated on the lowest rung of the occupational hierarchy, they were exploited by their employers and by the "padrone," the agent who acted as a middleman between the immigrants and the labor market. Moreover, the churches in the immigrant neighborhoods were staffed largely by Irish priests, who practiced a strange and harsh form of Catholicism, and had little sympathy for the Madonna and the local saints that the Italians respected. The caretaking agen-

cies and the political machines were run by Yankees and other ethnic groups. As a result of the surrounding strangeness, the immigrants tried to retain the self-sufficiency of the family circle as much as they could. They founded a number of community organizations that supported this circle, and kept away from the outside world whenever possible.

The major changes took place among the children, especially as a result of their contact with American schools. Since parochial schools were not yet in existence, the children were required to attend the public ones. Covello found that when the immigrants first arrived, there was considerable hostility toward the public school system. Not only did the schools take the children out of the job market and prevent them from contributing to the family income, but they also seemed to upset the Southern Italian conception of the child, and the child's own relation to the parents. The school's teaching—that the child has his own life, that he should study during school hours, and play afterwards—was foreign to the immigrants. They felt that by encouraging play, the schools were preventing the children from growing up, and that by keeping boys in school when they could be working, the schools were impairing their masculinity. Covello quotes one of his informants as saying: "The schools made of our children persons of leisure—little gentlemen. They lost the dignity of good children to think first of their parents, to help them whether they need it or not."[44]

Gradually, however, the immigrants accepted the fact that there was no work for young children in America. They also discovered that there were laws which not only prevented them from working but which required them to go to school. Consequently, they sent the children to school, and, except in case of family

[42]The most detailed description of this immigration is contained in R. F. Foerster, *The Italian Emigration of Our Times*, Cambridge: Harvard University Press, 1919. For brief summaries, see Paul J. Campisi, "Ethnic Family Patterns: The Italian Family in the United States," *American Journal of Sociology*, vol. 53 (1948), pp. 443–449; Francis Ianni, "The Italo-American Teenager," *The Annals*, vol. 338 (November, 1961), pp. 70–78; and Nathan Glazer, *Peoples of New York*, forthcoming.

[43]My account of the immigrants and their children is based on Covello's study in New York's East Harlem district. It is a detailed and sympathetic report, and although unpublished, the best source of information on the social structure and culture of the Italian immigrant in America. Covello, *op. cit.*, Parts II and III.

[44]*Ibid.*, p. 467.

need, permitted them to finish the elementary grades. Even so, there was considerable grumbling about the American laws. Covello quotes another immigrant respondent: "Someone decides not to allow the drinking of wine, so he makes a law without asking the people. Same with going to school. How can you respect such a law?"[45]

When the children were asked to go to high school, however, the immigrants rebelled. The family needed the extra income, and, since jobs were available for the boys, there was no reason for them to attend school. Thus, the immigrants had not really changed their attitude about education. They had merely adjusted it to fit American conditions.

The children themselves were caught between two cultures. While the school taught them to behave like American children, the parents demanded that they be useful and obedient family members. Covello has suggested that the outcome of the struggle between the two depended largely on the peer group. In neighborhoods where Italian children were a minority in the school population, they began to feel that the parental culture was inferior, and adopted the ways of the non-Italian majority. In predominantly Italian neighborhoods, however, the parents won out. The children of high-school age then decided that they should side with the family rather than remain in school. Since their peers supported this choice, the students took to widespread and frequent truancy—with the full support of their parents.

Consequently, the children who grew up in predominantly Italian neighborhoods were for the most part not weaned away from the Italian social structure. There are several reasons for this. First, the choice was clearly one between school and family, rather than between school and work, for even those children

who could not obtain jobs stayed away from school. Also, whereas the school treated them as children, the parents considered them to be adults. Had the children been interested in learning, they might have rebelled against their parents, but it is clear that they were not interested. They had grown up with the belief that education was children's activity and that it was irrelevant to getting or holding a job. Since unskilled jobs were still available, what they were learning in school was of no use occupationally. The longer they stayed in school, the greater the gap that developed between them and their parents.

Covello indicates clearly that the second generation did reject many of the culture patterns which parents had brought with them from Italy—the superstitions, the old styles of dress, the recreational activities, and all other rural traditions which were irrelevant in America. At the same time, however, they did not reject the family-centered social structure. Covello quotes one man about his youth: "I loathed Italian customs with all my heart, but I would never let anything stand between me and our family."[46]

Another change, which may have begun in the first generation but which was really visible only in the second, was an increase in the freedom and family influence of the woman. In Southern Italy, women were subservient to, and almost completely dependent on, the men. They could not work as laborers, and no other jobs existed. While daughters could help around the house, their major contribution to the family was to retain their virginity until the parents could arrange a marriage that might be economically or socially beneficial to them. Thus, father and brothers guarded them closely to make sure that their hymens and their reputations both remained inviolate.

[45]*Ibid.*, p. 603.

[46]*Ibid.*, p. 537.

In America, many of these restrictions fell away. Even in Italy, the girls had chafed at their lack of freedom of movement and of choosing a spouse. Consequently, the American school that seemed like a prison to the second-generation Italian boy was an avenue of escape for the girl. Also, as she was taught by women, she was able to adjust more comfortably to the dominant school culture, which was, after all, predominantly female. More important, the American economy did not discriminate sexually. Thus women were able to get jobs on their own, and could contribute to the family coffers. At the same time, the advantages of the arranged marriage evaporated. Now that a man could work to improve himself economically or socially, he no longer needed to depend on his daughter's marriage for such benefits. Moreover, the social and residential fluidity in the Italian neighborhood diminished in importance the union of two families through arranged marriage. It no longer meant what it had in the static small town of Southern Italy. Thus the girls were free to choose their own boyfriends and husbands. But they were still restricted in many other ways. Their virginity was guarded as closely as before, and they were expected to marry a man of Italian background, preferably of equal or higher status.

Once the girl was married, and the children came, she usually moved back quickly into the traditional role, for she could no longer work and was dependent once more on the man. Even so, her status in the family was not quite the same: jobs were available to her, and if the husband did lose his job, she could go to work temporarily. Moreover, even in childhood she had learned that much of American mass production was designed with her in mind, including the movies that put her on a pedestal. Thus, the American culture of school, church, and

consumer goods invited her more readily than it did the man. Indeed, the male's corner hangout, the streets, and the stag environments in which he spent his spare-time as a young man were not respected by the American climate of opinion. Much of the energy of Yankee caretakers and reformers, in fact, was devoted to persuading him to accept female-dominated institutions.

American culture, however, could not penetrate the family circle. Thus, whereas the children who became the adults of the second generation retained little of the Italian culture, they did retain most of its social structure. . . .

A comparison of the lives of the West Enders with those of the immigrants suggests a number of other changes. For the West Enders, life is much less of a struggle than it was for their parents. There are more jobs, more secure ones, and better paid as well. As economic conditions improve, the ethos which Banfield calls amoral familism has begun to recede in importance. Most West Enders, for example, no longer need to fear their neighbors and unrelated people as a threat to their own existence. These "others" are no longer competitors for a small number of scarce jobs, but people with whom one can associate. Consequently, social life and mutual aid are not entirely restricted to the family circle; West Enders can and do make friends more easily than their ancestors.[47]

Nor is the outside world as threatening

<hr/>

[47]A number of other changes between Italians and Italian-Americans are described as part of a larger study of drinking patterns in G. Lolli, E. Serianni, G. Golder, and P. Luzzatto-Fegiz, *Alcohol in Italian Culture*, New York: The Free Press of Glencoe and Yale Center of Alcohol Studies, 1958. This study notes, for example, that Italian-Americans go to church more than Italians (p. 22); that they report drinking for social reasons, rather than for their health (pp. 68–69); that they get drunk more often (p. 85); and that unlike Italians they get drunk in the presence of the opposite sex (p. 88).

as it was to immigrants. The second generation is not barred from it by language, and it can maneuver in the outside world if absolutely necessary. As a result, the attitude toward caretakers, the law, city government, and other phases of the outside world is no longer based on total incomprehension and fear.

The processes by which these generational changes came to be were of course not always painless. In too many cases, the family circle and other immigrant institutions could not cope with acculturation, poverty, and the other degradations forced on the newcomers and their children by the outside world. Some turned to delinquency, crime, and violence to resolve their difficulties; others were beset by individual and family breakdowns. Although these problems affected only a minority of the population, they too are a part of the transition from immigrant to second-generation status.

THE SLOWNESS OF CHANGE: THE BASIS OF THE PEER GROUP SOCIETY

Some aspects of a group's way of life change more rapidly than others. Moreover, the observer's perception of change is affected by his own perspective, by the indices he uses, and by his own value judgments about the desirability of change per se.

These considerations affect any attempt to summarize the comparison of the West Enders to the generations that preceded them. Clearly, there has been considerable change in the standard of living, and in certain patterns of culture. At the same time, however, the many parallels between Southern Italian society and the West Enders suggest that many basic features of the way of life have not changed. The old social structure has remained intact.

What accounts for the stability of the social structure in the face of what would seem to be a rather drastic change in environment? The static, poverty-stricken, and highly stratified rural society of Southern Italy bears little resemblance to the frequently changing, more prosperous, and comparatively open society of urban-industrial Boston. *A brief review of the three generations may suggest the answer: the environment has not really changed as drastically as it appears.* This review will also make it possible to outline more clearly the basis of the peer group society as a response to the opportunities and deprivations in the environment.

The Italians who came to America were not farmers or peasants, but town-dwelling farm laborers who worked for absentee owners and managers. Although there was some evidence of the existence of a clanlike extended family, the occupational role of the farm laborer made it impossible for the extended family to function as a unit. The farm laborer, who was paid in wages that barely supported even his wife and children, could exist only in a nuclear family household.

Since people lived under conditions of extreme poverty, and in a static social system from which escape—other than by emigration—was impossible, the overriding goal was the survival of the nuclear family. Moreover, as marriages were contracted to advance—or at least not to retrogress—the economic and social position of the families involved, they had to be arranged. Consequently, husband and wife were usually not as close as in partnerships based on love. Since children had to go to work at the earliest opportunity, they were raised to adult status as quickly as possible, which was accomplished by threating them as small adults from an early age.

The nuclear family is neither entirely self-sufficient nor independent; nor can it satisfy all the needs of daily life. It is particularly handicapped in dealing with emergencies. Consequently, other institutions must be available. But when every family was involved in a struggle to survive—as was the case with the Southern Italian farm laborer—few people could be called on for aid, or trusted to give it when their own families were equally in need. Nor could they be treated as friends and companions, for they might take advantage of this relationship to help themselves in the fight for survival. Moreover, in order to attract friends, one had to be able to make a good impression. This required a dwelling unit to which people could be invited without shame, money to pay the costs of entertaining, and a considerable amount of trust over a long period of time. As one of Covello's respondents put it: "Friends are a luxury we cannot afford." Community agencies, were they churches, schools, or welfare agencies, could not be trusted because they were controlled by the employer. It made no difference when they had been founded for beneficial purposes; they were rejected by their intended clients as a matter of pride.

Under such conditions, relatives were the only source of group life and mutual aid. Being tied to each other by what were felt to be irrevocable ties of blood, they could face each other without putting on appearances, without feelings of shame, and without suspicion that the relationship would be exploited. In a society where no one could afford to trust anyone else, relatives had to trust each other. Moreover, when survival depended on the ability to work strenuously for long hours, older people were at a disadvantage. Possessing no special skills or traditional knowledge not also available to younger people, they had little influence in the group once they had become too old to support themselves. In addition, since relatives had to double as friends, people naturally gravitated to family members with whom they had the most in common. Consequently, they were drawn to peers.

The Southern Italian farm laborers lived not simply in poverty, but in poverty in the midst of a visibly higher standard of living enjoyed by the artisans, the middle class, and the gentry. In some areas they resorted to strikes and to class conflict; in others, to emigration.[48] But until these solutions were possible, most farm laborers lived in a state of extreme relative deprivation, a state made even more painful because of the close proximity of more fortunate people. In such circumstances, the restriction of aspirations was emotionally a most functional solution—at least in the short range—since it prevented the development of frustrations, which were frequently harder to endure than physical deprivation. Parental lack of interest in education, detachment from the larger community, and unwillingness to fight the exploiting powers—all were practical solutions in a society in which mobility was so restricted that there was no reason to expect benefits from schooling, and where the oversupply of labor made it possible to starve out rebellious individuals. While these solutions were harsh and denying, they also reduced stress, and made life as bearable as possible. Since the achievement of object-goals was certain to be frustrated, children were reared to reject them. The development of empathy was also discouraged; too great a sensitivity to the problems of other people would have been hard to endure.

Many of the conditions that gave rise to this way of life accompanied the Southern Italians in their move to Amer-

[48]John S. MacDonald and Lea D. MacDonald, "Migration Versus Non-Migration: A Typology of Responses to Poverty," paper read at the 1961 meetings of the American Sociological Society.

ica. In Italy, they had labored from sunrise to sunset on the farms of landowners; in America, they worked long hours as laborers for factory owners or contractors. Moreover, since they did not gravitate to the highly mechanized and rationalized assembly line jobs, the nature of their work did not change radically either. Many worked with the earth—pick and shovel in hand—in both countries, although in America, they brought forth construction projects rather than farm products. In Italy, they had lived in densely built-up and overcrowded small towns, barren of vegetation; in America, they moved into equally overcrowded and barren tenement neighborhoods. Indeed, their trip across the ocean took them only from rural towns to urban villages.

Most of these parallels continued into the adulthood of the second generation. Not until World War II, in fact, and the subsequent prosperity of the postwar era, did their economic position differ radically from that of their forebears. Even then, many West Enders have been dogged by unemployment, layoffs, and other forms of economic insecurity. Since they—as well as their parents—have often been employed in marginal industries, they also have felt themselves to be exploited occupationally. Moreover, like their ancestors, they have been beset by serious illness, premature death, infant mortality, and by other of the sudden and unpredictable tragedies that so frequently hit low-income people.

Many other parallels exist between Southern Italy and Boston. The immigrants who settled in Boston found a society stratified not only by class but also by ethnic background and religion. In fact, in Boston—more so perhaps than in other cities—they encountered a hereditary aristocracy that at the time of the Italian influx still held considerable social, economic, and political power. Since then, its place has been taken by

the Irish and by other groups, all of them culturally different from the Southern Italians. In short, the world outside the home was and still is dominated by people different in class and culture, by outsiders to be suspected and rejected.

Thus, the environment that the immigrants and the West Enders have encountered in America has differed in degree rather than in kind; it is less hostile and depriving, of course, but it is otherwise still the same. There have been no radical changes in the position of the working class vis-a-vis other classes, or in the position of minority ethnic groups vis-a-vis the majority. As a result, there have been as yet no strong pressures or incentives among the West Enders for any radical change in the basic social structure with which they respond to the environment.

FROM SECOND TO THIRD GENERATION: SIGNS OF CHANGE [49]

In addition to the changes that have already taken place between the past and present generations, other changes are only now developing. Noticeable among a few West Enders today, they are likely to become more prevalent in the next generation. These changes are the result of processes in the larger society that are creating new opportunities for West Enders. They also will make it more difficult to maintain some of the traditional ways of life.

The major source of opportunities is occupational. A few West Enders are now beginning to move into white-collar technical jobs, actually the modern equivalents of skilled factory work. They are also

[49] This section is speculative, since it deals with a generation only now reaching adulthood. It is based on observations of West Enders, a few ex-West Enders who had left before redevelopment, and on additional observations made among a handful of Italian families in a suburban community near Philadelphia which I studied after I concluded my field work in the West End.

beginning to enter service occupations, notably in sales, in which their ability for self-display and for competitive group activity is helpful.[50]

The third generation will be able to respond to the new occupational opportunities partly because their parents believe in the need for education as a means of obtaining job security. Parents also can now afford to keep children in school at least until high school graduation. Whether or not the third generation actually will take up these opportunities will depend, of course, on their willingness to stay in school, and to learn what is necessary to compete for stable and secure jobs. I assume that an increasing number of third-generation adolescents will remain in school.

New occupational and educational attainments are likely to have repercussions on the structure of the family, and on the peer group society generally. For one thing, they will create more social and cultural differences between people. This, in turn, will affect the family circle, for relatives who have responded to the widening opportunities may begin to find that they have less in common, and are no longer compatible in their interests. At the same time, since people have fewer children than in previous generations, the number of potential family circle members will be reduced. Consequently, the family circle may be somewhat harder to maintain than in the second generation.

Although someday these trends may even decimate the circle, other changes are likely to attract new recruits. I have already noted that as unrelated people cease to be competitors in the struggle for survival, they can become allies in the search for companionship. Indeed, the

desire for companionship combined with the decreasing number of compatible kin can mean that friends and neighbors will begin to play a more important role in the social life of the peer group society.

Meanwhile, other changes are taking place in the nuclear family unit. The decimation of the family circle by differential mobility is one step in a larger social process that brings nuclear family members into a more intimate dependence on each other. For while friends can replace relatives in a number of functions, rarely do they help each other as fully or be as close as people bound by blood ties. Other changes are reinforcing the cohesion of the nuclear family. With the disappearance of arranged marriages, husband and wife are emotionally closer to each other than were their parents and grandparents. Moreover, the nature of the educational process—both in and out of the classroom—is such that husbands and wives now grow up with a more similar background than was true in previous generations. By and large, both sexes are exposed to the same subjects in school. In addition, they are taught by the school, and by American culture generally, that the man may participate in child-rearing and household duties and in sparetime activities with his wife with no reflection on his masculinity. Given the increasing influence of the wife, and the larger number of common bonds between the marriage partners, the segregation of roles now existing in the family is likely to decrease.

Moreover, as the economic functions of the child have disappeared completely, the child's need to become an adult as rapidly as possible has disappeared also. Indeed, as relatives become less close, parents are likely to discover that the child can help to draw husband and wife together. Thus will begin the shift from the adult-centered family to the child-centered one, and the eventual develop-

[50]Whether these opportunities will be available to the third generation in as plentiful amounts as I am suggesting depends on the consequences of automation on the labor market in the coming decades.

ment of the kind of nuclear family structure now prevalent in America.

Also, relations between parents and children are likely to become closer. With fewer ethnic differences between the second and third generation than existed between the first and second, parents will feel more capable of advising their children. This could result in increased family conflict, if only because questions which were never raised before between parents and children will now be thought of as proper subjects of discussion. Family conflict also may be engendered by the fact that children will make greater demands on their parents, not only for goods but also for freedom to participate in children's and teenagers' activities.

Such a family is also likely to increase its participation in the outside world. Reduced suspicion and a decrease in cultural differences will make it less necessary for the next generation to reject the outside world as strongly as did the second. With more economic security, installment buying will seem less risky, and changing tastes will attract people to the consumer products and services that are now rejected. Already, the desire for modernity has made itself felt among some pioneering West Enders. And while the postwar suburbs have attracted only a few, they are likely to seem less frightening to the next generation. Indeed, it is probable that young mothers who look askance on the life of the street and wish closer supervision over their children's activities will find the attractions of suburban life most advantageous, even should their husbands not share this enthusiasm or their urgency about the children. Even now, the bright and sometimes garish pleasures of California and Florida are luring some West End vacationers, and will do so increasingly in the next generation. I remember how intensely a West End mother in her early twenties spoke of her plan to move to California, if only she could persuade her husband to give up his ties in Boston.

By virtue of the women's greater receptivity to education, and their premarital employment in the white-collar world, they are likely to take the lead in the process of change. The husbands may resist their pressure, and will probably be more reluctant to give up the old ways, especially since these were designed—intentionally or not—to maximize their freedoms and privileges. But because the wife remains subordinate to the husband in most families, because she is thoroughly indoctrinated in her home-maker role, and because she is hesitant about leaving the house to go to work, she may be unable to implement many of the changes of which she dreams. Her traditional role could act as a brake on her aspirations and perhaps as an accelerator on her frustrations.

Moreover, the social forms of the outside world will continue to be less attractive than its products, for the unwillingness and inability to concern oneself with object-oriented ways of behaving is likely to remain, among women as well as men. Churches and formal organizations, civic associations, government agencies, and politicians—all will probably be suspect even in the next generation, and participation in such activities is likely to be notably less among people of Italian background than among others.

Most of the people who will be making these changes are routine-seekers. As life becomes more secure, they no longer need—or want—to live for the gratifications of the moment. Not only is the search for adventurous episodes losing its urgency, but the drawbacks of action-seeking now loom larger than they did before. The lulls between episodes, the depression that sometimes accompanies the waiting, and the negative consequences of action-seeking now make it seem much less desirable. The availability of more predictable forms of gratification within the family and the peer group also takes something away from the pleasures of successful action-seeking. Its attractiveness as a way of life is thus being reduced, especially after adolescence. The parental desire to have children grow up respectably encourages this development, as does the increasing influence of women, who are the more earnest advocates of routine-seeking.

Yet parental desires are not always achieved, and, indeed, parental behavior may contradict them. Thus, some third-generation people will pursue action as fervently as did their ancestors. But increasingly, they will be those people who have grown up in idiosyncratic or pathological surroundings. Therefore the search for action will be a consequence of distinctive—and increasingly deviant— childhood experiences, rather than a prevalent way of life that stems from the economic and social insecurity of an entire group.

STATUS PROCESSES IN COMMUNITIES

To this point, our consideration of status has been restricted to the processes involved in differentiating, ranking, evaluating, and rewarding a single social position. As we move to consider more complex social units such as communities, we find that various social positions are often grouped together and then ranked according to certain evaluative criteria. In a small group it is possible for each individual to occupy a unique social position with which is associated differentiated expectations and to which is attached differentiated evaluations. However, in complex collectivities, participants (and social analysts) find it necessary to simplify their social environments by treating certain groups of positions, which clearly vary in some ways, as though they were identical or, at least, similar in status. The grouping together and then the evaluative ranking of groups of social positions give rise to the phenomena of *social strata*.[1]

Bases of Community Status   In comparison with small groups and formal organizations, communities are at best loosely organized social collectivities. Participants in communities are linked primarily by geographical propinquity—sharing a limited territorial space for residence—and by some degree of economic and social interdependence. We have argued in our analysis of small groups that conformity to norms and contributions to group goals or values constitute the most important bases of evaluations leading to status distinctions. A similar argument was employed in our discussion of organizations, the process being facilitated in these relatively more complex systems by the introduction of formalized positions. Unlike formal organizations and informal task groups, communities lack a set of specific goals guiding the activities of participants. If community norms can be said to be present, they provide at best diffuse and ill-defined guides to behavior and to the evaluation of behavior. Given these characteristics of communities, what are we to conclude about the bases of status in such diffuse and ill-defined systems?

To begin, it is clear that differential evaluations leading to distinctions among social strata are in fact made by participants in communities. Hundreds of empirical studies of individual communities testify to the existence of differen-

---

[1]Although we did not emphasize this point in our earlier discussion, it should be noted that social strata are also present in organizations. That is, formal positions are often grouped into strata that are differentially evaluated; for example, distinctions are made between officers and enlisted men in armies, between higher executives and middle managers, between white-collar and blue-collar workers in industrial commercial firms, and between administrators and the professional staff in research agencies, universities, and hospitals. See for example, B. Anderson *et al.*, "Status classes in organizations," *Administrative Science Quarterly*, 11 (September, 1966), 164–283.

tial status in the community setting. On what grounds are such distinctions made? Bernard Barber suggests that the following criteria are employed:

The problems of each local community—its economic security and growth, its services to the young, its attractiveness as a place to realize one's interests and values, its conflicts and harmony, its continuity of tradition and change—are different from those of the larger society, though always related, of course. Individuals and families who serve the local community welfare more or less well earn a correspondingly higher or lower "local-community status."[2]

These criteria are somewhat vague, probably conflicting, and in any case clearly are more applicable to some types of communities than to others.

Realizing the tremendous diversity exhibited by communities in their goals or values and recognizing the diffuseness of the evaluative criteria employed, sociologists have tended to follow one of two strategies in exploring community status. These strategies may be labeled for convenience the "objective" and the "subjective" approaches. Both tend to ignore the problem of identifying the value criteria employed in the assignment of status, although the subjective approach permits an indirect attack on this problem. Let us consider each in turn.

The *objective* approach to community status systems sidesteps the problem of evaluative criteria (goals) by focusing instead on generalized means. Proponents of this approach argue in effect that whatever the goals of the community system, participants vary in their access to means or facilities for realizing them. Because the goals pursued are undetermined, emphasis is placed on generalized means—on facilities of value in pursuing a broad range of objectives. Such facilities may include wealth or education or possession of some other general resource, such as power.[3] The analyst himself determines which resources to emphasize and then stratifies the population according to degrees of possession of or access to these facilities. The analyst also determines the number of strata or levels of status to be distinguished, and they are not necessarily those recognized by the participants in the system under study. The Index of Status Characteristics, devised by W. Lloyd Warner and his associates, is at least in part such an objective measure of status that has been applied in many community studies.[4]

In the *subjective* approach, the investigator asks respondents from the community to describe the status groupings within the community as he perceives them. Ordinarily, the respondent is allowed to choose his own criteria of status placement, and he is allowed to posit the existence of as many strata as he pleases. Two variations are employed. In the first, respondents are asked to place themselves in the stratification system. In this approach, the type of question asked may be critical in determining the form of the status structure

²Bernard Barber, "Family status, local-community status, and social stratification: Three types of social ranking," *Pacific Sociological Review*, 4 (Spring, 1961), 8.

³Because these generalized means are not necessarily utilized in the pursuit of community goals, this approach is subject to Reiss' criticism that studies of community stratification often fail to show any connection between the strata described and the operation of the community qua community. See Albert J. Reiss, Jr., "The sociological study of communities," *Rural Sociology*, 24 (June, 1959), 125.

⁴This index consists of a weighted summation of scores assigned by the analyst to a person's occupation, source of income, house type, and dwelling area. Based on his score, each person is assigned to one of five or six strata. See W. Lloyd Warner, Marchia Meeker, and Kenneth Eells, *Social Class in America*, Chicago: Science Research Associates, 1949.

that emerges. For example, Gross has shown that respondents in an urban community placed themselves differently, depending on whether they or the analyst chose the labels for the various strata and on the type of labels chosen. Thus, when no labels were supplied, 31 percent of the respondents identified themselves as middle class; when the same respondents were given a choice of the labels "upper," "middle," "working," and "lower," 42 percent selected middle class; and when they were given a choice among the labels "upper," "middle," and "lower," 76 percent located themselves in the middle class.[5] In the second variation, sometimes referred to as the "reputational" approach, the investigator asks his respondents to place others, rather than themselves, in the stratification system. One variant of this technique is the Evaluated Participation approach developed by Warner. Warner's approach, like all reputational studies, is based on the assumption that

the people in the social system of a community judge the participation in that community; that they similarly judge the place in the system where each individual participates; and that they are consciously or unconsciously aware of such ratings of social class and can communicate them to an investigator. Thus, they are analytical techniques which identify the status values and rating systems used by the members of a community to class one another.[6]

We may take as examples of the subjective approach the research conducted by Warner and his associates, who have carried out detailed studies of the class structure of three American communities: Yankee City, a New England town of about 17,000 population; Old City, a Southern town of about 10,000; and Jonesville, a Midwestern town of about 6,000 population.[7] Employing primarily reputational approaches, Warner and his colleagues distinguished five or six strata in the communities studied. The strata are labeled upper-upper, lower-upper, upper-middle, lower-middle, upper-lower, and lower-lower. The number of strata varies because, according to Warner, an upper-upper stratum consisting of the "old-family aristocracy" exists only on the Eastern seaboard and in the deep South, not in the middle or far West because of rapid social changes in and the comparatively recent development of communities in the latter areas.[8] Warner insists that the strata described are not categories the investigators have imposed on the data, but are "real" in the sense that they are perceived by and affect the behavior of community members. The several studies by Warner and his collaborators attempt to show the variety of behavior and attitudes affected by strata membership, including the character of family life, the number and kinds of cliques and associations belonged to, church affiliation and participa-

[5]Neal Gross, "Social class identification in the urban community," *American Sociological Review*, 18 (August, 1953), 398–404.

[6]W. Lloyd Warner, *American Life: Dream and Reality*, Chicago: University of Chicago Press, 1953, p. 61. Note that Warner employs the term "social class" rather than "social strata." We shall distinguish between these concepts subsequently.

[7]All the town names are pseudonyms. The research on Yankee City is reported in a six-volume study of which the first three volumes are W. Lloyd Warner and Paul S. Lunt, *The Social Life of a Modern Community*, 1941; W. Lloyd Warner and Paul S. Lunt, *The Status System of a Modern Community*, 1942; W. Lloyd Warner and Leo Srole, *The Social System of American Ethnic Groups*, 1945; all published by Yale University Press; the research on Old City is reported in Allison Davis, Burleigh B. Gardner, and Mary R. Gardner, *Deep South*, Chicago: University of Chicago Press, 1941; and the study of Jonesville is reported in W. Lloyd Warner et al., *Democracy in Jonesville*, New York: Harper & Row, 1949.

[8]Warner, *American Life*, p. 59.

tion, the type of school attended, and the probability of graduating from high school and attending college.

As already noted, both the objective and the subjective approaches to community status structure leave aside the problem of identifying the bases of evaluation employed. The objective approach focuses on the evaluation of means rather than ends, and the subjective approach attempts to describe the resultant prestige structure, not the bases for its emergence. However, the subjective approach does move us closer to our goal: knowing how the various family groups and individuals are placed in the community allows the possibility of next determining *why* they are placed as they are. This is the problem pursued by Faunce and Smucker in Reading 37. After determining the location of families in three small communities by reputational techniques, Faunce and Smucker examine certain objective characteristics (including income, education, age, and sex) to determine the extent to which these variables are correlated with prestige in each of the communities. They also ask respondents to provide reasons for their high or low placement of other persons. In this manner it is possible to ferret out the underlying value criteria that serve as the bases of status assignment.

The research of Faunce and Smucker is instructive for another reason. Many studies of community status structure have been conducted in small, relatively isolated communities. Such communities still exist in this country, and it is important to understand status processes in such settings. But it must be recognized that the past several decades have wrought a great change in the American scene and, indeed, in the international scene. Fewer and fewer communities remain untouched by the great changes—industrialization, urbanization, centralization, and bureaucratization—that swirl around them. Faunce and Smucker carefully selected their communities to vary with respect to their exposure to such changes. Their cross-sectional study of three communities differentially exposed to the processes of industrialization provide some clues to the sorts of changes that may be expected to occur in the status structure of a community as it moves from isolation to involvement in these broader social patterns. Broadly speaking, these changes may be described as a move from ascribed to achievement criteria and from informal-personal to formal-positional characteristics as the bases of evaluation.

The Problem of Social Classes   There is a good deal of healthy controversy among sociologists concerning what social classes are and how they may best be studied. Karl Marx, the political polemicist and influential analyst of economic and social structure, argued that the single most important criterion for differentiating between social strata was relation to the means of production—in particular, ownership or nonownership of production facilities. However, Marx was not interested in social strata in the sense of prestige rankings, but in social classes. The basic condition for the emergence of a social class in the Marxian sense was the presence of a set of persons who performed a common function in the organization of production. Further, such persons must be aware of their common situation—the interests they hold in common.

But the existence of common conditions and the realization of common interests are in turn only the necessary, not the sufficient, bases for the development of a social class.

Only when the members of a "potential" class enter into an association for the organized pursuit of their common aims, does a class in Marx's sense exist.[9]

As is well known, the examination of social classes and class conflict was a central theme in Marx's interpretation of social change: social classes were, for Marx, the "engine of history."

The controversy to which reference has been made concerns the issue of whether or not classes in the Marxian sense—that is, self-conscious, interacting, purposeful groups—exist. The American sociologist W. Lloyd Warner defines social class differently from Marx. Social class, for Warner, consists of "two or more orders of people who are believed to be, and are accordingly ranked by all members of the community, in socially superior and inferior positions."[10] Nevertheless, he agrees with Marx that social classes are "real" groups: members of social classes identify themselves with distinctive labels, they interact with others in terms of these class designations, and members of a common class group often join together in efforts to gain advantage or to protect privileges they enjoy on the basis of their class position.

Other sociologists question the clarity of class lines and the extent of class consciousness in community behavior. They argue that even in small communities the prestige structure is a relatively ambiguous one, with persons in different strata locations perceiving varying numbers of classes and using differing criteria to distinguish among them. Because of such disagreements among respondents (which are present also in the Warner studies), the number of class groups is usually determined by the investigator and is somewhat arbitrarily imposed on the data.[11] In any case, the degree of class consciousness and the extent of social organization to pursue class interests are matters to be empirically determined in the study of any given community.

Some degree of consensus on status placement and some efforts on the part of class groups to protect their social standing are more likely to be characteristic of small, relatively stable communities than of urban centers. Many observers believe that Warner overgeneralized from his findings, particularly because in his early writings he insisted that his studies described the class structure of all American communities. As Kornhauser notes:

. . . the places studied by Warner and his collaborators have been relatively small, and findings based on them are not applicable to highly urbanized communities. The existence of the type of class structure Warner describes depends on the ability of most members of the community to make status evaluations of each other's conduct. . . .

In the large city contacts are mainly secondary rather than primary; hence the type of intimate participation patterns by which prestige class placement is effected in small towns in largely absent. . . .[12]

---

[9]Reinhard Bendix and Seymour Martin Lipset, "Karl Marx's theory of social classes," in Bendix and Lipset (eds.), *Class, Status, and Power* (2d ed.), p. 9. New York: Free Press, 1966, p. 9. For an extended analysis and critique of Marx's approach to social stratification, see Ralf Dahrendorf, *Class and Class Conflict in Industrial Society*, Stanford, Calif.: Stanford University Press, 1959.

[10]Warner and Lunt, *The Social Life*, p. 82.

[11]See, for example, Gerhard E. Lenski, "American social classes: Statistical strata or social groups?" *American Journal of Sociology*, 58 (September, 1952), 139–144.

[12]Ruth Rosner Kornhauser, "The Warner approach to social stratification," in Reinhard Bendix and Seymour Martin Lipset (eds.), *Class Status, and Power*, Glencoe, Ill.: Free Press, 1953, p. 247. See also Harold W. Pfautz and Otis Dudley Duncan, "A critical evaluation of Warner's work in community stratification," *American Sociological Review*, 15 (April, 1950), 205–215.

Kaufman adds two other factors that affect the ability of the residents of urban areas to make status evaluations:

First is the lack in the metropolis of "status equilibrium," e.g., the underworld operator who resides in the exclusive residential district. When incongruity in status becomes the rule rather than the exception, the conception of community rank tends to lose its scientific usefulness. Second, differential perception of status is common in the urban world. That is, the person being ranked will not only differ with observers concerning his status, but the observers will also disagree among themselves depending on the stratum to which they belong.[13]

Bendix and Lipset generally ascribe to these factors distinguishing rural from urban communities, noting, however, one important exception:

In cities like Dallas, Seattle, or Buffalo the only class of people who know and rank one another are Warner's "upper-uppers," i.e., those who are known as "society." The other "five classes" are much too numerous to permit that degree of personal acquaintance, which alone would make a system of interlocking status evaluations feasible.[14]

One sociologist in particular has attempted to document the existence of class behavior in the upper reaches of America's metropolitan centers. E. Digby Baltzell has studied the development, changing composition, and life style of Philadelphia's upper class. In his view:

The *upper class* concept . . . refers to a group of *families*, whose members are decendants of successful individuals (elite members) of one, two, three or more generations ago. These families are at the top of the *social class* hierarchy; they are brought up together, are friends, and are intermarried one with another; and finally, they maintain a distinctive style of life and a kind of primary group solidarity which sets them apart from the rest of the population.[15]

As an index of upper class membership, Baltzell employs listings in the *Social Register*.

It is Baltzell's thesis that the changes in the American economy associated with increasing centralization and urbanization and the growth of metropolitan centers have brought about changes in the character of the upper classes in this country. Specifically, beginning during the last decades of the nineteenth century, we have the development of "a *national* upper class with a similar way of life, institutional structure, and value system."[16] Institutions such as the New England boarding schools and the Ivy League universities supplement the efforts of families to confirm and perpetuate status across time (generations) and space (change of residence) ; the *Social Register* was founded to provide a reputable guide to this new intercity plutocracy.

Although the major focus of his analysis of the upper class is on the prestige dimension as demonstrated and validated by the maintenance of a distinctive style of life, Baltzell emphasizes the extent to which other stratification dimensions (wealth and power) are associated with prestige or status. He concludes:

Pomp without power paves the way for revolution. In the final analysis, social stratification is an outgrowth of, and ultimately dependent on, the differential distribution of social power within any community, and, of course, economic and political

[13]Harold F. Kaufman, "An approach to the study of urban stratification," *American Sociological Review*, 17 (August, 1952) , 434.

[14]Seymour M. Lipset and Reinhard Bendix, "Social status and social structure: A re-examination of data and interpretations: I," *British Journal of Sociology*, 2 (1951) , 168.

[15]E. Digby Baltzell, *Philadelphia Gentlemen: The Making of a National Upper Class*, Glencoe, Ill.: Free Press, 1958. Reprinted as *An American Business Aristocracy*, New York: Collier Books, 1962, p. 21. Emphasis in original.

[16]Baltzell, p. 24. Emphasis in original.

power are indivisible aspects of social power. In analyzing the growth of an upper-class way of life in metropolitan America, and especially in describing the social patina of Proper Philadelphia, there is a danger that we lose sight of the main function of an upper class: the perpetuation of its power in the world of affairs, whether in the bank, the factory, or in the halls of the legislature. Whenever an upper-class way of life becomes an end in itself, rather than a means for consolidating its power and influence, that upper class had outlived its function.[17]

[17]Baltzell, p. 405.

37   Industrialization and Community Status Structure*

William A. Faunce and M. Joseph Smucker

In urban, industrial communities, work is one of the primary factors determining the pattern of life experience. The importance of work in these communities is partly attributable to the fact that it is the primary determinant of a person's status or prestige within his community and within many of the organizations and groups in which he is a participant. Apparently, the assumption is often made that work is a *universally* important status criterion. Certainly the most common index of social status used in sociological research is a person's occupation or the occupation of his father.

While there is abundant evidence that work-related values are critical for urban status structures, the evidence is not so clear that this is the case for small towns. Studies suggest that, while income and occupation may be of importance in small towns in the United States, other variables, notably community organizational participation and personal attributes, are also important. These studies

indicate that as size of community increases, personal attributes tend to drop out as status assigning criteria while values related to work become of greater importance.[1]

The major premise in the present study

*Revised version of a paper presented at the annual meeting of the American Sociological Association, Chicago, 1965. The authors wish to express their appreciation to International Programs and the School of Labor and Industrial Relations at Michigan State University for support of the research on which this paper is based.

[1]The following studies are listed in order of size of community studied and by the emphasis given work-related values as major criteria in community status structures: James West, *Plainville, USA*, New York: Columbia University Press, 1945; Arthur Gallaher, Jr., *Plainville 15 Years Later*, New York: Columbia University Press, 1961; Harold Kaufman, "Prestige Classes in a New York Rural Community", in Reinhard Bendix and Seymour M. Lipset (eds.), *Class, Status and Power*, Glencoe: Free Press, 1953, pp. 190-203; Otis Dudley Duncan and Jay W. Artis, "Social Stratification in a Pennsylvania Rural Community", Bull. 543, State College, Pennsylvania: The Pennsylvania State College School of Agriculture, October, 1951; W. Wheeler, *Social Stratification in a Plains Community*, Minneapolis: Privately printed, 1949; Arthur J. Vidich and Joseph Bensman, *Small Town in Mass Society*, Princeton: Princeton University Press, 1958; William H. Form, "Status Stratification in a Planned Community", *American Sociological Review*, 10 (October, 1945), pp. 209-224; August Hollingshead, *Elmtown's Youth*, New York: John Wiley, 1949; John R. Seeley, Alexander Sim, and Elizabeth Loosly, *Crestwood Heights*, New York: Basic Books, 1956; W. Lloyd Warner and Paul S. Lunt, *The Status System of a Modern Community*, New Haven, Conn.: Yale University Press, 1947; Robert S. Lynd and Helen M. Lynd, *Middletown*, New York: Harcourt, Brace and World, 1929; William Dobriner, *Class in Suburbia*, Englewood Cliffs, N.J.: Prentice-Hall, 1963.

Reprinted from *American Sociological Review*, 31. (June, 1966), 390-399, by permission of the American Sociological Association and the authors.

is that the importance of work-related values for status assignment is determined by the extent to which there are social structural supports for such a system. In urban, industrial communities there is both a highly differentiated occupational structure and a system of social relationships that regularly involves people in interaction with others at different occupational status levels. This is obviously the case in the large, complex work organizations in which a substantial proportion of the labor force in these communities is employed, but it is equally the case for most of the rest who are involved in some form of employer-employee relationship. Outside the work organization, role relationships like doctor-patient, lawyer-client, voter-politician, banker-customer, and many others frequently involve the urbanite in interaction with others whose occupational status is either higher or lower than his own. Because these are functionally specific relationships among people who know little about each other, occupational prestige and related variables such as income or education provide the important cues regarding the behavior appropriate to these situations. In short, the structure of the urban, industrial community legitimizes and reinforces a status assignment system based principally upon work-related values.

Small towns in industrial societies are exposed to this same set of values. However, the social structure of the small town is much less supportive of a status assignment system based upon work. In these communities, the range of occupational status differences is generally narrower, there are fewer relationships involving people of unequal occupational status, and there is less organizational legitimation of occupational status differences. Also, and perhaps most important, relationships tend to be more functionally diffuse. For example, if the small town

doctor treating a patient is at the same time receiving expert advice about where to go fishing, the introduction of other valued status-assigning criteria into the relationship diminishes the force of occupational status differences. A status assignment system based upon occupation, income, and education is also potentially a very divisive system. Lipset, Trow, and Coleman, among others, have noted the importance of avoiding divisive issues in small, Gemeinschaft-like social systems.[2]

The point here is not that occupational status differences are either unrecognized or completely rejected by people in small towns. Relationships with prestigeful "outsiders" that implicate the person in the status structure of the total society are, for example, very likely to be regulated by urban, industrial values. At the level of the community and of subsystems within it, however, it appears that valued personal attributes may be of at least equal consequence for the allocation of social honor in small towns.

We have made reference so far to two conditions affecting the relationship of work and status: (1) exposure to urban, industrial status criteria and (2) the existence of a social structure which involves people in relationships to which these criteria are relevant. In industrial societies, the urban community is characterized by both of these conditions while in small towns there is exposure to urban, industrial values in the absence of a social structure appropriate to them.

The cross-classification of these two conditions yields two other types of communities. One of these is a community isolated from urban, industrial values but characterized by a social structure involving people of different occupational status levels in continuing interaction.

[2]Seymour Martin Lipset, Martin A. Trow, and James S. Coleman, *Union Democracy*, Glencoe: Free Press, 1956.

The fourth type of community is one in which neither of these variables is present.

It is with respect to these last two community types that the industrialization process is relevant to our concerns in this paper. The kind of community designated as "Type D" in Figure 37-1 is best exemplified by a traditional, isolated peasant village with a subsistence level agricultural economy. "Type C" in Figure 37-1 is found most often in economically underdeveloped areas where factory towns appear in an otherwise nonindustrial context.

FIGURE 37-1 A Typology of Communities

Exposure to Urban, Industrial Values:	Social Structure Supportive of Occupationally-Based Status Assignment System:	
	Yes	No
Yes	A (Detroit)	B (Michigan village)
No	C (Costa Rican village)	D (Guatemalan village)

This typology specifies stages in a sequence of developments accompanying industrialization in which work and community status become increasingly interrelated. In the course of industrialization the isolated, nonindustrial community either becomes a factory town or is integrated into industrial society and increasingly exposed to urban status criteria. There is the additional possibility that it may itself grow into or be incorporated into an urban, industrial center. Although this would seem to be a reasonable assumption, our data do not include information about change in communities over time and consequently they provide no direct evidence regarding the nature of this process.

The typology above was used in this study as a device for theoretically specifying differences among communities in the extent to which work-related values function in the status assignment process. The expectation is that work will have most consequence for status in "Type A" communities and least consequence in "Type D" communities. The hypothesized ordering of the other two community types is based upon the premise that a set of values has a limited effect upon human behavior in the absence of a supportive social structure. One of the structural supports for an occupationally-based status assignment system is a complex division of labor. Work is less likely to be the primary basis for ranking of persons in communities having a limited number of occupational roles. Another structural support is the extent to which there is an organizational framework that involves people of unequal occupational status in continuing interaction and legitimizes these status differences. In a small factory town, both types of social structural supports for a status structure based upon work are likely to be present. A non-industrial town, even though it is part of an industrial society, is less likely to have an elaborate division of labor. Also, formal organizations within the community are more likely to be occupationally homogeneous and to include only a small proportion of the population within any one organization. We expect then that "Type C" communities will rank second to the industrial city and that "Type B" communities will rank third in terms of the importance of work for status.

RESEARCH SETTING

Data were collected in three of the four types of communities described above. We proceeded from the assumption that further documentation of the extent to which the status structure of the urban industrial community (i.e., the "Type A" community) is occupationally-based was not necessary. Because size of community is an important variable affecting the status assignment process, three villages of approximately the same size—all under 1,000 inhabitants—were selected for study.

The "Type B" community studied is a small town in north central Michigan whose economic base is primarily tourism. There are no work organizations in the town involving more than four or five people and the largest proportion of household heads are either retired or self-employed. There are employer-employee relations and, in terms of urban, industrial values, there are clear occupational status differences between the town doctor, banker, other businessmen, and the rest of the community. It is obvious in observing these relationships, however, that they are relatively functionally diffuse. With the exception of some retired people who have recently moved to the town, nearly everyone knows everyone else well enough that a wide range of potential evaluative criteria are available in each instance of social interaction.[3]

While this town is somewhat isolated by comparison with other communities in Michigan, there is no lack of exposure to the kinds of values used in urban status assignment. Most of the people in town have lived or worked in urban areas at some time in their lives, many subscribe to city newspapers, almost all have radios and television sets, and during the summer months the permanent residents of the town constitute only a small fraction of the people in the area, most of whom are tourists from metropolitan centers in southern Michigan. In short, although the people in this town are continuously

confronted with the value placed upon occupational, income, and educational differences, there is neither the necessity for relying upon these differences as cues to appropriate behavior nor is there an organizational framework which involves these people in relationships in which occupational status and authority differences are important.

The town selected as representative of "Type C" in Figure 37-1 is a small factory town in the highlands of Costa Rica. It is relatively isolated from urban areas and is part of an essentially non-industrial society. Nearly all household heads in the village were either themselves peasants at one time or are the children of peasants. Almost all now are employed in a rope, bag, and fiber rug manufacturing plant or are field workers providing raw materials for the factory. The manufacturing operations involve modern machinery and there is an extensive division of labor including unskilled laborers, machine tenders, skilled tradesmen, clerical workers, first and second level supervisors, a general manager, and the factory owner. The occupational status and authority differences in both the field and factory sectors of the total work process provide an integrated, hierarchical structure involving nearly all household heads in the community. While the town is small enough to be characterized by functionally diffuse relations among people of unequal occupational status, the formal organizational structure of the plant provides a context for these relations to be dominated by an occupationally based status assignment system.

The "Type D" community studied is a small *ladino* village in Guatemala. There is no road going through this village— access is by a three-quarter-mile long footpath up a steep incline from the highway between Guatemala City and Antigua, Guatemala. The economic base of the community is subsistence level agriculture though there are a few skilled

[3]Cf. William H. Form and Gregory P. Stone, "Urbanism, Anonymity, and Status Symbolism," *American Journal of Sociology*, 22 (March, 1957), pp. 504–514.

tradesmen who work in Antigua and a few day laborers who work on nearby coffee plantations or on road construction. The village is for the most part, however, a traditional peasant community virtually isolated from the mainstream of events in the nation and the world. Instances of one villager employing another are rare. There are, in fact, almost no relationships with any continuity among villagers outside the nuclear family. The social structure of the community, with the exception of some patterned activities related to the church and village government, is best described as atomistic, involving little more than a collection of separate households.

METHOD

The specific hypothesis tested in this study is that work would have most consequence for community status in the Costa Rican village, next most consequence in the Michigan village, and would be least important in the Guatemalan village. Data bearing upon this hypothesis were collected through both field observation and formal interviewing techniques. A total of ten months was spent in the Guatemalan village and five months in the Michigan village. Although only one month of field observation was conducted in Costa Rica, a systematic ethnographic survey of the village was done by a Costa Rican anthropologist as part of the research project.

Intensive formal interviews were conducted with 123 of the 265 household heads in the Michigan community. The sample was drawn from a list using a table of random numbers. In addition, a brief census-type interview was conducted with all but eleven of the remaining household heads.

For a variety of reasons, it was possible to interview only 50 of the 80 household heads in the Guatemalan village although it was our intent to interview them all.

While it is possible that some systematic bias may have been introduced with a non-response rate of this size, our general knowledge of the village and of the 30 non-respondents did not suggest any relevant variables differentiating these people from those who were interviewed. We did, however, obtain some information about each household in the village. The Guatemalan census was conducted during the course of our field work there and we were able to obtain information on each household from this source.

In the Costa Rican village, there were 102 households as well as a number of relatively long-term residents of a dormitory-hotel owned by the hacienda. A randomly selected 25 per cent sample of the latter were added to the household heads for purposes of our study, making a total of 111 persons in our sample in this village. Interviews were completed with all but six of the people in this sample.

As part of the formal interviewing process, each respondent was asked to rate all household heads in the community on a ten-point status scale. The names of household heads were placed on 3 x 5 cards and the respondents sorted the cards on a ten-step "ladder." The instructions were to place each card on the step on the ladder, from ten at the top to one on the bottom, that indicated the person's standing or prestige in the community, or how he is generally rated or ranked in comparison with other villagers. There were two exceptions to this procedure. In the Michigan village, because of the large number of household heads, the cards were randomly divided and each respondent rated only half of the total. In the Guatemalan village, there is a high rate of illiteracy and pictures of heads of household were used in the sorting process rather than names on cards.

When the rating was completed, the respondents were asked to look through the cards they had placed at the top of the ladder and indicate why these people had high standing in the community. A similar procedure was used for people who had been placed at a step in the middle and on the bottom step of the status ladder.

There were several other questions in the interview. Respondents were asked to identify the kinds of persons that are respected and the kinds of persons that are not respected in the town. Two other questions were designed to identify and differentiate between two types of community elites. In one question, a situation was posed in which some villagers would have to meet with and represent the community to prestigeful outsiders who were representatives of the federal government or other political units larger than the village. The respondents were asked to name three people that they thought would be appropriate for this task and to give their reasons for selecting them. A second question posed a situation in which the respondents had been asked to nominate three residents of the community who they thought should be honored by having something in the town named for them. In the Michigan community, for example, the hypothetical situation involved the renaming of a county park located in the village. This question also asked for the reasons for selecting the three names. The intent of these questions was to discover what differences there might be between an elite having skills in dealing with the outside world with attributes valued in terms of the broader societal status structure, and a strictly honorific, internal elite.

The available data regarding status assignment in these communities permit two kinds of analysis of their status structures: (1) the *reasons* people give for status placements or the kinds of status criteria they *report* as being im-

portant in the community; and (2) actual attributes of people who are placed at different levels in the community status structure. In addition to average status rating, we have information about nearly all household heads in each community regarding their age, sex, education, occupation, income, length of residence in the community, and sociometric data, including number of times chosen as a friend and number of times identified as someone visited by others in the town.

RESULTS

Table 37-1 presents product-moment correlations between what have been identified as urban, industrial status criteria (income, occupation, and education) and the mean status rating of household heads in each village. Our hypothesis predicts high correlations for the Costa Rican village and low correlations for the Guatemalan village, with correlations for the Michigan village occupying an intermediate position. The data clearly support the hypothesis.

The average correlation of status with a series of other variables, however, is also higher in the Costa Rican village than in the other two villages. The multiple correlation between average status rating and all available information on household heads in each village was .90 in the Costa Rican village, .73 in the Michigan village, and .63 in the Guatemalan village. This finding is consistent with the rank ordering of these villages in terms of the degree of integration of their status assignment systems.

As an additional test of our hypothesis, we examine the rank order of the magnitude of correlations between average status and the other variables in each village. In the Costa Rican village, income ranked first, occupational prestige second, and education fourth among twelve variables correlated with status. The only

TABLE 37–1 Product-Moment Correlations between Mean Status Rating of Household Heads and Occupational Prestige, Income, and Education

Variable	Costa Rican Village	Michigan Village	Guatemalan Village
Income[1]	.78	.45	−.21
	(N = 98)	(N = 225)	(N = 79)
Occupational prestige[2]	.74	.43	−.07
	(N = 97)	(N = 138)[3]	(N = 80)
Education	.55	.24	.06
	(N = 104)	(N = 251)	(N = 79)

[1]The measures of income and occupational prestige used were somewhat different in each of the communities. Annual income was used in the Michigan village and monthly wage rates in the Costa Rican village. In the Guatemalan village, cash income is not a good index of wealth and size of total land holding was used instead.

[2]The measure of occupational prestige used in the Michigan village was North-Hatt Scale ratings. Prestige ratings corresponding to the authority structure of the factory were used in Costa Rica. Because of the narrow range of occupations found in the Guatemalan village, it was necessary to use a functional classification similar to the Edwards Scale.

[3]The lower N in this instance results from the exclusion from the analysis of retirees and housewives.

other variables with a high zero-order correlation with average status in this village were the number of times chosen as a friend, which ranked third (r=.68), and number of community organizations in which the person was a member, which ranked fifth (r=.51).

In the Michigan village, income ranked second, occupational prestige ranked third, and education ranked fifth among correlates of average status level. The variable most highly correlated with status (r=.50) was the number of community organizations in which the person was a member. The number of times the person was mentioned as someone others in the community visit ranked fourth (r=.44), and the number of times chosen as a friend by others in the village ranked sixth (r=.24).

The pattern in the Guatemalan village was quite different from the other two. Income level, measured in terms of total size of land holding, ranked sixth, number

of years of education ranked eighth, and occupational prestige ranked tenth among the ten variables that were correlated with mean status rating in the community. The most important correlate of status in this village was age (r=.49). Other variables with a higher-than-average correlation with status in this community were marital status (r=.27), number of times chosen by others as a friend (r=.27), number of times mentioned as someone others visit (r=.23), and length of residence in the village (r=.23).

The hypothesized rank order of the three villages in terms of the importance of work-related values for community status also obtains when other variables are controlled. Table 37–2 presents the partial correlation coefficients between mean status rating and selected variables for which comparable data were available in each village. While the differences in importance of educational level do not

TABLE 37–2 Partial Correlation Coefficients between Mean Status Rating and Selected Variables

Variable	Costa Rican Village	Michigan Village	Guatemalan Village
Occupational prestige	.44	.34	−.01
Income	.40	.28	.10
Education	.17	.12	.18
Number of times chosen as friend	.25	.14	.15
Number of times mentioned as someone others visit	.21	.35	.17
Length of residence in village	−.03	.14	−.02
Age	.14	.20	.42
Sex[1]	−.21	−.03	.22

Note: Although our data do not meet all the assumptions required for use of parametric statistics, we have elected to use a more powerful statistic since our concern is not so much with the absolute values as with rank ordering of the villages.

[1]Males were coded "1" and females "2." A negative correlation therefore indicates that males have a higher status rating than females.

follow the predicted pattern, occupational prestige and income are clearly most important in the Costa Rican village and least important in the Guatemalan village.

The general pattern suggested by Table 37-2 is that in an isolated peasant village with an essentially atomistic social structure typified by the community we studied in Guatemala, ascribed characteristics such as age and sex account for more of the variance in status level than any work-related values. In the Michigan village, while occupation and income are important, there are other variables of at least equal importance. We are treating the sociometric data (number of times chosen as a friend and number of times mentioned as someone others visit) as indexes of valued personal attributes. Field observation and the formal interview

data suggest that these attributes are particularly important status determinants in this village. In a community of the sort we studied in Costa Rica, with a highly integrated social structure that regularly involves people in interaction with others at different occupational status levels, occupation and income clearly predominate as status-assigning criteria.[4]

The characteristics of people who were named as appropriate representatives of the community to prestigeful outsiders and those named as worthy of an honor such as having something in the town named for them provide an additional

[4]For a comparative study of a farm village and two haciendas in Latin America with somewhat similar results, see Charles P. Loomis, Julio O. Morales, Roy A. Clifford, and Olin E. Leonard, *Turialba: Social Systems and the Introduction of Change,* Clencoe: Free Press, 1953.

TABLE 37-3 Ratio of Median Occupational, Educational, and Income Levels of Community Elites to Median Occupational, Educational, and Income Levels of All Household Heads

Type of Elite and Variable	Costa Rican Village	Michigan Village	Guatemalan Village
A. *Elites chosen for meeting outsiders*			
Occupational			
prestige	2.4	1.1	1.0
Income	2.7	3.0	1.4
Education	2.0	1.4	1.0
B. *Elites chosen for local honor*			
Occupational			
prestige	2.4	1.1	1.0
Income	3.0	2.6	1.4
Education	2.7	1.3	1.0

test of our hypothesis. By comparing the median occupational, educational, and income levels of these two types of elites with the medians for all household heads in each village, it is possible to assess the extent to which these variables differentially affect the selection of elites. The ratios resulting from this procedure are reported in Table 37-3. In the Guatemalan village, the median occupational prestige and educational levels for both types of elites are the same as the median for all household heads in the village (ratios of 1.0 in Table 37-3), and the median income of the elites is only slightly higher than the community median. In the Costa Rican village, the median for the elite groups is, in each instance, between two and three times higher than the median for the total community.

The only reversal of the rank order of the villages in Table 37-3 occurs for the ratios for income levels of elites chosen to meet prestigeful outsiders in the Costa Rican and Michigan communities. This reversal is not, however, inconsistent with predictions based upon the conceptual framework employed in this study. In the Michigan village, urban, industrial status criteria are relatively less important for community status than for the status structure of the total society of which the village is a part. The reverse is likely to be true for the Costa Rican village since it is an industrial town in an essentially non-industrial society. We might expect a difference between the two towns, then, in the kinds of values defined as appropriate to situations involving interaction with prestigeful outsiders. Comparison of the data regarding the two types of elites in Table 37-3 partially supports this expectation. In the Michigan village, income and education are *more* important determinants of elite status when this status involves meeting outsiders than when it refers to a strictly local or internal community allocation of social honor. In the Costa Rican village, the reverse is the case, that is, income and educational differences are greatest for the elite group that was selected without reference to broader societal values. We would expect

TABLE 37–4 Percentage Citing Given Reason for High and Low Status Placement

Reasons Given	Costa Rican Village	Michigan Village	Guatemalan Village
Reasons for high status placement:			
Occupation	23.4	20.1	1.3
Income	6.1	4.9	1.3
Education	8.2	3.4	2.6
Active in community affairs	11.7	25.9	16.9
Personal qualities	48.1	34.3	55.8
Age	0.0	0.3	16.9
Length of residence in village	0.4	4.6	1.3
Other	2.2	6.5	3.9
	100.1	100.0	100.0
	(N = 231)	(N = 324)	(N = 77)
Reasons for low status placement:			
Occupation	20.6	21.5	3.5
Income	5.0	15.6	0.0
Education	6.0	1.3	1.8
Inactive in community affairs	12.1	10.1	10.5
Personal qualities	44.2	44.7	59.6
Age	0.0	0.0	14.0
Length of residence in village	0.0	0.0	0.0
Other	12.1	6.8	10.5
	100.0	100.0	99.9
	(N = 199)	(N = 237)	(N = 57)

little or no difference between the two types of elites in a peasant community in a non-industrial society and our data from the Guatemalan village are consistent with this expectation.

The differences reported so far in the

attributes of elite and non-elite segments of these communities and in the attributes of people with different average status ratings suggest that the three villages differ considerably in the importance of work-related values for status assignment. We are also concerned, however, with the extent to which the community *ideologies* with respect to status assignment reflect these differences. The frequency with which occupation, income, or education are used to *explain* status differences was also expected to be highest in Costa Rica and lowest in Guatemala, with the Michigan village again in an intermediate position. Because these are all small communities, however, we did not expect explanations for status differences to be couched primarily in terms of divisive work-related values in any of the villages.

Table 37-4 reports the responses to the question regarding why people had been assigned a high or a low status. The data are generally consistent with our expectations. Occupational prestige is more important in both the Costa Rican and Michigan villages, while age is more important in the Guatemalan village. The striking thing about these data, however, is the extent to which personal qualities (like friendliness, honesty, dependability, morality, and other similar attributes) are used to explain status differences in *all three* communities.

Responses to a separate question asking for reasons why people are respected or not respected in each village followed a similar pattern except that there was an even higher frequency of responses referring to valued personal attributes. Approximately two-thirds to three-fourths of the reasons given for respect or disrespect in each of the communities were of this sort. In contrast to the questions asking for status ratings or the names of status elites, this one did not directly involve actual comparisons

among villagers in terms of status level. For this reason, it might be interpreted as representing a more idealized conception of the values regarded as appropriate in the status assignment process.

Additional data suggesting the importance of personal attributes for community ideologies regarding status differences are provided in the reasons given for naming people to the two types of elite statuses discussed previously. These data are presented in Table 37-5.

Personal qualities clearly predominate as an explanation for assigning elite status in these three villages. With some minor exceptions, notably education and activity in community affairs in the Costa Rican village and age in the Guatemalan village, the distribution of responses in panel A in each of the two Latin American communities is similar to that in panel B. In the Michigan village, however, the reasons given for choosing the two kinds of elites differ considerably from each other. Where the function of an elite involves interaction with prestigeful representatives of the larger urban, industrial society, occupation and personal qualities, particularly the possession of certain types of social graces, are of greater importance. For an exceptional honor involving only the status structure of the local community, activity in community affairs and length of residence in the town become more important values.

It is apparent that there is not a great deal of correspondence between the kinds of variables that account for most of the variance in average status rating and the kinds of explanations given for status differences in these three villages. While all three community ideologies regarding status assignment were framed primarily in terms of personality attributes, other variables served better to differentiate among people actually placed at different status levels. One possible interpretation of this finding is that our index of valued

TABLE 37–5 Percentage Citing Given Reason for Assigning Elite Status

Reasons Given	Costa Rican Village	Michigan Village	Guatemalan Village
A. *Reasons for choosing elites to meet outsiders:*			
Occupation	10.4	20.2	7.3
Income	2.8	0.5	7.3
Education	17.9	4.1	2.4
Active in community affairs	7.5	20.6	9.8
Personal qualities	55.7	41.7	48.8
Age	0.9	0.5	12.2
Length of residence in village	0.0	6.4	0.0
Other	4.7	6.0	12.2
	99.9	100.0	100.0
	(N = 106)	(N = 218)	(N = 41)
B. *Reasons for choosing elites for local honor:*			
Occupation	8.0	8.7	3.2
Income	1.8	0.7	3.2
Education	8.0	2.0	0.0
Active in community affairs	21.2	35.6	9.7
Personal qualities	54.9	19.5	51.6
Age	0.9	0.0	25.8
Length of residence in village	1.8	24.2	3.2
Other	3.5	9.4	3.2
	100.1	100.1	99.9
	(N = 113)	(N = 149)	(N = 31)

personal qualities (number of times chosen as a friend or as someone others visit) was not a particularly sensitive one and that with better measures we would have found greater correspondence between the attributes of people at different status levels and the explanations given for these differences. It was clear that status distinctions based primarily upon personality differences did occur, for example, among older people in the Guatemalan village or people at the same occupational and income levels in the Costa Rican village. Particularly in this latter community, however, the amount of the variance in mean status rating accounted for by occupational and income differences in contrast to the preponderance of "personal quality" responses among reasons given for status distinctions suggests that this lack of correspondence is not simply an artifact of the study design.

Another explanation of this difference was suggested earlier. An ideology which attributes valued personal qualities to people whose status may be based principally on other variables like age, occupation, income, or activity in community affairs is functional in the sense that it is a less divisive explanation of small town status structures. Neither old people in the Guatemalan village, the general manager of the factory in Costa Rica, nor the community activist in the Michigan village presumably have any monopoly on being trustworthy, loyal, thrifty, brave, clean, or reverent.

CONCLUSIONS

Two major differences among the communities we studied are the extent to which they are exposed to urban, industrial values and the extent to which they are characterized by a social structure that regularly involves people in interaction with others at different occupational prestige levels. Our data suggest that, while both of these variables may have some effect upon the relationship between work and community status, social structural factors have a more important bearing upon this relationship. Although there is considerably more contact with urban culture in the Michigan village, it is in the Costa Rican village that "urban" values have the greatest effect upon status. Regardless of the kinds of differences that exist among people at different status levels, however, the *explanations* for status distinctions, in small towns at least, are most likely to be couched in terms of differences in personal qualities. Under circumstances where the community status structure and the inclusive societal status structure are based upon different sets of values, *both* the actual attributes of people accorded elite status and the community ideology with respect to status differences will vary depending upon which of the two status structures is relevant.

One of the implications of these findings is that occupation should be used with some caution as an index of community status. It may not be the best indicator of status differences in small towns in industrial societies and may not be at all relevant in peasant villages in economically underdeveloped areas. Also, in attempting to characterize community status structures, it appears to make an important difference whether data regarding the actual attributes of people at different status levels or the explanations given for these differences are used. It is possible that ideologies with respect to status distinctions have some common elements in all small towns in which there are close, interpersonal relations. Our data indicate, however, that there are marked differences among such towns in the kinds of people who actually occupy high status positions.

Previous studies of community status have been interpreted as demonstrating that, as the size of the community increases, variables like personal qualities and participation in community activities become less important and work-related values become more important as status criteria. Although the three villages we studied are almost identical in size, the same differences were observed depending upon the presence or absence of certain attributes of community social structure. Size of community is often interpreted as an indicator of some of these same structural attributes. Most of the variables regularly used in sociological research, for example, occupation, income, education, ethnicity, age, and sex are, in fact, simply indicators in the sense that they neither appear as terms in nor are they logical derivatives of socological theory. Our finding that social structural attributes for which community size is presumably an index vary independently of community size suggests that a more careful examination and specification of the referents of indicators used in sociological research might produce more sensitive measures and pro-

vide a base for broader generalizations from empirical studies.

The relevance of our findings for the industrialization process rests upon the assumption that the types of communities we studied are most likely to be found at different stages in this process. If this assumption is accepted, it seems reasonable to infer, first of all, that neither economically underdeveloped nor mature industrial societies are likely to be homogeneous with respect to the function of work-related values for status assignment. However, to the extent that one of the concomitants of industrialization is the development of a more integrated, hierarchical community structure that involves people at different occupational prestige levels in regular interaction, one of the effects of the industrialization process is likely to be an increase in the interrelationship of work and community status.

POWER PROCESSES IN COMMUNITIES

Just as there is little agreement among sociologists as to the best way to conceptualize and examine social class in communities, so there are also interesting controversies raging as to the proper view of power processes in communities. Not only sociologists but also political scientists are participating in these intellectual debates. The two opposing positions in the controversy have been labeled the "elitist" and the "pluralist" positions and, as is typical of such disagreements, both theoretical and methodological differences separate the adversaries.

Two Conceptions of Community Power   The chief representatives of the *elitist* conception of community power are Floyd Hunter and Delbert Miller. Hunter concluded on the basis of his study of Atlanta that a small group of men—primarily business and industrial leaders—were in a position to dominate civic affairs in this Southern city of half a million persons.[1] Based on his study of a city in the Pacific Northwest[2] as well as the research of other investigators, Miller comes to the following conclusions:

1. Businessmen are over-represented in the institutional distribution of community interests and do dominate community policy-making in most communities.
2. Local government is a relatively weak power-center. . . .
3. The influence of certain persons, groups, and institutions is significantly curtailed and neutralized. This includes many corporation managers, professionals in government, education, religion, welfare, and mass communication.
4. Key Influentials are persons who are drawn from positions of first-rate power and influence. They are generally "economic dominants" in the community. . . .[3]

The conclusions reached by Hunter and Miller attracted considerable interest and attention because they called into question the comfortable assumption that power in communities is held by public officials elected or regulated by democratic procedures. In some ways it was suggested that civic officials were merely a facade screening the actions of powerful men operating "behind the scenes."

This view that most American cities possess a pyramidal, quasi-monolithic power structure dominated by a business elite is associated with the use of a particular research strategy known as the *reputational* approach.

---

[1]Floyd Hunter, *Community Power Structure*, Chapel Hill, N.C.: The University of North Carolina Press, 1953; reprinted by Anchor Books, Doubleday, New York, 1963.

[2]See William H. Form and Delbert C. Miller, *Industry, Labor, and Community*, New York: Harper & Row, 1960, pp. 589–97.

[3]Delbert C. Miller, "Democracy and decision-making in the community power structure," in William V. D'Antonio and Howard J. Ehrlich (eds.), *Power and Democracy in America*, Notre Dame, Ind.: University of Notre Dame Press, 1961, p. 61.

The reputational technique, which has, with many variations, become fairly wide-spread in use, seeks to get knowledgeable informants to select, from a list of leading figures in community organizations and institutional areas, those whom they considered most powerful in "getting things done." Those chosen were then interviewed to learn about the personal and social relations among them, and which people they would themselves solicit if they wanted something adopted or achieved.[4]

For example, in his study of Atlanta, Hunter gathered some 175 names from prominant business groups, government leaders, civic associations, and members of Society, used knowledgeable judges to pick the top 40 leaders from this group, and then interviewed these individuals to determine the core set of key influentials. On the basis of his study, Hunter concludes that without the consent and leadership of the members of this top leadership clique, groups would find it difficult to undertake any major innovations in the structure of the community.[5]

The second approach, the *pluralist* approach, has arisen largely in response to and as a critique of the elitist conception. The two major figures in promulgating this conception are the political scientists Robert Dahl, who bases his conclusions on a study of power in New Haven,[6] and Edward Banfield, who examined political decision-making in Chicago.[7] The view of the pluralists is that power is best studied by an actual examination of the political decision-making process rather than by simply asking people hypothetical questions about who has power. As Dahl comments:

. . . a reputation for power is not necessarily a valid index of power. An alternative way to determine who "runs things" is to study a series of concrete decisions in order to find out who specifically dominates those decisions. If this is done, you may or may not find a correlation with reputations.[8]

Polsby, another member of the pluralist school, criticizes the elitist assumption that power is held by a small clique of influentials and that all that is required of the researcher is to identify the members of this clique. He suggests instead that:

The first and perhaps most basic presupposition of the pluralist approach is that nothing categorical can be assumed about power in any community. It rejects the stratification thesis that *some* group necessarily dominates a community.[9]

The method proposed by the pluralists to study power in communities has come to be known as *event analysis.* This approach

is typically one of chronological narration of who did what, when, and what effect it had . . . supplemented by a more precise systematic tabulation of the kinds of people who held formal positions in the organizations concerned with the [issues examined] and of those who initiated or vetoed significant decisions.[10]

Because the focus of analysis is on decision making with respect to a specific set of issues, the problem of what issues are selected for examination becomes a

[4]William Spinrad, "Power in local communities," *Social Problems,* 5 (Winter, 1965) , 337.

[5]Hunter, pp. 11–12, 61–111. All page references are to the 1963 Anchor edition.

[6]Robert A. Dahl, *Who Governs? Democracy and Power in an American City,* New Haven, Conn.: Yale University Press, 1961.

[7]Edward C. Banfield, *Political Influence,* New York: Free Press, 1961.

[8]Robert A. Dahl, "Equality and power in American society," in D'Antonio and Ehrlich (eds.) , p. 76.

[9]Nelson W. Polsby, *Community Power and Political Theory,* New Haven, Conn.: Yale University Press, 1964, p. 113. Emphasis in original.

[10]Spinrad, p. 338.

crucial one. In his study of New Haven, Dahl focused on three issues: the selection of nominees for political office, public education, and urban redevelopment. Banfield's study of Chicago encompassed six specific community problems, including proposals for extending a particular hospital's facilities, reorganization of the welfare administration, the creation of a large Chicago branch of the University of Illinois, and the building of a large exhibition hall. The conclusions reached by Dahl and Banfield concerning the distribution of power in communities are quite similar. Dahl had no difficulty in identifying economic notables in New Haven but discovered that only a small proportion of them were involved in the decisions concerning urban renewal, that an even smaller number were influential in local politics, and that none of them were involved in the decisions made on public education. In short, he concludes that power in communities is highly decentralized and that the locus of power varies depending on the issue examined. Generalizing from his findings, Dahl **concludes:**

I would contend that in most American communities there isn't a single center of power. There is even a sense in which *nobody* runs the community. In fact, perhaps this is the most distressing discovery of all: typically a community is run by many different people, in many different ways, at many different times.[11]

In a similar vein, Banfield reports that the "richest men in Chicago are conspicuous by their absence" from the decision-making circles and that in fact "big businessmen are criticized less for interfering in public affairs than for 'failing to assume their civic responsibilities.' "[12] Also, Dahl and Banfield are in agreement that public officials are apt to exercise considerable influence over decisions made about a variety of community issues, in contrast with Hunter and Miller's view of their relative ineffectiveness.

What are we to conclude from our review of this controversy? First, we have here a clear case indicating the extent to which choice of methods can affect empirical findings. Investigators employing the reputational strategy almost invariably came out with a pyramidal view of the community power structure; analysts focusing on decision making and specific event analysis usually find factional coalitions and amorphous power structures.[13] Next, let us agree that individual reputations may often be an inaccurate guide to community power and that more valid data will be obtained by the study of actual influence on specific decisions affecting the community. On the other hand, conclusions reached from event analysis suffer from two defects. There is the difficult problem of what issues are to be selected, because one's conclusions about the distribution of power will be a function of the specific issues analyzed. Also, it is difficult to gather any kind of systematic data on who participates in decisions and with what consequences. The analysis of decisions typically generates long, narrative accounts that are difficult to analyze and from which it is difficult to generalize. Also, it seems to be unwarranted to reach any specific conclusions at this time as to the centralization or decentralization of power in American communities. It may well be that in some cities economic interests tend to dominate decision making across a broad spectrum of issues whereas in other

[11]Dahl in D'Antonio and Ehrlich (eds.), p. 75. Emphasis in original.
[12]Banfield, pp. 287-288.
[13]Walton has reviewed 33 studies of 55 communities and reports a strong correlation between methods used and substantive findings. See John Walton, "Substance and artifact: The current status of research on community power structure," *American Journal of Sociology*, 71 (January, 1966), 430-438.

cities economic influentials, for a variety of reasons, play a modest or insignificant role. In general, it appears that the two groups with the most potential for exercising power are businessmen and public officials; but whether they or other potentially powerful groups are in fact influential in a given community decision will be dependent on the type of issue involved and the extent to which group members perceive that their basic interests are at stake in the outcome.

The Fragmentation of Power and Authority in Communities   So much for the elitist-pluralist controversy. Using some of the terms developed in our previous discussions of power processes throughout this book, let us attempt to further explore power processes in the community. One point on which both the elitist and the pluralist camps agree is that in American communities

persons not elected to office play very considerable parts in the making of many important decisions. The differences among cities in this regard . . . are more in degree than in kind. Public affairs in New Haven and Chicago, although not "run" by tiny, informal "power elites," are nevertheless much influenced by persons who occupy no official position.[14]

In other words, *formal* power wielders in the community (mayors, city councilmen, city managers) do not typically exercise complete power in policy determination and management of the community but are obliged to share their power with *informal* power wielders—private citizens and groups, such as businessmen or professionals, whose power is based on their control of various kinds of resources (money, property, expertise). The participation of private parties in public business is not regarded as unusual in this country, but it is a distinctively American phenomenon. In most European countries, for example, it is assumed that civic affairs will be managed solely by elected or appointed officials.

What accounts for the relative weakness of formal power holders in American communities? Perhaps the most important factor is that Americans tend to hold their public officials in relatively low esteem.

Rightly or wrongly, local politicians and bureaucrats are seldom held in very high regard; the politician is often considered an "opportunist" at best and the bureaucrat is usually thought to lack enterprise and imagination. . . .

Since it is success in other than public service pursuits, especially business, that distinguishes the man of great capacity in our culture, it is not surprising that when a city wants assurance that its affairs are being managed efficiently it often turns to a businessman for "expert" opinion.[15]

To put it another way, formal community leaders are short on authority: norms held by residents do not go far in legitimating their attempts to exercise power. Another important consequence follows from the attitudes of the public toward their elected leaders. Because officials are not to be trusted, community laws are drawn up to assure that no one official will have very much power at his disposal. The power of public officials is highly fragmented: not only is little power bequeathed to public officials and much retained by private citizens, but what little power is granted to the public sector is itself highly decentralized. As Banfield and Wilson comment:

[14]Edward C. Banfield and James Q. Wilson, *City Politics*, New York: Random House Vintage Books, 1966, pp. 244-245 (originally published 1963 by the Harvard University Press).

[15]Banfield and Wilson, pp. 246-247.

The American city is not governed by a single hierarchy of authority in which all lines are gathered together at the top in one set of hands. On the contrary, from a purely formal standpoint, one can hardly say that there is such a thing as a local government. There are a great many of them. Or, more aptly bits and pieces of many governments are scattered around the local scene.[16]

The power of governmental officials is diffused because there is not one but many elected officials in most communities, each of whom has his own mandate from the electorate and, hence, can operate somewhat independently of other public officers. Moreover, each has only a temporary and fragile lease on power because his power base must be renewed at periodic intervals by the voters. Also, legal statutes in most communities see to it that voters retain considerable control over important policy decisions in municipal government: referenda are required to approve public expenditures, the setting of tax rates, and other policy questions. Some relatively recent efforts have been made to centralize power with a "strong mayor" form of government, but even in these cities the mayor must typically share power with dozens—and in large cities, with hundreds—of other elected officials. Most important, in most cities, the "city government" is only one of several governments within the city. "In most sizable cities and in many very small ones there are boards and commissions, councils, single officials, and special districts [for example, for schools, parks, sanitation] having little or no formal connection with the city government proper (i.e., the mayor and council)."[17] Because of such fragmentation, public officials must typically attempt to align themselves with a variety of private interest groups who are willing and able to mobilize broad support for a given policy. Public officials must enlist the support of private individuals and groups if they are to achieve any important or controversial goals.

Power in the Metropolitan Community   The complex arrangements for governing individual American cities are simplicity itself when compared with the political system—or, more accurately, the lack of system—characterizing metropolitan communities. There are now 212 areas defined by census standards as constituting metropolitan areas in this country, and none of them has a government enjoying jurisdiction over the entire area. The typical pattern is one of several county governments, dozens of city governments, and hundreds of special district governments.

Compounding the problem of fragmentation are the differences in composition and, hence, the differences in interests of these many governmental units. The most obvious and important distinction is that between the population occupying the central city and the population residing in its surrounding suburbs. The selection by Scott Greer is concerned with the analysis of these differences and their implication for the governance of the metropolitan community (see Reading 38).

One kind of attempt to solve the problem of geographical fragmentation is the creation of single-purpose district governments to handle special functions. Important examples include the New York Port Authority, the Metropolitan St.

---

[16]Banfield and Wilson, p. 76.

[17]Banfield and Wilson, pp. 81-82. The present discussion is much indebted to their consideration of "The distribution of authority within the city," pp. 76-86.

Louis Sewer District, and the Chicago Park District. In many areas, they constitute the only metropolitan governmental units. Another approach to the problems of the metropolis is to turn increasingly to the state or federal government to obtain assistance with such problems as schools and urban renewal. But such solutions have important consequences. As Greer comments:

> They are, for one thing, removed from the surveillance and control of the local voters, and may be largely inaccessible to the politician and governmental official. Thus they violate the norm of local self-rule and responsibility to the local voters. This is the very reason for their creation: they bypass the local political process. Money and powers guarded jealously from the central city and suburban municipalities are passed upwards to Washington, from which they return free of the political blame that local officials would have to bear. Ironically, the net result of the system which keeps government "close to the people" is its removal as far as possible from the people—to the United States Congress, a State agency, or a Federal agency. Or, as with special districts, the power is handed to agencies whose decisions are rarely ever known to their clients, much less controlled by them—agencies which have been dubbed "ghost governments."[18]

[18]Scott Greer, *Governing the Metropolis*, New York: Wiley, 1962, p. 132.

38   The Schizoid Polity and the Drive for Reunification

Scott Greer

The governmental dichotomy of the metropolis and fragmentation of suburbia have serious consequences for the total urban complex. First of all, the political processes are in no sense those of a unified metropolitan community. They are limited by the forces in play in each of the various subparts of the area, though the consequences of these forces may be very general. Furthermore, this fragmented polity confronts problems that are areawide in their origins, affecting all parts of the metropolitan area; they are problems which seem, logically and technically, to demand an areawide governmental response. Such a response, however, is difficult to imagine in an urban complex made up of a hundred or a thousand separate governmental jurisdictions. Let us look at this aspect of the metropolitan governmental structure in some detail.

CONSEQUENCES OF THE DICHOTOMY: I. THE POLITICAL PROCESS

We have already noted the most dramatic consequence of the dichotomy for urban politics: the separation of numbers and wealth. Those who live in the green neighborhoods of suburbia have saved their families and homes from the central city, at the price of valuable hostages left behind. Their property (if they are wealthy) is most likely to be located in the old center; banks and department stores, utilities and factories and transport facilities, have immense investments in the central city. The taxes they pay,

Reprinted from Scott Greer, *Governing the Metropolis*, New York: Wiley, 1962, pp. 107–128, by permission of the author and the publisher.

the governmental services they receive, their regulation and protection by government, are all decided in a political order of which they are not even citizens. Even if suburbanities are salaried managers and professionals, or wage workers, they still depend on the city for a workplace; but from the point of view of the central-city resident the suburbanites have abandoned the central city. They pay their property taxes on homes in Valhalla, Elm Village, Meadowlane. Meanwhile, they return to the city each day in droves, using the streets and sidewalks, claiming police and fire protection—demanding and getting a fair share of the central city's public services without paying the tax bill that the residents of the city must shoulder.

Thus the power of city government is in the hands of the central-city electorate, while great investments affected by government are owned, managed, and manned by suburbanites. What wonder that many suburban residents are concerned with central city government? Their concern stems also from another kind of investment—the pious dependence of suburbia upon the old central city as a clearinghouse, a symbol, a permanent center for the scattered metropolitan region. Though he only returns occasionally after work for the night life and the cultural events, the Loop, Manhattan, and the City of San Francisco still represent to the metropolitan citizen the social unity of the metropolis. If he sees it declining in looks, wealth, and activity, he is disturbed. Yet he is no citizen there; he has neither power nor responsibility for the center; he is a commuter.

As we have seen already, the governmental boundary lines between center and peripheries divide populations which differ on other counts. The variations result in a skewed distribution of both the central city and suburban electorates. Those who seek office in the center must

appeal to the ethnics, the nonwhites and the foreign-born, the Catholics and Jews. They must also appeal to the working class, the blue-collar manual laborers, those who ordinarily vote the Democratic Party's ticket. Thus the ethnic organizations, the National Association for the Advancement of Colored People, and the B'nai B'rith, are important in central-city politics, along with the Catholic Church, the A.F.L.-C.I.O. Central Labor Council, and the Democratic Party's ward and precinct officials. Appeal to such organizations and the interests they represent is quite different from an approach to the total range of urban voters. Somebody is missing.

The missing persons are, of course, the middle-class native white Protestants who moved to suburbia. Though they are still weighty factors in the outer wards of the city (they can, for example, change a Democratic mayor's winning percentage from 60 to 75) they are preponderantly in the suburbs and continue to move outwards. These folks were once the electoral base of the Republican Party in the city; they also provided the cadres for the party's organization, the men who were willing to invest time and energy and money in the party's fortunes. They are now involved in the country's politics, or those of their diminutive suburbs. Nobody takes their place in central-city politics.

The progressive withdrawal of the upper occupational, educational, and income levels from the central city has produced a governmental segregation by social class. Each of the two great divisions in American society, the middle class and the working class, has its own government in the metropolis, and the existence of these structures means that they are used for class interests. At the same time, the separation of the two prevents the development of a governmental process which would act as a clearinghouse, adjudicating the claims of different interests within the society, producing definitive decisions on conflicting and uncertain positions. The dichotomy makes it extremely difficult for any group of men to act for the area as a whole. The mutual suspicion between central city and suburb becomes a political platform for aspirants to office in each part of the metropolis, just as that between "downstate" and the "city" provides political fuel for campaigns at the state level. Even informal cooperation suffers in the process.

Yet the metropolitan area is in many respects an interdependent whole. Suburbia could not exist for a week without the continual transfer of value from the workplaces of the central city to the suburban households. The opposite is also true: key posts in the economic organization of the central city are manned by those who live in suburban villas. And the whole will continue to experience rapid and widespread change and major challenges. (The fantastic prediction of fifty million new residents in the next two decades, most of them suburban, the lion's share of them in urban complexes already large and old, guarantees a continuous series of challenges to the social and governmental order.) But it is difficult to see any concerted response from the scramble of governments we have described. Each will pursue its own interests and problems within its existing framework.

CONSEQUENCES OF THE DICHOTOMY: II. THE GOVERNMENTAL PROCESS

A useful way to approach the governmental process is to ask: What kinds of problems is it supposed to solve for the governed? We shall examine three types: (1) those resulting from the inescapable housekeeping problems of the city, (2) those produced in deciding the distribution of costs and benefits (or problems of equity) and (3) those deriving from the development of long-term control aimed at deciding the future shape of the metropolis. Each is radically affected by the dichotomy between central city and suburbs.

Most of the housekeeping problems of our metropolitan areas today are as old as cities. Julius Caesar struggled with the problems of transport in a growing Rome; city streets hardly wide enough for two carts to pass were forced to handle the flow of people and goods for a population rapidly approaching a million. Tenement dwellings were forever collapsing or catching fire because building contractors cheated, and because obsolete heating equipment was used in the housing of the poor. The streets at night were controlled by gangs of thieves and kidnappers, while sugar was sanded and milk was watered. The householders were apt to deposit their refuse in public places for others to walk through and carry away for them, while the supply of water was a perennial problem (leading to the construction of aqueducts which still stand and function in some places). In short, the urban problems of circulation, of energy input and waste disposal, and of public health and order emerged in Rome, as in Pittsburgh, and continue to appear wherever many live together in the interdependence of contiguity and exchange.

The tasks are clear. Political decisions arise with respect to such questions as these: How much service shall be provided, and how shall it be distributed among the citizens? The preconditions for answering these questions are (1) adequate technologies and (2) adequate resources of money and power. Our society of large and increasing scale has been fortunate in developing physical technologies; our potential power to control our environment is far greater than that of any previous society. However, the sheer volume and the rate of growth are also greater than they have been before. As for the resources needed to carry on the tasks we are, in some ways, poorer. In short, many of our metropolitan housekeeping problems exist because we do not pay enough to do a good job. In some degree, this results from dividing our public treasury (our "fisc") into too many bits and pieces, but in a large degree it results from parsimony. Our inadequate governmental powers, on the other hand, are more largely due to fractionated jurisdictions (though the Jacksonian dogma has kept a close curb on all expansions of governmental power). The political process does not allocate enough money and power to provide the kinds of services many urbanites expect from government.

The Problems of Providing Services

The provision of an efficient transportation grid for the metropolis requires a tremendous material investment. It also requires a unification of control patterns, so that traffic ordinances and police forces do not change every mile or two. It requires an areawide power, for the components of the problem situation are areawide in origin and effects. Traffic generated in the suburbs flows to the central city, while the central city's labor force pours back towards the suburbs in the evening. For instance, a change in the traffic ordinances of a suburban country town meant to improve the main street as a shopping street for that community, may result in serious snarls on the freeways of the central city. And the central city's express highway, ending on a suburban road, may suddenly funnel two or three times as much traffic through the village as had been expected by the village government. All efforts at control of circulation in the metropolis must include suburbs and central city, for the former usually provide the majority of the automobiles in movement. Such efforts, to be effective, must also take into account other aspects of transportation; terminals, public transport, parking arrangements and the like. Only broad areawide power can be effective.

The same holds true for water supply and waste disposal. Because water tends to organize its flow in a given depression (called a drainage basin), and because such a depression usually includes more than one governmental unit, the actions of one suburb affect another, and suburbs affect the drainage system of the central city. The St. Louis County municipality that empties its sewage into an open creek that runs through a neighboring town is, like the Roman burgher emptying his slops in the public square, an indication that the control system does not "fit" the interdependent populations. However, in the St. Louis County case, the "bad actor" was a government, standing for an entire municipal population. Solutions to such bad actions must obviously affect governments in their responses to housekeeping problems. The metropolitan household is in many respects one; but its housekeeping is organized in dozens or hundreds of families, each indifferent to (if not hostile to) the neighbors.

Thus the central city is perennially in need of close coordination of its services with those of the suburbs. Lying towards the waterways and the railroads (a heritage of its past in the Age of Steam), it is the ultimate recipient of many flowing waters. Including as it does the major part of the workplaces for the area, it is also the recipient of the densest traffic. Fanned out in the suburban fringes, traffic comes to a dense focus at the center of the arterials. Here, in the central city, the worst aspects of urban automobile traffic are continually on view. The central city resident, for whom the center is a "convenience shopping" area, must drive through the concentrated traffic of the entire metropolis in order to do his weekly shopping.

The suburbs also run into augmented problems as a result of their fragmentation. They suffer the consequences of spatial contiguity and resulting interdependence. Students of metropolitan government are fond of remarking that polluted air and water, crime and fire and hydrogen bombs, are no respecters of our divided jurisdictions. Indeed, fragmentation may increase our vulnerability; the juvenile gang which takes care never to be booked in the home community cannot be identified if no central records exist. It may with impunity commit depredations in other suburbs and return home safely. As for such growing governmental tasks as preventive public medicine or disaster control (a standby organization to handle the results of flood, tornadoes, and nuclear war), the governmental patchwork makes them utterly impractical. The municipalities in most cases simply cannot afford professional services of these kinds. Their legal autonomy can, however, effectively prevent the areawide organization essential to the evacuation of populations or the rapid identification of health menaces. In short, the housekeeping problems of the individual governments, suburban as well as central city, are greatly increased by the political fragmentation of metropolitan areas.

The Problem of Equity

A second kind of problem situation common in our metropolitan areas is that of equity. Because we have no areawide government, we have no areawide polity. As we have noted, this means that Negroes and other ethnics, union members, and wage workers tend to be represented most heavily in the central city;

white-collar workers are concentrated in suburbia, where they are represented by a plethora of tiny governments. But the problem arises when a given area must pay for services to another—when the taxing jurisdiction does not include those who benefit from the taxes. In such cases, the result is literally taxation without representation.

We have noted the central city's position, as workplace for the area and as central point of assembly. Important as its tasks are for the entire metropolis, it is not reimbursed by the villages of the fringe. It houses the poor, the unskilled and semiskilled laborers essential to many industries whose management lives in suburbia. These central-city populations produce far more than their share of the welfare and police problems of the area, just as they pay less than their share of taxes. They are net losses to the central-city government. At the same time the central city houses more of the areawide facilities of the metropolis— parks and museums and zoological gardens, convention halls and concert halls and theatres, universities and hospitals and trade schools. This land is ordinarily removed from the tax rolls; services must be provided for such sites, yet they cannot be taxed because they are non-profit public enterprises. A similar loss results from the increasing network of superhighways which center in the older city; such roadways usually are built at the cost of millions of dollars in taxable property. They make the center accessible to suburban residents and the city pays. In short, the cost of services stays the same or increases in the central city, while the sources of revenue are declining. The question arises: What is fair in this kind of situation? Who should pay, and how much should they pay? There is no polity which includes all interested parties: those who own property pay, those who choose to do so drive in and use the facilities.

All is not clear sailing in suburbia, either. In Robert Wood's felicitous phrase, the suburban fragmentation results in "the segregation of resources from needs." The industrial plant which provides jobs for thousands of suburban workers pays taxes only to the little village in which it stands. Its work force, however, may double the school enrollment in another municipality to which the plant pays nothing. The suburban governmental wall provides immunity to taxation which might represent the total social cost of private enterprise, just as it provides immunity to teen-age gangs. To be sure, the larger the municipality the less likelihood there is of such obvious segregation. As Wood remarks:

The larger a municipality . . . the more chance it may have to encompass a balanced blend of expenditure-inducing factors. . . . Hence the less vulnerable it becomes to decisions made in the private sector (i.e., the economy) .[1]

However, as we have noted, most suburbs are not very large in either population or statute miles. Under such conditions, "historical caprice, in the form of ancient boundary lines, disrupts the pattern of regularity . . . the location of a single industrial plant, the decision of a developer . . . insignificant elements in the total urban complex of the region—drastically affect the public fortunes of the jurisdiction."[2]

Such eccentricity in the location of boundaries and the composition of suburbs results in statistics which many find disturbing. In St. Louis County one school district has an assessed valuation (the basis for all property taxes) which is *twenty-eight times the tax base per capita of another.* The first suburb pays one of the lowest tax rates in the area, the second, one of the highest. But the school systems are far apart in quality. The first is a superior school system, the second is struggling to maintain its accreditation. In fact, suburban municipalities vary so greatly in the amount and quality of services provided that many protagonists of metropolitan government base their arguments on the need for enforcing a minimum standard of services in the suburbs. While some municipalities are as rich as Valhalla, many others are already paying higher taxes than the central city and providing poorer services. They can look forward to nothing but an astronomical increase in costs as the child population grows, settlement grows denser, and the school system, the street system, and police and fire protection become more expensive. For such suburbs, the question of equitable taxation is a pressing one indeed. But within the existing governmental framework they have no local resources beyond the taxes they can levy upon themselves.

The creation of an acceptable equity is, of course, a universal problem of government. It is usually solved through the adjudication of the political process which, within a framework of precedent (that is, a constitution), allocates costs and benefits in view of probable political repercussions. The peculiar nature of the problem in the metropolitan complex results from the governmental segregation caused by fixed boundary walls. The levying of taxes and use of social capital for social purposes can apply only to that segregated part of the population within the boundaries. The governmental redistribution of wealth which takes place wherever citizens pay unequal taxes and receive equal benefits (or vice versa) is

[1]Robert Wood, *1400 Governments, The Political Economy of the New York Metropolitan Region* (with the assistance of Vladimir V. Almendinger) Cambridge: Harvard University Press, 1961, p. 62.
[2]*Ibid.*, pp. 60-62.

also constrained by the boundaries. Instead of resulting from the political process it is ground out by the unequal units brought into being as the entrepreneurs incorporate municipalities on the fringe.

The Problem of Consensus: What Kind of City?

These effects of governmental fragmentation on the polity are clear. But in addition to the housekeeping problems and the moral problems of paying for them, we should also remember that the entire destiny of the metropolitan community is affected by its governance. Many aspects of the city which are today considered problems result from uncontrolled and unplanned development in the past. The tremendous investment of the past remains as the layout of the community. Thus the question arises: Are contemporary developments any less likely to create future problems? Is the development in one part of the area considered in its relation to another? Are both viewed as generators of the future city? Is that city one that we wish to create?

Those who raise such questions are sometimes social idealists, Utopians who can imagine a city different from and better than the historical facts among which we live. Some are oriented to the past; for them the true nature of the city lies in the highly centralized urban complex whose people all live within one polity and one community. Looking backwards to the days when the city was a whole, they aspire to a new version in the future. Other Utopians are committed to a version of the city as even more dispersed, one in which the density and indignity of crowded streets and sidewalks would give way to dispersed concentrations of workplaces, residences, shopping malls, and community centers, surrounded and separated from others by miles of green countrysides.

Perhaps there is a little of this idealism in the thought of anyone concerned with the future of his city. Many persons also worry about future developments because action is demanded *at this very moment.* Without knowing what will happen in other parts of the metropolis and in the following years it is not possible for them to make very dependable plans, yet they *must* try to plan. The massive program of urban redevelopment, which aims at rebuilding large segments of the central city, requires that its managers be able to guess what will happen in other parts of the metropolis: the suburban neighborhoods, the giant shopping centers in the outer wards, the industrial satellite cities. They need to know what the market will be for their redeveloped sites. Equally important, those who are pushing to the forefront of urban settlement in the suburbs need to know what is going to occur in the center. Both urban redevelopers and suburban housing developers need to know where the important sites of work will be tomorrow, where the commercial centers will be, and how the transportation network will develop.

Such problems become extremely specific and tangible to the decision makers. They know, for example, that the planning of a new thoroughfare to relieve traffic congestion is not an isolated act. The new thoroughfare will open new neighborhoods to settlement (it will change the space-time ratio from workplace to residence); the new neighborhoods will provide for new populations which will use the thoroughfare (and probably crowd it); they will also require streets, sidewalks, parks, playgrounds, sewerage systems, and (most expensive) school systems. Thus the building of an expressway is more than a means of solving a traffic problem; after it is in being, it affects the very structure of the city, and its consequences become the basis for the future actions of the planner. Similar examples could be given for the interdependence of other aspects of urban development. Inescapable interdependence is not limited to the population of one governmental unit; as we have shown in detail, growth and development cut across the mosaic of governments.

It is not possible to plan development in the present metropolis. The simple collecting of information is a difficult if not impossible task for the hundreds of governmental units. The exercise of control "across the board" is absolutely impossible. Thus neither the Utopians nor the practical planner have much basis for predicting the effects of their actions: but if they cannot do this, they cannot plan at all. The metropolis continues to grow as in the past at a rapid rate, and like Topsy, it "jest grows." The effects of today's expansion of the urban plant will be tomorrow's metropolitan problems.

THE DRIVE FOR REINTEGRATION

Many observers have noted the consequences of governmental fragmentation in the metropolis. Whether they are government officials facing serious problems in rising costs and declining revenues, party leaders who see their cohorts reduced to impotence, technicians who despair of achieving their missions, political scientists, or simply metropolitan citizens, they come to similar conclusions. The obvious solution is based upon the cause: the small-scale governments of suburbia. Most observers conclude that these must be integrated in a larger structure and the governmental dichotomy reduced to unity. In short, they prescribe a metropolitan area government.

There are three kinds of formulas typically invoked. First, there are those who imagine an urban county, with most of the municipal powers exercised through the encompassing structure of the county while cities as such disappear. Second, there are those who wish to keep as many municipal structures in existence as seems practical. They advise a metropolitan district government for the solution of metropolitan problems, a large-scale structure encompassing the area but leaving many tasks to the smaller units of suburbia and to the central city's existing government. Finally, there are those who take their stand in the city and fight for "irredentism," the return of the lost territories of suburbia to their rightful polity, the central city.

In general, it appears that those who prescribe an urban county focus their vision on the suburbs. The symbol of the county is an all-encompassing one, bypassing the schism between central city and suburbs. Those who recommend a metropolitan district are "realists" who try to allow for the suburban society already in being and incorporated, while integrating the governmental response to the inescapable tasks of the area as a whole. Those who fight for merger are, in general, patriots of the central city. For them there is no metropolis except that which rightfully centers in downtown St. Louis, Cleveland, San Francisco, or Miami.

Technical evaluation of these three alternatives is fairly consistent, from observer to observer and state to state. Within the provisions of most state constitutions the county is a very limited administrative arm; thus to create an urban county government is essentially to invent a new form of local government, and, having invented it, to insert it in the constitution. This is a complex and politically difficult task. The metropolitan "federal district" runs into similar difficulties; the division of tasks between area-wide government and the municipalities is a mare's nest of legal conundrums. How can traffic be divided between area-wide and local streets? They are interdependent. How can zoning become area-wide in its efficiency while leaving the power to protect the neighborhoods to the municipality? And so on. Such problems are not insoluble; they are merely complex and, again, politically difficult. The outright merger of all the urban area in one big city usually runs into only one purely technical difficulty—the spread of metropolitan complexes across county, state, and in some instances (such as El Paso-Juarez and Detroit-Windsor) national boundary lines. Could we merge all urban population in one municipality, however, it would then be relatively simple to adapt the existing legal rights of cities to the tasks created by the total metropolis.

The History of Metropolitan Government Plans

These are the most general recommendations of political scientists and other experts on metropolitan government. They are by no means new ideas. Writing in 1933, R. D. McKenzie noted the rapid growth of metropolitan areas and the increasing spread of population across existing political boundaries. He thought that "The larger cities of the country are becoming what might be termed regionally conscious."[3] He observed that even then efforts to reintegrate suburbs and central city in one government had been made in Pittsburgh, St. Louis, and Cleveland; he thought that, despite the failure of these attempts, they would be made again. He was right. The Governmental Affairs Foundation recently published a digest which summarized nearly a hundred surveys of metropolitan areas made in the past twenty years. And efforts have been made again and again in such cities as St. Louis, Cleveland and Pittsburgh.

The results have been failure, in city after city, time after time. This failure reflects the existing dichotomy of the

[3]"The Rise of Metropolitan Communities," in *Recent Social Trends, in The United States*, New York: McGraw-Hill Book Company, 1933, p. 451.

metropolis and the resulting political schizophrenia. In 1959, St. Louis held a referendum on a Metropolitan District Plan. It was a scheme developed by a Board of Freeholders and based largely upon the recommendations of the Metropolitan St. Louis Survey (a large-scale study of local government by social scientists); it was sponsored by many of the civic leaders of the community. It was well publicized by campaigns in the daily newspapers and was not vociferously opposed by the existing structures of government. Nevertheless, it lost by two to one in the central city, by three to one in the suburban county. The compromise solution had very little appeal.

There has, however, been one successful campaign for a metropolitan government. Perhaps we can learn something about resistance to such a government through looking at the campaign which, in 1957, resulted in a metropolitan Dade County government.

Dade County, the Greater Miami Metropolitan Area of Florida, is a new metropolis. At the time of the campaign for "Metro," half of the population had lived in the area for less than ten years. A medium-sized city, it had been flooded by migrants since World War II. As a result, the governmental machinery was overburdened, the revenues were inadequate to service the hundreds of thousands of new migrants, and such crucial services as sewerage disposal were nonexistent in many parts of the area. The political order was also rocked to its foundations; hundreds of new neighborhoods, dozens of communities, rose in a year or two without becoming integrated in the existing system. (The one-party regime also encouraged such looseness, for party discipline is still practically unknown in Dade County politics.) Under these circumstances there was little commitment to existing governments; the City of Miami came within eight hundred votes of being abolished as recently as the

1950's. Nor was there much loyalty to a discredited political order. The campaign for Metro was thus supported by all of the civic leaders and symbols of governmental virtue, while the opposition was practically silent. Yet, under such circumstances, the Metro plan won by only a few hundred votes.[4]

The campaign for Metro was, however, a costly one. In devising "a package that would sell" to the voters, the government that emerged was very weak. The Plan provided for little new revenue, though its backers promised that it would create all the governmental facilities needed in Dade County. It also failed to provide for any responsible governmental head: the Metro District was to be run by a County Manager, who served at the pleasure of an elected Council. The powers of the County were divided again and again with the existing municipalities; this created a potent source of centrifugal tendencies as each neighborhood or community jealously fought for its identity and privileges, making its voice heard through its elected representative. Then too, in the campaign for Metro one of the major selling points of its protagonists was economy: the Metro government was expected to do many more tasks than had ever been performed before, at a net saving in taxes. Needless to say, the price for getting the approval of citizens in referendum elections is now being paid by the Metro government. It appears that it may have been too great a price to result in amelioration of the various metropolitan problems the plan set out to solve.

The Barriers to Change

The difficulties of changing metropolitan governmental structure may be use-

[4]For a brief discussion of the campaign for Metro see Edward Sofen, "Problems of Metropolitan Leadership: The Miami Experience," *Midwest Journal of Political Science*, Vol. V, No. 1, pp. 18–38.

fully divided into three levels. These are (1) the underlying cultural norms of Americans concerning local government, (2) the resulting legal-constitutional structures, and (3) the political-governmental system built upon them. The underlying norms are those described earlier as the Jacksonian ideology, the dogma of the right to local self-government and the direct exposure of the governmental system to the veto of the voters. Shared by citizen and political leader alike, these norms are important because they specify *what is legitimate*. Based upon a deep distrust of governmental officials and a faith in the competence of the ordinary voter, they also lead to such corollaries as "that government is best which governs least" (and more important, *costs* least).

Translated into the legal provisions of the constitution, the norms set up the rules of the game. They validate the incorporation of municipalities for many purposes, including the trivial, spurious, and even socially injurious pursuit of self-interest. They also provide the mechanisms for changing the nature of local governments with the result that basic structural change must be submitted to the voters in referendum. In that referendum, the citizen does not act as an isolated, free-floating intelligence: he is, after all, an actor in an existing neighborhood, community, municipality. His political leaders are those who were elected through the present system, and are usually committed to it.

The existing political system is a major problem for any reform movement. Those who are committed to change are usually not the incumbents. Thus, reformers have to carry their message through the mass media and lectures, for they are disbarred from the political organizations. The "machine of the incumbents," however, can easily and quietly mobilize the existing system against change. Any change is a danger to the going concern, and those who benefit from existing arrangements see no gain in a radical departure. The public servant fears for his job; the contractor fears for his contract. Insofar as such persons are important reference points for voters, they encourage suspicion of anything new.

As for the ordinary voter, we can say something about his responses. In St. Louis a sample survey was taken immediately after the failure of the District Plan.[5] In general, it is clear that neither the protagonists nor the antagonists of reform "got through to the voter" very clearly. In the suburban sample, selected for past involvement in local elections, only 10 per cent of the voters had roughly correct notions of three most important provisions of the plan: its methods of governance, the effects on existing communities, and the tax rate authorized. Only about 20 per cent could state any of these major provisions correctly. Thus the ordinary voters were not even voting on the plan: nobody knows what they *were* voting on.

However, there is little evidence that the campaign against the plan was effective. The voters questioned afterward had never heard of most individuals for or against the plan (evidently civic leaders, the power elite, the economic dominants, talk chiefly to each other—and to social scientists studying the power structure). They were, if interested, more likely to know how the major mass media stood: still, only 49 per cent of them knew correctly the *Post-Dispatch's* position, after that dominant newspaper had put on an all-out three months' campaign for the plan.

The one major figure who seemed to have had an impact, and in the intended direction, was the mayor of the central

city. Even in the suburbs a majority knew his position, respected it, and in many cases said it helped them to make up their minds. The dominant symbolic position of the central city mayor in metropolitan affairs is thus demonstrated again. However, most individuals and organizations involved in the campaign were unknown to the voters, and their position on the plan (if the voter ventured a guess) was as likely to be reversed as correctly stated. The political system simply does not function for this type of campaign, not at least as its functioning is envisaged in the democratic dogma.

The lack of interest, involvement, and information among the voters should not lead us to ignore what did occur in their political discourse. There are strong indications that the campaign, the talk back and forth, while it did not increase competence, did produce a high degree of confusion among the voters. Rhetorical tricks, the exercise of the journalist's skills, and a certain amount of sharp practice on both sides, left the voter some basis for guessing that: "The District Plan would tax us fifty cents on the dollar," or "The District Plan would abolish all governments and create one big city."

The confusion resulted, chiefly, in the evocation of the basic political norms controlling local government. Governmental merger and the loss of local control was a bad business. On the other hand, increased coordination and cooperation among the scattered local governments were good; with increased size go efficiency and economy. The improvement in governmental services was a fine thing. But an increase in taxes was a dreadful prospect, and the addition of "another layer of government" brought chills to some people's spine. In short, confusion led to the evocation of norms. These norms are frequently contradictory. The average citizen, hardly educated to the real nature of the plan, evoked rules of

---

[5]This research was carried out by the Center for Metropolitan Studies of Northwestern University. It will be reported in detail in the volume *Metropolitics, A study of Political Culture*, Scott Greer and Norton Long.

thumb as old as government: "Better the evil that is known . . ." and "When in doubt do nothing." These phrases summarize the final response of a great many among both leaders and led to the plan for a metropolitan government.

The campaign attempted, in a few months' time, to propagandize a complex scheme for applied social science. It was further handicapped by dependence upon the mass media. No wonder the *status quo* was victorious. The norms evoked, however, are not transitory matters: the basic conflict between the norms for local government and the rising consumption norms for governmental services seems to be a permanent part of our public discourse. Local governing bodies are trusted with neither the powers nor the material resources to provide increasingly expensive services: at the same time, they are blamed for their failure to provide them. Such a campaign as that for the District Plan dramatizes this conflict in the normative structure of the American political community. Its results also become part of that structure, for the campaign resulted in a certain amount of social learning.

Many citizens learned something from both sides in the conflict. They learned, certainly, that much better services in the area of traffic facilities and transport could be provided for the metropolis. They also learned that efficiency, coordination, cooperation, were good things (as long as they cost nobody any taxes or local autonomy). In short, they learned some of the campaign slogans. The leaders of the campaign also learned. Some concluded that the District Plan, a compromise between the interests of central city and suburbs, satisfied nobody; it lacked "box office appeal." They decided that only an all-out campaign for one big city was capable of stirring the imaginations of the voters. But others (and probably the majority) decided that nothing could be done to create a metropolitan government through referendum elections.

When such an acknowledgement of defeat is common, the effort to restructure the government at the most general level is abandoned, often for a decade or more. That which exists, the snarl of polities, the multiplying suburbs, the slowly changing central city, becomes the given nature of things. It is a "traditional system" by default: it is impossible to change.

Section V

ADAPTIVE PROCESSES IN COMMUNITIES

Our previous consideration of adaptation processes has led us to the conclusion that a very significant counterpart of this process is structural differentiation. Thus, for example, in our analysis of adaptation processes in small groups, emphasis was placed on role differentiation. The association between adaptation and differentiation is seen even more clearly in the case of communities. Indeed, the key term to be used in describing all but the smallest and most isolated of communities is *differentiation*. Subgroups making up the community participate in a division of labor, each type of unit being allocated to a different spatial location by the competitive processes described by Bernard in Reading 35; and the community as a whole may be differentiated with respect to other communities, each specializing in some subset of activities.

One important basis for differences among communities are differences in the environment to which they must adapt. For this reason, there is a close relation between community location and function, as Duncan and his colleagues note:

What a city does depends so closely on where it is that function and location seem like the two sides of a coin. Deep-water ports are busy with commerce and trade. An urban concentration of chemical industries arises in a valley endowed by nature with bituminous coal deposits, pools of petroleum, pockets of natural gas, sources of brines, and an abundance of water. "Gateway" cities collect the produce of agricultural belts and distribute it over wide regions. The geometry of location, by itself, tells us something about function: the foci of trade and service industries in regions of the interior are likely to occur at approximately central points within those regions.[1]

This brief statement alludes to some of the major principles that have been used to explain the location of cities. Specifically, these include the "break in transportation" principle formulated by Cooley, who noted the tendency of cities to develop at the junction of land with water transportation, of one kind of water transportation with another, or of one kind of land transportation with another;[2] the "central-place" theory developed by Lösch, who emphasized the tendency of market towns to develop near the centers of the regions they serve;[3] and "special-function" cities, which develop to take advantage of specific site factors, such as the location of mineral deposits.

Note, however, that the influence of the environment on location is not a constant, unchanging factor. Cities that prospered and grew large in the early days of this country were invariably located on a sea or lake coast or a navigable

---

[1]Otis Dudley Duncan *et al.*, *Metropolis and Region*, Baltimore: The Johns Hopkins Press, 1960, p. 23.

[2]Charles Horton Cooley, "The theory of transportation," *Sociological Theory and Social Research*, New York: Holt, Rinehart and Winston, Inc., 1930 (first published 1894).

[3]August Lösch, *The Economics of Location*, translated by William H. Woglom, New Haven, Conn.: Yale University Press, 1954.

508

river (all 17 of the U.S. cities that reached a size of 100,000 or more prior to 1880 had such a location), but with the development of rail and air transportation, this environmental factor became less crucial for location. Form and Miller in Reading 39 note the effect on city location of changing technologies and sources of fuel.

In such discussions of the functions of cities and their relation to the environment, all the various activities carried on in cities are not considered. Rather, a distinction is made between two kinds of activities, *export* or *basic* functions and *maintenance* or *support* functions. Export activities are what create "an inflow of money to the community. Urban land economists and planners refer to this as the 'economic base' of communities. . . . The remaining economic activity in a community goes to satisfy local demand and may be said to constitute the maintenance activity of a community."[4]

There have been several attempts to classify cities in terms of their functions, that is, the extent to which they specialize in one or another kind of export activity. As an example of this approach to the typing of communities, we will consider the work of Duncan and Reiss.[5] Because information is not available on a national basis for the exports of communities, economic base is measured indirectly using data on labor force and production, under the following reasoning:

When a community has a high proportion employed or a high per capita output in a given industry, relative to other communities in the economy . . . it probably exports the products of that industry. . . . Statistics on the industrial composition of the labor force or on per capita volume of activity, analyzed comparatively, therefore, permit rough inferences as to export functions. For example, when a given community has a much larger proportion of its labor force engaged in manufacturing than the average of an appropriate group of communities, there is a presumption that it exports manufactured goods and, therefore, specializes in manufacturing.[6]

In addition to information on labor force and per capita output, the proposed typology takes account of differences in size and in metropolitan status (for example, independent cities located outside of the standard metropolitan statistical areas [SMSA] defined by the Bureau of the Census, central cities within the SMSA's, and suburbs within the SMSA's). That is, the criteria of functional specialization are varied according to community size and metropolitan location. Finally, it is possible for a given community to appear in more than one functional class—for example, to be both a trade center and a center of higher education.

The major functional types of cities identified by Duncan and Reiss are as follows:

1. Manufacturing specialization
2. Specialization in trade (a number of subtypes are identified here depending on the combination of retail-wholesale trade specialization)
3. Specialization in higher education
4. Public administration specialization

[4]Otis Dudley Duncan and Albert J. Reiss, Jr., *Social Characteristics of Urban and Rural Communities, 1950*, New York: Wiley, 1956, p. 216.

[5]Other comprehensive attempts to classify American cities by the functions they perform include that of Gunner Alexandersson, *The Industrial Structure of American Cities*, Lincoln, Nebr.: University of Nebraska Press, 1956; and O. D. Duncan *et al.*, *Metropolis and Region*.

[6]Duncan and Reiss, p. 217.

5. Specialization in transportation
6. Military specialization
7. Specialization in entertainment and recreation

The development of such a typology is the beginning, not the end, of the analysis. The hope is to show that certain other demographic, economic, and socioeconomic characteristics of communities vary with their functional classification. Duncan and Reiss provide ample evidence for the existence of important differences related to their typology of communities.[7] They conclude:

In sum, virtually every aspect of a community's structure is related to its basic functions. Reliable differences among the various types of communities are observed with respect to age and sex structure, mobility rates, labor force participation, industrial and occupational composition, educational attainment, income, and home ownership. This is not to state that each particular type of community has a distinctive pattern with respect to each of these characteristics, but rather, for each characteristic examined, at least one type of specialization was found to produce a considerable deviation from the average. The results warrant the conclusion that type of functional specialization, in addition to the factors of community size, spatial orientation, and population growth, must be included among the principal determinants of morphological differences among communities.[8]

The material reprinted from Form and Miller (Reading 39) is in keeping with this far-reaching summary statement of the association between a community's economic base and its structural characteristics. They specifically focus on industry's impact on city location, size, growth patterns, occupational composition, and the pattern of land usage.

[7]See Duncan and Reiss, pp. 253–345.
[8]Duncan and Reiss, pp. 15-16.

39   Industrial Relationships Which Shape the Community

William H. Form and Delbert C. Miller

INDUSTRY DETERMINES LOCATION OF COMMUNITIES

Location is Influenced by the Stages of Technology

Businessmen weigh many factors in deciding upon the location of industry. These factors are influenced by the given stage of technology. An historic view of industrial location reveals that the location of plants follows the requirements of four rather distinct stages of technology: the modern craft age, the machine age, the power age, and the atomic age.

IMPORTANCE OF WATER POWER TO THE EMERGENCE OF THE MODERN CRAFT AGE   The modern craft age was based on muscle and water power. The use of water wheels was a significant first step in the transition from animate to inanimate energy. The early growth of textile manufacturing occurred along the streams of New England. The largest developments were established at Lowell, Manchester, Lawrence, Holyoke,

Reprinted from William H. Form and Delbert C. Miller, *Industry, Labor, and Community* (New York, Harper & Bros., 1960), selections from Chapter 2, by permission of the authors.

and Lewiston before the Civil War.[1] Water power was not transportable, and the plants were forced to concentrate at the site itself. This greatly centralized industry about good water-power sites. Flour milling centered about such cities. Minneapolis and Buffalo testify to the early importance of water power.

Modern industrialization awaited the utilization of steam. The steam engine provided a means for converting fuel into mechanical energy and could be set up wherever fuel was obtainable.

IMPORTANCE OF COAL AND IRON TO THE EMERGENCE OF THE MACHINE AGE   Coal was the cheapest of the most effective fuels for the steam engine. Since the fuel could be transported, it was possible to locate industry more widely. Still, transportation costs could not be ignored. The locational effect was to concentrate industry on navigable water where it was cheap to transport coal or in the coal fields themselves. The application of steam power to the textile industry led to the rapid growth in the Fall River-New Bedford area after the middle of the nineteenth century. In the same period a rapid growth occurred in the Pennsylvania coal fields. As the processes of steelmaking became established an area of heavy industry arose. It was cheaper to bring the iron to the coal over the Great Lakes water route than to attempt the reverse, due to problems of transport. In addition, the large consuming market was already established in the East. With the coming of the steam locomotive and an elaborate rail system, a vast industrial area was shortly established. It covered an area which stretched along the Atlantic seaboard between Portland, Maine, and Baltimore, Maryland, extending westward across the Appalachians as far as the west side of Lake Michigan, and reaching from a line on the north through the lake ports of Toronto, Detroit, and Milwaukee, to the Potomac and Ohio Rivers on the south. Outlying districts may be identified particularly around Montreal and St. Louis. A separate region is found in the South Atlantic Piedmont. On the Pacific Coast, manufacturing is now increasing, but until recently it has been of relatively minor importance compared with lumbering, agriculture, and commercial activities.

Iron and coal exert a controlling influence on the location of manufacturing because extremely large amounts are required by many industries. The amount of iron consumed is greater than that of all other metals combined. The equipment of modern industrial civilization is largely made of iron and steel: machines, tools, commercial and manufacturing buildings, and transportation facilities are all made primarily of steel. Most power and heat for industry as well as for rail transportation is still obtained from coal, although oil and gas are being increasingly used.

The location of heavy industry identifies the heart of an industrialized nation. The industrial heart of America lies within a triangular area including the Pittsburgh coal field and the south shores of Lake Erie and of Lake Michigan. In this relatively small area are found most of the iron and steel industries of the continent and the great variety of other heavy and light industries associated with them. The development of this strategic district is based primarily on its accessibility to three things: iron, coal, and consuming markets. In addition, the coincidence of a rich agricultural area and nearness to sea routes is especially helpful to its sustained growth.[2]

Manufacturing stimulates commerce.

[1]T. R. Smith, *The Cotton Textile Industry of Fall River, Massachusetts—A Study of Industrial Localizations*, Kings Crown, Press, 1944, Table 8, p. 42; W. Fred Cottrell, *Energy and Society*, McGraw-Hill, 1955.

[2]Richard Hartshorne in Emerson P. Schmidt (ed.), *Man and Society*, Prentice-Hall, 1937, 359–372.

The great commercial centers rise on the ocean ports of the North Atlantic and North Pacific, on the Great Lakes, and on rail centers. Since most industries collect raw material from different areas and distribute their products to different regions, proximity to the major trade routes is of great importance. The exchange route between North America and Western Europe is the greatest trade route in the world.

IMPORTANCE OF ELECTRICITY TO THE EMERGENCE OF THE POWER AGE   The power age is identified with the widespread use of electricity. The steam engine remains important because it becomes a prime mover for the generation of electricity and for other reasons, too. Hydroelectric power has been increasingly employed, but steam plants generate the largest quantity of electric power. Electric power has had locational effects on industry that are important but far less revolutionary than those of steam. The ability to transmit electric energy as much as 1000 miles gives added flexibility. The Columbia and Tennessee River valleys are new recipients of industry based on hydroelectric power.

It has been thought that the availability of electric power would produce a general scattering of industry to small rural plants or even back into workers' homes, but no major shift has occurred. It is true that plants no longer need to huddle around giant steam engines close to rail lines. The large modern factory using electric motors is a long, one-story, shedlike structure which increasingly locates in suburban locations. The motor transport of products and workers and the transport of electrical energy make the new pattern possible. The rapid growth of satellite towns and cities is evidence of the pattern.

IMPORTANCE OF ATOMIC ENERGY TO THE EMERGENCE OF THE ATOMIC AGE   The atomic age provides a new fuel for steam power

stations. Heat can be developed and converted into electricity. The light weight of the fuel opens many new possibilities for airplane and marine engines. Use of atomic energy in the submarine *Nautilus* and its sister ships now operating for the United States Navy demonstrates an application of this superior fuel. The Atomic Energy Commission has announced successful "breeder" experiments which may eventually indicate the release of much greater energy at lower costs. Certainly, the development of economical atomic fuels and reactors which could be transported cheaply in an airplane to any point in the world would suggest revolutionary possibilities.

Perhaps another locational effect of the atomic age should be pointed out. The threat of the atomic bomb is encouraging dispersion of industry where feasible. In general, widespread dispersion of existing plants is considered so expensive as to be prohibitive, but the location of new plants may be increasingly influenced by the threat of atomic bombing. Many large corporations are placing new plants in or near small cities, away from heavily industrialized areas. A shift of B-52 bomber production from the Seattle plant of Boeing Airplane Company to Wichita, Kansas, was announced in June, 1957, after many previous encouragements from the United States Defense Department. New plants built by DuPont in recent years have been located near small cities or towns. Their nylon plant at Seaford, Delaware, is a good example. Many employees hired at the plant were born within a 40-mile radius. They tend to reside in their communities of birth and commute to Seaford daily to work. . . .

INDUSTRY INFLUENCES THE SIZE OF THE COMMUNITY

The Multiplication Factor

The size of a community depends mainly on the size of the industrial base which undergirds it. The industrial base may be considered as composed of two parts: the basic activities and the service activities. Basic activities refer to those producing goods and services for sale outside the community; service activities are those carried on for internal consumption only. Thus, the basic activities support the service activities. This is commonly measured by the number of basic employees (those working for an export activity) and number of service employees (those working for internal consumption). Economists, in analyzing the growth of an area, often speak of the "multiplication factor." They refer to the fact that any development that provides new jobs in basic activities also creates jobs in service activities. Table 39-1 shows the reproductive process which is set in motion by the creation of new jobs in manufacturing. It shows some of the many supporting jobs that are required as one new job is created in manufacturing. However, the ratio of basic to service activity varies according to city size and function and also according to the classification of basic activities and service activities. Indeed, there may be a great deal of variation within a given city over time. All that one can say as a generalization is that the multiplication factor arises because basic activities require

TABLE 39–1 Every 100 Jobs in Industry Create These Additional Jobs

Jobs	Percentage	Jobs	Percentage
Bus drivers	.42	Architects	.06
Department store clerks	2.5	Electricians	.22
Lawyers and judges	.44	Miners	2.2
Waitresses	1.6	Real estate agents	.16
Plumbers	.13	Nurses	1.0
Doctors	.57	Shoe repairmen	.16
Painters	1.0	Teachers	.50
Firemen	.30	Pharmacists	.25
Dressmakers	.44	Editors and reporters	.25
Bank clerks	.66	Florists	.13
Stenos, typists	2.2	Plasterers	.13
Cleaners, laundrymen	1.6	Mechanics, machinists	2.2
Carpenters	2.6	Postmen	.50
Musicians	.44	Bookkeepers	2.0
Truck and tractor drivers	4.0	Dentists	.20
Gas station attendants	.40	Telephone operators	1.0
Printers	.22	Technical engineers	.14
Beauticians, barbers	1.0	Shoe clerks	.20
Policemen	.57	Photographers	.14
Highway workers	.10	Entertainers	.13
Librarians	.14	Bakers	.33
Food clerks	1.3	Farmers	28.5
Cooks	.66	Tailors, Furriers	.40
Newsboys	.09	Hardware clerks	.44

This table is based on a ratio of civilian jobs in manufacturing to the number not in manufacturing. In the table that ratio is assumed to be 1 to 2.6. This is higher than the multiplication factors which are described because of the classification of all jobs *not in manufacturing* as supportive. Many nonmanufacturing jobs which produce goods and services for export are basic activities. See *Better Living*, Employee's Magazine of E. I. DuPont Co., May-June, 1954, p. 14.

**TABLE 39–2 Illustration of the Effect of the Multiplication Factor on Supporting
Workers and Population of a Community**

Population of the Community

Basic workers	100,000	Service workers	200,000
Dependents	200,000	Dependents	400,000
Total	300,000	Total	600,000
Grand total	900,000		

Estimated Number of Service Workers Required in Some Selected Occupations

Jobs	Number	Jobs	Number
Truck drivers	5,500	Gas station attendants	900
Department store clerks	5,500	Tailors, furriers	900
Stenographers, typists	5,000	Firemen	800
Mechanics, machinists	5,000	Welfare workers	800
Bookkeepers, cashiers	4,000	Cabinet makers	600
Teachers	4,500	Clergymen	500
Cleaners, laundrymen	3,500	Dentists	500
Waitresses	3,500	Printers	500
Food clerks	3,000	Shoe clerks	500
Carpenters	3,000	Real estate agents	400
Painters	2,800	Shoe repairmen	400
Beauticians, barbers	2,400	Florists	300
Postmen	2,300	Plasterers	300
Nurses	2,000	Roofers	300
Bank clerks	1,500	Librarians	300
Cooks	1,500	Photographers	300
Druggists	1,500	Conductors	250
Electricians	1,500	Writers, editors	250
Watchmen	1,500	Highway workers	220
Plumbers	1,300	Newsboys	200
Policemen	1,300	Entertainers	200
Insurance agents	1,200	Architects	100
Phone operators	1,200		
Musicians	1,100	*Outside Services Included:*	
Hardware clerks	1,000	Farmers	40,000
Bakers	1,000	Miners of raw materials in-	
Dressmakers	1,000	cluding fuel	5,000
Lawyers, judges	1,000	Federal and state employees	
Doctors	950	including armed forces	24,000

Source: Adapted from *Better Living*, May-June, 1954, pp. 10–14. Data represent estimates which are useful for illustrative purposes only.

service activities in a specialized industrial economy and that basic activities generally originate and support the service activities. Therefore the multiplication factor is not accidental; it is a product of the economy in a local area and has a definite range of values.

The search for values of the multiplication factor has led to an examination of the ratio between basic and service activities in many cities. The ratio for cities over 10,000 population appears fairly certain to be between 1 to .5 and 1 to 2. The larger the city, all other things being equal, the larger the service component should be, because a larger range of specialties will be supported by the larger market.[3] In small cities from 10,000 to 120,000 the ratios range between 1 to .6 and 1 to .9.[4] As larger cities are examined, the ratio of service employees to basic increases. Wichita, Kansas, with about 200,000 population, has averaged about 1 basic to 1.4 service workers from 1940 to 1950. Cincinnati, with 787,000, had a 1 to 1.7 ratio. New York City comes to about 1 to 2.[5]

In most middle-sized cities it may be concluded that approximately a 1 to 1 ratio appears. Thus for every employee in

a new factory in a town, ultimately one service job in the city would be created in various activities, particularly in retail trade and services; the result would be two new employees; if each of these two employees had an average family size of three, a sixfold increase in population would result. A new plant employing 100 would thus support 600 total new population.

For a large city with a ratio of basic to service employment of 1 to 2, a ninefold increase in population would take place, so that 100 new basic workers would have the effect of adding 900 to the population. Thus, if we imagine a mythical city of 100,000 basic workers, our city turns out to be a metropolis of 900,000 population comparable in size or scope to Buffalo, New York and its suburbs. Two hundred thousand (200,-000) service workers are providing the needs for their dependents, and for the basic workers and their dependents. As a result our city has an estimated total of 15,000 business establishments, 100 charitable organizations, and 150 professional athletes. There are 92 elementary and 19 high schools. Churches number more than 400. The municipal airport handles 40,000 flights a year with 500,000 passengers using the facilities. The city is governed by 9970 municipal employees (see Table 39-2).

Effect of the Multiplication Factor on Stability of the Community

The ratio of basic to service employment can vary rather widely in the same city depending on the business activities. In Wichita, Kansas, the ratio varied from 1 to 2.5 in 1939, to 1 to .6 in 1944. This variation is a large one and was brought about largely by fluctuation in airplane production. Figure 39-1 shows the basic (export) employment, total employment, and population of Wichita from 1939 to

[3]Edward R. Ullman, "The Basic-Service Ratio and the Areal Support of Cities," in David A. Revzan and Ernest A. Engelbert (eds.), *Proceedings, Western Committee on Regional Economic Analysis*, Social Science Research Council, University of California, June 25-27, 1953, pp. 110-123.

[4]Medford, Oregon (20,000 population), basic to service ratio, 1 to .8; Oshkosh, Wisconsin (42,000), basic to service ratio, 1 to .6; Albuquerque, New Mexico (100,000), basic to service ratio, 1 to .9; Madison, Wisconsin (110,000), basic to service ratio, 1 to .8; Brockton area, Massachusetts (120,000), basic to service ratio, 1 to .8.

[5]Ullman, "The Basic-Service Ratio . . . ," *op. cit.*, p. 120. Cf. the newly developed "minimum expectation method" as shown in Ullman's *Major Characteristics of the San Francisco Economic Base*, Discussion Paper No. 8, University of Washington, June 24, 1958.

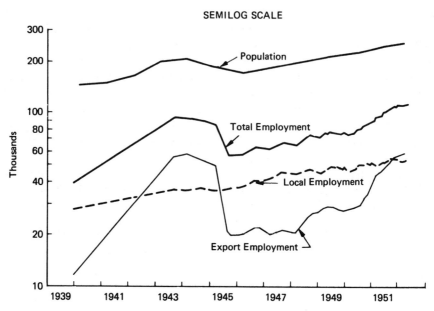

FIGURE 39-1. Employment and Population in Wichita, 1939-1952. On a
semilogarithmic graph, equal slopes indicate equal rates of change. The
population change appears small, even though it amounted to 80 percent,
because of the scale adopted to accommodate the wide fluctuations in
export employment. (Monthly Review, Agricultural and Business Conditions,
Tenth Federal Reserve District, Federal Reserve Bank of Kansas City,
September 30, 1952.)

1952. The impact of the war economy
and the rapid rise of basic (export)
employment can be seen. Its multiplying
effect on total employment and population appears small because of the semilogarithmic graph, but the population
change amounted to 80 percent over the
period 1939-1952.

This multiplication factor can be very
serious in the augmented impact of basic
activities in a community where one basic
industry provides the bulk of employment
in manufacturing. In Seattle, Washington,
the Boeing Aircraft Company is the largest employer of labor. It is an employer
whose principal product (Boeing bombers
and missiles) fluctuates with war and
defense needs of the nation. These
marked fluctuations in basic employment
have repercussions throughout the entire
community. The President of the Seattle
Chamber of Commerce, Mr. Thomas N.,
Pelly, in 1951 voiced feelings that have
been repeatedly emphasized.

Seattle furnishes one of the nation's prime
examples as to what might and could occur
if a single industry became the basis for our
entire living. I am speaking of the Boeing
Airplane Company, one of the city's really
great businesses. Eleven short years ago
Boeing employed a little more than 5,000
persons; seven years ago employment at
Boeing jumped to in excess of 45,733 but in
the following year, 1945, more than 35,000
workers suddenly found themselves without
a job. In 1947, employment went up again
to almost 17,000 but dropped within five
months to 6,740. These are violent fluctuations causing great instability, not only in
the lives of individuals and their families,
but in the activities of hundreds of related
businesses and their employees.[6]

Since 1951 the Boeing Airplane Company has continued to expand at a rapid
rate. The pay roll in 1954 was $6,000,000
a week.[7] Every community facility feels
the impact of the rise in basic employment. Hundreds of homes are needed

[6]*Seattle Times*, Sunday, August 19, 1951.
[7]*Ibid.*, June 14, 1957.

monthly for new workers. Over 500 rental units a month are required by the Boeing workers. Schools, churches, restaurants, stores, parks, garages, highways—all feel the demand for more services. Labor force figures show the addition of approximately one more service-supporting worker employed in Seattle for every new worker brought into the community for work in the airplane company.[8] Population is increasing sevenfold for each additional worker added in manufacturing. The threat of a possible cut-back in Boeing production is a threat that sends the same magnification of fears at the thought of the impact on the entire community. The present mayor, like his predecessors, keeps calling for new and diversified industry. Mayor Gordon S. Clinton has warned the community that "the aircraft industry has become synonymous with Seattle. The past year saw an accelerated program of new employees for industry. While this expansion is welcomed by the community it has the effect of throwing our economy still further out of balance. The fact is that we are not growing industrially with that type of balanced diversification which means stabilized growth."[9]

It may be concluded that industry determines not only size of the community, but also that the industrial base may greatly affect the stability of the community. Furthermore, industry plays a dominant role in the growth patterns of various communities.

INDUSTRY SHAPES THE GROWTH PATTERNS OF THE COMMUNITY

The Life Cycle of a Community

Most communities seem destined to live and to die. Some may have rebirths like Athens and Rome, but all cities are constantly expanding or contracting with the vicissitudes of geographic, biological, and social change. The life of some communities follows short cycles of life and growth; others have very long lives. A mining town, for example, appears with the discovery and demand for the resources its area possesses. When the resources vanish, only the ghostlike shadow of its former prosperity remains. This may happen in a decade or two. A community built on a sole resource which is exhausted very slowly or on a trade and industrial complex might well have a life cycle spanning centuries.

Paul Landis studied the three iron-mining towns of Virginia, Hibbing, and Eveleth, Minnesota, over a time period extending from 1895 to 1930.[10] He found that these towns characteristically experienced three phases of a relatively short life cycle. These were: (1) a rapid growth to maturity, (2) a period of relatively stable population, and then (3) a rapid decline. He found that the towns exhibited four kinds of synchronous cycles which he called physicosocial, cultural, biosocial, and psychosocial. The physicosocial cycle refers to an early period of quest and discovery of ore; the subsequent period of exploitation which soon brought shipments above discoveries and hastened the depletion of high-grade ore; and, third, a period of conservation of a rapidly diminishing resource.

The rhythm in cultural cycles is exhi-

[8]The Employment Security Department reported the county's average manufacturing employment increased 6100 between 1955 and 1956 in Seattle. Total wage and salary earners increased 12,200. This indicates one new job created outside of basic industry. Population increased in the county to 818,700, a gain of 44,800, between 1955 and 1956. This relation of the basic employment increase of 6100 to the total population gain of 44,800 represents a multiplication factor for population of approximately 1 to 7. E. B. Fussell, "Striking Gains in Western and Central State Areas Shown by New Population Studies," *Seattle Times*, March 20, 1957.

[9]*Seattle Times*, June 17, 1957.

[10]Paul H. Landis, *Three Iron Mining Communities*, Edwards, 1938.

bited in three stages of material culture of the community mores. The simple material culture gave way to a lavish material culture which faded into decay with the decline of the community. The mores developed around a tolerance of prostitution, gambling, fighting, and drinking, later to be succeeded by a reform of vice but an establishment of patronage and extravagance. As ore reserves declined, economy mores emerged.

The biosocial cycle refers to the growth of population. In the beginning the mining town is composed of adults, probably consisting chiefly of single young men, between the ages of 20 to 40, venturesome in temperament and full of vitality and courage. The second period is characterized by an abnormally large adult population. Declining opportunity will cause youth to leave for fields of opportunity elsewhere. The old will remain with vested interests in the community. The psychosocial cycle refers to the group attitudes as these changed from an early period of community integration when people worked together in the face of common dangers. This was followed by the ascendancy of the large mining company when conflict developed between the community and the mining company. High taxes were levied against the mining companies, and towns began a regime of spending that led the companies to institute lawsuits and various restraining actions against town building and recreation programs. This continued until companies became more powerful and made the communities bow to tax policies more advantageous to them. . . .

Four Patterns of Growth

These three iron-mining towns demonstrate a life cycle that can be observed in one generation. Thus, time is telescoped and it is possible to study the full cycle. This is ordinarily not possible because cities outlive the observer. But it is possible to observe cities in various stages of their growth pattern and to see how industry affects them. Over a given time period, growth patterns of communities may be of four major types. These include the pattern of *rapid growth*, the pattern of *continuous growth*, the pattern of *relatively stable growth*, and the pattern of *decline*. These are patterns which correspond to the phase of a cycle and any community might exhibit any of these phases in any sequence. A cross section of American communities at any given time will exhibit all of these patterns of growth. . . .

The rapid growth pattern in the United States is occurring largely in the cities located along the Gulf Coast, in the Southwest, and in the West. Here industry is booming because of increased discovery and use of oil and gas, the increase in such war industry production as shipbuilding and airplane manufacturing, and the growth of many new civilian industries. Available labor and space facilities have encouraged growth. Increasingly, amenities such as climate attract the sick and the healthy, the young and the old.

Intensive studies have been made of the boom pattern in some cities. Havighurst and Morgan report on Seneca, Illinois, a small town of 1235 in 1942 with a population of 6600 two years later. The boom was due to the location of a shipyard next to the village. Eighty-two million dollars were paid in wages in a little less than three years to the shipyard workers. To care for the inrush of workers, public housing projects were built; business, churches, and schools expanded; and the whole institutional complex of the village was transformed.[11] Carr and Stermer describe a similar process of boom in Willow Run, a village

[11]Robert Havighurst and H. Gerthon Morgan, *The Social History of a War Boom Community*, Longmans, Green, 1951.

transformed by the entry of airplane manufacture.[12]

The continuous growth pattern is appearing in cities that are developing new industries and expanding established industries. New industries especially stimulate rapid growth. The DuPont Company has adopted a policy of decentralizing its operations in relatively small cities over the United States, placing plants in 25 sites in 14 different states. At Montague, Michigan, the new neoprene plant is pumping a $2,000,000 annual pay roll into nearby communities. Carefully planned training programs, a month of tune-up operations, and dummy process runs have helped 200 new employees step from local farms, shops, and schoolrooms into a twentieth century chemical plant. These employees become the basic employment which sets the multiplication factor operating to increase service employment and population. New industry is one source of rapid growth, expansion of established industry is another. In an interdependent economy the demand of one expanding industry often sends repercussions throughout a large part of the entire economy. The supply requirements of the Boeing Airplane Company call upon every state in the nation for raw materials and parts.

Diversified cities with a broad base of industries create an especially stable economic base for the community. If these industries support systematic research and introduce new products, industry maintains its vitality and strengthens its position.

The slow or constant level growth pattern may be found where a city has developed an established economy which remains in a relatively stable position. A consumer goods industry like flour milling and food processing has a relatively

steady demand for its products. If the community is an agricultural service center it may continue for years with a slow growth pattern, since its hinterland is probably making a fairly steady demand for services. The community with a stable growth pattern may be facing a real decline. A shift in technology or in service may have placed it in a disadvantaged position.

The diminished or declining growth pattern is often associated with exhaustion of resources or a shift in technology. The cities with gross declines are in coal and iron mining areas where mechanization of production and decline in the richer or less costly produced ores have brought reductions in populations. Some cities die slowly, some rapidly. The standard metropolitan area of Scranton, Pennsylvania, demonstrates a declining growth pattern of long duration:

	Population	Percent Change
1910	250,570	
1920	286,311	10.3
1930	310,397	8.4
1940	301,243	−2.9
1950	257,396	

Scranton may be considered as in decline since 1910, when its growth was less than the average population growth in the United States. It may continue to decline, to stabilize at a lower level, or attract new industry and experience a stable growth pattern. With its large population, its immediate life is not threatened with extinction.

The West is dotted with mining towns that have disappeared. Many of the lumber producing towns have experienced decline due to depletion of the forests. The manager of the Elma, Washington, Chamber of Commerce has described the plight of his town:

In the beginning the forests ran like a green sea down to the little city. The great timber was fought like . . . an enemy. Pioneers hacked it, burned it, dissipated it

[12]Lowell J. Carr and James E. Stermer, *Willow Run, A Study in Industrialization and Cultural Inadequacy*, Harper, 1952.

in an effort to make a clearing. Loggers cut it ruthlessly and with no thought to perpetuate the stand. Yes, even worse than that— they utilized only the finest trees, and had no thought of the morrow. Everything was incidental to the logging and milling of the timber. Although Elma was situated in the great valley of the Chehalis, with rich and fertile soil at hand, farming was casual. The camps and mills offered a security of wage— the farm was merely a place of retreat. After a while men looked at the valleys and the hills and the timber was gone. By that time farming and dairying had attained a precarious dignity, there were substantial business buildings, churches, high schools; the country was gridironed with fine roads, with rural mail service—what's the use of continuing the story? It is that of several hundred communities west of the [Cascade] mountains. There had been the exhilaration, and then the sobering realization.[13]

Technological change is another factor constantly threatening the growth pattern of the community. Charles R. Walker in Steeltown[14] describes the impact of such a change on Ellwood City, Pennsylvania, when the national Tube Company announced that operations of its plant there would be moved to Gary, Indiana. The change was brought about in part by new technical requirements of continuous seamless tube mills. The company employed 4000 workers, two-thirds of the city's industrial workers, in a city of 14,000. The announcement brought first shock and resentment. Then a struggle to keep the plant followed. Finally, efforts were turned to acquiring new industry for the community.

In the Western part of the United States, Caliente, Nevada, a small railroad town, was also being faced with technical change. Cottrell describes how the introduction of the diesel locomotive brought new maintenance requirements. As the distance between servicing points was lengthened, Caliente was bypassed; and for Caliente this was death—death by

dieselization: "Those who have raised children see friendships broken and neighborhoods disintegrated. The childless more freely shake the dust of Caliente from their feet. Those who built their personalities into the structure of the community watch their work destroyed."[15]

Four growth patterns have been described. Each has implications for the life of the community. These patterns result from many different causes. Increasingly, all these growth patterns become dependent on events and the actions of people far removed from the immediate community. Yet it is the local community which must adjust to the economic forces which condition its growth or decline.

INDUSTRY DIFFERENTIATES THE COMMUNITY BY FUNCTIONAL TYPE AND OCCUPATIONAL COMPOSITION

Functional Types

The most widely accepted functional classification of cities was made by Chauncy D. Harris.[16] Nine principal types of cities are recognized, and each type is designated by a letter and definition (see p. 521).

These classifications reveal that one-fourth of the cities over 10,000 population in the United States are manufacturing cities; a little more than one-fifth are either industrial cities or diversified cities in which manufacturing predominates; one-eighth are diversified cities in which

---

[13]E. S. Avery in The Elma Survey, Washington State Planning Council, 1941, p. 1.

[14]Harper, 1950.

[15]W. F. Cottrell, "Death by Dieselization: A Case Study in the Reaction to Technological Change," American Sociological Review, June, 1951.

[16]Chauncy D. Harris, "A Functional Classification of Cities in the United States," Geographical Review, January, 1943, pp. 86-99; cf. Grace Kneedler Ohlson, "Economic Classification of Cities," Municipal Yearbook, 1949, pp. 31-39; Victor Jones, "Economic Classification of Cities and Metropolitan Areas," Municipal Yearbook, 1953, pp. 49-54, 69; Howard J. Nelson, "A Service Classification of American Cities," Economic Geography, July, 1955, pp. 189-210.

Type of City	Criteria
M'—manufacturing city (predominantly manufacturing)	Employment in manufacturing equals 74 percent or more of the total employment in manufacturing, retailing, and wholesaling. The manufacturing and mechanical industries contain at least 45 percent of the gainful workers.
M—manufacturing city (manufacturing with other characteristics)	Employment in manufacturing equals at least 60 percent of the total employment in manufacturing, retailing, and wholesaling. The manufacturing and mechanical industries contain between 20 and 45 percent of the gainful workers.
R—retail city	Employment in retailing is 50 percent or more of the total employment in manufacturing, wholesaling, and retailing, and at least 2.2 times that in wholesaling alone.
D—diversified city	Employment in manufacturing, wholesaling, and retailing, is less than 60 percent, 20 percent, and 50 percent, respectively, of total employment in these activities. No other special criteria apply. (Manufacturing and mechanical industries, with few exceptions, contain between 25 percent and 35 percent of the gainful workers.)
W—wholesale city	Employment in wholesaling is at least 20 percent of the total employment in manufacturing, wholesaling, and retailing, and at least 45 percent as much as retailing alone.
T—transportation city	Transportation and communication contain at least 11 percent of the gainful workers, and workers in transportation and communication equal at least one-third the number in manufacturing and mechanical industries, and at least two-thirds the number in trade.
S—mining town	Extraction of minerals accounts for more than 15 percent of the gainful workers (applied only to cities of 25,000 and over for which data are available).
E—university town	Enrollment in schools of collegiate rank (university, technical schools, liberal arts college and teachers colleges) equaled at least 25 percent of the city population (1940).
X—resort and retirement town	No satisfactory criterion found.

retailing predominates; one-sixth are residential cities; and the remaining cities have single functions, for example, mining, transportation, education, resort, or government.

Manufacturing, wholesale and retail trade, and transportation are the fundamental economic functions to keep in mind, for even the state capitals, educational, recreational, cultural, and religious centers are largely dependent upon these basic economic activities to furnish employment for the bulk of the labor force.[17] If cities were classified by the proportion of manufacturing, Gary, Indiana, would emerge as the manufacturing city par excellence. It has 68.9 percent of its workers engaged in industrial activities. Since Gary is one of Chicago's satellites,

[17]T. Lynn Smith, "The Functions of American Cities," in T. Lynn Smith and C. A. McMahan (eds.), *Urban Life*, Dryden, 1951, p. 102.

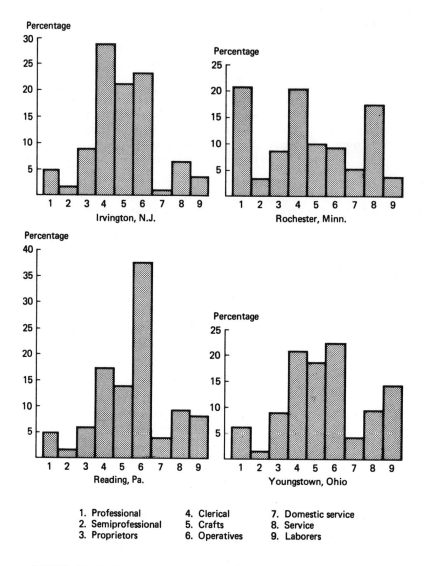

1. Professional   4. Clerical   7. Domestic service
2. Semiprofessional   5. Crafts   8. Service
3. Proprietors   6. Operatives   9. Laborers

FIGURE 39–2. The Occupational Profiles of Four Cities. (Paul Bates Gillen, The Distribution of Occupations as a City Yardstick, King's Crown, 1951, p. 24.)

a great many of the latter city's services and attractions are rather readily available to the people of Gary. Were it not for this fact it would probably not be possible for so large a proportion of the labor force to be engaged in manufacturing. Miami, Florida, Washington, D.C., and Sacramento, California each with manufacturing supplying employment to less than 11 percent, are cities which supply many services to their own population, to many visitors, and to persons outside the city.

Occupational Composition

Cities vary a great deal in their occupational structure. Some cities have a comparatively high proportion of professionals, for example, while others have relatively few employed persons of professional status. Such differences are also characteristic of other occupational groupings. An occupational profile of individual cities brings out these differences quite clearly. Figure 39-2 illustrates the occupational profiles of four cities: Irvington, New Jersey; Rochester, Minnesota; Reading, Pennsylvania; and Youngstown, Ohio.

These profiles suggest different industrial and social functions. Gillen believes that the chief factors which make for the differences between cities are the incomes of the people of the city and the amount of education they possess. His research led him to view the occupational distribution of the city as the single best indicator of these two chief factors.[18] This discovery makes possible an estimate of community character, as will be demonstrated in a following section.

INDUSTRY AFFECTS THE TOTAL LAND-USE PATTERN

Common Patterns

Urban ecology reveals a pattern of spatial and other needs for retailing, wholesaling, and manufacturing. The central business district is the predominant center of retail and wholesale activities and ancillary establishments that serve the needs of workers and shoppers and others who frequent the area. The large department stores are centered here as well as specialized retail shops, hotels, publishing firms, theaters and movie houses, concert halls, travel bureaus, and other establishments providing goods and services to the entire city and its tributary region. The warehouses are usually located close by.

Retail specialization may and does appear in various parts of the city. In the United States the proportion of retail service units outside central business districts tends to increase with size of

[18]Paul Bates Gillen, *The Distribution of Occupations as a City Yardstick*, King's Crown Press, 1951.

city. In the larger cities there are areas or districts devoted exclusively to certain types of stores.

Manufacturing is often divided into heavy industry, which requires a great deal of space and turns out bulky products, and light industry, which includes products of small size and weight and generally requires a small ground area per worker. Heavy industry includes such products manufactured as automobiles, airplanes, petroleum products, farm machinery, flour, sugar, lumber, steel, cement, meat products, railroad cars, and locomotives. Until the late nineteenth century, heavy industry in Europe and the United States tended to locate in the central portions of the cities, near wharves, docks, and railroad sidings and close to the center of supply.

During the twentieth century heavy industry has developed along railroad lines, river valleys, and ocean or lake fronts, commonly on the outskirts of the city or even well beyond the city's boundaries. River valley developments have occurred in the Youngstown, Pittsburgh, and Kansas City areas, while the tendency to locate on water fronts may be noted in the Chicago and Philadelphia districts.

Light industry is commonly at the edge of the central business district near the center of the city. Sometimes wholesaling and light manufacturing establishments are located in the same general area.

Both heavy and light industry may seek locations farther away from the central business district to positions toward the outskirts of the city or across a city's boundaries into peripheral areas. Among the reasons for such decentralization may be a need for more space, access to ground water, lower rentals, lower labor costs, lower tax rates, and freedom from zoning restrictions. Developments in transportation, particularly motor transport trucks and belt railroad lines linked with the regular railway systems, have helped to free industry of its direct dependence on central freight terminals. A survey by Woodbury and his associates presents considerable evidence of decentralization in the United States.[19] The yardstick used by Woodbury is the percentage change in production workers in central cities, satellite cities, and industrial peripheries (outside of the central city). From 1899 to 1947, there was a long-run decline from 39.5 percent to 32.2 percent of manufacturing workers found in the central city, with an increase of 14.6 percent to 19.8 percent in the periphery.

Residential areas are settled in accordance with the location of the industrial and commercial functions. While zoning restrictions may effectively bar the invasion of stores and factories, the prevalence of spot zoning and ribbon developments of business dispersion along streets, highways, and rail lines opens the residential district to invasion or the threat of invasion. Home owners, in a dynamic American city, are always on the move, seeking quiet and clean districts where residential property may be protected from the growth of business and industry.

Theories of City Growth

A number of urban ecologists have attempted to go beyond mere description of land patterns to the formulation of a set of theories or hypotheses concerning the ecology of the city. E. W. Burgess has

[19]Coleman Woodbury (ed.), *The Future of Cities and Urban Redevelopment*, University of Chicago Press, 1953, pp. 253-255.

suggested the concentric zone theory, which postulates an inner zone comprising the central business district, a zone of transition, a zone of workingmen's homes, a zone of middle-class dwellers, and a commuters' zone. Homer Hoyt has formulated a sector theory of urban development which recognizes the distinctive patterns which follow radial transportation lines connecting the central business district with outlying areas. These extensions reaching out into the peripheral zones give the city its star-shaped configuration. Industrial areas develop along river valleys, water courses, and railroad lines. The high-rent residential areas tend to be located along established transportation routes, usually on high ground and away from the "flats." The major highways which radiate out from the central city are commonly lined with commercial establishments.

There have been many criticisms of these theories as not fitting conditions in certain cities which have been studied, but they remain as useful guides to the understanding of land use in the community. Each theory recognizes the importance of industrial functions in determining the location of residential and other nonindustrial functions of the community. Paul Meadows has expressed the correlation of industry with urban life in these words: "Urbanization is the indispensable partner of industrialization, the measure of its growth, the mirror of its complexities, the interpreter of its values, and the matrix of its expansion."[20] . . .

[20]Paul Meadows, "The Industrial Way of Life," *Technology Review*, March, 1946.

Further Reading

Amos Hawley's *Human Ecology*, New York: Ronald, 1950, a book published some twenty years ago, still contains the best available treatment of the community from the ecological perspective. The latter half of this book is devoted to various aspects of community structure and to change and development processes within communities. The community is analyzed as a social organization or a social system in Roland L. Warren's, *The Community in America*, Skokie, Ill.: Rand McNally, 1963; and in Erwin

T. Sanders, *The Community: An Introduction to a Social System*, New York: Ronald, 1958. Jessie Bernard attempts to combine both the ecological and the social organization perspective in her book, *American Community Behavior* (rev. ed.), New York: Holt, Rinehart and Winston, Inc., 1962.

There are a great many well-known and revealing case studies of communities. Moving along the continuum from rural to urban, one of the best-known studies of a rural village is Robert Redfield, *Tepoztlán—A Mexican Village*, Chicago: University of Chicago Press, 1930. (Redfield's more general notions concerning the folk-urban continuum are contained in *The Folk Culture of Yucatan*, Chicago: University of Chicago Press, 1941, based on his study of four Mexican communities.) The study of Tepoztlán is of a particular interest because this same community was studied by another anthropologist 17 years later with somewhat conflicting results giving rise to a lively controversy as to the validity of Redfield's conclusions and the soundness of his theoretical framework. This latter study was conducted by Oscar Lewis and is reported in *Life in a Mexican Village: Tepoztlán Restudied*, Urbana, Ill.: University of Illinois Press, 1951. Certainly the most famous pair of studies of a small American community are those of Muncie, Indiana, conducted by Robert S. and Helen Merrell Lynd. The first study of this community (*Middletown: A Study in Contemporary American Culture*, New York: Harcourt, 1929) was carried out in the middle 1920s and provides a description of such everyday activities as getting a living, making a home, and training the young. The second study (*Middletown in Transition: A Study in Cultural Conflicts*, New York: Harcourt, 1937) was carried out during the depression years, and the Lynds report a sharpening of class distinctions, the arrival of absentee owner industries, and other changes of importance. We have commented earlier in this book on the important series of studies conducted by W. Lloyd Warner and his associates of Newburyport, Massachusetts, reported in six volumes: The "Yankee City Series" (New Haven, Conn.: Yale University Press). A major focus of this research was the stratification system of the community, but other aspects of community life were also closely examined. Appropriately enough, the most recent well-known study of a small community places great emphasis on the impact of changes in the larger society on life in the small community. This is the study reported by Arthur J. Vidich and Joseph Bensman, *Small Town in Mass Society: Class, Power, and Religion in a Rural Community*, Princeton, N.J.: Princeton University Press, 1958.

There now exist several interesting studies of suburban communities. These include Bennett M. Berger, *Working-Class Suburb*, Berkeley, Calif.: University of California Press, 1960; John R. Seeley, R. Alexander Sim, and Elizabeth W. Loosley, *Crestwood Heights: A Study of the Culture of Suburban Life*, New York: Basic Books, 1956; and Robert C. Wood, *Suburbia: Its People and Their Politics*, Boston: Houghton Mifflin, 1959.

Cities and metropolitan areas are sufficiently complex that investigators typically only explore selected aspects of their structure and operation. However, Scott Greer attempts to provide a comprehensive overview of the modern city in his book *The Emerging City: Myth and Reality*, New York: Free Press of Glencoe, 1962. Interesting comparative materials on early and contemporary non-western cities are explored in Gideon Sjoberg, *The Pre-Industrial City*, New York: Free Press, 1961. References to more specific studies of selected processes and structures within cities will be found in footnotes within this part.

Finally, some of the best articles on the community are conveniently available in several readers that focus on a variety of topics. The most comprehensive of these is Paul K. Hatt and Albert J. Reiss, Jr. (eds.), *Cities and Society* (rev. ed.), Glencoe, Ill.: Free Press, 1957. Sections of that volume are devoted to the spatial and temporal patterns of cities, the demographic structure, the stratification structure, institutions and organizational structures, and the characteristics of the urban dweller. The volume edited by George A. Theodorson, *Studies in Human Ecology*, Evanston, Ill.: Row, Peterson & Company, 1961, as the title suggests, concentrates on the ecological perspective and includes some of the most important papers within this tradition of research. In addition, this reader contains an excellent collection of articles reporting cross-cultural studies of community life and urban structure and contains a good selection of articles on the metropolitan community. A third reader, compiled by Roland L. Warren, *Perspectives on the American Community*, Skokie, Ill.: Rand McNally, 1966, places much greater emphasis on the social organization approach to the study of communities and includes sections devoted to such topics as planned community change and citizen participation in community affairs. Finally, a collection of articles by Rupert B. Vance and Nicholas J. Demerath, *The Urban South*, Chapel Hill, N.C.: The University of North Carolina Press, 1954, describes the changing patterns of community life and the development of a metropolitan system of communities in the Southern portion of the United States.

PART SEVEN

Social Processes in Societies

We cannot and shall not attempt to deal in the final section of this book with the full complexity that is society. Even to attempt a tentative definition of this phenomenon appears to be both premature and presumptuous. Suffice it to say that although societies are composed of the sorts of social units we have been analyzing (small groups, organizations, and communities), they are something more than the sum of these subunits. A society is itself a collectivity—an enormously complex social unit. Societies differ from other types of collectivities not only in degree of complexity but also in extent of self-sufficiency. As Parsons notes, ". . . a society is relatively the most self-sufficient type of social system."[1] This does not mean, of course, that a society is a closed system. On the contrary, societies are subject to the influences of their physical and social environment, and important and often vital exchange relations develop among societies. The assertion is a relative, not an absolute, one.

STRUCTURAL CHARACTERISTICS OF SOCIETIES

If a society is to be viewed as a collectivity, it should possess its own identifiable normative and social structure. The basic normative structures of societies are social institutions, and it is to these important elements that we now turn our attention.

Social Institutions　　Following Williams, we may define a social institution as a set of "norms that cohere around a relatively distinct and socially important complex of values."[2] Institutions, then, are not themselves collectivities but are normative elements—norms, values, and role expectations—interrelated so as to provide a set of guidelines for social behavior and structures. As Parsons notes,

[1]Talcott Parsons, *Societies: Evolutionary and Comparative Perspectives*, Englewood Cliffs, N.J.: Prentice-Hall, 1966, p. 3.
[2]Robin M. Williams, Jr., *American Society* (2d ed.), New York: Knopf, 1960, p. 31.

527

institutions are "a complex of patterned elements in role expectations which may apply to an indefinite number of collectivities."[3] To speak of the institution of "property," for example, is to refer to a set of norms defining role expectations concerning certain rights and duties with respect to the possession of various kinds of objects (for example, land, buildings, and other material commodities). These norms are applicable and binding on behaviors occurring within a broad range of specific kinds of collectivities.

Blau has suggested three criteria that help to distinguish institutions from other types of normative systems. He argues, first, that

> Institutionalization involves *formalized procedures* that perpetuate organizing principles of social life from generation to generation . . . . Formalized rules make an organized pattern of social relations and conduct independent of particular human beings, which is the first requirement of a social institution. Other requirements of institutionalization are that the rules of conduct be *legitimated by traditional values* and *enforced by powerful groups*, thereby being resistant against ready change.[4]

Blau goes on to suggest an interesting parallel between social structure and individual behavior on the one hand and social institutions and social structure on the other hand. He argues that just as a given social structure exerts certain constraints on the behavior of individuals within that structure, as we have seen in earlier sections of this volume, in the same manner social institutions exert constraints on particular social structures.

> Institutionalization involves *formalized procedures* that perpetuate organizing principles of social life from generation to generation . . . . Formalized rules make an organized pattern of social relations and conduct independent of particular human

This is not to suggest that the norms embodied in social institutions are unchanging and eternal. Just as human actions can, over time, change social structures, collective actions can bring about changes in social institutions, although the latter process is much more difficult and proceeds much more slowly. Blau argues:

> While the rebellion of children against their parents and, especially, the deprivations produced by political oppression or economic exploitation sometimes lead to the rejection of traditional values, only *selected* political or economic values are usually rejected. The major part of the cultural heritage tends to persist, even in periods of revolutionary transformations.[6]

A major problem confronting the student of institutions is how they are to be distinguished or classified. Williams' definition of institution suggests that this problem be approached by attempting to identify "relatively distinct and socially important" complexes of values. Williams provides some examples of the use of this principle of classification as follows:

> American society, for instance, like any other, must somehow deal with sexual activity, the care of dependent children, and the social relations established by sexual unions and the birth of children. The institutional norms concerned with these matters constitute the *familial* or *kinship institutions* of the society. Similarly, there is in every society a set of functional problems centering around the coercion of some individuals by others. The problem of power is a central fact of political life, and it is convenient to

---

[3]Talcott Parsons, *The Social System*, Glencoe, Ill.: Free Press, 1951, p. 39.
[4]Peter M. Blau, *Exchange and Power in Social Life*, New York: Wiley, 1964, pp. 273 274. Emphasis ours.
[5]Blau, p. 277.
[6]Blau, p. 275. Emphasis ours.

group together the norms regulating power as the *political institutions* of the society.[7]

Proceeding on this basis, Williams goes on to distinguish six types of institutions: kinship and family, social stratification, economic, political, educational, and religious institutions. Many such lists have been compiled, some longer and some shorter.[8]

Talcott Parsons has devoted a great deal of continuing effort toward developing a more abstract and general approach to the classification of societal institutions. Attempting to explicate the value distinctions implicit in the famous *gemeinschaft-gesellschaft* dichotomy,[9] Parsons developed five pairs of values as follows:[10]

Gemeinschaft Values	Gesellschaft Values	Description of Dimension
Affective orientation	Affectively neutral orientation	The extent to which an actor's interests are expected to be immediately gratified rather than postponed
Collectivity orientation	Self-orientation	The extent to which it is permissible for the actor to pursue interests private to himself or is expected to pursue collective interests
Particularistic orientation	Universalistic orientation	The extent to which the standards governing one actor's orientation to another are expected to be dependent on or independent of the particular relations that exist between them
Ascriptive orientation	Achievement orientation	The extent to which actors are expected to emphasize the characteristics or qualities versus the performances of others in relating to them
Diffuse orientation	Specific orientation	The extent to which an actor's orientation to another is expected to be specific and interest-segregated as opposed to one that is general and includes many types of interests

At about the same time Robert F. Bales was engaged in his work, described previously in this book, on the small group involved in problem solving. Parsons, Bales, and Edward Shils collaborated in a series of essays out of which emerged a set of abstract categories for classifying normative systems, including institutions.[11] Four of the five value dichotomies delineated by Parsons are combined to arrive at an abstract characterization of four functional sectors, as follows:

[7]Williams, pp. 31–32. Emphasis in original.

[8]See, for example, J. O. Hertzler, *American Social Institutions*, Boston: Allyn and Bacon, 1961; and Kingsley Davis, *Human Society*, New York: Macmillan, 1949.

[9]This distinction was first proposed by the German social theorist Ferdinand Tönnies in *Gemeinschaft und Gesellschaft* (1st ed., 1887), edited and translated by C. P. Loomis as *Fundamental Concepts of Sociology*, New York: American Book Co., 1940. A *Gemeinschaft* is a communal society in which people feel they belong together because they are of the same kind; ties of kinship are paramount. A *Gesellschaft*, by contrast, is an associational society in which the major social bonds are voluntary, based on the rational pursuit of self-interest and defined by contract.

[10]See Parsons, *The Social System*, pp. 58–67; and Parsons and Edward A. Shils, *Toward a General Theory of Action*, Cambridge, Mass.: Harvard University Press, 1951, pp. 76–88.

[11]Talcott Parsons, Robert F. Bales, and Edward A. Shils, *Working Papers in the Theory of Action*, Glencoe, Ill.: Free Press, 1953.

	Universalism Affective Neutrality	Particularism Affectivity
Specificity Achievement	Adaptation	Goal attainment
Diffuseness Ascription	Pattern maintenance	Integration

The four functional sectors so identified are given the following meaning by Parsons and his collaborators:

Adaptation: Attempts to maintain a generalized control over the external situation for the purpose of attaining desired goals

Goal attainment: Attempts to define and realize desired goals

Integration: Attempts to maintain solidarity and cohesion among the system units

Pattern maintenance: Attempts to create, preserve, and transmit the value system that is associated with and instrumental to the regulation of the system activities

The analytical schema devised by Parsons, Bales, and Shils is sufficiently abstract to be applicable to the full range of social systems, including collectivities like small groups and organizations and noncollectivities such as the economy or the stratification system. In their application to entire societies, the four functional sectors suggest appropriate complexes of institutional norms for each area. Thus, from the previous chart it is apparent that behaviors occurring within adaptative institutions, for example, are expected to be governed by norms that emphasize universalism, affective neutrality, specificity, and achievement.

Parsons labels these four areas "functional sectors" because he interprets them as defining four "independent functional imperatives or 'problems' which must be met adequately if equilibrium and/or continuing existence of the system is to be maintained."[12] We prefer not to view these sectors in this fashion because such a functionalist approach does not appear to us to be especially fruitful, as we have noted previously in this book. Instead, we propose to view Parsons' sectors as a useful typology, abstract and comprehensive, of social institutions.

Societal Social Structure   We move now from beliefs about behavior—social norms embodied in institutions—to behavior itself, or, rather, to the complex patterns of behavior that constitute social structures. And, make no mistake about it, the patterns are complex. Informal patterns and small groups do not disappear, but exist alongside formal organizations and institutional structures. As Homans notes:

Elementary social behavior does not grow just in the gaps between institutions; it clings to institutions as to a trellis. It grows everywhere—if only because the norms established as institutions and the orders given in instituted organizations can never

[12]Talcott Parsons and Neil J. Smelser, *Economy and Society*, Glencoe, Ill.: Free Press, 1956, p. 16.

prescribe human behavior to the last detail, even if they were obeyed to the letter, which they are not. Indeed the elementary behavior helps explain how and why they are disobeyed.[13]

Further, in addition to these many levels or layers of structure, there are also innumerable patterned relations between and among them.

Let us agree to studiously avoid this complexity in order to focus our attention exclusively on the institutional level, insofar as this is possible. Social institutions, we have argued, are complexes of social norms, but associated with each institution is an *institutional structure,* a complex of patterned relations and behaviors that is oriented to the norms. Blau provides us with an illustration of this distinction, often a difficult one to make, in his discussion of stratification.

On the one hand, the stratification system consists of a hierarchy of social positions, not the persons who occupy them, that yield differential rewards. On the other hand, the class structure consists of actual collectivities of individuals, not abstract positions, who differ in wealth, power, and prestige. The stratification system is an institution, while class structure is not.[14]

In fact, the social structure associated with the stratification system is even more complex than Blau's comments indicate. Norms embodied in the stratification system apply not only to social classes organized as collectivities, but also to aggregates of persons individually oriented to these norms. They apply not only to groups of persons consciously organized as status groups but also to certain aspects of all organized groups because, as we have seen, relations governed by status considerations develop in all such settings. This is the meaning of Parsons' statement quoted earlier to the effect that the role relations specified by institutional norms apply to an indefinite number of collectivities.

This being the case, we are faced by a considerable problem. How are we to identify the structures that are specifically oriented to one or another social institution? Obviously, we cannot do so in any definite or clear-cut way. Indeed, among the characteristics that distinguish institutions from other types of social norms are their generality and their pervasiveness—their applicability to a broad range of social behavior.

On the other hand, the situation is not as hopeless as it first appears. This, at least, is the view of Parsons, who argues that societies tend to become structurally differentiated along the lines of their functional systems. His basic argument is an evolutionary one in which differentiation occurs along functional lines, enhancing the adaptative capacity of society because the new units can perform their function more effectively. Discussing this process of differentiation, Parsons argues:

A unit, sub-system, or category of units or sub-systems having a single, relatively well-defined place in the society divides into units or systems (usually two) which differ in *both* structure and functional significance for the wider system. To take a familiar example . . . the kinship-organized household in predominantly peasant societies is both the unit of residence and the primary unit of agricultural production. In certain societies, however, most productive work is performed in specialized units, such as workshops, factories, or offices manned by people who are also members of family households. Thus two sets of roles and collectivities have become differentiated, and their functions separated . . . .

If differentiation is to yield a balanced, more evolved system, each newly differenti-

[13]George C. Homans, *Social Behavior: Its Elementary Forms,* New York: Harcourt, 1961, p. 391.

[14]Blau, pp. 278–279.

ated sub-structure (e.g., the producing organization in the above case) must have increased adaptive capacity for performing its *primary* function, as compared to the performance of *that* function in the previous, more diffuse structure. Thus economic production is typically more efficient in factories than in households. We may call this process the *adaptive upgrading* aspect of the evolutionary change cycle.[15]

Perhaps it is not clear why structural differentiation should occur along functional lines. To explain this tendency it is only necessary to recall Parsons' typology of social institutions based on differing combinations of norms. We need only argue that some norms are more appropriate for regulating some kinds of activities than are others. Using the same example—the tendency for productive enterprise to be separated from the family—we have in Parsons' schema the differentiation of productive arrangements which are better carried out under norms of universalism, affective neutrality, specificity, and achievement (the adaptative institution), from family and kinship relations, better carried out under norms of particularism, affectivity, diffuseness, and ascription (the integrative institution).

Pursuing this argument, advanced societies should exhibit considerable structural differentiation along functional lines. Associated with each of the functional sectors should be one or more types of specialized social structures. For Parsons, the *economy* is the institutional structure that is specialized in performing the adaptive functions for the society. Goal attainment functions are located in the *polity* composed of such "political" structures as the state, other organs of government, and certain aspects of financial systems. Social structures relatively specialized in integrative functions include the legal system, the structures of stratification, welfare organizations, a large variety of interest groups, and certain role components of the family (those having to do with the stabilization of the personalities of adult members—see Reading 41). Finally, pattern maintenance functions are primarily carried out by the social structures that are regarded as serving cultural, educational, or expressive functions, such as churches, schools, scientific research organizations, and the components of family structures having to do with the socialization of the young.

The attempt to assign specific roles or social structures to one or another of the functional sectors presupposes that the roles and structures are sufficiently specialized to permit such a classification, and this, in turn, presupposes a relatively advanced stage of societal differentiation. Further, no single person or collectivity is so specialized that he performs a single societal function: such units are always multifunctional. As Parsons notes, " . . . concrete structures do not follow the lines of differentiation of system-function exactly."[16] Nevertheless, with all its problems, this approach to the study of institutional structure is one of the more interesting attempts to begin to deal with the complexity that is society.

[15]Parsons, *Societies*, p. 22. Emphasis in original.
[16]Talcott Parsons, "A revised analytical approach to the theory of social stratification," in Reinhard Bendix and Seymour Martin Lipset (eds.), *Class, Status and Power*, Glencoe, Ill.: Free Press, 1953, p. 101.

Section I

INTEGRATIVE PROCESSES IN SOCIETIES

In our introductory discussion to this part, much emphasis has been placed on the role of certain norms and values—social institutions—in providing pattern and order in the society at large. Indeed, Blau has argued that such institutions constitute the "mediating mechanism" that guides and adjusts relations among the various types of social structures that make up the society. He argues:

> The cultural values and norms that prevail in a society are the matrix that forms the social relations among groups and individuals. These values and norms become institutionalized and perpetuated from generation to generation, although not without modification, and they shape the course of social life in the society and the social patterns that emerge in particular groups.[1]

The view that social institutions and institutionalized social structures function as the central integrating processes in modern societies has been severely challenged by another perspective—the view that modern society is increasingly a mass society.

The Concept of Mass Society   As Daniel Bell shows in Reading 40, mass society has been defined by many writers in many different ways. Probably the clearest statement on the subject is that of William Kornhauser. Kornhauser indicates that although the notion has two distinct intellectual sources—two very diverse groups critical of society—they can be reconciled and suggests that, indeed, both are required in order to provide a complete conception. The first intellectual source, termed the *aristocratic* tradition, was generated in the nineteenth-century reaction to revolutionary changes in European society, especially the French Revolution and the radical impetus it was continuing to provide. This view of mass society "found the decisive social process to be the loss of exclusiveness of elites and the rise of mass participation in cultural and political life."[2] These critics, chief among whom were Jacob Burckhardt[3] and Gustave Le Bon,[4] saw in these great social upheavals the loss of traditional authority and institutional control and the specter of rule by an incompetent and barbaric mass. In the critics' view, elites are the preservers and protectors of social and cultural values. The critics felt that when the untutored masses obtain high access to these governing groups (either through such procedures as direct elections or through the notion that public opinion should be sovereign), values are debased and destroyed.

[1]Peter M. Blau, *Exchange and Power in Social Life*, New York: Wiley, 1964, p. 253.
[2]William Kornhauser, *The Politics of Mass Society*, Glencoe, Ill.: Free Press, 1959, p. 21.
[3]Jacob Burckhardt, *Force and Freedom*, New York: Meridian, 1955 (first published 1905).
[4]Gustave Le Bon, *The Crowd*, London: Ernest Bonn, 1947 (first published 1895).

533

The second intellectual source, termed the *democratic* tradition, had its origin in the twentieth-century reaction to the rise of totalitarianism. Such writers as Emil Lederer[5] and Hannah Arendt[6] found the decisive social process giving rise to mass society to be "the loss of insulation of non-elites and the rise of elites bent on total mobilization of a population."[7] They see the conditions giving rise to a mass society not in the trends toward social equality but in the tendencies producing isolation and amorphous social relations within a society. They point to the growing atomization of relations—the loss of "community"—and see this as the seedbed of tyranny, in that people who lack community will settle for the pseudocommunity offered by totalitarianism. "In short, *people who are atomized readily become mobilized.*"[8]

Kornhauser argues that although the aristocratic and the democratic conceptions of mass society arose in response to differing social conditions and hence place emphasis on differing facets of the phenomena, they are not irreconcilable perspectives. He suggests that

these two versions of the mass society differ in their conception of freedom and the social foundations of freedom. One sees mass society as a set of conditions under which elites are exposed to mass pressure. The other conceives of mass society as a set of conditions under which non-elites are exposed to elite pressures. Nevertheless, they share a common image of mass society as the *naked society*, where the direct exposure of social units to outside forces makes freedom precarious.[9]

Further, each perspective requires the other:

The democratic criticism of mass society requires for its completion the notion of accessible elites provided by aristocratic critics . . . [and] the negative consequences of accessible elites envisioned by aristocratic critics are greatly increased when non-elites are available by virture of the loss of community.[10]

We arrive, then, at the following definition of the concept of *mass society:*

Mass society is a social system in which elites are readily accessible to influence by non-elites and non-elites are readily available for mobilization by elites.[11]

As we shall discuss subsequently, a mass society is often a transitory state of the social system. It is a volatile state that is likely to be transformed in the direction of totalitarianism.

The Structure of Mass Society   Having defined the concept of mass society, we may examine more carefully its structural characteristics, implicit in the preceding discussion. It is useful to view the social relations that together comprise society as existing at three levels: personal or primary relations; relations that link all members of the population to the state or other embodiment of the total society; and relationships that are at an intermediate level between primary relations and relations at a societal level. The latter set of relations include those that link individuals in voluntary associations, in occupational groups and organizations, and in local government and community. In Kornhauser's view, the structure of mass society is characterized by " (1) the

[5]Emil Lederer, *State of the Masses*, New York: Norton, 1940.
[6]Hannah Arendt, *The Origins of Totalitarianism* (2d ed.), New York: Meridian, 1958 (first published by Harcourt, 1951).
[7]Kornhauser, p. 22.
[8]Kornhauser, p. 33. Emphasis in original.
[9]Kornhauser, p. 23. Emphasis in original.
[10]Kornhauser, p. 37.
[11]Kornhauser, p. 39.

weakness of intermediate relations, (2) the isolation of primary relations, and (3) the centralization of national relations."[12]

The first structural feature (the weakness of intermediate relations) accounts for the "nakedness" within a society: elites and nonelites confront one another directly, without the complex of mediating links and substructures that stabilize relations and provide appropriate channels of communication and influence. Lipset, Trow, and Coleman argue that "the struggles of various groups—class, religious, sectional, economic, professional, and so on—against one another and against the group which controls the state" gives rise to tolerance if no one group is strong enough to gain complete power.[13]

Further,

These organizations serve as channels of communication among different groups in the population, crystallizing and organizing conflicting interests and opinions. Their existence makes more difficult the triumph of such movements as Communism and Fascism, for a variety of groups lay claim to the allegiance of the population, reinforcing diversity of belief and helping mobilize such diversity in the political arena.[14]

The second and third structural features—the isolation of primary relations and the centralization of national relations—require little elaboration. Primary relations can continue to exist in the mass society if they do not become the basis for social or political organization on a broader scale. In the absence of healthy, independent, intermediate units—characteristic of a *pluralistic* society—the state can and does expand to fill the vacuum in the interest of preserving unity and order.

The social conditions that tend to give rise to mass society include the following: severe social discontinuities that undermine the legitimacy of authority; discontinuities that disrupt community ties, such as rapid urbanization or rapid industrialization; and other types of discontinuities, such as economic depressions and wars.[15] It is of more than passing interest to note that Germany, the major Western country to undergo a totalitarian regime in this century, experienced *all* these types of disruptions virtually simultaneously. Kornhauser argues: ". . . major discontinuities in social process produce mass movements by destroying pre-established intermediate relations and by preventing the formation of new associations aligned with the social order."[16] In other words, some social upheavals may be sufficiently severe that older institutionalized social structures are rendered useless and provide no satisfactory guidelines for behavior. Individual members of the society are cut loose from their social moorings. The old patterns no longer work; the society is in a state of normlessness or *anomie*.

It has been claimed that the United States is, or is well on the way toward becoming, a mass society. Those who make this claim point to the increasing industrialization and urbanization of this country with their disruptive effects on community, the increasing reliance on mass communication techniques, the

---

[12]Kornhauser, p. 75.

[13]Seymour Martin Lipset, Martin A. Trow, and James S. Coleman, *Union Democracy*, Glencoe, Ill.: Free Press, 1956, p. 15.

[14]Lipset, Trow, and Coleman, p. 16.

[15]See Kornhauser, pp. 129–174.

[16]Kornhauser, p. 128.

increasing centralization of power at the national level, and so on. In Reading 40, Daniel Bell examines the evidence for and against this thesis. Bell, writing in the mid-1950s, may be a bit more sanguine about the condition of our society than he would be if he were viewing this topic in the light of the tumultuous changes of the 1960s. Based on the advantages of fifteen more years of experience, we may disagree with some of his answers to the questions he poses. Nevertheless, the questions themselves remain a valuable guide to inquiry in this complex area.

The Characteristics of Totalitarian Society   A mass society is not a totalitarian society, but it does provide the conditions under which one is likely to develop. Socially isolated and disoriented individuals are more likely to turn for guidance to leaders with emotional appeals and quick and easy solutions to the problems of the society. As Arendt comments:

Totalitarian movements are mass organizations of atomized, isolated individuals. Compared with all other parties and movements, their most conspicuous external characteristic is their demand for total, unrestricted, unconditional, and unalterable loyalty of the individual member. . . . Such loyalty can be expected only from the completely isolated human being who, without any other social ties to family, friends, comrades, or even mere acquaintances, derives his sense of having a place in the world only from his belonging to a movement, his membership in the party.[17]

A totalitarian society emerges to the extent that new elites arise and consolidate their power in ways that involve direct and centralized control over the population. In short, in Kornhauser's terms, a totalitarian society is one in which there is an *inaccessible* elite that sustains a system of total control from above over an *available* nonelite.[18]

It might be supposed that totalitarian societies merely supplant differentiated social institutions and their related social structures with a single set of institutionalized norms and values supporting a monolithic social structure. Although this description may fit some of the autocratic regimes of the past, it apparently does not accurately describe totalitarian societies of this century. Rather than developing a fixed set of social institutions, totalitarian societies are more likely to espouse "laws of movement" that are presumably "laws of nature" or "laws of history." Friedrich and Brzezinski explain the nature and uses of such laws.

The totalitarian ideology tends to dissolve the normative in the existential realm, and to consider all ordinary laws merely as expressions of laws of nature and history. "All history is the history of class struggles," for example, would be such a law in terms of which the positive legal order must be structured; it provides the standard by which to measure positive laws, to interpret and if necessary to alter and break them. All laws become fluid when they are treated merely as the emanation of such laws of movement, and their very multiplicity testifies to their normative weakness. Such fluidity makes them incapable of serving as standards of responsible conduct, since every violation can be argued away by the rulers as merely an adaptation to the higher laws of movement.[19]

By refusing to provide a stable set of norms and values, leaders hope to keep the

[17]Arendt, pp. 323–324.
[18]Kornhauser, pp. 40–41.
[19]Carl J. Friedrich and Zbigniew K. Brzezinski, *Totalitarian Dictatorship and Autocracy*, New York: Frederick A. Praeger, 1961, p. 5 (originally published by the Harvard University Press, 1956).

masses off balance and uncertain—"both Hitler and Stalin held out promises of stability in order to hide their intention of creating a state of permanent instability"[20]—and at the same time preserve maximum freedom of action for themselves. This instability in the institutional sphere, in the laws and norms that regulate behavior, is reflected also in the actual structures of totalitarian society. As Arendt notes:

> What strikes the observer of the totalitarian state is certainly not its monolithic structure. On the contrary, all serious students of the subject agree at least on the co-existence (or the conflict) of a dual authority, the party and the state. Many, moreover, have stressed the peculiar "shapelessness" of the totalitarian government.[21]

"Shapeless" and indeterminate structures have their functions, as Arendt points out:

> One should not forget that only a building can have a structure, but that a movement—if the word is to be taken as seriously and as literally as the Nazis meant it—can have only a direction, and that any form of legal or governmental structure can be only a handicap to a movement which is being propelled with increasing speed in a certain direction.[22]

In short, in the case of totalitarianism, we are dealing not with a particular kind of social institution but with the absence of social institutions; and, rather than the presence of a particular kind of social structure, we see what is more nearly the absence of structure. Put in other terms, leaders of totalitarian systems apparently prefer coercive power to authority—and for what is, to them, a very good reason. Authority is power supported by an appropriate normative structure; but at the same time, as we have noted earlier in this book, it is power that is regulated and circumscribed by these same social norms. Totalitarian rulers prefer to gamble for total power rather than to settle merely for authority that is restricted and stabilized by social norms.

The attempts of an elite group to achieve and retain total power over an entire population is one basis for the "integration" of a society. Friedrich and Brzezinski have argued that this type of integration is something "new under the sun" in that its success depends upon a highly developed technology. The types of control that are required—a system of terroristic police control, a near monopoly of control of all means of mass communication, a monopoly of the means of effective armed combat, and a central control and direction of the basic productive arrangements—presume a highly advanced state of technology in these areas for their success.[23]

We can perhaps take some comfort from the knowledge that the two most conspicuous examples of large-scale totalitarian systems—Nazi Germany and Stalinist Russia—no longer exist. The one was crushed by external forces mobilized to deny Hitler's imperialist ambitions, while the other has apparently been the victim of moderating forces within Russia seeking greater internal stability. Nevertheless, factors giving rise to mass societies are ever with us, and we have too recently witnessed the rapidity and ease with which mass societies can be transformed into totalitarian systems to be completely sanguine regarding the future.

[20] Arendt, p. 391.
[21] Arendt, p. 395.
[22] Arendt, p. 398.
[23] Friedrich and Brzezinski, pp. 9–12.

40   America as a Mass Society: A Critique*

Daniel Bell

The sense of a radical dehumanization of life which has accompanied events of the past several decades has given rise to the theory of "mass society." One can say that, Marxism apart, it is probably the most influential social theory in the Western world today. While no single individual has stamped his name on it—to the extent that Marx is associated with the transformation of personal relations under capitalism into commodity values, or Freud with the role of the irrational and unconscious in behavior—the theory is central to the thinking of the principal aristocratic, Catholic, or Existentialist critics of bourgeois society today. These critics—Ortega y Gasset, Karl Mannheim, Karl Jaspers, Paul Tillich, Gabriel Marcel, Emil Lederer, and others—have been concerned, less with the general conditions of freedom, than with the freedom of the *person*, and with the possibility for some *few* persons of achieving a sense of individual self in our mechanized society.

The conception of "mass society" can be summarized as follows: The revolutions in transport and communications have brought men into closer contact with each other and bound them in new ways; the division of labor has made them more interdependent; tremors in one part of society affect all others. Despite this greater interdependence, however, individuals have grown more

*This article is based on a paper presented before the Conference on the Future of Freedom held in Milan in September 1955 and sponsored by the Congress for Cultural Freedom.

estranged from one another. The old primary group ties of family and local community have been shattered; ancient parochial faiths are questioned; few unifying values have taken their place. Most important, the critical standards of an educated elite no longer shape opinion or taste. As a result, mores and morals are in constant flux, relations between individuals are tangential or compartmentalized rather than organic. At the same time greater mobility, spatial and social, intensifies concern over status. Instead of a fixed or known status symbolized by dress or title, each person assumes a multiplicity of roles and constantly has to prove himself in a succession of new situations. Because of all this, the individual loses a coherent sense of self. His anxieties increase. There ensues a search for new faiths. The stage is thus set for the charismatic leader, the secular messiah, who, by bestowing upon each person the semblance of necessary grace, and of fullness of personality, supplies a substitute for the older unifying belief that the mass society has destroyed.

In a world of lonely crowds seeking individual distinction, where values are constantly translated into economic calculabilities, where in extreme situations shame and conscience can no longer restrain the most dreadful excesses of terror, the theory of the mass society seems a forceful, realistic description of contemporary society, an accurate reflection of the *quality* and *feeling* of modern life. But when one seeks to apply the

Reprinted from *Commentary*, 22 (July, 1956), 75–83, by permission of the author and the publisher; Copyright © 1956 by the American Jewish Committee.

theory of mass society analytically, it becomes very slippery. Ideal types, like the shadows in Plato's cave, generally never give us more than a silhouette. So, too, with the theory of "mass society." Each of the statements making up the theory, as set forth in the second paragraph above, might be true, but they do not follow necessarily from one another. Nor can we say that all the conditions described are present at any one time or place. More than that, there is no organizing principle—other than the general concept of a "breakdown of values"—which puts the individual elements of theory together in a logical, meaningful—let alone historical—manner. And when we examine the way the "theory" is used by those who employ it, we find ourselves even more at a loss.

As commonly used in the term "mass media," "mass" implies that standardized material is transmitted to "all groups of the population uniformly." As understood generally by sociologists, a *mass* is a heterogeneous and undifferentiated audience as opposed to a *class*, or any parochial and relatively homogeneous segment. Some sociologists have been tempted to go further and make "mass" a rather pejorative term. Because the mass media subject a diverse audience to a common set of cultural materials, it is argued that these experiences must necessarily lie outside the personal—and therefore meaningful—experiences to which the individual responds directly. A movie audience, for example, is a "mass" because the individuals looking at the screen are, in the words of the American sociologist Herbert Blumer, "separate, detached, and anonymous." The "mass" divorces—or alienates"—the individual from himself.

As first introduced by the late Ortega y Gasset, however, in his *Revolt of the Masses*, the word "mass" does not designate a *group* of persons—for Ortega, workers do not constitute the "masses"—but calls attention to the *low quality* of modern civilization resulting from the loss of commanding position by an elite. Modern taste, for Ortega, represents the judgment of the unqualified. Modern culture, since it disowns the past, seeks a "free expression of its vital desires"; it becomes, therefore, an unrestrained "spoiled child," with no controlling standards, "no limit to its caprice."

Still another meaning is given to the concept by some German writers, for whom mass society is *mechanized* society. Ernst Jünger asserts that society has become an "apparatus." The machine impresses its style on man, making life calculable, mathematical, and precise; existence takes on a mask-like character: the steel helmet and the welder's face-guard symbolize the individual's disappearance into his technical function. The "regulated man" emerges as a new type, hard and ruthless, a cog in the technological process.

Less romantic, but equally critical, are those theorists who see extreme rationalization and bureaucratization—the *over-organization* of life—as the salient features of the mass society. The idea of "rationalization" goes back to Hegel and Marx, and along with it the notions of "estrangement" or "alienation," "reification," and the "fetishism of commodities"—all of which express the thought that in modern society man has become a "thing," an object manipulated by society, rather than a subject who can remake life in accordance with his own desires. In our time, Georg Simmel, Max Weber, and Karl Mannheim have developed and elaborated these concepts. In Mannheim's work—notably in his *Man and Society in an Age of Reconstruction*—the diverse strands are all brought together. Mannheim's argument, put schematically, runs as follows: modern large-scale organizations, oriented exclusively toward efficiency, withdraw all decisions from the shop floor and concentrate direction and planning at the top. This concentration of decision-making not only creates conformity, but stunts the initiative of subordinates and leaves them unsatisfied in their personal needs for gratification and esteem. Normally, the routinization of one's job dulls the edge of frustration and provides some security. But when unemployment looms, one's sense of helplessness becomes sharpened, and self-esteem is threatened. Since individuals cannot rationally locate the source of their frustration (i.e., the impersonal bureaucratic system itself), they will under these circumstances seek scapegoats and turn to fascism.

While for Mannheim mass society is equated with monolithic bureaucratization, for Emil Lederer and Hannah Arendt it is defined by the elimination of difference, by uniformity, aimlessness, alienation, and the failure of integration. In Lederer's view, society is made up of many social groups which, so long as society is stratified, can exercise only partial control over the others. As long as this situation obtains, irrational emotions are thus kept within some bounds. But when the lines dividing social groups break down, then the people become volatile, febrile "masses" ready to be manipulated by a leader. Similarly, for Hannah Arendt, the revolt of the masses is a revolt against the "loss of social status along with which [is] lost the whole sector of communal relationships in whose framework common sense makes sense. . . . The masses [become] obsessed by a desire to escape from reality because in their essential homelessness they can no longer bear its accidental incomprehensible aspects." Because modern life sunders all social bonds, and because the techniques of modern com-

munication have perfected the conditions under which propaganda can sway masses, the "age of the masses" is now upon us.

What strikes one first about these varied uses of the concept of mass society is how little they reflect or relate to the complex, richly striated social relations of the real world. Take Blumer's example of the movie audience as "separate, detached, and anonymous." Presumably a large number of individuals, because they have been subjected to similar experiences, now share some common psychological reality in which the differences between individual and individual become blurred; and accordingly we get the sociological assumption that each person is now of "equal weight," and therefore a sampling of what such disparate individuals say they think constitutes "*mass* opinion." But is this so? Individuals are not *tabulae rasae*. They bring varying social conceptions to the same experience, and go away with dissimilar responses. They may be silent, separate, detached, and anonymous while watching the movie, but afterward they talk about it with friends and exchange opinions and judgments. They are once again members of particular social groups. Would one say that several hundred or a thousand individuals home alone alone at night, but all reading the same book, constitute a "mass?"

One could argue, of course, that reading a book is a qualitatively different experience from going to a movie. But this leads precisely to the first damaging ambiguity in the theory of the mass society. Two things are mixed up in that theory: a judgment as to the *quality* of modern experience—with much of which any sensitive individual would agree—and a presumed scientific statement concerning the disorganization of society created by industrialization and by the demand of the masses for equality. It is the second of these statements with which this essay quarrels, not the first.

Behind the theory of social disorganization lies a romantic notion of the past that sees society as having once been made up of small "organic," close-knit communities (called *Gemeinschaften* in the terminology of the sociologists) that were shattered by industrialism and modern life, and replaced by a large impersonal "atomistic" society (called *Gesellschaft*) which is unable to provide the basic gratifications and call forth the loyalties that the older communities knew.[1] These distinctions are, however, completely riddled by value judgments. Everyone is against atomism and for "organic living." But if we substitute, with good logic, the term "total" for "organic," and "individualistic" for "atomistic," the whole argument looks quite different. In any case, a great weakness in the theory is its lack of history-mindedness. The transition to a mass society, if it be such, was not effected suddenly, explosively, within a single lifetime, but took generations to mature. In its sociological determinism, the hypothesis overlooks the human capacity for adaptiveness and creativeness, for ingenuity in shaping new social forms. Such new forms may be trade unions whose leaders rise from the ranks—there are 50,000 trade union locals in this country that form little worlds of their own—or the persistence under new conditions of ethnic groups and solidarities.

Because romantic feeling colors critical judgment, the attacks on modern life often have an unduly strong emotional charge. The image of "facelessness," for example, is given a metaphysical twist by Gabriel Marcel: "The individual, in order

[1] This antithesis, associated usually with the German sociologist Tönnies, is central in one way or another to almost every major modern social theory: Weber's traditional-rational behavior, Durkheim's mechanical-organic solidarity, Redfield's folk-urban society, and so on.

to belong to the mass . . . has had to . . . divest himself of that substantial reality which was linked to his initial individuality. . . . The incredibly sinister role of the press, the cinema, the radio has consisted in passing that original reality through a pair of flattening rollers to substitute for it a superimposed pattern of ideas, an image with no real roots in the deep being of the subject of this experiment." Perhaps terms like "original reality" and "real roots in the deep being" have a meaning that escapes an empiricist temper, but without the press, the radio, etc., etc.—and they are not monolithic—in what way, short of being everywhere at once, can one learn of events that take place elsewhere? Or should one go back to the happy ignorance of earlier days?

Some of the images of life in the mass society as presented by its critics border on caricature. According to Ernst Jünger, traffic demands traffic regulations, and so the public becomes conditioned to automatism. Karl Jaspers has written that in the "technical mass order" the home is transformed "into a lair or sleeping place." Even more puzzling is the complaint against modern medicine. "In medical practice . . . patients are now dealt with in the mass according to the principle of rationalization, being sent to institutes for technical treatment, the sick being classified in groups and referred to this or that specialized department. . . . The supposition is that, like everything else, medical treatment has become a sort of manufactured article."

The attack on the mass society sometimes widens into an attack on science itself. For Ortega, "the scientific man is the prototype of the mass-man" because science, by encouraging specialization, has made the scientist "hermetic and self-satisfied within his limitations." Ortega draws from this the sweeping conclusion that "the most immediate result of this unbalanced specialization has been that today, when there are more 'scientists' than ever, there are much less 'cultured' men than, for example, about 1750." But how is one to verify such a comparison between 1750 and the present. Even if we could establish comparable categories, surely Ortega would have been the first to shy away from statistical comparisons. Moreover, can we assume that, because a man specializes in his work, he is unable in his leisure, and in reflection, to appreciate culture? And what is "culture"? Would not Ortega admit that we have more knowledge of the world than in 1750—knowledge not only of nature, but of the inner life of man? Is knowledge to be divorced from culture, or is "true culture" a narrow area of classical learning in which eternal truths reside?

But more than mere contradictions in usage, ambiguities in terminology, and a lack of historical sense are involved in the theory of the mass society. It is at heart a defense of an aristocratic cultural tradition—a tradition that does carry with it an important but neglected conception of liberty—and a doubt that the large mass of mankind can ever become truly educated or acquire an appreciation of culture. Thus, the theory often becomes a conservative defense of privilege. This defense is so extreme at times as to pose a conflict between "culture" and "social justice." The argument (reminiscent of the title of Matthew Arnold's book, *Culture and Anarchy*) is made that any attempts at social betterment must harm culture. And while mainly directed against "bourgeois" society, the theory also strikes at radicalism and its egalitarian notions.

The fear of the "mass" has its roots in the dominant conservative tradition of Western political thought, which in large measure still shapes many of the political and sociological categories of social the-

ory—i.e., in authoritarian definitions of leadership, and in the image of the "mindless masses." The picture of the "mass" as capable only of violence and excess originates with Aristotle's *Politics*. In his threefold typology, democracy is equated with the rule of *hoi polloi*—who are easily swayed by demagogues—and must degenerate into tyranny. This notion of the masses as developed in Hellenistic times was deepened by the struggles between *plebs* and aristocracy in the Roman republic and by the efforts of the Caesars to exploit mob support; the image of the insensate mob fed by "bread and circuses" became deeply imprinted in history. Early Christian theory justified its fear of the masses with a theory about human nature. In the religious terms of Augustine—as later in the secularized version of Hobbes—the Earthly City bore an ineradicable stain of blood: property and police were the consequences of the Fall of Man; property and police were evidence, therefore, not of man's civilization, but of his corruption. In heaven there would be neither private property nor government.

It was the French Revolution that transplated the image of the "mindless masses" into modern consciousness. The destruction of the *ancien régime* and the rallying cry of "equality" sharpened the fear of conservative, and especially Catholic, critics that traditional values (meaning political, social, and religious dogma) would be destroyed.[2] For a Tocqueville and an Acton, there was an irreducible conflict between liberty and equality; liberty guaranteed each man the right to be different, whereas equality meant a "leveling" of tastes to the lowest common denominator. For a Max Scheler,

[2]Nazism, in the view of modern conservative and Catholic critics, is not a reaction against, but the inevitable end-product of, democracy. Hitler was a new version of the classical demagogue, leading the mindless masses in nihilistic revolt against the traditional culture of Europe.

as well as an Ortega, the mass society meant a "democracy of the emotions" which could only unleash irrational forces. For the Catholic de Maistre, as for the Anglican T. S. Eliot, the equality of men meant the destruction of the harmony and authority so necessary to a healthy, integrated society.

Important as these conceptions are as reminders of the meaning of excellence, and of liberty, they reflect a narrow conception of human potentialities. The question of social change has to be seen against the large political canvas. The starting point of modern politics, as Karl Mannheim has pointed out, came after the Reformation when chiliasm, or religiously inspired millennial striving to bring about heaven on earth, became an expression of the demands for social and economic betterment of the lower strata of society. Blind resentment of things as they were was thereby given principle, reason, and eschatological force, and directed to definite political goals. The equality of all souls became the equality of all individuals and the right of everyone, as enlightened by progressive revelation, to make a judgment on society. Comte, the father of modern sociology, expressed great horror at the idea of this universal right to one's own opinion. No community could exist, he wrote, unless its members had a certain degree of confidence in one another, and this, he said, was incompatible with the right of everyone to submit the very foundations of society to discussion whenever he felt like it. In calling attention to the dangers of free criticism, Comte pointed to the decline in public morals as evidenced by the increase of divorces, the effacement of traditional class distinctions, and the ensuing impudence of individual ambitions. It was part of the function of government, he thought, to prevent the diffusion of ideas and the anarchic spread of intellectual freedom.

Modern society, apparently, does not bear Comte out: though the foundations of privilege go on being challenged in the name of justice, society does not collapse. Few moralists would now uphold the bleak view once expressed by Malthus that "from the inevitable laws of human nature some human beings will be exposed to want. These are the unhappy persons who in the great lottery of life have drawn a blank." The most salient fact about modern life—capitalist and Communist—is the ideological commitment to social change. And by change is meant the striving for material economic betterment, greater opportunity for individuals to exercise their talents, and an appreciation of culture by wider masses of people. Can any society deny these aspirations?

It is curious that in these "aristocratic" critiques of modern society, refracted as they are through the glass of an idealized feudal past, democracy is identified with equality alone. The role of constitutionalism and of the rule of law which, with universal suffrage, are constituent elements of the Western democratic structure, are overlooked. The picture of modern culture as debauched by concessions to popular taste—a picture that leaves out the great rise in the general appreciation of culture—is equally overdrawn. If it is granted that mass society is compartmentalized, superficial in personal relations, anonymous, transitory, specialized, utilitarian, competitive, acquisitive, mobile, status-hungry, etc., etc., the obverse side of the coin must be shown too—the right to privacy, to free choice of friends and occupation, status on the basis of achievement rather than of ascription, a plurality of norms and standards rather than the exclusive and monopolistic social controls of a single dominant group, etc., etc. For if, as Sir Henry Maine once put it, the movement of modern society has been from status to contract, then it has been, in that light, a movement from a fixed place in the world to possible freedom.

The early theorists of the mass society (Ortega, Marcel) focussed attention on the "deterioration of excellence," while the later theorists (Mannheim, Lederer, Arendt) called attention to the way in which the over-organization and, at the same time, the disruption of the social fabric facilitated the rise of fascism. Recently, in the light of Communist successes, the argument has been advanced that the mass society, because it cannot provide for the individual's real participation in effective social groups, is particularly vulnerable to Communist penetration, and that the mass organization, because it is so unwieldy, is peculiarly susceptible to Communist penetration and manipulation. (See Philip Selznick's study, *The Organizational Weapon*.) Certainly, the Communists have scored enormous successes in infiltration, and their "front" organization may be counted one of the great political inventions of our century. But without discounting Communist techniques, the real problem here lies less with the "mass society" as such (aside from the excuse it affords disaffected intellectuals for attacks on modern culture) than in the capacity or incapacity of the given social order to satisfy the demands for social mobility and higher standards of living that arise once social change is under way. This is the key to any radical appeal.

It is not poverty *per se* that leads people to revolt; poverty most often induces fatalism and despair, and a reliance, embodied in ritual and superstitious practices, on supernatural help. *Social tensions are an expression of unfulfilled expectations*. It is only when expectations are aroused that radicalism can take hold. Radical strength is greatest (and here the appeal of Communism must be seen as a variant of the

general appeal of radicalism) in societies where awareness of class differences runs deep, expectations of social advancement outstrip possibilities, and the establishments of culture fail to make room for aspiring intellectuals.

It is among industrial workers rather than apathetic peasants (in Milan rather than Calabria), among frustrated intellectuals rather than workers long unionized (e.g. India), that radicalism spreads. Resentment, as Max Scheler once noted, is among the most potent of human motives; it is certainly that in politics. It is in the advanced industrial countries, principally the United States, Britain, and Northwestern Europe, where national income *has* been rising, where mass expectations of an equitable share in that increase are relatively fulfilled, and where social mobility affects ever greater numbers, that extremist politics have least hold. It may be, as the late Joseph Schumpeter pessimistically believed, that, in newly awakened societies like Asia's, the impatient expectations of key social strata, particularly the intellectuals, may so exceed the actual possibilities of economic expansion that Communism will come to look like the only plausible solution to the majority.[3] Whether this will happen in India and Indonesia is one of the crucial political questions of the next decade. But at any rate it is not the mass society, but the inability, pure and

[3] As Morris Watnick has pointed out in a pioneering study (in the University of Chicago symposium *The Progress of Underdeveloped Areas*), the Communist parties of Asia are completely the handiwork of native intellectuals. The history of the Chinese Communist party from Li Ta-Chao and Ch'en Tu-hsu, its founders, to Mao Tse-tung and Liu Shao-Chi, its present leaders, "is virtually an unbroken record of a party controlled by intellectuals." This is equally true of India, "where in 1943, 86 of 139 [Communist] delegates were members of professional and intellectual groups." The same pattern also holds true "for the Communist parties of Indochina, Thailand, Burma, Malaya and Indonesia, all of which show a heavy preponderance of journalists, lawyers and teachers among the top leadership."

simple, of any society to meet impatient popular expectations that makes for a strong response to radical appeals.

From the viewpoint of the mass society hypothesis, the United States ought to be exceptionally vulnerable to the politics of disaffection. In our country, urbanization, industrialization, and democratization have eroded older primary and community ties on a scale unprecedented in social history. Yet, though large-scale unemployment during the depression was more prolonged and more severe here than in any country in Western Europe, the Communist movement never gained a real foothold in the United States, nor has any fascist movement on a European model arisen. How does one explain this?

It is asserted that the United States is an "atomized" society composed of lonely, isolated individuals. One forgets the truism, expressed sometimes as a jeer, that Americans are a nation of joiners. There are in the United States today at least 200,000 voluntary organizations, associations, clubs, societies, lodges, and fraternities with an aggregate (but obviously overlapping) membership of close to eighty million men and women. In no other country in the world, probably, is there such a high degree of voluntary communal activity, expressed sometimes in absurd rituals, yet often providing real satisfactions for real needs.

"It is natural for the ordinary American," wrote Gunnar Myrdal, "when he sees something that is wrong to feel not only that there should be a law against it, but also that an organization should be formed to combat it." Some of these voluntary organizations are pressure groups—business, farm, labor, veterans, trade associations, the aged, etc., etc.— but thousands more are like the National Association for the Advancement of Colored People, the American Civil Liberties Union, the League of Women Voters, the American Jewish Committee, the Parent-Teachers Associations, local community improvement groups, and so on, each of which affords hundreds of individuals concrete, emotionally shared activities.

Equally astonishing are the number of ethnic group organizations in this country carrying on varied cultural, social, and political activities. The number of Irish, Italian, Jewish, Polish, Czech, Finnish, Bulgarian, Bessarabian, and other national groups, their hundreds of fraternal, communal, and political groups, each playing a role in the life of America, is staggering. In December 1954, for example, when the issue of Cyprus was first placed before the United Nations, the Justice for Cyprus Committee, "an organization of American citizens," according to its statement, took a full-page advertisement in the New York *Times* to plead the right of that small island to self-determination. Among the groups listed in the Justice for Cyprus Committee were: The Order of Ahepa, the Daughters of Penelope, the Pan-Laconian Federation, the Cretan Federation, the Pan-Messian Federation, the Pan-Icarian Federation, the Pan-Epirotic Federation of America, the Pan-Thracian Association, the Pan-Elian Federation of America, the Dodecanesian League of America, the Pan-Macedonian Association of America, the Pan-Samian Association, the Federation of Sterea Ellas, the Cyprus Federation of America, the Pan-Arcadian Federation, the GAPA, and the Federation of Hellenic Organizations.

We can be sure that if, in a free world, the question of the territorial affiliation of Ruthenia were to come up before the United Nations, dozens of Hungarian, Rumanian, Ukrainian, Slovakian, and Czech "organizations of American citizens" would rush eagerly into print to plead the justice of the claims of their respective homelands to Ruthenia.

Even in urban neighborhoods, where anonymity is presumed to flourish, the extent of local ties is astounding. Within the city limits of Chicago, for example, there are eighty-two community newspapers with a total weekly circulation of almost 1,000,000; within Chicago's larger metropolitan area, there are 181. According to standard sociological theory, these local papers providing news and gossip about neighbors should slowly decline under the pressure of the national media. Yet the reverse is true. In Chicago, the number of such newspapers has increased 165 per cent since 1910; in those forty years circulation has jumped 770 per cent. As sociologist Morris Janowitz, who studied these community newspapers, observed: "If society were as impersonal, as self-centered and barren as described by some who are preoccupied with the oneway trend from 'Gemeinschaft' to 'Gesellschaft' seem to believe, the levels of criminality, social disorganization and psychopathology which social science seeks to account for would have to be viewed as very low rather than (as viewed now) alarmingly high."

It may be argued that the existence of such a large network of voluntary associations says little about the cultural level of the country concerned. It may well be, as Ortega maintains, that cultural standards throughout the world have declined (in everything—architecture, dress, design?), but nonetheless a greater proportion of the population today participates in worthwhile cultural activities. This has been almost an inevitable concomitant of the doubling—*literally*—of the American standard of living over the last fifty years. The rising levels of education have meant rising appreciation of culture. In the United States more dollars are spent on concerts of classical music than on baseball. Sales of books have doubled in a decade. There are over a thousand symphony orchestras, and several hundred museums, institutes, and colleges

purchasing art in the United States today. Various other indices can be cited to show the growth of a vast middlebrow society. And in coming years, with steadily increasing productivity and leisure, the United States will become even more actively a "consumer" of culture. (These changes pose important questions for the development of a "high culture," but that problem lies outside the scope of this essay—see Clement Greenberg's "The Plight of Our Culture," COMMENTARY, June and July 1953.)

It has been argued that the American mass society imposes an excessive conformity upon its members. But it is hard to discern who is conforming to what. The *New Republic* cries that "hucksters are sugar-coating the culture." The *National Review*, organ of the "radical right," raises the banner of iconoclasm against the liberal domination of opinion-formation in our society. *Fortune* decries the growth of "organization man." Each of these tendencies exists, yet in historical perspective, there is probably less conformity to an over-all mode of conduct today than at any time within the last half-century in America. True, there is less bohemianism than in the twenties (though increased sexual tolerance), and less political radicalism than in the thirties (though the New Deal enacted sweeping reforms). But does the arrival at a political dead-center mean the establishment, too, of a dead norm? I do not think so. One would be hard put to it to find today the "conformity" *Main Street* exacted of Carol Kennicott thirty years ago. With rising educational levels, more individuals are able to indulge a wider variety of interests. ("Twenty years ago you couldn't sell Beethoven out of New York," reports a record salesman. "Today we sell Palestrina, Monteverdi, Gabrielli, and Renaissance and Baroque music in large quantities.")

One hears, too, the complaint that

divorce, crime, and violence demonstrate a widespread social disorganization in the country. But the rising number of divorces, as Dennis Wrong pointed out (COMMENTARY, April 1950), indicates not the disruption of the family, but a freer, more individualistic basis of choice, and the emergence of the "companionship" marriage. And as regards crime, I have sought to demonstrate (in *Fortune*, January 1955) that there is actually much *less* crime and violence (though more vicarious violence through movies and TV, and more "windows" onto crime, through the press) than was the case twenty-five and fifty years ago. Certainly, Chicago, San Francisco, and New York were much rougher and tougher cities in those years. But violent crime, which is usually a lower-class phenomenon, was then contained within the ecological boundaries of the slum; hence one can recall quiet, tree-lined, crime-free areas and feel that the tenor of life was more even in the past. But a cursory look at the accounts of those days—the descriptions of the gang wars, bordellos, and street-fighting in San Francisco's Barbary Coast, New York's Five Points, or Chicago's First Ward—would show how much more violent in the past the actual life of those cities was.

At this point it becomes quite apparent that such large-scale abstractions as "the mass society," with the implicit diagnoses of social disorganization and decay that derive from them, are rather meaningless without standards of comparison. Social and cultural change is probably greater and more rapid today in the United States than in any other country, but the assumption that social disorder and *anomie* inevitably attend such change is not borne out in this case.

This may be owing to the singular fact that the United States is probably the first large society in history to have change and innovation "built into" its culture. Almost all human societies, traditionalist and habit-ridden as they have been and still are, tend to resist change. The great efforts to industrialize under-developed countries, increase worker mobility in Europe, and broaden markets—so necessary to the raising of productivity and standards of living—are again and again frustrated by ingrained resistance to change. Thus in the Soviet Union change has been introduced only by dint of wholesale coercion. In the United States—a culture with no feudal tradition; with a pragmatic ethos, as expressed by Jefferson, that regards God as a "workman"; with a boundless optimism and a restless eagerness for the new that has been bred out of the original conditions of a huge, richly endowed land— change, and the readiness to change, have become the norm. This indeed may be why those consequences of change predicted by theorists basing themselves on European precedent find small confirmation.

The mass society is the product of change—and is itself change. But the *theory* of the mass society affords us no view of the relations of the parts of the society to each other that would enable us to locate the sources of change. We may not have enough data on which to sketch an alternative theory, but I would argue that certain key factors, in this country at least, deserve to be much more closely examined than they have been.

The change from a society once geared to frugal saving and now impelled to spend dizzily; the break-up of family capitalism, with the consequent impact on corporate structure and political power; the centralization of decision-making, politically, in the state and, economically, in a group of large corporate bodies; the rise of status and symbol groups replacing specific interest groups

—indicate that new social forms are in the making, and with them still greater changes in the complexion of life under mass society. With these may well come new status anxieties—aggravated by the threats of war—changed character structures, and new moral tempers.

The moralist may have his reservations or give approval—as some see in the break-up of the family the loss of a source of essential values, while others see in the new, freer marriages a healthier form of companionship—but the singular fact is that these changes emerge in a society that is now providing one answer to the great challenge posed to Western—and new world—society over the last two hundred years: how, within the framework of freedom, to increase the living standards of the majority of people, and at the same time maintain or raise cultural levels. American society, for all

its shortcomings, its speed, its commercialism, its corruption, still, I believe. shows us the most humane way.

The theory of the mass society no longer serves as a description of Western society, but as an ideology of romantic protest against contemporary society. This is a time when other areas of the globe are beginning to follow in the paths of the West, which may be all to the good as far as material things are concerned; but many of the economically underdeveloped countries, especially in Asia, have caught up the shopworn self-critical Western ideologies of the 19th century and are using them against the West, to whose "materialism" they oppose their "spirituality." What these Asian and our own intellectuals fail to realize, perhaps, is that one may be a thorough going critic of one's own society without being an enemy of its promises.

Section II

SOCIALIZATION PROCESSES IN SOCIETIES

Primary Socialization   The importance of the family as an agent of socialization is uniformly recognized. Whether or not the task of socialization is universally associated with this particular social institution need not concern us. It is sufficient for our purposes that in most times and places the family carries heavy responsibility for this task. This is clearly the case in the United States.

It is frequently asserted that the American family is rapidly disintegrating, that it is in an advanced state of social disorganization. Critics point for evidence to the high divorce rate, to the progressive decline in birth rates (prior to 1946), and to the residential mobility of family units. However, Talcott Parsons, examining these arguments, comes to a different conclusion:

... in spite of divorces and related phenomena, Americans recently have been marrying on an unprecedented scale. They have been having children, not on an unprecedented scale, but on one which by contrast with somewhat earlier trends is unlikely to be without significance and, third, they have been establishing homes for themselves as family units on a very large scale.[1]

Rather than being in a state of decline, Parsons argues, the family is undergoing important changes; specifically, it is becoming "a more specialized agency than before, probably more specialized than it has been in any previously known society." (See Reading 41) Like all units in our complex industrialized society, the family has become a more highly differentiated unit of the social structure, concentrating on certain activities while giving up other activities to other specialized units. But the socialization of young children remains as one of the central activities performed by the nuclear family in our society.

Our previous consideration of the socialization process has suggested the importance of analyzing the characteristics of the social structure within which this process is carried out. This is precisely the direction taken by Parsons in his examination of the role structure of the nuclear family as a socialization context. (See Reading 41) Parsons points to several special features of family structure in contemporary America, all of which have significance for the socialization of children. To begin, there is the isolation of the nuclear family: families are typically composed only of parents and children, the family unit typically being separated from close association with others, both relatives and nonrelatives. Also, reduction of the birth rate means that the typical American family is smaller today than in the past. This in turn means that more intense interaction—in terms of both frequency and level of affectivity—occurs among family mem-

---

[1]Talcott Parsons, "The American family: Its relations to personality and to the social structure," in Talcott Parsons and Robert F. Bales, *Family, Socialization and Interaction Process,* Glencoe, Ill.: Free Press, 1955, p. 8.

bers. Further, as already noted, the family operates as a more specialized structure than in the past, no longer typically serving as a basic unit of economic production or as a center of political or religious activities. Finally, the family, as a differentiated unit of the larger society, is itself internally differentiated. Drawing on his own previous work and that of Robert Bales, with which we are now familiar, Parsons argues that

(1) power within a family becomes differentiated, so that some members have more influence than others; (2) there is not one, but at least two, distinct power structures; (3) one of these two power structures focuses more on instrumental performance (such as making economic decisions, providing support for the family, managing the family farm or business) and the other focuses more on expressive leadership (such as nurturant behavior, child-rearing, expression of affiliation); and (4) that the two forms of power are allocated according to sex and age, the husband-father being more instrumental, the wife-mother more expressive, and the children subordinated in both dimensions.[2]

Parsons views the socialization process as occurring within and being profoundly affected by these structural characteristics. In the early socialization stages, the child's experience is restricted to contacts with immediate family members, the relative isolation of the family providing a simplified and stable environment to which the child can respond. The child's earliest experiences are with the mother, who emphasizes the expressive role, abiding by the particularistic and quality norms appropriate to that role. This process begins with the stage of mother-child identity before the child is able to differentiate himself from his mother. Only gradually does such differentiation occur and does the child learn to abide by the particular expectations appropriate to his subordinate role. The father, playing the instrumental role and abiding by the norms of universalism and performance, introduces a new set of role demands to which the child must adapt. The child's interaction with his siblings provides yet other roles for him to learn and perform. In sum, Parson's views socialization as occurring as the child is sequentially confronted with and must respond to differentiated expectations defining for him a continually expanding set of social roles he is expected to perform.

Looked at in socialization terms, there is always one, or a team of "socializing agents," the alters who, at the end of the process under consideration become players of the critical roles complementary to that of ego [the child undergoing socialization] in the system of social interaction into which he is being socialized. But he will be functioning as a full member of that system, in a stable state, only at the end of the process in question.[3]

Parsons' view of the role of parents as primary socializing agents is of particular interest. He argues that the success of the socialization process is dependent on their simultaneous participation in two systems: the larger social system of which they are members and which the child must be prepared to enter, and the subsystem of the family in which they serve as the primary agents of socialization. The parents' secure grounding in the larger social system is indispensable for their own mental health and for their awareness of the demands of the larger system for which the child must be prepared. At the same

[2]Morris Zelditch, Jr., "Family, marriage, and kinship," in Robert E. L. Faris (ed.), *Handbook of Modern Sociology*, Skokie, Ill.: Rand McNally, 1964, p. 703.

[3]Talcott Parsons, "Family Structure and the Socialization of the Child," in Parsons and Bales, p. 58.

time, they must participate within the family in roles that are adjusted to take account of the stage of development of the child, scaling their activities and expectations to fit his present level of maturation.[4]

Parsons' analysis of the consequences of the structural characteristics of the family system for the socialization process is extremely suggestive, and considerable research has been carried out to explore the adequacy of his conceptions.[5] In general, these studies substantiate what one would expect: that there is not a perfect one-to-one relation between functions and structures, that, in particular, specific individuals do not play a single role. For example, the father does not invariably play the instrumental role or the mother the expressive role, but role-taking varies as a function of the situation and the specific content of the interaction. Nevertheless, most studies reveal a tendency toward the type of role differentiation to which Parsons points, and this differentiation is found to have an impact on the conduct of the socialization process.

Secondary Socialization   A question of some consequence for every society is the extent to which there exists some continuity in the socialization process across types of socialization contexts. That is, are the "products" of one socialization context usable inputs in subsequent contexts? Benedict argues, based on her studies of numerous cultures, both primitive and modern, that U.S. society is plagued by serious socialization discontinuities.[6] Specifically, Benedict asserts that American children are trained within the family context to behave nonresponsibly and submissively, and that their sexuality as children is denied. As young adults they suddenly are confronted with diametrically opposed expectations: they are expected to assume responsibilities, to be assertive, and to assume appropriate sex roles. Benedict suggests that this lack of continuity creates severe social and personal problems for adolescents in American society. In many societies

the cultural institutions furnish adequate support to the individual as he progresses from role to role. . . . The contrast with arrangements in our culture is very striking, and against this background of social arrangements in other cultures, the adolescent period of *Sturm und Drang* with which we are so familiar becomes intelligible in terms of our discontinuous cultural institutions and dogmas rather than in terms of physiological necessity. It is even more pertinent to consider these comparative facts in relation to maladjusted persons in our culture who are said to be fixated at one or another pre-adult level.[7]

The problems that Benedict pointed to in 1938 may perhaps have become less severe, as more and more American children stay in schools for longer and longer periods, many now completing college. The role of student intervenes and provides a transition between that of child and adult. As recently as 1940

---

[4]Parsons, "Family Structure and the Socialization of the Child," in Parsons and Bales, pp. 58-62.

[5]See, for example, R. O. Blood and D. M. Wolfe, *Husbands and Wives*, Glencoe, Ill.: Free Press, 1960; W. F. Kendel, "Influence differentiation in family decision-making," *Sociology and Social Research*, 42 (1957), 18-25; M. L. Kohn and Eleanor E. Carroll, "Social class and the allocation of parental responsibilities," *Sociometry*, 23 (1960), 372-392; and D. Wolfe, "Power and authority in the family," in D. Cartwright (ed.), *Studies in Social Power*, Ann Arbor, Mich.: University of Michigan Press, 1959, pp. 99-117. For a comprehensive review of these and related studies of role differentiation in the family, see Zelditch, pp. 699-707.

[6]Ruth Benedict, "Continuities and discontinuities in cultural conditioning," *Psychiatry*, 1 (1938), 161-167.

[7]Benedict, p. 67.

the total number of students enrolled in colleges comprised only about 15 percent of the college age group; by 1954 the proportion was up to 30 percent, and in 1960 it was near 38 percent. The reason for these changes is not difficult to find.

The change in the economy from agriculture to manufacturing and then to service industry that takes place with advancing industrialism affects deeply the nature of the educational institution, for the shift in labor from manual to mental and from low to high degree of skill markedly alters the educational requirements of work. Literacy is required for the mass of workers, at first a literacy of the most elementary reading and writing, and then at later stages of industrialism a rising "functional literacy" of more advanced capability, for example, the reading ability necessary to comprehend employment forms, written tests, and blue-prints. For a constantly growing sector of the labor force, work requires educational preparation measureably beyond this minimal level, including lengthened general education for the sophistication useful in much white-collar work and particularized education in an occupational speciality. In short, as industrialism advances, the educational threshold of employment rises across the labor force, and educational preparation is markedly lengthened for fields based on advanced mental skills.[8]

So again we see the process of differentiation at work. Rather than occupational socialization occurring within the family, with a child learning his father's trade or a boy joining an industrial firm and receiving on-the-job training, we have the development of specialized institutional structures—secondary schools, colleges, and universities. It is their task to provide students with generalized skills that will equip them to move into occupations or into technical or professional schools where they will receive more specialized training. During this process of differentiation, secondary schools have undergone two important transformations. Up to approximately 1870, only a very small proportion of adolescents graduated from high school. These schools offered a classical education, and most of the graduates went on to some institution of higher learning.[9] After 1870, with the creation of a mass secondary educational program, secondary schools increasingly turned their efforts to terminal—vocational—rather than preparatory training. But today we are observing a shift back toward preparatory education, as secondary schools increasingly serve as launching pads to advanced training institutions rather than directly to occupational positions.[10]

In examining various types of socialization contexts throughout this volume, we have concentrated somewhat heavily on the structural characteristics of these settings. Our final paper, by John Meyer (reading 42), dealing with colleges as socializing institutions, changes this emphasis by suggesting that an organization's impact on the person being socialized "may be less affected by the structure of the organization itself than by its relation with and definition in its larger social context." He introduces the concept of the organization's *charter* to denote the definition that the larger environment puts on the products of the socializing organization. He argues that the power that such institutional structures have over their members is in large measure a function of the value of the statuses that these organizations are empowered to confer upon their students.

[8]Burton R. Clark, "Sociology of education," in Faris (ed.), *Handbook of Modern Sociology*, p. 736.

[9]Martin Trow, "The second transformation of American secondary education," *International Journal of Comparative Sociology*, 2 (1961), 144–166.

[10]Trow, pp. 154–157.

Central to Meyer's argument is the notion that the impact colleges have on their students may not be primarily one of changing their attitudes, values, or personal characteristics, but, rather, of changing their social positions. Students who spend four years in a college may not be less authoritarian or more intellectual or may not even, necessarily, possess greater knowledge than their peers who did not attend college. But one characteristic clearly differentiates them: they have attained the position of "college graduate"; and to the extent that this is a valued status in the society, they will be relatively advantaged in terms of the opportunities open to them.

In short, socializing institutions may have their impact not only through modifying the abilities, knowledge, or motivations of their clients. They may also affect individuals profoundly by the power that they have to confer or not to confer certain kinds of status on their graduates. We have previously noted that an important determinant of our behavior is the way in which we are treated by others and the expectations that they hold for us. Socializing institutions perhaps bring about some of their most important effects not by changing persons but by changing *expectations* about persons.

41   The American Family: Its Relations to Personality and to the Social Structure

Talcott Parsons

It is a striking fact of sociological discussion that there has been no settled agreement on either of two fundamental problems. One is the problem of the structural and functional relations between the nuclear family on the one hand, and the other elements of the kinship complex in the same society. Structural analysis of kinship is, we feel, just reaching a point where the importance of clear discriminations in this field is coming to be appreciated. Second, there has been no clear conception of what are the important "functions of the family." Procreation and child care are always included, as is some reference to sexual relations, but in addition there are frequent references to "economic" functions, religious functions and various others.

There has been little attempt to work out the implications of the suggestion that there are certain "root functions" which much be found wherever there is a family or kinship system at all, while other functions may be present or not according to the *kind* of family or kinship system under consideration, and its place in the structure of the rest of the society.

The aspect of this problem in which we are particularly interested concerns its relations to the problem of structural differentiation in societies. It is well known that in many "primitive" societies there is a sense in which kinship "dominates" the social structure; there are few concrete structures in which participation is independent of kinship status. In comparative perspective it is clear that in the more "advanced" societies a far greater part is played by non-kinship structures. States, churches, the larger business firms, universities and professional associations cannot be treated as mere "extensions" of the kinship system.

The process by which non-kinship units become of prime importance in a social structure, inevitably entails "loss of function" on the part of some or even all of the kinship units. In the processes of social evolution there have been many stages by which this process has gone on, and many different directions in which it has worked out.

Our suggestion is, in this perspective, that what has recently been happening to the American family constitutes part of one of these stages of a process of differentiation. This process has involved a further step in the reduction of the importance in our society of kinship units other than the nuclear family. It has also resulted in the transfer of a variety of functions from the nuclear family to other structures of the society, notably the occupationally organized sectors of it. This means that the family has become *a more specialized agency than before,* probably more specialized than it has been in any previously known society. This represents a decline of *certain* features which traditionally have been associated with families; but whether it represents a "decline of the family" in a more general sense is another matter; we think not. We think the trend of the evidence points to the beginning of the relative stabilization of a *new* type of

family structure in a new relation to a general social structure, one in which the family is more specialized than before, but not in any general sense less important, because the society is dependent *more* exclusively on it for the performance of *certain* of its vital functions.

We further think that this new situation presents a particularly favorable opportunity to the social scientist. Because we are dealing with a more highly differentiated and specialized agency, it is easier to identify clearly the features of it which are essential on the most general level of cross-cultural significance. The situation is methodologically comparable to the relation between the emergence of the modern type of industrial economy and the problems of economic theory. The high level of differentiation of economic from non-economic processes under modern conditions, has made possible a kind of natural experimental situation which has been crucial to the development of modern economic theory.

THE AMERICAN FAMILY IN THE TOTAL SOCIETY

From this perspective, then, let us review some of the most essential features of the structure of the American family-kinship system in its relation to the rest of the society.

The first feature to be noted is on the level of kinship organization as anthropologists ordinarily treat this; namely the "isolation" of the nuclear family and its relation to "bilaterality" with respect to the lines of descent. This "isolation" is manifested in the fact that the members of the nuclear family, consisting of parents and their still dependent children, ordinarily occupy a separate dwelling not shared with members of the family of orientation of either spouse, and that this household is in the typical case economically independent, subsisting in the first instance from the occupational earnings of the husband-father.[1] It is of course not uncommon to find a surviving parent of one or the other spouse, or even a sibling or cousin of one of them residing with the family, but this is both statistically secondary, and it is clearly not felt to be the "normal" arrangement.[2]

Of course with the independence, particularly the marriage, of children, relations to the family of orientation are by no means broken. But separate residence, very often in a different geographical community, and separate economic support, attenuate these relations. Furthermore, there is a strong presumption that relations to one family of orientation will not be markedly closer than to the other (though there is a certain tendency for the mother-married daughter relation to be particularly close). This bilaterality is further strongly reinforced by our patterns of inheritance. In the first place the presumption is that a newly married couple will "stand on their own feet," supporting themselves from their own earnings. But so far as property is inherited the pattern calls for equal division between children regardless of birth order or sex, so that the fact or expectation of inheritance does not typically bind certain children to their families of orientation more closely than others. Furthermore, though it is not uncommon for sons to work in their fathers' businesses—almost certainly much less common than it was fifty years ago—this tendency is at least partially matched by the phenomenon of "marrying the boss's daughter," so that no clear unilateral structure can be derived from this fact.

It has been noted that the primary source of family income lies in occupational earnings. It is above all the presence of the modern occupational system and its mode of articulation with the family which accounts for the difference between the modern, especially American, kinship system and *any* found in nonliterate or even peasant societies. The family household is a solidary unit where, once formed, membership and status are ascribed, and the communalistic principle of "to each according to his needs" prevails. In the occupational world, status is achieved by the individual and is contingent on his continuing performance. Though of course this is modified in varying respects, there is a high premium on mobility and equality of opportunity according to individual capacity to perform. Over much of the world and of history a very large proportion of the world's ordinary work is and has been performed in the context of kinship units. Occupational organization in the modern sense is the sociological antithesis of this.

This means essentially, that as the occupational system develops and absorbs functions in the society, it *must* be at the expense of the relative prominence of kinship organization as a structural component in one sense, and must also

---

[1] Cf. R. M. Williams, *American Society*, Chapter IV (New York: Alfred A. Knopf, Inc., 1951). Also T. Parsons, "The Kinship System of the Contemporary United States," *Essays in Sociological Theory* (rev. ed., Glencoe, Ill.: The Free Press, 1954).

[2] "Sixty-four per cent of husband and wife families in 1940 had no adult relatives eighteen years old and over living in the home. Very few, about one-eighth, of the families in which the husband was under thirty-five years of age contained any of these additional adults. . . . Nearly three-fifths of these (adult relatives) were single sons or daughters of the couple who had not left home, of whom most were between eighteen and thirty-four years old. . . . About one-eighth of the adult relatives were married, widowed or divorced parents of the husband or his wife. . . . Thus, all but one-fifth of the adult relatives were children or parents (own or in-law) of the family head and his wife."

Source: P. C. Glick, "The Family Cycle," *American Sociological Review*, Vol. 12, No. 2, April, 1947.

be at the expense of many of what previously have been *functions* of the kinship unit. The double consequence is that the same people, who are members of kinship units, perform economic, political, religious and cultural functions outside the kinship context in occupational roles and otherwise in a variety of other types of organization. But conversely, the members of kinship units must meet many of their needs, which formerly were met in the processes of interaction within the kinship unit, through other channels. This of course includes meeting the need for income with which to purchase the goods and services necessary for family functioning itself.

In this type of society the basic mode of articulation between family and the occupational world lies in the fact that the *same* adults are both members of nuclear families and incumbents of occupational roles, the holders of "jobs." The individual's job and not the products of the cooperative activities of the family as a unit is of course the primary source of income for the family.

Next it is important to remember that the *primary* responsibility for this support rests on the one adult male member of the nuclear family. It is clearly the exceptional "normal" adult male who can occupy a respected place in our society without having a regular "job," though he may of course be "independent" as a professional practitioner or some kind of a "free lance" and not be employed by an organization, or he may be the proprietor of one. That at the bottom of the scale the "hobo" and the sick and disabled are deviants scarcely needs mentioning, while at the other end, among the relatively few who are in a position to "live on their money" there is a notable reluctance to do so. The "playboy" is not a highly respected type and there is no real American equivalent of the older European type of "gentle-man" who did not "work" unless he had to.

The occupational role is of course, in the first instance, part of the "occupational system" but it is not only that. It is an example of the phenomenon of "interpenetration" which will be extensively analyzed below. In this connection it is both a role in the occupational system, *and* in the family; it is a "boundary-role" between them. The husband-father, in holding an acceptable job and earning an income from it is performing an essential function or set of functions for his family (which of course includes himself in one set of roles) as a system. The status of the family in the community is determined probably more by the "level" of job he holds than by any other single factor, and the income he earns is usually the most important basis of the family's standard of living and hence "style of life." Of course, as we shall see, he has other very important functions in relation both to wife and to children, but it is fundamentally by virtue of the importance of his occupational role *as a component of his familial role* that in our society we can unequivocally designate the husband-father as the "instrumental leader" of the family as a system.[3]

The membership of large numbers of

[3]Comparative data confirm this interpretation. We now have a good deal of evidence about social situations where there is neither a strong "lineage" structure in the kinship field nor a developed "industrial" type of occupational structure. One of the first perceptive studies of this type was made by E. F. Frazier in his *Negro Family in the United States* (Chicago: University of Chicago Press, 1939). This has more recently been supplemented and refined by studies of kinship in the British West Indies. See F. Henriques, *Family and Color in Jamaica*, 1953; Lloyd Braithwaite, "Social Stratification in Trinidad," *Social and Economic Studies,* October, 1953; and especially the as yet unpublished study by R. T. Smith, *The Rural Negro Family in British Guiana* (Doctoral dissertation, University of Cambridge, 1954). Dr. Smith shows very clearly the connection between the "mother-centered" character of the lower-class rural negro family in the West

women in the American labor force must not be overlooked. Nevertheless there can be no question of symmetry between the sexes in this respect, and we argue, there is no serious tendency in this direction. In the first place a large proportion of gainfully employed women are single, widowed or divorced, and thus cannot be said to be either taking the place of a husband as breadwinner of the family, or competing with him. A second large contingent are women who either do not yet have children (some of course never will) or whose children are grown up and independent. The number in the labor force who have small children is still quite small and has not shown a marked tendency to increase. The role of "housewife" is still the overwhelmingly predominant one for the married woman with small children.[4]

But even where this type does have a job, as is also true of those who are married but do not have dependent children, above the lowest occupational levels it is quite clear that in general the woman's job tends to be of a qualitatively different type and not of a status which seriously competes with that of her husband as the primary status-giver or income-earner.

It seems quite safe in general to say that the adult feminine role has not

ceased to be anchored primarily in the internal affairs of the family, as wife, mother and manager of the household, while the role of the adult male is primarily anchored in the occupational world, in his job and through it by his status-giving and income-earning functions for the family. Even if, as seems possible, it should come about that the average married woman had some kind of job, it seems most unlikely that this relative balance would be upset; that either the roles would be reversed, or their qualitative differentiation in these respects completely erased.[5]

THE PRINCIPAL FUNCTIONS OF THE NUCLEAR FAMILY

Within this broad setting of the structure of the society, what can we say about the functions of the family, that is, the isolated nuclear family? There are, we think, two main types of considerations. The first is that the "loss of function," both in our own recent history and as seen in broader comparative perspective, means that the family has become, on the "macroscopic" levels, almost completely functionless. It does not itself, except here and there, engage in much economic production; it is not a significant unit in the political power system; it is not a major direct agency of integration of the larger society. Its individual members participate in all these

---

Indies (his study deals with British Guiana) and the "casual" character of most of the available employment and income-earning opportunities. This is a sharp modification of the typical American pattern, but must not be interpreted to mean that the husband-father has, at the critical periods of the family cycle, altogether lost the role of instrumental leader. Dr. Smith shows that this is not the case, and that the impression to the contrary (which might for instance be inferred from Henriques' discussion) arises from failure to consider the development of the particular family over a full cycle from the first sexual relations to complete "emancipation" of the children from their family of orientation.

[4]Two tables showing "population and labor force by age and sex" and "labor forces status of women by marital status" have been omitted in this reprinting. [Ed.]

[5]The distribution of women in the labor force clearly confirms this general view of the balance of the sex roles. Thus, on higher levels typical feminine occupations are those of teacher, social worker, nurse, private secretary and entertainer. Such roles tend to have a prominent expressive component, and often to be "supportive" to masculine roles. Within the occupational organization they are analogous to the wife-mother role in the family. It is much less common to find women in the "top executive" roles and the more specialized and "impersonal" technical roles. Even within professions we find comparable differentiations, e.g., in medicine women are heavily concentrated in the two branches of pediatrics and psychiatry, while there are few women surgeons.

functions, but they do so "as individuals" not in their roles as family members.[6]

The most important implication of this view is that the functions of the family in a highly differentiated society are not to be interpreted as functions directly on behalf of the society, but on behalf of personality. If, as some psychologists seem to assume, the essentials of human personality were determined biologically, independently of involvement in social systems, there would be no need for families, since reproduction as such does not require family organization. It is because the *human* personality is not "born" but must be "made" through the socialization process that in the first instance families are necessary. They are "factories" which produce human personalities. But at the same time even once produced, it cannot be assumed that the human personality would remain stable in the respects which are vital to social functioning, if there were not mechanisms of stabilization which were organically integrated with the socialization process. We therefore suggest that the basic and irreducible functions of the family are two: first, the primary socialization of children so that they can truly become members of the society into which they have been born; second, the stabilization of the adult personalities of the population of the society. It is the combination of these two functional imperatives, which explains why, in the "normal" case it is both true that *every adult* is a member of a nuclear family and that every child must begin his process of socialization in a nuclear family. It will be one of the most important theses of our subsequent analysis that these two cir-

cumstances are most intimately interconnected. Their connection goes back to the fact that it is control of the residua of the process of socialization which constitutes the primary focus of the problem of stabilization of the adult personality.

In subsequent chapters we shall develop, in a variety of applications and ramifications, the view that the central focus of the process of socialization lies in the internalization of the culture of the society into which the child is born. The most important part of this culture from this focal point consists in the patterns of value which in another aspect constitute the institutionalized patterns of the society. The conditions under which effective socialization can take place then will include being placed in a social situation where the more powerful and responsible persons are themselves integrated in the cultural value system in question, both in that they constitute with the children an *institutionalized* social system, and that the patterns have previously been internalized in the relevant ways in their own personalities. The family is clearly in all societies, and no less in our own, in this sense an institutionalized system.[7]

But it is not enough to place the child in any institutionalized system of social

---

[6]In terms of our technical analytical scheme we interpret this to mean that the family belongs in the "latency" or "pattern-maintenance—tension-management" subsystem as seen in functional terms. We so interpreted it in *Working Papers*, Chapter V, Sec. viii. (T. Parsons, R. F. Bales, and E. A. Shils, *Working Papers in Theory of Action* [Glencoe, Ill.: The Free Press, 1953], hereinafter referred to as *Working Papers*.)

[7]It is important not to confuse this sense of institutionalization with the usage of Burgess and his associates when they distinguish the "institutional family" from the "companionship" family. To contrast the institutional and companionship family, Burgess and Locke characterize the institutional as a family with "family behavior controlled by the mores, public opinion and law." It is a family "in which its unity would be determined entirely by the social pressure impinging on family members." The companionship form of the family has "family behavior arising from the mutual affection and consensus of its members . . . and intimate association of husband and wife and parents and children." E. W. Burgess and H. J. Locke, *The Family* (New York: American Book Co., 1950), pp. 26–27.

From the present point of view *both* types of family are institutionalized. The statuses of marriage and parenthood are most definitely linked to expectations and obligations, both legal and informal, which are not simply discretionary with the individuals concerned.

relationships. He must be placed in one of a special type which fulfills the necessary psychological conditions of successful completion of the process we call socialization, over a succession of stages starting with earliest infancy. One of the principal tasks of the subsequent discussion is to explore some of these conditions. A few of them may, however, be noted here, while the reasons for their importance will be discussed as we go along. In the first place, we feel that for the earlier stages of socialization, at least, the socialization system must be a *small* group. Furthermore, it must be differentiated into subsystems so the child need not have an equal level of participation with all members at the same time in the earlier stages of the process. We will show that it is particularly important that in the earliest stage he tends to have a special relation to one other member of the family, his mother.

In this connection a certain importance may well attach to the biological fact that, except for the relatively rare plural births, it is unusual for human births to the same mother to follow each other at intervals of less than a year with any regularity. It is, we feel, broadly in the first year of life that a critical phase of the socialization process, which requires the most exclusive attention of a certain sort from the mother, takes place. Furthermore, it is probably significant that in our type of society the family typically no longer has what by other standards may be considered to be large numbers of children. Partly, in earlier times the effects of higher rates of birth have been cancelled by infant mortality. But partly, we feel the large family—say over five or six children—is a different *type* of social system with different effects on the children in it. We will not try to analyze these differences carefully here.

Another very important range of problems in the larger setting concerns the impact for the outcome of the socializa-tion process of the role of relatives other than members of the nuclear family. Particularly important cross-culturally are siblings of the parents, the role of whom varies with the type of kinship structure. Some of the setting for consideration of these problems will be given by Zelditch in Chapter VI [of *Family, Socialization and Interaction Process*]. In the conclusion there will be a brief discussion of their general character, but it will not be possible to deal at all adequately with them in this volume.

We should like to suggest only that what we have called the "isolation of the nuclear family" for the contemporary American scene, may, along with reduction in the average size of family, have considerable significance for the character of the contemporary socialization process. This significance would, we think, have something to do with the greater sharpness of the *difference* in status, from the point of view of the child, between members of the family and nonmembers. It will be our general thesis that in certain respects the modern child has "farther to go" in his socialization than his predecessors. There seem to be certain reasons why the number of fundamental steps of a certain type is restricted. If this is true, each step has to be "longer" and it is important that the "landmarks" along the way, the "cues" presented to the child, should involve extremely clear discriminations.

A primary function and characteristic of the family is that it should be a social group in which in the earliest stages the child can "invest" *all* of his emotional resources, to which he can become overwhelmingly "committed" or on which he can become fully "dependent." But, at the same time, in the nature of the socialization process, this dependency must be temporary rather than permanent. Therefore, it is very important that the socializing agents should not themselves be *too* completely immersed in their family ties. It is a condition equally important with facilitating dependency that a family should, in due course, help in emancipating the child from his dependency on the family. *Hence the family must be a differentiated subsystem of a society, not itself a "little society" or anything too closely approaching it.* More specifically this means that the adult members must have roles other than their familial roles which occupy strategically important places in their own personalities. In our own society the most important of these other roles, though by no means the only one, is the occupational role of the father.

The second primary function of the family, along with socialization of children, concerns regulation of balances in the personalities of the adult members of both sexes. It is clear that this function is concentrated on the marriage relation as such. From this point of view a particularly significant aspect of the isolation of the nuclear family in our society is again the sharp discrimination in status which it emphasizes between family members and nonmembers. In particular, then, spouses are thrown upon each other, and their ties with members of their own families of orientation, notably parents and adult siblings, are correspondingly weakened. In its negative aspect as a source of strain, the consequence of this may be stated as the fact that the family of procreation, and in particular the marriage pair, are in a "structurally unsupported" situation. Neither party has any other adult kin on whom they have a right to "lean for support" in a sense closely comparable to the position of the spouse.

The marriage relation is then placed in a far more strategic position in this respect than is the case in kinship systems where solidarity with "extended" kin categories is more pronounced. But for the functional context we are discussing, the marriage relationship is by no means alone in its importance. Parenthood acquires, it may be said, an enhanced significance for the emotional balance of the parents themselves, as well as for the socialization of their children. The two generations are, by virtue of the isolation of the nuclear family, thrown more closely on each other.

The main basis of the importance of children to their parents derives, we think, from the implications of problems which psychoanalytic theory has immensely illuminated but which also, we think, need to be understood in their relation to the family as a social system, and the conditions of its functional effectiveness and stability. The most general consideration is that the principal stages in the development of personality, particularly on its affective or "emotional" side, leave certain "residua" which constitute a stratification (in the geological sense) of the structure of the personality itself with reference to its own developmental history. Partly these residua of earlier experience can constitute threats to effective functioning on adult levels, the more so the more "abnormal" that history and its consequences for the individual have been. But partly, also, they have important positive functions for the adult personality. To express and in certain ways and contexts "act out," motivational systems and complexes which are primarily "infantile" or "regressive" in their meaning is, in our view, by no means always undesirable, but on the contrary necessary to a healthy balance of the adult personality. At the same time the dangers are very real and regulation of context, manner and occasion of expression is very important.

We shall attempt later to mobilize evidence that a particularly important role in this situation is played by the erotic elements of the personality constitution, because of the great importance of eroticism in the developmental process.

We suggest then that children are important to adults because it is important to the latter to express what are essentially the "childish" elements of their own personalities. There can be no better way of doing this than living with and interacting on their own level with *real* children. But at the same time it is essential that this should not be an unregulated acting out, a mere opportunity for regressive indulgence. The fact that it takes place in the parental role, with all its responsibilities, not least of which is the necessity to renounce earlier modes of indulgence as the child grows older, is, as seen in this connection, of the first importance. The circumstantially detailed analysis which alone can substantiate such a set of statements, will be presented in the subsequent chapters. The general thesis, however, is that the family and, in a particularly visible and trenchant way, the modern isolated family, incorporates an intricate set of interactive mechanisms whereby these two essential functions for personality are interlocked and interwoven. By and large a "good" marriage from the point of view of the personality of the participants, is likely to be one with children; the functions as parents reinforce the functions in relation to each other as spouses.

If this be true, it would be surprising if the marital relation itself were, even in the more direct interaction of the spouses with each other, altogether dissociated from those aspects of the personality which benefit from the role of parent. It will be suggested later[8] that genital sexuality, which in a sense may be regarded as the primary "ritual" of marital solidarity, is in its symbolic significance, for *both* parties in the first in-

stance a reenactment of the preoedipal mother-child relationship, when the love-relationship to the mother was the most important thing in the child's life. Thus it also may be regarded as "regressive" in an important sense. But like the parental relationship, it takes place in a context where its expressive or indulgent aspect is balanced by a regulatory aspect. The most important part of this is the contingency of sexual love on the assumption of fully adult responsibilities in roles other than that of marriage directly. Put very schematically, a mature woman can love, sexually, only a man who takes his full place in the masculine world, above all its occupational aspect, and who takes responsibility for a family; conversely, the mature man can only love a woman who is really an adult, a full wife to him and mother to his children, and an adequate "person" in her extrafamilial roles. It is this "building in" to a more differentiated personality system on both sides, and to a more differentiated role system than the child possesses or could tolerate, which constitutes the essential *difference* between preoedipal child-mother love and adult heterosexual love.

SEX ROLE AND FAMILY STRUCTURE

It goes without saying that the differentiation of the sex roles within the family constitutes not merely a major axis of its structure, but is deeply involved in both of these two central function-complexes of the family and in their articulation with each other. Indeed we argue that probably the importance of the family and its functions for society constitutes the primary set of reasons why there is a *social* as distinguished from purely reproductive, differentiation of sex roles.

We will maintain that in its most essential structure the nuclear family consists of four main role-types, which are differentiated from each other by the

[8]Cf. Chapter III [of *Family: Socialization and Interaction Process*], pp. 150–151.

criteria of generation and sex. Of these two, generation is, in its social role-significance, biologically given, since the helplessness of the small child, particularly of course the infant, precludes anything approaching equality of "power" between the generations in the early stages of socialization. This biological "intrinsicness" does not, however, we feel apply in at all the same way to sex; both parents are adults and children of both sexes are equally powerless. We will argue that the differentiation of sex role in the family is, in its sociological character and significance, primarily an example of a basic qualitative mode of differentiation which tends to appear in *all* systems of social interaction regardless of their composition. In particular this type of differentiation, that on "instrumental-expressive" lines, is conspicuous in small groups of about the same membership-size as the nuclear family, as Bales had already shown,[9] and he and Slater develop further in Chapter V [of *Family, Socialization and Interaction Process*]

We suggest that this order of differentiation is generic to the "leadership element" of small groups everywhere and that the problem with respect to the family is not *why* it appears there given the fact that families as groups exist, but why the man takes the more instrumental role, the woman the more expressive, and why in detailed ways these roles take particular forms. In our opinion the fundamental explanation of the allocation of the roles between the biological sexes lies in the fact that the bearing and early nursing of children establish a strong presumptive primacy of the relation of mother to the small child and this in turn establishes a presumption that the man, who is exempted from these biological functions, should specialize in the alternative instrumental direction.

However the allocation may have come

[9]"The Equilibrium Problem in Small Groups," *Working Papers,* Chap. IV.

about in the course of bio-social evolution, there can be little doubt about the ways in which differentiation plays into the structure and functioning of the family as we know it. It is our suggestion that the recent change in the American family itself and in its relation to the rest of the society which we have taken as our point of departure, is far from implying an erasure of the differentiation of sex roles; in many respects it reinforces and clarifies it. In the first place, the articulation between family and occupational system in our society focuses the instrumental responsibility for a family very sharply on its one adult male member, and prevents its diffusion through the ramifications of an extended kinship system. Secondly, the isolation of the nuclear family in a complementary way focuses the responsibility of the mother role more sharply on the one adult woman, to a relatively high degree cutting her off from the help of adult sisters and other kinswomen; furthermore, the fact of the absence of the husband-father from the home premises so much of the time means that she has to take the primary responsibility for the children. This responsibility is partly mitigated by reduction in the number of children and by aids to household management, but by no means to the point of emancipating the mother from it. Along with this goes, from the child's point of view, a probable intensification of the emotional significance of his parents as individuals, particularly and in the early stages, his mother, which, there is reason to believe, is important for our type of socialization.

Hence, it is suggested that, if anything, in certain respects the *differentiation* between the roles of the parents becomes more rather than less significant for the socialization process under modern American conditions. It may also be suggested that in subtle ways the same is true of the roles of spouses vis-à-vis each other. The enhanced significance of the marriage relationship, both for the structure of the family itself and for the personalities of the spouses, means that the *complementarity* of roles within it tends to be accentuated. The romantic love complex and our current strong preoccupation with the emotional importance of the "significant person" of opposite sex strongly suggests this. Indeed there has been, we think, a greatly increased emphasis on the importance of good heterosexual relations, which overwhelmingly means *within* marriage. Such disorganization within this field as there is, apart from premarital experimenting, takes primarily the form of difficulties with the current marriage relationship and, if its dissolution is sought, the establishment of a *new* one. It does not mainly take the form of centering erotic interests outside the marriage relation.

All of this seems to us to indicate that the increased emphasis, manifested in all sorts of ways, on overt, specifically feminine attractiveness, with strong erotic overtones, is related to this situation within the family. The content of the conceptions of masculinity and femininity has undoubtedly changed. But it seems clear that the accent of their differentiation has not lessened.

It seems to us legitimate to interpret the recent and, to what extent we do not know, continuing, high level of the divorce rate in this light. It is not an index that the nuclear family and the marriage relationship are rapidly disintegrating and losing their importance. The truth is rather that, on the one hand, the two roles have been changing their character; on the other, their specific importance, particularly that of marriage, has actually been *increasing*. Both these aspects of the process of change impose additional strain on family and marriage as systems, and on their members as personalities. We suggest that the high rates of divorce are primarily indices of this additional

strain. When the difficulty of a task is increased it is not unreasonable to expect that a larger proportion of failures should result until the necessary adjustments have been better worked out. In this case we feel that the adjustments are extremely complex and far-reaching.

In this context two other conspicuous and related features of our modern society, which are closely related to marriage and the family, may be called to mind. The first of these is the enormous vogue of treating "human" problems from the point of view of "mental health" and in various respects of psychology. There has been and there is much faddism in these fields, but in the perspective of a couple of generations there can be no doubt of the magnitude of this movement. The United States is a society in which technological-organizational developments closely related to science have taken hold over a very wide front. It is, one might suggest, the "American method," to attempt to solve problems in foci of strain by calling in scientifically expert aid. In industry we take this for granted. In human relations it is just coming to the fore. The immense vogue of psychiatry, of clinical psychology and such phenomena are, we suggest, an index of the importance of strain in the area of the personality and the human relations in which persons are placed. In the nature of our society much of this strain relates to family and marriage relations.[10]

The second, and related, phenomenon,

[10]It has been suggested in other connections that illness should in certain respects be treated as a form of "deviant behavior" and medical practice, even if not explicitly psychotherapy, as a "mechanism of social control." This viewpoint will be very important in the subsequent analysis in this volume. See Parsons, "Illness and the Role of the Physician" in Kluckhohn, Murray and Schneider, eds., *Personality in Nature, Society and Culture*, New York: Alfred A. Knopf, Inc., 1953. For certain relations to the family, see T. Parsons and Renée Fox, "Illness, Therapy and the Modern American Urban Family," *Journal of Social Issues*, Vol. 8, pp. 31-44.

is what is sometimes called, with reference to child training, the "professionalization" of the mother role. It is, starting with the elementary matters of early feeding and other aspects of physical care, the attempt to rationalize, on the basis of scientific—though often pseudo-scientific—authority, the technical aspects of the care of the children. The breakdown of traditionalism which has long since been taken for granted in many other areas, has now penetrated far into this one. It is not surprising in these circumstances that psychology plays a prominent part.

This involvement of applied science in so many aspects of the intimate life of personalities, as in the mother's care of her children and in the marriage relationship, suggests an important aspect of the developing American feminine role

which should not be overlooked. This is that, though the tendency in certain respects is probably increasing, to specialize in the expressive direction, the American woman is not thereby sacrificing the values of rationality. On the contrary, she is heavily involved in the attempt to rationalize these areas of human relations themselves. Women do not act only in the role of patient of the psychiatrist, but often the psychiatrist also is a woman. The mother not only "loves" her children, but she attempts to understand rationally the nature, conditions and limitations of that love, and the ways in which its deviant forms can injure rather than benefit her child. In this, as in other respects, the development we have been outlining is an integral part of the more general development of American society.

42 The Charter: Conditions of Diffuse Socialization in Schools*

John W. Meyer

Research on the ways in which organizations socialize people has been primarily concerned with one major problem: What features of the structure of organizations which process people, and of the interaction that goes on within them, lead to diffuse changes in the values or orientation of the people being processed? Thus the independent variables are such properties as the size or isolation of colleges. The dependent variables typically include diffuse attributes of students such

as their liberalism, their tolerance, or their authoritarianism.[1]

This concern with organizational socialization as major restructuring of the individual through the internal impact of

[1] In this respect, American colleges are studied more often than other institutions in this general category. Theodore Newcomb's famous Bennington study provided much impetus. See his *Personality and Social Change*, New York: Dryden Press, 1943, and his "Attitude development as a function of reference groups," in Maccoby et al., eds, *Readings in Social Psychology*, New York:

*Work on this project was partially supported by a grant from the U.S. Office of Education through the Stanford Center for Research and Development in Teaching.

Reprinted by permission of the author.

the organization alone has led to an odd emphasis in the research literature. Interest focuses, to an unusual degree, on extreme and total organizational settings as loci of socialization. Thus, the studies most commonly referred to cover a concentration camp, a prisoner of war camp, a military academy, an isolated and politicized college, two medical schools, and a mental hospital.[2] This is true in a historical period in which socializing organizations (schools in particular) are moving in just the opposite direction—becoming more open, more flexible, integrated and interpenetrated with their surroundings.

A previous paper commented on the *dependent* variable in the research equation—the inclination to study diffuse aspects of the organization's clients (such as their values) as the central outputs of the socialization process.[3] It was argued that some of the crucial consequences of the socialization of students in complex societies involve their allocation to various specialized roles in the social order, and that these decisions as to where a given student will be socially located may be more significant than the changes in his values or tastes, and may be affected by quite different processes.

In this paper, we reconceptualize the nature of the *independent* variable in the standard research equation. Our central argument is that an organization's *impact on the values* (or, for that matter, on other properties) *of the people it processes may be less affected by the structure of the organization itself than by its relation with and definition in its larger social context.* In particular, we argue that the effectiveness of a socializing organization is dependent on its *charter*—the agreed on social definition of its products. For example, a school whose graduates are generally understood to become members of an elite with broadly-defined powers will have much greater impact on the values of its students than will a school whose graduates are defined as eligible for more limited technical roles.

We go on, then, to consider the consequences for diffuse socialization of the social *charter* of a school or other socializing organizations. Before we take up this major problem, however, we need briefly to define (a) what we mean by diffuse socialization, and (b) what significant motivational features we need to attribute to socializees.

A. Diffuse Socialization

It is conventional to distinguish three kinds of broad or diffuse socialization—shifts in an individual's (1) values, or cultural desiderata; (2) personality needs or drives, and (3) significant social roles, or identities, or self-conceptions. These distinctions, of course, rest on established distinctions between the cultural system, the personality system, and the

---

Henry Holt and Co., 1958, pp. 265-275. The research which followed this lead is briefly reviewed in Philip Jacob, *Changing Values in College*, New York: Harper and Brothers, 1957, and very completely summarized in a thorough, new review by Theodore Newcomb and Kenneth Feldman, *The Impact of Colleges Upon Their Students*, a report to the Carnegie Foundation for the Advancement of Teaching, 1968.

[2] Bruno Bettelheim, "Individual and mass behavior in extreme situations," and Edgar Schein, "The Chinese indoctrination for prisoners of war: a study of attempted brainwashing," in Maccoby et al., *op. cit.*, pp. 300–334; Sanford M. Dornbusch, "The military academy as an assimilating institution," *Social Forces*, 33 (1955), pp. 316–321; Newcomb, *op. cit.*, Robert K. Merton, George G. Reader, M. D., and Patricia Kendall, *The Student-Physician*, Chicago: Free Press, 1957; Howard S. Becker, Blanche Geer, and Everett C. Hughes, *Boys in White: Student Culture in the Medical School*, University of Chicago Press, 1961; Erving Goffman, "The characteristics of total institutions," in Goffman, *Asylums*, Garden City, New York: Doubleday Anchor, 1961, pp. 1–124.

[3] John Meyer, *Some Non-Value Effects of Colleges*, Columbia University: Bureau of Applied Social Research, 1965.

social system. Intellectually, they make sense. For most research purposes they seem at present to be unnecessary, since the processes by which they are affected are thought to be very similar. More important, methodologically it is difficult to distinguish among them. Thus, Plant finds reductions in the level of authoritarianism of San Jose State College students over their four years of attendance.[4] This could reflect changes in the features of the *personality system* which authoritarianism scales were originally constructed to measure. The finding could reflect *value changes* in the students as they came in contact with, and identified with the tolerance languages and ethics of middle-class American culture. The finding could also reflect adaptation by the students to the role-perspectives of the middle-class Americans they are becoming, or even simply the adults and full-fledged members of society they are becoming. This latter possibility is suggested by Plant's finding that applicants to San Jose State College who did not attend the school also lowered their scores on authoritarianism.

Any of these changes may be captured by empirical findings of changes in authoritarianism, liberalism, and so on. In measurement, there is no way to sharply separate value components from personality components or role-taking. Further, sociological thinking about these components suggests they are constructed and changed by similar socialization processes.[5]

[4]Walter T. Plant, *Personality Changes Associated with a College Education*, U.S. Office of Education, Cooperative Research Project #348, 1962.

[5]For example, see the various essays on socialization by Talcott Parsons: "Family structure and the socialization of the child," in Parsons and Bales, *Family, Socialization and Interaction Process*, Glencoe, Ill.: Free Press, 1955, chapter 2; or "Social structure and the development of personality," in Bert Kaplan, ed., *Studying Personality Cross-Culturally*, New York: Harper & Row, 1961, pp. 165–199; and others. In his

Thus, in our discussion, we consider these types of socialization under a common heading—diffuse socialization—and do not talk about them separately. From our perspective the taking on of allocated roles is the crucial feature of organizational socialization. Value and motivational components clearly go along with this process and there is no need to distinguish them.

By *diffuse socialization*, then, we mean the acquisition by individuals of qualities which will guide a considerable range of their behavior—behavior in differing contexts and vis-à-vis different social others. We use this idea in contrast to specific or technical learning.

B. Motivational Features of Socializees

In order to discuss the conditions under which clients will take on diffuse qualities, we need to describe briefly the two motivational orientations which we (in common with most of the literature) attribute to them. (1) Individuals are motivated to adopt those qualities which are associated with more valued definitions of themselves and which are associated with more valued futures. Thus greater prospective gains in social status or value lead to more socialization. This idea, of course, is related to the sociological tradition of thinking of the individual as *maximizer* of social profit. (2) Individuals are motivated to take on those qualities which are related to widely-legitimated definitions of themselves and of their futures. Thus, the more clearly defined an individual's future position, and the more it is socially agreed that he will acquire that position, the more likely he is to take on the attributes of that position. This idea is associated with the intellectual tradition of conceiving of the

thinking, value, motivational, and role or positional attributes of individuals are socialized in similar ways and at roughly the same points in time.

individual's action as oriented to social order—as conforming to the definitions of himself and his proper behavior held by others.

With these two motivational ideas in hand, we go on to discuss how individuals acquire from socializing organizations those qualities which the organizations are socially chartered to confer upon them.[6]

I. SOCIETAL CONDITIONS: THE CHARTER

Discussions of the effects of socializing organizations often make some hidden assumptions. They look for effects of internal organizational features such as rates of interaction, social climate, or size. Interaction between socializers and socializees in these settings, however, is enormously conditioned by the understanding both parties have of the wider standing of the institution in society— what social position it can guarantee its clients in society, or what future it can hold out to them. Thus thinking and research about organizational effects include effects the organization has by virtue of its charter in the larger society.

Thus, in studies of "college effects," a great many possibilities are simply evaded by bringing in the highly significant but unanalyzed word *college* into the picture. The word signifies that by virtue of their social charters (*not* their internal interaction) all of these institutions can offer their students guaranteed entry into the American middle-class occupational structure. Any qualities the students take on as a result of their prospective entry into these futures have resulted from the *charter* of the college, not its internal structure.[7] It is further true that American colleges typically can *only* offer students entry into the occupation world. Broader social and cultural elites are almost absent or are so lacking in clear definition that colleges are not chartered to confer these memberships. We will later suggest that this lack of clearly defined elites in society rather than weaknesses of internal structure may account for the general failure of American colleges to produce much broad socialization.

We can visualize this point by imagining what the Bennington Study would have discovered about value changes created by the school if everyone involved—students, teachers, parents, and

---

[6]Obviously, the discussion above by no means covers the problem of the social psychology of the socializee. For example, under the heading of *anticipatory socialization*, there have been some discussions in the literature on reference groups of how an individual may acquire qualities of desirable groups of which he is not, but hopes to become, a member. See Robert K. Merton and Alice S. Rossi, "Contributions to the theory of reference group behavior," in Merton, *Social Theory and Social Structure*, 2nd ed., Glencoe, Ill.: Free Press, 1957, especially pp. 265–268. We consider this problem from the point of view of the larger social order, which allocates various futures to socializees. By the assumptions above, we take it as given that socializees will anticipatorily adopt the qualities they are allocated. This perspective is also related to another point made by Merton—that social statuses are arranged in structured *sequences*, with connections between statuses being made, not only by the individuals holding them, but also by others. See, for example, Merton, *op. cit.*, p. 385.

[7]Thus, the charter is an attribute of an organization's relation to its environmental context, not its internal structure. This distinction is developed in Allen H. Barton, *Organizational Measurement*, New York: College Entrance Examination Board, 1961. Such properties have not been emphasized much in discussions of organizational socialization. Their effects are usually seen to be mediated by internal features of the organization. Prestige and resources, for example, are usually thought to operate by providing higher quality socializers and greater organizational capability. The idea that they might operate directly, by defining the value of the organization's products, has not been given much discussion. See, for example, the thorough discussion of organizational socialization by Stanton Wheeler, "The structure of formally-organized socialization settings," in Orville G. Brim, Jr., and Stanton Wheeler, *Socialization After Childhood: Two Essays*, New York: Wiley, 1966. At several points (e.g., p. 81, and pp. 93-95) this study considers the organization's relation to its environment, but only as this affects such mediating variables as the amount and type of internal interaction.

the wider community—had believed Bennington College to be a reform school for delinquent girls, from which the students would eventually graduate to a stigmatized social status. Even with the same students, the same teachers, and the same organization, it is obvious that the effects of the school would have been very different. The girls would probably have withdrawn in various ways from their status as members—perhaps into a defensive counter-culture—and would have been disinterested in the larger issues of national and world politics.

How does this general effect occur? In this discussion we focus on its operation in schools or systems of schools, as specific and major instances of socializing organizations. The ideas are applicable to all kinds of socializing organizations.

Any socializing organization has crucial features which lie largely outside its own structure and which constitute its relationship with its social setting. One such feature—perhaps the most important—is the social definition of the products of the organization. If, for example, everyone knows that a particular school or class of schools (i.e., "colleges") produces successful people, and if they know that others—employers, professional gatekeepers—know and accept this, then the school has acquired an invaluable social resource in transforming its products. First, the holding power of a school which has desirable futures to offer is very great. Second, the steps in the required socialization process which the school presents to its students do not need to be legitimated with novel ideas located in the school, but can be defended with reference to the already validated futures to which they lead.

The power of a socializing organization or class of organizations to transform students depends on the increase in social value and the type of social posi-

tion which it is chartered to confer on them. Schools which can provide entry into social elites have more power or leverage over their students than those which can confer less success. The status gain from a given school may be greater for students who come from lower status backgrounds, so the proposition must be formulated in terms of status *gain* conferred by the organization. This is a minor point, since practically no young people in modern societies are *themselves* of high status.[8]

In the rest of this paper we apply this generalization in two ways. First, in this section, we consider how variations in school charters *among societies* will affect the kind of socialization which takes place within them. And second, in the last part of the paper, we consider how variations among school organizations may affect the implementation of any given charter.

Now we turn to two specific problems in the relation between societal characteristics and diffuse socialization: (a) Under what societal conditions will a school or class of schools have power to offer

[8]Even if they come from high status families, their own positions are much lower, since they contain only probabilities of future success, not established certainties, and these probabilities—even if conceived quite realistically by themselves and their associates—certainly add up for young people of any given generation to figures centered more closely around the status average than would be true of the range of defined status positions achieved by their parents. Also, and to some extent independently, membership in the adult world is conferred by the school system. Those who have not completed their education are still dependent on this system and in this sense of low status.

For these reasons, it seems likely that the simplest way of defining the status gain a school offers students is to take into account the social definition it is chartered to offer its products. Even though a reform school or prison may seem (to an observer) to offer great future gains to its devalued client, it is likely, compared to the alternative definitions of themselves and associated possible futures which they hold, that these organizations are quite weak.

students entry into elites? (b) Under what societal conditions will this power be utilized to induce students to adopt new diffuse characteristics?

A. The Structural Conditions of School Influence

In order to have great power over its students as a result of the status gains it can offer them, it is important that a school in fact be able to offer and implement the success of its students. But a closely related aspect is even more important. The students must *believe*, and think others believe, that the school has this power. The more it is widely understood and clearly symbolized that passage through a given school will ensure entry into an elite—and the more this power is seen widely legitimated— the more power the school will have over its students.

A number of societal features which increase the power of schools are involved here:

(1) *The prestige and visibility of the elites to which schools lead:* It is easier for schools to establish their authority if they can transform students into members of distinctive elites with special names, styles of behavior, and legitimated prestige. Conversely, schools may be quite efficient in producing social mobility, as in American society, but if the classes and social positions into which their students go are not dramatized, their power is reduced. (In this respect American schools suffer from the same weaknesses as all American non-economic elites.)

In particular, the prestige of elites, and presumably the socializing power of the schools is influenced by the *relative size* of the elite to which given schools lead. If the elite is small, and positions in it are scarce relative to the number of aspirants, the power of the schools is increased. However, this power is again diffused if only a few of the students in the schools will succeed in attaining elite positions, as we shall note later on.

(2) *The degree to which the schools monopolize entry into all social elites:* If any kind of success to which a student or his family may aspire implies success in the schools, then failure in the schools immediately will be seen as blocking off other possibilities for success. On the other hand, if it is true (or believed) that non-academic virtues (strength, hard work, perseverance, piety, or courage) may readily produce success in the institutional order, the student is less dependent on the schools for the validation of his success. He may instead refer to, emphasize, or invent other virtues in himself, and thus retain on a non-academic basis his possibilities for success.

(3) *The directness of the publicly-understood association between the schools and elite entry:* If completion of a given school is seen as almost by definition producing entry into an elite, the power of the school is, of course, greater. This is the case with entry into many professions in the United States, and entry into the civil service in many other countries. The directness of the relation between schools and elites is marked by the use of academic titles, definitions, and achievements in defining elite positions.

One special way in which a society may minimize an association between schools and elite entry should be emphasized. It is possible culturally to agree to view much success (especially economic success) as achieved and defined not in social institutions but vis-à-vis the natural order, or naturally-established markets. This pretense, common in the United States, automatically removes some of the power which schools might otherwise have. The schools can still be thought to provide educations which lead to success in the "natural" order, but they cannot automatically provide and define the success itself.

(4) *The social legitimacy of successful elite entry*: Societies differ on the extent to which success in the institutional structure is valued and seen as legitimate. If it is not greatly valued, or if it is seen as of dubious worth to anyone other than the individual obtaining it, the schools will have less power over their students' significant futures. This is a more important point than it may seem, because societies in which there is the least potential for diffuse socialization (i.e., in which elites and non-elites are most similar) are just those societies with the greatest inclination to legitimize success. If elites are very different from ordinary members, the latter are less likely to legitimize the elites or elite entry. These two factors work against each other.

(5) *The integration and unification of the market in schools*: No matter how powerful a given class or system of schools is in terms of its overall ability to offer valued futures, this power is lost to each specific school if there is no integration among them. If a student, despite any particular failure, can always enter a competing school with his record almost unblemished, as has practically been the situation in the United States, then much of the power of the schools is lost. The student can reject, and anticipate rejecting, his own failure, claiming that it was produced by some undesirable features of the school itself, rather than his own inadequacy.

Thus, if there are many different kinds of schools with different and uncoordinated rules of admission, performance, and graduation, all producing products with a generally similar social definition, it will be difficult for any of them to have great power over their students. On the other hand, if admissions procedures and performance standards are highly coordinated, and if a student who fails in any one school has failed in the entire system, this monopolistic feature of the market of schools will add greatly to the influence of each individual school. That is, to the extent that the route to success within the educational institutional structure is unique and singular, each school gains power over its students.

B. The Conditions of Efforts toward Diffuse Socialization

We have discussed above the conditions under which schools, or classes of schools, will be socially chartered with more or less power over students, presumably to change them in various ways. Now we turn to discuss the conditions under which the influence the schools have—whatever its amount—will be directed toward creating diffuse changes in the individual. That is, under what circumstances will the schools produce the reconstitution of the students' values, needs, or personal styles of behavior? Of course, schools can greatly change students without being *organized* (or allocated the function) to do so. But by and large, for systematic and large-scale effects to be possible, it seems likely that those involved (students, teachers, administrators and groups outside the institution) must be aware of them as functions. The Bennington Study, for example, did not find everyone unaware of the political climate and intentions of the school. And one of the mechanisms by which the school affected its students was precisely through their *awareness* of the valued styles of thought.

The essential societal attribute which determines whether or not schools or classes of schools will devote their power over students to attempts at diffuse changes in them is *the character of the elites for which they confer membership*. If these elites are defined, as typically in

America, to have specific and technical functions for the society, and if their status and authority is seen to rest on this *technical competence and orientation*, then the schools will be chartered, in everyone's eyes, to produce it. If, however, the social status of these elites is defined in a more diffuse way, as involving competence, authority, and responsibility over a wider range, the schools will be chartered to produce broad changes in their students. The students, the groups and communities from which they come, will all understand that the schools are inducting them into a new social world, with new styles of action, new values and virtues, and perhaps new attributes of character. As they proceed through the schools, and year by year are given new standing, they adopt and acquire these new properties.[9]

Thus it happens that students in scientific or technical curricula are less broadly affected by the colleges they attend than students in the social sciences and humanities.[10] It is only partly the formal curricula that are involved—such things play a secondary role in these processes. It is much more what the students and others expect to be acquired in the school, and this in turn is constructed largely out of what they will become. In America, college students in the humanities and social sciences will become *college graduates*—members of a rather low level elite with at least some diffuse functions which are thought to require generally educated people. Students in the sciences will become *engineers* or *chemists*—members of technically-defined occupational groups.

[9]For example, for studies of the relation between the broadly-defined English elite and the public schools which confer membership in it, see Rupert Wilkinson, *British Leadership and the Public School Tradition*, and Ian Weinberg, *The English Public Schools*, New York: Atherton Press, 1967.

[10]See Newcomb and Feldman, *op. cit.*

The general idea discussed above suggests a number of more specific ones:

(1) *The more a society is modernized in structure, the less diffuse will be the impact of its schools on their students.* Modern societies tend to have highly differentiated, technically-defined elites, particularly in their economies, and their schools are thus chartered with creating these specific roles.

(2) *The more a society is organized around economic institutions, the less diffuse will be the impact of its schools.* Economic institutions are, more than others, organized around technical and specific roles, especially at elite levels.

(3) *The more a society places moral emphasis on status, or on ascription, in defining given elite positions, the more diffuse will be the impact of the schools.* On the other hand, elite positions whose public definition is linked closely only with specific performances will not lead to emphasis, in their socialization, on producing or validating broad capabilities in the individual. Thus, societies which emphasize many features of elite class and estate—distinctive forms of expression, distinctive modes of association and recreation, distinctive tastes and consumption—will have school systems which tend to produce broader effects. Of course, American society without a developed or "high" culture, and without networks of communications which form and embellish such a culture, confers exceptionally little power on its schools to create broad changes in their students.

This idea leads to a more general point:

(4) *The more similar a society's elites and non-elites are in their culture and styles of action, the less diffuse will be the impact of its schools.* In other words, where an elite is a separate and distinct culture, the mere entry into it will be associated with taking on attributes of this culture and rejecting attributes of the

mass, or tribal, or folk culture. This situation might be typical of many new and developing nations. It would be less likely in an integrated modern society; but even among modern societies there are important differences in the degree of integration of popular and elite cultures and institutions, which should be reflected in differences in the foci of the schools.

It is of course true that as elite and popular culture diverge, the former may seem increasingly illegitimate to students coming from the latter. Thus the schools may have less and less total power [see above, A (4)]. But our point here is that whatever power is available will increasingly create diffuse socialization under these "missionary-school" conditions.

C. Directions for Research

The analysis above suggests some new types of research. Present studies usually look at value changes in students in one or several American schools. We are suggesting the importance of broader comparisons, and in particular, two sorts of studies:

(1) *Societies* should be classified by the characteristics of their elites and by the social arrangements which lead from given classes of schools to these elites. Then the impact on student values of schools which are organizationally similar, but which exist in different types of societies should be compared. In this way it would be possible to find out, for example, whether schools have more diffuse impact on students in societies with ascriptively defined elites [B (3) above]. Because the comparison would be made between *organizationally similar* schools, it would isolate those effects which did not occur through the organization of the school. In this way, the research could begin to locate the distinctive impact of the *charter* of the schools.

(2) In the same way, within any given society it would be useful to compare the impact of schools or types of schools which are internally similar but which are differently chartered. How much difference, for example, does *prestige* make [related to A (1) above] independent of internal organizational resources and interaction? Or are the effects of technical schools on values weaker than those of broader schools with similar students in similar curricula and activities [B (1) and (2) above]?

The essential characteristics of these two types of studies would be their attempt to measure, and to assess the consequences of, characteristics of social elites and of the connections of the schools with such elites. Schools would be defined in terms of what we are considering their most important resource —the right to confer socially-validated qualities upon students.

II. ORGANIZATIONAL CONDITIONS OF DIFFUSE SOCIALIZATION

As we noted at the outset, there is an extensive sociological literature on the internal structural features of schools (and similar organizations) which are thought to increase their effects on diffuse characteristics of students. If students are isolated from extra-organizational positions and relationships; if they are subordinated to a powerful status order built around the values of the school; if they are prevented from developing or maintaining a defensive counter-culture and indeed are integrated into a peer structure which reinforces the values of the school; and if they are involved in high rates of interaction structured around the appropriate values and with themselves acting in ways which exemplify these values; then, the students will tend to take on the values of the school This is a much-discussed subject, and it is understood that there are a number of ways in which these effects may occur.

Essentially, the literature stresses the impact schools may have by managing the *present* experienced by the student, and by disconnecting him from the past. In this paper we concentrate on the effects schools may have by manipulating the students' potential *futures*: (A) The larger social charter of the school to transform students reaches and affects the student in part through the organizational structure of the school itself. (B) This organization is constantly at work to change and redefine the charter as it is experienced by the student, and also by other members of the community. We deal, in turn, with these two specialized processes, leaving aside those which are better understood.

A. Organization Conditions as Implementing the Charter

Students do not usually have a very clear idea of where in the social and occupational structure they will be allocated. Nor do they know much about a more complex structure—the distribution of probabilities of various social futures which could be attached to them. They do not even know whether they are likely to complete the particular school or class of schools they are entering. (All these things change a little at the level of professional training. There students are more realistic about the social status they will enter, but even so there seems to be considerable unclarity about likely social circumstances—incomes, organizational settings, social contacts, style of life, and so on.)

Thus, whatever the charter which a school or class of schools may have established vis-à-vis various significant parties—legally and socially established gatekeepers, other elements of the system of schools, and even students' fam-

ilies—much depends on whether it can establish this same charter with its students. Unless they *know* how dependent they are on the school for future gains, and unless they know how widely the school's charter is accepted, much of its effect will be lost. For socialization depends heavily on the willing and motivated adoption of appropriate characteristics by the individual, and all this depends on the (a) perceived gains the future offers, and (b) the perceived legitimacy of accepting these gains.

A school must persuade its students, then, that it *can* offer desired futures, and also that its right to do so is widely legitimated, so that they can in safety assume characteristics of these futures.[11]

Some of the classically-discussed features of socializing organizations help here. High rates of interaction around desired values and roles help convince the students that they are likely to have significant associated futures. Attractive and established role-models can *demonstrate* possible futures. Isolation from other social institutions combined with the equalization in status of the students

[11]Wallace, for example, finds sharp changes in the freshmen he studied in their first few months of college. Many more planned to engage in graduate study than planned to do so upon entry into the college. Wallace finds this shift is sharper among the freshmen who interact with upperclassmen (who, by and large, plan on graduate study). He interprets it as peer group influence, but this may play a secondary and mediating role. What is happening may be that the freshmen are finding out from the upperclassmen what the charter of the school is, and how it is to be implemented. Fellow students could be important as additional examples of the charter, not a source of intrinsically-valued influence. See Walter Wallace, *Student Culture*, Chicago: Aldine, 1966. Becker and his colleagues clearly conceive of the peer culture as helping students to adapt to medical school and to retain their highly-valued futures. See Becker et al., *op. cit.*, and Howard S. Becker and Blanche Geer, "Fate of idealism in medical school," *American Sociological Review*, 23, (1958), pp. 50–56, and "Student culture in medical school," *Harvard Educational Review*, 28, (1958), pp. 70–80.

at any level can help commit them to an expectation of a common future created for them by the school.

Some characteristics of schools take on changed significance when seen in terms of their capacity to implement a school's charter with its students. *Prestige*, for instance, which has sometimes been seen as important only because it is associated with socializing resources, becomes important in its own right. Prestigious schools can offer students both general status gains and the knowledge that these gains will be legitimated at many points in the system.

The *social isolation of students* from positions and relationships outside the school, which has commonly been seen as an aid to diffuse socialization, has important defects in its impact on the implementation of the charter. Unable to see themselves and their changes from outside the school, and unable to discover by interaction and experience their changing value and how much the outside world legitimates their internal changes, isolated students must always entertain the hypothesis that their experience is all a game, and that it has little meaning so far as the future is concerned. This idea, privately or publicly held, greatly weakens the impact of the school's charter. To combat it, isolated schools must constantly dramatize the successful career lines which they claim to open up—calling attention to successful alumni, and so on.

Small schools face problems similar to those of isolated schools. Again our reasoning is at odds with the common emphasis in this field, on the virtues of small institutions in socialization. Precisely because they are involved in a network of inter*personal* relationships rather than in a massive and formal status structure, students are less certain of the significance to the outside world of the steps through which they are

passing. They see less clearly the formal status of their teachers in the outside world. Courses, curricula and majors seem more personal—more associated with particular tastes and particular teachers—and less connected with established career lines. As with isolated schools, students in smaller schools (if everything else is held constant) are torn between the idea that their particular college experience is a central part of their development (i.e., is externally validated) and the thought that it is all a game. Large schools tend to be more convincing. Courses, requirements and curricula are more formal and impersonal. It would seem unreasonable to students to believe that such a massive institutional apparatus is not well connected to futures which are validated by the wider status order. In other words, large schools, by virtue of their size, impersonality, and bureaucratization, may seem to the students to have more valid charters than small ones.

It should not be ignored here, of course, that most of the other processes by which school size might affect diffuse socialization operate the other way from ours (i.e., such schools can involve students more and make them more dependent) —they suggest small schools might be more effective. We are not denying that those processes operate, but simply suggesting an additional one which runs counter to them.[12]

[12]Kamens, in a major study of the contextual sources of college dropout, finds substantial evidence related to this point. He shows that, holding the general quality of a college constant, small colleges tend to produce more dropout among students with any given background than larger colleges. This finding runs counter to most sociological thinking on the point and is of great interest. See David H. Kamens, *Institutional Stratification and Student Commitment: College Effects on Dropout*, unpublished doctoral dissertation, Columbia University, 1968, especially Chap. 3. Also see his "College size and student commitment," Russell B. Stearns Study, Northeastern University, 1968.

THE ORGANIZATION OF THE INTERNAL CAREER

Whatever future a school is chartered to confer on its successful graduates it faces a choice about *when* to confer it. If the school chooses to admit large numbers of students and graduate only a few, then the future status of the graduates tends to be conferred only upon completion of their programs. Each student is made unsure about his relation to the charter of the school—whether he is going to be one of the few who succeed or one of the many who fail.

On the other hand, if the school admits only a few students, and graduates almost all of them, then the charter of the school tends to become attached to the students *early* in their career. They are marked out from their other peers at the start and share a common future with their classmates.[13]

It is possible to argue that either of these kinds of systems would have greater impact on the student. The competitive system, in which many are admitted but few succeed, establishes in one sense great power over its students. Their success in improving their degree of conformity to the requirements of the system carries a potentially maximal payoff. A whole career line depends on their acceptance of socialization. On the other hand, this system has great defects as a socializer. Each student must hedge his commitment—if it gets too high, failure would be too costly, and failure is a very realistic possibility. So in protecting himself, each student tends to adopt as behaviors and orientations a set of characteristics which represent a realistic

combination of the probable futures which at that moment attach to him. This is also made necessary by his relationships with peers and others, who also understand his high probability of failure, and who would regard over-eager attempts on his part to adopt the charter of the school illegitimate grasping and aping of his betters. In this way, the peer culture tends to resist the pressures of the institutions.[14]

On the other hand, in a school where a student is given a high probability of success upon entry, adoption of the chartered attributes by the student tends to be safer and more legitimate, even though the school itself might have lost some power over him by having so greatly reduced the scarcity of the success it offers. The student knows that he is set apart by virtue of his admission, and that it is both safe and proper in the eyes of peers and relatives to begin to take on the qualities of the positions to which he is being given entry. In such schools, it is also true that the student or peer culture tends to reinforce each student's adoption of the charter.

THE INTERNAL PROVISION OF OPPORTUNITIES TO ACT

Even if a school is clearly chartered to confer many broad changes on its stu-

---

[13]The distinction between these kinds of systems corresponds in part to Turner's distinction between sponsored and contest mobility. See Ralph Turner, "Modes of social ascent through education: sponsored and contest mobility," in A. H. Halsey et al., eds., *Education, Economy and Society*, New York: Free Press, 1961. But there is no evidence that the organizing principles Turner discusses are closely related to systems and rates of admission and graduation.

[14]Thus Stinchcombe finds that high school students who do not intend to pursue future careers which require high school graduation tend to resist and decline to legitimate high school rules and requirements. See Arthur Stinchcombe, *Rebellion in a High School*, Quadrangle Books, 1964. It is possible to argue that the general resistance of peer groups to efforts at broad socialization which American researchers find arises precisely because such broad socialization is not and cannot be legitimated on the basis of the social futures toward which the students are moving. See, for example, James Coleman, *Adolescent Society*, New York: Free Press, 1961. If this interpretation is taken, student culture is seen as helping the student maintain his career line in the face of relatively arbitrary pressures from the school. This is the view taken, of course, in the Becker medical school studies, *op. cit.* It is also discussed by Ralph Turner, *The Social Context of Ambition*, San Francisco: Chandler, 1964.

dents, it makes a great deal of difference whether or not the students have opportunities to act and interact on the basis of the qualities they are to assume. If they have such opportunities to act and interact, they are of course much more likely to assume the appropriate qualities, and by complying, to control the behavior of other students. One of the difficulties with very prestigious universities in America and elsewhere is that students are chartered with great prestige and future success but little present opportunity to adopt these qualities in action because of the size of the school, the distraction of the faculty, and the scarcity of opportunities to act *per talented and chartered student*. Faced with this situation, they often construct their own networks of action around political orientations and around peripheral student organizations and educational ventures.

B. Organizational Conditions as Constructing the Charter

We have discussed the cases in which schools have broad social authority and legitimacy to confer massive changes on students. Now we turn to discuss the areas in which schools have little by way of such a charter. For example, most of the over two thousand American colleges and universities have little distinctive standing with the law and various other publics through which to transform students. Thus an average school which is trying to assume some larger power over the lives of its students must do so with the force, not of a public charter, but of its own internal structures. This can happen in many ways, which are extensively discussed in the literature. But one process by which it can happen is *through the construction by the school in the minds of its students of a charter which is in fact not socially validated.*

That is, the school can create a picture of an outside world which expects, legitimates, and has distinctive career lines to organize the unique features with which the school can endow its graduates.

In order to create this picture in the minds of students when in fact its charter is narrow and similar to that of other schools, a school must have some of the features which have sometimes been thought of, probably erroneously, as requisites of *any* kind of diffuse organizational socialization. It should be *isolated,* socially and perhaps physically, so the contrast between the internal description of their status and future and that obtaining in the outside world will not overwhelm students. It must have *very high rates of internal interaction,* so as to construct and sustain without external support a novel definition of reality. It needs to *control the norms of the student culture* which are a potential source of skepticism. And it needs, at least to some extent, *a distinctive ideology* to justify without much cultural support the changes it claims to be producing in the characters of the students.

Schools without institutionalized charters also need an ideological base to support the idea that the broad changes they are producing in students will lead these students to success in society even if their significance is not acknowledged by the society. If a school is built around a slightly distinctive moral perspective, it can claim that the virtues it inculcates will lead its alumni, by a structurally mysterious or invisible career line, to success. A school in this situation is trying to base its charter in part on some other moral authority than that of the society itself. Religious schools and some politicized schools have this quality.

All these characteristics of schools are linked together, particularly in societies which do not commonly charter schools to greatly remold students. Thus, among the great majority of American colleges which are not distinctively chartered, those which aim at broadly changing students emphasize social isolation, high rates of interaction, and the long-run significance for the success of present students and past alumni of the virtues of character they claim to produce.

Causal processes here do not move only in one direction—from the design or interest of the college to its actual structure. It is also true that small and isolated schools with high rates of internal interaction tend to create in their students the belief that personal attributes are being constructed in them which will have long-run significance, and which may even be recognized—that is, chartered—by influential gatekeepers in the wider world. In small schools with little renown in which students are isolated from the career lines they hope to follow, and uncertain about the degree to which their educations will actually entitle them to entry, the larger beliefs about the moral significance of their educations are almost essential balancing mechanisms if they are to retain their commitment. Of course, many students in such schools do not retain their membership in the face of this situation.[15] The required faith may be too much to accept and maintain.

C. Some Research Possibilities

Research on the problems discussed above is made more difficult by the fact that a number of different processes connect the variables—suggesting different kinds of relationships between them. Distinguishing these empirically becomes a problem. But two types of studies can be suggested as relatively unambiguous:

(1) The charter of schools or systems of schools should greatly affect the relationships between the size or structural iso-lation of a school and diffuse changes in its students. Research should distinguish schools (or societies) on the basis of the extent to which their social charters involve diffuse socialization. We argue that the size and isolation of a school should be a much more important determinant of diffuse socialization in the absence of such charters.

(2) Researchers can investigate directly the student's perception of the charter of his school. Under what organizational conditions will students (in schools with given charters in fact) be more likely to believe that they are being allocated distinctive futures in the social order? Here the dependent variable is not value change, but student beliefs about the properties of the "alumnus," both in reality and as socially acknowledged. Do students *of given qualities* see themselves as having futures involving broader leadership rights if they attend more prestigious schools, or schools involving them in more intense interaction? And if they have these views, do they acquire them early in their period of membership, suggesting the adaptation to a charter by the student, rather than what is traditionally seen as socialization?[16]

III. CONCLUSION

We conceive of schools or classes of schools as possessing *charters*—institutionalized social definitions of their products. Schools will be more able to create broad changes in the values or attributes of their students if their charters give them the right and power to (a) greatly elevate the social standing of the students and to (b) move them into diffusely defined social positions. Obviously, then, the capacity of a school to change students is greatly dependent on the wider society in which it exists and which charters it. In the United States, for

---

[15]Kamens, *op. cit.*

[16]W. Wallace, *op. cit.*

example, specific schools have less power to control the future standing of their students than is the case in other societies. Further, schools are chartered more to confer occupational and technical future roles on their students than to confer membership in broadly-defined elites. Thus, American schools are likely to be peculiarly weak in their ability to broadly transform students in comparison to schools of similar internal structure in other societies.

The impact of the charter of a school is partly mediated for a student by his information and social relations outside the school—family, friends, community, and mass media. But partly it is transmitted by the organizational structure of the school itself, which can more or less convincingly provide for him the kind of futures which lead him to change in diffuse ways. Sometimes it is even possible for schools to construct broad charters in the minds of their students when the social validity of these charters is weak or non-existent. In part this explains the emphasis, in American education, on broad socialization as occurring under stringent conditions of isolation and control.

STATUS PROCESSES IN SOCIETIES

Positional Prestige   Personal prestige is a significant factor in determining status in the small community, in the suburban neighborhood, and also in the rarified atmosphere of the metropolitan upper class groups, as we have seen. But in the context of a complex industrial society, where individuals are much more apt to relate to others whom they know only casually or with whom they have only occasional contact, status is usually structured in terms of the prestige associated with a person's position in society. And in industrial societies, there is one overriding position that affects prestige: *occupation.*

Occupation as an indicator of prestige tends to cut across our previous classification of the techniques by which status is measured.[1] It is "objective" in the sense that investigators have relatively little difficulty determining a rank ordering of occupations, being aided by such factors as income and education, which are highly correlated with occupational position. It is also both "subjective" and "reputational" in the sense that individuals often employ occupational differences as the basis on which they rank themselves and others in terms of relative prestige. Occupation is a highly salient variable in industrialized societies, and its use as an indicator of status by social scientists and laymen alike is widespread.

A great many empirical studies have been conducted that demonstrate the great similarity in the prestige rankings individuals attribute to occupations.[2] Certainly the most persuasive of these is a study of the rankings given by a representative sample of the U.S. population conducted by the National Opinion Research Center.[3] This study found high agreement among the sample as to the relative prestige ranking of 90 occupations, the ratings being little influenced by the respondent's regional location, size of city in which he lived, his own occupation,[4] his age, sex, education, or economic level. This survey conducted in 1947 was replicated by the National Opinion Research Center in 1963 using similar sampling procedures and an identical questionnaire.[5] The extremely high stability over time of these occupational ratings is dramatically

---

[1]See p. 472.

[2]For a summary of many of these studies, see Bernard Barber, *Social Stratification*, New York: Harcourt, 1957, pp. 100–108.

[3]National Opinion Research Center, "Jobs and occupations: A popular evaluation," *Public Opinion News*, 9 (1947), 3-13; reprinted in Reinhard Bendix and Seymour Martin Lipset (eds.), *Class, Status, and Power*, Glencoe, Ill.: Free Press, 1953, pp. 411–426.

[4]There was, however, a marked tendency for a respondent to rank his own occupation, or one similar to it, considerably higher than the average evaluation of the position.

[5]See Robert W. Hodge, Paul M. Siegel, and Peter H. Rossi, "Occupational Prestige in the United States, 1925-63," *American Journal of Sociology*, 70 (November, 1964), 286–302.

summarized in the product-moment correlation coefficient of .99 between the scores assigned by respondents to occupations in 1947 and the scores in 1963. Results from the 1963 study were also compared with those obtained from a somewhat similar survey carried out in 1925 by Counts.[6] A correlation of .93 again attests to the remarkable stability of occupational ratings over a 38-year period. Hodge and his colleagues appear to be on safe ground in concluding that "there have been no substantial changes in occupational prestige in the United States since 1925."[7]

Similar surveys have been conducted in a large number of countries, both Western and non-Western. A recent summary of 24 of these studies indicates a high degree of correlation ($r^2=.83$) between these rankings and those obtained in the U.S. sample.[8] Of course, the occupations rated are those common to societies of divergent levels of industrial development, and the number of occupations rated varied from study to study—from a high of 90 for the United States to a low of 13 for Soviet Russia. In explaining the high degree of similarity across societies, the authors conclude, "Gross similarities in occupational-prestige hierarchies can be accounted for on the basis of gross uniformities in social structure across societies, whatever the particulars of different societies may be."[9] This conclusion concerning the impact of structure on the evaluation of occupations is, however, somewhat tempered by the authors' later analysis that reveals great similarities across societies regardless of their stage of economic development as measured by gross national product. The latter finding suggests to Hodge and his collaborators an important causal link in just the opposite direction. They propose:

. . . structural similarities may in part be the product of similarities in occupational evaluation. Development hinges in part upon the recruitment and training of persons for the skilled, clerical, managerial, and professional positions necessary to support an industrial economy. Thus, acquisition of a "modern" system of occupational evaluation would seem to be a necessary precondition to rapid industrialization, insofar as such an evaluation of occupations insures that resources and personnel in sufficient numbers and of sufficient quality are allocated to those occupational positions most crucial to the industrial development of a nation. In one important regard, then, adoption of an occupational-prestige hierarchy similar to that of industrial nations may be a prerequisite for development, notwithstanding the fact that increased development may in turn induce further similarities in occupational prestige evaluations.[10]

This latter line of reasoning is consistent with the functional theory of stratification proposed by Kingsley Davis and Wilbert Moore, who explain the "universal presence of stratification" by noting the necessity faced by all societies of motivating qualified persons to seek positions of importance.[11] They argue that two factors determine the relative rank of occupational positions: differential functional importance and differential scarcity of personnel. Their position has

---

[6]George S. Counts, "Social status of occupations," *School Review*, 33 (1925), 16–27.

[7]Hodge, Siegel, and Rossi, p. 296.

[8]Robert W. Hodge, Donald J. Treiman, and Peter H. Rossi, "A comparative study of occupational prestige," in Reinhard Bendix and Seymour Martin Lipset (eds.), *Class, Status, and Power* (2d ed.), New York: Free Press, 1966, pp. 309–321.

[9]Hodge, Treiman, and Rossi, p. 312.

[10]Hodge, Treiman, and Rossi, p. 320.

[11]Kingsley Davis and Wilbert E. Moore, "Some principles of stratification," *American Sociological Review*, 5 (April, 1945), 242–249.

come under severe attack by such critics as Melvin Tumin, who points out the vagueness of the term "functional importance" and questions the validity of assumptions made concerning the scarcity of personnel, arguing that "the more rigidly stratified a society is, the less chance does that society have of discovering any new facts about the talents of its members."[12] As we noted in our earlier discussion of status processes,[13] the debate concerning the necessity of stratification systems continues to rage among sociologists and indeed, implicitly, among all members of all societies and gives little indication of being resolved in the near future.

Social Mobility   To this point, we have completely neglected one of the most important social processes associated with stratification: social mobility. Looking at human society across time and space, three general types of stratification systems may be distinguished. One system is the *caste system*, a stratification order marked by closed social groups, membership in which is characterized by ascribed characteristics, endogamy, and the absence of mobility between strata.[14] A second system is the *estate system*, typically found in connection with feudal societies, where the social organization revolves around a specific form of land tenure. In feudal society there are generally three well-defined strata: the nobility, the clergy, and the peasants. Some mobility occurred within this society, because the clergy never became a closed strata, celibacy among its members preventing its becoming hereditary. The estate system crumbled with the rise of the merchant and artisan classes, these groups having discovered important alternatives to land ownership as a means to wealth and power.[15]

In both the caste and the estate systems, social mobility—the process by which individuals or groups of individuals move either "upward" or "downward" as they occupy differentially evaluated social positions—is either severely restricted or absent. By contrast, we have the third type of stratification system—the *open strata system*—which "assumes that inequalities will exist, and simply stresses equal opportunity to take advantage of them."[16] Unlike the caste and estate systems, these strata have no legal standing; indeed, societies with open strata typically do not attempt to justify or support status differences, and they often attempt to deny their existence. In short, differentially evaluated strata or social positions are in no official way sanctioned or legitimated by the state. Another important distinction among types of stratification systems is the extent to which the three dimensions of status—economic position or wealth, prestige, and power—are intercorrelated. In caste and estate systems these three dimensions tend to be highly correlated, persons highly ranked on one dimension being highly ranked on the other two. In the open strata system, however, the rankings of the various dimensions are much more likely to become out of

[12]Melvin M. Tumin, "Some principles of stratification: A critical analysis," *American Sociological Review*, 5 (August, 1953), 387–394.

[13]See p. 175.

[14]For descriptions of this type of stratification system, see Kingsley Davis, *Human Society*, New York: Macmillan, 1948, pp. 378–386; and Mason Olcott, "The caste system of India," *American Sociological Review*, 9 (December, 1944), 648–657.

[15]For a description of the estate system within feudal society, see Marc Bloch, *Feudal Society*, Translated by L. A. Manyon, London: Routledge, 1961.

[16]Davis, p. 386.

phase, giving rise to the phenomena of rank imbalance. For example, an individual may acquire great wealth but lack the prestige associated with elite status (see Reading 8).

Mobility is possible, then, in open strata systems, but how much mobility in fact is there? Lipset and Rogoff examine this question, using as data the extent to which sons move above the occupational position held by their fathers—an index of *intergenerational mobility* (see Reading 43). Only a crude indicator of positional mobility is employed: the amount of movement between manual (skilled, semiskilled, and unskilled) and non-manual (clerical, managerial, semiprofessional, and professional) occupations. The authors find, contrary to popular belief, that the amount of mobility in American society is approximately of the same level as that found in two selected European countries, France and Germany.[17] On the basis of their analysis of the data, Lipset and Rogoff conclude:

. . . in the United States, France, and Germany, somewhere between a fifth and a quarter of those with fathers in white-collar occupations become manual workers, whereas about one-third of those whose fathers are manual workers rise to a non-manual position, and . . . this has been the state of affairs since before the First World War.

More complex studies of intergenerational mobility, based on movement across ten occupational categories rather than on the simple manual-nonmanual dichotomy, support the conclusions of Lipset and Rogoff. Blau and Duncan compared intergenerational mobility in Sweden with that in the United States and concluded that "there is about as much occupational inheritance in the United States as in Sweden."[18]

Lipset and Rogoff go on to explore some of the reasons that may account for the widespread belief that the United States is the "land of opportunity"—that the possibilities for mobility are greater in this country than in Europe. They propose that these varying beliefs may stem from the American ideology of egalitarianism and the "20th century fact of the greater economic productivity and more equal distribution of income and prestige symbols" characteristic of U.S. society. The presence in the United States of open strata and an ideology of egalitarianism, however, also creates problems for individuals within the society. The ideology encourages *all* members of the society to have mobility aspirations, but does not provide equal access to success for all. The fact that many do experience upward mobility does not mean that all do, or that all can, or that all have an equal chance to do so. For example, whether or how far an individual can rise in this society depends to a considerable extent on the education he is able to get, which in turn depends greatly on his father's socioeconomic status.[19]

[17]A more elaborate study comparing mobility rates in the United States with those in four European countries and Japan resulted in similar conclusions. See Reinhard Bendix and Seymour Martin Lipset, *Social Mobility in Industrial Society*, Berkeley, Calif.: University of California Press, 1960, pp. 11–38.

[18]Peter M. Blau and Otis Dudley Duncan, "Some preliminary findings on social stratification in the United States," *Acta Sociologica*, 9 (1966), 6. Data for the United States utilized in this study were collected partly by the U.S. Bureau of the Census in March, 1962, in the course of its regular "Current Population Survey," and partly through a supplementary self-administered questionnaire administered to a sample of 20,700 American men between the ages of 20 and 65. As such, it represents the most reliable and valid data available to date on this subject. A full report of this study is contained in Peter M. Blau and Otis Dudley Duncan, *The American Occupational Structure*, New York: Wiley, 1967.

[19]See Blau and Duncan, pp. 7–8.

Although the balance is probably gradually moving toward greater emphasis on ability, as recently as 1961 a nation-wide survey indicated that family status and student ability played about equal roles in determining students' aspirations to go on to college.[20]

Ethnicity also continues to play a role in determining the possibilities for social mobility. Negroes, for example, have had far less educational opportunity than whites: over twice the proportion of Negroes compared to native whites have had less than eight years of school, the percentages being 37 and 18, respectively. Although the foreign born are nearly as poorly educated as the Negroes, the education of second-generation Americans hardly differs from that of other native whites.[21] In other ways, too, with respect to mobility, foreign-born and second-generation Americans fare much better than native black Americans. Blau and Duncan present evidence to demonstrate that

Even when education is held constant, the occupational status of Negroes is far inferior to that of whites in the United States. . . . [In twenty of twenty comparisons between Negroes and whites, the occupational score of whites is higher, and the average difference represents] nearly a full step in the rank order of major occupational groups. . . . In sum, Negroes are handicapped by having less education and by having lower social origins than whites. But even if these handicaps are controlled statistically— asking, in effect, what the chances of Negroes would be if they had the same education and social origins as whites—the occupational attainments of Negroes are still considerably inferior to those of whites.

Foreign-born Americans and their children, the second-generation Americans, in sharp contrast to Negroes, do not differ in occupation attainments from the native white of native parentage on the same educational levels.[22]

Aspirations that are encouraged when adequate means for fulfilling them are not provided create tragedies for disadvantaged individuals and groups and sow the seeds of strife and torment for the whole society. (See also the discussion of expectations associated with status processes, pp. 171–175.)

The Problem of Social Classes Revisited   We have previously considered some of the major problems associated with the concept of social class.[23] If we take the Marxian definition of social classes as comprised of sets of persons in similar economic positions who are aware of their common interests and organize to pursue them, then it is clear that there are no viable social classes in modern industrial societies. As Wrong notes:

. . . modern societies are unmistakably moving in the direction of maintaining considerable institutionalized inequality in the absence of a class system, a condition that the Polish sociologist, Stanislaw Ossowski, has characterized as "non-egalitarian classlessness." This condition has not yet been fully achieved even in the United States, much less in Western Europe. But the steady approach toward it increasingly transforms social classes into "ghost" communities preserving a fitful and wavering identity rooted in historical memories. . . .[24]

[20]Natalie Rogoff, "Local social structure and educational selection," in A. H. Halsey, Jean Floud, and C. A. Anderson (eds.), *Education, Economy, and Society*, New York: Free Press, 1961, pp. 241–251.

[21]Blau and Duncan, p. 8.

[22]Blau and Duncan, p. 9.

[23]See p. 474–477.

[24]Dennis H. Wrong, "Social inequality without social stratification," *Canadian Review of Sociology and Anthropology*, 1 (February, 1964), 9. The quotation is from Stanislaw Ossowski, *Class Structure in the Social Consciousness*, New York: Free Press, 1963, pp. 100–118.

Perhaps the disappearance of classes from the social scene should be cause for general celebration, but Wrong is not so certain:

American sociologists have failed to see that the absence of classes may both in ideology and social fact more effectively conceal existing inequalities than a social structure clearly divided into recognizable classes.[25]

In short, classes may be disappearing, but the phenomenon of socially evaluated differences and differential distribution of rewards among men show no signs of weakening. The present evidence suggests that inequalities among men have existed, exist today, and will continue to exist.

We spoke earlier of the increasing reliance on ability and other achieved characteristics and the decreasing emphasis on ascribed characteristics in determining an individual's place in society. Even this transformation is perhaps not to be viewed as an unmixed blessing. Michael Young, in his social science-fiction essay on the rise of the meritocracy between the years 1870 and 2033, suggests some of the problems associated with the merit criterion of social mobility if it is carried to its limit. He writes:

Now that people are classified by ability, the gap between the classes has inevitably become wider. The upper classes are, on the one hand, no longer weakened by self-doubt and self-criticism. Today the eminent know that success is just reward for their own capacity, for their own efforts, and for their own undeniable achievement. They deserve to belong to a superior class. They know, too, that not only are they of higher calibre to start with, but that a first-class education has been built upon their native gifts. . . . What can they have in common with people whose education stopped at sixteen or seventeen. . . . How can they carry on a two-sided conversation with the lower classes when they speak another, richer, and more exact language? . . .

As for the lower classes, their situation is different too. Today all persons, however humble, know they have had every chance. They are tested again and again. If on one occasion they are off-colour, they have a second, a third, and fourth opportunity to demonstrate their ability. But if they have been labelled "dunce" repeatedly they cannot any longer pretend; their image of themselves is more nearly a true, unflattering, reflection. Are they not bound to recognize that they have an inferior status—not as in the past because they are denied opportunity; but because they are inferior? For the first time in human history the inferior man has no ready buttress for his self-regard.[26]

The problem of social class apparently just will not go away.

[25]Wrong, p. 13.
[26]Michael Young, *The Rise of the Meritocracy, 1870–2033*, London: Thames and Hudson, 1958. Paperback edition, Baltimore, Md.: Penguin Books, 1961, pp. 106–108.

43 Class and Opportunity in Europe and the U.S.

Seymour Martin Lipset and Natalie Rogoff

The new sociology has in recent years effectively destroyed a number of hallowed myths. Studies of election campaigns have demolished the civics-textbook image of the independent voter who decides the election after weighing all the arguments—we now know that the "independent voters," the men who make up their minds at the last moment, are for the most part the least informed and least interested section of the electorate, as Paul F. Lazarsfeld, Bernard Berelson, and Hazel Gaudet show in their book *The People's Choice* (Columbia University Press). In a recently published study, *Psychosis and Civilization* (The Free Press), Herbert Goldhammer and Andrew Marshall indicate that the almost universally accepted belief that insanity has increased during the past century is untrue. And in the November 1953 issue of *Commentary*, William Petersen assembled the evidence from a number of studies to demolish the myth that opportunity to rise in the social scale in the United States is shrinking. Examining, among other things, the survey data on the relation between the occupational status of fathers and sons, Mr. Petersen concluded that the rate of social mobility is probably at its all-time high today, with more people rising above the occupational status of their fathers than ever before in American history.

I

If one were to find fault with Mr. Petersen's demonstration that America is still a land of opportunity, we think it

would be in his implicit assumption that the United States has a higher rate of social mobility than other countries. High mobility is a relative term; we call the American rate "high" in comparison with what is assumed to be the "low" rate obtaining in the rigid, closed societies of Europe. But is this assumption, traditional and universal though it be, justified, or is it another one of those myths waiting to be destroyed by sociological analysis?

Until recently we simply did not have the data to answer this question. In the last few years, however, sociologists in Germany, France, Great Britain, Finland, Italy, The Netherlands, Sweden, and Japan have made studies of social-mobility rates based on random samples of national populations. Unfortunately, it is not easy to compare these studies with one another, for in almost every country different systems of classifying occupations were employed. But every study (except the British) does differentiate between manual and nonmanual (white collar, professional, managerial, etc.) occupations, and most (except the British and the Italian) separate rural from urban occupations.

Thus broad comparisons are possible; and having made them, we can hardly doubt that all of the European societies for which we have data, except Italy, actually have "high" rates of social mobility, if by a high rate we mean one comparable to the American. In each country, a large minority is able to rise above the occupational position of their fathers, while a smaller but still substan-

Reprinted from *Commentary*, 18 (1954), pp. 562–568, by permission of the author and the publisher; Copyright © 1954 by the American Jewish Committee.

tial minority falls in occupational status. Indeed, the data indicate hardly any substantial difference in the rates of mobility among France, Great Britain, Germany, Finland, Sweden, *and* the United States. In our opinion, even if the data were completely comparable, they still would not show a great difference among these six countries. The Italian data, it is true, indicate a somewhat lesser rate of mobility in that country than in the other six, but even here the difference does not appear to be great.

Three of the studies—the American, French, and German—permit a statistical comparison if we reduce the occupational classifications to three groupings: manual, non-manual, and farm.[1] The table below compares the proportion of sons in each country who remained in the occupational groupings of their fathers, and the proportion that shifted into different groupings—that is, it compares the occupational "destinations" of men of similar origins in each society. Thus, the first column of the table shows that of 100 sons of American non-manual workers, 71 are themselves engaged in non-manual work, 25 in manual work, and 4 in farming. Notice how similar are the figures for non-manual workers' sons in France and the United States and that the pattern of movement of manual workers' sons in all three countries is well-nigh identical.

Father's	*Son's Occupation*		
Occupation	*Non-Manual*	*Manual*	*Farm*
United States			
Non-Manual: 100%	71	25	4
Manual: 100%	35	61	4
Farm: 100%	23	39	38
France			
Non-Manual: 100%	73	18	9
Manual: 100%	35	55	10
Farm: 100%	16	13	71
Germany			
Non-Manual: 100%	80	20	—
Manual: 100%	30	60	10
Farm: 100%	12	19	69

There can be no doubt that the data from these three studies refute any claim that social mobility in the United States is on the whole markedly greater than in Europe, where family status allegedly limits positions open to sons.[2]

There is, however, a significant difference revealed in the above table between the United States and the other countries: while the majority of the sons of American farmers have shifted to non-agricultural occupations, in France and Germany seven farmers' sons out of ten stay on the land. That is, the American urban economy has offered many more opportunities than the European, drawing large numbers of people from rural areas into cities, with the result that the number of people engaged in farming in the United States has declined at a far greater rate than in France or Germany. But this is not so much a reflection of the difference in the rate of social mobility between America and Europe, of any severer limitations imposed by class origins in Europe—after all, the pattern of

<hr>

[1] The American study "Jobs and Occupations: A Popular Evaluation" was made by the National Opinion Research Center and appears in its bulletin *Opinion News* for September 1947. The French survey "Mobilité sociale et dimension de la famille" was made by the Institut National d'Etudes Démographiques, and appears in *Population*, Vol. V, No. 3. The German data are from the files of the German Institut für Demoskopie. We assume for all three countries that a man's going from a manual to a non-manual job constitutes upward social mobility. For a justification of this assumption, see S. M. Lipset and Reinhard Bendix, "Social Mobility and Occupational Career Patterns," in *American Journal of Sociology*, 57 (1952), pp. 366–374, 494–504.

[2] Pitirim Sorokin reached similar conslusions in the 1920's in his comprehensive survey of the then existing mobility data, *Social Mobility*, New York: Harpers, 1927. A recent survey, *Mobility in Britain*, edited by David V. Glass, also concludes that Britain, France, and the U.S. have about the same rates of social mobility.

occupational distribution for the sons of manual and non-manual workers remains approximately the same in France, Germany, and the U.S.; rather it reflects a difference in what is called the "opportunity structure" in these countries.[3] Not the alleged rigidity of European class lines—Europe's supposed lower rate of social mobility—but the ability of the expanding American urban economy to absorb much larger numbers of the sons and daughters of the American countryside, explains why America is more of a land of opportunity than Europe.

We have looked at the different social "destinations" of men of the same social origins. Now let us consider the different social origins of men who have arrived at the same destination. This is the conventional approach to the study of social and political elites, but it is just as enlightening when used to examine the origins of *all* strata in society.

We find that there is more movement from the manual worker and farm class into clerical, managerial, and professional jobs in the U. S. than abroad. A larger proportion (52 per cent) of American non-manual workers have manual or farm

backgrounds than do their French and German counterparts (35 per cent and 30 per cent respectively) . But this is only the other side of the above-mentioned decline of the proportion of Americans engaged in agriculture. The larger movement of Americans into the class of non-manual workers is due, again, not to *a higher rate of social mobility as such*, but to a greater increase in the proportion of non-manual "opportunities" in the U. S., which have expanded at a faster rate than in Europe.[4]

Returning again to the comparison of social mobility patterns, we should like to buttress our conclusion that much of

Son's Occupation	Father's Occupation			
	Aarhus, Denmark			
	I	II	III	IV
I—Professionals, Bus. Execs. and Self-Employed	38%	23%	14%	32%
II—Clerical and Sales	20	28	12	12
III—Manual	41	48	73	52
IV—Farm	1	1	1	4
	Indianapolis			
I	33%	21%	10%	11%
II	29	42	17	15
III—Manual	41	48	73	52
IV	—	—	1	4

[3]Country A may have more social mobility than Country B, and still enjoy less equality of opportunity because of variation in the opportunity structure. For example, if a country's economy requires 90 per cent of a population to be peasants, even though absolute equality of opportunity prevails, most children of peasants must remain peasants; that is to say, even if every non-peasant position is filled by a peasant's son, only 10 per cent at best can change their occupations. On the other hand, if a country undergoes rapid economic change and the proportion of non-manual positions rises from 10 to 25 per cent—i.e., its "opportunity structure" changes —then even if every son of a non-manual father is provided a non-manual position, a large group must be recruited from some other occupational stratum. Thus one society may have very little inheritance of socio-economic privilege and still have little social mobility, while another society may place a great stress on the inheritance of privileged status and have a great deal of mobility. In any given situation, the "opportunity structure" must be taken into account.

[4]The Finnish data show origins only, and suggest an extremely high rate of social mobility. For example, 29 per cent of the "middle class" (white-collar people) have "working-class" fathers, and an equal percentage have "farmer" fathers. "Upper-class" sons (business and industrial leaders and persons in positions which require a university degree) reported that 15 per cent of their fathers were workers, and 17 per cent farmers. The data are unfortunately not comparable with those from other countries, but they suggest that Finland may have an even higher rate of social mobility, as judged by destination, than the United States. (See Tauno Hellevuo, "Poimintatutkimus Säätykierrosta" [A Sampling Study of Social Mobility], *Suomalainen Suomi*, No. 2, 1952.)

Western Europe has as open a class structure as the U. S. with data from two provincial cities, Indianapolis, Indiana, and Aarhus, Denmark.[5]

It is clear that there is no substantial difference in the social mobility patterns of Aarhus and Indianapolis. The sons of manual workers have about the same chance of rising in both communities.

The Indianapolis study was primarily designed to find out whether mobility in the U. S. has decreased over time. As Mr. Petersen notes in his article, it demonstrates conclusively that the rate of social mobility in Indianapolis remained constant between 1910 and 1940.[6] Happily, we have a somewhat similar comparison for a European city. One of the earliest quantitative studies of social mobility (Federico Chesaa, *La Transmissione Ereditoria delle Professione*, Fratelli Bocca, 1912) was made in Rome using marriage license statistics for 1908. In 1950 another survey of Rome was made using a representative sample of the population. (This study by Alessandro Lehner is reported in a paper presented to the 1953 meeting of the International Sociological Association.) These two studies suggest the same conclusion as the Indianapolis study: mobility rates have hardly varied in the forty-year period.

There are also a number of studies, made during the 20's, of social mobility

[5]The Indianapolis data are taken from Natalie Rogoff, *Recent Trends in Occupational Mobility*, Glencoe, Ill.: The Free Press, 1953. The late Theodor Geiger made the Aarhus survey, which was published under the title of *Soziale Umschichtungen in einer Dänischen Mittelstadt* (University of Aarhus, 1951).

[6]An excellent study of the social origins of the American business elite in 1870, 1900, and 1950 demonstrates that the amount of movement from the lower classes into the "upper crust" of business leadership is about the same today as it was in 1870 (Suzanne Keller, *The Social Origins of Three Generations of American Business Leaders*, an unpublished doctoral dissertation, Columbia University, 1953).

in Germany, and these, too, indicate a rate of social mobility (both upwards and downwards) which is not much below contemporary findings. The largest single study was made by the German white-collar workers' union, which secured questionnaire data from over 90,000 white-collar workers in the late 1920's. Almost a quarter of the males in this group, 23.9 per cent, came from working-class families.

To sum up, our evidence suggests that in the United States, France, and Germany, somewhere between a fifth and a quarter of those with fathers in white-collar occupations become manual workers, whereas about one-third of those whose fathers are manual workers rise to a non-manual position, and that this has been the state of affairs since before the First World War.

II

Two questions present themselves. First, why do all the countries for which we have data exhibit similar patterns of social mobility? And second, why did everyone agree in seeing great differences in social mobility between Europe and America when the data in fact show none?

The answer to the first question is relatively simple. In each of these countries, the so-called new middle (white collar) class has grown at the expense of the rural population, and to a lesser extent of the manual working-class population, though this development has gone very much further and faster in the U. S. than in Europe. The "second industrial revolution" has brought about an increase in administrative, office, and paper work rather than in the number of industrial workers. More and more people are needed in each country to manage industry, distribute goods, provide the services required for leisure activities, and run the welfare state. Thus there has to be "upward" mobility within each society.

A second factor that tends to produce upward mobility is a differential fertility—the tendency of those with more money to have fewer children. While shifts in the economic structure have expanded the proportion of the non-manual prestige occupations, the families in such occupations have not been begetting their proportionate share of children. Consequently, even if every son of a high-status family keeps that status, room is left for others to rise into it.

There is also the fact that the ever growing cities in modern industrial countries cannot replenish and enlarge themselves except by receiving a steady stream of migrants from the countryside who take the least desirable positions. The implications of this fact emerge clearly from two studies, one of Stockholm, and the other of a San Francisco area.

In the first study ("Social Mobility in Sweden," a paper presented to the International Sociological Association at Liege in August 1953), two Swedish social scientists, Gunnar Boalt and Carl-Gunnar Jannsson, determined the name and father's occupation of every boy in the fourth grade of the Stockholm public schools in 1936. By checking these same names against the Stockholm electoral register for 1949, they were able to discover the occupations of 94 per cent of the 1936 schoolboy group. To their surprise, 69 per cent were employed in non-manual occupations; over half of the sons of manual workers had entered non-manual work, though the group was only about twenty-four years old in 1949.

The question naturally arose as to where the manual workers of Stockholm came from, since most of the children of manual workers were no longer in that

class. To answer this, Boalt and Jannsson went back to the electoral register and recorded the occupations of all males born in 1925, the year in which their original group had been born. Comparing "natives" (those in Stockholm schools in 1936) with "migrants" (those who had *not* been in Stockholm that year), they found that over two-thirds of the "migrants" were manual workers, as compared with less than one-third of the "natives." Comparable findings are also reported for Finland.

This clearly suggests the existence of a cycle in which the children of workers in metropolitan areas are able to climb higher on the occupational ladder while their places below are taken by migrants from smaller communities and rural areas. A similar pattern in the U. S. was detected in a study of social mobility in Oakland, California, conducted by the Institute of Industrial Relations of the University of California. The smaller the community in which one was brought up, the greater the likelihood of remaining a manual worker. (In the U. S., the migrants taking up the lower positions in the rapidly growing cities come from Puerto Rico, Mexico, and Canada, as well as from the smaller American cities and the countryside.)

Since urban expansion is also characteristic of Western Europe, this pattern of migrants taking up the lower positions is probably uniform. No wonder the rate of social mobility differs so little at the present time among these countries.

III

Given the evidence that the social structure of the U.S. is actually no more fluid than that of Western Europe, the problem remains of explaining why everyone thinks that it is. This is a complex question. We have answered it in part by distinguishing between social mobility as such, and fundamental changes in the "opportunity structure" caused by the rapidly expanding American economy. Thus the precipitous decline in the absolute and relative size of the American farm class, the other side of which is a sharp increase in the number and proportion of non-manual urban occupations, has been mistakenly attributed to a more fluid class structure in the U. S. But this is only part of the answer. The rest of the answer is to be sought in two things: the differences in total national income and its distribution between the U.S. and Western Europe, and the different value systems of the American and European upper classes.

Income, in every class, is so much greater in America, and the gap between the living styles of the different social classes so much narrower that in effect the egalitarian society envisaged by the proponents of high social mobility is much more closely approximated here than in Europe. While Europeans rise in the occupational scale as often as we do, the marked contrast between the ways of life of the different classes continues to exist. Thus, in the United States, workers and middle-class people have cars, while in Europe only the middle class can own an automobile. In the world as a whole, the wealthier countries tend to have a more equitable distribution of income among their social and occupational groups than do the poorer ones, contrary to the view that sees the rich getting richer and the poor poorer under capitalism. (This more equal distribution of income has nothing to do with social mobility, strictly defined: a high rate of social mobility is compatible with wide discrepancies in standards of living, as we find in India and the Soviet Union today.)

This is what one might call the real, or material, explanation of the impression that the European class structure is rigid and the American fluid. However, there is also an "ideological" explanation, and this has not perhaps been given its due weight.

Until the emergence of the Communist societies, the U. S. was the only country in which the predominant conservative as well as liberal ideology asserted the equality of all men. Ideological egalitarianism in the U.S. has not denied or even challenged existing differences in rank and authority. It has, however, insisted that such differences are only justifiable as a reward for demonstrated ability: able men can and should rise. While family background and inherited social position play a role in the U. S., eminent businessmen of even upper-class background point in self-justification to the humble youthful origins from which they have risen. Walter Chrysler entitled his autobiography *The Story of an American Workman*, and a recent magazine advertisement by the Crown-Zellerbach Corporation, one of the largest West Coast businesses, boasts that it started in a pushcart in the streets of San Francisco in 1870.

In Europe, on the other hand, the conservatives, at least until the present century, have rejected egalitarianism. Aristocratic values and patterns of inherited privilege and position are still upheld by much of the upper class of Great Britain, Germany, France, and many other countries. Thus the European conservative would wish to minimize the extent of social mobility. We would hazard that in much of Europe successful individuals of lower-class provenance would seek to conceal rather than publicize their origins.

In the previously cited French survey of social mobility, this motive is considered a problem affecting the very data. The author of the survey says that "it is precisely among those who have experienced the greatest social mobility that reticence [in the interview] may be of most significance. One interviewer, commenting on the refusal of an interview by a respondent, adds: 'I think it was a question of self-esteem; though he is an industrialist, his father was a white-collar worker, and his grandfather's origins were humble.' "

Then, too, advocacy of equality in European society has largely been the function of the left, whose chief charge against capitalist society is that equal opportunity does not exist and class mobility is not possible. Thus European conservatives and radicals both find it to their interest to deny the existence of significant opportunity to rise out of one's class in Europe. In America, on the other hand, the conservatives argue that it has existed and still exists, and the radicals disagree with them solely as to whether there is sufficient opportunity, or whether the rate of mobility is declining.

This is undoubtedly an illustration of W. I. Thomas's sociological dictum, "If men define things as real, they are real in their consequences." Whatever the actual rate of social mobility has been in Europe, it has been *experienced* by Europeans (and Americans) as low; and this illusory conviction of a lack of mobility has served as one of the major stimuli to political activity.

Is it possible that occupational mobility means less in Europe because there is more snobbery there, and one does not move up *socially* as fast, or as far, as one moves *occupationally*? Such data as we have do not support this view. We have German and American data[7] on marriages between persons classified according to their occupations, the former being based on all marriages in the state of Bavaria in 1927, and the latter on Philadelphia marriage licenses for the years 1913 to 1916.

One would have expected that the differences between the value systems of the European and American upper classes discussed above would make for higher barriers to inter-class marriage in Europe. In fact, however, if the limited and partly non-comparable data for Bavaria and Philadelphia are typical of European and American patterns, such differences do not exist. Indeed, the similarities in inter-class mobility patterns revealed by the above table are in some ways more startling than the similarities in occupational mobility patterns considered earlier.

Other evidence also suggests that social snobbery in Europe is perhaps not as

[7]The German material is contained in *Sozialer Auf und Abstieg im Deutschen Volk*. The American material is drawn from Donald Marvin, "Occupational Propinquity as a Factor in Marriage Selection," *Publications of the American Statistical Association*, 1918, one of the first and in many ways the best American study of social mobility.

Occupations of Marriage Partners, Bavaria and Philadelphia

Husband's Occupation	Bavaria 1927 Wife's Occupation		Philadelphia 1913–1916 Wife's Occupation	
	Non-manual	Manual	Non-manual	Manual
Non-manual	59%	21%	60%	23%
Manual	41	79	39	77

strong a barrier as many believe. A recent British study reports little differences in the rates of marriage across class lines between Great Britain and America when occupations of the fathers of husbands and wives are compared. (David V. Glass, editor, *Mobility in Britain*, Routledge and Kegan Paul, 1954.) The fact that inter-marriage between Jews and Gentiles tends to be higher in Western Europe than in America (see "Jewish-Gentile Intermarriage: Facts and Figures," by Herschel Shanks, in *Commentary*, October 1953) also suggests that status restrictions may be lower under certain conditions abroad than in this country. It may be argued, in fact, that the more aristocratic and secure an upper-status group, the less emphasis it places on exclusiveness. Thus the patterns of rigid upper-class exclusion of *nouveau riche* families, which W. L. Warner has suggested is characteristic of the highest status groups in American society, may reflect the insecurity which is felt in a highly mobile society where no one can feel that he has a permanent and irrevocable place in the upper class.

But why is it that successful Americans, who are more open about their lower-status origins than successful Europeans, nevertheless seem to show great concern about origins in evaluating a man's status? The answer may lie in the ability of men and groups successfully to uphold contradictory values in different life contexts. In economic contexts, ability is on the whole the criterion; in social contexts, inherited qualities. A recent study of race tensions among automobile workers exposes clearly this human ability to maintain "contradictory" attitudes. Dietrich Reitzes reports (in *Journal of Social Issues*, Vol. IX, No. 1, 1953) that many of the workers who strongly favored equal job rights for Negroes took part in organized efforts to keep Negroes out of their residential neighborhoods.

IV

Our finding that no significant differences exist between the rates of occupational mobility in America and industrially advanced European countries suggests a need to modify the long held assumption that a large socialist movement and class-conscious proletariat have not developed in the U. S. because of the high rate of American social mobility as compared with the presumed low European rate. Ambitious sons of lower-class fathers are able to rise in *all* Western societies.

What then makes for the difference in political behavior? Apparently, for one thing, the differences in total income as between America and Europe and the degree to which the different classes share equally in that income, and the different definitions of the class structure. Socialism developed in countries whose dominant groups traditionally accepted rigid class differentiation as a basic social value. Marxist doctrine, with its emphasis on class differences, reflected the realities of European society; it reflected less and less of the realities of the American status system as the productivity of the American economy surged upwards. The socialists in Europe did not have to underline the large variations in rewards for different services; this was, and is, an obvious feature of most non-American societies. It is the American assumption of egalitarianism, combined with the 20th-century fact of the greater economic productivity and more equal distribution of income and prestige symbols, that prevents the building up of proletarian class-consciousness in this country.[8]

[8]Many sociological studies have been dismissed as "painful elaborations of the obvious." If the comparative studies cited in this article had shown that the U.S. had a much higher rate of social mobility than Europe, they too would have fallen under this general condemnation. But their results happen to challenge popular consensus

Further evidence for this general thesis may be found in the fact that there was greater working-class radicalism and class-consciousness in 19th and early 20th-century America than exists today. In the 19th century, the income and consumption gap between the urban classes was much greater than at present. And we find that workers were much more likely to respond to class appeals

than today. The slogan, "a rich man's war and a poor man's fight," arose during the Civil War, not during the First or Second World Wars. Local labor and radical parties had greater success between 1865 and 1914 then they have had since. Trade unions were much more outspokenly anti-capitalist in the earlier period. The assembly line and mass production, with the higher wages and more equal distribution of wealth that they make possible, are thus probably more responsible for the development of the American "classless" society than trends in social mobility.

---

and therefore are exciting. It should be obvious, however, that studies which validate popular opinion are as significant as those which suggest it is wrong—there is no way of telling beforehand: before, that is, a scientific determination of the truth has been made.

POWER PROCESSES IN SOCIETIES

If it is difficult to describe and analyze power processes as they operate within the community, and we have seen that it is, how much more difficult it is to examine the operation of these processes on the larger canvas of a society. At this point in time, it must be confessed that social scientists have yet to produce even adequate descriptive accounts of the operation of societal power processes. It is, we believe, fair to say that at the present time the best we have to offer in this area are some impressionistic observations.

Pluralist and Elitist Conceptions   When we turn to writings on power in American society, we find once again writ large the same controversy we encountered among students of power at the community level. Some observers, most notably, Riesman,[1] Parsons,[2] and Dahl,[3] report that power in American society is widely dispersed and that no one group or coalition of groups occupies a dominant position. Other observers, led by C. Wright Mills[4] and including such writers as Fred Cook,[5] point to the existence of a small, interrelated group acting as a power elite. The views of the two leading spokesmen for these opposing positions, Riesman and Mills, are carefully summarized and compared by Kornhauser (see Reading 44). We have little to add to his excellent discussion, but will re-emphasize one of his points and add one or two of our own.

Kornhauser comments that both Riesman and Mills are "inclined toward a negative response to power." There is the implicit view of power as illegitimate, the notion that in an "ideal" society power would not play any role at all. Parsons has noted that such views are common, being shared by groups as different as utopian liberals and socialists. Their view is

that *both* individual and collective rights are . . . promoted only by *minimizing* the positive organization of social groups. Social organization as such is presumptively bad because, on a limited, short-run basis, it always and necessarily limits the freedom of the individual to do exactly what he may happen to want. The question of the deeper and longer-run dependence of the goals and capacities of individuals themselves on social organization is simply shoved into the background.[6]

[1]David Riesman, *The Lonely Crowd*, New Haven, Conn.: Yale University Press, 1950.
[2]Talcott Parsons, "The distribution of power in American society," *Structure and Process in Modern Societies*, Glencoe, Ill.: Free Press, 1960, pp. 199–225.
[3]Robert A. Dahl, "Equality and Power in American Society," in William V. D'Antonio and Howard J. Ehrlich (eds.), *Power and Democracy in America*, Notre Dame, Ind.: University of Notre Dame Press, 1961, pp. 73–89.
[4]C. Wright Mills, *The Power Elite*, New York: Oxford, 1956.
[5]Fred J. Cook, *The Warfare State*, New York: Macmillan, 1962.
[6]Parsons, p. 222. Emphasis in original.

Both Riesman and Mills appear to refuse to acknowledge the necessity of power processes operating in a society. Perhaps this is the case because both tend to focus attention on *intermember* power—the ability of one actor (individual or collective) to attain dominance over other actors—and to neglect what we may refer to as *systemic* power (the capacity to set, pursue, and implement goals for the system as a whole).[7] The distinction between these two types of power is chiefly an analytical one at the level of the small group: the leader appears sometimes to be acting as one member enforcing his will on another member or other members, and he sometimes appears to be exercising power on behalf of the entire group. However, as we move up the scale of structural complexity to the level of the society, we see a differentiation of structure not only along vertical lines (for example, institutionalized division of labor) but also along horizontal lines, with the institutionalization of various levels of power. That is, some social units, such as the state, become structurally differentiated so that they are legitimately empowered to act in behalf of the larger group; they specialize in the exercise of power in the name of the system as a whole. This is one of the important ways in which power processes at the macrosociological level are differentiated from power processes at the microsociological level.[8]

In this connection, both Parsons[9] and Bell[10] comment that particularly Mills' analysis of power in American society strangely neglects the importance of the role played by political parties, governmental officers, and elected political leaders. Political power, particularly at the national level, has greatly increased in our society in this century. Given this development, Bell finds Mills' analysis, which purports to deal with power but which rarely considers politics, to be "curious, indeed."

A public opinion survey is the last way in which one might appropriately decide to resolve the controversy between the elitist and the pluralist views of power. Nevertheless, Form and Rytina demonstrate that something can be learned about this controversy through this medium.[11] They asked a sample of 354 respondents in Muskegon, Michigan, to report their views on the distribution of power in American society, permitting them to choose among the pluralist views of Reisman, the elitist views of Mills, and the Marxian view that it is big businessmen who really run the country. About three fifths of the respondents were found to agree with the pluralist view of power, and about one fifth each agreed with the position of Mills and that of Marx.

Of more interest was the finding that respondents' views were affected by their own social position: poor white and middle-income Negro respondents were somewhat less likely to agree with the pluralist position than white respondents of middle and higher income. Also, Negroes were much more likely to select the Marxian position than whites. Responses were also affected by the respondent's education, the more highly educated respondents being more likely

[7]Edward W. Lehman, "Toward a macrosociology of power," *American Sociological Review*, 34 (August, 1969), 455, 459-463.

[8]Lehman, p. 460.

[9]Parsons, pp. 206-214.

[10]Daniel Bell, "Is there a ruling class in America?" *The End of Ideology*, New York: Columbia University Press, pp. 59-67.

[11]William H. Form and Joan Rytina, "Ideological beliefs on the distribution of power in the United States," *American Sociological Review*, 34 (February, 1969), 19-31.

to agree with the pluralist position.[12] Given a list of 12 interest groups and asked
to pick those with the "most influence in Washington," almost half the poor and
middle income families, both whites and blacks, selected either "big business" or
"rich people." High income respondents deviated from this response pattern,
over half of them indicating that unions are most influential. Finally, respondents were asked which of the 12 groups listed *ought* to have the most power.
Over 40 percent of the sample refused to select any one group, insisting that all
should have equal power. Poor and middle income blacks and whites were most
likely to take this position; higher income whites were less likely than these
groups to state that all should have power (although the largest plurality took
this position), and were more likely to state that big business should be most
influential.[13]

Two conclusions may safely be drawn from this study. First, perceptions of
the distribution of power in American society are affected by the respondent's
position in the stratification system. Second, precisely what position is taken
appears to vary according to how the question is asked. Economically advantaged groups chose the pluralist description over that of Mills and Marx when
given a choice among the three positions; but the same respondents were more
likely than others to respond that big businessmen ought to have most influence.
As Form and Rytina comment:

. . . respondents with highest income and education are most likely to think the
Riesman description of the distribution of power best when they hear it, but they are
least likely, left to their own devices, to think that this is the way things ought to be . . .
the *ideal* of pluralism received least support from the most economically advantaged.[14]

We see, then, an important drawback to the study of power processes via
perception. The respondent's own position will affect his views of both what is
actual and what is ideal. In our earlier review of the literature on community
power, we also saw the problems associated with relying on reputation. Reputation for power is not the same thing as wielding power. Again, what seems to be
required are studies that focus on the actual decision-making process. As Bell
comments: "Ultimately, if one wants to discuss power, it is more fruitful to
discuss it in terms of types of decisions rather than elites."[15] What one needs to
know is what types of decisions are made by what persons or types of positions
and to what sorts of influences they are subject as they make decisions, with
what kinds of consequences. There are precious few studies of this kind now
available on the exercise of power at the societal level.[16] Many more studies of
this type are required if the discussion of power processes in society is to be
raised above the level of ideological dispute and value-laden controversy.

[12]Form and Rytina, p. 23.
[13]Form and Rytina, pp. 24–27.
[14]Form and Rytina, pp. 26, 29. Emphasis in original.
[15]Bell, p. 64.
[16]Decision making in state legislatures has been studied systematically in a comparative
framework by J. C. Wahlke *et al.*, *The Legislative System: Explorations in Legislative Behavior*,
New York: Wiley, 1962; and various aspects of the decision-making process in the U.S. Congress
have been examined. See, for example, S. Bailey, *Congress Makes a Law*, New York: Columbia
University Press, 1950; J. A. Robinson, "The role of the rules committee in regulating debate in
the U.S. House of Representatives," *Midwest Journal of Political Science*, 1 (1961), 59–69; and
David B. Truman, *The Congressional Party*, New York: Wiley, 1959.

44 "Power Elite" or "Veto Groups"?

William Kornhauser

Recently two books appeared purporting to describe the structure of power in present-day America. They reached opposite conclusions: where C. Wright Mills found a "power elite," David Riesman found "veto groups." Both books have enjoyed a wide response, which has tended to divide along ideological lines. *The Power Elite* has been most favorably received by radical intellectuals, while *The Lonely Crowd* has found its main response among liberals. Mills and Riesman have not been oblivious to their differences. Mills is quite explicit on the matter: Riesman is a "romantic pluralist" who refuses to see the forest of American power inequalities from the trees of short-run and discrete balances of power among diverse groups.[1] Riesman has been less explictly polemical, but he might have had Mills in mind when he spoke of those intellectuals "who feel themselves very much out of power and who are frightened of those who they think have the power," and who "prefer to be scared by the power structures they conjure up than to face the possibility that the power structure they believe exists has largely evaporated."[2]

I wish to intervene in this controversy just long enough to do two things: 1) locate as precisely as possible the issues upon which Reisman and Mills disagree; and 2) formulate certain underlying problems in the analysis of power which have to be considered before such specific disagreements as those between Riesman and Mills can profitably be resolved.

I

We may compare Mills and Riesman on power in America along five dimensions:

1. structure of power: how power is distributed among the major segments of present-day American society;
2. changes in the structure of power: how the distribution of power has changed in the course of American history;
3. operation of the structure of power: the means whereby power is exercised in American society;
4. bases of the structure of power: how social and psychological factors shape and sustain the existing distribution of power;
5. consequences of the structure of power: how the existing distribution of power affects American society.

1) Structure of Power

It is symptomatic of their underlying differences that Mills entitles his major consideration of power simply "the power elite," whereas Riesman has entitled one

[1]C. Wright Mills, *The Power Elite* (New York: Oxford University Press, 1956) ; p. 244.

[2]David Riesman, *The Lonely Crowd* (New York: Doubleday Anchor Edition, 1953) ; pp. 257–258.

Reprinted with permission of the author and The Macmillan Company from *Culture and Social Character*, by Seymour Martin Lipset and Leo Lowenthal, (eds.) © The Free Press of Glencoe, Inc., 1961.

of his discussions "Who has the power?" Mills is quite certain about the location of power, and so indicates by the assertive form of his title. Riesman perceives a much more amorphous and indeterminate power situation, and conveys this view in the interrogative form of his title. These contrasting images of American power may be diagrammed as two different pyramids of power. Mills' pyramid of power contains three levels:

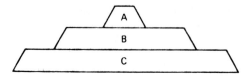

The apex of the pyramid ("A") is the "power elite": a unified power group composed of the top government executives, military officials, and corporation directors. The second level ("B") comprises the "middle levels of power": a diversified and balanced plurality of interest groups, perhaps most visibly at work in the halls of Congress. The third level ("C") is the "mass society": the powerless mass of unorganized and atomized people who are controlled from above.

Riesman's pyramid of power contains only two major levels:

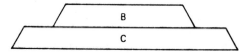

The two levels roughly correspond to Mills' second and third levels, and have been labeled accordingly. The obvious difference between the two pyramids is the presence of a peak in the one case and its absence in the other. Riesman sees no "power elite," in the sense of a single unified power group at the top of the structure, and this in the simplest terms contrasts his image of power in America with that of Mills. The upper

level of Riesman's pyramid ("B") consists of "veto groups": a diversified and balanced plurality of interest groups, each of which is primarily concerned with protecting its jurisdiction by blocking actions of other groups which seem to threaten that jurisdiction. There is no decisive ruling group here, but rather an amorphous structure of power centering in the interplay among interest groups. The lower level of the pyramid ("C") comprises the more or less unorganized public, which is sought as an ally (rather than dominated) by the interest groups in their maneuvers against actual or threatened encroachments on the jurisdiction each claims for itself.

2) Changes in the Structure of Power

Riesman and Mills agree that the American power structure has gone through four major epochs. They disagree on the present and prospective future in the following historical terms: Mills judges the present to represent a fifth epoch, whereas Riesman judges it to be a continuation of the fourth.

The first period, according to Mills and Riesman, extended roughly from the founding of the republic to the Jacksonian era. During this period, Riesman believes America possessed a clearly demarcated ruling group, composed of a "landed-gentry and mercantilist-money leadership."[3] According to Mills, "the important fact about these early days is that social life, economic institutions, military establishment, and political order coincided, and men who were high politicians also played key roles in the economy and with their families, were among those of the reputable who made up local society."[4]

The second period extended roughly from the decline of Federalist leadership

[3]Ibid., p. 239.
[4]Power Elite, p. 270.

to the Civil War. During this period power became more widely dispersed, and it was no longer possible to identify a sharply defined ruling group. "In this society," Mills writes, "the 'elite' became a plurality of top groups, each in turn quite loosely made up."[5] Riesman notes that farmers and artisan groups became influential, and "occasionally, as with Jackson, moved into a more positive command."[6]

The third period began after the Civil War and extended through McKinley's administration in Riesman's view,[7] and until the New Deal according to Mills.[8] They agree that the era of McKinley marked the high point of the unilateral supremacy of corporate economic power. During this period, power once more became concentrated, but unlike the Federalist period and also unlike subsequent periods, the higher circles of economic institutions were dominant.

The fourth period took definite shape in the 1930's. In Riesman s view this period marked the ascendancy of the "veto groups," and rule by coalitions rather than by a unified power group. Mills judges it to have been so only in the early and middle Roosevelt administrations: "In these years, the New Deal as a system of power was essentially a balance of pressure groups and interest blocs."[9]

Up to World War II, then, Mills and Riesman view the historical development of power relations in America along strikingly similar lines. Their sharply contrasting portrayal of present-day American power relations begins with their diverging assessments of the period beginning about 1940. Mills envisions World War II and its aftermath as marking a new era in American power relations. With war as the major problem, there arises a new power group composed of corporate, governmental, and military directors.

The formation of the power elite, as we may now know it, occurred during World War II and its aftermath. In the course of the organization of the nation for that war, and the consequent stabilization of the warlike posture, certain types of man have been selected and formed, and in the course of these institutional and psychological developments, new opportunities and intentions have arisen among them.[10]

Where Mills sees the ascendancy of a power elite, Riesman sees the opposite tendency toward the dispersal of power among a plurality of organized interests:

There has been in the last fifty years a change in the configuration of power in America, in which a single hierarchy with a ruling class at its head has been replaced by a number of "veto groups" among which power is dispersed (239). The shifting nature of the lobby provides us with an important clue as to the difference between the present American political scene and that of the age of McKinley. The ruling class of businessmen could relatively easily (though perhaps mistakenly) decide where their interests lay and what editors, lawyers, and legislators might be paid to advance them. The lobby ministered to the clear leadership, privilege, and imperative of the business ruling class. Today we have substituted for that leadership a series of groups, each of which has struggled for and finally attained a power to stop things conceivably inimical to its interests and, within far narrower limits, to start things.[11]

We may conclude that both Mills and Riesman view the current scene as constituting an important break with the past; but where one finds a hitherto unknown *concentration* of power, the other finds an emerging *indeterminacy* of power.

[5]*Power Elite*, p. 270.
[6]*Lonely Crowd*, p. 240.
[7]*Ibid.*, p. 240.
[8]*Power Elite*, p. 271.
[9]*Ibid.*, p. 273.

[10]C. Wright Mills, "The Power Elite," in Arthur Kornhauser (ed.), *Problems of Power in American Society* (Detroit: Wayne University Press, 1958), p. 161.
[11]*Lonely Crowd*, pp. 246-247.

3) Operation of the Structure of Power

Mills believes the power elite sets all important public policies, especially foreign policy. Riesman, on the other hand, does not believe that the same group or coalition of groups sets all major policies, but rather that the question of who exercises power varies with the issue at stake: most groups are inoperative on most issues, and all groups are operative primarily on those issues which vitally impinge on their central interests. This is to say that there are as many power structures as there are distinct spheres of policy.[12]

As to the modes of operation, both Mills and Riesman point to increasing *manipulation* rather than command or persuasion as the favored form of power play. Mills emphasizes the secrecy behind which important policy-determination occurs. Riesman stresses not so much manipulation under the guise of secrecy as manipulation under the guise of mutual tolerance for one another's interests and beliefs. Manipulation occurs, according to Riesman, because each group is trying to hide its concern with power in order not to antagonize other groups. Power relations tend to take the form of "monopolistic competition", "rules of fairness and fellowship [rather than the impersonal forces of competition] dictate how far one can go."[13] Thus both believe the play of power takes place to a considerable extent backstage; but Mills judges this power play to be under the direction of one group, while Riesman sees it as controlled by a mood and structure of accommodation among many groups.

Mills maintains that the mass media of communication are important instruments of manipulation: the media lull people to sleep, so to speak, by suppressing political topics and by emphasizing entertainment. Riesman alleges that the mass media give more attention to politics and problems of public policy than their audiences actually want, and thereby convey the false impression that there is more interest in public affairs than really exists in America at the present time. Where Mills judges the mass media of communication to be powerful political instruments in American society,[14] Riesman argues that they have relatively less significance in this respect.[15]

4) Bases of the Structure of Power

Power tends to be patterned according to the structure of interests in a society. Power is shared among those whose interests converge, and divides along lines where interests diverge. To Mills, the power elite is a reflection and solidification of a *coincidence of interests* among the ascendant institutional orders. The power elite rests on the "many interconnections and points of coinciding interests" of the corporations, political institutions, and military services.[16] For Riesman, on the other hand, there is an amorphous power structure which reflects a *diversity of interests* among the major organized groups. The power structure of veto groups rests on the divergent interests of political parties, business groups, labor organizations, farm blocs, and a myriad of other organized groups.[17]

But power is not a simple reflex of interests alone. It also rests on the capabilities and opportunities for cooperation among those who have similar interests, and for confrontation among those with opposing interests. Mills argues in some detail that the power elite rests not merely on the coincidence of

[2]*Ibid.*, p. 256.
[13]*Ibid.*, p. 247.

[14]*Power Elite*, pp. 315–316.
[15]*Lonely Crowd*, pp. 229–231.
[16]*Power Elite*, p. 19.
[17]*Lonely Crowd*, p. 247.

interests among major institutions but also on the "psychological similarity and social intermingling" of their higher circles.[18] By virtue of similar social origins (old family, upper-class background), religious affiliations (Episcopalian and Presbyterian), education (Ivy League college or military academy), and the like, those who head up the major institutions share codes and values as well as material interests. This makes for easy communication, especially when many of these people already know one another, or at least know many people in common. They share a common way of life, and therefore possess both the will and the opportunity to integrate their lines of action as representatives of key institutions. At times this integration involves "explicit co-ordination," as during war.[19] So much for the bases of power at the apex of the structure.

At the middle and lower levels of power, Mills emphasizes the lack of independence and concerted purpose among those who occupy similar social positions. In his book on the middle classes,[20] Mills purports to show the weakness of white-collar people that results from their lack of economic independence and political direction. The white-collar worker simply follows the more powerful group of the moment. In his book on labor leaders,[21] Mills locates the alleged political impotence of organized labor in its dependence on government. Finally, the public is construed as composed of atomized and submissive individuals who are incapable of engaging in effective communication and political action.[22]

Riesman believes that power "is founded, in large measure, on interpersonal expectations and attitudes."[23] He asserts that in addition to the diversity of interest underlying the pattern of power in America there are widespread feelings of weakness and dependence at the top as well as at the bottom of the power structure: "if businessmen feel weak and dependent they do in actuality become weaker and more dependent, no matter what material resources may be ascribed to them."[24] In other words, the amorphousness of power in America rests in part on widespread feelings of weakness and dependence. These feelings are found among those whose position in the social structure provides resources which they could exploit, as well as among those whose position provides less access to the means of power. In fact, Riesman is concerned with showing that people at all levels of the social structure tend to feel weaker than their objective position warrants.

The theory of types of conformity that provides the foundation of so much of Riesman's writings enters into his analysis of power at this point. The "other-directed" orientation in culture and character helps to sustain the amorphousness of power.

The other-directed person in politics is the "inside-dopester," the person who possesses political competence but avoids political commitment. This is the dominant type in the veto groups, since other-direction is prevalent in the strata from which their leaders are drawn.

Both within the [veto] groups and in the situation created by their presence, the political mood tends to become one of other-directed tolerance.[25]

However, Riesman does not make the basis of power solely psychological:

---

[18]*Power Elite*, p. 19.

[19]*Ibid.*, pp. 19-20.

[20]C. Wright Mills, *White Collar* (New York: Oxford University Press, 1951).

[21]C. Wright Mills, *The New Men of Power* (New York: Harcourt, Brace, 1948).

[22]*Power Elite*, 302ff.

[23]*Lonely Crowd*, p. 253.

[24]*Ibid.*, p. 253.

[25]*Ibid.*, p. 248.

This does not mean, however, that the veto groups are formed along the lines of character structure. As in a business corporation there is room for extreme inner-directed and other-directed types, and all mixtures between, so in a veto group there can exist complex "symbiotic" relationships among people of different political styles. . . . Despite these complications I think it fair to say that the veto groups, even when they are set up to protect a clearcut moralizing interest, are generally forced to adopt the political manners of the other-directed.[26]

Riesman and Mills agree that there is widespread apathy in American society, but they disagree on the social distribution of political apathy. Mills locates the apathetic primarily among the lower social strata, whereas Riesman finds extensive apathy among people of higher as well as lower status. Part of the difference may rest on what criteria of apathy are used. Mills conceives of apathy as the lack of political meaning in one's life, the failure to think of personal interests in political terms, so that what happens in politics does not appear to be related to personal troubles.[27] Riesman extends the notion of apathy to include the politically uninformed as well as the politically uncommitted.[28] Thus political indignation undisciplined by political understanding is not a genuine political orientation. Riesman judges political apathy to be an important *basis* for amorphous power relations. Mills, on the other hand, treats political apathy primarily as a *result* of the concentration of power.

5) Consequences of the Structure of Power

Four parallel sets of consequences of the structure of power for American society may be inferred from the writings of Mills and Riesman. The first concerns the impact of the power structure on the interests of certain groups or classes in American society. Mills asserts that the existing power arrangements enhance the interests of the major institutions whose leaders constitute the power elite.[29] Riesman asserts the contrary: no one group or class is decisively favored over others by the cumulated decisions on public issues.[30]

The second set of consequences concerns the impact of the structure of power on the quality of politics in American society. Here Mills and Riesman are in closer agreement. Mills maintains that the concentration of power in a small circle, and the use of manipulation as the favored manner of exercising power, lead to the decline of politics as public debate. People are decreasingly capable of grasping political issues, and of relating them to personal interests.[31] Riesman also believes that politics has declined in meaning for large numbers of people. This is not due simply to the ascendancy of "veto groups," although they do foster "the tolerant mood of other-direction and hasten the retreat of the inner-directed indignants."[32] More important, the increasing complexity and remoteness of politics make political self-interest obscure and aggravate feelings of impotence even when self-interest is clear.[33]

The third set of consequences of the American power structure concerns its impact on the quality of power relations themselves. Mills contends that the concentration of power has taken place without a corresponding shift in the bases of legitimacy of power: power is still supposed to reside in the public and its elected representatives, whereas in reality it resides in the hands of those who direct the key bureaucracies. As a consequence,

[26]*Lonely Crowd*, p. 249.
[27]*White Collar*, p. 327.
[28]David Riesman and Nathan Glazer, "Criteria for Political Apathy," in Alvin W. Gouldner (ed.), *Studies in Leadership* (New York: Harper, 1950).

[29]*Power Elite*, 276ff.
[30]*Lonely Crowd*, p. 257.
[31]*White Collar*, pp. 342–350.
[32]*Lonely Crowd*, p. 251.
[33]"Criteria for Political Apathy," p. 520.

men of power are neither responsible nor accountable for their power.[34] Riesman also implies that there is a growing discrepancy between the facts of power and the images of power, but for a reason opposite to Mills': power is more widely dispersed than is generally believed.[35]

Finally, a fourth set of consequences concerns the impact of the power structure on democratic leadership. If power tends to be lodged in a small group which is not accountable for its power, and if politics no longer involves genuine public debate, then there will be a *severe weakening of democratic institutions*, if not of leadership (the power elite exercises leadership in one sense of the term in that it makes decisions on basic policy for the nation). Mills claims that power in America has become so concentrated that it increasingly resembles the Soviet system of power:

> Official commentators like to contrast the ascendancy in totalitarian countries of a tightly organized clique with the American system of power. Such comments, however, are easier to sustain if one compares mid-twentieth-century Russia with mid-nineteenth-century America, which is what is often done by Tocqueville, quoting Americans making the contrast. But that was an America of a century ago, and in the century that has passed, the American elite have not remained as patrioteer essayists have described them to us. The "loose cliques" now head institutions of a scale and power not then existing and, especially since World War I, the loose cliques have tightened up.[36]

If, on the other hand, power tends to be dispersed among groups which are primarily concerned to protect and defend their interests, rather than to advance general policies and their own leadership, and if at the same time politics has declined as a sphere of duty and self-interest, then there will be a

severe weakening of leadership. Thus Riesman believes that "power in America seems to [be] situational and mercurial; it resists attempts to locate it."[37] This "indeterminacy and amorphousness" of power inhibits the development of leadership:

> Where the issue involves the country as a whole, no individual or group leadership is likely to be very effective, because the entrenched veto groups cannot be budged. . . . Veto groups exist as defense groups, not as leadership groups.[38]

Yet Riesman does not claim that the decline of leadership directly threatens American democracy at least in the short run: the dispersion of power among a diversity of balancing "veto groups" operates to support democratic institutions even as it inhibits effective leadership. The long-run prospects of a leaderless democracy are of course not promising.

In the second part of this paper, I wish to raise certain critical questions about Riesman's and Mills' views of power. One set of questions seeks to probe more deeply the basic area of disagreement in their views. A second set of questions concerns their major areas of agreement.

Power usually is analyzed according to its distribution among the several units of a system. Most power analysts construe the structure of power as a *hierarchy*—a rank-order of units according to their amount of power. The assumption often is made that there is only one such structure, and that all units may be ranked vis-à-vis one another. Units higher in the hierarchy have power over units lower in the structure, so there is a one-way flow of power. Mills tends to adopt this approach to the structure of power.

Riesman rejects this conception of the power structure as mere hierarchy:

> The determination of who [has more power] has to be made all over again for

[34]*Power Elite*, pp. 316–317.
[35]*Lonely Crowd*, pp. 257–258.
[36]*Power Elite*, p. 271.

[37]*Lonely Crowd*, p. 257.
[38]*Ibid.*, pp. 257, 248.

Two Portraits of the American Power Structure

Power structure	Mills	Riesman
Levels	a) unified power elite b) diversified and balanced plurality of interest groups c) mass of unorganized people who have no power over elite	a) no dominant power elite b) diversified and balanced plurality of interest groups c) mass of unorganized people who have some power over interest groups
Changes	a) increasing concentration of power	a) increasing dispersion of power
Operation	a) one group determines all major policies b) manipulation of people at the bottom by group at the top	a) who determines policy shifts with the issue b) monopolistic competition among organized groups
Bases	a) coincidence of interests among major institutions (economic, military, governmental) b) social similarities and psychological affinities among those who direct major institutions	a) diversity of interests among major organized groups b) sense of weakness and dependence among those in higher as well as lower status
Consequences	a) enhancement of interests of corporations, armed forces, and executive branch of government b) decline of politics as public debate c) decline of responsible and accountable power— loss of democracy	a) no one group or class is favored significantly over others b) decline of politics as duty and self-interest c) decline of effective leadership

our time: we cannot be satisfied with the answers given by Marx, Mosca, Michels, Pareto, Weber, Veblen, or Burnham.[39]

The image of power in contemporary America presented [in the *Lonely Crowd*] departs from current discussions of power which are usually based on a search for a ruling class.[40]

Riesman is not just denying the existence of a power elite in contemporary American society; he is also affirming the need to consider other aspects of power than only its unequal distribution. He is especially eager to analyze common responses to power:

If the leaders have lost the power, why have the led not gained it? What is there about the other-directed man and his life situation which prevents the transfer? In terms of situation, it seems that the pattern of monopolistic competition of the veto groups resists individual attempts at power aggrandizement. In terms of character, the other-directed man simply does not seek power; perhaps, rather, he avoids and evades it.[41]

Whereas Mills emphasizes the *differences* between units according to their power, Riesman emphasizes their *similarities* in this respect. In the first view, some units are seen as dominated by other units, while in the second view, all units are

[39]*Lonely Crowd*, p. 255.
[40]*Ibid.*, p. 260.

[41]*Ibid.*, p. 275.

seen as subject to constraints which shape and limit their use of power *in similar directions.*

The problem of power is not simply the differential capacity to make decisions, so that those who have power bind those who do not. Constraints also operate on those who are in decision-making positions, for if these are the places where acts of great consequence occur so are they the foci for social pressures. These pressures become translated into restrictions on the alternatives among which decision-makers can choose. Power may be meaningfully measured by ascertaining the range of alternatives which decision-makers can realistically consider. To identify those who make decisions is not to say how many lines of action are open to them, or how much freedom of choice they enjoy.

A major advance in the study of power is made by going beyond a formal conception of power, in which those who have the authority to make decisions are assumed to possess the effective means of power and the will to use it. Nor can it be assumed that those not in authority lack the power to determine public policy. The identification of effective sources of power requires analysis of how *decision-makers are themselves subject to various kinds of constraint.* Major sources of constraint include 1) opposing elites and publics, and 2) cultural values and corresponding psychological receptivities and resistances to power. A comparison of Mills and Riesman with respect to these categories of constraint reveals the major area of disagreement between them.

Mills implies that both sources of constraint are inoperative on the highest levels of power. 1) There is little opposition among the top power-holders. Since they are not in opposition they do not constrain one another. Instead, they are unified and mutually supportive. Further-

more, there are few publics to constrain the elite. Groups capable of effective participation in broad policy determination have been replaced by atomized masses that are powerless to affect policy since they lack the bases for association and communication. Instead, people in large numbers are manipulated through organizations and media controlled by the elite. 2) Older values and codes no longer grip elites nor have they been replaced by new values and codes which could regulate the exercise of power. Top men of power are not constrained either by an inner moral sense or by feelings of dependence on others. The widespread permissiveness toward the use of expedient means to achieve success produces "the higher immorality," that is to say, the irresponsible exercise of power.

In sharp contrast to Mills, Riesman attaches great importance to constraints on decision-makers. 1) There is a plethora of organized groups, "each of which has struggled for and finally attained a power to stop things conceivably inimical to its interests."[42] Furthermore, there is extensive opportunity for large numbers of people to influence elites, because the latter are constrained by their competitive relations with one another to bid for support in the electoral arena and more diffusely in the realm of public relations. 2) The cultural emphasis on "mutual tolerance" and social conformity places a premium on "getting along" with others at the expense of taking strong stands. People are disposed to avoid long-term commitments as a result of their strong feelings of dependence on their immediate peers. "Other-directed" persons seek to maximize approval rather than power.

In general, the decisive consideration in respect to the restraint of power is the presence of multiple centers of power. Where there are many power groups, not

[42]*Lonely Crowd,* p. 247.

only are they mutually constrained; they also are dependent on popular support, and therefore responsive to public demands. Now, there are many readily observable cases of regularized constraint among power groups in American society. Organized labor is one of many kinds of "countervailing power" in the market place.[43] In the political sphere, there is a strong two-party system and more or less stable factionalism within both parties, opposition among interest blocs in state and national legislatures, rivalry among executive agencies of government and the military services, and so forth.

Mills relegates these conflicting groups to the middle levels of power. Political parties and interest groups both inside and outside of government are not important units in the structure of power, according to Mills. It would seem that he takes this position primarily with an eye to the sphere of foreign policy, where only a few people finally make the big decisions. But he fails to put his argument to a decisive or meaningful test: he does not examine the pattern of decisions to show that foreign policy not only is made *by* a few people, but that it is made *for their particular interests.* Mills' major premise seems to be that all decisions are taken by and for special interests; there is no action oriented toward the general interests of the whole community. Furthermore, Mills seems to argue that because only a very few people occupy key decision-making *positions,* they are free to decide on whatever best suits their particular interests. But the degree of *autonomy* of decision-makers cannot be

[43]Riesman notes that "the concept of the veto groups is analogous to that of countervailing power developed in Galbraith's *American Capitalism,* although the latter is more sanguine in suggesting that excessive power tended to call forth its own limitation by opposing power. . ." (Riesman and Glazer, "The Lonely Crowd: A Reconsideration in 1960," in S. M. Lipset and Leo Lowenthal, editors, *Culture and Social Character,* New York: The Free Press of Glencoe, 1961, p. 449).

inferred from the *number* of decision-makers, nor from the *scope* of their decisions. It also is determined by the character of decision-making, especially *the dependence of decision-makers on certain kinds of procedure and support.*

Just as Mills is presenting a distorted image of power in America when he fails to consider the pressures on those in high positions, so Riesman presents a biased picture by not giving sufficient attention to *power differentials* among the various groups in society. When Riesman implies that if power is dispersed, then it must be relatively equal among groups and interests, with no points of concentration, he is making an unwarranted inference. The following statement conjures up an image of power in America that is as misleading on its side as anything Mills has written in defense of his idea of a power elite.

One might ask whether one would not find, over a long period of time, that decisions in America favored one group or class . . . over others. Does not wealth exert its pull in the long run? In the past this has been so; for the future I doubt it. The future seems to be in the hands of the small business and professional men who control Congress, such as realtors, lawyers, car salesmen, undertakers, and so on; of the military men who control defense and, in part, foreign policy; of the big business managers and their lawyers, finance-committee men, and other counselors who decide on plant investment and influence the rate of technological change; of the labor leaders who control worker productivity and worker votes; of the black belt whites who have the greatest stake in southern politics; of the Poles, Italians, Jews, and Irishmen who have stakes in foreign policy, city jobs, and ethnic, religious and cultural organizations; of the editorializers and storytellers who help socialize the young, tease and train the adult, and amuse and annoy the aged; of the farmers—themselves a warring congeries of cattlemen, corn men, dairymen, cotton men, and so on—who control key departments and committees and who, as the living representatives of our inner-directed past, control many of our memories; of the Russians and, to a lesser degree, other foreign powers who control much of our agenda of attention; and so on.[44]

It appears that Riesman is asking us to believe that power differentials do not exist, but only differences in the spheres within which groups exercise control.

If Riesman greatly exaggerates the extent to which organized interests possess equal power, nevertheless he poses an important problem that Mills brushes aside. For Riesman goes beyond merely noting the existence of opposition among "veto groups" to suggest that they operate to smother one another's initiative and leadership. It is one thing for interest groups to constrain one another; it is something else again when they produce stalemate. Riesman has pointed to a critical problem for pluralist society: the danger that power may become fragmented among so many competing groups that effective general leadership cannot emerge.

On Mills' side, it is indisputable that American political institutions have undergone extensive centralization and bureaucratization. This is above all an *institutional* change wrought by the greatly expanded scale of events and decisions in the contemporary world. But centralization cannot be equated with a power elite! There can be highly centralized institutions and at the same time a fragmentation of power among a multiplicity of relatively independent public and private groups. Thus Riesman would appear to be correct that the substance of power resides in many large organizations, and that these organizations are not unified or coordinated in any firm fashion. If they were, surely Mills would have been able to identify the major mechanisms that could produce this result. That he has failed to do so is the most convincing evidence for their nonexistence.

To complete this analysis, we need

[44] *The Lonely Crowd*, p. 257.

only remind ourselves of the fundamental area of agreement between our two critics of American power relations. Both stress *the absence of effective political action* at all levels of the political order, in particular among the citizenry. For all of their differences, Mills and Riesman agree that there has been a decline in effective political participation, or at least a failure of political participation to measure up to the requirements of contemporary events and decisions. This failure has not been compensated by an increase in effective political action at the center: certainly Riesman's "veto groups" are not capable of defining and realizing the community's general aspirations; nor is Mills' "power elite" such a political agency. Both are asserting the inadequacy of political institutions, including public opinion, party leadership, Congress, and the Presidency, even as they see the slippage of power in different directions. In consequence, neither is sanguine about the capacity of the American political system to provide responsible leadership, especially in international affairs.

If there is truth in this indictment, it also may have its source in the very images of power that pervade Mills' and Riesman's thought. They are both inclined toward a negative response to power; and neither shows a willingness to confront the idea of a political system and the ends of power in it. Riesman reflects the liberal suspicion of power, as when he writes "we have come to realize that men who compete primarily for wealth are relatively harmless as compared with men who compete primarily for power." That such assertions as this may very well be true is beside the point. For certainly negative consequences of power can subsist along with positive ones. At times Riesman seems to recognize the need for people to seek and use power if they as individuals and the society as a whole are to develop to the fullest of their capacities. But his dominant orientation towards power remains highly individualistic and negative.

Mills is more extreme than Riesman on this matter, as he never asks what the community requires in the way of resources of power and uses of power. He is instead preoccupied with the magnitude of those resources and the allegedly destructive expropriation of them by and for the higher circles of major institutions. It is a very limited notion of power that construes it only in terms of coercion and conflict among particular interests. Societies require arrangements whereby resources of power can be effectively used and supplemented for public goals. This is a requirement for government, but the use of this term should not obscure the fact that government possesses power— or lacks effectiveness. Mills does not concern himself with the *ends* of power, nor with the conditions for their attainment. He has no conception of the bases of political order, and no theory of the functions of government and politics. He suggests nothing that could prevent his "power elite" from developing into a full-blown totalitarianism. The logic of Mills' position finally reduces to a contest between anarchy and tyranny.[45]

[45]Mills' narrow conception of power has been discussed by Talcott Parsons in his review of *The Power Elite* [Talcott Parsons, "The Distribution of Power in American Society," *World Politics*, X (October, 1957), 123–143]. Parsons notes that Mills uses a "zero-sum" notion, in that power is interpreted exclusively as a fixed quantity which is more or less unequally distributed among the various units in society. Power, however, also has a more general reference, to the political community as a whole, and to government as the agency of the total community. Viewed from this standpoint, power is a function of the integration of the community and serves general interests. Parsons argues, I think correctly, that Mills' sole concern

The problem of power seems to bring out the clinician in each of us. We quickly fasten on the pathology of power, whether we label the symptoms as "inside-dopesterism" (Riesman) or as "the higher immorality" (Mills). As a result, we often lose sight of the ends of power in the political system under review. It is important to understand that pivotal decisions increasingly are made at the national level, and that this poses genuine difficulties for the maintenance of democratic control. It is also important to understand that a multiplicity of relatively autonomous public and private agencies increasingly pressure decision-makers, and that this poses genuine difficulties for the maintenance of effective political leadership. But the fact remains that there are many cases of increasingly centralized decision-making *and* democratic control, and of multiple constraints on power *and* effective leadership. There is no simple relationship between the extent to which power is equally distributed and the efficacy of democratic order. For a modern democratic society requires strong government as well as a dispersal of power among diverse groups. Unless current tendencies are measured against both sets of needs, there will be little progress in understanding how either one is frustrated or fulfilled. Finally, in the absence of more disciplined historical and comparative research, we shall continue to lack a solid empirical basis for evaluating such widely divergent diagnoses of political malaise as those given us by Mills and Riesman.

for how power is used by some against others is associated with his tendency to exaggerate both the weight and the illegitimacy of power in the determination of social events.

Section V

ADAPTIVE PROCESSES IN SOCIETIES

Adaptation—the securing and conserving of control over the environment—in societies occurs primarily within the province of economic institutions and structures. It is clear that in the United States, as in other Western societies, economic institutions are the dominant institutions. Indeed, it is no accident that most of the adjectives used to differentiate Western societies from most other societies—adjectives such as "advanced," "developed," "industrialized"—refer specifically to the state of the economic institutions and structures. We cannot pretend to anything like a complete treatment of the development and present characteristics of economic institutions in advanced societies in this brief discussion, but let us attempt to point to some of their more salient features.

Private Property and the Corporation   "Property consists, first, not of things, but of rights; it is not a concrete object of reference, but a socially recognized claim."[1] Wilbert Moore has defined *property* as an institutionalized right of persons or other social units to scarce values.[2] In former times, when the most important type of property consisted of land, property rights included both the right to control the use of the land and the right to whatever benefits were associated with the use of the land, including sale of produce and land rent. However, with the rise of the modern corporation, important changes have occurred in the concept of property. There has been a "dissolution of the old atom of ownership into its component parts, control and beneficial ownership."[3] That is, ownership resides in a set of shareholders who are entitled under specified conditions to a return from funds that they have placed at the disposal of the corporation. On the other hand, effective control resides not with this group but typically with a set of hired managers who are empowered to make decisions governing the operation of the corporate enterprise.

The emergence of the corporation as the dominant form of business enterprise has caused further transformations. The corporation is a legal entity that permits a number of individuals to pool their resources and abilities to carry on business, and that at the same time limits the liability of each individual for the common enterprise to the amount of his original investment. As such, it is an important mechanism for collecting the large amounts of capital required for today's complex and expensive equipment and facilities. Moreover, the corporation

---

[1] Robin M. Williams, Jr., *American Society* (rev. ed.), New York: Knopf, 1960, p. 187.

[2] Wilbert E. Moore, "The emergence of new property conceptions in America," *Journal of Legal and Political Sociology*, 1 (April, 1943), 34–35.

[3] A. A. Berle and Gardner C. Means, *The Modern Corporation and Private Property*, New York: Macmillan, 1934, p. 8.

itself has become the prime source of capital accumulation, a substantial proportion of corporate profits typically being plowed back into the enterprise. The result is that the corporation has become by far the largest property-owner. As Lerner comments:

Private property has not been abolished, either by Big Government or the Big Corporation: it has taken new forms. It is still private in the sense that it is not statist, but it has ceased to be individualist and has become corporate, institutional, and managerial.[4]

Technology and Planning   Following Galbraith, we may define *technology* as the "systematic application of scientific or other organized knowledge to practical tasks."[5] Such tasks are typically subdivided into component parts because only in this way can such organized knowledge be brought to bear on performance. Galbraith has argued that among the important consequences of the widespread use of technology are the following: (1) a sizable and increasing amount of time separates the beginning of a task from the completion of a given task; (2) the capital that is committed to production increases; (3) specialized manpower is needed; and (4) organization must bring to a coherent result the work of the many specialists. Associated with these is a further consequence:

From the time and capital that must be committed, the inflexibility of this commitment, the needs of large organization and the problems of market performance under conditions of advanced technology, comes the necessity for planning.[6]

In short, as the technical requirements of production become more complex, planning is not something in which a firm may or may not choose to engage—it is of necessity thrust upon the company if it is to survive. Further, the definition of "planning" rapidly becomes enlarged. "Much of what the firm regards as planning consists in minimizing or getting rid of market influences."[7] Individual firms may seek to overcome market uncertainties in several ways: by taking over buyers or sellers, a technique known as vertical integration; by attempting to reduce or control or influence the actions of related companies; or by entering into specific contracts with other companies to buy their products or to sell to them at a specified price for a specified period of time.[8]

It is not only the individual firm, however, that has moved to restrict the market economy. Government has also done so. Economic liberals have always placed their faith in the operation of a market economy. They argued that the market was a harsh but just judge of economic performance: given the creation of a demand, new firms would rise to meet the demand most economically, hence selling at the lowest prices. Labor and capital should similarly be free to move as demand required. Americans retained their faith in the unrestricted operation of the market long after Europeans had moved toward a more controlled economy. Polanyi has argued that this American faith was bolstered by a special set of circumstances. He writes:

Up to the 1890's the frontier was open and free land lasted; up to the Great War the

[4]Max Lerner, *America as a Civilization*, New York: Simon and Schuster, 1957, p. 302.
[5]John Kenneth Galbraith, *The New Industrial State*, New York: New American Library (Signet Books), 1968, p. 24 (originally published by Houghton Mifflin, Boston, 1967).
[6]Galbraith, p. 28.
[7]Galbraith, p. 37.
[8]Galbraith, pp. 33–45. See also Thompson's closely related discussion reprinted in this book, Reading 34.

supply of low standard labor flowed freely; and up to the turn of the century there was no commitment to keep foreign exchanges stable. . . .

As soon as these conditions ceased to exist, social protection set in. As the lower ranges of labor could not any more be freely replaced from an inexhaustible reservoir of immigrants, while its higher ranges were unable to settle freely on the land; as the soil and natural resources became scarce and had to be husbanded; as the gold standard was introduced in order to remove the currency from politics and to link domestic trade with that of the world, the United States caught up with a century of European development: protection of the soil and its cultivators, social security for labor through unionism and legislation, and central banking—all on the largest scale—make their appearance.[9]

In the years since these early governmental actions to restrict the operation of the free market, this nation has moved much further along the path toward a managed economy. Tariffs have been established to protect home industries; subsidies in the form of land grants, special tax shelters, and outright monetary grants have been widely employed; and government increasingly provides the venture capital to explore new techniques and products. With the advent and widespread acceptance of Keynesian economics we have entered a new phase of governmental regulation with the use of tax policies, credit controls, and close surveillance of economic cycles, trends, and needs. Max Lerner in Reading 45 attempts to assess the current situation in which a balance is sought between freedom and regulation, between public and private ownership, and between capitalism and socialism. He concludes, in essence, that our present situation represents "a mixed economy, with large areas of freedom and varied techniques of regulation, control, and some forms of planning."[10]

Means and Ends   The scientific and technological revolution has created vast changes in our society. These changes are particularly apparent in the economic sector where the creation and exploitation of new knowledge creates a succession of far-reaching changes that occur at an ever increasing rate. There is some question as to whether other institutions and structures can adjust to—either keep up with or regulate in some manner—the rate of technological change.

There is also the question of the relative emphasis or value placed on participation in the various institutional sectors. Tumin, for example, has suggested that the present emphasis on economic institutions in our society has created a serious institutional imbalance. He writes:

. . . as a result of the great emphasis placed upon job-achievement and its correlates, it becomes difficult to give enough socially rewarding meaning to the values of other institutions to enable them to compete successfully on their own terms. There is relatively inadequate reward for conscientious role performance in other institutions. As a result, values from the economic institution invade other institutions. . . . This invasion is dysfunctional to the extent that the entering values are inappropriate to the roles to which they become attached.[11]

As an example of such invasion, we may cite Elliot Liebow's descriptions of Negro fathers in an urban slum area who, being unable to find jobs that will

[9]Karl Polanyi, *The Great Transformation*, Boston: Beacon, 1957, pp. 201–202 (first published by Holt, Rinehart and Winston, Inc., New York, 1944).

[10]Lerner, p. 341.

[11]Melvin M. Tumin, "Some dysfunctions of institutional imbalances," *Behavioral Science*, 1 (July, 1956), 218–223.

pay a living wage, are unable to perform their roles of husband and father in other respects as well. They are unable even to show concern and affection for their children because

The more demonstrative and accepting he is of his children, the greater is his public and private commitment to the duties and responsibilities of fatherhood; and the greater his commitment, the greater and sharper his failure as the provider and head of the family. To soften this failure, and to lessen the damage to his public and self-esteem, he pushes the children away from him, saying, in effect, "I'm not even trying to be your father, so now I can't be blamed for failing to accomplish what I'm not trying to do."[12]

Technology is, of course, concerned with the appropriate selection of means of human action. It is an attempt to rationalize behavior in the sense that it provides techniques for determining the most effective and efficient means for reaching some predetermined objective. According to Jacques Ellul, ours is a progressively technical civilization. Merton has summarized Ellul's arguments as follows:

. . . the ever-expanding and irreversible rule of technique is extended to all domains of life. It is a civilization committed to the quest for continually improved means to carelessly examined ends. Indeed, technique transforms ends into means. What was once prized in its own right now becomes worthwhile only if it helps achieve something else. And, conversely, technique turns means into ends. "Know-how" takes on an ultimate value.[13]

According to Ellul and others, technicism is now well established in the economic sector and is spreading to others, most particularly into the political arena. Technicians and administrators working in and for the government perceive the nation as simply another sphere in which to apply their expertise. They are apt to view the state as "an enterprise providing services that must be made to function efficiently"[14] rather than as a political entity responsive to the will of the people or as an instrument for effecting social justice.

Ellul has perhaps overstated his case, but the problems he points to are real ones. The modern economy and the modern state are sufficiently complex that great reliance must be placed on the expertise of the technical specialist. However, specialists, by reason of their specialization—their narrowness—are not well equipped to take into account the full range of relevant factors in arriving at decisions. On the other hand, the generalist may be handicapped by his lack of knowledge of the specifics. Wheeler summarizes this dilemma as follows:

The world of the scientific revolution has become so complex that only men of general wisdom and knowledge can run it properly. But its problems are so specialized that the generalist cannot understand them. The experts and scientists who do understand lack the general knowledge made politically necessary by the discord produced by their proliferating specialities.[15]

This is the new world in which we "half-men" must struggle. Finding ways to harness our technology in the service of human ends is perhaps the greatest challenge facing our society today.

---

[12]Elliot Liebow, *Tally's Corner: A Study of Negro Streetcorner Men*, Boston: Little, Brown, 1967, p. 86.

[13]"Foreword" by Robert K. Merton to Jacques Ellul, *The Technological Society*, New York: Random House (Vintage Books), 1964, p. vi (originally published as *La Technique ou l'enjeu du siècle*, Librairie Armand Colin, 1954).

[14]Merton, p. vii.

[15]Harvey Wheeler, "Means, ends, and human institutions," *The Nation*, 204 (January 2, 1967), 15.

45 Capitalist Economy and Business Civilization

Max Lerner

1. AMERICAN CAPITALISM: TRIAL BALANCE

Given this culture of science and the machine, how about the system of American capitalism which organizes it? The appraisal of American capitalism as a going concern must be made largely in terms of a balance sheet. Whoever embraces its achievements should not flinch from acknowledging its costs; whoever condemns the costs should be candid enough to recognize the achievement.

The record of achievement is clear enough: a continuously rising curve of man-hour productivity; a high rate of capital formation; steadily rising profits which have made a corpse of the Marxist predictions about profits under capitalism; employment levels which in the mid-1950s were at their top peacetime pitch; a wilderness of available commodities and a strong "propensity to consume," reflecting the spread of high and increasing living standards even among middle- and low-income levels; a steadily increasing growth in real wages; a continuing secular increase in the national product; a production record which has provided the military production for two world wars and the current "readiness economy" for defense, while increasing the products available for civilian consumption; a capacity to take in its stride an ever-heavier tax structure without destroying freedom of economic movement and decision within the economy; a continuing sense of economic dynamism, and finally an economy with the capacity for changing its forms under pressure so that it could

in the mid-1950s lay claim to being a "people's capitalism" even while being to a high degree a corporate and monopoly capitalism.

The debit side is also clear: a haste for profits which has used up too rapidly the land and resources of the continent and built unplanned cities; an economy which made heavy productive gains (especially in World War II) through the expansion of war industries and seems still to be buttressed by a government budget for arms which runs to 15 or 20 per cent of the Gross National Product; one which has lived like a fever-chart patient by constantly taking its pulse and has not been able to control firmly the periodic swings of prosperity and depression; one in which the Big Enterprise corporations create private empires challenging the state itself; one in which the chances for a competitive start in the race for the Big Money are less open to small businessmen and depend more upon upward movement in a corporate bureaucracy; an economy in which, despite its production levels, much remains to be done in distributing the final product more fairly.

The observer is tempted to say (with Hamlet): "Look at this picture, and here at this one."

The defense of American capitalism runs largely in broad abstractions like "the American system" or "the free-enterprise economy," or in epithets like "serfdom" or "totalitarian" applied to noncapitalist systems. Underlying these catchwords are some basic arguments.

One is the *argument from incentive:* that men's brains and energy work best when they have no hampering restrictions, and when they see an immediacy of relation between effort and reward. The second is the *argument from a free market:* that an economy runs best as the result of millions of individual decisions made through the operations of a free production, wage and price system; that when it goes off kilter, it can generally set itself right again by individual adjustments within a frame of government spurs and checks; and that even government regulation is best accomplished by the indirect methods of inducements and pressures on the free market, rather than the direct method of planning and control. The third is the *argument from managerial efficiency:* that the corporate managerial group is recruited from the men with the best skills, who deal with the problems of industrial production more flexibly than a governmental bureaucracy could.

The arguments, though vulnerable, are basically valid. True, the free market no longer exists in anything like its historic form, and Big Enterprise and the giant corporation, with prices largely reached by administrative decision, have in part taken its place. Yet the economy has developed its own distinctive forms of freedom, and the decisions reached in it are still freer than in a cartelized or largely government-directed economy. The system of profit and property incentives has been transformed in the giant corporation; yet new incentives have emerged that keep the corporate managers alert and drive the productive system on. The argument from corporate efficiency has much in its favor, provided we do not forget that a corporate bureaucracy has a strong inner impulse toward conformism of spirit and, like government bureaucracies, runs the danger of stagnation.

Some corollaries of these doctrines that emerge in the capitalist apologia are more open to question: the argument that the big corporations and their managers administer their power *as a trust* for the people as a whole; and the argument that there is a *harmony of interests* which ties labor and the farmers to business prosperity and therefore business decisions. While most Americans are too realistic to accept the view that Big Property is being held in trust for them, they do not resent the power of the possessing groups because they hope themselves someday to be secure enough to "take it easy." As for the harmony of interests, they may have some skepticism about it, yet they have never been caught by the European idea that class cleavages must deepen until the whole system breaks.

The real problems of capitalism, however, are not the doctrinal struggles but the operational strains—the periodic breakdowns, the sense of insecurity, the shadow of monopoly, the dependence upon war expenditures, the question of distributive justice. The American economy, because of its power and prosperity, has become the last, best hope of free economies in the world. But by the same token the issues of its capacity for survival, its social costs, and its impact on the human spirit have called in question the nature and survival value of the system of capitalism itself.

What are the elements of American capitalism as a going concern, distinguishing it from other going systems? It is customary to say that capitalism is organized as a "private-enterprise system," for private (individual or corporate) profit, with the resulting rewards protected by the state as private property. This is valid enough, except for the fact that far-reaching changes have taken place in the structure and functioning of American capitalism. The profit incentive, for example, does not operate in corporate management as it used to operate in individual enterprise, since ownership and management have split apart: it still holds, however, if it is rephrased as the drive within the manager to make the best possible profit record for the corporation. The idea of private property has also suffered a change, since industrial ownership is now widely scattered in the form of stock ownership, some of the stocks being owned by trust funds, investment trusts, other corporations, life insurance companies, and even trade-unions. The earlier picture of capitalism as a competitive system has also had to be changed. To some extent competition has been inhibited by price agreements and "oligopoly"—the control of an industry by a handful of big corporations competing only partly in price and mainly in packaging, advertising, and brand names, as in meat packing, automobiles, or cigarettes. Yet the impressive fact about the American economy is the extent to which it has effectively resisted the monopoly tendencies. The concept of bigness is not the same as the concept of monopoly, and something that can fairly be called competition is still a power regulator of the economy.

The core of capitalism then is still present. It is in essence concerned with decision-making within a profit-competitive framework. Under communism the decisions are made by a small group of political functionaries assigned to strategic industrial posts. Under democratic socialism they are made by technicians operating largely within government corporations, responsible ultimately to the people. Under American capitalism the decisions on production, pricing, advertising, and sales policies are private decisions—that is to say, they are made by individual businessmen or heads of small corporations, whether they be producers, middlemen, or retailers, and in the case of big corporations they are made by the managers to whom the power of decision is delegated by the stockholders; the decisions on wages and labor policy are generally made through collective bargaining by the managers and trade-union leaders. Obviously there are restrictions placed on these decisions by price and wage legislation, sometimes by priorities and the allocation of scarce materials in a defense economy. But within these limits the decisions are linked with ownership and management, and they are made always with a view to profit and in competition with other enterprises. At the other end of the capitalist process there are millions of decisions made by the consumer: production and investment policies are guided not by governmental decisions or by what might be considered socially necessary production but in the light of consumers' decisions about how they will spend their money and for what.

Thus at one end American capitalism is guided by decisions made by businessmen, managers, and trade-union leaders, at the other end by consumer decisions. This decision-making operates within a frame in which there are strong surviving elements of private property, private and corporate profits, and competition.

In assessing American capitalism as a going concern, one important test is the test of *productivity.* Here American capitalism shows the most impressive facet of its record. Socialists might argue that, given the resources of America and the accidents of its history, some other system of organization, ownership, and power could have attained the same productivity with a better distribution of the products. This is one of those iffy questions that will never be resolved. On the other hand it is hard to sustain the claim that the creative force in the American record of increased productivity is the capitalist entrepreneur and manager, and he alone. Science, technology, the legal and governmental framework, and the skill of the worker—all belong in the larger pattern along with the supplier of risk capital and the business organizer. Yet the American record of an increase of productivity running between 2 per cent and 3 per cent a year must be counted one of the over-all achievements of capitalism. Nor has this production record been only a matter of technology and resources. The drive toward productivity has also been due to the elements within the social structure which have invested the whole productive process with the *élan* of freedom. This is as true today as it was a century ago, as John Sawyer has shown, basing himself on the accounts of European travelers in America in the 1840s and 1850s.

All this brings us to the question of *incentive*, which is more troublesome. Those who contend that profit alone has furnished the effective incentive for industrial production must plead guilty to a lower view of human motive than applies even in an imperfect world. The fact is that the managerial function in the big corporation has been performed through incentives quite· different from those of ownership profits or dividends, and more closely related to competitive performance and pride in a job well done. Through a complex mingling of profit, salary, bonus, and craftsmanship incentives, capitalism as a going concern has enlisted considerable talents in the processes of production and selling; and it has plowed back into increased production a steady portion (recently around 7 per cent) of the national product, keeping the process of capital formation an active and growing one.

It is on the test of *stability* that American capitalism is most vulnerable. American economic thought is crisscrossed by conflicts of opinion about the underlying causes of the periodic swings and breakdowns of the system, resulting in cycles of prosperity and recession, boom and depression. There are still die-hard critics of the system who believe that boom and bust are inherent in the system and will never yield to anything short of full-scale socialism. There are also True Believers of another stripe who feel, as their forerunners felt in the boom days of the 1920s, that Americans have somehow found the golden key to perpetual prosperity.

Aside from these two groups there is fairly general agreement, however, that, while the swings in the "business cycle" may not yet have been mastered, American business, labor, and government leaders have learned to detect the danger signals and put in motion some preventive measures, and have learned also—once the cycle is on its way—how to cut the length and severity of the downward swing and cushion its impact. In the mid-1950s there was an upsurge of conviction that the cycle had to a large extent been mastered and need never again operate drastically. The bitter experience after 1929 taught the nation's leaders how to use "counter-cyclical" measures in the form of tax and fiscal policies, rediscounting rates, Federal expenditures for defense and public works, state and Federal programs for building roads, schoolhouses, and hospitals. The President's Council of Economic Advisers, working with a committee of Congress, is now accepted under Republican as well as Democratic administrations. Its reports, carefully studied in business, labor, and government circles, are in effect· an embryonic form of corrective and preventive planning. The government's massive role in a war-geared "readiness economy" has also given it a leverage in guiding, checking, and stimulating business activity and as such it is a form of indirect planning.

America has thus characteristically used an indirect approach to the control of the swings of business activity, aiming at stability without embracing a direct program of planning and without transferring the crucial decisions from the corporate managers and the consumers to government managers. The specter of Depression is, of course, always present. At the close of World War II there were widespread prophecies of economic ca-tastrophe, yet the real danger proved to be not mass unemployment but inflation, not a paralysis of production but a boom induced by high demand and sustained by the armament race. This mood has lasted into the mid-1950s. Obviously there is a serious problem in the steady inflationary movement of American prices, year after year, largely due to the pressure of rising consumer demand, with its tragic effect in wiping out much of the substance and meaning of savings. Yet, while Americans are still far from solving the basic problem of boom and bust, they have at least a heightened awareness of what is involved and are willing to take decisive action. There are few economists who would accept the European notion, seemingly as widespread among scholars as among the people, that American capitalism will once again in the calculable future be as helpless as it was in the years following 1929.

On the test of *security and insecurity* American capitalism has made steady if reluctant progress. So far from interfering with prosperity, it is now accepted that effective, well-administered insurance programs make the economy more stable as well as adding to personal security. Every person must confront the tragic elements in life, but the pathetic elements can be whittled down by common action. To the degree that America has become a welfare state it is not because of effeminacy or the importation of "foreign" ideas, but of practical grappling with a deeply felt need to make the individual fate more secure.

Judged by another test—that of *income spread and distribution*—the going economy has in the past evoked strong self-criticism from American writers, if not from the economists. Especially in the decade before World War I, and in the 1920s and 1930s, they unsparingly subjected the economy to the test of equity. The extremes of wealth and poverty, the discrepancies between the Babylonian living at the top of the pyramid and the scrimping and degradation at its base, became staples of the American self-portrait. There was a time when the prospects of the future for many Americans seemed precarious. Any European or Asian who thinks that Americans need to be prodded about this should read the almost unparalleled record in which sensitive Americans have made their own indictment of their own vaunted system. But the note of self-criticism has recently grown fainter because of the overwhelming evidence of American living standards. These have improved all through the class system as productivity has increased and the trade-unions have been able to claim a share of it for their members. The problem of poverty in America is now circumscribed within the lower fourth of the population.

One could argue, of course, that the depressed groups in backward areas in other countries are far worse off than this lower fourth in America. This would be sound if American living standards were judged by productivity in other areas of the world, but they must be judged by American productivity. In every economy, as Sumner put it, "there are dinners without appetites at one end of the table, and appetites without dinners at the other." The American economy as a production miracle has evoked life claims in America not roused in the underdeveloped economies: what would be a full meal elsewhere is a skimpy one at the table of the American business system.

The final test of a going economy is the *creativeness* it evokes and makes possible. Few systems in history have attracted so much talent and put it to use, and in no other economy have men's business abilities been so continuously tapped. The problem is not whether the economy gives scope to creativeness, but what kind of creativeness it gives scope to. The question asked is always whether a new idea or a new insight is "practical"—that is, whether it can be translated into dollar-and-cents terms. The creativeness that is not vendible is likely to be ignored and to wither. Yet within this pecuniary framework there has been broader scope for the creation of use values and life values than the critics of the money calculus have been ready to admit.

This then would be a rough trial balance of American capitalism as a going concern: that it has done brilliantly in productivity and national product; that it has done less will with the swings of the business cycle and with boom and bust, but that substantial steps have been taken to meet this; that its greatest weakness on this score lies in the dependence of the recent prosperity on the war-geared economy; that its growth in the areas of concentrated economic power has been at the expense of small business; that in its income distribution it is a good deal better than its opponents would admit but not nearly as good as its apologists claim, good enough to retain the faith of those who are fulfilled by it but not good enough to exact the loyalty of those who feel left out; that it allows for creativeness but within a limited sense of that word; that as a whole it is an economy which has wrested from the world its envy along with a grudging respect, but not its imitation.

Further Reading

There are an enormous number of writings concerned with the analysis of societies, institutions, and institutional structures, so that our suggestions for further reading in this area must be highly selective.

Several sociologists have attempted to develop somewhat general conceptual schemes for approaching the study of society. An early and influential attempt is that of Max Weber, *Theory of Social and Economic Organization*, Glencoe, Ill.: Free Press, 1947; another early attempt is represented by the work of Charles H. Cooley, *Social Organization*, New York: Scribner, 1910. More recent efforts include those of Talcott Parsons, *The Social System*, Glencoe, Ill.: Free Press, 1951; and Marion J. Levy, Jr., *The Structure of Society*, Princeton, N.J.: Princeton University Press, 1952.

General treatises on social institutions as well as analyses of a variety of specific institutional complexes have been written by S. N. Eisenstadt, *Essays on Comparative Institutions*, New York: Wiley, 1965; and edited by Arnold M. Rose, *The Institutions of Advanced Societies*, Minneapolis: University of Minnesota Press, 1958. An extensive collection of excerpts from books and articles dealing with the analysis of societies has been edited by Talcott Parsons, Edward Shils, Kaspar Naegele, and Jessie Pitts, *Theories of Society*. New York: Free Press, 1961. Works focused on the American case include those of Robin M. Williams, Jr., *American Society* (rev. ed.), New York: Knopf, 1960; and Max Lerner, *America as a Civilization*, New York: Simon and Schuster, 1957.

Turning briefly to analyses of specific institutions, Emile Durkheim in *The Division of Labor in Society*, Glencoe, Ill.: Free Press, 1947 (first published in France in 1893), examined the changing bases of social integration, noting a shift from mechanical to organic solidarity. And Seymour Martin Lip et has recently examined the contributions of religious and political institutions to the integration of American society in *The First New Nation*, New York: Basic Books, 1963. For another treatment of the relation between institutional differentiation and the social functions of religion in American life, see Peter L. Berger, *The Noise of Solemn Assemblies*, Garden City. N.Y.: Doubleday, 1961.

The family as a social institution and as the basic context of socialization has been much studied. Recent representative works include William N. Stephens, *The Family in Cross-Cultural Perspective*, New York: Holt, Rinehart and Winston, Inc., 1963; and William J. Goode, *The Family*, Englewood Cliffs, N.J.: Prentice-Hall, 1964. Collections of articles dealing with various aspects of family functioning include Norman W. Bell and Ezra F. Vogel (eds.), *A Modern Introduction to the Family*, Glencoe, Ill.: Free Press, 1960; and Rose L. Coser (ed.), *The Family: Its Structure and Functions*, New York: St. Martin's, 1964.

Recent studies examining colleges and universities as socialization contexts include Burton Clark, *Educating the Expert Society*, San Francisco: Chandler Publishing Company, 1962; Nevitt Sanford (ed.), *The American College*, New York: Wiley, 1962; and Theodore Newcomb and Kenneth Feldman, *The Impact of Colleges upon Their Students*, a report to the Carnegie Foundation for the Advancement of Teaching, 1968.

Two texts comprehensively examine stratification systems in modern society: Bernard Barber, *Social Stratification*, New York: Harcourt, 1957; and Joseph A. Kahl, *The American Class Structure*, New York: Rinehart, 1957. Recent notable studies of social stratification include Albert J. Reiss *et al.*, *Occupations and Social Status*, New York: Free Press, 1961; Peter M. Blau and Otis Dudley Duncan, *The American Occupational Structure*, New York: Wiley, 1967; and Gerhard Lenski, *Power and Privilege*, New York: McGraw-Hill, 1966. An outstanding collection of recent writings giving a comparative view of social stratification is that of Reinhard Bendix and Seymour Martin Lipset (eds.), *Class, Status, and Power* (rev. ed.), New York: Free Press, 1966.

Political institutions and behavior have been much analyzed by political scientists and political sociologists. Among the better overall treatments are David Truman, *The Governmental Process*, New York: Knopf, 1951; and Samuel Lubell, *The Future of American Politics* (2d ed.), New York: Doubleday, 1956. A comprehensive reader on political institutions has been edited by Reinhard Bendix, *State and Society*, Boston: Little, Brown, 1968. The structure and functioning of political parties are presented in comparative perspective by Maurice Duverger, *Political Parties* (tr. Barbara and Robert North), New York: Wiley, 1954. A number of selections dealing further with parties has been collected by Seymour M. Lipset and Stein Rokkan (eds.), *Party Systems and Voter Alignments*, New York: Free Press, 1967. The role of public opinion and the electorate is analyzed in Angus Campbell *et al.*, *Elections and Political Order*, New York: Wiley, 1966; and in William McPhee and William Glaser, *Public Opinion and Congressional Elections*, New York: Free Press, 1962.

Finally, there are many highly readable sources treating the American economic system, its growth and development, and its implications for the larger society. On the changing concept of property, see Adolf A. Berle, Jr., and Gardiner C. Means, *The Modern Corporation and Private Property*, New York: Macmillan, 1934; and A. A. Berle, Jr., *Power Without Property*, New York: Harcourt, 1959. The structure and internal processes of the corporation are discussed in Edward S. Mason (ed.), *The Corporation in Modern Society*, Cambridge, Mass.: Harvard University Press, 1959; and in Robert A. Gordon, *Business Leadership in the Large Corporation*, Washington, D.C.: The Brookings Institution, 1945. Studies focusing on the concentration of economic resources in America include the report of the National Resources Committee, *The Structure of the American Economy*, Washington, D.C.: U.S. Government

Printing Office, 1939; and David Lynch, *The Concentration of Economic Power*, New York: Columbia University Press, 1946. The latter is a summary and analysis of materials collected in the investigations of the Temporary National Economic Committee. An important description of new sources of economic competition in our society is that of John Kenneth Galbraith, *American Capitalism: The Concept of Countervailing Power*, Boston: Houghton Mifflin, 1952. Turning to the implications for the larger society of the operation of our economic institutions, we have the penetrating analyses by A. A. Berle, Jr., *The 20th Century Capitalist Revolution*, New York: Harcourt, 1954; Robert A. Brady, *Business as a System of Power*, New York: Columbia University Press, 1943; Karl Mannheim, *Man and Society in an Age of Reconstruction*, New York: Harcourt, 1950; and John Kenneth Galbraith, *The New Industrial State*, Boston: Houghton Mifflin, 1967.

NAME INDEX

SUBJECT INDEX

Academic achievement, and adolescent values, 37–46
and I.Q., 41–43
Acceptance and conformity, 232–234, 252–253
Acculturation, 452–454, 457–470
defined, 452
of Italian-Americans, 457–470
and socialization, 452
See also Assimilation; Socialization
Adaptation, 200–211
defined, 201, 203
and differentiation, 201–202, 286–287, 290–301, 508
genetic and somatic, 204–205
individual and communal, 201, 204–211
and integration, 287–288, 290–301
and maladaptation, 206
See also Adaptive processes
Adaptive processes, in communities, 508–524
in formal organizations, 410–429
in small groups, 286–310
in societies, 609–618
Administrative staff, conflicts within, 356–366
in formal organizations, 314–315, 318–319, 328–339, 417
size of, in formal organizations, 318–319, 331–334
in universities, 399–409
See also Bureaucratic organization; Bureaucratization
Adolescents, as a subculture, 37–46
Alienation (see Anomie; Apathy)
Anomie, 108, 119, 127–139
defined, 129
Durkheim's theory of, 128–129
and mass society, 535, 538, 540–541, 547
Merton's theory of, 129–130
Apathy, and bureaucratic rules, 327–329
and oligarchic processes, 389–391
political, and power, 602
Assimilation, 343–350, 452–453, 457
defined, 343
in a military academy, 343–350
See also Acculturation; Socialization; Socialization processes
Association, differential, 127, 130–139
Attraction, social, 115–118, 195–196, 198, 252
Authority, 197–198, 385–388, 392–398
in communities, 494–495
and evaluation, 386–388, 392–398
of faculty, in universities, 399–409
in formal organizations, 385–388, 392–409
of line officers in industrial organizations, 360–366

and managerial ideologies, 334–339
and professionals, 389
systems, 396
in totalitarian societies, 537
See also Control, social; Legitimation; Power
Autonomy, of communities, 436–437
of organizations, 411–412
of professionals in organizations, 402–409, 418–419

Bargaining, and goal-setting in organizations, 413–414
Biological drives, and family roles, 562–564
and norms, 33
and socialization, 156, 558
Black power, 186, 188–192
Blacks, employment opportunities for, 456–457
migration of, 455–457
and Negroes, 186–187
prejudice toward, 173–175, 232
and "Sambo" personality type, 241–251
segregation of, 190–192, 444–445, 456–457
and slavery, 61–62, 241–251
social mobility of, 583
as status, 63, 173–175, 180–181, 185–192
See also Ethnic groups
Boundaries, system, 72, 122–123, 200, 213–214, 238, 411, 419–429
Bureaucratic organization, 328–339
Coast Guard Academy as a, 346–347
and community structure, 439
and routine tasks, 417–418
university as a, 399–409
Weber's description of, 314–315, 319
See also Organizations, formal
Bureaucratization, 318–319, 328–339
and changes in managerial functions, 328–334
and changes in managerial ideology, 334–339
defined, 318
and integration, 319
and mass society, 539–540
and power, 607

Capitalism, 613–618
Caste system of stratification, 581
Characteristics, social
as basis for role assignment, 66, 171–175
and resources, 274–276
and rewards, 354–356, 366–383
and social status, 62, 170–175, 255–256
Charter, organizational, 552, 565–578
Child-rearing (see Socialization)
City planning, 448–451, 502–503